D1355257

Museums and their Communities

Museums and their Communities brings together a collection of readings from practitioners and researchers, working across a range of disciplines, which explore and illuminate the complex and evolving relationships between museums and the diverse communities they represent, serve and with which they engage.

This collection of high quality, provocative and stimulating readings draws together thinking, practice and case studies relating to many different kinds of museum. Through wide-ranging, international contexts it examines the ways in which museums operate as sites of community representation, identity and memory.

The Reader considers the shifting institutional priorities of the museum from a focus on collections to a growing concern for audience needs and expectations. It reflects on areas of contestation and addresses a number of timely questions which increasingly are challenging museum practitioners and scholars:

* Who are the museum's communities? What needs and challenges do these constituencies present?
* What is the impact upon the museum of competing community interests?
* How do issues of power and control affect communities and influence the messages museums attempt to communicate?

Museums and their Communities provides a focused consideration of the challenges and opportunities facing museums that wish to engage with their community responsibilities.

Sheila Watson is a lecturer in the Department of Museum Studies, University of Leicester.

Leicester Readers in Museum Studies
Series editor: Professor Simon J. Knell

Museums

and

their

Communities

Edited by

Sheila Watson

Routledge
Taylor & Francis Group

LONDON AND NEW YORK

First published 2007
by Routledge
2 Park Square, Milton Park, Abingdon, Oxon OX14 4RN

Simultaneously published in the USA and Canada
by Routledge
270 Madison Ave, New York NY 10016

Routledge is an imprint of the Taylor & Francis Group, an informa business

© 2007 Sheila Watson

Typeset in 11.5/12.5 pt Perpetua by Graphicraft Limited, Hong Kong
Printed and bound in Great Britain by The Cromwell Press, Trowbridge, Wiltshire

British Library Cataloguing in Publication Data
A catalogue record for this book is available from the British Library

Library of Congress Cataloging in Publication Data
A catalog record for this book has been requested

ISBN10: 0-415-40259-X (hbk)
ISBN10: 0-415-40260-3 (pbk)

ISBN13: 978-0-415-40259-0 (hbk)
ISBN13: 978-0-415-40260-6 (pbk)

Dedication

To my parents, with love

Contents

List of Contributors

Stephen Alsford is website manager for the Canadian Museum of Civilization Corporation. He joined the Task Force set up to design the museum in 1982 and since then he has been involved in a variety of projects relating to the museum. He co-authored this chapter with George F. MacDonald and it appeared in *Cultural Dynamics* 7 (1) London, Sage Publications, 15–36 in 1995.

Josie Appleton writes about politics and culture for *spiked* and a range of publications: *Spectator, Times Literary Supplement, The Times* and *Blueprint* magazine. This chapter appeared in, *Museums for the 'People'? Conversations in Print*, London, Institute of Ideas, 14–26, in 2001.

Susan Ashley is a postgraduate student in the Communication and Culture program at Ryerson University in Toronto, Canada. This chapter was published in *Museum and Society*, March 2005 3 (1) 5–17.

Matt Barnard is a freelance journalist. This chapter, 'Kist and Tell' appeared in *Museums Journal* Feb. 2002, 36–7.

Peter Beresford is Professor of Social Policy and Director of the Centre for Citizen Participation at Brunel University. Before becoming a professor he spent twelve years as a mental health service user including time in a psychiatric hospital. This chapter is taken from *Openmind* (91), May/June 1998, 12–13.

Roger Bordage was arrested by the Gestapo for resistance activities in France in 1943. He survived two years in Oranienburg-Sachsenhausen concentration camp and was freed in 1945 by the Allies. Subsequently he studied in France and the

United States and then worked for over thirty years training personnel in rural literacy programmes in Asia, Africa and Latin America. His chapter was published in *Museums International* 177, vol. XLV, no. 1, 26–31 in 1993.

Annette van den Bosch taught in the Department of Visual Culture, Monash University, Australia and this chapter was published in *Third Text*, volume 19, issue 1, January 2005, 81–9.

Alison K. Brown is Research Manager (Human History) at Glasgow Museums and was formerly a researcher at the Pitt Rivers Museum and Junior Research Fellow at Wolfson College, University of Oxford. This extract appears from her co-authored introduction in Peers, L. and Brown, A.K., 2003, *Museums and Source Communities*, London, Routledge, 1–16.

Dawn Casey was appointed Director of the National Museum of Australia in 1999. She left the museum in December 2003. Before her appointment she was Chief General Manager of the Acton Peninsula Project Task Force, the body responsible for the construction of the new National Museum. This chapter appeared in *Curator*, vol. 44, no. 3, Walnut Creek, Altamira Press, 230–36 in 2001.

Elizabeth Crooke is a senior lecturer in Museum and Heritage Studies at the University of Ulster. This chapter appeared in Littler, J. and Naidoo, R. (eds) (2005) *The Politics of Heritage: The Legacies of 'Race'*, London, Routledge, 69–81.

Andrew Crosby was visiting Research Fellow in Pacific archaeology at the University of Southampton. This chapter appeared in *World Archaeology*, vol. 34, no. 2, 363–78 in 2002.

James Cuno has been Director of the Harvard University Art Museums and Professor of History of Art and Architecture at Harvard, Director of the Courtauld Institute of Art, London, and is currently Director and President of The Art Institute of Chicago. This chapter appeared in *Art Bulletin*, vol. 79, 6–9 in 1997.

Peter Davis is Professor of Museology at Newcastle University, England. His research interests include natural history museums and environmentalism, and ecomuseums. His books include *Ecomuseums: a sense of place* (1999; from which this extract is taken, pp. 24–43). His recent work on ecomuseums has led him to a close involvement with developments in East Asia, particularly Japan and China, including Taiwan. He was appointed as the first Guest Professor of Museology in Museion, University of Gothenburg (Sweden) in 2005, a role which he carries out in tandem with his post in Newcastle.

Steven C. Dubin was Director of the Media, Society, and Arts program at the State University of New York, Purchase. This is a chapter from *Displays of Power*, New York and London: New York University Press, 227–45, published in 1999.

Terence Duffy taught Peace Studies at the University of Ulster, Magee College, in Northern Ireland and was Director of the Irish Peace Museum Project. This chapter appeared in *Museum International*, vol. 49, no. 1, 54–8 in 1997.

Cressida Fforde completed her PhD at the University of Southampton in 1997 on 'Controlling the Dead: an analysis of the collecting and repatriation of Aboriginal human remains' upon which part of this extract is based. She is currently an independent researcher and consultant. She is co-editor of *The Dead and Their Possessions: Repatriation in Principle, Policy and Practice* (2002), 34–46, from which this chapter is taken.

Viv Golding is lecturer in Museum Studies and Education at the University of Leicester. Before taking up her post at Leicester in 2001 she had ten years' experience developing educational opportunities at the Horniman Museum in London. This chapter was presented at *Museums and Intangible Heritage*, ICOM 2004 general conference, Seoul, Korea, October 2004 and has subsequently been published in *the International Journal of Intangible Heritage*, vol. 1, Seoul, Korea, 83–93.

Nelson Graburn has been Professor of Anthropology at the University of California, Berkeley, since 1964 and, from 1972, Curator of North American Ethnology at the Hearst Museum of Anthropology. This chapter appeared in *Museum International* in 1998 vol. 50, no. 3, Blackwell, Oxford, 13–18.

Anna Green is head of the School of Social Sciences at Auckland University of Technology, New Zealand. This chapter was first presented at the US Oral History Association conference in October 1996. This version is taken from Perks, R. and Thomson, A. (eds) *The Oral History Reader*, London: Routledge, 2006, 416–24.

Marjorie M. Halpin was the curator of Ethnology at the Museum of Anthropology and associate professor in the Department of Anthropology and Sociology, University of British Columbia, where she taught courses in museology and about Canada's aboriginal inhabitants of the North Pacific coast. This article appeared in *Museum International*, vol. 49, no. 2, 52–6 in 1997.

Richard W. Hill, Sr., is the former Director of the North American Indian Museum Association and has been involved with repatriation issues for nearly three decades. He has also taught Native American Studies at the State University of New York. This chapter appeared in Bray, T.L. (ed.) *The Future of the Past*, New York, Garland Pub Inc, 2001, 127–38.

Eilean Hooper-Greenhill is Professor of Museum Studies at the University of Leicester. Her teaching experience spans schools, museums and universities. She is editor (with Flora Kaplan) for the Routledge *Museum Meanings* series. A former Head of Department and Director of the Research Centre for Museums and Galleries, she is currently focussing on writing and research, with a new book on museums and education in preparation. These extracts are taken from *Museums and the Interpretation of Visual Culture*, 119–23, 151–62, published in 2000.

Tiffany Jenkins is the arts and society Director at the London-based Institute of Ideas. This chapter was published in *Museums Journal*, May 2005, 22–3, 25.

Steven Lubar is Professor of American Civilization and History and Director, John Nicholas Brown Center for the Study of American Civilization. This is taken from Anderson, A. and Kaeppler, A.L. (eds) *Exhibiting Dilemmas: Issues of Representation at the Smithsonian*, Washington DC, London, Smithsonian Institution Press, 15–27, published in 1997.

Timothy W. Luke is University Distinguished Professor in the Department of Political Science at Virginia Polytechnic Institute and State University. This is a chapter from his book: *Museum Politics: Power Plays at the Exhibition*, Minneapolis, University of Minnesota Press, 19–36, published in 2002.

George F. MacDonald is Director Emeritus of the Canadian Museum of Civilization having begun his career there in 1960. He became Museum Director in 1983. He co-authored this chapter with Stephen Alsford and it appeared in *Cultural Dynamics* 7 (1) London, Sage Publications, 15–36 in 1995.

Sharon Macdonald is Professor of Social Anthropology in the School of Social Sciences at the University of Manchester, and was previously Professor of Cultural Anthropology at the University of Sheffield. This chapter is from her book *The Politics of Display: Museums, Science, Culture*, London and New York, Routledge, 1–24, published in 1998.

Charmaine McEachern wrote this chapter while a member of the Department of Anthropology at the University of Adelaide, Australia. It appeared in *Social Identities*, vol. 4, no. 3, 1998, 499–521.

Peter C. Marzio is Director of the Museum of Fine Arts, Houston, Texas. This chapter appeared in Karp, I. and Lavine, S.D. (eds) *Exhibiting Cultures: The Poetics and Politics of Museum Display*, Washington and London, Smithsonian Institution Press, 2001, 121–7.

Nick Merriman is Director of the Manchester Museum and was formerly Reader in Museum Studies at University College London. This chapter appeared in Hooper-Greenhill, E. (ed.) *Cultural Diversity: Developing Museum Audiences in Britain*, London, Leicester University Press, 1997, 119–48.

Barbara Misztal is Professor of Sociology at the University of Leicester. This extract is taken from her book *Theories of Social Remembering*, Maidenhead, Open University Press, 9–26, published in 2003.

Hamzah Muzaini is a Research Associate in the Department of Geography, Durham University. From 2000 to 2002 he worked as a curator in the Changi Chapel and Museum in Singapore. This co-authored chapter appeared in *Australian Geographer*, vol. 36, no. 1, 1–17, March 2005.

Laura Peers is curator for the Americas Collection, Pitt Rivers Museum, lecturer in the School of Anthropology, and fellow of Linacre College at the University of Oxford. This extract appears from her co-authored introduction in Peers, L. and Brown, A.K., *Museums and Source Communities*, London, Routledge, 2003, 1–16.

Richard Sandell is deputy head of the department of Museum Studies in the University of Leicester. His research is concerned with the social role and agency of cultural organisations and, in particular, the museum's potential to combat prejudice and inequality. His most recent book is *Museums, Prejudice and the Reframing of Difference*, Routledge, 2006. This chapter appeared in Sandell, R. (ed.) *Museums, Society, Inequality*, Routledge, 2002, 3–23.

Moira Simpson is based in the Department of English and Cultural Studies at Flinders University in Adelaide, South Australia. She has written extensively about museums, indigenous cultural politics, and repatriation. Her publications include *Making Representations: Museums in the Post-Colonial Era* (Routledge: 1996/2001) from which this extract is taken (107–9, 112–15, 118, 119–22, 126–8, 133).

Viv Szekeres began work in the Migration Museum in Adelaide, South Australia, in 1984 and was appointed Director in 1987. She originally presented this chapter at the University of Leicester's conference on *Inclusion* in 2000 and it subsequently appeared in Sandell, R. (ed.) *Museums, Society, Inequality*, London: Routledge, 2002, 142–52.

Kevin Walsh co-directs the MA in Archaeological Heritage Management at the University of York. His chapter appeared in *International Journal of Heritage Studies*, vol. 7, no. 1, 83–98, in 2001.

Joe Watkins (part Choctaw Indian) has worked as Agency Archaeologist for the Bureau of Indian Affairs in Oklahoma. This chapter appears in Bray, T.L. (ed.) *The Future of the Past*, New York, Garland Pub Inc, 2001, 57–68.

Stephen Weil was a scholar emeritus at the Smithsonian Institution's Centre for Education and Museum Studies and a deputy director of the Hirshhorn Museum and Sculpture Garden. He spoke widely about the ways in which museums could improve peoples' lives and wrote on the role of museums in society. His publications include Weil, S. *Making Museums Matter*, Washington, London, Smithsonian Institution Press, 2002, 195–213, from which this extract is taken.

Andrea Witcomb was a curator at the Australian National Maritime Museum and at the Australian National Museum. She was formerly a senior lecturer at the Research Institute for Cultural Heritage at Curtin University of Technology in Perth and is now employed at Deakin University, in Melbourne. This extract is from her book, *Re-Imagining the Museum, Beyond the Mausoleum*, published in 2003 by Routledge in the Museum Meanings series, edited by Eilean Hooper-Greenhill and Flora Kaplan, 79–101.

Brenda S. A. Yeoh is a senior lecturer in the Department of Geography, National University of Singapore. This co-authored chapter appeared in *Australian Geographer*, vol. 36, no. 1, 1–17, March 2005.

Herlinda Zamora is a graduate student in museum studies at the University of Texas at Austin, and a museum educator at the Mexic-Arte museum, Austin, Texas. This chapter appeared in *Museum News*, vol. 81, no. 3, 36–41 in 2002.

Series Preface

Leicester Readers in Museum Studies provide students of museums – whether employed in the museum, engaged in a museum studies programme or studying in a cognate area – with a selection of focused readings in core areas of museum thought and practice. Each book has been compiled by a specialist in that field, but all share the Leicester Department's belief that the development and effectiveness of museums relies upon informed and creative practice. The series as a whole reflects the core Leicester curriculum which is now visible in programmes around the world and which grew, forty years ago, from a desire to train working professionals, and students prior to entry into the museum, in the technical aspects of museum practice. In some respects the curriculum taught then looks similar to that which we teach today. The following, for example, was included in the curriculum in 1968: history and development of the museum movement; the purpose of museums; types of museum and their functions; the law as it relates to museums; staff appointments and duties, sources of funding; preparation of estimates; byelaws and regulations; local, regional, etc. bodies; buildings; heating, ventilation and cleaning; lighting; security systems; control of stores and so on. Some of the language and focus here, however, indicates a very different world. A single component of the course, for example, focused on collections and dealt with collection management, conservation and exhibitions. Another component covered 'museum activities' from enquiry services to lectures, films and so on. There was also training in specialist areas, such as local history, and many practical classes which included making plaster casts and models. Many museum workers around the world will recognize these kinds of curriculum topics; they certainly resonate with my early experiences of working in museums.

While the skeleton of that curriculum in some respects remains, there has been a fundamental shift in the flesh we hang upon it. One cannot help but think that the museum world has grown remarkably sophisticated: practices are now regulated by equal opportunities, child protection, cultural property and wildlife conservation laws; collections are now exposed to material culture analysis, contemporary documentation projects, digital capture and so on; communication is now multi-media, inclusive, evaluated and theorized. The museum has over that time become intellectually fashionable, technologically advanced and developed a new social relevance. *Leicester Readers in Museum Studies* address this change. They deal with practice as it is relevant to the museum today, but they are also about expanding horizons beyond one's own experiences. They reflect a more profession-alized world and one that has thought very deeply about this wonderfully inter-esting and significant institution. Museum studies remains a vocational subject but it is now very different. It is, however, sobering to think that the Leicester course was founded in the year Michel Foucault published *The Order of Things* – a book that greatly influenced the way we think about the museum today. The writing was on the wall even then.

Simon Knell   2007
Series Editor

Acknowledgements

The editor is indebted to a number of individuals and organisations for making this book possible. I would like to thank the following for permission to reproduce copyright material.

While every effort has been made to trace copyright holders and obtain permission, this has not been possible in all cases. Any omissions brought to our attention will be remedied in future editions.

1. Changing roles of museums over time and current challenges

Weil, S. (2002) 'The Museum and the Public' in Weil, S. *Making Museums Matter*, Smithsonian Institution Press, 195–213. Reproduced with permission.

Halpin, M.M. (1997) '"Play it again, Sam": reflections on a new museology' *Museum International*, vol. 49, no. 2, 52–6, Blackwell Publishing. Reproduced by permission of the publisher.

Davis, P. (1999) 'Place exploration: museums, identity, community' in Davis, P. *Ecomuseums: A Sense of Place*, Leicester University Press, 24–44. Reproduced by kind permission of the Continuum Publishing Group.

Hooper-Greenhill, E. (2000) 'Objects and interpretive processes' 119–23, 172, 'The rebirth of the museum' 151–62, 174–5, 176–90 in *Museums and the Interpretation of Visual Culture*, Routledge. Reproduced with permission.

Sandell, R. (2002) 'Museums and the combating of social inequality: roles, responsibilities, resistance' in ed. Sandell, R. *Museums, Society Inequality*, Routledge, 3–23. Reproduced with permission.

Appleton, J. (2001) 'Museums for "The People"?' in Appleton *et al. Museums for 'The People'?* Conversations in Print, Institute of Ideas, 14–26. Reproduced by permission of the publisher.

Graburn, N. (1998) 'A quest for identity' *Museum International*, vol. 50, no. 3, 13–18, Blackwell Publishing. Reproduced by permission of the publisher.

Witcomb, A. (2003) 'A place for all of us? Museums and communities' in Witcomb, A. *Re-imagining the Museum: Beyond the Mausoleum*, Routledge, 79–101, 172–3 (footnotes), 175–85 (bibliography). Reproduced with permission.

Simpson, M.G. (1996) 'From treasure house to museum . . . and back' in Simpson, M.G. *Making Representations, Museums in the Post-Colonial Era*, Routledge, 107–9, 112–15, 118, 119–22, 126–28, 133 (271–88 plus bibliography). Reproduced with permission.

2. Who controls the museum?

Macdonald, S. (1998) 'Exhibitions of power and powers of exhibition: an introduction to the politics of display' in ed. Macdonald, S. *The Politics of Display: Museums, Science, Culture*, Routledge, 1–24. Reproduced with permission.

Luke, T.W. (2002) 'Nuclear reactions: The (re)presentation of Hiroshima at the National Air and Space Museum' in Luke, T.W. *Museum Politics: Power Plays at the Exhibition*, Minneapolis, University of Minnesota Press, 19–36 (plus footnotes). Copyright © 2002 Timothy W. Luke. Reproduced by permission of the publisher.

Dubin, S.C. (1999) 'The postmodern exhibition' in Dubin, S.C. *Displays of Power*, New York and London, New York University Press, pp. 227–45, 281–2. Copyright © 2000 Steven C. Dubin. Reproduced by permission of the publisher and author.

Bordage, R. (1993) 'Sachsenhausen: a flawed museum' *Museum International*, 177, vol. XLV, no. 1, 26–31, Blackwell Publishing. Reproduced by permission of the publisher.

Szekeres, V. (2002) 'Representing diversity and challenging racism: The Migration Museum' in ed. Sandell, R. *Museums, Society, Inequality*, Routlege, 142–52. Reproduced with permission.

Fforde, C. (2002) 'Collection, repatriation and identity' in eds Fforde, C., Hubert, J. and Turnbull, P. *The Dead and their Possessions: Repatriation in Principle, Policy and Practice*, Routledge, 34–46. Reproduced with permission.

Watkins, J. 'Yours, mine, or ours?' Copyright © 2001 from *The Future of the Past* by ed. Bray, T.L. New York, Garland Pub Inc., pp. 57–68. Reproduced by permission of Routledge/Taylor & Francis Group, LLC.

3. Museums and Identities

MacDonald, G.F. and Alsford, S. 'Canadian museums and the representation of culture in a multicultural nation' reproduced with permission from *Cultural Dynamics*, 7 (1) London, Sage Publications, copyright © 1995, pp. 15–36. By permission of Sage Publications Ltd.

Casey, D. (2001) 'Museums as agents for social and political change' *Curator*, vol. 44, no. 3, Walnut Creek, Altamira Press, 230–6. Reproduced by permission of the publisher.

Crooke, E. (2005) 'Museums, communities and the politics of heritage in Northern Ireland' in eds Littler, J. and Naidoo, R. *The Politics of Heritage: The Legacies of 'Race'*, Routledge, 237–55 (bibliography). Reproduced with permission.

Hill, R.W. (2001) 'Regenerating identity: repatriation and the Indian frame of mind,' copyright © 2001 from *The Future of the Past: Archaeologists, Native Americans and Repatriation* in ed. Bray, T.L. New York, Garland Pub Inc., pp. 127–38. Reproduced by permission of Routledge/Taylor & Francis Group, LLC.

Zamora, H. (2002) 'Identity and community, a look at four Latino museums' *Museum News*, vol. 81, no. 3, 36–41. Reproduced by permission of the publisher, American Association of Museums.

Marzio, P.C. (1991) 'Minorities and Fine-Arts museums in the United States' in eds Karp, I. and Lavine, S.D. *Exhibiting Cultures: The Poetics and Politics of Museum Display*, Smithsonian Institution Press, 121–7. Reproduced with permission.

Merriman, N. (1997) 'The Peopling of London project' in ed. Hooper-Greenhill, E. *Cultural Diversity: Developing Museum Audiences in Britain*, Leicester University Press, pp. 119–48. Reproduced by kind permission of the Continuum Publishing Group.

Golding, V. (2005) 'Inspiration Africa!' paper presented for ICME at Museums and Intangible Heritage ICOM 2004 general conference, Seoul, Korea, October 2–8, 2004. Reproduced with kind permission of the author and the National Folk Museum on behalf of the Korean Ministry of Culture.

4. Communities remembering and forgetting

Misztal, B.A. 'Memory experience', from Misztal, B.M. *Theories of Social Remembering*, copyright © 2003 Open University Press, 9–26, 162–80. Reproduced with the kind permission of the Open University Press/McGraw-Hill Publishing Company.

Lubar, S. (1997) 'Exhibiting Memories' in eds Henderson, A. and Kaeppler, A.L. *Exhibiting Dilemmas: Issues of Representation at the Smithsonian*, Smithsonian Institution Press, 15–27. Reproduced with permission.

Beresford, P. 'Past Tense'. Copyright © 1998 Mind, reprinted from *Openmind* issue 91 May/June 1998 by permission of Mind (National Association for Mental Health).

Green, A. (2006) 'The exhibition that speaks for itself: oral history and museums' in eds Perks, R. and Thomson, A. *The Oral History Reader*, 416–24, Routledge. Reproduced with permission.

Muzaini, H. and Yeoh, B. (2005) 'Contesting "local", commemoration of the Second World War: the case of the Changi Chapel and Museum in Singapore' *Australian Geographer*, March, vol. 36, no. 1, 1–17, http://www.tandf.co.uk/journals. Reproduced with permission.

Walsh, K. (2001) 'Collective amnesia and the mediation of painful pasts: the representation of France in the Second World War' *International Journal of Heritage Studies*, vol. 7, no. 1, 83–98, http://www.tandf.co.uk/journals. Reproduced with permission.

Jenkins, T. (2005) 'Victims remembered' *Museums Journal*, May, 22–23, 25. Reproduced by kind permission of the author.

Duffy, T. (1997) 'The Holocaust museum concept' *Museum International*, vol. 49, no. 1, 54–8, Blackwell Publishing. Reproduced by permission of the publisher.

McEachern, C. (1998) 'Mapping the memories: politics, place and identity in the District Six Museum, Cape Town' *Social Identities*, vol. 4, no. 3, 499–521, http://www.tandf.co.uk/journals. Reproduced with permission.

5. Challenges: museums and communities in the twenty-first century

Ashley, S. (2005) 'State authority and the public sphere: ideas on the changing role of the museum as a Canadian Social Institution' *Museum and Society*, vol. 3, no. 1, 5–17. Reproduced by kind permission of the author.

Van den Bosch, A. (2005) 'Museums constructing a public culture in the Golden Age' *Third Text*, issue 1, January, 81–9, http://www.tandf.co.uk/journals. Reproduced with permission.

Cuno, J. (1997) 'Money, power and the history of art' *Art Bulletin*, vol. 79, 6–9. Reproduced by kind permission of the author.

Peers, L. and Brown, A.K. (2003) 'Introduction' in eds Peers, L. and Brown, A.K. *Museums and Source Communities*, Routledge, 1–16, 252–73 (bibliography). Reproduced with permission.

Crosby, A. (2002) 'Archaeology and *vanua* development in Fiji' *World Archaeology*, vol. 34, no. 2, 363–78, http://www.tandf.co.uk/journals. Reproduced with permission.

I would also like to thank Professor Simon Knell of the Department of Museum Studies at the University of Leicester and Matthew Gibbons of Routledge for organising and facilitating the Reader. I am particularly grateful to Simon for his supportive comments throughout the development of this book, in particular for reading drafts of the introduction and for his invaluable insights. I would also like to thank my students and colleagues at the Department of Museum Studies for all their ideas and encouragement. Particular thanks go to Yoshiko Nishigori and Sarah King who undertook much of the work of locating suitable papers and to Susan Dixon, production editor, and Julene Knox, copy editor, who was also responsible for gathering all the permissions.

Museums and their Communities

Museum communities in theory and practice

MUSEUMS[1] 'possess a power to shape collective values and social understandings in a decisively important fashion' (Luke 2002: xiii).

Such shaping of ideas depends not only on visitors' individual senses of themselves and prior knowledge but also upon the perspectives, values and understandings of the communities to which they belong. Above all, however, it depends on the attitudes of those who work in museums towards the communities they serve.

Museums 'are living institutions' (Spalding 2002: 23). As such they are constantly changing and regularly revisiting their purposes. Weil has pointed out that in the United States (and one might add in many other countries) there is currently a shift in attitude towards museums. A museum is no longer only measured by its internal possessions such as collections, endowments, staff and facilities, but by 'an *external* consideration of the benefits it provides to the individuals and communities it seeks to serve' (Weil 2003: 42). For example, many museums within the United Kingdom are the beneficiaries of a range of extra funding sources from the Heritage Lottery Fund to Renaissance in the Regions (the Museums, Libraries and Archives Council's programme to invest money from central government in England's regional museums). None of these funds can be accessed without specific, demonstrable and measurable benefits to the public.

The shift in attitude towards museums by external public funders is summarised thus: 'The museum that does not prove an outcome to its community is as socially irresponsible as the business that fails to show a profit. It wastes society's resources' (Weil 2003: 43). This outcome should be no less than 'the positive and intended differences that it makes in the lives of the individuals and communities that constitute its target audiences' (Weil 2003: 53). While this accountability is to be welcomed there are inherent dangers within this approach as Weil himself acknowledges. All too often it is what can be measured that counts, not the long-term and important work on collections (Knell 2004: 11), or the difficult to define qualitative and incremental effects of museums upon individuals and groups. In England great strides have been made recently in the evaluation of educational and learning outcomes by using qualitative and quantitative methods (Hooper-Greenhill *et al.* 2004 and 2006) but these are mainly focussed on school-age children. While those seeking funding will often claim community benefits this is rarely demonstrated with detailed summative evaluation.

In the twenty-first century the word community has often become synonymous with goodness and moral standards but the term is infrequently defined. For example, the United Kingdom's Museums Association's *Code of Ethics*, to which all registered or accredited museums subscribe, provides an interesting snapshot of thinking about museums' relationships with their publics at the beginning of the twenty-first century. It states that 'Society can expect museums to: consult and involve communities, users and supporters', and 'promote a sense of shared ownership in the work of the museum' (Museums Association 2002: 12) and, at the same time, 'involve partners in decision-making' (ibid.: 13). However, it is not entirely clear what is meant by the term communities in this context.

The chapters in this volume consider the concept of the community in its various forms, national, regional and local, and explore some key issues relating to ownership, power, identity and memory that help us understand the complexities of the relationship between museums and the societies they serve.

First, a word about the title of the book. In his introduction to Karp, Mullen Kreamer and Lavine's *Museums and Communities: The Politics of Public Culture* (1992), Karp discussed how the original title to a conference 'Museums and *Their* Communities' (own emphasis) rested on the false assumption that the politics of 'museums and communities had easy solutions' and implied an 'acquisitive relationship' (Karp 1992: 2–3). Both the conference and the subsequent book were therefore renamed to avoid reproducing a relationship they had been designed to challenge. On reviewing and selecting chapters for this volume it became clear that such an 'acquisitive relationship' exists and it would be unrealistic to deny it.

Research and museum practice over the last decade and a half has served to demonstrate that this relationship is more difficult to understand and change than was, perhaps, once thought. For example, the sensitivity of museums to the pressures by vocal and well-organised members of a few communities has made some institutions understandably anxious to avoid public controversy and keen to consult with such groups. Thus the museum may well offer to share decision making with effectively led and managed pressure groups, or with communities that have a sense of grievance, understand museum politics, or are just easily identifiable and have formal structures with which museums can work. The issue that thus remains unresolved, and with which many chapters in this volume wrestle, is how can museums establish transparent, inclusive and fair relationships with all communities?

Thus the title of this book, while not intended to imply in any way 'an easy solution' to the relationships between museums and communities, acknowledges that many museums, however constituted, particularly those in receipt of public funding, still identify the communities they wish to work with and they exercise the power to represent *their* communities. The title also reflects a conscious decision to focus this volume mainly on museums that work with and for a variety of communities rather than those that arise from, belong to, and are controlled by, one particular community or group. It thus, on the whole, examines the relationship of the paid professional with communities.

The term museum is now used to include a wide range of heritage projects and community initiatives that bear little resemblance to the concept of an institution established to collect, conserve and exhibit material culture within its walls, and often includes intangible heritage and the natural and historic built environment (Davis 1999, this volume pp. 53–75, 2005). This extends the idea of the museum so that it is seen to be embedded in the lives of people (Tegomoh 2006). While some of the chapters in this volume refer to other ways of interpreting the idea of the museum (for example, Crooke 2005, Crosby 2002, Davis 1999, Hooper-Greenhill 2000), this reader is mainly concerned with the Western model of institutions with collections of material culture.

There are three themes that can help us disentangle some of the misunderstandings and assumptions that arise when museums and their stakeholders attempt to work with and for communities:

- the concept of the community and how this affects the way museums engage with their audiences
- knowledge and who controls it
- the museum as an institution in society and its purposes.

The three themes are complementary and interdependent. All five parts of the book deal with them in one way or another and the introduction to each part will attempt to provide an overview of these interlinking concepts and ideas.[2]

The concept of community

Museums in the twenty-first century often find it difficult to identify communities and their representatives. In what way does the community differ from the public, or a target audience? A sociological dictionary states that the term 'community is one of the most elusive and vague in sociology and is by now largely without specific meaning' (Abercrombie *et al.* 2000: 64). Davis agrees stating that '"the museum community" is . . . an almost meaningless expression', and that what we consider to be the community 'is hugely complex, a constantly changing pattern of the tangible and intangible' (Davis 1999: 30, this volume pp. 59–60).

However, for our purposes, let us accept that the essential defining factor of a community is the sense of belonging that comes to those who are part of it (Kavanagh 1990: 68) and that, through association with communities, individuals conceptualise identity. Such identities are relational and depend on a sense not only of self but also of others (Woodward 2002). Thus a community is essentially self-determined. As such, it may well have characteristics that are 'frequently idiosyncratic, even contradictory. As such it may well be defined simply in the eye and mind of the beholder or participant and will almost inevitably be multi-layered' (Kavanagh 1990:

68). It is not a target audience as such, though a museum may identify members of a community or communities as a target audience; nor is it 'the public', which is too general a term and within which there may be many different communities. We all belong to many different communities and our membership of these will change with time and circumstances. Some communities are ours by choice, some are ours because of the way others see us.

One useful way of conceptualising communities in order to understand the multiple meanings they make has been extended by Hooper-Greenhill (2000, this volume pp. 76–94), who has, within a museum setting, explored how collective public meanings depend on the interpretive communities to which individuals belong. These communities are 'located in relation to interpretive acts' (2000: 121, this volume p. 78) and are 'recognised by their common frameworks of intelligibility, interpretive repertoires, knowledge and intellectual skills' (2000: 122, this volume p. 79). Such communities are fluid and unstable, and people belong to more than one at any one time. Nevertheless, despite the difficulties inherent in identifying such communities, this concept is a useful one for museums. Witcomb's example of the Portuguese community exhibition in Perth, Australia, provides an interesting example of the way the community had different interpretation objectives and methodologies from those of the museum staff (Witcomb 2003, this volume pp. 133–56). It was, in effect, an interpretive community that had different conceptual frameworks from those of the museum professional.

Mason (2005: 206–7) suggests six ways of extending the concept of interpretive (interpretative) communities:

1   'Communities defined by shared historical or cultural experiences'
2   'Communities defined by their specialist knowledge'
3   'Communities defined by demographic/socio-economic factors'
4   'Communities defined by identities (national, regional, local or relating to sexuality, disability, age and gender)'
5   'Communities defined by their visiting practices'
6   'Communities defined by their exclusion from other communities'.

These definitions serve as a useful starting point for analysing the definition of the community and the role museums fulfil in society and with communities in particular.

1.   'Communities defined by shared historical or cultural experiences'

Such shared historical or cultural experiences depend on memory and the ordering of the act of remembrance. It is here that museums play a key role in not only preserving memories but also in re-ordering them and making sense of them for later generations. The role of museums in supporting individual and community memory is so important that there is a whole section of this book dedicated to this idea (Part Four).

If we take one experience, the Second World War, which remains one of the defining experiences of an older generation who lived through it, we can see the many ways in which individuals with shared memories use museums to validate their lives. The *Enola Gay* episode in the Smithsonian in 1995 (Luke 2002, this volume pp. 197–212) demonstrated very clearly a continuing sense of ownership by veterans over public interpretations of their wartime activities, and their desire to see the bombing of Hiroshima presented as commemoration of sacrifice and a victory rather than a time of suffering and the beginning of the Cold War. Here a community who had experienced the war consciously articulated their protest against those they saw as belonging to a different generation that did not understand their values and national narratives. Yet such community remembering is not dependent on personal experiences. Individuals born after the war can use museums as places where they remember their relatives' experiences of the war and contribute to a collective national memory (Lubar 1997, this volume pp. 397–405). The Holocaust and other wartime atrocities are remembered within museums as ways of articulating not only terrible past events so they are not repeated but also as ways of articulating community identity through suffering and oppression (Jenkins 2005, this volume pp. 448–51).

2. 'Communities defined by their specialist knowledge'

Many museums are devoted to subjects or events that appeal to a particular audience. While open to all, and usually keen to attract a wide section of society, these museums serve communities of interest who share specialist knowledge. Museums with a wide range of collections will often plan temporary exhibitions for target audiences with particular interest in, and knowledge of, the material culture or general theme that will be displayed. Such knowledge is often accompanied by preferred interpretive strategies that museums adopt, thus re-enforcing the separation of those who have such knowledge and those who do not. Bourdieu and Darbel's survey of visitors who frequent art galleries is a classic study of this phenomenon. They investigated why art galleries tend to attract visitors from a wealthier and better-educated background and they used theories of educational advantage and cultural capital to help to explain this (Bourdieu and Darbel 1997, originally 1969). Thus many museums seek to develop programmes and exhibitions to include those without the appropriate interpretive strategies and specialist knowledge, though this can be resented by those who already possess this understanding (O'Neill 2002a).

3. 'Communities defined by demographic/socio-economic factors'

This is the way many museums continue to identify their visitors: investigating age profiles, and general social groupings such as families, couples and social/economic background. Much of the research in this area is marketing led and linked directly to a better understanding of existing audiences to enable more effective targeting of publicity. These visitor profiles tell museums some basic information about the people they attract. However, while demographics and socio-economic factors can help museums target their audiences and understand why certain displays appeal to some and not others, it is doubtful whether this form of categorisation helps museums understand the complexities of the communities they serve.

4. 'Communities defined by identities (national, regional, local or relating to sexuality, disability, age and gender)'

The role museums play in supporting and defining community identity is so important that, as with memory, there is a whole section of this book devoted to an exploration of this topic (Part Three). One interesting issue explored by Witcomb, developing ideas from Bennett (1990, 1995, 1998), is whether museums, acting as agents of civic reform, construct community identity, whether in fact they are institutions 'which actually *produce* the very notion of community and culture' (Witcomb 2003: 80, this volume p. 134).

Identities are complex and difficult to define. When we begin to consider the multiple ways in which individuals and communities privilege a range of common factors that define the way they see themselves and are seen by others then we find that Mason's list is a useful starting point but is by no means exclusive. For example, identities are also linked to factors relating to social class, ethnicity and religion. MacDonald and Alsford (1995, this volume pp. 276–91) look at the issue of ethnicity and identity, and elsewhere this topic attracts considerable attention (for example, Littler and Naidoo 2005). Locating articles about religious identity in museums has, however, been more difficult.[3] In a secular Western society we rarely prioritise religious identities although in some areas such as Northern Ireland these Roman Catholic and Protestant community identities have been inescapably foregrounded in political disputes for generations, and museums have long had to work with Christian identities in conflict (Crooke 2001, 2005, this volume pp. 300–12). All too often this religious identity is made manifest by a few extremists who behave violently. For example, in the twenty-first century, 9/11 in America and terrorism in London in July 2005 have brought to the attention of the public and the media in a negative way a strong and complex version of Muslim identity that can transcend national boundaries. It is not surprising, given the history of Christian and Muslim extremism, that we are sometimes uncomfortable with the notion that religious belief can be a powerful agent of identity and community cohesion, particularly when it becomes politicised.

National identity has been one of the preferred and privileged forms of identity in the modern world and continues to exert a powerful influence on the way museums represent communities. Indeed museums are tools by which nations 'imagine' themselves (Anderson 1983). The museum as a means of supporting identity formation of nations was exported across the world by colonial powers. Globalisation has affected the way communities in different nations are encouraged to view themselves and museums are part of this process of global identity making (Prösler 1999). Some of the most bitter museum controversies in the last few years have centred around ways in which the histories of the hitherto excluded or marginalised have been incorporated into the national story (Casey 2001, this volume pp. 292–9). As nations become more multicultural and governments struggle to balance the need for national unity with the idea of the toleration of difference, museums become arenas where concepts of what it is to belong within a nation are explored and made explicit. Attitudes towards multiculturalism vary from nation to nation and are changing as the complexities of maintaining social cohesion and civic acceptance of differences become increasingly apparent in the twenty-first century. While 'multiculturalism has brought the natives home in the post-imperial countries, occasioning a need for the redefinition of citizenship' (Pieterse 1997: 124), that redefinition is constantly held up to scrutiny. One of the greatest challenges facing museums in the twenty-first century is how to exhibit the nation in an inclusive way and to recognise other forms of privileging identities such as religion. At the same time they frequently have to struggle to reconcile different ideas as to how the nation should present its actions to the world (Luke 2002, this volume pp. 197–212).

5. 'Communities defined by their visiting practices'

Hooper-Greenhill's analysis of the way the West commonly accepts the existence of five senses and yet privileges sight is useful here. Other peoples interact with objects in ways that allow them to use other senses such as intuition and emotion. For example, some Maori people regard objects as animate, and take them out of museums to participate in family and tribal rituals (Hooper-Greenhill 2000: 113). MacDonald and Alsford point out that the presentation of heritage artefacts and 'their isolation in display cases is in contradiction to the Native belief that such objects have no value or meaning except when employed in traditional expressions of a living culture' (MacDonald and Alsford 1995: 19, this volume p. 280).

6. 'Communities defined by their exclusion from other communities'

In the United Kingdom the term 'social exclusion' is used to refer to the way in which some groups or individuals suffer from multiple deprivation and are marginalised. Such people are often infrequent visitors to cultural and heritage sites. Museums have been encouraged to see themselves as agents of social inclusion (Sandell 1998, 2002, this volume pp. 95–113) and to develop programmes and exhibitions to support such communities in a range of imaginative ways, and this concept of the museum as an agent of the state promoting inclusiveness in society is considered further on pages 15–17 (this volume). Within this category of exclusion across the globe, we can, perhaps, place a range of communities, for example, mental health service users, who are often marginalised wherever they live. Beresford (1998: this volume p. 406) illustrates the complex issues surrounding museums' representation of such communities.

In addition to these useful categories we can add one other.

7. Communities defined by location

This is the way in which many museums define their communities. They often see themselves as working within and for a geographical place whether it is a region, city, town or rural district. This idea that the museum's community can be located in a defined space is so common that it is worth exploring it further. The more we think about it the more complex this idea of location appears to be. Some people can live in a place for a long time but still associate themselves with, and feel part of, a community in which they no longer live. The expatriate community during the British Empire lived out their lives in places far from Britain but many felt more part of the community of national origin than the community in which they lived and worked and among whom they often died. People continue more than ever before to move across the globe, living and working in places to which they feel only temporary affiliation. Home is somewhere else. With numerous opportunities to network internationally through the digital revolution, communities can be worldwide. In addition the development of media technology has provided museums with opportunities to support the creation of 'virtual communities' that have been defined as 'social aggregations that emerge from the Net when enough people carry on those public discussions long enough, with sufficient human feeling, to form Webs of personal relationships in cyberspace' (Rheingold 1994 cited in von Appen *et al.* 2006: 6).[4]

However, there are many people who associate themselves with the place in which they currently live. They express this sense of community in a variety of ways, which might include supporting a local football team or taking pride in something that makes their village, town, city or nation unique. Their identities are embedded in a sense of place (Ashworth and Graham 2005). While museums may well decide to collect material culture from those who live in a specific locality, their collecting policy might preclude this type of collecting if it specifies (as many collecting policies do) that objects should have a specific local significance, for example, manufacture, before being accepted into the collections. However, people pick up material possessions from all over the place. When a museum wishes to represent a community in a specific location it will need to be flexible about its collecting policies as the Tyne and Wear Museums in the North of England were when they asked people to donate five items to represent 'significant events, people or moments in their lives' (Findlay 2000: 10).

The idea of location is frequently linked to time. Communities identify themselves by the length of time they have resided in a particular place, and museums help support this type of community identity by constructing displays of groups of people located within a particular period or time frame.

Knowledge and power

There are some museums that develop directly from the community they serve. They may represent particular groups who feel ignored or misrepresented elsewhere. Examples include some of the African American museums such as the Anacostia Museum, which 'emerged from efforts on the part of that community to create a museum to serve their specific needs' (Crew 1996: 83). Others are created out of a desire to save some elements of a vanishing life or industry within a specific location. One such is True's Yard Fishing Heritage Museum in King's Lynn, Norfolk, which opened in 1993. It was founded to collect and store objects and stories relating to a fishing community in the North End of King's Lynn. Led by a charismatic volunteer, a small group of enthusiasts worked tirelessly to raise funds and develop a museum in their midst, a museum that provided a range of services to the community, including education courses, and opportunities to participate in saving something that the community perceived as being lost. Other museums are run by communities of interest, such as the Narrow Gauge Railway Museum in North Wales. Many such museums receive state or local government funding; others do not. Some have a curator or manager, others run entirely without any formal professional or paid help. They are testimony to the desire of people not only to preserve some-thing that means a great deal to them but also to display it to others. Those who work professionally in the sector sometimes support them with advice rather than working directly for them. However, many of these museums, whatever their com-munity origins, depend on some kind of external funding. The Anacostia Museum was set up by the Smithsonian. True's Yard Museum, supported from the start by the local authority, now has a professional museums manager funded, in part, by the Borough Council. The Narrow Gauge Railway Museum receives grants from a variety of sources including the National Assembly for Wales. Once such museums move beyond self-sufficiency their links with their communities of origin usually remain strong but power often shifts from the community to the museum as an institution when paid staff undertake some of the work previously done by volunteers. This shift of power does not always happen but it is a common con-sequence of a museum's need to be sustainable once the initial enthusiasm and driving force of the founder members have waned. Thus much of this reader is con-cerned with the notion of the museum as a powerful institution, how museums often struggle to understand the relationships they have with their communities and how difficult they find it to share the power they have.

The relationship museums have with their communities must be based on the recognition that this is an unequal one, with the balance of power heavily tipped in favour of the institution. Understanding the nature of that authority goes some way towards helping us understand the relationships museums have with their publics. Museums have influence far beyond their walls. They support and help to create cultural identity and make explicit values for individuals, communities and nations (Davis 1999, this volume pp. 53–75; Prösler 1999; Newman and McLean 2002; Macdonald 1998, this volume pp. 176–96 and 1999; Hooper-Greenhill 2001; Mason 2004; Weil 2002, this volume pp. 32–46; Halpin 1997, this volume pp. 47–52; Durrans 1993). Thinking about museums has been greatly influenced by the work of Derrida and Foucault. Derrida questioned the stability of meanings and postu-lated that these are multiple and always conditioned by past interpretations and pre-sent conditions (Green and Troup 1999: 299, after Patterson 1989, Kamuf 1991, Sarup 1993). Foucault examined the way in which power operates throughout society to provide 'official or dominant knowledges which impart power to those who know and speak them' (Green and Troup 1999: 302; Foucault 1984). These theories encouraged museums to engage critically with some fundamental assump-tions about their presumed impartiality. 'It has been argued that systems of power and authority, and validated forms of artistic and cultural expression traditionally affirm the dominant ideology' (Harrison 1993: 172). Macdonald asserts that '"Knowledge" here does not only mean that which is displayed in an exhibition as formal knowledge, of course. It also includes the knowledges (including unreflected upon assumptions) of different parties involved in exhibition-making, their attempts to, for example, gather knowledge about visitors, and the under-standings of visitors themselves' (Macdonald 1998: 3, this volume p. 178). Appleton (2001, this volume pp. 114–26) has pointed out that such ideas, expressed through a variety of forms, for example, as post-colonialism and postmodernism, are rarely challenged. To her, Foucauldian theories are 'especially pernicious' (Appleton 2001: 16, this volume p. 116), and damaging of museum professionals' confidence in scholarship and the pursuit of knowledge. 'For the cultural left, the claim to objective knowledge was no more than an attempt by the establishment to assert its intellectual hegemony' (Appleton 2001: 15, this volume p. 115).

Appleton's views are a useful reminder that the dominant thinking in museum literature about power and objectivity is not accepted by all. Nevertheless there is widespread agreement that museums are political. They are understood to represent those who have privileges in society, i.e., the educated, the relatively wealthy, those who are in control either through their status, such as museum owners, governors, trustees, professionals and consultants, or through their direct political power, such as elected councillors or representatives of grant-giving bodies managed by the state. Yet, as Macdonald points out, politics is more than the role of individuals or groups within a decision-making process but lies in 'the architecture of buildings, the classification and juxtaposition of artefacts in an exhibition', and the methods of display (Macdonald 1998: 3, this volume p. 178). Hooper-Greenhill sums it up thus: 'Subjectivity, meaning, knowledge, truth and history are the materials of cultural politics and especially in their inter-relationships with power; the power to name, to represent common sense, to create official versions, to represent the social world and to represent the past' (Hooper-Greenhill 2001: 2). It is not surprising that some people in society, and some groups and communities, are either not represented at all in museums or find that the objects and the stories they tell in some museums depict only part of their view of the world, or misunderstand it.

Museums may no longer be seen by academics as the purveyors of objective truth (MacDonald and Alsford 1995: 15, this volume p. 276) but in practice they still command great respect. Anyone who has dealt with general enquiries in a museum soon learns that the museum is perceived to be the repository not only of objects but also of uncontested knowledge. In a postmodern world the curator's expertise will sometimes be challenged but such challenges usually come from within the museum profession and academia rather than from the communities museums serve. There are exceptions, for example, the controversies that surrounded exhibitions such as The Last Act about the Enola Gay (Luke 2002, this volume pp. 197–212), The Spirit Sings and Into the Heart of Africa (MacDonald and Alsford 1995, this volume pp. 276–91), and they usually relate to curatorial power to represent communities in a specific way. Indigenous communities, concerned with the manner in which Western museums represent them and their culture, pose a particular challenge to museum professionals. The conflicts that occur illustrate how difficult it can be for the latter to understand how communities see themselves and wish to be perceived by others. Sensitive methodologies for consulting and working with community groups are needed if museum staff are to understand and respond to the way meanings are constructed and developed.

We should not underestimate the very real difficulties museums have when they seek to change the balance of power in the relationship they have with communities (Witcomb 2003, this volume pp. 133–56). Communities can feel that museums are not relevant to them if they do not find within them a sense of their own history, identity and belonging, because they have not been invited to contribute to the collecting and exhibiting process or because museums are geographically distant. Working with communities either inside museum walls or in the form of outreach activities can be seen as some kind of way of broadening the power sharing and of making museums more relevant to more people. However, the process of such museum practice is fraught with practical and theoretical problems and does not necessarily shift power to the community in any realistic manner. Sometimes it merely provides a privileged group within the community with control and excludes others.

Any such power sharing is negotiated and the museum usually retains overall control of the messages and the medium delivering them. There is always the temptation to edit community input to make it more coherent, less controversial or more commercial. Merriman, in the Museum of London's Peopling of London Project, raises the problem of working with 'a large number of communities and a huge time-span' and argues that 'a reasonably strong degree of direction and central editorial control was required to co-ordinate the many different aspects of the project' (Merriman 1997: 131, this volume p. 344). He acknowledges that while there was a great deal of positive comment, some communities were disappointed that there was no specific section of the exhibition devoted to them. They preferred a separatist rather than an inclusive approach (1997: 144, this volume p. 354). Communities wanted to emphasise their positive contribution and did not want negative or contentious ideas explored (1997: 130, this volume pp. 343–4). For them the museum was an opportunity to celebrate their identity publicly. In the Canadian Museum of Civilization there is an open acknowledgement that the museum will present a particularly positive view of group identities. 'To date it has focused on presentations of a celebratory character, in the belief that an individual's first experience of his or her cultural heritage in a museum should be a positive one that fosters cultural self-esteem, confidence in the institution and motivation for further learning' (MacDonald and Alsford 1995: 29, this volume p. 288).

It can be very difficult to negotiate between competing versions of histories among communities and across generations (Szekeres 2002: 145, this volume p. 237). Dubin (1999, this volume pp. 213–27) considers the difficulties experienced in America by museums when they encounter strong objections from specific community groups to exhibitions. He considers the argument that while curators are not impartial, once they have consulted with interested parties, they should be allowed to curate exhibitions as they like. There is a great deal to be said for the curator as the individual who negotiates meanings and attempts to act as an independent arbiter, otherwise the strongest view will prevail and some groups, individuals and communities will be disenfranchised. Yet, this curatorial control and belief in im-partiality is not without contestation. Who decides whose version and voice will be included and whose excluded? It is easier when there is a consensus but even then this might not result in dispassionate and objective curatorial decisions.

Empowerment of one group to allow them to control not only knowledge (the stories told and the manner of their telling) but also access to that knowledge can result in other groups being disempowered. There are laudable attempts by museum professionals to support indigenous peoples' rights to control material culture originally from their ancestors as a way of dealing with the legacy of colonisation, 'bolster cultural identity and foster healing' (Peers and Brown 2003: 5–6, this volume p. 524). However, occasionally this results in the restriction of material.

Denial of access can be made on the grounds of ethnicity, gender, status or all three factors. For example, in Australia certain indigenous materials can now only be seen by 'senior male figures with kinship claims' (Jones 1998: 35). There is little debate as to whether such restrictions are acceptable to those upon whom they are placed and some women may be uncomfortable with these controls, although for some male indigenous Australians the decision to deny women access to this material is an important part of their sense of identity and acknowledges their cultural values. It also goes some way towards providing them with some power over the representation of themselves by others.

Szekeres (2002, this volume p. 234) offers a model where museum staff hand over a temporary exhibition space to community groups for them to create their own representations of themselves in a Community Access Gallery. Yet, even handing over a gallery to a community group does not necessarily result in the empowerment of more than a few individuals. One of the challenges facing museums working with communities is how to determine that the spokespeople for the group represent the majority view. 'Museums which exhibit community histories – such as the histories of immigrant groups in America or Britain – are not beyond contestation. Even though they may reflect community values more adequately than any outsider view no community is homogeneous. Different generation cohorts, for instance, hold different perspectives' (Pieterse 1997: 134). An American curator, Ed O'Donnell, writing from experience, comments that 'there's a segment that has a strong sense of itself, and begins to speak for the group. Those subgroups tend to be more motivated and more organized while most [other] people are out there trying to put food on the table and go through everyday life. [This privileging of identity] is not their burning passion' (Dubin 1999: 238, this volume p. 220). There is a temptation to work with such people, if only because they are accessible and usually want to work with museums. They do not necessarily represent the views of others but only themselves.

The institution of the museum

Reflections on knowledge and power have influenced thinking about the way in which museums function as social institutions and thus help us understand their relationship with communities. It is accepted that museums mirror the beliefs of the society in which they have developed as well as influencing that society's view of itself. Collections and their interpretation imply a 'set of social relations' (Duncan and Wallach 1980: 456). They also operate within a society that is organised through a range of other institutions and associations besides those of the community in what has been described as 'civil society' (Karp 1992: 4). Museums, as Davis (1999, this volume p. 53) reminds us, are places in which cultural identity is exposed and debated. Exhibitions reveal as much about those who create and curate them as their subjects. The idea that museums represent impartial knowledge is, as we have seen, discredited.

The Western concept of the museum is not necessarily relevant to many communities both within the developed world and outside it. However, Simpson (1996, this volume p. 157) examines the way in which indigenous peoples in Australia and

New Zealand have developed the concept of the museum to benefit their own lifestyles and support their own cultures and identities. For some Australian Aboriginal communities the museum offers an opportunity to tell a story of 'cultural genocide' (Simpson 1996: 127) and dispossession. Simpson's chapter suggests that this story is relatively uncontentious when it is confined within the parameters of Aboriginal museums (although there were some complaints). It is interesting to contrast this apparent acceptance of this version of the founding of modern Australia with the furore caused when a similar version was included in the National Museum of Australia (Casey 2001, this volume p. 292).

Within the developed world it sometimes appears as though an awareness of the need for museums to take account of a range of communities is relatively new, dating from social changes after the Second World War. The radical politics of the 1960s encouraged museum professionals to be more aware of the social purpose of museums and to examine their role in society generally (Davis 1999: 52). This shift in attitudes is complex and is sometimes described as 'new museology'. While definitions of this term vary from country to country, at its simplest, if we understand 'old museology' to be characterised by an emphasis on the professional collection, documentation and interpretation of objects, then 'new museology' is community focussed with the emphasis on community needs (Vergo 1989; Harrison 1993; Witcomb 2003: 79, this volume p. 133; Mason 2004: 60). 'The new museology specifically questions traditional museum approaches to issues of value, meaning, control, interpretation, authority and authenticity' (Van Mensch 1995 from Stam, quoted in Davis 1999: 55). One consequence of this change in thinking was the rise of the concept of the ecomuseum, particularly in France, where power, in theory, is devolved to the local population and the emphasis is on community ownership and the wider environment (Davis 1999: 75).

However, museums have been engaged with communities for a long time. The idea that museums should and can act in the service of different communities within society for their greater good has a long and honourable history. There have been many experiments testing and exploring the role museums can play for the communities they serve. For example, in the early twentieth century, community museums engaged with their constituents in a wide variety of innovative ways in America (Alexander 1996; Halpin 1997, this volume p. 47). We do not have to look too hard to go further back in time than this.

Museums reflect the concerns of the society in which they are located, and their relationship with the communities they serve is renegotiated and reinvented as their purposes develop and change, as the following case study illustrates. In the United Kingdom one of the earliest public art galleries was established during the 1740s, in the Foundling Hospital in London, through the endeavours of William Hogarth. The Foundling Hospital was the idea of his colleague, a philanthropist, Thomas Coram, who was shocked to see babies abandoned and dying in London's streets. Most of these children were illegitimate. Few wished to support Coram's endeavours to set up a refuge for them, such was the stigma of illegitimacy and the fear that any charitable endeavour aimed at relieving the destitute mothers and children would encourage immorality. If the enterprise were to succeed it would need the support of wealthy patrons who at first shunned it. However, Hogarth matched the need for a public exhibition space among living artists with the hospital's need for society's acceptance. He persuaded many of his contemporaries in the art world such as Gainsborough and Reynolds to donate their pictures, which formed the nucleus of a contemporary art collection to which the public flocked in large numbers. Once in the hospital they not only admired the art, they also donated money. At the same time the hospital raised money through concerts in its chapel, many of which were organised and conducted by Handel. The art gallery and the concerts were established for the purpose of supporting the weakest and most vulnerable outcasts in society. The collection remained largely intact, and much of it can be seen in the Foundling Museum, opened in 2004, to provide 'a testament to the vulnerability of children and the imperative for their care, through history and into the future' (Harris 2004: 5).

Art on the walls of the Foundling Hospital was not exhibited for the purpose of educating the foundlings in the principles of fine art appreciation. Their education was basic and designed to render them fit for their lives of serviceable toil. Indeed, the children themselves became, in time, objects. An engraving from *The Illustrated London News* of 7 December 1872[5] depicted wealthy families visiting the Foundling Hospital on Sundays to view the pictures, and the children having lunch. Nevertheless, art was there to serve a purpose beyond those of being seen and for artists to be acknowledged. Hogarth understood the political power of museums. Art helped to make the foundlings respectable. It also brought in much-needed income (Uglow 1997). As such it was an unusually early example of the ways in which museums can provide tangible and intangible benefits to communities (here the foundlings). However, it is also an example of the way in which institutions (here a mixture of museum and children's home) represent communities without consultation. Here the foundlings were to be seen as the product of immorality to be redeemed through Christian charity and a life of patient but lowly service in society. Only in the most recent reincarnation of Coram's and Hogarth's vision, the new Foundling Museum, is there an attempt through oral testimony from some of the last foundlings from the 1940s and 1950s, literally to allow these children a voice so they can represent themselves.

While we applaud the constructive way in which the arts were used to support the poorest in society we now find it shocking to exhibit living children in this manner, and to display them overtly as an educational experience, a moral example. Similarly museums now try to avoid displays which represent people as stereotypes or examples of backwardness, immorality or other unattractive attributes. Over the last few decades many museums have become much more aware of the way they represent individuals and groups, particularly those from indigenous communities, including them in exhibition and collecting processes so that they become equal partners and not the exoticised 'other' (Peers and Brown 2003, this volume p. 519). Minority community groups and indigenous peoples are also increasingly assertive in demanding that this representation is not undertaken without their consent and only with their input.

While museums increasingly consult with such groups, power, as we have seen, still rests firmly with the museum. Moreover, some museums rarely consider it important or necessary to consult with majority communities. While many local history museums in the United Kingdom show sensitivity towards their local communities and engage in various types of consultation when developing their displays, others do not. At best they obtain some oral history stories on topics pre-determined by a display team meeting. Hooper-Greenhill's concept of the post-museum with its 'many voices and many perspectives', where 'the voice of the museum is one among many', is difficult to realise, but optimistically she argues that solutions will result in new ways of working (Hooper-Greenhill 2000: 152, this volume p. 82). Certainly there are some exceptional museums now engaging with varied communities and sharing the decision-making processes.

For all the new museological theory, professionally run museums rarely relinquish all power to their stakeholders, although some are exhibiting increased willingness to do so (Ashley 2005: 11, this volume p. 493). It is here that we can see the political nature of museums, for all publicly funded museums in the developed world reflect the aspirations of the state. For example, they are expected to construct rather than just represent a culturally diverse society and produce 'the notion of community' (Witcomb 2003: 82, this volume p. 136). Until recently any community in the UK wishing publicly to express itself as opposed to multi-culturalism would be unlikely to be given a museum platform in which to do so. However, at the time of writing in 2006 Ruth Kelly, Labour's Secretary of State for Communities and Local Government, has queried whether multiculturalism 'is encouraging separateness' (Woodward 2006: 7) and it will be interesting to see how such debates are reflected by museums. Nevertheless, before we ascribe too much power to museums in their role in constructing societies, let us remember, as Sandell points out, citing Hooper-Greenhill, visitors may resist or question purposefully inclusive displays and make contrary meanings (Sandell 2002: 15, this volume pp. 104–5). Until further research is carried out into this, it is unlikely that we will understand whether museums significantly influence community cohesion or not.

Sandell points out that in the nineteenth century there was a notion of the museum as an 'instrument for positive social change' (Sandell 1998: 408), but he also comments that notwithstanding this imperative, museums excluded certain groups and continue to do so. The gathering momentum for museums to demonstrate their responsibilities towards society, and thus to identify and support a range of community groups that might otherwise be reluctant or unable to access their services, is a direct result of political pressure, linked to financial incentives. Museums in the developed world argue among themselves about the relative merits of this approach to museum purposes. Some of the most acrimonious debates are about the prioritisation of resources. Visitors to British museums are still predominantly from the relatively prosperous and more highly educated social classes (MLA 2004). The need to widen access to museums has long been a concern within the museum profession and in 1997 British political agendas prioritised poorer individuals and groups. The Labour government in 2000 published policy guidance on social inclusion for all DCMS (Department of Culture, Media and Sport) funded and local authority museums in England, highlighting the role the government anticipated museums playing in combating social exclusion (DCMS 2000). Social exclusion occurs 'when individuals or areas suffer from a combination of linked problems such as unemployment, poor skills, low incomes, poor housing, high crime environments, bad health and family breakdown' (Social Exclusion Unit 2004: 1). Such individuals inevitably find it difficult to benefit from educational and cultural opportunities.

Sandell provides some examples of ways in which museums can 'engage with and impact upon social inequality, disadvantage and discrimination' (Sandell 2002: 4, this volume p. 96) working with individuals, communities and for society as a whole in an attempt to create a more inclusive society, thus foregrounding 'the value of community diversity (Sandell 2002: 10, this volume p. 102).

Museums have been encouraged to support the Labour government's attempts to combat social exclusion through funding sources such as the Heritage Lottery Fund and Resource[6] (now MLA) (Resource 2001). They are also encouraged to enter into partnerships with other organisations to help regenerate deprived areas (Resource 2002). Cultural projects have long been integral to urban regeneration schemes designed to support communities whose economies have been devastated by de-industrialisation or by the changing economic consequences of globalisation. Cultural regeneration has embraced the concept of the museum as a means of attracting middle-class visitors into areas of poor housing and high unemployment. Such schemes can be seen as a way of raising the low self-esteem of local residents. Some museums are linked directly to a lost industry and its devastated community. Big Pit, the National Coal Museum in Wales, uses ex-miners to interpret working practices lost when the mine was closed. Art galleries, such as the Guggenheim, Bilbao, provide flagship icons of a city's determination to develop a tourist economy and rebrand itself. Museums are partners in regeneration schemes across the globe and, as such, at best, they represent the aspirations not only of the organisations promoting regeneration but also of the people living where they are sited. At worst they are imposed upon communities already fragmented and dislocated by change.

Not all regeneration projects involve landmark buildings and large-scale economic regeneration. In Fiji community groups worked with museums and other regeneration partners to develop archaeological eco-tourism. Although the process of consultation and community collaboration was not straightforward, nevertheless progress was made in providing the communities of the islands with a sense of ownership and pride in their history and archaeology, along with improved economic prospects (Crosby 2002, this volume p. 538). Glasgow's Greater Pollock Kist scheme, part of the city's strategy of regeneration through culture, provided opportunities for communities to curate exhibitions in their own localities (Barnard 2002, this volume p. 554).

Changes to museum priorities have evoked some anxiety and much debate, not just among those concerned with income targets (O'Neill 2002b; Appleton 2001, this volume p. 114). Articles in the British national press question the validity of what is seen as 'politically correct' museum policies (Delingpole 2006: 5). Many within the museum sector still continue to regard the 'processes of collection, preservation and display, not as functions through which the organisation creates social value, but as outcomes in their own right' (Sandell 2002: xvii). Some museum professionals remain defensively protective of their traditional expertise and their roles and are reluctant to change their customary curatorial practices. They fear excluding their existing audiences if they include new ones (Butler 2001). Some writers condemn this as self-seeking. 'Currently, curators tend to think of collections in terms of their own interests, not those of their visitors' (Spalding 2002: 80). One would like to think that this was not true of most museum professionals. Within the museum community itself there is considerable support for focussing on the purpose of the museum rather than the interest of those who work within it. There is also a realisation that a debate that pitches objects against people is unproductive and is a perspective based on 'a utopian curatorial past which never existed' (O'Neill 2002b: 20).

Future challenges

Museums throughout the world face similar challenges when they seek to work with their communities. Even those museums that are established and run by volunteers with little or no professional input face difficulties. Trustees and other volunteers are often representative of a small section of the population, often older, wealthier and with higher formal levels of education than many of the rest of the community.

Yorkshire Museums, Libraries and Archives Council produced a Toolkit for improving practice.[7] It identifies a number of principles of involvement relating to access to archives that provide a useful starting point for considering how museums can also best manage these challenges.

- The necessity of understanding the community/communities you are working with – composition, needs, priorities, tensions, strengths, existing networks, etc.
- The need for partnership working and resourcing participation at all stages of the process and the need for recognition of long-term involvement.
- Sensitivity around accountability and representation structures – building groups/structures that strengthen communities rather than divide them.
- The need for a wider range of ways in which people can participate – creating some community ownership and control.
- The need for clarity and recognition of influence, e.g., evidence that communities have been heard.
- The recognition that people participate from a variety of starting points and cultural experience and that this has implications for how people learn and contribute. (CAAP 2004: 41)

However, such a list is only a beginning. Practitioners know how difficult this work can be. Identifying and working with one community can lead to alienation and exclusion of others. Traditionally in the United Kingdom museums have adopted a variety of methods of representing communities. Temporary exhibitions and special events often focus on groups not perceived to be represented in permanent displays. Building on marketing ideas, museums tend to segment their offers. They believe that they have a product which needs to be packaged and sold to the target group or groups. This policy is now being questioned as possibly divisive.[8] Merriman and Poovaya-Smith have pointed out the difficult balancing act that museums undertake when they seek to redress previous neglected communities with targeted exhibitions and in so doing they 'can also run the risk of institutionalizing their marginalization as "the other"' (Merriman and Poovaya-Smith 1996: 183). Museums, more than ever before, have to work carefully with all their constituencies.

In a world where mobility is more common there are often areas where there is 'a continuing exodus of more established residents alongside newcomers making social relations far more uncertain' (CAAP 2004: 29). Communities become fragmented. Old allegiances compete with new ones. It is not always the existing communities that exclude the newcomers. New groups, whether they are defined by wealth, poverty, ethnic group, class, religion or interests, can marginalise existing groups, which leads to tensions, confusion, disillusionment with political systems and demoralisation. Targeting some communities and not others can lead to resentment. Wealthy, majority, socially powerful and articulate groups as well as poorer, minority ones can feel excluded and marginalised by some types of programmes and exhibitions. Antagonism towards the museum and the incomers can result (Szekeres 2002: 150, this volume p. 242). Shifting perspectives and attitudes within communities are equally complex and potentially divisive. Museums are often on the front line of these changes. They are the public face of power struggles and can validate claims to resources, re-enforce or ignore community identities and have to negotiate carefully between competing groups.

In 1992 Karp raised some of the issues museums faced when working with communities and posed a question about the moral dilemma that confronts museums when one community makes a request that 'will inevitably oppress another community' (Karp 1992: 10). This question has not been resolved and is a cause of pain (Bordage 1993, this volume p. 228). What oppresses or offends a community is complex and dependent on power relations not only between the museum and its communities but also between those communities and the nation state in which they reside. As we have seen, identity is about difference, and one community's identity will often foreground past or present disputes with others. For many museum workers such complex issues require not only good consultation skills but also, inevitably, some exercise of power over community representation. Such issues require visionary leadership and good management.

Communities are fluid and change regularly. Increasingly, museums recognise they need to respond quickly to community needs and they cannot always work effectively alone. Liaison and collaboration with a range of other organisations with skills and expertise, as well as links to specific communities often widen museum access to different social groups and vice versa. However, exhibitions, outreach programmes and similar activities all require a relatively long run in time particularly if they are to be developed in partnership with formal groups that will often have different agendas from the museum.

Moreover, working with all kinds of communities takes time and patience. Very often a museum professional visiting a group will reap no immediate reward for the museum nor for the community the group represents. Developing good relationships takes years and requires patience and good listening skills. Implicit in all this is the issue of social relationships. Museums do not work with communities but with individuals within those communities. Those individuals do not establish partnerships with the museum but with individuals within that institution. Writing about indigenous Australians working with museums, Field points out that 'social relationships are very important and for people undertaking consultations or short term projects, establishing their personal credentials over time may exceed the life of their project and their resources' (Field et al. 2000: 43).

Working with existing formal groups may not be enough. They are self-selecting and often politically active and do not necessarily reflect the needs and aspirations of the majority. Consultation with individuals, whether brought together in groups, or on a one-to-one basis, will help museums understand the needs of the communities they serve (Watson 1999, 2000).

No one reading the chapters in this volume will underestimate the problems museums face in the twenty-first century in their attempts to work effectively with communities, supporting diverse identities and satisfying multiple needs and expectations, many of which are economic and political as well as social. The fact that such issues are debated so fiercely suggests that solutions are difficult and rarely uncontested. Despite these challenges, or perhaps because of them, museums are some of the most dynamic and interesting institutions to study and in which to work.

Notes

1   Museums and art galleries are the subject of this book. The word museum should be understood to embrace both the traditional museum and the art gallery and art museum.

2   There are certain areas relating to museums' relationships with their communities that this book does not attempt to explore in depth, although they are considered in various chapters. These include the repatriation of human remains, restitution of cultural materials and the development of community and educational outreach programmes. These topics are covered by other volumes in this series of readers.

3   There are, of course, exceptions that prove the rule. Anyone interested in religious identities and communities will find several useful papers in Paine (2000). Paine is also one of the editors of *Material Religion: the Journal of Objects, Art and Belief*, first published in March 2005.

4   This concept of virtual community and museums, and new technologies are covered by another reader in this series.

5   Illustrated in Wedd (2004: 34) from whom much of the information about the history of the hospital has been taken. See also Uglow 1997: 430.

6   Resource, renamed the Museums, Libraries and Archives Council (MLA) in 2004, is the lead strategic agency working for and on behalf of museums, libraries and archives, which advises government on policy and priorities for the sector.

7   'Community Involvement in MALs (Museums, Archives and Libraries): Toolkit for improving practice', COGS for Yorkshire Museums Council, 2002, cited in *Final Report, Community Access to Archives Project* (CAAP), October 2004: 41.

8   *Diversify* Programme, May 2005, Museums Association training day, Birmingham, posed this question.

References

Abercrombie, N., Hill, S. and Turner, B. (2000) *The Penguin Dictionary of Sociology*, London: The Penguin Group.

Alexander, E.P. (1996) 'The Museum as cultural center and social instrument', in E.P. Alexander *Museums in Motion: An Introduction to the History and Functions of Museums*, Walnut Creek, California: Altamira Press, 215–29.

Anderson, B. (1983) *Imagined Communities: Reflections on the Origin and Spread of Nationalism*, London: Verso.

Appleton, J. (2001) 'Museums for "The People"?' in Appleton *et al. Museums for the People?* London: Institute of Ideas, 14–26.

Ashley, S. (2005) 'State authority and the public sphere: ideas on the changing role of the museum as a Canadian Social Institution', *Museum and Society*, vol. 3, no. 1, March 2005, 5–17.

Ashworth, G.J. and Graham, B. (2005) 'Senses of place, senses of time and heritage' in G.J. Ashworth and B. Graham (eds) *Senses of Place: Senses of Time*, Aldershot: Ashgate, 3–12.

Barnard, M. (2002) 'Kist and tell', *Museums Journal*, vol. 102, no. 2, February 2002, 36–7.

Bennett, T. (1990) 'The political rationality of the museum', *Continuum*, vol. 3, no. 1, 35–55.

Bennett, T. (1995) *The Birth of the Museum: History, Theory, Politics*, London: Routledge.

Bennett, T. (1998) *Culture: A Reformer's Science*, London: Routledge.

Bordage, R. (1993) 'Sachsenhausen: a flawed museum', *Museum International*, 177, vol. XLV, no. 1, 26–31.

Bourdieu, P. and Darbel, A. (1997) *The Love of Art: European Art Museums and their Public*, Cambridge: Polity Press (first published 1969).

Butler, T. (2001) 'Man of the people', *Museums Journal*, vol. 101, no. 1, January 2001, 18–19, 21.

CAAP (2004) *Community Access to Archives Project Final Report*, October 2004, National Archives.

Casey, D. (2001) 'Museums as agents of social and political change', *Curator*, vol. 44, no. 3, July 2001, 230–6.

Crew, S. (1996) 'African Americans, history and museums: preserving African American history in the public arena', in G. Kavanagh (ed.) *Making Histories in Museums*, London: Routledge, 80–91.

Crooke, E. (2001) 'Confronting a troubled history: which past in Northern Ireland's museums?' *International Journal of Heritage Studies*, vol. 7, no. 2, 2001, 119–36.

Crooke, E. (2005) 'Museums, communities and the politics of heritage in Northern Ireland', in J. Littler and R. Naidoo (eds) *The Politics of Heritage: The Legacies of 'Race'*, London: Routledge, 69–81.

Crosby, A. (2002) 'Archaeology and *vanua* development in Fiji', *World Archaeology*, vol. 34, no. 2, October 2002, 363–78.

Davis, P. (1999) *Ecomuseums: A Sense of Place*, London: Leicester University Press.

Davis, P. (2005) 'Places, "cultural touchstones" and the ecomuseum', in G. Corsane (ed.) *Heritage, Museums and Galleries*, Abingdon: Routledge, 365–76.

DCMS (2000) *Centres for Social Change: Museums, Galleries and Archives for All*, London: DCMS.

Delingpole, J. (2006) 'Ouch! Is this the direction our museums have to go?' *The Times*, 18 March 2006, 25 (full text available on www.timesonline/comment).

Dubin, S.C. (1999) 'The postmodern exhibition', in S.C. Dubin *Displays of Power: Memory and Amnesia in the American Museum*, New York and London: New York University Press, 227–45.

Duncan, C. and Wallach, A. (1980) 'The universal survey museum', *Art History*, vol. 3, no. 4, 448–69.

Durrans, B. (1993) 'Cultural identity and museums', in E. Southworth (ed.) *Picking up the Pieces, Adapting to change in Museums and Archaeology*, special issue of *The Museum Archaeologist*, vol. 18, Conference Proceedings, Sheffield, 1991, Liverpool: Society of Museum Archaeologists, 42–55.

Field *et al.* (2000) '"Coming back". Aborigines and archaeologists at Cuddie Springs', *Public Archaeology*, vol. 1, 35–48.

Findlay, G. (2000) 'Making history: your story, your lifetime', in *Social History Curators Group News*, 46, April, 10–12.

Foucault, M. (1984) 'Truth and power', in P. Rabinow (ed.) *The Foucault Reader*, London: Penguin Books, 51–75.

Green, A. and Troup, K. (eds) (1999) *The Houses of History: A Critical Reader in Twentieth-Century History and Theory*, Manchester: Manchester University Press.

Halpin, M.M. (1997) '"Play it again, Sam", reflections on a new museology', *Museum International*, vol. 49, no. 2, 1997, 52–6.

Harris, R. (2004) 'Introduction', in K. Wedd *The Foundling Museum*, London: The Foundling Museum, 3–5.

Harrison, J.D. (1993) 'Ideas of museums in the 1990s', *Museum Management and Curatorship*, vol. 13, 160–76.

Hooper-Greenhill, E. (2000) *Museums and the Interpretation of Visual Culture*, London: Routledge.

Hooper-Greenhill, E. (2001) 'Museums and Cultural Politics', University of Leicester, Department of Museum Studies, online paper http://www.le.ac.uk/ms/profdev/culturalpolitics.pdf.

Hooper-Greenhill, E., Dodd, J., Phillips, M., Jones, C., Woodward, J. and O'Rian, H. (2004) *Inspiration, Identity, Learning: The Value of Museums*, Leicester: RCMG.

Hooper-Greenhill, E., Dodd, J., Gibson, L., Phillips, M., Jones, C. and Sullivan, S. (2006) *What Did you Learn at The Museum Today? Second Study*, Leicester: RCMG.

Jenkins, T. (2005) 'Victims remembered', *Museums Journal*, May 2005, 22–3, 25.

Jones, S. (1998) 'Walkabout with me', *Museums Journal*, vol. 98, no. 10, 34–5.

Kamuf, P. (ed.) (1991) *A Derrida Reader: Between the Blinds*, Hemel Hempstead: Harvester Wheatsheaf.

Karp, I. (1992) 'Introduction: Museums and communities: the politics of public culture', in I. Karp, C. Mullen Kreamer and S. Lavine (eds) *Museums and Communities: the Politics of Public Culture*, Washington, DC: Smithsonian Institution Press, 1–17.

Karp, I., Mullen Kreamer, C., Lavine, S. (eds) (1992) *Museums and Communities: the Politics of Public Culture*, Washington, DC: Smithsonian Institution Press.

Kavanagh, G. (1990) *History Curatorship*, Washington, DC: Smithsonian Institution Press.

Knell, S. (2004) *Museums and the Future of Collecting*, second edition, Aldershot: Ashgate.

Littler, J. and Naidoo, R. (eds) (2005) *The Politics of Heritage, The Legacies of 'Race'*, Abingdon: Routledge.

Lubar, S. (1997) 'Exhibiting memories', in A. Henderson and L. Kaeppler (eds) *Exhibiting Dilemmas: Issues of Representation at the Smithsonian*, Washington, DC and London: Smithsonian Institution Press, 15–27.

Luke, T.W. (2002) *Museum Politics*, Minneapolis: University of Minnesota Press.

MacDonald, G.F. and Alsford, S. (1995) 'Canadian museums and the representation of culture in a multicultural nation', *Cultural Dynamics*, vol. 7, no. 1, 15–36.

Macdonald, S. (1998) 'Exhibitions of power and powers of exhibition', in S. Macdonald (ed.) *The Politics of Display: Museums, Science, Culture*, London and New York: Routledge, 1–24.

Macdonald, S. (1999) 'Theorizing museums: an introduction', in S. Macdonald and G. Fyfe (eds) *Theorizing Museums: Representing Identity and Diversity in a Changing World*, Oxford: Blackwell, 1–18.

Mason, R. (2004) 'Conflict and complement: an exploration of the discourses informing the concept of the socially inclusive museum in contemporary Britain', *International Journal of Heritage Studies*, vol. 10, no. 1, March, 49–73.

Mason, R. (2005) 'Museums, galleries and heritage: sites of meaning-making and communication', in G. Corsane (ed.) *Heritage, Museums and Galleries*, Abingdon: Routledge, 200–14.

Merriman, N. (1997) 'The Peopling of London Project', in E. Hooper-Greenhill (ed.) *Cultural Diversity: Developing Museum Audiences in Britain*, London: Leicester University Press, 119–48.

Merriman, N. and Poovaya-Smith, N. (1996) 'Making culturally diverse histories', in G. Kavanagh (ed.) *Making Histories in Museums*, London and New York: Leicester University Press, 176–87.

Museums Association (2002) *Code of Ethics for Museums*, London: Museums Association.

MLA (2004) *Visitors to museums and galleries 2004*, London: Museums, Libraries and Archives Council.

Newman, A. and McLean, F. (2002) 'Architectures of inclusion: museums, galleries and inclusive communities', in R. Sandell (ed.) *Museums, Society, Inequality*, London: Routledge, 56–68.

O'Neill, M. (2002a) 'The good enough visitor', in R. Sandell (ed.) *Museums, Society, Inequality*, London: Routledge, 24–40.

O'Neill, M. (2002b) 'The people versus', *Museums Journal*, vol. 102, no. 2, February, 20–21.

Paine, C. (ed.) (2000) *Godly Things: Museums, Objects and Religion*, London and New York: Leicester University Press.

Patterson, T.C. (1989) 'Post-structuralism, Post-modernism: Implications for Historians', *Social History*, vol. 14, 83–8.

Peers, L. and Brown, A.K. (2003) 'Introduction', in L. Peers and A.K. Brown (eds) *Museums and Source Communities*, London and New York: Routledge, 1–16.

Pieterse, J.N. (1997) 'Multiculturalism and museums: Discourse about others in the age of globalization', in *Theory, Culture and Society*, vol. 14, no. 4, November, 123–46.

Prösler, M. (1999) 'Museums and globalization', in S. Macdonald and G. Fyfe (eds) *Theorizing Museums: Representing Identity and Diversity in a Changing World*, Oxford: Blackwell, 21–44.

Resource (2001) *Renaissance in the Regions: A New Vision for England's Museums*, London: Resource.

Resource (2002) *Neighbourhood Renewal and Social Inclusion: The Role of Museums, Archives and Libraries*, Newcastle-upon-Tyne: Northumbria University.

Rheingold, H. (1994) *The Virtual Community: Homesteading on the Electronic Frontier*, New York: Harper Perennial.

Sandell, R. (1998) 'Museums as agents of social inclusion', *Museum Management and Curatorship*, vol. 17, no. 4, December, 401–18.

Sandell, R. (ed.) (2002) *Museums, Society, Inequality*, London: Routledge.

Sarup, M. (1993) *An Introductory Guide to Post-structuralism and Post-modernism*, New York, London: Harvester Wheatsheaf.

Simpson, M.G. (1996) 'From treasure house to museum. . . . and back', in M.G. Simpson *Making Representations, Museums in the Post-Colonial Era*, London: Routledge, 107–33.

Social Exclusion Unit (2004) 'Welcome to the Social Exclusion Unit', http://www:socialexclusionunit.gov.uk (accessed 21 April 2004).

Spalding, J. (2002) *The Poetic Museum: Reviving Historic Collections*, Munich, London and New York: Prestel Verlag.

Szekeres, V. (2002) 'Representing diversity and challenging racism: the Migration Museum', in R. Sandell (ed.) *Museums, Society, Inequality*, London: Routledge, 142–52.

Tegomoh, N.E. (2006) 'Sacred objects, cultural change and the museum: the case of the Mbum people of northern Cameroon', paper presented at the Department of Museum Studies, University of Leicester Conference, The Museum: A World Forum, April 2006.

Uglow, J. (1997) *Hogarth: A Life and a World*, London: Faber and Faber Limited.

Van Mensch, P.J.A. (1995) 'Magpies on Mount Helicon', in Scharer, M.R. (ed.) *Museum and Community*, ICOFOM Study Series, 25, 133–8.

Vergo, P. (1989) 'Introduction', in P. Vergo (ed.) *The New Museology*, London: Reaktion Books Ltd, 1–5.

Von Appen, K., Kennedy, B. and Spadaccini, J. (2006) 'Community sites & emerging sociable technologies', in J. Trant and D. Bearman (eds) *Museums and the Web 2006: Proceedings*, Toronto: Archives & Museum Informatics, published March 1, http://www.archimuse.com/mw2006/papers/vonappen.html (accessed 24 March 2006).

Watson, S. (1999) 'Using focus groups: the Great Yarmouth Experience', *Social History Curators' Group Newsletter*, vol. 44, 6–9.

Watson, S. (2000) 'The Great Yarmouth Experience', *Significant Others: Society of Museum Archaeologists, special issue of The Museum Archaeologist*, vol. 25, 35–8.

Wedd, K. (2004) *The Foundling Museum*, London: The Foundling Museum.

Weil, S. (2002) 'The museum and the public', in S. Weil *Making Museums Matter*, Washington: Smithsonian Institution Press, 195–213.

Weil, S. (2003) 'Beyond big & awesome: outcome-based evaluation', *Museum News*, November/December, 40–45, 52–3.

Witcomb, A. (2003) 'A place for all of us? Museums and communities', in A. Witcomb *Re-imagining the Museum: Beyond the Mausoleum*, London: Routledge, 79–101.

Woodward, K. (2002) 'Concepts of identity and difference', in K. Woodward (ed.) *Identity and Difference*, London: The Open University, Sage, 7–50.

Woodward, W. (2006) 'Kelly vows that new debate on immigration will engage critically with multiculturalism', *The Guardian*, 25 August, 7.

Changing Roles of Museums over Time and Current Challenges

Introduction to Part One

MUSEUMS ARE EVER CHANGING, adapting to the pressures of the society in which they exist and which they seek to serve. Museums are increasingly expected to be responsive to their audiences and to justify and actively develop the roles they play within society. There are visitors and museum workers who find these changes exhilarating, while, for others, they are threatening. Some museum professionals are anxious lest what is perceived to be the functional work of the museum, the collecting, researching and documenting of material culture, is swamped by pressures that range from financial to political and social. At the same time there is in some quarters a feeling that challenges to old certainties about knowledge and the ordering of things has gone too far, in others that it has not gone far enough.

The first four authors explore the changing meaning of museums in the last century and a half and serve as a general introduction to the whole reader. Weil, Halpin, Davis and Hooper-Greenhill provide different perspectives on museum development and the challenges facing an institution in society attempting to become more responsive towards individuals and community groups. All four authors present different but complementary ideas of what museums might become. All foreground the responsibility of the museum towards its communities.

Weil's concept of museum development is optimistic and visionary. For Weil museums have infinite possibilities. Placing the development of the museum within a historical framework he traces how museums developed in the nineteenth century to express a particular view of the world. They were didactic, espousing an understanding of the way nature was organised and how people evolved (or not in the case of some so-called primitive societies). They also promulgated the idea that history and success were synonymous and therefore celebratory. Museums were morally uplifting. They were controlled by those who saw themselves as superior to many of their visitors who, in turn, were expected to consider themselves fortunate to be allowed to visit such treasure houses of educational opportunities. At the same time, as Weil points out, these museums were perceived by themselves and their audiences to be 'disinterested, neutral and objective' (Weil 2002: 202, this volume p. 37).

It is now recognised that museums are not necessarily inherently and un-questionably benevolent nor are they neutral. Weil considers why this change in attitude has come about and considers how museums might develop as a result of the financial and ideological pressures they are currently facing. He adopts a positive view of the museum of the future, arguing that it will be 'ideologically neutral . . . available to the supporting community to be used in pursuit of its com-munal goals' (Weil 2002: 200, this volume p. 35).

Weil recognises that for individuals, museums and their objects have par-ticular meanings that are unique and allow them to experience something about themselves and their own individual identities. He notes that in a postmodern world the visitors' experiences and their expectations can be seen as being as important as those of the curators. At the same time, museums, he believes, are places that can 'contribute importantly to the health of human communities' (2002: 208, this volume p. 42), where people can not only be safe but where they can also engage with 'interchange' (ibid.) and debate. Weil challenges all those who study, write about and work in museums to think in a creative and forward-thinking way about the potential of museums for individuals and communities. His writing sets the scene for all the chapters that follow.

Halpin's survey of developments in museological thinking complements Weil's, and both consider different ways in which museums can conceptualise their futures as being in service to their communities.

Davis's analysis of what a community is illuminates the difficulties museums face when they try to define the meaning of the communities they serve. Starting with a consideration of cultural identity and the importance of iconic objects to a community's sense of itself, he discusses both the limitations and possibilities of objects as agents of identity formation within communities. Davis uses the term ecomuseum, an idea originating in France in the 1960s and one that has spread across the globe. In a survey carried out in 1998 he identified some 166 eco-museums in twenty-five countries (Davis 1999). While this does not constitute a large number compared with the total number of museums worldwide, never-theless, ecomuseums represent an interesting and dynamic development in museum thinking. The idea of the ecomuseum is an evolving one and the chapter selected only indirectly explains it, so it is worth spending a little time here considering what is so special about them. Davis has argued that one key element distinguishes ecomuseums from others. 'In the ecomuseum the local population *must* have prim-ary and ultimate responsibility for their museum: the people are the curators' (Davis 1999: 75). Other distinguishing factors appear to be a sense of territory (the museum is more than a building) and the sense of ownership by the community. In addition ecomuseums embrace far more than objects collected for display or stored within a building. They can include 'intangible local skills, behaviour patterns, social structure and traditions . . . . (as well as) the tangible evidence of landscapes, underlying geology, wildlife, buildings and objects, people and their domestic animals' (Davis 2005: 370). Davis points out that implicit within the concept of the ecomuseum is the idea that the local community is responsible and empowered to take control of all heritage resources within their local environment, and that the community itself has a strong sense of place. In the introduction we noted the many ways in which people conceptualise communities and how location or place is but one of many ways communities identify themselves. Perhaps the complexities of community identity are one of the reasons why the idea of the ecomuseum is difficult to implement in practice, and these complexities, along with museum reactions to them, are explored by Davis in the extract chosen for this reader.

Davis also considers briefly the issue of cultural property and its restitution, a topic that will be dealt with in more detail in another reader in this series, but one that nevertheless reminds us that there is a conflict of interest between material culture that is seen as universal in significance and the claims of the local people from which such culture originated. Hooper-Greenhill and Appleton both consider, albeit from different perspectives, The Ghost Dance Shirt as a case study of restitution and its relevance to its source community.

All the authors suggest that museums can no longer rely on interpreting objects inside buildings in a traditional manner. Museums have to think beyond their existing interpretation strategies, and work hard to develop new relationships with communities both within the museum walls and beyond. At the same time we recognise that in a postmodern world the ideas and attitudes people bring with them to the museum affect not only their interpretation of what they see, but also the experiences they take away with them. Some of these ideas and attitudes will have been developed by the communities to which these individuals belong, and Hooper-Greenhill's use of the concept of interpretive communities offers us a theory of understanding how communities relate to material within museums. At the same time her post-museum concept challenges some existing assumptions about what museums are and can aspire to be in the future.

Museum relationships with their communities are overtly political. Sandell considers to what extent museums can and should attempt to combat prejudice, social inequality and discrimination. Social exclusion is both about individuals being excluded from society and thus from relevant communities, and also about groups that find themselves isolated and excluded from a range of opportunities and benefits that accrue to most people living in society. Like Weil he views the potential of museums for individuals and communities in positive and life-changing ways, and he considers the theoretical issues that underpin such activities and cites specific examples as to how museums can make a difference. Museums in the United Kingdom have developed a very wide range of initiatives to support the Labour government's social inclusion agenda. Public grants such as the Single Regeneration Budget Challenge Fund and the Heritage Lottery Fund all require museums to demonstrate how they are responding to community needs.

Appleton takes issue with some of the views held by Weil, Sandell and others in this section and provides us with a reminder that there is no consensus about the role of museums and their relationship with their communities. She surveys the impact of Thatcherism and 'cultural leftism' on museums in the United Kingdom from a radically different perspective from Sandell's. We can compare her opinion on the restitution of The Ghost Dance Shirt with that of Hooper-Greenhill's to see how contentious the issue of community ownership of material culture can be. For her and her supporters, debates about the objectivity of knowledge and social inclusion have led to a crisis of confidence in museums and a dumbing down of intellectual debate. Her call to respect collections and curatorial expertise is a call to a lost mythical golden age of museums. However, although she overstates her case, some of her demands for a return to a respect for collections perhaps reflect some disquiet among the museum profession in the United Kingdom that objects and their curation have been undervalued in recent years, as exemplified by the Museums Association report *Collections for the Future* (Museums Association 2005).

Graburn considers tourists, a group of visitors that museums traditionally target in their marketing and whose needs can sometimes override those of local people. Although he does not use the term community as such, preferring the word 'group', he considers the complementary and sometimes competing needs of tourists and the local inhabitants of a place and looks at the responsibilities museums have towards the tourist. He reflects on how this community of interest (tourists) has impacted on the way museums present themselves and their communities of location to the outside world. He reminds us that, to a certain extent, with the rise of travel opportunities and the increased importance of the tourist industry, museums belong to 'all of us'. Both he and Davis suggest that some art and heritage have become of universal importance and cannot be claimed as being only of special significance to one community or another, although this universal ownership is becoming increasingly contested by communities of origin.

These authors assume that museums have a primary responsibility towards society and that it is incumbent on those working in the museum to identify this purpose and direct their energies towards supporting this. The exception here is Appleton, who sees museums abandoning a duty to knowledge and scholarship as they engage more with their publics and communities. Museums have always served as agents of the state (Weil 2002). The role they are expected to play has changed over time as new imperatives within society require public validation. Witcomb examines both Bennett's ideas that the museum is an agent of civic reform, working with communities to foster cultural diversity, and also Clifford's (1997) concept of the museum as a contact zone. She writes as a museum practitioner and an academic, providing interesting examples of the way theory can help inform practice and, at the same time, be tested by museum case studies. Drawing on her experiences in Australia and using examples from Canada, Witcomb suggests that some theories, although useful in helping us understand some of the key issues facing museums, when applied to practical examples of museums engaging with communities, expose the complexities of the relationships between different groups within communities. Her case study of the Portuguese in Australia illustrates all too well Davis's argument that communities are complex and very difficult to understand. Her chapter exposes some struggles relating to power and these issues will be considered more fully in Part Two.

Finally Simpson considers whether or not museums are a Western concept and suggests that we can be too eager to impose our idea of what a museum is and can be on indigenous groups. Her chapter suggests that museums can come in many forms and have a variety of roles for communities. However, in common with previous authors, she finds that community needs are complex and sometimes a cause of contention within communities themselves.

These chapters raise issues that will be explored further in later sections. They illustrate that, as fashions in museum thinking come and go, debates continue about the purposes of museums, who are the museum communities and how best to serve their needs.

References

Clifford, J. (1997) 'Museums as contact zones', in J. Clifford *Routes: Travel and Translation in the late Twentieth Century*, Cambridge, MA: Harvard University Press, 188–219.

Davis, P. (1999) *Ecomuseums: A Sense of Place*, London and New York: Leicester University Press.

Davis, P. (2005) 'Places, "cultural touchstones" and the ecomuseum', in G. Corsane (ed.) *Heritage, Museums and Galleries*, Abingdon: Routledge, 365–76.

Museums Association (2005) *Collections for the Future*, London: Museums Association.

Weil, S. (2002) 'The museum and the public', in S. Weil *Making Museums Matter*, Washington, DC: Smithsonian Institution Press, 195–213.

Chapter 1

The Museum and the Public

Stephen Weil

FOR THE SAKE OF SIMPLICITY in addressing the topic of 'The Museum and The Public,' I will be using those two big words – 'museum' and 'public' – as if each had behind it some single, monolithic, sharply defined reality. Neither, of course, does. Museums are almost infinite in their variety and occupy a field with fuzzy edges. The public is not singular but plural, in no way sharply bounded but perceived and defined differently from one observer to the next. Likewise, from time to time I may employ that always slippery pronoun 'we' in a way that seems too encompassing. Feel free to disassociate yourself from any such use. In general, 'we' will be intended to refer to a majority – or at least plurality – of the people who spend substantial time thinking, talking, or writing about the museum and its situation.

I will propose that the relationship between the museum and the public must be understood as a revolution in process, a revolution in the most fundamental sense of that term. At the museum's birth – some two hundred years ago in Europe and only a little more than one hundred years ago in America – its position vis-à-vis the public was one of superiority. Commonly used spatial metaphors made this relationship clear: The museum was established to 'raise' the level of public understanding, to 'elevate' the spirits of its visitors, and to refine and 'uplift' the common taste. There was no ambiguity in this. Museums were created and maintained by the high for the low, by the couth for the uncouth, by the washed for the unwashed, by those who knew for those who didn't but needed to know and who would come to learn. The museum was established to 'do'; what was to be 'done' was the public. The museum was a place of inculcation. At some point – probably not more than forty to fifty years into the twenty-first century – the relative positions of the museum and the public will have revolved a full 180 degrees. In their emerging

Source: *Making Museums Matter*, Washington: Smithsonian Institution Press, 2002, pp. 195–213.

new relationship – already to be glimpsed in a myriad of ways – it will be the public, not the museum, that occupies the superior position. The museum's role will
have been transformed from one of mastery to one of service. Toward what ends
that service is to be performed, for whom it is to be rendered, and how, and when
– those are all determinations that will be made by the museum's newly ascendant
master, the public.

What follows is in three parts. First, I would like to look briefly at the museum
as it was in its earliest days, and particularly at the ways it was thought to relate
to the public. Then I will turn to consideration of the museum of the near future,
which we can begin to discern as emerging from the worn and hollowed-out husk
of that old museum. Finally, I will look back at some of the factors that account
for the loss of the museum's initially superior position and then examine some
phenomena that seem to me symptomatic of the ongoing metamorphosis through
which the public is succeeding to the museum's formerly commanding position.
My basic contention is that we – and again readers are free to disassociate themselves from that 'we' – are engaged in a process of adaptive reuse. What we have
inherited was once a grand and imposing structure. With most of its ideological
foundations long since rotted away, that structure can no longer function in all the
ways its builders intended. Few of us, though, are prepared to tear it down or even
just to walk away and leave it to collapse. It still provides value and, properly adapted,
it could provide far greater value still. Although this work of adapting the museum
to better serve the public's needs is far from successfully accomplished, the
museum community shows heartening signs that it is well under way.

To begin, then, with some beginnings. The Museum of Fine Arts in Boston
was established in 1870. In arguing for its establishment, Charles Callahan Perkins
– destined to serve as one of its first trustees – was explicit in describing what such
an institution might offer to the public at large: 'There exists a modicum of capacity for improvement in all men, which can be greatly developed by familiarity
with such acknowledged masterpieces as are found in all great collections of works
of art. Their humblest function is to give enjoyment to all classes; their highest, to
elevate men by purifying the taste and acting upon the moral nature.'

Beyond the capacity to elevate the taste and purify the morals of its visitors,
the museum was also envisioned by its founders as providing a wholesome alternative to the seamier forms of diversion that might otherwise tempt the working-
class inhabitants of those burgeoning nineteenth-century cities where the earliest
museums were established. The original program for the Metropolitan Museum of
Art – also founded in 1870 – proposed that the new institution not only cultivate
a 'pure taste in all matters connected with the arts' but also provide the people of
New York City with a 'means for innocent and refined enjoyment.' As for uplift,
William Cullen Bryant said that the new museum would provide 'entertainment
of an . . . improving character.' Discussing the advantages of adding evening hours
for the public at London's South Kensington Museum (subsequently to be renamed
the Victoria & Albert Museum) Sir Henry Cole, the museum's superintendent, projected the following scene:

> The working man comes to this Museum from his one or two dimly
> lighted, cheerless dwelling rooms, in his fustian jacket [fuschen: an

inexpensive cloth combining cotton and flax] with his shirt collar a little trimmed up, accompanied by his threes, and fours, and fives of little fustian jackets, a wife, in her best bonnet, and a baby, of course, under her shawl. The looks of surprise and pleasure of the whole party when they first observe the brilliant lighting inside the Museum show what a new, acceptable, and wholesome excitement this evening entertainment affords to all of them. Perhaps the evening opening of Public Museums may furnish a powerful antidote to the gin palace.

On another occasion, Sir Henry suggested that keeping the South Kensington Museum open on Sundays as well as evenings might be a way, in his phrase, of 'defeating Satan.' As it was in New York and London, so too in Paris: The conversion of the Louvre from a palace to a museum in the years immediately following the French Revolution was multiple in its purposes. It was intended to provide a facility for training artists who would subsequently employ their talents on behalf of the state. It was also intended to symbolize the newborn freedom of the people, in which access to what had once been exclusive to the aristocracy and clergy would now be universal for every citizen. Such access, as George Heard Hamilton has written, 'was not solely for aesthetic pleasure, but for the inculcation of political and social virtue. Though Napoleon's imperial ambition eroded the earlier artistic morality, there remained a strong belief that acquaintance with great art improves the morals as it does the taste of the individual and thus contributes to the general welfare of society.'

Founded on a somewhat different premise from the art museum was the natural-history museum. There the goal was not so much to inculcate virtue as to locate the place that its Western and predominantly Caucasian visitors occupied in the terrestrial order of things. And that place, beyond any doubt, was at the top of things, certainly above the dinosaurs – sometimes portrayed as bird-brained losers – seashells, tigers, and swordfish, but also above the little red, brown, and yellow people who appeared in dioramas or scale models with their quaint but primitive hunting weapons, clothing, shelter, and cookpots. In an evolutionary twist, the societies that these people inhabited were not presented as self-sustaining and functional responses to the particular circumstances in which their members lived. These societies were depicted, rather, as passing through one of advanced society's earlier stages of development, as living examples of civilization's long-gone past. Consider the following extract from the British Museum's *Handbook to the Ethnographic Collections*, all the more shocking because it was first published within the twentieth century, in 1910, and republished almost within our lifetimes – mine, anyway – in 1925. It reads:

> The mind of primitive man is wayward, and seldom capable of continuous attention. His thoughts are not quickly collected, so that he is bewildered in an emergency; and he is so much the creature of habit that unfamiliar influences such as those which white men introduce into his country disturb his mental balance. His powers of discrimination and analysis are undeveloped, so that distinctions which to us are fundamental, need not be obvious to him. Thus he does not distinguish between

similarity and identity, between names and things, between the events that occur in dreams and real events, between the sequence of ideas in his mind and of things in the outer world to which they correspond. His ideas are grouped by chance impressions, and his conclusions often based on superficial analogies which have no weight with us.

Key to understanding the art and natural-history museums in their earliest manifestations is that they were both celebratory: The art museum celebrated 'acknowledged masterpieces'; the natural-history museum celebrated Western humankind's place in nature. No less celebratory in its founding days was the history museum. In its European version what it tended to celebrate was military victory. Almost invariably, it was founded and maintained by the state. At the extreme end of the scale was the Gallery of Battles opened by Louis-Philippe at Versailles in 1837. Some 400 feet (122 meters) long, it is hung with huge canvases depicting the glory of French arms. With each new war – win or lose – new paintings were to be added.

In the United States, history museums evolved somewhat differently. Although also celebratory, they were initially private in their inception, tended to grow out of local historical societies, were frequently located in historic houses, and were as much concerned with civic virtue as with military valor. Civic virtue, in turn, was largely defined by success in politics, the professions, or business. The subject matter ultimately celebrated in most of these museums (at least in the East; a somewhat different tradition developed in such populist Midwestern states as Wisconsin and Minnesota) was the community's first families. Those who principally supported these museums, served on their boards, worked in them, or even directed them were often none other than the descendants of those same first families. The stories that these museums told were invariably success stories. The greatest success story of all, and the model for many others, was that of George Washington. Campaigning in the mid-1850s for the establishment of Mount Vernon as a historic-house museum, South Carolina's Ann Pamela Cunningham called for it to be a 'shrine' where 'the mothers of the land and their innocent children might make their offering in the cause of [the] greatness, goodness, and prosperity of their country.'

Let us turn to the museum of the near future. Will it too be celebratory? Perhaps, or perhaps not. What will be important and what will be different are not so much what particular stance the museum may take but how the decision to take that stance is to be made. In that museum, it will be primarily the public, and not those inside the museum, who will make those decisions. And what, in turn, can those museum insiders be expected to bring to the table? The answer, I think, is their astonishing technical expertise. As I wrote in another context, 'Museum workers are fundamentally technicians. They have developed and passed along to their successors systematic ways in which to deal with the objects (and with information about those objects) that their museums collect and make accessible to the public. Through training and experience they have developed a high level of expertise as to how those objects ought properly be collected, preserved, restored, classified, catalogued, studied, displayed, interpreted, stored, transported, and safeguarded.'

The museum of the near future, as thus envisioned, will in itself be an ideologically neutral organization. It will in essence be one of a range of organizations

– instruments, really – available to the supporting community to be used in pursuit of its communal goals. As an intricate and potentially powerful instrument of communication, it will make available to the community, and for the community's purposes, its profound expertise at telling stories, eliciting emotion, triggering memories, stirring imagination, and prompting discovery – its expertise in stimulating all those object-based responses.

And how might the community choose to use the museum? In as many ways, certainly, as different communities at different times might have different needs. We know already that the museum has proven itself to be a remarkably flexible instrument. The history museum, for example, has shown that beyond being celebratory, it can also – as Professor Joyce Appleby of UCLA has pointed out – be compensatory, and that beyond praising history's winners, be they military, political, professional, or economic, it can also seek to soothe the pain – or at least recognize, memorialize, and try to understand the losses – of history's victims. Our repertory of museum types has expanded enormously in just the past two decades. Consider, for example, the Famine Museum that opened in Strokestown, Ireland, in 1994, or the U.S. Holocaust Memorial Museum in Washington, D.C., or the Yad Vashem Memorial in Jerusalem. In much the same way that Maya Lin's Vietnam Memorial differs from the celebratory war memorials of earlier conflicts, these new museums are places of memory, places for inward and sober reflection. Likewise, the art museum and the natural-history museum have cloned off variants of themselves, which can serve a multiplicity of public purposes.

How was this revolution set into motion? How was the museum so unceremoniously dethroned from the sovereign position in which it was first established? One factor, certainly, was money. As the report submitted to the White House in February 1997 by the President's Committee on the Arts and Humanities made clear, the dependence of the America's museums on government for their support exceeds that of other arts institutions by a ratio of almost four to one. In the case of museums, just under 30 percent of their 1995 income was from governmental sources; for the other groups surveyed, nonprofit theater was the highest at 6.5 percent, and symphony orchestras and opera companies were each at 6 percent. So disproportionately great a dependence on governmental support requires that museums, far more than other cultural organizations, keep themselves at all times finely tuned as to how they are being perceived, not merely by their visitors and potential visitors but also by the larger, tax-paying public upon whose goodwill and at least tacit approval they have made themselves so dependent. In those bygone days when museums were supported largely by the contributions of their well-to-do trustees, a touch of royal arrogance might not have been wholly unexpected. With so radical a shift in their sources of support – only 22.8 percent of their support was received through private contributions in 1995, when every other group surveyed by the president's committee received between 30 and 40 percent – whatever arrogance the museum may have once displayed toward the public has long since been converted to deference.

In accounting for the public's growing ascendancy, money figures in a second way as well. Given the recurring fear that levels of governmental support might fall victim to budget balancing, museums have become ever more intense in their pursuit of earned income, whether through increased admissions revenue and/or the net proceeds from such auxiliary activities as on-site and off-site gift shops, mail-order catalogs, restaurants, facilities rentals, and foreign travel tours. Consider this irony: Sir Henry Cole originally envisioned the museum as a wholesome alternative to the gin mill, but given the innumerable social events for which museums rent themselves out these days, it is by no means clear that the museum itself has not *become* the gin mill. In its pursuit of earned income, the museum has inevitably – kicking and screaming, certainly, but nonetheless inevitably – put itself in a marketing mode. In planning special exhibitions, and in creating the special merchandise it hopes to sell in conjunction with such exhibitions, the degree to which these will appeal to the public is necessarily taken seriously into account.

The American Museum of Natural History's exhibition *Endangered! Exploring a World at Risk* is a case in point. According to the *New York Times* (March 13, 1997), the American Museum spent an estimated two hundred to three hundred thousand dollars to publicize the exhibition. Asked whether he thought such an expenditure for a single, five-and-a-half month exhibition was unusual, New York City's commissioner of cultural affairs Schuyler C. Chapin said, 'I think the American Museum is increasingly moving in a new, more visible direction, using the tools of modern marketing in a precise way. And I think the museum is trying to bring in a larger family audience.' Among the special gift shop items that the family audience could buy were a fifty-five-cent pencil with the exhibition's logo, a seventy-five-hundred-dollar chessboard made of Cambrian slate with gold and silver chess pieces in the forms of endangered species, exhibition-relevant plush toys, and a CD-ROM, *The Encyclopedia of Endangered Species*. By yet another metamorphosis, museum visitors, once the people to be 'done,' have been transformed into customers. And as customers – like those legendary people who pay the piper – they can with increasing frequency call the tune. Money, or the need for it, does not wholly account for the loss of the museum's former superiority. Contributing to that loss as well has been a general and ongoing decline in the respect generally accorded to institutions of every sort, from the presidency of the United States down to the local day-care center. Museums, although relatively untouched by scandals and touched only modestly by mismanagement, are in no way exempt from this loss of public trust. As University of Chicago historian Neal Harris observed in 1986, the 'museum's voice is no longer seen as transcendent. Rather it is implicated in the distribution of wealth, power, knowledge and taste shaped by the larger social order.'

With the loss of the museum's transcendent voice, the public's confidence in the museum as a disinterested, neutral, and objective agency has also been lost, or at least tarnished. In a dozen different contexts, identity and interest groups of every kind insist that the mainstream museum is neither empowered nor qualified to speak on their behalf. Increasingly, such groups are creating their own museums from which to speak in their own voices and address what they consider to be their own issues. In recent years, Native Americans, Asian Americans, and African Americans have been particularly active in the establishment of specialized museums. The Mashantucket Pequot Museum and Research Center on the Pequots' tribal reservation in Connecticut, with its 316,000 square feet (29,000 square meters), is among the largest museums in New England. The expanded Museum of African American History in Detroit has quadrupled its former space. It displays materials relating to slavery, a topic – compensatory, not celebratory – that is scarcely touched in any depth at most mainstream history museums. In Los Angeles, the Japanese American National Museum tells the story of the wartime detention centers in which innocent American citizens were held and treated as prisoners.

Consistent with this distrust of the museum's objectivity has come a growing recognition that the museum, in and of itself, is a morally neutral entity. The nineteenth-century view was different. As Carol Duncan describes the situation that prevailed in Europe, 'public art museums were regarded as evidence of political virtue, indicative of a government which provided the right things for its people . . . [E]ducated opinion understood that art museums could demonstrate the goodness of a state or show the civic-mindedness of its leading citizens.' In the United States, of course, it was the latter part of Duncan's formulation that applied: The museum stood as tangible evidence of the civic-mindedness of the community's leading citizens. In the century since, we have come to understand that museums can be used just as easily for malevolent purposes as for benevolent ones, that the same technical skills that might be called upon to create a museum of tolerance could as easily be employed to create one of intolerance, and that the museum is simply an instrument. What really matters is in whose hands it is held and for what purposes it is intended to be used. Just as we recognize today that 'art' is simply a noun and not a value judgment – those judgments come through such qualifying adjectives as sublime, terrible, interesting, disgusting, charming, and dull – so too is 'museum' simply a noun. Whatever positive values it acquires must come through the appropriate qualifying adjectives.

Beyond these factors – beyond money, loss of public confidence, and the recognition that they are not inherently virtuous organizations – perhaps the greatest single factor contributing to the loss of the museum's once-superior position has been the bankruptcy of the underlying ideologies upon which it was founded. Where this can most clearly be seen is in the case of the art museum. No sooner had their founders begun to establish such museums in the United States than the link between art and moral uplift began to unravel. New ways of painting began to take hold, with painting intended to be looked at for its own sake and not because it depicted some character-forming scene from history, mythology, or the prevailing religious tradition. In time, new ways of looking at older paintings would also take hold. Instead of appreciating paintings for their moral probity or elevating sentiment, visitors were encouraged to value them only in terms of such formal elements as line, color, composition, and painterly skill. And what of the argument that the link between art and morality need not necessarily be broken? That line, color, and composition – even in their most abstract manifestations – might still be the stuff of moral uplift? 'We know in our hearts,' writes Robert Hughes, 'that the idea that people are morally ennobled by contact with works of art is a pious fiction. The Rothko on the wall does not turn its lucky owner into Bambi.' And what of Sir Robert Peel's observation to Parliament in 1832 when, in discussing London's proposed new National Gallery, he suggested that in times of political turmoil 'the exacerbation of angry and unsocial feelings might be much softened' by exposure to works of fine art. Nobody believes that any longer, either.

In the case of the natural-history museum, the ideology that went bankrupt was that which placed Western Caucasians at the pinnacle of creation. Being required to share that pinnacle with the former diorama and scale-model people was humbling enough. Much worse, though, was the discovery that far from having transcended the rest of the natural world, the people on the pinnacle, the whole lot of them, Caucasians and diorama-folk alike, were locked into a profound inter-dependence with that world, and that for better or for worse their futures were inextricably intertwined. Over the past several decades the center of interest for the natural-history museum, and that of many zoological parks as well, has shifted from taxonomy to ecological and environmental issues. To the extent that the natural-history museum has defined, as its principal purpose, an increase in public awareness and activism with respect to those issues, it appears today to be far more focused as an institution than either the art or the history museum.

For the history museum – founded primarily on a 'great man' and a celebrat-ory approach to its subject matter – it was not so much the case that its underly-ing ideology was repudiated as that such an approach simply became just one, and by no means the dominant one, out of a great many different ways to do history. Whereas a historic house in New York City had once meant something on the order of the Morris-Jumel Mansion or Edgar Allan Poe's Cottage in the Bronx, it just as easily today can mean those three circa-1863 buildings that make up the Lower East Side Tenement Museum on Orchard Street. History museums that focused on political leaders were apt to take for their subject such tried, true, and golden oldies as Jefferson or Lincoln, but today we can find history museums operating in the thicket of everyday contemporary life. Consider, for example, the Wing Luke Asian Museum in Seattle, which is named for and celebrates the life of Seattle's first elected city councilman of Chinese descent, or, a hemisphere away, the newly established museum on Robben Island where Nelson Mandela and other leaders of the African National Congress were held as prisoners.

The Smithsonian Institution announced in February 1997 that it would assist in the establishment of a National Museum of Industrial History in Bethlehem, Pennsylvania. The museum would occupy a massive, abandoned steel mill that still stands on the 160-acre (64-hectare) site. How very different is that new museum from the earlier museums we associate with steel-making: the Morgan Library and Frick Collection in New York, or the Carnegie in Pittsburgh. That its frame can be enlarged to include not merely those who financed the making of steel or captained its great companies, but also those whose labor actually produced the steel, is symptomatic of how very far the history museum has evolved from its original approach.

Another example: When the Whitney Museum mounted an exhibition about the landscape architect and urban planner Frederick Law Olmstead in 1972, it was cast in the conventional hagiographic mode. Olmstead was portrayed as a heroic figure, who triumphed over whoever or whatever might have frustrated the full flowering of his talents. From a New York perspective, his greatest triumph, of course, had to be the creation of its beloved Central Park. Unmentioned, beyond vague references to 'some shanties' that had to be moved and some 'squatters' to be sent on their way, was the fact that there was a small town – Seneca Village, comprising poor African American and Irish American communities located toward the western edge of the park near Eighty-sixth Street – that had to be destroyed to make way for Olmstead's new construction. In January 1997 the New-York Historical Society opened the exhibition *Before Central Park: The Life and Death of Seneca Village*. In a manner more compensatory than celebratory, it tells the story of this lost community and its all-but-forgotten citizens. Included as part of the exhibition is a study center where visitors can consult files pertaining to those inhabitants of Seneca Village who can still be identified and explore the possibility of finding some family relationship. In that connection, the New-York Historical Society also presents several workshops on genealogical research; such an example might seem to suggest that the museum of the near future, which will conceive itself wholly in terms of its ability to serve the public, might be even nearer than first appeared.

Not quite, though. These are still only isolated examples, and a great deal of hard work remains to be done. In all fairness, one might ask why so much work should be undertaken at all. If the original premises upon which the museum was founded no longer appear valid, why are we struggling so hard to wrestle it onto some other foundation? Why not just let it go? Let me suggest two answers. The first has to do with the all-but-unique power of objects.

Although the museum as we know it has been with us for some two hundred years, we are only in the foothills of learning about the ways in which the museum's visitors respond to the objects it shows. Some things we already know: that the response to a real, three-dimensional object, be it a moon rock, George Washington's false teeth, or an original painting by Rembrandt, is entirely different from our response to a photograph, video image, or verbal description of that same object. Whether this response is attributable to some Benjaminian 'aura' or to the power of association – the moon rock, as tangible proof that there really is a moon, is more than just a rock; it is a souvenir of a truly grand adventure; and it makes a claim to be 'true' in a way that words or pictures can never be – the fact remains that authentic objects displayed in a museumlike setting can trigger powerful cognitive and affective responses. In an effort to sort such responses into some sensible pattern, the touring exhibition that marked the Smithsonian Institution's 150th anniversary in 1996 was divided into three sections, *Remembering*, *Discovering*, and *Imagining*. Even those categories barely scratch the surface.

What we are learning about visitor response has come as something of a surprise. That museums serve an educational function has long been a basic rubric of the field. It has also long been supposed that the way they serve that function is through exhibitions, in which the curator, by the artful arrangement of objects and placement of labels, spells out a lesson in such a way that the visitor, having carefully visited the exhibition, will have learned some or all of the lesson that the curator was trying to teach. In a paper published in 1996, Zahava Doering, who directs the Office of Institutional Studies at the Smithsonian, argued that this might not be the case at all. Rather than communicating new information, she says, the primary impact of visiting a museum exhibition is to confirm, reinforce, and extend the visitor's existing beliefs. The 'most satisfying exhibition[s] for visitors,' she says, 'are those that resonate with their experience and provide new information in ways that confirm and enrich their [own] view of the world.'

A parallel conclusion was drawn by Russel J. Ohta of Arizona State University West, who studied visitor responses to the admittedly controversial exhibition *Old Glory: The American Flag in Contemporary Art* when it was shown in Phoenix in 1996. Although each of the visitors he studied experienced 'rich moments filled with deep personal meaning,' none of those meanings resembled each other. The meaning in each case was forged from the visitor's own personal identity. What they primarily experienced was neither about art nor about the flag, he concluded, it was primarily about themselves. 'In essence,' he writes, 'the exhibition became a looking glass for visitors. They experienced what they were capable of experiencing. They experienced who they were.' He concluded by quoting David Pilbeam's dictum that, in looking at things, we tend not see them as they are but as we are. This research suggests that, among the services a museum is able to offer to its community is this capacity to provide the individual visitor with an important degree of personal self-affirmation. Although some religious organizations may perform a similar function, it is difficult to identify many other secular institutions that can play so communally valuable a role for an adult population. It is also difficult to identify many other secular institutions that play such a conservative role. As Doering points out, the museum, when understood in this mode of providing individual self-affirmation, functions far more strongly as an instrument for social stability than as any kind of a lever for radical change. To what extent might just such an insight serve to justify the continued funding of museums by government at its current, or even a higher, level?

A second answer as to why museums might justify all the effort required for their readaption might be based on what is a relatively new concept for museums: They have a vital role to play in building what a Baltimore-based consulting organization, the Museum Group, calls 'healthy human communities.' A related idea has been advocated for some time now by Elaine Heumann Gurian, a member of the group and well known for her work over many years at the Boston Children's Museum, the Smithsonian, and the Holocaust Museum. During the winter of 1996–1997, Gurian proposed that the American Association of Museums (AAM) expand its official statement of principles – which seeks to encapsulate the educational, stewardship, and public-service roles that museums play, and to do so within a framework of diversity – to include the notion that one of the museum's core functions was to be 'a place of safety.' In an increasingly atomized and even hostile environment, she argued, the museum ought to emphasize the fact that it has traditionally been and still remains one of the few public spaces in which people of every background can gather together for peaceful exchange in a secure surrounding. In that mode, the museum might be understood as a contemporary descendent of such earlier public gathering places as the Roman bath, the medieval cathedral, and the New England village green. Although the AAM's leadership was not prepared to adopt Gurian's proposal, it did engender considerable discussion and, as they say on Wall Street, it certainly remains in play.

During a spring 1997 meeting at the North Carolina Museum of Art, Releigh architect-artist Thomas Sayre expressed a similar idea. Discussing the various ways that public space might be conceptualized, two of his examples seemed particularly relevant to the museum: one to the museum that once was, the other to the museum of the near future. The example relevant to the museum that once was, the Museum of Inculcation, was this: 'Public space as the display of "civic virtue." This is a space which has traditionally had the large equestrian statue proclaiming a host of attitudes and emotions about seminal events in the culture. [The p]otency of this kind of public space comes from the extent to which the public agrees or "buys into" the civic virtues, themselves. Nowadays, this kind of space is losing its potency. We don't agree so readily on what is civic virtue.'

In contrast to that, Sayre proposed another kind of public space, one that seems in its way only a slight variant on Gurian's notion of the museum as a place of safety and is also akin to Duncan Cameron's vision of a quarter century ago, that the museum, in addition to what it already was, ought properly to be a site for community confrontation, interchange, and debate. Sayre's description: 'Public space [as] a confluence of voices, as [a] forum for exchange. This admittedly utopian vision sees public space as a place where our multi-cultural society orchestrates its many voices into a dynamic whole. It is a place where the melting pot melts. Its function is something like fluid dynamics.'

To be a place for personal self-affirmation, to contribute importantly to the health of human communities, to be a place where the melting pot melts: All in all, and combined with what we already think to be of value about the museum, those seem reasonably powerful arguments to justify this ongoing effort to build the museum of the near future.

At this point, let me describe a few of the phenomena occurring in and around museums, phenomena that in some instances seem to resonate with one another and seem to me symptomatic of this changing relationship between the museum and the public. One involves a toning down of that omniscient and impersonal voice in which the museum of yesteryear was accustomed to address its public. This change is particularly evident in natural-history museums. Consider the renovated Dinosaur Halls at the American Museum of Natural History. In contrast with the scientifically authoritarian tone of the museum's old galleries, humility is now the order of the day. The labels make clear that the book on dinosaurs is far from closed. 'So far,' the labels seem to say, 'this is what we think we know and this is why we think so; but we're just people and we've been wrong before, and we may well be proven wrong again. Moreover, there are some things – like what color the dinosaurs were – that we may just never find out.' At the Think Tank building at the National Zoo in Washington, D.C., the public can watch and interact with scientists who are studying animal intelligence. The methodologies are all experimental. Asked by members of the public why one approach is being used rather than another, the scientists openly acknowledge the experimental nature of their work. That, they say, is how science is. At the Field Museum of Natural History in Chicago, Michael Spock made it a practice to include in each exhibit hall photographs of the curators and preparators who had been responsible for its installation. It is important, he believes, for the public to understand that its interaction with the indubitably authentic specimens on view is in no way inevitable but has been shaped and mediated by real human beings, with all the possibilities for error and/or bias that any such human undertaking might entail.

Also symptomatic of change are several recent instances in which museums have reformulated their missions entirely in an effort to connect more directly with their visitors and potential visitors. Two recent examples are the Strong Museum in Rochester, New York, and the Glenbow Museum in Calgary, Alberta. Established just two years apart in the mid-1960s, both museums were created by the gifts of very large private collections, in the case of the Glenbow some 1.2 million objects. Both were provided with substantial funds to underwrite their operations, by a very considerable private bequest in the case of the Strong and by public funding from the Province of Alberta in the case of the Glenbow, and both were left relatively free to develop their own missions. They both also found it necessary, some twenty to twenty-five years after first opening their doors, to rethink what they were doing. In its original conception the Strong, which concentrates on the history of the northeastern United States, chose the year 1940 as the end date for its collecting and interpretive activities. With the passage of time, the museum came to recognize that its ties to the community were becoming progressively weaker. Attendance was in decline, public interest appeared scant, and nobody below the age of fifty could any longer make much of a connection with the museum's cut-off date of 1940. The Strong Museum gathered its collective courage and did what very few museums have ever dared to do. It went to the community to ask if there was something else, something different from a museum concentrating on history up to 1940, that the community might find more useful. There was: The community wanted a museum oriented toward contemporary issues and family visits, a museum where parents might take their children to learn important lessons not fully taught in school. Since 1992, the Strong has mounted exhibitions dealing with AIDS, the cold war, bereavement, racism, alcohol, and drugs. It is also working with the Children's Television Workshop on an exhibition that will be built around the characters from *Sesame Street*.

The Glenbow experienced what its director, Robert Janes, calls a 'philosophic shift.' Whereas the collection and its management had previously been at the core of its operations, that focus was shifted instead to public service and communication. 'Museums,' he writes, 'exist to communicate and in the process provide answers to the question . . . What does it mean to be a human being? Although collections are the indispensable means to that end, they are not the end in themselves.' Reflecting that shift of focus is the Glenbow's new statement of its mission. Unlike traditional mission statements, filled with such museum-specific verbs as 'collect,' 'preserve,' and 'exhibit,' the Glenbow's new statement concentrates on the response of its visiting public: 'to be a place where people find meaning and value, and delight in exploring the diversity of the human experience.'

In contrast with these older museums making midcourse corrections in order to place greater emphasis on the public-service aspects of their operation, new museums are being established that provide this emphasis from the outset. At a symposium held in Washington, D.C., in September 1996 in celebration of the Smithsonian's 150th anniversary, Irene Hirano of the Japanese American National Museum in Los Angeles described how her own museum had been founded in 1985. Members of the local Japanese American community, she said, had become aware that the experience of the World War II detention camps in which they and their families had been incarcerated was slowly being forgotten. Sensing the need, in her phrase, to 'give their history a home' and fearful that their story would never be properly told if the telling was left to others, the community itself determined to take on the responsibility to 'ensure that [its] history and culture was documented.' Of the various means by which this might have been done, a museum was the community's instrument of choice. At that same symposium, Maria de Lourdes Horta of the Museu Imperial in Brazil talked about the remarkable cluster of small history museums that are springing up in Brazil's rural countryside:

> Under the stress of development and the need to survive, communities
> are taking hold of the idea of a 'museum,' whatever that may be in their
> minds, and are starting to take the job in their own hands. This is the
> case of some projects developed with the assistance of . . . educators
> and museologists in the south of Brazil. . . . Working with teachers and
> children, the process involves . . . old people and field workers, who
> start to dig into their past, looking for their roots, recovering self-pride
> and a sense of belonging to a given group with a unique history. A museum
> without walls, a true virtual museum, is being born in some of those
> communities that look in wonder to their own process of self-discovery
> and recognition. . . . For the moment, in my country, [museums] are
> being used in a new way, as tools for self-expression, self-recognition
> and representation, as spaces of power negotiation among social forces,
> as strategies for empowering people so [that] they are more capable to
> decide their own destiny.

The art museum is changing too, if not as dramatically. One of the factors driving
its change is simply the unavailability to new museums of the 'Old Master' art —
or even not-so-old-master art — that was once collected by the great urban museums
such as those in Boston, New York, Cleveland, Philadelphia, and Chicago. Most
of that art is already in museum collections. With the explosion in art prices over
the last two decades, what is not already in museum collections is prohibitively
expensive. Concurrently, increasingly restrictive ethical codes and the worldwide
spread of export controls have made it virtually impossible for these new museums
to collect the once-so-cheerfully plundered art of other cultures. Nor is it likely
that many will inherit important private collections. The era of heroic collecting
may well be on the wane. Accordingly, these new museums have had to learn to
do more with less. And many of them have done so with remarkable ingenuity. Of
necessity, their energies are directed at public programming rather than collection
care. That, in turn, has required that their focus be more outward than inward.

In the southwestern corner of Virginia, the William King Regional Art Center
in Abingdon lacks a single work of art that a major New York City museum would
consider fit to hang in its galleries, but it provides a broad range of community and
school programming that would, pound for pound, knock the socks off anything
to be found in New York City. Closer to home, the James A. Michener Museum
of Art in Doylestown, Pennsylvania — a museum that limits its program to Bucks
County — seamlessly supplements its rather slender collection of Bucks County paintings with masterfully designed displays about the writers and other creative individuals who have been associated with the county, including individuals such as
S.J. Perelman, playwrights Kauffman and Hart, writer Jean Toomer, and lyricist
Oscar Hammerstein. In so doing, it has evolved from what was originally a museum
of visual art into a novel form: a museum of human creativity. Often for the new
art museum, the strength of its imagination and not the strength of its collection
may be its only hope for distinction.

Also influencing how the museum and the public interact, or at least on how
they may be perceived to interact, is an idea implicit in postmodernism. It is the
proposition that no text is completed except through the act of 'reading' it, and

that every text, accordingly, has as many versions – all equally correct – as it has readers. Translated into museum terms, that would suggest that the objects displayed in the museum do not have any fixed or inherent meaning but that 'meaning-making,' or the process by which those objects acquire meaning for individual members of the public, will in each case involve the specific memories, expertise, viewpoint, assumptions, and connections that the particular individual brings. It may be noted that this notion has considerable resonance with some of the visitor research considered earlier. Indeed, adherents of this meaning-making paradigm claim that it is unduly restrictive to conceive of the museum's relationship to the public purely in terms of its educational potential. Lois Silverman of Indiana University argued, 'Hindered by [their] historical focus on a nearly exclusively educational mission, other potentialities of museums lie seriously underutilized in exhibitions and institutions alike. Museums in a new age can become places that actively support and facilitate a range of human experiences with artifacts and collections – social, spiritual, imaginal, therapeutic, aesthetic, and more.'

Among the interesting implications that Silverman draws from the meaning-making model is that a museum visit made in company, whether that be the company of partners, family, or friends, is likely to produce a richer harvest of meanings than a visit made by an individual alone. 'Often,' she writes, 'visitors learn new things through the past experience and knowledge of their companions. Thus . . . people create content and meaning in museums through the filter of their interpersonal relationships.' Again, some resonance may be sensed between this and the experience of the Strong Museum, where the community expressed its interest in having a museum that encouraged family visits. From this postmodernist perspective, the relationship of the museum to its visiting public in one sense seems clear. They are partners in giving a meaningful voice to objects that, according to a previous generation of museum practitioners, were once said to speak for themselves.

One final symptom of change: at a Smithsonian-wide exchange of ideas held in Washington, D.C., in March 1997, Doering astonished some participants with her radical suggestion that museum visitor studies might become more useful to museums if they focused, at least in part, on whether the visitor's expectations with respect to a display had been satisfied rather than on whether the expectations of the display's curator had been met. Underlying this suggestion was a recognition of the disconnect between what curators have traditionally expected of the display medium – that visitors will learn the lesson the curator has set out to teach – and the emerging reality that visitors may inevitably bring their own agendas to the museum and that, from their point of view, the satisfaction of those agendas constitutes the essence of a successful museum visit. As she noted in the abstract for her session: 'The visitor paradigm most commonly found among museum staff today is the "baby bird" model, which sees the visitor as a relatively undeveloped appetite needing our wise and learned feeding. The staff expects to provide these visitors with motivation and with learning experiences. The actual range of visitor expectations is more sophisticated, more complex, and more challenging than most of us suspect.'

Is not that precise shift of focus, subordinating a concentration on the museum's expectations of the public to a concentration on the public's expectation of the museum, at the very center of the revolution under consideration? I would submit that it is.

Finally, then, when that revolution has run its course and when the museum of the near future is firmly established, what might we expect it to be like? In the glorious phrase that Northrup Frye once used to describe the potentialities of an open society, there will be a 'reservoir of possibilities.' From that very rich reservoir, it will be the public – voting with its feet, voting with its credit cards, and acting through its elected representatives – that will determine which of those many possibilities and in what combinations best meet its needs and wants. No longer the passive body of the museum's first conception, doomed to be raised, elevated, refined, and up-lifted, in short, to be 'done' – the public will have succeeded to active control of this quite remarkable and uniquely powerful instrument. The museum will still do, but this time it will be the public, in all its plurality, that determines what it does. By then, perhaps, that might not even seem like such a revolutionary idea.

Note

Stephen Weil was a scholar emeritus at the Smithsonian Institution's Center for Education and Museum Studies and a deputy director of the Hirshhorn Museum and Sculpture Garden.

Chapter 2

'Play It again, Sam': Reflections on a New Museology

Marjorie M. Halpin

O N 17 SEPTEMBER 1773, the following notice appeared in some English newspapers, signed by Sir Ashton Lever:

> This is to inform the Publick that being tired out with the insolence of the common People, who I have hitherto indulged with a sight of my museum [at Alkrington], I am now come to the resolution of refusing admittance to the lower classes except they come provided with a ticket from some Gentlemen or Lady of my acquaintance. And I hereby author-ize every friend of mine to give a ticket to any orderly Man to bring in eleven Persons, besides himself whose behaviour he must be answer-able for, according to the directions he himself will receive before they are admitted. They will not be admitted during the time of Gentlemen and Ladies being in the Museum.[1]

More than a century later in New York, anthropologist Franz Boas wrote that

> the value of the museum for popular entertainment must not be under-rated, particularly in a large city where every opportunity that is given to the people to employ their leisure time in healthy and stimulating surroundings should be developed, where every attraction that coun-teracts the influence of the saloon and of the race-track is of great social importance.[2]

By Boas's time, of course, museums were enjoying the patronage of the modern nation state, in partnership with the social élite. Hence the shift to a rhetoric of museum visiting as culturally uplifting and in the public interest.

Source: *Museum International*, vol. 49, no. 2, 1997, pp. 52–6.

The democratization of museums continued throughout the present century, and is still expanding, notably in collaboration between museums and local communities and First Nations (as aboriginal communities in Canada are called) that is now resulting in exhibitions. What is not continuing is the patronage of the state. Now that governments in the West are withdrawing financial support from museums, it occurs to me to question why they supported us in the first place.

I am influenced by the work of anthropologist Richard Handler and art historian Carol Duncan on the role museums play in maintaining the cultural hegemony of the élite. Duncan explains the current contestations over museum representations as follows:

> To control a museum means precisely to control the representation of a community and its highest values and truths. It is also the power to define the relative standing of individuals within that community. Those who are best prepared to perform its ritual – those who are most able to respond to its various cues – are also those whose identities (social sexual, racial, etc.) the museum ritual most fully confirms. It is precisely for this reason that museums and museum practices can become objects of fierce struggle and impassioned debate. What we see and do not see in art museums – and on what terms and by whose authority we do or do not see it – is closely linked to larger questions about who constitutes the community and who defines its identity.[3]

My title, 'Play It Again, Sam', which has come to be associated with the unforgettable theme song of the film classic, *Casablanca*, is borrowed from cultural theoretician Homi Bhabha, who calls the song 'perhaps the Western world's most celebrated demand for repetition . . . an invocation to similitude, a return to eternal verities':[4]

> You must remember this,
> a kiss is still a kiss,
> a sigh is but a sigh.
> The fundamental things apply
> as time goes by.

It is in the interest of the state, itself the representation of representations, that meanings be 'fixed' and eternal, deriving from an authentic and idealized past.

How do we 'entify' the state and stabilize meaning in the contemporary museum? The first and most obvious way is that we inscribe an institutional voice on the walls. Science or history or archaeology speaks. Not as they speak to the initiated – in footnoted, contested and intertextual ways – but authoritatively, unambiguously, anonymously.

Less obviously, we also 'entify' the state by eliminating the distasteful, the ugly, the diseased, the disturbing objects that reveal cultural loss and brutalization. Our narrative is at once authoritative and romantic. Museums exhibit aboriginal peoples, for example, as noble and homogeneous carriers of cultures of great beauty, at harmony with their surroundings. (Paradoxically, this works to the advantage of First Nations, who are adopting an ideology of nationhood in their struggle for land and self government.) Still less obviously, we 'entify' the state by banishing hybridity, poetry, ambiguity, irony, complexity, dissent. Our narratives, by and large, are realist and boring. Fortunately, I think, the Western state is now too much in debt and too unstable to want to speak, and some of us are already choosing new partners and finding new messages, informed by what is being called the 'new museology'.

Engaging the community

There are several new museologies. In places in Quebec and in Europe, the new museology museumizes the community, throughout which its functions are dispersed. In the Netherlands, Peter van Mensch, a lecturer in theoretical museology at the Reinwardt Academy, in his comment on the Internet, defined a 'critical museology' in which exhibition design emphasizes authorship, replacing the former anonymous institutional voice. In this approach, he writes, 'uncertainty and ambiguity should play a role'. In the United Kingdom, Peter Vergo defines the new museology as a 'state of widespread dissatisfaction with the "old" museology, both within and outside the museum profession', and writes that 'what is wrong with the "old" museology is that it is too much about museum *methods*, and too little about the purposes of museums'.[5]

Concern with museum methods was appropriate during the years of state support, and while we were developing as a profession, which is now accomplished. In the absence of our previous function of stabilizing the values of the nation state, what are we to do? My concern is with how we engage the new and rapidly changing urban communities within which most of our buildings are situated. My primary reason is practical and simple: we have to increase admissions to pay the bills.

And, as Vergo argues, that means looking carefully at what we are doing, especially, I think, at the centuries-old assumptions that people visit museums in order to commune silently with objects on display, and that our professional function is to care for and present such objects. Anthropologist Richard Handler recently defined museums as social arenas. 'It is not at all clear', he writes, 'that the viewing of objects is the main activity that takes place in museums.' If a Martian anthropologist were to drop into one of our museums, he continues, the Martian would see 'administrative meetings, study and research, conservation activities, maintenance work, parties and celebration, eating and drinking, buying and selling, coming and going – many people doing many things'. He also contends that, however altruistic our mission statements, it is 'commonplace of the literature on cultural hegemony' that museums 'function to bolster the authority of élites'.[6] Carol Duncan refers to this as 'the space between what museums say they do and what they do without saying'.

To stimulate discussion, I shall refer to the work of John Cotton Dana, the founder of the Newark Museum in the United States ('a museum of museum experiments'), whom Duncan calls a 'museum maverick' and 'the greatest master of anti-aesthetic, anti-ritual, pro-educational polemic'. He was also defining a new museum movement (the word 'museology' was not yet coined) in the early years of this century. In 1917 he wrote a book entitled *The New Museum*, in which he estimated that there were only some fifty museums in the United States that could be called 'live museums' (out of a total of some 600 institutions by then using that name) by which he meant museums 'supposed to produce beneficial effects on their respective communities'.[7] The purposes of the New Museum movement that he espoused were community entertainment and 'visual instruction', or as we might say today, visual literacy. Moreover, he advocated 'branch institutes', such as 'store-rooms on business streets' as 'veritable teaching centers'; the lending to 'individuals, groups and societies, for any proper use and for any reasonable time, any of the museum's objects, whenever it is clear that the things thus lent will be of more service to the community than when they are resting, relatively unseen and unused, in the museum's headquarters'; and the display of objects 'which are products of the community's activities in field, factory and workshops'. The new museums he advocated would be 'museums properly so-called – homes and work-shops of the Muses'. Museums of 'the old kind', he contended, 'are not truly museums at all. They are "collections"'.

Dana's New Museum would exhibit the community itself, 'with, of course, suggestions to old and young as to specific things they can do to make the town a better place in which to live and do business'. The New Museum idea, he writes, is 'the idea of a definitely useful museum'. As such, its 'purposes and methods change daily, as do all other community enterprises in these days. Therefore, do not try to develop a museum after a plan. Learn what aid the community needs: fit the museum idea to those needs.' He cautions us to 'beware of "experts" in the museum field', and to remember, always, 'that the very essence of the public service of a public institution is the public's knowledge of the service that institutions can give; therefore advertise, advertise, and then advertise again. Advertising is the very life-blood of all the education a museum can give.'

The exhibition as process rather than product

Most museum professionals are trained in both the categories of professional museology and some university discipline. We regard it as our responsibility to teach the visiting public some version, suitably popularized, of academic discourse, whether history, ethnology, archaeology, art history or natural science. Let us think for a moment about the kind of exhibit we might create if it were not necessary for us to speak for a discipline. I am not advocating that we forget what we know, but that we use it for genuine museum purposes, not for disciplinary ones. Would we be perhaps more playful, personal, ironic, challenging, interesting?

Let me give a recent example of what happened when I departed from the now quarter-century-old tradition of exhibiting First Nations art on the Pacific coast of Canada in terms of quite well-established ethnological and art-market categories. In 1995 a former student and I exhibited the poems and drawings of a First Nations (Nuuchah-nulth) historian, dancer, singer, speaker, carver, etc. (he does not use the word 'artist' when referring to himself), Ron Hamilton. We managed to find sixty-four of the images that he draws incessantly, on napkins, place-mats, envelopes – any scrap of paper. A few he keeps, most he gives away, some are merely left behind in restaurants. The works are not made or edited for others and, indeed, it is stretching the matter to call even the poems 'composed', for we presented them just as he wrote them for himself in his journal. None of this work had ever been sold or even offered to the market (I dare say they have market value now, although he talks about giving those he owns away in a potlatch).

Because we are a museum, we had to frame these pieces of paper – as described, pieces of paper bags, restaurant doilies and place-mats, anything to hand. We also put on the wall Hamilton's narratives about the circumstances and stories that lay behind the poems and drawings – political meetings, the naming of his new son, an encounter with a cousin, sexual abuse in his childhood, his mother's can of bacon grease kept near the stove, myths of the Nuuchah-nulth cosmos. Two students and I transcribed these stories and sent them back to him for editing and corrections.

The exhibition was so successful that the editor of the University of British Columbia Press invited us to turn it into a book, and I want to make it into a CD-ROM so as to include Hamilton's taped voice and parts of the hour of video we made at the opening of the exhibit, at which twenty-four members of his family sang and danced, and friends and relatives spoke about what he means to their lives. We also have dozens of pages of visitor comments responding to Hamilton's request for dialogue and commending his honesty, political candour and cultural knowledge.

Including the opening feast and celebration, the exhibition cost only a few thousand dollars, will live on in a book and perhaps a CD-ROM, and marked the most eloquent and moving introduction to Nuuchah-nulth culture that I have seen anywhere. Its strength lies in its collaborative nature: instead of presenting the standard 'curated' museum introduction to Nuuchah-nulth culture – borrowing pieces from the world's great collections and doing the ethno-historical and ethnological research such an exhibition would require – the artist and I, along with other museum staff, engaged in a process to allow Hamilton's drawings and words to speak for themselves and the man. As a result, his intensely personal experience was (and continues to be) shared by museum staff and visitors alike. It is unlikely that the state would have funded such an exhibition in the first place, but perhaps we are better off free of the constraints such funding would impose.

In conclusion, the new or critical museology about which I am speaking might be a useful museology in service to a community, instead of the state and the élite. A museology practised by named, committed and creative professionals who know that people other than themselves are also cultural experts. A museology without a five-year plan, one that continuously examines its community and responds to what it sees and hears. A museology that, now in its maturity, can challenge, play with, and separate itself from the always serious academic voice.

A final word from Handler: 'The purpose of a museum is to survive.' Whether or not museums ought to survive is a question that our constituencies will, in the long or short run, answer for us.

Notes

Marjorie M. Halpin was the curator of Ethnology at the Museum of Anthropology and associate professor in the Department of Anthropology, University of British Columbia.

1   Alma Wittlin, *Museums: In Search of a Usable Future*, p. 76. Cambridge, Mass, MIT Press, 1970.
2   Franz Boas, 'Some Principles of Museum Administration', *Science*, 14 June 1907, pp. 921–2.
3   Carol Duncan, *Civilizing Rituals: Inside Public Art Museums*, pp. 8–9. London/New York, Routledge, 1995.
4   Homi Bhabha, *The Location of Culture*, p. 182. London/New York, Routledge, 1994.
5   Peter Vergo, 'Introduction', in P. Vergo (ed.), *The New Museology*, p. 3. London, Reaktion Books, 1989.
6   Richard Handler, 'An Anthropological Definition of the Museum and Its Purpose', *Museum Anthropology*, vol. 17, no. 1, 1993. pp. 33–4.
7   J.C. Dana, *The New Museum*, Part I, pp. 9–39. Woodstock, Vt., Elm Tree Press, 1917.

Chapter 3

Place Exploration: museums, identity, community

Peter Davis

MUSEUMS ARE IMPORTANT because they serve to remind us of who we are and what our place is in the world. Their power is due to their ability to operate at a variety of levels: they are significant to us as individuals, as a member of a community, even as a statement of nationhood. To begin to understand the idea of the ecomuseum, it is necessary to explore the concepts of cultural identity and community as they relate to museums in general. Museum professionals, with reference to their visitors, frequently use the expression 'museum community', but can this be defined? We also need to discover how museums interact with their community, and the community with its museums, and place this in a historical perspective. The influences of postmodernity and new museology have seen the emergence of new practices and attempts by museums to develop new audiences and engage with different communities in order to actively include all members of society. There is also a need to understand how the physical aspects of the environment that are valued by a community mesh with other factors to create a sense of place.

Museums and identity

When the ancient manuscripts *Flateyjarbók* and *Codex Regius* were returned to Iceland by Denmark in April 1971:

> There were 15,000 Icelanders cramming the quayside; but throughout the rest of Iceland it was as if a plague had struck. No one moved in the streets. Shops and schools were closed. The whole nation, just over 200,000 souls in those days, was listening to the radio or watching television for a live account of the historic event. (Magnusson 1989)

Source: *Ecomuseums: A Sense of Place*, London: Leicester University Press, 1999, pp. 24–44.

The return of the Stone of Scone to Scotland in November 1996 also created widespread media coverage, although not quite on the same scale. Indeed, it appeared that the British press were primarily interested in the questionable authenticity of the ancient coronation stone of Scottish kings, and in the timing of the exercise. That the then Secretary of State for Scotland engineered the removal of the stone from Westminster Abbey a few months before a general election was considered a 'pre-election sop' (Boggan 1996) by most observers. The political agenda was clear for all to see, a message amplified two days later as Alex Salmond, leader of the Scottish National Party, began a campaign for the return to Scotland of the ninth-century *Book of Deer* from the University of Cambridge and the Uig Chessmen from the British Museum (Cusick 1996).

These two examples demonstrate first the significance of cultural identity (and its tangible manifestation as 'cultural property') to nations, and perhaps more importantly the political dimension that plagues debates about the restitution of cultural objects. Provincial museums are not immune from such controversies either, as the example of the Lindisfarne Gospels demonstrates. In the summer of 1996 the Laing Art Gallery in Newcastle upon Tyne opened *Treasures from the Lost Kingdom of Northumbria*, a temporary exhibition that brought together some 250 objects from Anglo-Saxon Northumbria, including the wonderful illuminated manuscript known as the Lindisfarne Gospels. Written and illustrated by monks on Holy Island (Lindisfarne) off the coast of Northumberland in the late seventh century, the Gospels had been loaned by the British Library. The collections on display provided a statement of the past cultural and political achievements of the north-east of England, and the exhibition proved a huge success, attracting some 7,000 visitors during the final weekend alone. The treasures were made available to the public at a time when the call for the devolution of political power to the region (in the form of a Northern Assembly) was growing. As this campaign grew, so did the call for the return of the Gospels to the North of England from the British Library. It was evident that the manuscript had assumed a new layer of meaning as a potent symbol for the region. The campaign (in 1998) is well organized and vociferous, and plans are being laid to display the manuscript at alternating venues in Durham and Northumberland, including Holy Island itself, should the Trustees of the British Library relent. Inevitably, the British Library is firmly defending its position as the repository for one of Europe's greatest art and religious treasures; however, attempts to assuage the demands from the North with replicas, and even a digital version with pages that can be turned, have so far met with a frosty response.

Why is cultural property, as an element of 'cultural identity', such a powerful force? UNESCO (Viet 1980) defines cultural identity as 'the correspondence between a community (national, ethnic, linguistic, etc.) and its cultural life, as well as the right of each community to its own culture'. Objects are not specifically mentioned in this definition, yet for UNESCO, as well as for all museum professionals, the concept of ownership of cultural property is a major ethical issue, and arguably the most significant aspect of cultural identity. Objects have the ability to communicate either directly or by association. These aspects of reality which transcend time or space have special significance and are therefore sought after and protected. Perhaps it is not surprising, therefore, that the museums that guard these cultural icons are also recognized as symbols of power (Anderson 1991), and as aides to the creation

of national identity (Boylan 1990). The implication of the UNESCO definition is
that the meanings endowed by the original creator or owner of an object have
the greatest significance. But in the case of 'The Treasures of Troy', removed
from Berlin by the Russians following the Second World War, who should assume
ownership:

> the Germans who found and preserved it on the Museum Island in Berlin,
> or the Greeks whose alleged ancestors plundered fallen Troy, or the
> Turks whose forefathers conquered both the site of Troy and the Greeks?
> Even Rome might put in a claim, since Virgil tells us the city was founded
> by the descendants of exiles from Troy. (Almond 1991)

Similar arguments regarding ownership might be asked of the Parthenon or 'Elgin'
Marbles or the Benin Bronzes, which over time have also assumed new meanings
and significance.

There are growing attempts within the museum world to escape from the shack-
les of ownership, and this has largely been achieved in the fine arts. International
exhibitions of paintings by Impressionists, Pre-Raphaelites and Surrealists travel widely,
displayed in the art galleries of the world irrespective of ownership and nationality. Such works have assumed the status of 'global heritage'. It has been suggested
that other cultural objects (ethnographic or archaeological) could be treated in the
same manner, that there are certain objects or collections that are of such great
significance that they should transcend national barriers. There are parallels here
to the designation of World Heritage Sites[1] – would it be possible to give international status to certain objects or collections, with suitable financial incentives
for their conservation, mobility and security? The moral dilemma here is that the
recognition of certain collections as 'global heritage' conveniently justifies both the
retention of displaced antiquities, works of art and natural history collections in
North American or Western European museums and subsumes global culture into
a 'Western' paradigm. Despite these ethical drawbacks, attempting to circumvent
ownership must be a significant route to enabling wider access to major cultural
objects.

Although UNESCO has provided a workable definition of cultural identity, it
is evident that the terms identity, cultural identity and community are regularly
used in a seemingly interchangeable manner in museological and sociological literature. For example, the authors of the collected papers in Hall and Du Gay (1996)
Questions of Cultural Identity mainly use the word identity, not cultural identity. Bauman
(1996) describes identity as an escape from uncertainty, 'the thing we turn to when
unsure of ourselves', a view supported by Spielbauer (1986): 'Identity has become
increasingly popular as an expressive term for the need to find stability and order
in a rapidly changing world.' Hall (1996) prefers to use the term 'identification'
rather than identity, suggesting that this reflects 'a recognition of some common
origin or shared characteristics with another person or group, or with an ideal, and
with the natural closure of solidarity and allegiance established in this foundation'.
He also suggests that identification 'can be won or lost, sustained or abandoned
. . . identification is in the end conditional, lodged in contingency'. In other words,
identity is not fixed, but changes with time and circumstance. Arguments as to whether

identity is rooted in geographic locality, nation, politics, religion, education, ethnic background or genealogy are not irrelevant of course, but it is important to recognize that they are dynamic, not concrete, factors. Even ethnicity can be diluted. Circumstances which influence a cultural identity based on territory, including the dominance of certain cultural groups, migration, the formation of new societal groupings and communications technology are part of this dynamic. Indeed, any fixed concept of identity, itself a construct of modern Western society, is totally at odds with postmodern views, where the main problem of identity is how to avoid permanence and keep one's options open.

So where does postmodernist thought, with its emphasis on change, leave the museum, which is a permanent institution dedicated to the long-term care of durable objects? As Šuler (1986) suggests, 'If history were a flowing river museum exhibits would be the stones standing out in the water'; even ephemeral objects can assume a state of permanence with the right museological approach, as Robert Opie's Museum of Packaging demonstrates (Elsner and Cardinal 1994). So are museums and museum objects symbols of solidity in an age of change and uncertainty, places where absolute truth and the keys to our identity are preserved? Is this why cultural property is seen to be so important, that it represents past glories, status and lifestyle – a previous, now lost, identity? There is a real paradox here. Can museums be recognized as part of postmodern society with the labels of permanence that their collections and monumental buildings imply? The answer to this riddle lies in the ways that museums and collections are exploited, the ways that new meanings have been attributed to objects, or at the extreme, to interpret themes without reference to real objects at all. Approaches to objects, to interpretation, to exhibitions, to museums; are all being redefined and deconstructed to enable museums to escape from their late-nineteenth-century fixed identity and to create a new image, one more in tune with today's society.

But just how important are objects, and hence museums, in defining our cultural identity as an individual or as part of a community? We need to be a little cautious in assigning anything other than political significance to the Stone of Scone, for example. It is difficult to imagine either that the Scottish nation has an identity crisis or that a large block of stone, genuine or not, has a major influence on the identity of the individual Scot. Similarly, although the Lindisfarne Gospels attracted 7,000 individuals to the Laing Art Gallery in one weekend, more than 38,000 supported Newcastle United for ninety minutes on the Saturday afternoon. Dress codes, song and ritual proudly state their cultural identity as supporters of their football club, known as 'The Magpies', and as 'Geordies'. It is important then to put the significance of objects into perspective in any discussion of cultural identity. An object requires additional information or interpretation to determine its place or role and hence its significance to individual or group identity. This 'added value' can enable objects to be recruited into situations when the manipulation of identity is useful, with political expediency frequently providing the motivation for the addition of new meanings or values to objects to further restitution claims. Whatever value is added to objects (and museums), it is still difficult to quantify their role in the formation of identity in comparison to other cultural influences.

Diop (1982) suggested that there are three essential building blocks of culture: language, attitudes and history. Museums have assumed cultural significance because they have formed collections of objects in which history and attitudes are reflected; however, the traditional approach of museums, and their emphasis on form (objects) rather than content (meanings), has meant that their role in preserving cultural iden- tity has been rather limited. The classic approach of museums has been object- centred rather than concept-centred (Cannon-Brookes 1984; Taborsky 1982), and it is still possible to visit museums where cultures (e.g. Neolithic peoples, the Maori) are exclusively defined by the form and decoration of their material culture. The challenge for museums is to 'look behind forms to make indigenous values appear' (Burgess, quoted in Bellaigue 1986) and 'to prove we are not connected to the past only through myths and mementoes' (Sola 1986). Other limitations are imposed by collecting and exhibition policies: what is not collected, researched, documented or exhibited does not exist – for the museum or its public – and 'as a consequence museums are full of invisible objects documenting invisible groups' (Van Mensch 1986). A museum visitor would (until recently) have assumed that women played a merely decorative role in history, that the history of the American continent began when Europeans arrived, that immigrants from India or the West Indies had nothing to do with English history, and that art produced by non-Western artists is displayed only in anthropology museums.

The debate surrounding museums and issues of national identity and the return of cultural property (including art, archaeological and ethnographic items, sacred religious objects and the remains of ancestors) has been widely documented in museo- logical literature (see, for example, San Roman [1992] and the essays in Kaplan [1994]). With the social emancipation of minority cultures, the subjugation or dis- play of the culture of 'others' – the politics of representation – has also received considerable coverage (see, for example, Carter [1994]; Herle [1997]; Merriman [1992]; and the essays in Karp and Levine [1991]). Involvement in the represent- ation of minority cultural identity also requires the museum to assume the role of self-appointed advocate. Both demands are potentially troublesome for museums, primarily because it is difficult for a member of one (usually dominant) social group (the curator) to abandon their own set of values and to describe another culture without projecting their own fears, frustrations or hopes. The curator as advocate (with the high moral objective of presenting another culture to promote under- standing) is therefore very exposed. It is only through mutual confidence and co- operation between museum and minority cultures that advocacy can be successful: in other words, a major input is required from the community itself. Despite these difficulties, the celebration of cultural difference is an essential feature of post- modernism, and there is a firm belief among museum professionals (e.g. Boylan 1995) that exhibiting other 'cultures' can promote tolerance and understanding, and is an essential role for museums to play. Roth (1992) suggests that we extend this tolerance not just to different ethnic groups but also to disadvantaged social groups, because 'Le musée d'aujourd'hui doit être capable d'intégrer des ruptures. Il doit aussi oser reconnaître ce qui est ruiniforme dans notre société, tolérer les maintes identités différentes et leur ouvrir un espace d'exposition.'

However we try and define cultural identity and what it means for museums, it is apparent that issues relating to the restitution or ownership of major cultural objects, and the representation of other cultures, will continue to be debated. If society is to appreciate cultural differences, and grow stronger as a result, further reflection is desirable. Postmodernism, or more correctly its manifestation as new museology, has ensured that the ethical, moral and practical concerns of individuals, communities, museums and curators are being openly discussed. At a meeting in Mexico City in 1982 a major statement was prepared by UNESCO (UNESCO 1982) – the 'Declaration on Cultural Policies' – which clearly illustrates how the concept of cultural identity is incorporated into global cultural policy. The key paragraphs in this document make a useful summary of the significance of the meaning of cultural identity for museums; although it inevitably has a 'national' emphasis, many of the points made are relevant to communities at every scale:

- Every culture represents a unique and irreplaceable body of values since each people's traditions and forms of expression are its most effective means of demonstrating its presence in the world.
- The assertion of cultural identity therefore contributes to the liberation of peoples. Conversely, any form of domination constitutes a denial or the impairment of that identity.
- Cultural identity is a treasure that vitalizes mankind's possibilities of self-fulfilment by moving every people and every group to seek nurture in its past, to welcome contributions from outside that are compatible with its own characteristics, and so to continue the process of its own creation.
- All cultures form part of the common heritage of mankind. The cultural identity of a people is enriched through contact with the traditions and values of others. Culture is dialogue, the exchange of ideas and experiences and the appreciation of other values and traditions; it withers and dies in isolation.
- The universal cannot be postulated in the abstract by any single culture: it emerges from the experience of all the world's peoples as each affirms its own identity. Cultural identity and cultural diversity are inseparable.
- Special characteristics do not hinder, but rather enrich the communion of the universal values that unite people. Hence recognition of the presence of a variety of cultural identities wherever various traditions exist side by side constitutes the very essence of cultural pluralism.
- The international community considers it its duty to ensure that the cultural identity of each people is preserved and protected.
- All of this points to the need for cultural policies that will protect, stimulate and enrich each people's identity and cultural heritage and establish absolute respect for and appreciation of cultural minorities and the other cultures of the world. The neglect or destruction of the culture of any group is a loss to mankind as a whole.
- The equality and dignity of all cultures must be recognized, as must the right of each people and cultural community to affirm and preserve its cultural identity and have it respected by others.

Such a declaration places an obligation on museums to reconsider the ways in which they operate, and to carefully explore the academic and moral grounds under which they hold and exhibit collections. It is fair to say that in some cases restitution of major cultural artefacts and the return of ancestral remains has taken place, and that greater care, humility and respect is being demonstrated by museums when

exhibiting artefacts of other cultures. More efforts are being made to involve people in the interpretation of their cultural heritage. All museums can learn from these
changes in attitudes and practices, and they are as pertinent to provincial museums
as they are to the great national collections. On the national-provincial-local cline
of museums, none is free from the theory, ethics, politics and practice of cultural
policy.

However, it is important in the context of ecomuseums to make a distinction between national and provincial museums that hold historical collections from
world cultures and the more recently founded small, sometimes rural, 'community' museums. The latter operate at a different geographical scale and with a local,
sometimes introspective, political agenda. They are more concerned about collecting,
conserving and displaying what is important to the people of their geographical area:
in other words, acting on behalf of their immediate local community. It might be
argued that the smaller and more rural the museum, the less the influence of the
major national issues of repatriation and restitution, and the closer is the link to
the community. The proximity of a museum to its community and its cultural identity gives special relevance to the opening and closing sentences of the UNESCO
statement.

Defining the museum community

The *Collins English Dictionary and Thesaurus* (Makins 1997) gives the following definition
of community: '1a. the people living in one locality; b. the locality in which they
live; c. (as modifier) *community spirit*. 2. a group of people having cultural, religious or other characteristics in common; *the Protestant community*. 3. a group of nations
having certain interests in common. 4. the public, society. 5. common ownership.
6. similarity or agreement; *community interests*. 7. (in Scotland and Wales) the
smallest unit of local government. 8. *ecology* – a group of interdependent plants
and animals inhabiting the same region.' A shorter definition provided in *Chambers
Twentieth-Century Dictionary* (Macdonald 1977) reads, 'People having common
rights etc.; the public in general; a body of persons in the same locality; a body of
persons leading a common life, or under socialistic or similar organisation.' Here
then are the essential shared elements of community. Geographical locality (with
its influence on landscape, natural resources and the economy), shared religions,
political systems and ownership, a common culture (which includes material
objects, traditions, song, language and dialect), interdependence, common needs
and the notion of 'community spirit' (with its close tie to community identity) help
to make a community what it is.

It is evident that what we consider 'the community' is hugely complex, a constantly changing pattern of the tangible and intangible. Any individual within the
geographical region that we loosely (and probably inaccurately) refer to as the museum
community may also belong to several different sub-communities. These may occur
as a result of the influences of their ethnic background, work, income level, mar-
ital status, age, leisure interests or the street they live in, among others. Hence
at the macro-level an individual may receive their (ascribed) identity, often in the
form of a geographical (a Scot, a Glaswegian) or functional (a professor, a plumber)

label and its associated stereotype. In reality he or she (self-identity) is not attached to a single community, and may move freely in and out of sub-communities as circumstances and interests change. It is also possible to think of sub-communities or groups in two ways – as groups formed by a kind of patterned interaction, or those that are bound together by a 'we' feeling – that are also subject to change. Wasserman (1995) attempts to encapsulate these notions in her definition of community:

> A population living in an area, conscious of the affinities and the differences which characterise its elements, as well as the conflicting relationships between these and their environment and to whom at least the future is common. Communities may depend on institutional, political, technical or economic structures . . . or be based on spontaneous structures: groups of individuals . . . with a freely chosen social objective, unrelated to material profit or the will of legislators or administrators. Even in the case of small communities, more or less local or at least with a definite location, a community may be of various dimensions; village, country, region, nation, company, country, religious grouping, academic, immigrant, professional, family. Everybody belongs to a community, while at the same time crossing several others; an individual chooses certain communities, while others are imposed on him by law, events or birth.

The 'museum community' is therefore an almost meaningless expression, as the Museum of London discovered during its 'Peopling of London project' when attempting to change its audience profile to reflect more accurately the racial mix of the city (Merriman 1995). Here, the task of involving the community has proved far from easy, because 'people do not just form themselves into homogeneous groups called communities . . .' (Carrington 1995). However, through their marketing operations museums can target parts of the local community – their target audience – knowing that certain sections of the population will be more receptive than others to their exhibitions or activities. This fact is clearly demonstrable in the profile of museum visitors – the community served by an art gallery is identifiably different from that sector of the community who visit a railway museum. Even the type of exhibition mounted by a single museum may attract a certain element within the community. For example, the Hancock Museum, a natural history museum in Newcastle, found through its visitor monitoring programme that *Dinosaurs Alive* appealed to family groups and young children, while *Star Trek* attracted an older, specialized audience, many of whom were first-time visitors.

Museums must therefore relate to, serve and interact with several communities, and through their actions define for themselves what their 'museum community' is. The status, collections and location of museums will inevitably affect their choice of 'community'. Thus, a national institution such as the Louvre in Paris has a truly international and worldwide audience. A large provincial museum may serve only the people within the city or region (and could therefore be defined as 'local'), but the quality of the collections and its proximity to tourist routes may attract a different community. Generally speaking a local museum – that is, a small museum

with limited collections that serves those people in a defined geographical area –
should be able to qualify its museum community more readily. It is these museums
that can most easily capture the identity of places. The worldwide growth in
the numbers of such 'identity museums' (the heimatmuseums in Germany, or folk
museums in the USA, for example), both in towns or in rural areas, has been
considerable in the last decades of the twentieth century. Maure (1986) indicates
that there is a perfectly normal need for small communities to be aware of those
attributes that make them different: 'L'identité d'un groupe se définit et est vécue
par rapport à l'existence d'autres groupes qui sont "différents".' In other words,
to be part of an identifiable community we need to know that there are other, different, communities out there.

However, even within small towns and villages, the nature of the 'museum
community' is difficult to grasp. Such places are frequently introspective and reflective,
and with a population that is all too aware of the foibles and passions of their neighbours it is difficult to assign an outward appearance of harmony to an individual
'community'. Macqueen (1998) cites numerous examples of community tensions
and rivalries in Argyll and Bute; Rachel Clough of Kilmartin House (pers. comm.,
July 1997) confirmed that such tensions came to the fore when the Kilmartin Centre
was being planned, with pro and anti factions emerging within the village.

Defining the 'museum community' is therefore very difficult; it can, however,
be best understood through the realization that communities and sub-communities
are dynamic. A pool of individuals within any geographical locality will form into
groups due to a variety of social influences (immigration, economics and cultural
change); some of these groups will become part of the museum community. The
fact that only some will be attracted by what the museum has to offer implies
that other social groups are excluded from museums. In his essay 'The end of the
museum?' Goodman (1992) compared the relative problems that faced museums
and libraries:

> while most users of a library know how to read the books there many
> visitors to a museum do not know how to see, or to see in terms of,
> the works there; and second, that the works in a museum must be viewed
> under severe and stultifying restraints. Unless the museum . . . finds ways
> of inculcating the ability to see and of aiding and abetting the exercise
> of that ability, the other functions of the museum will be pointless and
> its works as dormant as books in an unreadable language or in locked
> bindings.

The remodelling of museum philosophies and practices from the 1970s has attempted
to address this major issue, and has rapidly gathered pace.

Museum and community interactions – an ecological approach

It is clear that defining identity, cultural identity or the museum community with
any conviction is not a simple matter. However – and this is especially relevant to
the ecomuseum debate – it is clear that the traditional museum's relationship to

its community demands that it is perceived as a separate entity. There is a build-ing, called a museum, housing experts, collections, knowledge and exhibitions that is both physically and philosophically a discrete entity; it allows the public – its community – access on a limited basis, but essentially it is separated from that community. Terms used by museums such as 'outreach' or 'outstation' (with etymological links to 'outcast') reinforce this separation.

The interaction between the museum and the community occurs through exhibitions and educational and other activities. This can be expressed in a simple model of overlapping circles representing museum and community (Figure 3.1), to which can be added an 'environment' circle to represent interaction between museum and environment, and community and environment (Figure 3.2). The amount of overlap of these three circles could provide a simple measure of a museum's commitment to its community and to the environment [discussed further in rela-tion to the philosophy of the ecomuseum in Davis, Ch. 3; not reproduced here].

. . . the science of ecology has developed its own specialized vocabulary that provides a definition of what constitutes a community in biological terms. Thus, any organism (species) has a specific ecological niche (a role or 'profession') and the variety of species occupying a specific geographical area makes up its biotic

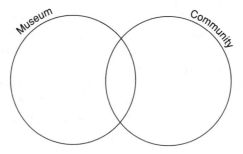

Figure 3.1   The relationship between museum and community

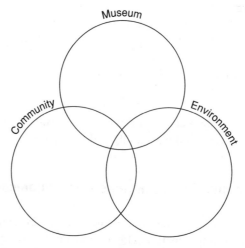

Figure 3.2   The relationship between museum, community and environment

community. For instance, a rabbit will occupy the grazing niche in a grassland community, or a fungus will perform a decomposing role in a woodland community.
The range of communities makes up the ecosystem. Using this parallel we can place
the species we call 'museum' within the cultural community, which is inhabited
by other closely related species such as theatre, dance, music, literature and cinema. The niches occupied by these species are relatively easy to identify as trans-
mitters of culture, as entertainers. Although niche separation occurs, there is
considerable overlap. The museum species, as a more complex organism, occupies
a number of additional niches – collector, guardian, educator and technician, among
others. In many ways it is easier to think of the museum occupying a recycling niche:
it absorbs and collects objects, specimens, ideas and skills, and recycles them back
into the community as exhibitions, activities or publications. This recycling takes
place within the cultural community, but also within the ecosystem – society as a
whole. Although many museum professionals might be horrified at the thought of
being compared to fungi or bacteria, they might be heartened by the realization
that the planet's ecosystems would grind to a halt without such organisms – they
are indispensable.

Like all species, the museum is in competition with its close relatives, as
well as those occupying the adjacent communities of sport and media. In nature
animal species compete for resources in terms of energy and living space, and both
competitive exclusion and coexistence occur. In the cultural community the
museum species competes for resources in terms of financial support and visitors
and although coexistence is the norm, exclusion and even local extinction has been
known to occur. Competition and variety are the cornerstones of evolution, however, and like all species the museum has evolved through time, adapting to the
needs of society. However, it is important to realize that community involvement
has always been important to museums in the past, but also that the scale and nature
of the involvement has waxed and waned.

The local museum and its community – a historical perspective

From a late-twentieth-century view it would be relatively easy to suggest that
museums are more in tune with their communities than ever before. Yet the
development of museums in the nineteenth century was in part a response to the
utilitarian view of education that identified the museum as a means of delivering
knowledge to communities; it is a strong indication that local museums have always
been community oriented. For example, in the UK, museums were considered the
'universities of the people' (Hooper-Greenhill 1994) and were created as a result
of a heady combination of 'private philanthropy and civic pride' (Museums and Galleries
Commission 1986). Thus, the first public museum to open in Scotland, founded
on the collections bequeathed by William Hunter to the University of Glasgow in
1807, demonstrated not only civic pride and philanthropy but also strong educational goals, being readily accessible to students and the general public. The many
museums founded throughout Britain by literary and philosophical societies, natural history or antiquarian societies were the end result of a passion for knowledge
and self-improvement which was frequently directed to the immediate locality. This

is not to suggest that such societies were inward looking – their ethnographic and worldwide natural history collections inform us otherwise – only that they served the local community well both geographically and socially. Emphasis on the local area can frequently be seen in references to the formation of such societies, such as the notice in the *Campbeltown Courier* (Kintyre, Scotland) in 1890 which read:

> while recognising the repeated efforts of individuals to organise and estab-
> lish A SCIENTIFIC INSTITUTION OR ASSOCIATION in our midst and the partial
> success resulting therefrom, we think the time has now come when the
> public might be asked to assist in the formation and establishment of an
> Association for the purpose of Collecting, Preserving and Classifying
> Specimens of the various products of Kintyre and its surrounding waters.
> We, the undersigned, being residenters in the district of Kintyre there-
> fore respectfully submit the matter to your favourable consideration and
> request . . . a public meeting of those favourable to such an Associa-
> tion . . . (Quoted in Macqueen 1998)

The subsequent formation of the association and the patronage of James Macalister Hall (1823–1904) eventually led to the building of the town museum and library, which opened in 1899. This is an excellent example of community action for community benefit, and provides an interesting parallel to current developments.

The societies were often quick to realize the educational value of their collections for the wider community, and gradually began to open their doors to non-members. For example, the Natural History Society of Northumberland, Durham and Newcastle upon Tyne opened its museum to the general public of Newcastle for the first time in 1835. Visitors were allowed access on one evening each month, and the society minutes record that 'the interest was so great, and the people came in crowds so large, as to fill the whole building, and totally defeat the end your Committee had in view' (Goddard 1929). In 1836 schools were admitted for the first time, and by 1838 annual attendance was in the region of 20,000. As the nineteenth century progressed, many of the collections formed by society museums became the cornerstones of local authority museums, and their value to the community was widely recognized.

'Civic pride' is in itself an interesting yet rather intangible phenomenon, a demonstration of commitment to a geographical area and its people akin to community spirit, but with political overtones. The opening of new museums in the nineteenth century was frequently greeted with acclaim. The *Argyllshire Herald* for 28 January 1899 described the opening of the Campbeltown Public Library and Museum as an 'important epoch in the history of the town . . . a new era in providing opportunities for improvement and culture', while the museum building was regarded with great pride 'from an architectural point of view but also [for] the treasures contained within' (Macqueen 1998).

This close link between the local museum and its community in Britain – so readily identified in the middle and late nineteenth century and demonstrated by the activities of museums and the clear expressions of pride in them – began to erode in the early twentieth century. The Miers Report (1928) suggested that museums were set apart from communities:

to put it bluntly, most people in this country do not really care for
museums or believe in them; they have not played a significantly important part in the life of the community to make ordinary folk realise what
they can do . . . The museum should be one of the best-recognised forms
of public service and should attract the enthusiasm of the community.
(Quoted in Chadwick 1980)

Museums had evolved into elitist establishments in which curators pursued their
academic interests without public interference or accountability. Sir Henry Miers
believed that museums needed to re-examine their community involvement, cooperate more fully, develop travelling exhibitions and educational services, and,
most importantly, communicate their function to the public, so breaking down the
barriers which had been erected between museums and the community they served.
It is fascinating to consider that we can read the same sentiments being expressed
seventy years later. For example, Carter (1992) suggests that museums need to
revise their aims and policies in order to 'put the community back into museums'.
Although the above examples refer to the situation in the UK, similar patterns of
development were observed throughout Europe.

Expanding the museum community – audience development

Museums, especially throughout the twentieth century, have been noted for the
ways in which they have excluded many factions of society. Such 'social exclusion'
has not necessarily been deliberate; rather, it has been a less than active attempt to
include certain (often disadvantaged) groups. However, the realization by museums
that their public is composed of a variety of interest groups or sub-communities
(some of whom are culturally and ethnically distinct minorities) is gradually beginning to change the ways that they function, and as a consequence public perceptions
of museums have also altered. The driving force for this new vision of the public
has been societal change. Not always altruism, but sometimes political expediency,
economics and survival have caused museums to be aware of the needs of their
communities; more revenue, and hence larger (and different) audiences are required,
as is the need to be seen to be publicly accountable and politically correct. New
visions, new audiences, access and outreach, even new museums, have been
central to this reappraisal. Miles (1994) notes that

as a body, Western Europe's museums have undergone profound
changes in the last twenty years. These have tended to affect all aspects
of their existence and operation, and are imperfectly captured in
bald statistics such as the doubling of the number of museums in the
last thirty-five years . . .

These changes in museum attitudes and practice, the critical reappraisal of their
roles and responsibilities is evidence for the new museology, and the demand
for new approaches and new challenges within the profession is helping to create
a new identity for museums. Museums' professionals are, however, among the first

to recognize that the rate of change is slow, and that it will be a long road from cosmetic change to complete metamorphosis (Cameron 1992).

Highlighting past cultural injustices has been a feature of museum activity in the last two decades, with the museological literature benefiting from accounts that detail the efforts museums have made to re-establish the cultural identity and cultural achievements of (for example) native Australians and the North American Indians. In Europe, the case of the Sami posed similar issues, as Magga (1995) explains:

> From 1850 onwards museums played a part in the growth of the Norwegian nation . . . Sami history was not regarded as part of this national consciousness, but instead belonged to a 'foreign' people. Objects collected from Sami culture were generally consigned to the ethnographic archives. The Sami past was seen as a homogeneous, frozen and static culture rather than as a part of the nation's history; and the museum displays confirmed the dominant society's stereotype of the Sami culture and way of life.

The catalyst for change in Norway was the call for the creation of an independent Sami parliament, following land-claim debates that occurred during the development of the Guovdageaidnu/Alta River hydroelectric dam project. The Sami Act of 1987 made it a responsibility of state authorities to recognize that the Sami should secure and develop their own culture on their own terms. Central to this change was the establishment of Sami museums and the preservation and use of Sami heritage sites. These initiatives are to be welcomed, although there are still several problems to be overcome. The small Sami museums are poorly staffed and have few resources, and opening up cultural sites to visitors in fragile environments is fraught with difficulties, especially when sacred landscapes can lose spiritual meaning if heavily used.

In the USA the civil rights movement brought issues of opportunity and equality to communities whose histories had largely been ignored by conventional museums – the middle and working classes, the poor, immigrants and non-white races. Many urban museums have dramatically changed the ways they work, and have redefined their communities. Benson (1995), influenced and inspired by the Museum of London's 'Peopling the City' and the Migration Museum in Adelaide, devised a programme to reach out to non-traditional audiences at the Museum of New York. Here a gallery was designated as a 'Community Gallery' and has operated as a bridge between the museum and the residents of East Harlem. Activities and exhibitions have been mounted with the assistance of local community groups, and the subjects have ranged from serious social issues to traditional street games.

Dickerson (1995) referring to the museum of the Chicago Historical Society notes that

> the challenge is to synthesise the many component histories, the many stories that give depth and breadth and face to our definition of Chicago history, then we must find within these stories a common ground among the divergent voices, values and perspectives. Finally we must offer ourselves as welcoming space for the public to come and see themselves

and to consider our collective possibilities for the future. That is museums
as a resource for ideas, innovation and experimentation. We see ourselves as working across numerous borders. Borders of perception
and experience, borders of tradition and change, borders of past and
future, of color and race and nationality, borders of our institutional
culture and public or civic culture.

This refocused mission for the museum has changed its approach in all areas, but
none more so than in exhibition design, where 'community members, lay scholars,
elders and museum staff come together to develop the themes, temporal parameters and content for an exhibition'. This theme is echoed by Jenkinson (1994),
who argues that museum professionals must 'regard people not just as consumers
and spectators, who tramp past the turnstiles for their subliminal swish past a fixed
culture, but as critics and creators. We should welcome partnership and collaboration as the source of new energy, new ideas and new museum meanings.'

In *A Common Wealth* (Anderson 1997) it was suggested that UK museums needed
to ensure access to their collections, scholarship, expertise and skills to provide
opportunities for learning. 'Access' has become a key word of the late 1990s. Museums
and art galleries have made increasing efforts to encourage all members of the local
community to use their galleries. This has resulted not only in better provision for
people with disabilities but also in more innovative use of collections and expertise via lectures, demonstrations and outreach activities. Initiatives such as 'the Open
Museum' in Glasgow, which allows community groups to 'borrow objects and exhibitions from the world's biggest civic museum collection for display in their own
communities' (Anon, n.d.), is just one example that reflects the trend of increasing access, enabling museums to reach audiences who might never consider visiting a museum. 'The Open Museum' is committed to 'working with communities
that are under-represented, deprived, or otherwise marginalised' (Carrington 1995).
Another example of outreach work carried out in Glasgow was the creation of *Hotel
Caledonia*, an exhibition based on the experience of the city's homeless. Increasingly, efforts have been made to reach across cultural boundaries to ethnic minorities, and to ensure representation of all cultures. There are many examples (see
Hooper-Greenhill 1997), including the work of Walsall Museum with the Sikh community (Cox and Singh 1997) and the Geffrye Museum's developing link with the
Chinese community in Hackney (Hemming 1997). Aygeman and Kinsman (1997)
have referred to museums and heritage sites as micro-environments, and make an
interesting parallel between the exclusion of ethnic minorities from them and the
macro-environment, the wider environment, including the countryside.

Ideas and practices to engage a wider community and to develop the social
role of museums have included exhibitions, outreach and educational programmes.
Attempts have been made to pinpoint geographical or social sectors within the
community to break down not just ethnic barriers but also other cultural barriers,
including those of education and elitism. The phenomenon of the 'People's Show'
(Lovatt 1997), where members of the public are given opportunities to exhibit their
private collections in their local museum, has been widely adopted. There have been
a number of variants on this theme. For example, members of the public in disadvantaged neighbourhoods were asked by Tyne and Wear Museums to make their

own choice of paintings and artwork from the permanent collections to mount the exhibitions *From the Vaults* at the Laing Art Gallery and *People's Choice* at Sunderland Museum and Art Gallery. *Clothes from the Closet* was an exhibition held at the Discovery Museum, Newcastle, and arranged by a class of primary schoolchildren, who selected items from the museum's costume collections. According to Education Officer Paul Swift (pers. comm., January 1997):

> The idea behind these projects is that the museum becomes more than just a place to passively visit, it actually becomes a place where local people can work alongside museum staff and participate in the develop-ment of a real exhibition, open to the public. We are attempting to address their interests as well as those of museum staff, thereby ensur-ing that the museum becomes more relevant to local communities. Active participation within the museum is our aim during these projects and they also help to show [to communities] the work that goes on behind the scenes in the museum.

In *Clothes from the Closet II* Paul Swift and Keeper of Costume Caroline Imlah worked with young people in the care of NACRO (National Association for the Care and Resettlement of Young Offenders), many of whom had experienced consid-erable difficulties at school or with the police. None of them had visited a museum before becoming involved in the project. The concept was to enlist their help in designing and creating a temporary exhibition in the Fashion Works gallery at Newcastle's Discovery Museum. Communication was difficult, meetings were cancelled, the group membership fluctuated constantly, but thanks to persistence on behalf of NACRO and museum staff, selections of objects were made. The costume-handling sessions became a social occasion; the group began to see it as their exhibition and felt relaxed working together. The exhibition opened on time, accompanied by collages and clothes designed by the group that had been inspired by their contact with genuine historical costume. It is attractive, informative and something of which the group and the museum staff are justifiably proud. One of the large labels, written by a NACRO youngster, states: 'At the end of this, we hope that our ideas will give much pleasure to you and maybe bring back fond memories . . .' That the exhibition was a success in its own terms is undeniable. Although few of the young people attended the official opening, they are now regularly seen in the gallery with friends.

Engaging new communities is not an easy option for museums. In devising a project to work with four neighbourhood areas in Chicago that crossed a variety of ethnic, class, geographical and generation boundaries, Dickerson (1995) recalls:

> One of the most important lessons learned was the need for strong community-based links . . . to establish the continuity and sense of trust central to the success of such an effort, as well as to achieve a full under-standing of the social and political dynamics of that community.

There is always going to be a sense of mistrust and apprehension among members of a community who are not traditional museum visitors – what are they going to gain by the experience? The museum gains a great deal, of course, and not just a sense of pride in reaching a different audience, but frequently good press coverage, strong political support and new contacts. As individuals museum staff undoubtedly learn much about themselves, their attitudes and perspectives.

It might be argued that if museums wish to engage with diverse communities, and involve them with museum activities, then they must radically alter the ways they work. Thus, aspects of personnel recruitment, staffing and training need to be re-examined, and attitudes to customer care and collections management revised. Weil (1990) advocates this view, stressing that 'we must envision a higher professionalism, one in which museum staff members become as expert and as skilful in responding to community needs and desires as they are today in collecting, preserving, studying, exhibiting and interpreting collections'.

Museums, tourism and economics

In many countries the significance of tourism to museums and to the economics of its community is considerable. In New Zealand, for example, museums have become stopping-off points on the tourist trail, and are now regarded as 'crucial to audiences and revenue' (Legget 1995). Although research on the direct effect of museums on the local economy, and especially on employment, appears inconclusive (Johnson and Thomas 1991a), there is a symbiotic relationship where the tourist as visitor is contributing to the economic well-being of the museum and the museum provides the tourist with cultural enrichment. In addition, museums provide the possibility for interaction between local community and tourist, and enable locals to demonstrate pride in their region's environment, heritage and culture. As Johnson and Thomas (1991) have noted: 'In the case of Beamish (the North of England Open Air Museum), the availability of the "Beamish Experience" has stimulated a greater sense of regional identity, awareness, and pride in the area's industrial heritage.' This is also true for other smaller UK museums, such as those at Easdale Island and Kilmartin. Museums can provide a powerful combination of economic advantage and a sense of pride in the locality, even in areas that have suffered economic decline.

The founding of the Fortress of Louisbourg, a 'living-history' site based around an eighteenth-century French stronghold in Cape Breton, Nova Scotia, was motivated 'with primarily economic benefits in mind' (Kell 1991). Although the fortress had been recognized as a historic site in 1928, and had a museum from 1930, it was only when the local coal industry went into rapid decline that any real interest was shown in developing the site. The project made a direct bid to increase the tourism potential of the area, while injecting a ray of hope into the community: 'What is proposed will be not only of economic benefit to the Island; it will introduce elements to regenerate its life and outlook, dissolve the climate of drabness and let into human hearts and intelligence the light of new interests, hopes and ambitions' (Rand, quoted in Kell 1991). The site is now recognized as a great success in professional terms, with an impressive programme of events, but 'it is clear that the operation comes nowhere near paying its own way . . . in this sense the project has failed to create self-sustaining employment'. However, it has become the best-known historic site in Canada, and its impact on tourism in the area has been considerable; the local community also gains some direct

employment, despite the fact that much of the expertise (especially costumed interpretation) is brought in from outside. Kell (ibid.) suggests that:

> The only level on which this economic plan has failed is in selling the
> vision of Louisbourg to the people of the local community not as a
> single employer but as the creator of an interest and investment which
> reaches far beyond the walls of the Fortress and into the private econ-
> omy of the community and the communal national psyche.

It appears that although the site has been saved and developed, and that there are
some economic benefits, the local community has been almost totally marginalized,
their sense of ownership of what was 'theirs' has been lost. This heritage development provides a warning not only of the unproven impact of musealization on the
local economy but also more importantly of the need to ensure that local people
can identify with the project, that their community identity is an integral part of it.

The significance of place – community identity

It is clear that the terms identity, cultural identity and community must be considered as dynamic concepts; it is also apparent that the factors which give us a sense
of identity, whether it be our self-, national or community identity are many and
complicated. Some of them are also subject to change. With all these variables how
can we begin to understand what the most significant features of our community,
our place or territory are? Although physical surroundings are important (landscapes,
habitats, buildings), place is much more: it is a web of understanding between
people and the environment, between people and their neighbours, between people
and their history. And it has to change, and be permeable to new ideas, new practices and new people. Cultural identity demands that in a changing world we try and
hold on to what is important from the past and adopt the best features of the new.
    Common Ground use the term 'local distinctiveness' to try and encapsulate
what is special about a geographical area.[2] They suggest that little things (detail)
and fragments of previous lives and landscapes (patina) are the attributes that 'breath
significance into the streets or fields'. To Common Ground:

> local distinctiveness is about everywhere, not just beautiful places; it
> is about details, patina and meaning, the things which create identity.
> Importantly it focuses on locality, not on the region. It is about accum-
> ulation and assemblages . . . accomodation and change . . . it includes
> the invisible as well as the physical; dialect, festivals, myths, may be as
> important as hedgerows, hills and houses. (Common Ground 1996)

Common Ground have mainly applied this approach to small geographical areas,
producing 'illuminated alphabets' to list the 'cultural touchstones' that help us to
define, or identify, our place. These may be significant landscape features, or small
things – the design of farm gates, the type of stile encountered on a footpath. Such
a methodology can be used on a larger scale, although the touchstones themselves

are also larger. Tyneside, an area in the North of England with strong cultural traditions, can be taken as an example. When 'brainstorming' with my students the range of cultural factors that make Newcastle 'special' as a place, a range of factors emerged as being important to the Geordie identity. Some of the factors that give Tyneside a 'cultural distinctiveness' are listed as an 'alphabet' below:

A – Armstrong, Sir William (inventor and engineer); Angel of the North (Anthony Gormley sculpture). B – Blaydon Races (traditional song); Bewick, Thomas (engraver). C – coal, collective memories; coastline; Central Station. D – dress codes (old and new); Dobson, John (architect). E – enjoyment, especially F – Friday evenings in the Bigg Market. G – Geordie accent; Geordie warmth and friendship; Grainger Street; glass and ceramics. H – history; Hoppings (fair on Town Moor). I – industrial past (coalmining, shipbuilding, engineering). J – Jesmond Dene (local park). K – keep (of the New Castle). L – leek growing; Literary and Philosophical Society; Laing Art Gallery. M – Magpies (see NUFC); Metrocentre (shopping mall); monument (to Earl Grey); Maritime heritage. N – Newcastle Brown Ale; Newcastle United Football Club (Magpies); Northumberland Street. O – objects which reflect the rest of this alphabet. P – pigeon-racing; people. Q – Quayside. R – River Tyne; railways and railway history. S – shopping; stottie cake (local delicacy); Stephenson, Robert (railway engineer); scientific heritage. T – Tyne Bridge; Town Moor; traditions and tragedies. U – unemployment and hardship. V – verve for life. W – walls (city, Roman, Byker); Whitley Bay; whippets. X – Exhibition Park; Exhibition Ale. Y and Z – and all the rest.

It must be taken into account that this list is based on the views of people new to the area and not local people, so it is rather artificial and in some respects it reads like a list of features compiled by the local tourist board. It would be interesting to compare this alphabet to ones compiled by residents of Wallsend, with their close connections to the River Tyne and its industries, or the Asian community of Benwell in the inner city. Despite its shortcomings, it is the concept that is important, and the range of features that emerge from the exercise that is fascinating. The above list includes architecture, structures, art, buildings, dress, accent, pastimes, food and drink, societies, behaviours, attitudes, people, past achievements, natural features, traditions, events, song and a sense of history. Buried within this list is a unique combination of past and present, of traditions and new ideas, of appearance and language, the potent symbols and tangible structures that help to provide a specific identity. Museums can embrace, reflect and celebrate all of these through their activities, and hence their significance to cultural identity.

A new community approach

A close and permanent interaction between museums and communities rarely takes place in larger institutions, and the limitations imposed by traditional attitudes, large and historic collections, academic specialists and monumental buildings are clear. Small provincial museums, open-air and folk museums are not bound by such strictures and have developed ways to work closer with their communities. However, it requires a total change in circumstances, as well as philosophy and organization, for museums to become fully integrated with and driven by their communities. Perhaps it is no surprise that such circumstances were more likely to occur in rural locations with a strong sense of identity. However, it required a combination of factors in addition to geography – social, economic, cultural and museological – to come together to show a new way ahead. This happened in France in the late 1960s and early 1970s, when the slate depicting the strong and precise lines of the traditional museum, its organization and functions, was wiped clean and redrawn with the vague shadows and dotted connections of the ecomuseum.

Notes

Peter Davis is Professor of Museology at Newcastle University, England. He was appointed as Guest Professor of Museology in Museion, University of Gothenburg (Sweden) in 2005.

1   The world Heritage Convention is itself a very 'Western' concept, and tends to separate natural and cultural sites in a way that is alien to many cultures. Peter Stone (pers.comm., October 1998) suggests that attempts are being made to make the designation of sites more internationally appropriate.

2   'the charity which encourages you to stand up for your place. Our localities need our constant attention, and our task here is to excite people – as locals or visitors – with ways of getting under the surface of places, offering a way of looking at the local, a kind of evolving celebration along with ideas for effecting change. This will develop, so please return often, but we have made a start, a few ways of navigating the great common wealth of nature, landscapes, buildings, settlements, histories, myths and stories, always on the move, which in their interweaving give us the rich and varied particularity of our surroundings', http://www.england-in-particular.info (accessed 11 February 2007).

References

Almond, M. (1991) 'Nine-tenths of the law?', *The Times*, 26 March.
Anderson, B. (1991) *Imagined Communities*, Verso, London.
Anderson, D. (1997) *A Common Wealth: Museums and Learning in the United Kingdom*, Department of National Heritage, London.
Anon (n.d.) *The Open Museum*, Glasgow Museums, Glasgow.
Aygeman, J. and Kinsman, P. (1997) 'Analysing macro- and microenvironments from a multicultural perspective', in E. Hooper-Greenhill (ed.) *Cultural Diversity: Developing Museum Audiences in Britain*, Leicester University Press, London and Washington, pp. 81–98.
Bauman, Z. (1996) 'From pilgrim to tourist – or a short history of identity', in S. Hall and P. Du Gay (eds) *Questions of Cultural Identity*, Sage Publications, London, pp. 18–36.

Bellaigue, M. (1986) 'Museums and identities', in V. Sofka (ed.) *Museums and Identity*, ICOFOM Study Series 10, pp. 33–8.

Benson, K. (1995) 'Community connections', *Curator*, 38 (1), 9–13.

Boggan, S. (1996) 'Scots get the Scone, but Major wants the jam', *The Independent*, Saturday 16 November, p. 3.

Boylan, P. (1990) 'Museums and cultural identity', *Museums Journal*, 90 (10), 29–33.

Boylan, P. (1995) 'Thinking the unthinkable', *ICOM News*, 48 (1), 3–5.

Cameron, D.F. (1992) 'Getting out of our skin: museums and a new identity', *Muse*, Summer/Autumn, 7–10.

Cannon-Brookes, P. (1984) 'The nature of museum collections', in J.M.A. Thompson *The Manual of Curatorship*, Butterworths, London, pp. 115–26.

Carrington, L. (1995) 'Power to the people', *Museums Journal*, 95 (11), 21–4.

Carter, J. (1994) 'Museums and the indigenous peoples in Canada', in S. Pearce *Museums and the Appropriation of Culture*, The Athlone Press, London and Atlantic Highlands, NJ, pp. 213–26.

Carter, J.C. (1992) 'Escaping the bounds: putting the community back into museums', *Muse*, Winter, 61–2.

Chadwick, A.F. (1980) *The Role of the Museum and Art Gallery in Community Education*, Nottingham studies in the theory and practice of the education of adults, University of Nottingham, Nottingham.

Common Ground (1996) *Promotional Leaflet: Common Ground*, Common Ground, London.

Cox, A. and Singh, A. (1997) 'Walsall Museum and Art Gallery and the Sikh community: a case study', in E. Hooper-Greenhill (ed.) *Cultural Diversity: Developing Museum Audiences in Britain*, Leicester University Press, London and Washington, pp. 159–67.

Cusick, J. (1996) 'Scots open new chapter in fight to reclaim past', *The Independent*, Monday 18 November, p. 5.

Dickerson, A. (1995) 'Museums and cultural diversity: the new challenges', in *Museums and Communities*, International Council of Museums, Paris, pp. 19–22.

Diop, C.A. (1982) 'The building blocks of culture', *UNESCO Courier*, August/September.

Elsner, J. and Cardinal, R. (1994) 'Unless you do these crazy things – an interview with Robert Opie', in J. Elsner and R. Cardinal (eds) *The Cultures of Collecting*, Reaktion Books, London, pp. 25–48.

Goddard, T.R. (1929) *History of the Natural History Society of Northumberland, Durham and Newcastle upon Tyne, 1829–1929*, Andrew Reid, Newcastle.

Goodman, N. (1992) 'The end of the museum?' in L. Aagaard-Mogenson (ed.) *The Idea of the Museum: Philosophical, Artistic and Political Questions*, Problems in Contemporary Philosophy, Vol. 6, The Edwin Mellen Press, Lewiston/Queenston, Lampeter, pp. 139–55.

Hall, S. (1996) 'Who needs identity?' in S. Hall and P. Du Gay *Questions of Cultural Identity*, Sage Publications, London, pp. 1–17.

Hall, S. and Du Gay, P. (1996) *Questions of Cultural Identity*, Sage Publications, London.

Hemming, S. (1997) 'Audience participation: working with local people at the Geffrye Museum, London', in E. Hooper-Greenhill (ed.) *Cultural Diversity: Developing Museum Audiences in Britain*, Leicester University Press, London and Washington, pp. 168–82.

Herle, A. (1997) 'Museums, politics and representation', *Journal of Museum Ethnography*, 9, 65–78.

Hooper-Greenhill, E. (1994) 'Museum education: past, present and future', in R. Miles and L. Zavala (eds) *Towards the Museum of the Future: New European Perspectives*, Routledge, London, p. 138.

Hooper-Greenhill, E. (1997) *Cultural Diversity: Developing Museum Audiences in Britain*, Leicester University Press, London and Washington.

Jenkinson, P. (1994) 'Museum futures', in G. Kavanagh (ed.) *Museum Provision and Professionalism*, Routledge, London, pp. 51–4.

Johnson, P. and Thomas, B. (1991) 'Museums: an economic perspective', in S. Pearce (ed.) *Museum Economics and the Community*, The Athlone Press, London, pp. 5–40.

Johnson, P. and Thomas, B. (1991a) 'Museums and the local economy', in G. Kavanagh (ed.) *The Museums Profession: Internal and External Relations*, Leicester University Press, Leicester, London and New York, pp. 101–23.

Kaplan, F.E.S. (1994) *Museums and the Making of 'Ourselves': The Role of Objects in National Identity*, Leicester University Press, London and New York.

Karp, I. and Levine, S.D. (eds) (1991) *Exhibiting Cultures: The Poetics and Politics of Museum Display*, Smithsonian Institution Press, Washington and London.

Kell, P.E. (1991) 'Reflections on the social and economic impact of the Fortress of Louisbourg', in S. Pearce (ed.) *Museum Economics and the Community*, The Athlone Press, London and Atlantic Highlands, NJ, pp. 118–31.

Legget, J. (1995) 'Tourism – the new saviour?' *Museums Journal*, 95 (12), 25.

Lovatt, J.R. (1997) 'The People's Show Festival 1994: a survey', in S.M. Pearce (ed.) *Experiencing Material Culture in the Western World*, Leicester University Press, London and Washington, pp. 196–221.

Macdonald, A.M. (ed.) (1977) *Chambers Twentieth Century Dictionary*, Chambers, Edinburgh.

Macqueen, E. (1998) 'Museums and Their Communities: A Case Study in Argyll and Bute', unpublished M.Phil. thesis, University of Newcastle upon Tyne.

Magga, O.H. (1995) 'Museums and cultural diversity: indigenous and dominant cultures', in *Museums and Communities*, International Council of Museums, Paris, pp. 16–18.

Magnusson, M. (1989) Introduction, in J. Greenfield *The Return of Cultural Treasures*, Cambridge University Press, Cambridge, pp. 1–9.

Makins, M. (ed.) (1997) *Collins English Dictionary and Thesaurus*, HarperCollins, Glasgow.

Maure, M. (1986) 'Identites et cultures', in V. Sofka (ed.) *Museums and Identity*, ICOFOM Study Series 10, pp. 197–9.

Merriman, N. (1992) 'The dilemma of representation', in *Les Cahiers de publics et musées: la nouvelle Alexandrie*, Ministère de la Culture et de la Francophonie, DMF, Paris, pp. 135–40.

Merriman, N. (1995) 'Hidden history: the peopling of London project', *Museum International*, 47 (3), 12–16.

Miles, R. (1994) Introduction, in R. Miles and L. Zavala (eds) *Towards the Museum of the Future: New European Perspectives*, Routledge, London, pp. 1–3.

Museums and Galleries Commission (1986) *Museums in Scotland: Report by a Working Party 1986*, HMSO, London.

Roth, M. (1992) 'Encore une fois: musée et identité', in *Les Cahiers de publics et musées: la nouvelle Alexandrie*, Ministère de la Culture et de la Francophone, DMF, Paris, pp. 171–5.

San Roman, L. (1992) 'Politics and the role of museums in the rescue of identity', in P.J. Boylan (ed.) *Museums 2000: Politics, People, Professionals and Profit*, Museums Association/Routledge, London and New York, pp. 25–41.

Sola, T. (1986) 'Identity – reflections on a crucial problem for museums', in V. Sofka (ed.) *Museums and Identity*, ICOFOM Study Series 10, pp. 15–18.

Spielbauer, J.K. (1986) 'Introduction to identity', in V. Sofka (ed.) *Museums and Identity*, ICOFOM Study Series 10, pp. 273–82.

Šuler, P. (1986) 'The role of museology', in V. Sofka (ed.) *Museums and Identity*, ICOFOM Study Series 10, pp. 283–6.

Taborsky, E. (1982) 'The sociological role of the museum', *International Journal of Museum Management and Curatorship*, 1, 339–45.

UNESCO (1982) 'Mexico City Declaration on Cultural Policies', adopted by the World Conference on Cultural Policies, Mexico, 6 August 1982. In *World Conference on Cultural Properties, Mexico City, 26 July–6 August 1982, Final Report*, UNESCO, Paris, pp. 41–6.

Van Mensch, P.J.A. (1986) 'Museums and cultural identity', in V. Sofka (ed.) *Museology and Identity*. ICOFOM Study Series 11, pp. 201–9.

Viet, J. (ed.) (1980) *The International Thesaurus of Cultural Development*, Clearing House and Research Centre for Cultural Development, UNESCO, Paris.

Wasserman, F. (1995) 'Museums and otherness: community challenges and the ecomuseum of Fresnes', in *Museums and Communities*, International Council of Museums, Paris, pp. 23–8.

Weil, S.E. (1990) 'Dry rot, woodworm and damp', in S.E. Weil *Rethinking the Museum and Other Meditations*, Smithsonian Institution Press, Washington, DC, p. 24.

Chapter 4

Interpretive Communities, Strategies and Repertoires

Eilean Hooper-Greenhill

Interpretive communities, strategies and repertoires

. . . **M**EANING IS ACTUALISED, brought into being, by the negotiation of objects by the viewer.[1] These negotiations, however, are not the act of detached atomistic individuals but are the products of both individuals and communities;[2] personal interpretations are forged through social and cultural frameworks. Culture is concerned with the production and exchange of meanings; 'the giving and taking of meaning' between members of a society or a group.[3] Individual meaning-making is forged and tested in relation to communities of meaning-making, which establish frameworks of intelligibility within which individual subjects negotiate, refine and develop personal constructs. How the present and the past is understood, and how objects are interpreted, depends on personal biography, cultural background, and interpretive community.

The concept of 'interpretive communities' has been an influential one in media and communication research for the last two decades and more,[4] although very little has been written in relation to museums.[5] The way the expression has been used has varied, as has the focus of analysis.

Fish offers a definition of interpretive community which focuses on the interpretation of textual meaning:

> Interpretive communities are made up of those who share interpretive strategies for writing texts, for constituting their properties and assigning their intentions.[6]

Fish is working against the formalist assumption that there are observable facts that can be first described and then interpreted. Fish suggests that an interpreting subject,

Source: *Museums and The Interpretation of Visual Culture*, London: Routledge, 2000, pp. 119–23, 172; 151–62, 174–5, 176–90.

endowed with purposes and concerns, is, by virtue of this very operation, determining what counts as the facts to be observed, and that since this determining is not a neutral marking out of a valueless area, but the extension of an already existing field of interest, it *is* an interpretation.[7] If meaning develops in dynamic relationship with the expectations, conclusions, judgements, and assumptions of the interpreter, then these activities are not merely instrumental and mechanical, used to extract meaning, but are essential in the construction of meaning.[8] In the quotation above, he uses the word 'writing' to refer to the activity of reading a written text. For Fish this activity is a form of writing, as each reader constructs their own meaning and therefore 'writes' their own text. Fish goes on:

> Systems of intelligibility constrain and fashion us and furnish us with categories of understanding with which we fashion the entities to which we then point.[9]

And further: 'Readers make meanings, but meaning make readers.'[10]

The significant element of Fish's argument is that systems of intelligibility are not individual but collective. Individuals share interpretive strategies with others who share the same frames of reference, the same cultural references and the same positions within history. Learning is social.

Some interesting applications of the concept of 'interpretive communities' can be found, although again not in relation to making meaning in museums. Radway[11] studied a specific identifiable community, a small group of sixteen women romance readers clustered about a bookshop in 'Smithton'. Although not formally constituted as a reading group, she found that, as readers, the women were united by common purposes, references and interpretive procedures. In the interpretation of stories of male/female relationships (historical romances) the women operated from a transparent view of language (where words had fixed and definite meanings) that enabled the heroine of the romances to be constructed as strong, intelligent, and self-reliant. Writers always initially presented their heroine as such, but the subsequent story did not confirm this presentation; however, through their interpretive strategies, the readers constructed a powerful heroine who was always perceived as converting the frequently recalcitrant hero to her feminine values. Radway identified specific textual and interpretive strategies, and also identified the uses of these strategies to the women readers. By picking up a book, the readers signalled a detaching from the everyday world of middle-class mother and wife. By reading romances, these women found temporary release from the demands of their defining social role, and psychological gratification of the needs created by that role. In that all the women in the study followed the same interpretive strategies for the same purposes, Radway was able to identify an interpretive community.

Zelizer[12] undertook a wider study which focused on American journalists to review how far the notion of 'interpretive community' might explain how journalists constituted themselves as a group which shared interpretive strategies. Looking beyond conventional analyses of journalists as a profession, and incorporating the shared journalistic discourses around key public events, she found informal networking, narrative and storytelling (about the past and present of the practice of journalism) and what she calls 'the trappings' of professionalism which all contributed to the ways in which journalists shaped meaning about themselves. These shared strategies contributed to the construction of the establishment and maintenance of the frame of mind necessary to become a journalist in America; journalists, she proposes, do constitute a definable interpretive community.

Mitra[13] studied a group of users of the World Wide Web. This group of Indian immigrants to the West was in no sense a community that met face to face, as their only common point of contact was through the Web. Mitra studied a specific website that spoke both to what he describes as an 'in-group', an interpretive community that had the interpretive history and strategies to make sense of the web pages, and an 'out-group' that visited the site by chance. The stylistics of the site, the formatting, use of language, use of images and sound, and type of textual content itself created two groups of meaning-makers – those who had the skills and predispositions to make sense out of the site and its hypertextual links, and those who did not. Such skills included language, histories of past affiliations, appreciation of the intricacies of Indian culture, and familiarity with ongoing events and changes in India. For Indians outside of India, who are frequently split up from family and community members, the Web, to those who could use it, offered a way of affirming their cultural origins. As Mitra puts it, in the relevant web pages 'the alienated and isolated immigrant can find a friendly cyber-community which acknowledges the residual cultural attributes of the diasporic individual'.[14] The use of the Web itself constituted and constructed the community.

The concept of 'interpretive community', although widely familiar in the theory of media and communication studies, is a complex and slippery concept in practice, and it has been called under-theorised.[15] It has been used in a number of ways. Radway's work can be seen as a classic audience study, which describes a small group of geographically delimited women all reading very similar books. Zelizer's study is rather more unusual in that it addresses media producers – a group of journalists – rather than consumers, and the group, although meeting together at conferences and through other professional networks, is geographically dispersed. Mitra's work addresses a group that is not a group in any sense of the word except through its coming together in acts of interpretation, when common cultures and histories can be deployed. The function of these interpretive acts is to affirm the cultural frameworks of the individual meaning-makers through the collective character of the repertoires and strategies used.

Interpretive communities are located in relation to interpretive acts. It is only through the common repertoires and strategies used in interpretation that such communities can be recognised. The communities are not necessarily communities in any other sense. Radway's women did not necessarily know each other; their only concrete connection with each other was anonymous in that they all took the advice of the bookshop assistant who advised them what to buy. The Indian users of the Web might, during the course of using it, meet, but were not in communication with each other outside this activity. The journalists, although all using similar interpretive strategies and belonging to the same profession, might not meet at all throughout their professional lives. All these communities, therefore, can only be called communities because of their constitution through the media, either as media audiences or consumers (text readers), or as media producers (journalists), or in the case of the Indian Web users, both producers and consumers at the same time.[16]

Interpretive communities cannot be mapped onto socio-economic positions, demographic groupings, or kinship structures.[17] Specific class, gender, or racialised positions do not determine how meaning is made, although position in the social structure may delimit the availability of the discursive repertoires and meaning-making strategies available.[18]

Interpretive communities are fluid and unstable. Their membership changes as individuals revise their affiliations and redirect their interests. Each individual may typically belong to more than one interpretive community at any one time.

> Interpretive communities grow larger and decline and individuals move from one to another; thus while alignments are not permanent, they are always there, providing just enough stability for interpretive battles to go on, and just enough shift and slippage to ensure that they are never settled.[19]

Interpretive communities are recognised by their common frameworks of intelligibility, interpretive repertoires, knowledge, and intellectual skills.[20] These will include specific uses of words and things, and particular textual and artefactual strategies. Attitudes, values, and beliefs will become evident in those recurrently used systems of terms deployed to characterise and evaluate actions and events.[21]

The concept of interpretive communities is significant for several reasons. First, in relation to theories of knowledge, it insists that interpretation is not based in the individual but is a shared occurrence. Although each individual actively makes sense of their own experience, the interpretive strategies and repertoires they use emerge through prior social and cultural events. Fish spells out the implications of this, by pointing out that repertoires and strategies exist prior to the encounter with the text. They:

> proceed not from [the reader] but from the interpretive community of which he is a member; they are in effect, community property, and insofar as they at once enable and limit the operations of his consciousness, he is [community property] too . . . The claims of objectivity and subjectivity can no longer be debated because the authorising agency, the centre of interpretive authority, is at once both and neither. An interpretive community is not objective because as a bundle of interests, of particular purposes and goals, its perspective is interested rather than neutral; but by the very same reasoning, the meanings and texts produced by an interpretive community are not subjective because they do not proceed from an isolated individual but from a public and conventional point of view.[22]

The concept of interpretive communities thus undermines the argument that a constructivist understanding of the character of knowledge inevitably leads to an extreme epistemological relativism. Fish subtitles his book 'The *authority* of interpretive communities'; the power he has in mind is the *collective* power to produce publicly acceptable meaning. The depth or breadth of the acceptance of specific ideas will depend on the size and influence of the specific interpretive community. Thus, as Fish points out, it is possible to move beyond the subjective/objective knowledge debate to examine how knowledge and power interrelate.

Second, in relation to the interpretation of visual culture, the concept of interpretive community can be used to explain difference in response to specific objects. Merton Russell-Cotes, for example, can be described as belonging to a different interpretive community from that of Makereti. Different systems of intelligibility, different frames of reference, and different interpretive repertoires are used to construct diverse meaning from objects that were of the same type – Maori cloaks, clubs, staffs, and carvings. On one level the interpretations were personal because of the biographies of the individuals concerned, but these interpretations were also deeply rooted in the ways of thinking of the cultural and historical communities to which each belonged.

Third, in relation to the significance of the concept of interpretive communities for the interpretation of visual culture in museums, it begins to suggest explanations for the difficulties some visitors have in grasping the meanings and relevance of certain displays. If exhibitions speak only to the interpretive community to which the curator belongs, then unless visitors share these interpretive frameworks, they will not feel comfortable. And fourth, in planning exhibitions and displays, the interpretive strategies and repertoires of the interpretive communities to which intended audiences belong should be anticipated (through audience research) and enabled.

A range of issues relate to the interpretive processes that characterise encounters between subjects and objects. In museums, these encounters are in part shaped in advance by the ways in which objects are selected and displayed. The museum display or exhibition sets an agenda and provides a framework within which the interpretive strategies of the visitor must be deployed. Any encounter with an object in a museum will therefore involve the articulation of the interpretive processes of museum visitors with the pedagogic provision of the museum.

[. . .]

The rebirth of the museum

This chapter summarises the character of the modernist museum and considers further the idea of the post-museum. Most of the chapter is taken up with a final case-study that enables the discussion of the interpretation of visual culture using the concepts that this study has sought to elaborate.

The modernist museum – an enduring model

The modernist museum represents a nineteenth-century European model. In contrast to earlier princely cabinets and royal collections it was conceived to play a public role as part of the nation-state, a major part of which concerned the education of large sections of society. The collection and classification of artefacts and specimens, frequently from territories under the control of the collecting nation, were drawn together to produce an encyclopaedic world-view, understood from a Western perspective. The modernist museum emerged gradually to become a fully established and very powerful institutional form by the end of the nineteenth century. It has remained the idea of what a museum is for most of the twentieth century, and is still today, at the dawn of the twenty-first, what springs to mind when the word 'museum' is used.[23]

The modernist museum collected objects and placed them on display. Visual statements, constructed through objects placed in carefully fixed relationships, presented aspects of a European world-view. The power of display as a method of communication lies in its capacity to produce visual narratives that are apparently harmonious, unified, and complete. These holistic and apparently inevitable visual narratives, generally presented with anonymous authority, legitimised specific attitudes and opinions and gave them the status of truth. Display is a one-way method of mass communication – once it is completed and opened to the public it is very difficult to modify. In the modernist museum, the voice of the visitor was not heard.

The modernist museum was and is imagined as a building, which might have a classical form with columns and a pediment; might equally be the white cube of the modernist art museum; or, in recent years, might have the more unusual and dynamic appearance of museums such as the Guggenheim Museum in Bilbao. Although the form might vary, the processes of museum-making, and the museum/audience relationship, remain the same.

The post-museum – a new museum concept

Born in the nineteenth century, the modernist museum is still a force to be reckoned with. But the idea of the museum is being reborn and some of its characteristics and challenges are becoming clear. The post-museum will retain some of the characteristics of its parent, but it will re-shape them to its own ends.

The great collecting phase of museums is over. The post-museum will hold and care for objects, but will concentrate more on their use rather than on further accumulation. In addition, the post-museum will be equally interested in intangible heritage. Where the tangible material objects of a cultural group have largely been destroyed, it is the memories, songs, and cultural traditions that embody that culture's past and future.

In the modernist museum display is the major form of communication. This transmission approach to pedagogy has severe limitations . . . In the post-museum, the exhibition will become one among many other forms of communication. The exhibition will form part of a nucleus of events which will take place both before and after the display is mounted. These events might involve the establishments of community and organisational partnerships; the production of objects during educational programmes which then enter the collections; periods of time when specific community groups use the museum spaces in their own way; writers, scientists and artists in residence; or satellite displays set up in pubs and shops.[24] During these events, discussions, workshops, performances, dances, songs, and meals will be produced or enacted.

The production of events and exhibitions as conjoint dynamic processes enables the incorporation into the museum of many voices and many perspectives.

Knowledge is no longer unified and monolithic; it becomes fragmented and multi-vocal. There is no necessary unified perspective – rather a cacophony of voices may be heard that present a range of views, experiences, and values. The voice of the museum is one among many.

There are difficult issues to be resolved here about the continued respons-ibility of the museum for the production of knowledge, the care of its tangible and intangible collections, the need to balance opportunities to speak for all who wish to do so, and the question of when, whether, and how to take a stand in relation to moral and ethical matters. There are no easy answers. Many museums, espe-cially those with ethnographic collections, are already working with their various communities to negotiate their own provisional solutions to each issue as it arises. Together, the solutions will add up to new processes and ways of working.

Where the modernist museum was (and is) imagined as a building, the museum in the future may be imagined as a process or an experience. The post-museum will take, and is already beginning to take, many architectural forms. It is, how-ever, not limited to its own walls, but moves as a set of process into the spaces, the concerns, and the ambitions of communities.

The development of the post-museum will represent a feminisation of the museum. Rather than upholding the values of objectivity, rationality, order, and distance, the post-museum will negotiate responsiveness, encourage mutually nurturing partnerships, and celebrate diversity. It is likely too, that much of the intellectual development of the post-museum will take place outside the major European centres which witnessed the birth of the modernist museum.

The remainder of this chapter is taken up with a final case-study which is based on the life-story (so far) of one object, a Lakota Sioux Ghost Dance Shirt. The narrative tracks the movement of one single object into a museum and out again. It shows how and why objects were collected and why they may be repatriated; it also shows how change can, on the one hand, be long and slow, but, on the other, very rapid and dramatic. The story of the Ghost Dance Shirt presents some of the dilemmas that face museums in the West today, and shows how one museum negotiated this dilemma through working together with its visitors and with other stakeholders to arrive at a provisional resolution.

I do not present this case-study to take a stand on matters to do with repatri-ation as a whole. These matters are complex and, today, highly politicised. Each issue must be treated on its own merits. My interest in the Ghost Dance Shirt is in terms of its meaning to a number of diverse interpretive communities. The themes of narrative, difference, identity, interpretive procedures, and museum pedagogy run through the account.

The Ghost Dance Shirt: public visual culture or sacred talisman?

The life-stories of artefacts take place within a series of local circumstances, and interpretive and artefactual frameworks, which may remain stable for a long period of time, or change very rapidly. Each local circumstance will involve specific individual actors and communities, and will be linked in a range of ways to broad signifying systems. An artefact may find itself in a number of geographical and institutional sites. In each site, it will be positioned within a group of related objects that together form a meaningful set. Within each local circumstance, specific meanings will be mobilised that have provisional significance within the site concerned. These meanings may change radically as the object is moved from one site of semiosis to another. As the moves take place in time and across space, earlier meanings may be lost or recovered, overlaid by new significations, or reinterpreted by different interpreters. Meanings, as we have seen, are constructed through a range of semiotic frameworks, which include texts, artefacts, actions, events, and which involve active individuals within interactive communities. It is the issue of meaning that will form one of the main forces behind the development of the post-museum.

On 19 January 1892, Kelvingrove Museum and Art Gallery in Glasgow acquired a substantial body of Native American material.[25] The Accessions Register briefly describes each object and records what can be surmised to be comments that were made as the objects joined the collection:[26] '2a: Pair of Buckskin Leggins [sic], embroidered with beads worn by "Calls-the-name" Squaw Chief of the Brulé Sioux in 1876; Waistcoat of buckskin covered with beadwork worn by "Rain-in-the-face" the Mineconjou Sioux warrior . . .' Listed along with other donated objects is 3c: ' "Ghost Shirt" of cotton cloth with feather ornament, blessed by "Short Bull" the High Priest to the Messiah, and supposed to render the Wearer invulnerable. Taken from a Sioux Warrior killed at the battle of Wounded Knee, 30th Dec. 1890.' The Ghost Dance Shirt entered the museum already imbued with affiliations which were significant at the time and are so again today, although for the period of one hundred years the significance seems to have been almost lost.

The entries in the museum Register read like a roll-call of heroes: Sitting Bull, Rain-in-the-Face, Short Bull, Lone Bull, Big Foot. Four of the items are associated with Wounded Knee: the Ghost Dance Shirt, and in addition, a 'War necklace of hide fringe made from sections of deer's hoof' (92–2i); a 'Pair of Moccasins of buckskin embroidered with beadwork. Taken from "Across the room" son of Big Foot . . .' (92–3b); and a 'Sioux cradle' (92–3d).[27] During 1891–92, Buffalo Bill's Wild West Show had toured Britain. Calls The Name, Short Bull, and Lone Bull were with the Show as performers;[28] and the Show was in Glasgow at the time of the acquisition of the objects.[29] The objects may have seemed attractive to the museum as examples of an exotic way of life, and as objects that would be both educational and at the same time popular with the public, who had possibly just seen some of them used in the Wild West Show.

George Crager, who acted as translator and manager for the Native American group working for the Show, offered the objects to the museum, describing them as his 'collection'.[30] It is not known how these objects were acquired, although it is clear that Crager was at Wounded Knee shortly after the massacre; as a man who acted on many occasions as a Lakota Sioux interpreter[31] he had secured a job as special correspondent for the New York World.[32] It would appear that as the bodies of those killed were buried together in a trench at the site, they were stripped of any potential mementoes by some of the white soldiers in the burial party and by civilians.[33] Crager was in the area within one month of the event, and was photographed with 'Buffalo Bill and Sioux leaders at Pine Ridge Agency'.[34] It is certainly possible that the Ghost Dance Shirt could have been acquired by Crager shortly after the massacre at Wounded Knee.

The Accessions Register refers to the 'battle of "Wounded Knee"'. The events that took place have been well documented, and to refer to the event as a 'battle' is inaccurate.[35] Sitting Bull had been killed on 15 December 1890 during the process of his arrest[36] and by 28 December the members of his band, the Hunkpapa, accompanied by some of Big Foot's Miniconjou, were encamped at Wounded Knee creek, surrounded by soldiers of the 7th Regiment of the United States Army.[37] The Native American group was made up of 120 men and 250 women and children, and most of the men were disarmed. During the removal of their remaining weapons, a shot was fired and the surrounding soldiers opened fire indiscriminately; 153 people were killed at the site, and others died later from wounds: altogether close to 300 of the 370 at the camp were killed.[38]

At the camp, the men had been wearing Ghost Dance shirts, sacred and thought to be imbued with protective qualities.[39] The medicine man had protested at the removal of the weapons by dancing some Ghost Dance steps and chanting one of the holy songs, assuring the men that the soldiers' bullets could not penetrate their shirts: 'The bullets will not go toward you . . . The prairie is large and the bullets will not go toward you.'[40] The Ghost Dance religion offered hope to the Lakota tribes, who in 1890 were verging on cultural breakdown due to loss of tribal lands and the imposition by the US Government of an alien way of life.[41] A holy man, Wovoka, living in Nevada, promised a return to a traditional way of life in a land without white people, and the return of dead friends and relatives, if his faith was embraced and the Ghost Dance performed.[42] Ghost Dance shirts, worn during the Dance, were sometimes produced as a group by dancers after having been inspired by the visions.[43]

The Ghost Dance Shirt in Glasgow, prior to its acquisition by the museum, had been a sign of hope and the revival of Lakota values, of invulnerability, and strength. It had possibly been worn during a performance of the Ghost Dance, a religious event, and, assuming that its provenance is correct, had been worn as a protection against betrayal and attack. It was understood as a religious object, a protective talisman with magic powers.

Crager's collection was sometimes placed on display for visitors to the Wild West Show,[44] and the latter should be examined as the background against which the objects were acquired. The Wild West Show was already in existence by the time of Wounded Knee. In 1884, William F. Cody (Buffalo Bill), in partnership with Nate Salsbury, opened the Wild West Show in St Louis, Missouri. The Show quickly became fashionable, and a performative format was evolved that would remain largely the same for the next thirty years. One of the biggest attractions were the Native Americans, the 'Indians'.[45] The formula that Cody developed presented the American West as the 'frontier', a land of heroes and glorious battles. His Show was one of what would turn out to be a large number of media events that constructed the enduring myth of the 'West'.[46]

Cody produced a master narrative of the West,[47] partly through working with real historical events and real historical figures. After Wounded Knee, a large number of Native Americans went on tour with the Wild West Show in lieu of jail.[48] Sioux who had charged Custer at Little Bighorn later charged him nightly in the Show.[49] Cody, Buffalo Bill, presented himself as having lived through the events he depicted, as indeed he had, and continued to do so as the Show developed. During the Custer Campaign and the Ghost Dance period, Cody worked intermittently for the army and each time incorporated elements of his experience into the Show.[50] Through the intermingling of history and performance he created a mythic code that presented the 'Indians' as savage attackers and the whites as vulnerable victims. The role of the 'Indians' in the Show was to attack whites. Audiences were in no doubt that this is what 'Indians' were 'actually like'.[51] Set pieces, such as the 'Capture of the Deadwood Mail Coach by Indians', were devised;[52] they presented Native Americans as aggressive killers and whites as victims who were then forced to defend themselves.[53] In this inversion of history, Buffalo Bill exploited an iconography of white victimisation that can be traced back to Puritan captivity narratives;[54] the trope transferred to the frontier was construed by audiences as 'real' through the ambiguity between history and performance.[55]

The Wild West Show and its several imitators, and dime novels (some stories were based around Cody's experiences) which presented a romanticised version of events for a mass audience, together generated an image of what Francis calls 'the Imaginary Indian'.[56] The Plains Indians represented all 'Indians' in the minds of the public. The complexity of North American native cultures, and diverse groups, was reduced to a single image – that of the mounted, war-bonneted Plains chieftain.[57] This unified and simplified stereotype had one major characteristic – its savagery. Cody, although himself sympathetic to the plight of the Native Americans, created his show in the form of an allegory: the triumph of civilised values over the barbarity of the wilderness. The more savage the wilderness, the greater the power of civilisation. The apparent reflection of history in the making underlined these values even more. Within the context of the Wild West Show, the Ghost Dance Shirt is reduced to one of the signs that sustained the stereotypical 'Imaginary Indian'. It had already attained the status of 'visual culture'.

The Ghost Dance Shirt on display

It is not known whether the Ghost Dance Shirt was placed along with the other acquisitions on display when it entered Kelvingrove Museum in January 1892, although it is possible that it has been on display continuously since that date.[58] What is sure is that it was one of the objects on display in the Ethnography Gallery at the museum, which was set out as it still is today during the late 1950s or early 1960s.[59] In a single room, objects from North America, Asia, Africa, Australia, and New Zealand are gathered together. The largest groups of cases contain 'Indian' material, grouped geographically: South West Indian, North West Coast Indian, Eastern Woodland Indian (Cree, Chippewa), North West Coast Indian (Haida, Tlingit, Kwakuitl), and South American Indian (i.e. Mexico). There are two cases containing Plains Indian material, and here objects from several groups can be found, including the Brulé band of Dakota, Blood, Blackfoot, Comanche. No dates are mentioned, except in connection with the Ghost Dance Shirt. The North American section of the gallery is the most visited part, with the Plains Indian material the most popular of all.[60] One reason for this is the study of the Plains Indian at primary school level.

The Ethnography Gallery at Kelvingrove has characteristics that are recognisable as typical of galleries of this date; material drawn from wide areas of the world is grouped together, diverse and fragmented specific cultures are assembled to form a unified narrative; the narrative is timeless. The result is an exotic story — sometime in the past and somewhere in space.

One of the characters in this story, the Imaginary Indian, would already be familiar to visitors in the 1960s from children's books, John Wayne Westerns, films and Cowboy and Indian games, and the Boy Scouts.[61] The Ghost Dance Shirt might have spoken of camp-fires, wigwams, Hiawatha, beautiful Indian princesses, and bows and arrows. Little in the gallery encouraged a more critical reading — the myths were left to be recycled rather than decoded. The text: 'Neck ornament of hide with deer's hoof fringes. Both men and women wore necklaces and ear ornaments. Taken from a warrior after the battle of Wounded Knee', echoes the Accession Register closely.

In 1992, one hundred years after the Ghost Dance Shirt had been acquired by the museum, it was loaned to Home of the Brave, a temporary exhibition in Glasgow. Here it was seen by John Earl, a lawyer from Atlanta, Georgia, who recognised it as other than a signifier of the 'Imaginary Indian'. He contacted the Wounded Knee Survivors Association, and set in train a series of events that resulted in the Shirt being repatriated in 1999. During the debates over whether the shirt should be 'returned home' or not, a number of interpretive strategies, some old and some new, came into play.

The Shirt itself was redisplayed twice during the period. By 1995 it had been taken out of the Ethnography Gallery and placed in the large main hall of the museum. This was clearly an attempt to respond to public interest by putting the Shirt in a more accessible position, but it was also a way of detaching it from its ethnographic significance and moving it into a new framework for making meaning. The temporary positioning had limited effectiveness — the display case dated back to about the 1930s, the Shirt was draped over a headless dressmaker's dummy, and the light was extremely poor. A large page-sized typed label was attached to the elderly wooden display case which visually obscured the object within, but did serve to highlight the moral and political dilemma. The details of the history of the Shirt, as it was known then, the nature of the claim from the Wounded Knee Survivors Association, and the position of the museum (which at that stage was to retain the Shirt in Glasgow for educational reasons) were all spelt out. Comments were invited on how the dilemma should be resolved: 'Please give us your comments on whether you think the shirt should be returned.' This was the beginning of what would be an extraordinary episode in the museum's history, one that opened museum issues to public scrutiny and took a course that was actively discouraged both by prevailing professional practice and by specific professional advice from British and American curators.

Interpreting the Ghost Dance Shirt

The demands for the return of the Shirt and the first visit of the Wounded Knee Survivors Association to Glasgow in 1995 generated a considerable amount of media coverage, and much of it recycled the old stereotypes. Predictably, it was the tabloids that used the most extreme language, revealing the crude and simplistic ideas of 'unschooled minds';[62] 'Indians in heap big row for shirt: a tribe of Red Indians are on the warpath . . . to claim back a sacred shirt from a Scots museum';[63] 'Sioux pow-wow for the return of Ghost Shirt: In a different age they would have arrived painted for war to hurl themselves on the guns of the white men intent on killing their race.'[64] However, even more sober newspapers could barely resist the opportunity. Headlines included 'Lakota Sioux raid Glasgow to seek return of 'ghost shirt',[65] and 'Sioux on the warpath'.[66]

The *Daily Mail* gave a few clues to its readers to place the story within existing frames of reference: 'to generations of Scots bred on John Wayne Westerns', and 'the Lakota Sioux – the Indians made famous by Kevin Costner's *Dances With Wolves* blockbuster'. However, having established a visual picture the *Daily Mail* presented a human and sympathetic, if romantic, story:

> To Scots . . . it is just another dry museum piece, an artefact of a people long gone. To the Lakota Sioux . . . it is, literally, symbolic of the death of their race . . . Lawyer John Earl, a Cherokee, said . . . 'I can't describe how I felt . . .' On his return he contacted . . . Marcella Lebeau, the Lakota granddaughter of Rain-In-The-Face . . . The curator of history for Glasgow museums said: 'We are sympathetic. I wouldn't close the door on its repatriation.'[67]

Glasgow Museums had asked for comments from the public about whether the Shirt should be returned. Letters sent to the museum and published in the press were almost unanimously of the view that the Shirt should be returned. In spite of the extreme language used by some of the newspapers, the letters were carefully and thoughtfully written. A number of interpretive strategies were used in constructing meanings for the Shirt. The debate was almost always placed within a moral framework: 'Please give it back to the rightful owners from whom it was stolen. The North American Indians have the same rights as us to have their stolen property returned to them.' Frequently Scottish complicity in the exploitation of the Sioux, and a present-day responsibility to atone for this, was mentioned: 'I may be wrong, but I am sure that I've read somewhere that the commanding officer on that dreadful day in 1890 was a Scot'; 'Prominent among our European thugs were the Spanish and British; prominent among the British were the Scots.'

Affinity between the Scots and the Sioux was a further strong theme. One writer noted 'a subtle analogy between the Sioux and the Scots . . . a clear parallel . . . between the fates of a talisman of the Sioux nation and the physical symbol of the mythical origins of the Scots, the Stone of destiny . . .'. Links were made with the Highland Clearances and the loss of Sioux lands: 'We all in Scotland feel the pain when we think of the highland clearances, a pain felt in the soul . . .' Links were also made between Scottish and Sioux cultural deprivation: 'We as a nation have witnessed our own culture being ravaged and treated with disrespect and contempt . . . the Shirt should have been handed back immediately.'

The museological argument made by Glasgow Museums in initially refusing the request for repatriation on the grounds that it would create a precedent that could prove difficult for other museums at a later date (what became known as the 'floodgates' argument) was roundly dismissed: 'A precedent for what –

compassion?' A parallel argument that the item should be retained on educational grounds was equally firmly rebuffed: 'Your claim . . . is repellent'; 'I can see no better demonstration of education purpose than a publicised return of this arte-fact.' This writer spoke to the museum on its own terms, pointing out how the situation was of relevance to 'current dialectics in the nature of the contemporary museum . . . at an international and national level'.[68]

Many of the associations and arguments made by the writers echoed points made in newspaper stories quoting the lawyers accompanying the Wounded Knee delegation to Glasgow. Mario Gonzales was reported as pointing out 'Our history is like yours; you had your massacre in a glen, ours was in a creek. You had the Highland clearances, we lost our land.' He further pointed out that the Shirt was a funerary object, 'stolen from a dead person'. Gonzales even pointed out that he himself was part Scottish on his great-great grandmother's side.[69]

The second redisplay, in time for the public hearing in 1998, moved the Shirt upstairs into its own separate gallery where three new matching display cabinets were used to show the Ghost Dance Shirt and other items with attributed Wounded Knee provenance: the necklace and moccasins, and the baby cradle. The move upstairs represented a move from a timeless ethnography to a period within living memory; a move that can be seen as from culture to history. This was rein-forced by an elaborate three-screen video presentation that presented portraits of Lakota heroes past and present, and the story of Wounded Knee and the events that took place there through images, photographs, and words. Images of the Shirt itself were used in the video to show the movement of the Shirt while being worn, as for example during the massacre itself, where the Shirt was lit as though by gunfire. The video positioned the Shirt clearly within its sacred, religious framework, and in relation to the struggles of the Lakota against colonial aggression. The museum here attempted to invoke the framework for the very first meanings for the shirt in order to go beyond the simplistic stereotypical interpretations that journalists and possibly others were prone to slip into. It presented the historical events as a preliminary to understanding the contemporary demands for return, which were also laid out clearly.

By 1998, changes in museum personnel,[70] support from the City Council and a uniquely open approach to the situation, had led to a public hearing where the arguments for and against the return of the Shirt were fully aired. By this time, the request for repatriation was heard by Glasgow residents in a very different way. Although the result of the hearing was not a foregone conclusion, the Shirt was no longer a mere document of the past with no cultural significance apart from a reference to childhood games and macho movies. It had become part of a known history and tradition that could be used to underpin new ways of thinking and acting. In some sense, a new interpretive community had been established, able to use newly learnt interpretive strategies.

The Shirt, in conjunction with the other artefacts, the museum displays, and the public letters and debates in Glasgow, had become part of a network that generated, through interpretation, both new interpretive communities and new inter-pretive possibilities.[71] The events in Glasgow linked into other media events, such as the six fifty-minute programmes *History in Action: the Wild West*, screened dur-ing the autumn of 1996, where Marie-Not-Help-Him, who had become a familiar name in the Glasgow events, was seen talking about her history. One year later, in September 1997, a second event was given a high media profile; the body of Long Wolf, who had travelled with Cody and the Wild West Show, and who had died of pneumonia before returning home, was exhumed from Brompton Cemetery in west London. The newspaper story was moving, and showed how close history is to the present. As Long Wolf lay ill, he drew a wolf and asked for it to be carved on his gravestone. It was this carving that enabled the grave to be located. Once Long Wolf's family had been found, they came to take him home. The party included his granddaughter, aged 87, who could remember her mother's story of the death of her father when she (her mother) was 12 years old, travelling with him and the Wild West Show. One newspaper report was headed by a half-page colour portrait of Long Wolf's great-grandson in full feathered war-bonnet.[72]

Eight months after the decision to repatriate the Shirt,[73] a party from Glasgow took it back to where it had come from. Prior to this, comments from visitors in a book placed close to where it stood, once again, in the main hall at Kelvingrove, described it as 'going home', which was 'the right thing to do'. On 31 July 1999, at HVJ Lakota Cultural Centre, Cheyenne River Reservation, the Ghost Dance Shirt was carried in procession by tribal elders wearing feather bonnets and speeches, singing and drumming followed. Written accounts of memories of the events at Wounded Knee were read by descendants. The next day, the Shirt was taken back to the site of the massacre at Wounded Knee and prayers and further ceremonies took place. The Shirt is now in the care of the South Dakota Historical Society, pending the building of a museum at Wounded Knee.[74]

Over the 110 years or so of the life of the Ghost Dance Shirt, its significance has been summoned to serve the causes of religion, war, entertainment, display, and reconciliation. It has been used to construct narratives of heroism, massacre, sensationalism, colonial justification, scientific study, media drama, humanitarianism,[75] and historical change. It acted as a marker and an instigator of both old and new ways of thinking. There will be more uses for the Shirt as time passes. There is no one way in which objects 'mean'. There is no essential truth of the object. Their meaning is fluid, changeable, relational, and contextual. As circumstances and contexts change around them, they are seen in different ways and mean new things. Viewers in museums, and elsewhere, are social creatures, and the personal meanings they construct are influenced by their particular social contexts, by their 'interpretive communities'[76] and their 'interpretive repertoire'.[77] The meanings of the object are created through the personal and social processes of interpretation.

Towards the post-museum

The ideas on which this [extract] has been based are not very new, and in many intellectual fields they are not very controversial; however, when they are considered in relation to the modernist museum they become both of these things. They throw up in a stark way the need for a cultural change within museums. Although there is much dynamic and exciting innovative work being done, much of this is challenged by the forces of conservatism, and in many museums the need for change is refused. The issues concern the articulation of ideologies with the prioritisation of resources. Museums are frequently large and always complex, with many key stakeholders who will have divergent views on most matters; wholesale change is rarely possible or desirable in such circumstances.

The post-museum faces considerable challenges. The character of these challenges is beginning to become clear, but the modernist values, relations and practices on which most museums are based, and which are not regarded as contentious by everyone, are deeply imbedded. Visual culture within the museum is a technology of power. This power can be used to further democratic possibilities, or it can be used to uphold exclusionary values. Once this is acknowledged, and the museum is understood as a form of cultural politics, the post-museum will develop its identity.

Notes

Eilean Hooper-Greenhill is Professor of Museum Studies at the University of Leicester.

1   Fish 1980: 2.
2   Burnett 1995: 21.
3   Hall 1997: 2.
4   See Schroder 1994; Lindlof 1988; Jensen 1991: 42.
5   References to interpretive communities are appearing in the museum studies literature; see for example Appadurai and Breckenridge 1992; Perin 1992; Hooper-Greenhill 1999. Csikszentmihalyi and Robinson 1990, although not undertaken from this specific perspective, does support it rather well.
6   Fish 1980: 171.
7   Ibid.: 94.
8   Ibid.: 2.
9   Ibid.: 332.
10   Ibid.: 336.
11   Radway 1984.
12   Zelizer 1993.
13   Mitra 1997.
14   Ibid.: 177.
15   Radway 1984: 8; Schroder 1994: 337.
16   The Web users can be seen as consumers in that they used specific identifiable websites, but also producers, in that they produced web-based texts through emails and chat-rooms. In addition, they produced their own texts through their navigation of the various pages and hyperlinks . . .
17   Schroder 1994.
18   Morley 1992: 70.
19   Fish 1980: 172.
20   Lindlof 1988: 89.
21   Potter and Wetherell 1987: 138–57.
22   Fish 1980: 14.
23   The Museums and Galleries research report *Cultural Diversity: Attitudes of Ethnic Minority Populations Towards Museums and Galleries* shows how the image of the museum

is common across ethnic groups in Britain. This image is the image of the modernist museum, with 'old buildings' and 'posh people' (Desai and Thomas 1998: 1).

24 See Merriman 1997 for a description of an exhibition that was event among many on a specific theme – The Peopling of London one.

25 Maddra 1999.

26 Accessions Register, pp. 226–8, 1892, Kelvingrove Art Gallery and Museum, Glasgow. Fourteen objects, listed 92–2a–n, were purchased for £40. The name of the seller, in accordance with the museum's practice, is not recorded. Immediately following in the Register is a further set of objects listed 3a–n, which must have been donated, as the names of donors were recorded (O'Neill 1999: 10). The name given is George C. Crager. The Ghost Dance Shirt is listed at 3c, signifying that it must have been donated.

27 Accessions Register, 1892: 226–7; Maddra 1996: 2244.

28 Ibid.

29 The letter offering the objects to the museum is written on notepaper headed Buffalo Bill's Wild West Co. It is dated as in 'Glasgow Dec. 19th 1891'. It reads: 'Mr. Paton, Curator, Calvin Grove Museum, Glasgow. Dear Sir, Hearing that you are empowered to purchase relics for your museum, I would respectfully inform you that I have a collection of Indian Relics (North American) which I will dispose of before we sail for America. Should you wish any of them after inspection I would be pleased to have you call at my Room at the East End Exhibition Building – Please answer when you can come. Yours Resp. Geo. C. Crager, Incharge of Indians'. Kelvingrove Art Gallery and Museum Archives.

30 Crager letter to Paton, 1891.

31 Maddra 1995: 2.

32 Crager's Clipping Book, quoted in ibid.: n.30.

33 Maddra 1996: 49.

34 Utley 1963, photo 21, quoted by Maddra 1996: 49. Crager is listed as J.C. Craiger.

35 Brown 1991; Utley 1963.

36 Utley 1993.

37 Brown 1991: 441.

38 Maddra 1995: n.27, quotes *Nebraska History* 62 (2), 1981, and interviews concerning oral accounts of the event. Brown 1991, cites the *US Bureau of Ethnology 14th Report, 1892–93*, Part 2, p. 885.

39 Utley 1993: 311.

40 Brown 1991: 442.

41 Utley 1993: 281.

42 Ibid.: 282.

43 O'Neill 1999: 14.

44 Personal communication from Sam Maddra, 4 January 2000.

45 Royal Armouries 1999: 11.

46 Ibid.: 13.

47 White 1994.

48 Francis 1992: 92. Francis says there were thirty people, but Maddra suggests twenty-three (personal communication, 4 January 2000).

49 White 1994: 32.

50 Ibid.: 32.

51 Francis 1992: 92–3.

52   Members of the audience could ride in the stage as it was attacked (ibid.: 93).
53   White 1994: 27.
54   Ibid.: 29.
55   Francis 1992: 89, quotes a reporter for the *Toronto Globe* who on 22 August 1885, wrote: 'The Indians have been so isolated from the outside world that they are today precisely the same in manner, dress, habits and ways of thinking as they were when first taken from their reserves.'
56   Francis 1992.
57   Ibid.: 94.
58   Interview with Antonia Lovelace, Curator of Ethnography, at Kelvingrove Museum, 28 November 1995.
59   Ibid.
60   Ibid.
61   See Francis 1992: ch. 7, for an extended discussion of this point; see also Deloria 1999.
62   See Gardner 1991: 29, n.81, ch. 5.
63   Bendoris 1995.
64   McBeth 1995a.
65   Mullin 1995.
66   McBeth 1995b.
67   McBeth 1995a.
68   All excerpts are from letters held in the Ghost Dance Shirt file in the Kelvingrove Museum Archive. I am grateful to Mark O'Neill for making them available to me.
69   Donnelly 1995.
70   During the years between the first Lakota visit in 1995 and the second in 1999, many local authority museums in Britain were subject to reorganisation. In Glasgow, museum staff were cut by one-third between 1996 and 1998.
71   Markus 1987: 144.
72   Garner 1997.
73   These events were watched eagerly by museums in Britain; see *Museums Journal*, 1998; Harvey 1998, 1999.
74   O'Neill 1999: 16–17.
75   Glasgow Council's Media Release announcing the decision to return the Shirt quoted the Arts and Council Committee convener: 'We have been impressed by the Lakota during their visit to Glasgow. They have set an example in the way they have listened to different views about the fate of the shirt, and Glasgow has lived up to its reputation as a humanitarian city' (Forbes 1998).
76   Fish 1980: 15.
77   Jensen 1991: 42.

References

Appadurai, A. and Breckenridge, C. (1992) 'Museums are good to think: heritage on view in India', in Karp, I., Kreamer, C. and Lavine, S. *Museums and Communities: the Politics of Public Culture*, Smithsonian Institution, Washington, DC, 34–55.
Bendoris, M. (1995) 'Indians in heap big row for shirt', *Daily Record*, 8 April.

Brown, D. (1991) *Bury my Heart at Wounded Knee: An Indian History of the American West*, Vintage, London.

Burnett, R. (1995) *Cultures of Vision: Images, Media and the Imaginary*, Indiana University Press, Bloomington and Indianapolis.

Csikszentmihalyi, M. and Robinson, R. (1990) *The Art of Seeing: An Interpretation of the Aesthetic Encounter*, J. Paul Getty Museum and the Getty Center for Education in the Arts, Malibu, Calif.

Deloria, P. (1999) *Playing Indian*, Yale University Press, New Haven, Conn.

Desai, P. and Thomas, A. (1998) *Cultural Diversity: Attitudes of Ethnic Minority Populations towards Museums and Galleries*, Museums and Galleries Commission, London.

Donnelly, J. (1995) 'Museum reluctant to part with sacred tribal shirt', *Scotsman*, 10 April.

Fish, S. (1980) *Is There A Text in this Class? The Authority of Interpretive Communities*, Harvard University Press, Cambridge, Mass. and London.

Forbes, A. (1998) Media release: Glasgow City Council to Return Ghost Dance Shirt, Glasgow City Council, 20 November.

Francis, D. (1992) *The Imaginary Indian: The Image of the Indian in Canadian Culture*, Arsenal Pulp Press, Vancouver.

Gardner, H. (1991) *The Unschooled Mind: How Children Think and How Schools Should Teach*, Fontana Press, London.

Garner, C. (1997) 'London to Wounded Knee: Custer's conqueror goes home', *The Independent*, 23 September, 1.

Hall, S. (ed.) (1997) *Representation: Cultural Representations and Signifying Practices*, Sage Publications, London in association with the Open University, Milton Keynes.

Harvey, S. (1998) 'Repatriation', *Museums Journal*, 98 (12), 5.

Harvey, S. (1999) 'Letting go', *Museums Journal*, 98 (12), January: 34–5.

Hooper-Greenhill, E. (1999) 'Education, communication and interpretation: towards a critical pedagogy in museums', in Hooper-Greenhill, E. (ed.) *The Educational Role of Museums*, 2nd edition, Routledge, London, 3–27.

Jensen, K.B. (1991) 'Humanistic scholarship as qualitative science: contributions to mass communication research', in Jensen, K. and Jankowski, N. (eds) *A Handbook of Qualitative Methodologies for Mass Communication Research*, Routledge, London and New York, 17–43.

Keys, D. (1993) 'House saved villagers from volcano', *The Independent*, 30 November, 28.

Lindlof, T. (1988) 'Media audiences as interpretive communities', *Communication Yearbook*, 11, Sage Publications, Beverly Hills, Calif., 81–107.

Maddra, S. (1995) 'The Wounded Knee Ghost Dance Shirt', unpublished paper for Glasgow Museums.

Maddra, S. (1996) 'The Wounded Knee Ghost Dance Shirt', *Journal of Museum Ethnography*, 8, 41–58.

Maddra, S. (1999) *Glasgow's Ghost Dance Shirt*, Glasgow Museums, Glasgow.

Markus, G. (1987) 'Diogenes Laertius contra Gadamer: universal or historical hermeneutics?' in Fekete, J. *Life after Post-modernism: Essays on Value and Culture*, New World Perspectives, Montreal, Canada.

McBeth, J. (1995a) 'Sioux pow-wow for the return of Ghost Shirt', *Daily Mail*, 10 April, 3.

McBeth, J. (1995b) 'Sioux on the warpath', *The Scotsman*, 8 April.

Merriman, N. (1997) 'The "Peopling of London" project', in Hooper-Greenhill, E. (ed.) *Cultural Diversity: Developing Museum Audiences in Britain*, Leicester University Press, London and Washington, 119–48.

Mitra, A. (1997) 'Diasporic web sites: ingroup and outgroup discourse', *Critical Studies in Mass Communication*, 14, 158–81.

Morley, D. (1992) *Television, Audiences and Cultural Studies*, Routledge, London and New York.

Morley, D. (1996) 'Populism, revisionism and the "new" audience research', in Curran, J., Morley, D. and Walkerdine, V. (eds) *Cultural Studies and Communications*, Arnold, London and New York, 279–93.

Mullin, J. (1995) 'Lakota Sioux raid Glasgow to seek return of "ghost shirt"', *The Guardian*, 11 April.

O'Neill, M. (1999) 'The Glasgow Ghost Dance Shirt: a case study in repatriation', unpublished working paper, Glasgow Museums.

Perin, C. (1992) 'The communicative circle: museums as communities', in Karp, I., Kreamer, C. and Lavine, S. (eds) *Museums and Communities*, Smithsonian Institution Press, Washington, DC and London, 182–220.

Potter, J. and Wetherell, M. (1987) *Discourse and Social Psychology: Beyond Attitudes and Behaviour*, Sage Publications, London.

Radway, J. (1984) 'Interpretive communities and variable literacies: the functions of romance reading', *Daedalus*, 113 (3), 49–73.

Royal Armouries (1999) *Buffalo Bill's Wild West*, Royal Armouries, Leeds.

Schroder, K. (1994) 'Audience semiotics, interpretive communities and the "ethnographic turn" in media research', *Media, Culture and Society*, 16, 337–47.

Utley, R. (1963) *Last Days of the Sioux Nation*, Yale University Press, New Haven, Conn.

Utley, R. (1993) *The Lance and The Shield: The Life and Times of Sitting Bull*, Ballantine Books, New York.

White, R. (1994) 'Frederick Jackson Turner and Buffalo Bill', in Grossman, J. (ed.) *The Frontier in American Culture*, University of California Press, Berkeley, Los Angeles and London, 7–65.

Yung, K.K. (1981) *National Portrait Gallery Complete Illustrated Catalogue 1856–1979*, National Portrait Gallery, London.

Zelizer, B. (1993) 'Journalists as interpretive communities', *Critical Studies in Mass Communication*, 10, 219–37.

Chapter 5

Museums and the Combating of Social Inequality: roles, responsibilities, resistance

Richard Sandell

MUSEUMS AND GALLERIES of all kinds have both the potential to contribute towards the combating of social inequality and a responsibility to do so. Though by no means entirely new,[1] such claims to social influence and agency are still likely to elicit challenges from both within and outside the museum. Within the museum and wider cultural sector, there are many who remain uncomfortable with the assignment of overtly social roles; roles that are perceived as imposed, extraneous and unnecessary. For the majority of those working in social, welfare and health agencies – those whose day-to-day work is concerned with issues of inequality and disadvantage – museums' roles in terms of education and leisure are more likely to be acknowledged than their potential contributions to social equity. Museums are viewed as unlikely partners[2] whose goals are discretely cultural rather than social.

Claims to social agency – the ability to influence and affect society – may not be new, but in recent years these are taking on both a new form and a new confidence. First, claims are moving from the more abstract, theorised and equivocal to become more concretised and more closely linked to contemporary social policy and the combating of specific forms of disadvantage. For example, whilst there has been a burgeoning literature that explores the political effects of representation and the generative potentials of culture, this has focused largely on processes of *construction* within the museum, rather less on processes of *reception* and the tangible impact on audiences.[3] Here, the social impact of the museum is linked to outcomes such as the creation of cultural identity or the engendering of a sense of place and belonging (as well as negative outcomes such as the subjugation of minorities). These complex outcomes that are difficult to measure have been based, for the most part, on theoretical assumptions around the signifying power of culture. Alongside increasingly sophisticated conceptual development in the area of representation there are

Source: *Museums, Society, Inequality*, London: Routledge, 2002, pp. 3–23.

now increasingly bold and explicit claims that are beginning to explore the museum's impact on the lives of individuals and communities and the role that cultural organisations are playing in tackling specific manifestations of inequality – such as racism and other forms of discrimination, poor health, crime and unemployment.[4]

Second, within the cultural sector, fundamental questions about the social purpose and role of museums and galleries, which have for many decades been marginalised, have more recently been foregrounded and have achieved a currency and confidence that has proved difficult to ignore, even by the most entrenched and traditional sections of the museums and arts community.[5] Those who work within and with museums and those who fund and support them are increasingly asking: What kind of difference can museums make to people's lives and to society in general? What evidence exists to support this view?

This chapter draws on recent empirical and conceptual research to posit a framework within which the social agency of museums can be further explored. It argues that museums can contribute to the combating of the causes and the amelioration of the symptoms of social inequality and disadvantage at three levels: with individuals, specific communities and wider society. It is recognised that the arguments are presented from a British perspective, though examples of museum initiatives in Australia and the US are cited. The concepts discussed and the conclusions reached are by no means confined to the British context. It is then argued that, whilst not all organisations have the resources or the mandate to deliver benefits at all three levels, nonetheless, *all* museums and galleries have a social responsibility. The argument for acknowledgement of a social responsibility emerges from discussion around the interplay between the notions of social inequality[6] and cultural authority.[7] The chapter concludes by suggesting that all museums have an obligation to develop reflexive and self-conscious approaches to collection and exhibition and an awareness and understanding of their potential to construct more inclusive, equitable and respectful societies.

Museums and inequality: roles and outcomes

In what ways can museums engage with and impact upon social inequality, disadvantage and discrimination? The framework posited below (see Figure 5.1) has emerged from recent conceptual and empirical research and a range of international and UK examples are presented to illustrate the roles described.[8]

The framework suggests that museums can impact positively on the lives of disadvantaged or marginalised *individuals*, act as a catalyst for social regeneration and as a vehicle for empowerment with specific *communities* and also contribute towards the creation of more equitable *societies*. It is this latter role that will receive greatest attention here, as it is argued that it is through the thoughtful representation of difference and diversity that all museums, regardless of the nature of their collections, the resources available to them, their mission and the context within which they operate, can contribute towards greater social equity. The framework purposefully challenges the notion that the museum's contribution to the combating of social inequality is confined to its outreach or education work with specific groups and communities. It attempts to illustrate the wide-ranging outcomes museums can

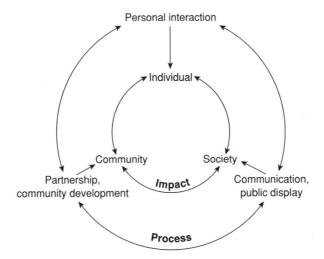

Figure 5.1   Museums and the combating of social inequality: impact and process

deliver and the most commonly deployed means or processes through which these are achieved. It is, however, necessarily schematised and it is recognised that, in practice, the categories of impact and process are neither so distinct nor discrete.

Individual

This category concerns the impact that museums can have on the lives of individuals. Here the potential outcomes are wide-ranging, from the personal, psychological and emotional (such as enhanced self-esteem or sense of place) to the pragmatic (such as the acquisition of skills to enhance employment opportunities).[9] In some instances, these outcomes are unintended, peripheral or at least are not always articulated within the goals of the museum or specific programme. For example, projects that may be motivated at the outset by a desire to encourage members of a specific group, under-represented in the museum's visitor profile, to make use of its services, have later resulted in unexpected positive outcomes for individuals (Sandell 1998). In such cases, the impact on individuals' lives may only emerge informally through anecdote or remain undisclosed or unevaluated. In recent research undertaken into the contribution of large local authority museums to social inclusion, one gallery described a project with visually impaired and blind people:

> The visually impaired group – now just a group of friends – have real rapport with staff and feel at home in the building. One blind person told us how she learned to handle public places through coming to the museum, which took her out of her shell. You only get that kind of feedback from individuals themselves, as evidence from group leaders is always second hand. I hope we are doing that for others too. (GLLAM 2000: 25)

Another project at Nottingham Museums initially sought to enhance access to its programmes and facilities for users of mental health services in the city (Dodd and Sandell 1998). Over time, the partnership between the museum and the health service developed to include new goals, based around using the museum programmes as a vehicle to deliver skills and confidence that would enhance the quality of life for individuals.

In other instances, museums are purposefully designing programmes that position access to, or use of, the museum, not as a goal in itself but as the means of helping to bring personal and practical benefits to individuals. Though the exact nature of that benefit or outcome is not always known at the outset, crucially the programmes are developed with a focus on bringing benefit to the individual and enhancing their equality of life, rather than the museum.[10] Such programmes reflect a belief in the social utility of museums.

An example can be found in the training projects established by the Living Museum of the West, Melbourne, Australia. The museum has provided the setting for a number of projects that have sought to provide training for long-term unemployed people:

> In Australia, such job creation schemes have frequently been criticised as merely providing cheap labour pools, and for failing to deliver meaningful long-term benefit to the participants . . . However, for the Living Museum of the West, such schemes offer an opportunity to provide valuable training and skills development for local people, in particular those from disadvantaged groups with few opportunities to gain employment . . . For example, the Koorie Garden Project . . . aims to provide culturally relevant employment for indigenous people within the locality combined with horticultural training. The project enables the participants . . . to develop skills to help them gain employment after the lifetime of the project. The original members of the Koorie Garden Project have now moved on to form a separate company in which all participants are shareholders and run a gardening business within the region. (Sandell 1998: 413)

Finally, recent research into the role that small museums can play in relation to social inclusion highlights the potential significance for some individuals of voluntary work.

> The research [also] highlighted the significance of volunteering as a means by which individuals gained benefit. At the Ragged School Museum in London, volunteers come from many backgrounds and for many reasons. As well as benefiting the museum, volunteers can also gain. Through volunteering, unemployed people can learn new skills, people with mental health problems learn to develop confidence and elderly people can develop a social network and combat isolation and loneliness. (Dodd and Sandell 2001: 27)

The processes by which these individual outcomes are delivered are, for the most part, characterised by face-to-face interaction between museum staff or representatives and members of, for example, a community group. In larger museums, they are often developed by the museum's education or outreach section. In many instances the most effective of these are developed in partnership with the agencies that have direct links with, and knowledge of, the group with which the museum is engaged (Silverman 1998).

Community

What role can museums play in delivering benefits to specific, geographically defined communities? Within this category we might consider museums' contributions to regeneration and renewal initiatives in, for example, deprived inner city or rural neighbourhoods. Specific outcomes include enhanced community self-determination, and increased participation in decision-making processes and democratic structures. Though empirical data is limited, it appears that cultural organisations, in comparison with other agencies, might be uniquely positioned to act as catalysts for community involvement and as agents for capacity building. An international conference on the role of culture in regeneration initiatives concluded that: 'Cultural initiatives are inclusive, and have an unsurpassed capacity to open dialogue between people and engage their enthusiasm and commitment to a shared redevelopment process.' Furthermore, 'culture and the development of creativity has a major part to play in helping to develop the capacity of local communities to address their own needs' (Matarasso and Landry 1996: v).

Although little formal evaluation of the museum's role in community empowerment and capacity building has been undertaken, those project experiences that have been documented point to the potential for museums to engage and enable groups that have previously been deprived of decision-making opportunities. Museums have provided an enabling, creative, perhaps less threatening forum through which community members can gain the skills and confidence required to take control and play an active, self-determining role in their community's future. Nancy Fuller, in her account of the Ak-Chin Indian community's ecomuseum project, provides further insight into the specific role that museums can play and the methods and techniques they can employ in empowering a community. She suggests that the ecomuseum model offers,

> a new role for community museums: that of instrument of self-knowledge and a place to learn and regularly practice the skills and attitudes needed for community problem solving. In this model the museum functions as a mediator in the transition from control of a community by those who are not members of the community to control by those who are. (Fuller 1992: 361)

In the categories of individual and community impact outlined briefly so far, the role of face-to-face engagement, partnerships with non-museum agencies and approaches and working practices that might be likened to those used by, for example, social, health or community development workers can be identified. This perhaps goes some way to explaining the perception that the museum's role in combating social inequality is equated solely with the outreach and education function. Furthermore, this may also account, in part, for reticence and resistance on the part of some museums' staff who feel that they are ill equipped to embark on projects of this kind, lacking the skills and resources to work directly with communities.

However, what role might museums play in tackling inequality through their ubiquitous and long-established functions of collection and display? The growing body of literature that explores the generative potential of museum representations focuses largely on its negative consequences and the museum's part in excluding, stereotyping or silencing difference through the selection, arrangement and public display of objects. In what ways then are museums reversing processes of exclusion and othering, to include and to celebrate, rather than stereotype, difference? Where this is happening, what impact does it have on the perceptions and actions of those who visit and on the creation of more equitable, tolerant societies?

Society

Claims that museums can change society can appear inappropriately immodest and naïve, a sentiment reflected in Stephen Weil's cautionary scepticism.

> Museums might [also] be more modest about the extent to which they have the capability to remedy the ills of the communities in which they are embedded. We live, all of us, in a society of startling inequalities, a society that has badly failed to achieve community, and a society that seems determined to lay waste to the planet that is its sole source of support. Museums neither caused these ills nor – except for calling attention to them – have it within their power alone to do very much to cure them. (Weil 1995: xvi)

Indeed, it is problematic to establish a direct, causal relationship between museum practices and contemporary manifestations of social inequality or their amelioration. On the other hand, museums and other cultural organisations cannot be conceived as discretely cultural, or asocial – they are undeniably implicated in the dynamics of (in)equality and the power relations between different groups through their role in constructing and disseminating dominant social narratives. What then of the political role that museums might play, alongside other organisations within civil society,[11] in promoting equality of opportunity and pluralist values?

Constructing equality

> The ways in which objects are selected, put together, and written or spoken about have political effects. These effects are not those of the objects *per se*; it is the use made of these objects and their interpretive frameworks that can open up or close down historical, social and cultural possibilities. By making marginal cultures visible, and by legitimating difference, museum pedagogy can become a critical pedagogy. (Hooper-Greenhill 2000: 148)

As a medium for mass communication and with a powerful, perceived cultural author-ity or 'weight' (Macdonald 1998: xi) the museum's potential as an agent of change is, perhaps, underestimated. Within the framework illustrated in Figure 5.1, the role that museums can play at a societal level is based on the notion of culture as generative. As Eilean Hooper-Greenhill states:

> Culture is frequently conceived as *reflective*. However, this is less accurate than the idea of culture as *constitutive*. Cultural symbols have the power to shape cultural identities at both individual and social levels; to mobilise emotions, perceptions and values; to influence the way we feel and think. In this sense, culture is generative, constructivist. (2000: 13)

This understanding of culture therefore suggests a critical role for museums in picturing and presenting inclusive, equitable societies. However, despite many examples of ways in which museums have sought to implement a 'critical pedagogy', to redress previous misrepresentations or exclusions, to legitimise difference, celebrate community diversity and challenge stereotypes, there is a dearth of empir-ical audience studies that attest to the influence of these projects on people's atti-tudes and actions towards others.[12] The following examples pose more questions than they answer about the social agency of museums and the effects of display on people's values, perceptions and social actions. They do, however, begin to sug-gest a possible role that museums might play in the combating of inequality and serve to highlight issues relating to the relative efficacy of different modes of exhibi-tion and display.

At Nottingham Castle Museum and Art Gallery, a display dating from the 1970s insensitively contrasted, on one side of a gallery, 'ethnographic' objects and on the other the military collections of the Sherwood Foresters Regiment. The display's overtly colonial interpretation angered many local communities and was eventu-ally replaced with The *Circle of Life* exhibition in 1994. The gallery, like others of its kind, set out to replace an unequivocal 'us and them' message with one that gives equal attention to sameness as it does to difference. The gallery explores the ways in which people from different cultures mark their outward appearance through different stages in their lives and uses objects from the collections alongside mater-ial loaned by local communities, including Lithuanian, Hindu, Ghanaian and Jewish groups. As the introductory panel states:

The Circle of Life

Life is a journey, a road upon which we all must travel from the cradle to the grave. We all share the experiences of life; good fortune or bad, success or failure, youth, maturity or old age and finally death.

We mark these changes in our lives, these steps along the road, in our outward appearance. Our clothes, jewellery, hairstyles and body decoration all proclaim to others our status, beliefs, attitudes, sex, occu-pation or origin.

Different cultures in different times have all found ways of saying 'Look, this is me. This is who I am!'

So, British military uniforms that were once displayed symbolically and physically in stark opposition to objects from non-western cultures now share a case with them and an interpretive framework that no longer prioritises one over another. The objects displayed were selected to represent the diversity of communities that currently live within the city.

Though redisplays, such as *The Circle of Life*, represent a conscious attempt to engage with ideas of equality and to foreground the value of community diversity, there are very few examples where the impact of the exhibition on visitors' perceptions and values has been researched. What cognitive, psychological and emotional reactions can occur during or following the visitor–exhibition encounter? How might cultural representations of those perceived as 'other' be received and decoded by visitors when difference is no longer exoticised, but rather integrated within and alongside the familiar? Does the cultural authority of the museum play a part in challenging visitors' beliefs and values about, for example, a specific community or group?

It can sometimes seem as if cultural organisations are uncertain about asserting their value in constructing and imagining inclusive societies. On the other hand, where the political implications and social consequences of culture are negative, these can be more confidently expressed. The relationship between processes of cultural production and manifestations of racial prejudice is clearly pointed out in *The Parekh Report* on *The Future of Multi-Ethnic Britain*:

> Acts of racism, racial violence, racial prejudice and abuse do not exist in a vacuum. They are not isolated incidents or individual acts, removed from the cultural fabric of our lives. Notions of cultural value, belonging and worth are defined and fixed by the decisions we make about what is or is not our culture, and how we are represented (or not) by cultural institutions. (The Commission on the Future of Multi-Ethnic Britain 2000: 159)

The political consequences of representation have received most attention in relation to displays and redisplays of collections traditionally categorised as anthropological or ethnographic (Hooper-Greenhill 2000; Macdonald 1998; Karp 1992). Though these museums have been subject to most scrutiny, as Eilean Hooper-Greenhill comments,

> the points that are made perhaps most forcibly in the anthropological museums are of more general relevance. Displayed objects of all types are made meaningful according to the interpretive frameworks within which they are placed, and the historical or cultural position from which they are seen. (2000: 8)

Similarly, Karp asserts that 'Art, history, and ethnography displays, even natural history exhibitions, are all involved in defining the identities of communities – or in denying them identity' (1992: 19).

What implications does this have for the social responsibility of *all* museums and for exhibition and collection practices in particular? Are different kinds of museum and different modes of display more authoritative, better positioned to influence and shape attitudes, more powerful agents of change than others? Though, as stated earlier, there exists little in the way of formal, in-depth research with which to test out these hypotheses, the following examples serve to highlight ways in which museum exhibitions can potentially contribute towards the combating of discrimination, intolerance and social inequities.

In 1998, during the final phase of a major refurbishment of Nottingham Castle Museum and Art Gallery, an exhibition of decorative arts, *Every Object Tells a Story*, opened on the ground floor, adjacent to the foyer and main entrance. The exhibition represents a departure from previous exhibitionary styles for the decorative arts collections within the museum. The formerly distinct and separate galleries of ceramics, silver and glass have been merged to take a thematic look at the stories attached to different objects. The gallery employs a number of interpretive devices: activities and displays aimed at very young children, reflexive texts and videos by artists that explore the colonial histories of collections[13] and the personal accounts and responses of individuals from different communities to the objects displayed. The museum is perhaps the best-known and most prestigious cultural venue in the city. *Every Object Tells a Story* is the first exhibition that most of the museum's 400,000 visitors each year will encounter. The museum attracts large numbers of local families as well as tourists and is run by the local authority. One section of the exhibition, *Stories of Love*, includes just three objects displayed together in the same case. The text panel states:

Stories of Love

Objects have the power to evoke strong emotions in people.

The objects in this section are symbols of the most powerful human emotion – love.

Different objects – different kinds of love.

Do you have any object that you treasure as symbols of love?

The three objects displayed are a pocket watch and love poem that belonged to Private John Batty, a soldier who died in the Battle of Waterloo in 1815, a child's jacket made by the Rabari people from the Kutch area of Gujerat and a large, decorative ceramic bowl, entitled 'Lovers'. The text that accompanies the bowl is the moving testimony of Andrew who explains that the bowl was created as a memorial to his partner Neil who died in 1993.

> The design of the bowl really came from myself and what I got to know of Neil over the five years that we were together – the fact that he loved ceramics and loved Karen Atherley's work . . . My definition of real love? Neil was the love of my life and we were very close and shared a hell of a lot. I used to work in my shop a lot more than I do now, but I had other things to look forward to then, so that didn't seem so bad. I used to work until 5 o'clock and Neil would come to the shop whenever he could. I just remember the happy hours at the end of the day, and Neil's little face coming past the shop window.

Though no research has been undertaken into visitor responses to the bowl, and its place within a mainstream, family-oriented exhibition, the example poses interesting questions about the political implications and consequences of display. Whilst the controversial nature of many temporary exhibitions often evokes mixed public reactions and even media controversy,[14] the placing of an object representing a gay relationship, within one of the museum's main galleries alongside those which tell the story of a historical/heterosexual relationship and that between a mother and child has, to date, produced no formal complaints or adverse comment (Wood 2001). The extent to which this is a consequence of the naturalising effects of the museum's cultural authority is uncertain.

In the *Stories of Love* exhibit, sameness is once more conferred equal status to difference. Karp and Kratz[15] state that:

> In museum exhibits as much as in other cultural forms, the construction of cultural identity is achieved through two simultaneously occurring processes: (1) the use of exaggerated differences or oppositions that can be alternately a mode of exploration and understanding or an act of discrimination and (2) the use of varied assertions of sameness or similarity between audience and the object of contemplation. (2000: 194)

They further argue that:

> Stressing similarities produces an assimilating impression creating both familiarity and intimacy with representations and their subjects. Assertions of unbridgeable difference, on the other hand, exoticise by creating relations of great spatial or temporal distance, perhaps the thrill of the unknown. (ibid.: 198)

In this example, does the placement of objects, and the relations established between them, offer a preferred reading to visitors, one that encourages empathy, acceptance and respect? How might visitors receive such messages?

Shaping the unpredictable: visitor reception and response

It is, of course, naïve to imagine that purposefully inclusive museum displays can guide visitors, without resistance or question, towards preordained opinions and engender within them specific values. The way in which processes of communication within the museum are now understood challenges the transmission model of pedagogy in which the messages received and decoded by the audience are those intended, prescribed and predicted by the curator (Hooper-Greenhill 2000: 133). Instead, communication is now understood in a way that gives much greater emphasis to the audience or visitor.

> In this approach to communication, the focus is on how meaning is constructed through social life by active individual agents, within social networks . . . The task for communicators – or, in the museum, curators,

educators and exhibition developers – is to provide experiences that invite visitors to make meaning through deploying and extending their existing interpretive strategies and repertories, using their prior knowledge and their preferred learning styles, and testing their hypotheses against those of others, including experts. (ibid.: 139)

What are the implications of this understanding of communication for discussions about the social responsibility of museums? Since the prior knowledge, experiences and value systems of visitors are so central to the communication process, what role can the museum play in shaping their attitudes and values? The constructivist view of museum pedagogy requires us to acknowledge the complex and unpredictable nature of the visitor response (Hooper-Greenhill 2000: 124). Messages, intended by museum staff to evoke feelings of respect, empathy, understanding and insight may instead evoke equally strong negative responses. As Eilean Hooper-Greenhill states:

> Exhibitions are produced to communicate meaningful visual and textual statements, but there is no guarantee that the intended meaning will be achieved. Visitors to museum exhibitions respond in diverse ways. They may or may not perceive the intended messages, and, perceiving them, they may or may not agree with them, find them interesting, or pay attention to them. (ibid.: 4)

This unpredictability of response is exemplified in a letter of complaint, recently sent to Nottingham Castle Museum and Art Gallery. Alongside the permanent displays of *The Circle of Life* and *Every Object Tells a Story*, previously discussed, a recent temporary exhibition of work by artist Alison Lapper, organised by the museum, clearly presented its aims in the introductory text panel. Here the artist stated:

> My work reflects and responds to other people's attitude to me. I hope to question and change society's ideas about physical beauty, normality, disability and sexuality. As a disabled person, I am generally perceived as ugly, sexless, inert, helpless and miserable.
>
> I know I am not.
>
> My work gives me the opportunity to represent myself to the world on my own terms . . .

Visitor responses to the exhibition were largely positive and the artist herself found the experience of exhibiting in a 'mainstream' cultural organisation an empowering one.

> I was in the gallery when a group of pretty robust, straight-talking children came in and we got into a conversation. They wanted to know how I got dressed, what it was like being a mum with no arms, they were inquisitive and accepting, they wanted to use their feet as I do. It was spontaneous and accidental but it seemed to me what this is all about – it was about difference, about diversity, about my disability, my life. (quoted in Dodd and Sandell 2001)

One formal complaint however, about the visitor's experience of the whole museum, was received from a local resident and illustrates not only a general resistance to museums engaging with contemporary social issues but a reading of the exhibition that is in direct opposition with its stated aims. The visitor stated:

> Only one room remained as we had remembered it and that was full of old uniforms and war memorabilia. The remaining rooms were disorganised mazes of what I can only describe as rubbish. We were particularly offended by the display of photographs of a disabled woman and her baby, which I can only compare to the old 'freak show'. I know we live in the age of 'political correctness' but I do not think that the Castle was the place to display such items of so called modern art.

Such responses may be seen to challenge the view that museums can and should exploit their cultural authority. As Hilde Hein comments:

> Like a literary text, an object represents a potential effect that is realized only in an act of apprehension equivalent to the act of reading. That act may concur with, but can also resist, the author's act of writing or the judgement of a curator. Meaning is not 'put into' a text or object to be 'taken away' by someone who 'finds' it here, but comes into being through intersubjective participatory experiences. (2000: 63)

With this understanding of communication, claims that a museum visit might transform an individual's entrenched and oppositional views and values appear both problematic and naïve.

However, Eilean Hooper-Greenhill's discussion of learning theory and the work of Gadamer on the encounter between object and viewer points to a way forward:

> Gadamer suggests that experiences, objects and other materials such as texts are approached with what he calls prejudices, or foreknowledge, given by our own historicity, and with a certain openness. This receptiveness to the objects creates a balance or dialectic between prejudice (what is already known) and openness. This dialectic permits revision of prejudices towards a greater 'truth' but this truth is still relative, historical and socially determined. (2000: 117)

This might suggest that, whilst a single museum visit is unlikely to overturn the most entrenched attitudes, nonetheless, more inchoate values and perceptions may be open to challenge, question, modification. At the very least, it can be argued that, alongside other mass media, museums can play a role in the promulgation of values based on social equity.

Whilst the ways in which visitors decode purposeful attempts to promote social equality are under-researched and poorly understood, research that has been undertaken lends support to this argument. In 'Harnessing the power of history', Ruth Abram (2002) describes a project to challenge misconceptions and stereotypical attitudes amongst schoolchildren:

Teaming up with private and public schools, and with Lyndhurst, a National Trust Site, the Museum is developing a programme with a simple message – a person's worth cannot be measured by calculating his/her material wealth. As a first step, nine-year-olds were invited to write down words they associated with the word 'poor' both before and after a visit to the Tenement Museum. The number of negative associations with the word 'poor' (including 'mean', 'dangerous', 'dishonest') plummeted from 90 before the visit to 20 after it.

Similarly, evidence from evaluation undertaken at the Australian Museum, Sydney into the impact of the *Indigenous Australians* exhibition that opened in 1997 suggests that it has successfully achieved significant shifts in some visitors' attitudes.

Focus group interviews were held with adults and children six months after they had visited the exhibition to investigate long-term learning, impact and change. Participants in this study gave many examples of gaining greater understanding through relating what they had seen in the exhibition to their own experiences and knowledge . . . Participants also talked about thinking differently after seeing the exhibition: '*I thought differently. I've met Aboriginal people . . . and it didn't click with the way that, as a child, when you grew up and everything you heard [was negative] and then you see an exhibition like this, well then you see a lot more of the story.*' (Kelly and Gordon 2002)

Whilst the way in which visitors will respond to exhibitions cannot be predicted with certainty, the museum's role and efficacy could be both better understood and, as a result, enhanced through a greater understanding of the processes of audience reception. As Hilde Hein states, 'learning theorists and environmental psychologists have concluded that certain conceptual and developmental commonalities do exist and that knowledge of these would enable museums to shepherd the experience of their audience to achieve some degree of uniformity' (2000: 112).

These brief examples go some way to supporting the view that museums might purposefully employ their cultural authority to broader social ends. Despite a growing recognition that museums have often reproduced and reinforced social inequalities through their collecting and exhibitionary practices, many museum staff are uncomfortable with the notion of relinquishing their pursuit of perceived objectivity and neutrality in favour of adopting an active, political stance on equality issues. What obligations might be placed on museums to do so?

Museums and social responsibility

The arguments presented so far have focused on two key issues: the relationship between museums and social inequality and the notion of cultural authority. Where these intersect and are brought together, questions of social responsibility emerge most strongly. Within the museum context, social responsibility requires an acknowledgement not only of the potential to impact on social inequality, but also of the organisations' obligation to deploy their social agency and cultural authority in a way that is aligned and consistent with the values of contemporary society.

In the UK, where the concept of social inclusion has become embedded throughout central government policy, critics have argued that the assignment of social goals to cultural organisations is tying them too closely to the state and eroding their autonomy. This, it is argued, is reducing the arts to a tool for governmental social control (Thorpe 2000: 9). However, issues of social responsibility require museums to become responsive, not to short-term, party political objectives but rather to longer-term, paradigmatic shifts in thinking and what Hein calls the 'prevailing moral spirit' of society as a whole (2000: 92). Museums' principles and practices are no longer in step with contemporary, dominant value systems and ways of thinking. As Eilean Hooper-Greenhill states:

> The museum of the modernist period, the modernist museum, which emerged in the nineteenth century, developed characteristics which were shaped in relation to the ideas and values of the period . . . Since this time, however, these ideas and values have been challenged, modified, put away. (2000: 21)

Social responsibility requires an acknowledgement of the meaning-making potential of the museum and an imperative to utilise that to positive social ends. From her perspective as a philosopher, Hein describes this as 'institutional morality'.[16] She is critical of professional codes of ethics that have focused on the behaviour of individuals whilst neglecting the agency of the museum as an institution.

> The suggestion that institutions might originate and express moral agency appears to personify and invest them with suprahuman consciousness. We tend to believe that because morality entails intentionality, it therefore requires consciousness. I am claiming that moral character does not imply consciousness, but rather the capacity to create meaning. Institutions possess that capacity to an extent exceeding that of any individual. (2000: 103)

Alongside these moral and ethical arguments, there are also those who would argue that museums have obligations to deliver benefits to society by virtue of their status as publicly funded institutions. Edmund Barry Gaither argues that,

> Museums have obligations as both educational and social institutions to participate in and contribute towards the restoration of wholeness in the communities of our country. They ought to increase understanding within and between cultural groups in the matrix of lives in which we exist. They ought to help to give substance, correction and reality to the often incomplete and distorted stories we hear about art and social history. They should not dodge the controversy that often arises from the reappraisal of our common and overlapping pasts. If our museums cannot muster the courage to tackle these considerations in ways

appropriate to their various missions and scales then concern must be raised for how they justify the receipt of support from the public. (1992: 58)

Of course, acceptance of the social and moral agency of the museum as an institution raises innumerable complex issues for those who work within them. Issues of balance, partiality and moral judgement are those that many museums are already grappling with.[17] Similarly, there are tensions between the notion of 'institutional morality' (as a force for positive change) and the potential for its misuse. Furthermore, some critics are sceptical of the museum's ability to effectively challenge the dominant narratives and power relations with which it is inextricably linked (Marcus 2000; Hallam and Street 2000: 151). These concerns again raise questions for museum practice and the need for a methodology that adequately responds to a diverse and rapidly changing society. Increasingly museums are looking to discard exhibitions with a single, authoritative voice in favour of multiple voices, speaking in their own words and on their own terms.[18] Stephen Levine articulates some of these concerns, and the possible way forward:

> Museum officials, accustomed to speaking authoritatively, must recognize that their choice of whom to hire and whom to listen to retains for them the cultural power to cast the terms of discourse about people and history. Even when museums consult representatives of minority cultures or bring them onto their staff, they still must consider how and on what basis their selections of such representatives have been made . . . a solution is likely to be found only in an adequate process of dialogue, one that can transform the voice of authority on which museums have traditionally relied into the voice of a pluralistic society. (1992: 145)

Social responsibility is not a new concept to the museum. It can be linked, for example, to the new approaches to social history curation that gained momentum in the early 1980s and that sought to present the histories of previously marginalised groups (Fleming 2001). Indeed, over fifteen years ago, Edward Chappell wrote,

> Millions of people visit history museums each year. This vast audience is ready to be thoughtfully engaged, to be challenged to think about major issues, past and present . . . decent museums must not be passive or regressive. They should be accessible and – just as important – they should have things to say that ultimately advance the discussion about social relations and economic structure. (1989: 265)

Similarly, museums have been urged to adopt a political stance in their exhibitions that explore contemporary social problems (Ellis 1995) and to accept that they cannot be impartial observers in clashes over contested identities (Karp 1992: 15).

However, despite a growing recognition of the social agency of museums, (both positive and negative), there remains a marked reluctance to acknowledge the obligations that accompany it and to explore the possibilities and limitations in practice. Some of the most entrenched views can be found in the art museum where the belief in 'art for art's sake' remains, for some, strongly resistant to social and political influence. This resistance is exemplified by comments made by Mark Ryan:

> When the new elite says we must tackle 'social exclusion', such a state-
> ment could mean a lot of different things . . . The museum or gallery
> that is not prepared to turn its collection into a children's playground
> is being exclusive . . . Although the precise meaning is unclear, there
> is never a doubt as to what the new language intends. The artistic direc-
> tor who is concerned only with the merit of his work, when he hears
> that he must tackle social exclusion, knows that he is being warned.
> Perhaps he is thinking too much about art and not enough about The
> People. (2000: 17)

The concept of responsibility – individual, institutional, professional and shared – is an increasingly significant feature of contemporary society.[19] Social responsibility is receiving increasing attention in many professional arenas (ranging from business to architecture, mass media to engineering)[20] and in academic contexts exploring, for example, the social responsibility of science. Many museums, in their desire for autonomy, resistance to change, and disengagement from societal concerns run the risk of becoming increasingly irrelevant and anachronistic in their values.

Acknowledgement of a potential to contribute to social change brings many challenges as well as possibilities. However, the concept of social responsibility does not imply that the combating of inequality becomes the sole aim of all museums,[21] nor that disadvantage and discrimination are problems that museums alone must tackle. Similarly, social responsibility does not require museums to become govern-ment tools for social engineering and control. The reality, much less threatening and radical than many traditionalists assume, is based on the idea that museums, alongside many other institutional and individual agents, must consider their impact on society and seek to shape that impact through practice that is based on contemporary values and a commitment to social equality.

Notes

Richard Sandell is deputy head of the Department of Museum Studies in the University of Leicester.

1   The social purpose and goals of many museums established in the nineteenth century have been widely discussed (see, for example, Davies 1994). Though these museums had a clear social purpose, the motivations behind them are generally understood as paternalistic and based on notions of civilising and fac-ilitating the governance of the masses (Hein 2000: 44 and Hooper-Greenhill 2000: 11).

2   For example, Margaret Mackechnie (2001: 117) comments, 'In the past, with a background in residential social work, I have generally thought of museums as places to take children for a day out and that was about the extent of it. Museums did not figure in terms of thinking about childcare, I really didn't think they

had much to offer. I am sure that these perceptions echo those of many who are working in the social sector.'

3   The dearth of empirical audience studies and associated delay in conceptual development is discussed by Hooper-Greenhill (1995: 9).

4   Such claims are being supported by a growing body of qualitative research into the social impact of museums. See, for example, GLLAM 2000 and Dodd and Sandell 2001.

5   In the UK, the election of New Labour in 1997 has seen the concepts and terminology of social inclusion become embedded in not only social and welfare but also cultural policies. Such policy developments have helped to highlight and bring into focus the questions of social purpose and value facing cultural organisations. A lively debate has ensued in professional journals, seminars and conferences as well as national newspapers.

6   Social inequality is understood here in terms of not only the forms of disadvantage experienced by different groups and individuals but also the dynamic social processes and power relations that operate to deny those groups opportunities, rights and access to resources.

7   Cultural authority is understood here to refer to the museum's capacity to make meaning and, in doing so, to influence and shape visitors' perceptions.

8   The framework presented here is developed from concepts originally put forward in Sandell 1998 and developed in Dodd and Sandell 2001.

9   See, for example, GLLAM 2000.

10   See for example, Silverman 1998; 'Mandy's story' in Dodd and Sandell 2001.

11   Karp (1992: 5) states that 'Civil society includes such diverse forms of organization as families, voluntary associations, ethnic groups and associations, educational organizations and professional societies. These are the social apparatuses responsible for providing the arenas and contexts in which people define, debate and contest their identities and produce and reproduce their living circumstances, their beliefs and values and ultimately their social order.'

12   This lack of empirical research into visitors' responses to exhibitions is highlighted by Hooper-Greenhill (1995: 9) and, in relation to science exhibitions, Macdonald (1998: 2).

13   One text panel reads, 'The silver candlesticks have been displayed in the museum since 1968 as purely decorative objects. Made in 1757 at the height of the slave trade, they depict African slaves, yet this provocative subject was neither acknowledged nor interpreted. Video makers Dan Saul and Joules Ayodeji explore the wider history of the candlesticks. Take a closer look . . .'

14   It might be argued that temporary exhibitions are more likely (by virtue of their sometimes controversial content and higher profile) than their more permanent exhibitionary counterparts to provoke debate and public reaction, both positive and negative. On the other hand, they may perhaps be perceived as less authoritative, more open to scrutiny and question than more permanent displays. Sharon Macdonald, citing Roger Silverstone, suggests that the cultural authority of different media might be usefully explored in relation to the space they occupy and their degree of permanency. 'An emphasis on time and space would direct us to consideration of such matters as the authority effects of the temporal stability of most museum exhibitions, many of which are in place for years' (Macdonald 1998: 5).

15   Drawing on the ideas of Barthes 1984.

16   She also uses the term 'moral leadership' (2000: 103).

17   See, in particular, Szekeres, this volume.
18   The text that accompanies the bowl within *Every Object Tells a Story*, described earlier, is just one example of this.
19   See, for example, Strydom, P. (1999) 'The challenge of responsibility for sociology', *Current Sociology*, 47(3), London: Sage Publications.
20   See, for example, Bussel, A. (1995) 'The (social) art of architecture', *Progressive Architecture* 76, January: 43–6; Wilson, I. (2000) 'The new rules: ethics, social responsibility and strategy', *Strategy and Leadership*, 28(3): 12–16.
21   In a recent article about the under-representation of ethnic minorities on British television, Gurbux Singh, chair of the Commission for Racial Equality, considers the shared nature of responsibility. 'It helps no one that young people still grow up looking at the world and themselves through a television screen that hides much of the reality that it does not distort. It is not television's fault that the world out there is infested by racism and discrimination, but television needs to play its part in helping to deal with the problem instead of compromising with it' (2001: 17).

References

Abram, R. (2002) 'Harnessing the Power of History' in R. Sandell (ed.) *Museums, Society, Inequality*, London: Routledge.

Barthes, R. (1984) 'The great family of man', in *Mythologies*, New York: Hill and Wang.

Chappell, E.A. (1989) 'Social responsibility and the American history museum', *Winterthur Portfolio* 24, Winter: 247–65.

The Commission on the Future of Multi-Ethnic Britain (2000) *The Future of Multi-Ethnic Britain: The Parekh Report*, London: The Runnymede Trust and Profile Books.

Davies, S. (1994) 'A sense of purpose: rethinking museum values and strategies', in G. Kavanagh (ed.) *Museum Provision and Professionalism*, London and New York: Routledge.

Dodd, J. and Sandell, R. (1998) *Building Bridges: Guidance for Museums and Galleries on Developing New Audiences*, London: Museums and Galleries Commission.

Dodd, J. and Sandell, R. (eds) (2001) *Including Museums: Perspectives on Museums, Galleries and Social Inclusion*, Leicester: Research Centre for Museums and Galleries, Department of Museum Studies.

Ellis, R. (1995) 'Museums as change agents', *Journal of Museum Education*, Spring/Summer: 14–17.

Fleming, D. (2001) 'The politics of social inclusion', in J. Dodd and R. Sandell (eds) *Including Museums: Perspectives on Museums, Galleries and Social Inclusion*, Leicester: Research Centre for Museums and Galleries, Department of Museum Studies.

Fuller, N.J. (1992) 'The museum as a vehicle for community empowerment: the Ak-Chin Indian Community Ecomuseum Project', in I. Karp, C. Kreamer and S. Levine (eds) *Museums and Communities: The Politics of Public Culture*, Washington and London: Smithsonian Institution Press.

Gaither, E.B. (1992) '"Hey! That's mine": thoughts on pluralism and American museums', in I. Karp, C. Kreamer and S. Levine (eds) *Museums and Communities: The Politics of Public Culture*, Washington and London: Smithsonian Institution Press.

GLLAM (2000) *Museums and Social Inclusion – The GLLAM Report*, Leicester: Research Centre for Museums and Galleries, Department of Museum Studies.

Hallam, E. and Street, B.V. (eds) (2000) *Cultural Encounters: Representing 'Otherness'*, London and New York: Routledge.

Hein, H. (2000) *The Museum in Transition: A Philosophical Perspective*, Washington: Smithsonian Institution.

Hooper-Greenhill, E. (ed.) (1995) *Museum, Media, Message*, London and New York: Routledge.

Hooper-Greenhill, E. (2000) *Museums and the Interpretation of Visual Culture*, London and New York: Routledge.

Karp, I. (1992) 'On civil society and social identity', in I. Karp, C. Kreamer and S. Levine (eds) *Museums and Communities: The Politics of Public Culture*, Washington and London: Smithsonian Institution Press.

Karp, I. and Kratz, C.A. (2000) 'Reflections on the fate of Tippoo's Tiger: defining cultures through public display', in E. Hallam and B.V. Street (eds) *Cultural Encounters: Representing 'Otherness'*, London and New York: Routledge.

Kelly, L. and Gordon, P. (2002) 'Developing a community of practice', in R. Sandell (ed.) *Museum, Society, Inequality*, London: Routledge.

Levine, S.D. (1992) 'Audience, ownership and authority: designing relations between museums and communities', in I. Karp, C. Kreamer and S. Levine (eds) *Museums and Communities: The Politics of Public Culture*, Washington and London: Smithsonian Institution Press.

Macdonald, S. (ed.) (1998) *The Politics of Display: Museums, Science, Culture*, London and New York: Routledge.

Mackechnie, M. (2001) 'Partnerships and a shared responsibility', in J. Dodd and R. Sandell (eds) *Including Museums: Perspectives on Museums, Galleries and Social Inclusion*, Leicester: Research Centre for Museums and Galleries, Department of Museum Studies.

Marcus, K. (2000) 'Towards an erotics of the museum', in E. Hallam and B.V. Street (eds) *Cultural Encounters: Representing 'Otherness'*, London and New York: Routledge.

Matarasso, F. and Landry, C. (eds) (1996) *The Art of Regeneration*, Stroud: Comedia and Nottingham City Council.

Ryan, M. (2000) 'Manipulation without end', in M. Wallinger and M. Warnock (eds) *Art for All?: Their Policies and Our Culture*, London: Peer.

Sandell, R. (1998) 'Museums as agents of social inclusion', *Museum Management and Curatorship*, 17(4): 401–18.

Silverman, L. (1998) *The Therapeutic Potential of Museums: A Guide to Social Service/Museum Collaboration*, Indiana: Institute of Museum and Library Services.

Singh, G. (2001) 'Any colour, as long as it's white', *Guardian*, 9 April.

Szekeres, V. (2002) 'Representing diversity and challenging racism: the Migration Museum'.

Thorpe, V. (2000) 'Labour using art as "tool of social control"', *Observer*, 3 December.

Weil, S. (1995) *A Cabinet of Curiosities: Inquiries Into Museums and Their Prospects*, Washington and London: Smithsonian Institution Press.

Wood, P. (2001) Personal communication to the author.

Chapter 6

Museums for 'The People'?

Josie Appleton

'The position [on culture] staked out by some conservatives, which has changed little over time, speaks for itself; they sanction fortifying the dykes. The position staked out by liberals and leftists, which has changed, raises questions. Once upon a time they believed in a new and better culture for people. No longer. In the name of democracy they anoint the daily fare of entertainment and movies; their confidence in a transformed future has evaporated . . . They ratify the status quo in the name of democracy.'

Russell Jacoby, *The End of Utopia*[1]

'Plenty of people will try to give the masses, as they call them, an intellectual food prepared and adapted in the way they think proper for the actual condition of the masses.'

Matthew Arnold, *Culture and Anarchy*[2]

Introduction

LAST YEAR, during the screening of the TV programme *Big Brother*, an exhibition was built around the show in the newly opened Wellcome Wing of the Science Museum London. The exhibition posed questions such as whether or not the contestants would be harmed by their experiences, then asked visitors: 'would you like to be a guinea pig in the Big Brother house?' Three options were given, Yes/No/Don't know. Votes were clocked up in large electronic numbers. Upstairs on the floor 'Who am I?' visitors could explore the principles of genetic fingerprinting on a mock fruit-machine, matching up the DNA bands of father, mother and offspring. On the floor 'Digitopolis' they could create digital music or set up their own website. The wing was semi-dark, bathed in spacey sounds and moving lights. Here was a museum: but not as we know it.

Source: *Museums for 'The People'?*, Appleton *et al.*, London: Institute of Ideas 2001, pp. 14–26.

An interview with one of the Wellcome Wing project leaders, Heather Mayfield, illustrates the thrust behind the project. When some of the interactive machines broke down, Mayfield's direct telephone number was flashed up 'for all those dissatisfied visitors'.[3] The focus of the wing seems less to produce exhibitions with high-quality scientific or intellectual content, than to attract and engage its visitors. The exhibitions on the ground floor of the Wellcome Wing change frequently, according to whatever the curators think will excite interest at the time. Many of the interactive machines ask visitors what they think about current scientific controversies, such as the use of drugs to treat depression, foot-and-mouth disease, or the male pill. The museum is anxious to assure its visitors that their views are important and will be taken very seriously by scientists, though what happens to all the Yesses/Noes/Don't knows is not clear.

The Wellcome Wing is not alone. In recent years, a new generation of museum professionals, backed by the New Labour government, has begun to create a new type of museum. In this people-centred museum, the visitor has become the focus of the museum's activity: everything, from the physical layout to the choice of exhibition to the organisation of the collection is assessed in terms of how it will appeal to and stimulate people. Like politicians and media moguls, museum officials also love The People, so much so, that the original purpose of museums, the collection, study and exhibition of objects, is now subordinate to a vast array of other social activities.

Turning museums towards The People in this way is not just a change of direction or an embellishment of what went before. It is a total reversal of the meaning and purpose of the museum and puts in question the existence of museums as such. For 200 years, from the creation of the Louvre by the French republican government as the first national museum open to the general public, the central concern of curators was the collection, preservation and study of objects deemed to be of artistic, historic or scientific interest. The museum was organised around its collections. Because these collections were held in perpetuity on behalf of the public, museums have always had a concern with, and sense of obligation to, society at large. Whatever the ideological bent of those who ran the museum, the fact that it was bound by a clearly defined professional obligation gave its activity some rational purpose. The new museum, by contrast, organised around the ever-changing presumed needs of people, lacks any rational foundation whatsoever. Its function bends and twists to fit perceived demands, most of which are arbitrarily chosen by the government or the museum authorities themselves, and which often have no connection with the original core activity of the museum.

We can identify two key trends which have led to this state of affairs. These trends can be summarised briefly as the ascendancy over a period of 20–30 years of two seemingly opposed, yet ultimately compatible ideologies: the ideology of the economic right on the one side, and of the cultural left on the other.

Cultural leftism has gained supremacy in academic and intellectual circles since the 1960s. The enduring legacy of the cultural left has been its hostility to the idea of objectivity itself. For the cultural left, the claim to objective knowledge was no more than an attempt by the establishment to assert its intellectual hegemony. Expressed in various forms – postcolonial and feminist theories, post-modernism, Foucauldian theories of power relations – the cultural left undermined every attempt

at objective truth and universality. Foucauldian theories had an especially pernicious influence within the museum profession: the acts of collecting, categorising
and interpreting objects came to be seen not as the disinterested pursuit of knowledge, but as the striving for power on the part of the Western elite. The very act
of building collections was seen as an affirmation of Western racism and imperialism. Collections were deemed no longer to have any meaning distinct from the
subjective interpretations imposed on them by scholars and curators. The result
was a loosening of the bonds which tied the scholar and curator to their objects.
If all interpretations were subjective, then why privilege the one which laid false
claims to objectivity? Freed from the discipline of objective knowledge, those in
museums now had unprecedented scope for the exercise of whim and fancy.

The intellectual nihilism of the cultural left was compounded by the attack on
traditional institutions from the economic right. Under the Conservative government of Margaret Thatcher, public arts bodies were forced to justify their existence by proving that they could give value for money. Under the new market
criteria, arts bodies became service delivery organisations. 'The customer always
comes first' was the new mantra. If the arts could not find customers, then they
would have to go to the wall. Having lost their intellectual bearings, museum
professionals were now pushed decisively in a new direction – towards the new
market ideology of customer satisfaction. At the same time, they could justify
this move in pseudo-democratic terms: 'The People have been excluded from
museums for too long – time to give them a say in what we do.' Thatcherism saved
the cultural left by giving a focus and a rationale to its activities: having lost the
rigour he once found in his professional work, the museum official could now fall
back on one overriding criterion of judgement, 'does the customer like it?' The
peculiar mixture of economic rightism and cultural leftism explains the odd jargon
of the new official. He speaks with a leftish social conscience (The People, social
inclusion, accessibility, raising self-esteem), but delivers all these as services which can
be measured, audited and justified in hard-nosed market terms (such as 'benchmark-
ing', 'best value' and so on). Just as the New Economy business speaks of meeting
the diverse needs of its customers, so the new museum speaks of meeting the diverse
needs of The People.

This coming together of two seemingly opposed forces reached its triumphant
apogee in the election of the New Labour government in 1997. For the first time,
the state, big business and culture all spoke the same language – empowerment,
inclusiveness, diversity and customer satisfaction. The new orthodoxy was churned
out from the new super-ministry at the Department for Culture, Media and Sport
(DCMS).

Most new museum professionals have grasped this moment with enthusiasm.
No longer simple curators or scholars, now they are social campaigners, out there
on the frontline, fighting for The People, raising health/environmental/gender/
identity awareness. The heady effects of the new orthodoxy can be seen throughout the profession. David Fleming, director of Tyne and Wear museums and
convenor for Group for Large Local Authority Museums (GLLAM), told the 2000
Museums Association conference: 'I came into museums because it was my way of
trying to change the world'. An admirable aim, of course, but maybe Fleming should
have become a politician or a social worker rather than a museum director.

A GLLAM report on museums and social inclusion[4] offers some examples of museums which now function as composite health, education and social service centres. An Asian women's textile project at the Birmingham Museum and Art Gallery is run in collaboration with social services and targets isolated Asian women with mental health problems. Describing the benefits of the project, the report states: 'Not only does this project enable the women to improve their skills and self-confidence, but it also provides a safe space for mental health issues to be confronted and discussed.' Tyne and Wear Museum worked with Michael – 'a real tearaway [who] became involved in the production of a CD-ROM for the museum, and gained enormously in self-esteem'. Once museums are freed from the core obligation to their collections there are almost no limits to their functions.

As their functions become more loose and wide-ranging, so the sense of their own importance becomes more grandiose. The Museums Association draft code of ethics, 'Museums for People',[5] lists in its obligatory mission statement 'key museum values', all of which, we are told, are founded on the 'expectations of the public'. (How the Museums Association worked out the public's expectations is not made clear.) Each section begins with the clause 'Society expects that museums will . . .'. Instead of simply saying, 'Museums will do such and such', the Museums Association constitutes itself as Society, then proceeds to submit to the demands of its alter ego.

Museums, which once concentrated on organising and classifying objects, now, with the active encouragement of government, are much more interested in classifying, segmenting and categorising the public. The visitor is always treated as a group-member, never as an individual. Artefacts are no longer seen to have universal appeal, but are divided up on the basis of the particular social group to which they are deemed to be of interest. Exhibitions on African art or slavery are seen to be of interest to black British communities; the Science Museum constructed an exhibition on sport to appeal to teenage boys.

Museums vie with each other in drawing in the key target groups: the young, ethnic minorities and the economically marginalised. The DCMS suggests that museums identify an excluded group and their 'distribution', then 'engage them and establish their needs'.[6] In keeping with the new market-driven spirit, all museums funded by the DCMS now have to publish access targets and detail measures by which they are 'widening access to a broad cross-section of the public for example by age, social class, and ethnicity'.[7] Museum exhibitions, it suggests, should consciously attempt to appeal to the young as well as the old, Asian as well as white, working class as well as middle class. The diverse needs of all these different groups of people should be at the forefront of curators' minds, and inform every aspect of their work.

Good for the collection?

The collection in decline

Once a museum puts the perceived needs of the people at the heart of its work, the collection will quite naturally lose its importance and value. A collection is no longer seen as valuable in itself – because it is rare or beautiful, or because it represents something important within a particular field. Instead, its value is embodied in something external to itself: the immediate relationship it is able to establish to the public, how it will help the museum and its officials connect with the public, or how it will lead to observable changes in the lives of visitors.

The loss of collections' value can be observed in many aspects of museum practice. Sometimes collections are left to gather dust while museums get on with more exciting and socially responsible activities. In the GLLAM case studies of best practice, museum projects involved awareness-raising about teenage pregnancy, or setting up a football team with young vandals. The report argues that a reorientation towards social ends will show why collections 'are worth having in the first place'. But in practice the desired social ends are more easily achieved without bringing artefacts into it. If they are used, the objects become no more than props for the wider social project to which they have no necessary connection.

Sometimes interactive exhibits replace objects. If the main concern of a museum is to engage the public in particular ways, these aims might be better achieved with animation or interactive technologies than with the raw object. The simple object allows for an open encounter with no predetermined outcome – the visitor can make of it what he likes. Interactive technology only allows for closed outcomes because the encounter is all programmed in advance by the museum. For museums geared towards building relationships with the people, an open-ended encounter between visitor and object leaves far too much to chance. Likewise, animated contraptions, which sometimes replace original specimens, are calculated to elicit a desired effect. The animated tyrannosaurus rex at the Natural History Museum, for example, elicits the 'Wow, scary' effect. In the most extreme cases, collections can be broken up and dispersed. The new Commission for Museums Libraries and Archives put forward the argument that accessibility would be increased by 'deaccessioning' collections, i.e., dispersing parts of them to targeted community centres that a museum may deem to be particularly worthy recipients. Paradoxically, the effect of such measures would be to make collections accessible only to those communities chosen by the museum, while making them increasingly inaccessible to the population as a whole.

Forming links with specific communities is taken to its logical extreme by simply giving objects back. Influenced by similar cases in the USA, Glasgow Museums repatriated the Lakota Ghost Dance Shirt to a tribe of Native Americans. Mark O'Neill, of Glasgow Museums, told a Museums and Galleries Commission conference in 2000 that the loss of the shirt was outweighed by the benefits of 'bringing healing to a sad people'. Unusual as this case is (there has been much talk of restitution, but little action, so far), it nevertheless reveals an important shift. Some museum professionals seem to value the demonstration of empathy and social responsibility more highly than they value the collections they are supposed to protect.

Increasingly, the aim of exhibitions seems aimed more at drawing in a particular audience, by creating a deliberate shock effect. In the summer of 2000, the Victoria and Albert Museum (V&A) staged an exhibition of modern design by Ron Arad next to medieval religious icons. Curator Susan Lambert told me that the exhibition was 'going for a slightly different audience' that was not 'on top of

Christian symbolism'. She 'wanted a visual spectacle', that would get new people looking at old objects.

Curators and scholarship

Advocates of the people-centred museum argue that collections have no intrinsic value anyway. Their value lies instead in their relationship to The People. At best, this is a statement of the obvious. Without society, without thought and knowledge, there would be no museums and objects would have no value in any meaningful sense of the word. It is true also, that society's understanding and appreciation of objects changes through time. Charles Saumarez Smith has traced the V&A's treatment of the Mark Lane doorway, which started out as the carved wooden front for a late seventeenth-century London house. In the late nineteenth century it was acquired by the museum for the quality of its woodwork, and in the late twentieth century was placed in the V&A shop. As time passed, the same object was seen by turns to have a decorative, historical, aesthetic and commercial value.[8]

However, just because different societies might bring to light different or even conflicting aspects of the same object does not mean that the aesthetic or scientific value of those objects is arbitrary. Society might impose its tastes upon museum collections – classifying, organising and interpreting in its own way. But that is only one side of the relationship, because objects also impose themselves upon society. The Parthenon Marbles did not gain their importance from the whim of Lord Elgin or the British Museum. They hold their exalted place today because of their artistic greatness, the perfection of the craftsmanship and their unique historical significance in relation both to the art of Periclean Athens and to the entire Western tradition.

It is the task of scholarship to assess the relative importance of objects, for what they are in themselves and for the broader artistic, scientific or historical context within which they are to be placed. Collections are evidence – of past societies, of different cultures, species of bird, forms of rock, etc. Collections are the raw material of our knowledge on so many subjects. The study of works of art develops our ideas about art as such, just as the study of the products of nature develops our ideas about the natural world, or the study of the artefacts of past societies develops our ideas about history. Knowledge is not some arbitrary ideological construct within our minds. In the specific context of museums, knowledge comes from the critical encounter between the scholar and his raw material.

It is rare for the core activities of curatorship and scholarship to be done away with altogether. Instead, they are swamped by an ever-expanding array of 'audience-related' activities. In the last 30 years there has been a remorseless growth in education, helpdesk and marketing functions. A survey on museum research and scholarship documented the sense among many curators that their research function was under threat.[9] Eighty percent said that they were not as active in research as they would like to be, and most said the time available for research had declined in the past ten years. However, even these figures do not fully convey the depth of the malaise. Much of what now passes for research would have been done in the past by the marketing department (if there even was one). Many curators now spend an increasing amount of their time researching the public and the attitudes of the public towards their work.

Often a museum's small numbers of curators are expected to double up as PR officers and managers. In London's Science Museum scientists are asked to go to the galleries to talk to the public about their work. The aim of these sessions seems less to help the public understand science, than to help curators build relationships with their visitors (or to pretend to include the public in the process of making science). Many museums emphasise the importance of management training – the Cultural Heritage National Training Organisation now produces courses in management for museum professionals.

Fewer people entering the museum profession today have the specialist training necessary to study and care for collections. Many enter the profession, not by gaining a doctorate in art history or palaeontology, for example, but by doing a one-year Museums Studies MA (this is especially the case for those working in local and independent museums). A small proportion of the Museums Studies course is concerned with the conservation and interpretation of artefacts – most is concerned with the study of audiences and cultural theory analyses of power in exhibitions. In response to this training gap, University College London has created a separate Artefact Studies MA. Expertise in objects, it seems, is just one of the many functions of the new curator. Even when curators have studied their collections, they are often asked to defer to non-specialists when organising exhibitions – administrators, PR officers or members of the public themselves. Tyne and Wear museum has encouraged the display of works which 'may not necessarily be famous or highly regarded, but instead have been chosen by members of the public simply because they like them or because they arouse certain emotions or memories'.[10]

Underlying all these changes is the declining authority of scholarship itself. The advance of cultural relativism throughout the Western academic system had already shattered the belief among scholars that there was anything intrinsically valuable held by museums, or that their understanding of objects was any more valuable than anybody else's. Now, the elevation of the emotional well-being of the visitor put scholars further on the defensive, making them feel guilty that they would value dead objects over living people.

For scholarship to flourish, scholars must be allowed some degree of separation from the immediate demands of politicians, bureaucrats and even from the public. They must be allowed to study their subject and to follow the demands of their own discipline without having to wonder all the time whether it is directly relevant to the public. The question of how to communicate the results of their research to the public will come at the stage of creating exhibitions. But in the process of original research, intellectual concentration necessarily means the exclusion of concerns external to the matter in hand. If scholars are forced to listen to the clamour of discordant voices outside their profession, the chances of profound insights are slim indeed.

If scholarship in museums is neglected, our knowledge will suffer. Museums cannot simply rest on the expertise they have built up over the years. There must be a constant replenishment of that knowledge by scholars who keep up with the latest research and who are ready always to reassess the significance and meaning of objects. If this central task falls into neglect, it will be very difficult to repair the damage done. If, for example, the expert in fossil reptiles has been redeployed to study how people react to fossil reptiles, he is less likely to concentrate on new discoveries in the field. At worst, whole branches of knowledge could go into decline through wilful neglect.

The socially responsible museum

While the core function for which museums were created is downgraded to an ancillary activity, a vast range of spurious functions are loaded on to them for which they are entirely unsuited. For the new orthodoxy, museums must reflect the concerns and experiences of our society and of everyday life. They must become relevant, and inclusive, and should talk to 'real people'. Sociology professor Tony Bennett complains that nineteenth-century museums were exclusive, as they showed no interest in the lives and habits of working people.[11] He praises the People's Palace in Glasgow for talking to real living people because it allows them to recognise themselves in public life. Most museums offer something similar to Tyne and Wear's commitment 'to try to reflect and involve the whole community in its exhibitions and activities'.[12]

Museums try to make themselves relevant in two different ways. The first method is to cling to the appeal of mass entertainment. The logic here is crude, but occasionally effective: lots of people watch TV (for example); therefore museums should use TV in their exhibition to pull in the crowds. Exhibitions based around this principle include the museum for popular music in Sheffield, the *Brand.new* exhibition at the V&A and the video games in the Wellcome Wing. The second approach is to target specific groups, such as women, youth or ethnic minorities. This strategy is far less effective because it almost always involves some massive presumption on the part of the museum as to what appeals to these groups.

Social inclusion is another crusade aimed at transforming the function of the museum. In the improbable circumstances of his 1999 budget speech, chancellor Gordon Brown committed museums to the struggle against social exclusion.[13] The DCMS had the vision of museums becoming 'centres for social change', improving people's self-esteem and improving community relations, while the GLLAM social inclusion report defined seven social ends to which museums should gear themselves, such as personal growth and development, community empowerment and tackling unemployment and crime.

More widespread concerns about social cohesion and the decline of the traditional bonds of church, family and political parties have led commentators to search for alternative sources of social bonding. This concern was no doubt heightened by the apathy implied by the historically low turnout in the recent general election. Museums are seen as 'cultural meeting places' that could fill the gaps left by the decline of the old institutions and bring cohesion to a fragmented society. New Labour thinkers Charles Leadbeater and Kate Oakley write that 'art, culture and sport create meeting places for people in an increasingly diversified, fragmented and unequal society', meeting places that were once 'provided by work, religion or trade unions'.[14] This explains the interest with which government watched the crowds bustling at Tate Modern in London.

There is nothing new about using museums and cultural institutions for social purposes. In the early nineteenth century Prime Minister Sir Robert Peel stated that one of the purposes of the new National Gallery would be to 'cement the bonds of union between the richer and poorer orders of the state'.[15] Such a sentiment would chime with those of our present cultural elite. The crucial qualification, however, was that the National Gallery would give access to great works of art. Museums can be used for all sorts of purposes, some good, some bad. Conveying the insights of art and science is a mighty social task. Using art and science to prop up the existing ruling caste is a less glorious cause. But as long as the core functions of the museum – the preservation, study and display of collections – are not interfered with and retain their central role, the added contribution of politicians and bureaucrats can be dispensed with by the visitor.

In the people-centred museum, however, social ends tend to take over. Much of the activity of museum staff is now indistinguishable from that of a host of social, health or educational services. Most of the DCMS or GLLAM case-studies of best social inclusion practice could have been performed by any charity or social service. The collection and the specialist knowledge required to understand it are pushed to the margins. In its efforts to provide every sort of service, from health to social support, the people-centred museum tends to undermine the distinctive character and eventually the very rationale of the museum as such. This is compounded by efforts to dissolve the museum into its community, to break down any barriers with the world around. Outreach programmes, attempts to involve local communities in the museum's activities, and the outright dispersal of the collection into community centres; all these blur the museum out of existence. When the newly appointed head of Resource Matthew Evans suggested in February 2000 that museums get away from the idea that they are constrained by physical walls and that they should get their collections into shops, clubs and pubs, many in the profession reacted at first with surprise. 'We're already there, we're doing it', said Simon Thurley, director of the Museum of London.

A good museum will give the visitor the opportunity to withdraw from the mundane cares and concerns of everyday life and to contemplate instead something which may be remote from his own experience. A good museum will of necessity be different and separate from the world, not because it deliberately and pretentiously sets out to be different, but because its contents (one hopes) will not be everyday things. On the other hand, a museum that tries only to replicate the world around, and dissolve itself into it, has lost both its reason and its will to exist.

Good for the people?

Advocates of the new museum say that because museums are public institutions funded by public money, they must answer to all the people and not just to a cultural elite. This seems a reasonable argument. So let us examine how well the people-centred museum fulfils its obligations. Perhaps a categorical distinction might guide us here. The distinction is between 'The People' as imagined by the museum profession, and the older concept of the public. The public forms itself, independently of any guiding authority from above, such as the state. It is an amorphous and ill-defined entity, typically made up of abstract individuals. The People, on the other hand, is formed by the state or one of its institutions. It is a projection on the part of those in authority on to those over whom it has authority, an attempt to define, classify and categorise according to its own needs. Joe Public does not exist among The People. He is far too vague an individual. The People is made up of many different categories of people, all well defined (by the state). Diversity is the great buzzword among supporters of The People. Because of the talk about diversity and difference, it appears more individualistic. But this individual does not make himself, he is always created from above, by authority.

In the case of the new museum, The People that they are so anxious to follow are a pure projection, a creation by the museums themselves. Nobody outside the cultural elite ever demanded that museums become more accessible, relevant, inclusive, diverse and interactive. All these views were hatched within government and the museums world itself and then projected out on to the public.

The consequences of orienting the museum towards The People are two-fold. As the Millennium Dome in London proved beyond doubt, when the new cultural elite start second-guessing what people want, they invariably underestimate them and try to go for the lowest common denominator. Reaching for the lowest common denominator explains the growing tendency in museums to treat all visitors as children. It is strange how, for all the talk of different needs, the child tends to provide the universal model for the public. Secondly, the people focus also leads museums to build manipulative and invasive relationships with their visitors. When the purpose of an exhibition lies in its relationship to the visitor, the museum will, quite naturally, want to check to see if the relationship is working. People become the objects of study, their interests and responses catalogued and catered to. In the new museum the observation of the masses has replaced the study of things.

Direct address and forced chumminess are favoured to assist the visitor; impersonal and abstract terms are now considered too cold and too user-unfriendly. Both the Science Museum and the Natural History Museum use the second person in their exhibitions on human biology: 'This is your brain', 'Have you ever wondered where your relatives came from?', as if people would not be interested if the model was of the human brain, in the abstract. At a Natural History Museum exhibit on leaf structure and function, a voiceover announces: 'Welcome to the leaf factory. You are an 8,000th of your normal size and are inside the leaf.' An intellectual regression seems to be taking place here. Making the abstraction from the particular 'me' to the general human is not only fundamental to thought itself, but is something that children grasp at school. This shift in style of presentation, trivial as it is, is still very revealing. On a visit to the *High Street Londinium* exhibition in the Museum of London, I overheard the following exchange between a member of staff dressed in a toga and a visitor:

> Actress: 'My husband has gone to the amphitheatre. Come in and help yourself to food. There's some nice cheese over there . . .'
>
> Visitor: 'How do you know they made cheese?'
> Actress: 'What do you mean *they*? This is me you're talking about'.

'Me', 'you', not 'they'. Don't question, don't try to stand back, says the new museum.

The new museum aims to help people understand through fabricated feelings and experience rather than by reason. Full-scale reconstructions such as the Jorvik Viking Centre, York, UK, and *High Street Londinium* at the Museum of London are presented with the claim that visitors gain an authentic experience of the past. 'Visit the Jorvik Viking Centre, step aboard a time car and be whisked back through the centuries to real-life Viking Britain . . . You can experience in sight, sound and smell exactly what it was like to live and work in Viking-age Jorvik.' 'Leave year 2000, and enter *High Street Londinium*, first century AD . . . You enter Londinium early in the morning.' Both of these reconstructions are based on actual archaeological digs; they are representations and interpretations of the evidence uncovered. Why does this evidence need to be presented as a 'real' picture of the past, rather than what it is, archaeological evidence? Any opportunity for the visitor to exercise his imagination is severely curtailed.

At the Museum of Verulamium in St Albans a complete Roman skeleton lies in a battered but elaborate lead coffin. From tooth-wear studies we know that he ate high-quality soft foods, and the style of his coffin suggests a high social class. His face can be reconstructed from skull shape and from the calcification of his skeleton we can guess his age. Twenty years ago, the solution would probably have been to present this information next to the skeleton, leaving visitors to make their own image of the man. So much of the fascination of this exhibit is that we do not know what this man was like. Unfortunately, today's visitors cannot be left alone to make these imaginative leaps. A video next to the skeleton conjures up the man. The dark shadow of the past is transformed into an upper-middle-class man poncing around the streets of St Albans in a toga, narrating the story of his life and death: 'My coffin, as befits my status, had the highest quality detail!'

Many museums seem to think the public has the most limited capacity for concentration and little need for quiet. The proliferation of gadgets and interactive displays, flashing lights, talking exhibits, music and sound effects tells us more about museums' view of the public than it does about the public itself. Children have limited concentration and are still at the stage of 'learning through play'. But adults can read books for hours on end; they can sit and concentrate on ideas without moving their body, without playing or physically engaging in any way. Indeed, concentration in stillness is the only way most adults can think in a sustained manner.

A common refrain from the new museums and their government backers is that many of the visitors they want to attract are from marginalised social groups and are therefore easily intimidated – a patronising and rather strange perception of the public. One of the 'barriers to access' identified by the DCMS is 'attitudinal', that is 'museums not making all of their visitors feel welcomed and valued'.[16] To draw in the shy masses, museums now create spaces for public participation. In order to bolster people's confidence, some museums – such as the Tyne and Wear Museum and the People's Gallery in Birmingham – show community exhibitions chosen and curated by local people. Other museums help their visitors to feel valued by asking their opinion in the exhibition, such as the 'Tell us what you think' exhibits in the Science Museum's Wellcome Wing.

Museums were once places where individuals could go in and be left alone to reflect on something that had nothing to do with their everyday lives. Now, in their every move the public are watched and examined, giving the relationship of museums to their public a predatory aspect – museums feed off the shifting source of public opinion and reaction. Officials debate how architecture affects the way visitors move around buildings. Questionnaires and focus groups analyse visitor response to exhibits, or their understanding of a particular label. Visitor figures are monitored to see what ethnic group, what age or gender group is underrepresented and the missing groups can then be targeted.

While making few intellectual demands, exhibitions set up to engage visitors can be very demanding in other ways. People are not left to wander through the museum with their own thoughts, looking at an object or reading a label as they choose. To obtain information visitors often must press a button. This seems less a means to an end than an end in itself – the temperature and pressure of the planets of the solar system, for example, could be printed on a card, yet the Natural History Museum has interactive exhibits that provide these basic facts. Action is often demanded just to see an object. In the Jersey Maritime Museum some of the text accompanying exhibits is hidden away in models of shells, boats and bottles that the visitor must open up if they wish to see it.

We arrive then at a paradox. The curator who is concerned with The People, who loudly professes his respect for every ethnic, class, age and gender group and who builds his exhibition around what he perceives to be their needs, almost inevitably ends up expressing disdain for the public. On the other hand, the curator who is concerned above all with his collection, is more truly respectful towards the public. In his fidelity to his own work, he assumes that visitors are intelligent enough to understand what he has done and to appreciate the effort he has invested. 'The People's' curator is motivated (or is proclaimed so) by a concern not to look down on people, but ends up doing just that. The objects' curator starts with an unabashed belief in the superiority of expertise, but nevertheless treats all as equals.

In the new museum, the honest scholar, the curator with a genuine love for his subject is pushed to the margins, or might be redesignated as a helpdesk assistant. In his place comes the service delivery manager with his social conscience on permanent display. For this type of person, the visitors are his subjects, in every sense of the word.

Conclusion

Museums should stick to what they do best – to preserve, display, study and where possible collect the treasures of civilisation and of nature. They are not fit to do anything else. It is this single rationale for the museum that makes each one unique, which gives each its own distinctive character. It is the hard work of scholars and curators in their own areas of expertise that attracts visitors. Everybody knows that the harder you try to win friends and ingratiate yourself with people, the more you repel them. It would seem however that those running our new museums need to learn afresh this simple human lesson.

Notes

Josie Appleton writes about politics and culture for *spiked* and a range of publications.

1   Jacoby, Russell, *The End Of Utopia*, Basic Books, 1999.
2   Arnold, Matthew, *Culture and Anarchy*, Yale University Press, 1994.
3   *Museums Journal*, September 2000.
4   GLLAM, October 2000, *Museums and Social Inclusion*.
5   Museums Association, Draft code of Ethics, *Museums for People*, October 2000.
6   DCMS, *Centres for social change: museums, galleries and archives for all*, 2000.
7   DCMS, *Museums for the many*, 1999.
8   Saumarez Smith, Charles, 'Museums, artefacts and meanings', in Peter Vergo, *The New Museology*, Reaktion Books, 1989.
9   Gunn, Ann V. and Prescott, R.G.W., *Lifting the Veil: Research and Scholarship in United Kingdom*, Museums and Galleries, 1999.
10 DCMS, *Museums for the many*, 1999.
11 Lumley, Robert, *The Museum Time Machine: putting cultures on display*, Routledge, 1988.
12 DCMS, *Museums for the many*, 1999.
13 The Social Exclusion Unit defines social exclusion as 'what can happen when people or areas suffer from a combination of linked problems such as unemployment, poor skills, low incomes, poor housing, high crime environments', DCMS, *Centres for social change: museums, galleries and archives for all*, 2000.
14 Leadbeater, Charles and Oakley, Kate, *The Independents*, Demos, 1999.
15 Cited in Richard Sandell, 'Museums as Agents of Inclusion', in *Museum and Management Curatorship* 17 (4), 1998.
16 DCMS, *Museums for the many*, 1999.

Chapter 7

A Quest for Identity

Nelson Graburn

Museums and tourism are among the fastest growing institutions in the modern world. From 1960 to 1995 the number of international tourists grew from 70 million to over 500 million a year. Their expenditures rose from $6,900 million to $334,000 million (in 1992 dollars). The World Tourism Organization expects international travel of 750 million people spending $720,000 million by the year 2000, rising to 1 billion people by 2010.

Twenty years ago the American futurologist Herman Kahn predicted that by the end of this century tourism would be one of the largest industries in the world. When expenditure on world domestic tourism is added to international tourism, we already have an industry with expenditures of over $2,000 billion a year. As cultural and heritage tourism are among the fastest growing segments of tourism,[1] we expect the numbers of museum visitors to increase well into the next century.

Since the 1960s the number of museums in the United States has grown more than fifteenfold, and the same is probably true in Japan and other industrialized countries. More people in the United States now go to museums every week than to sporting events such as football and baseball. There has been a frenzy of museum building as well as a continual upgrading and renewal of museums in Europe too, in cities such as Groningen in the Netherlands, Aachen, Bremen, Dresden and Frankfurt in Germany, and Barcelona and Seville in Spain. Perhaps there have been proportionately fewer entirely new museums opened in France and Italy because these countries are already so richly endowed. The numbers of museums in Third World countries has grown even faster, responding to the needs of tourism and for the expression of local and national identities.[2]

Broadly speaking, both museums and tourism, except for the most hedonistic kinds, appeal to the middle classes all over the world. Although it is difficult to

Source: *Museum International*, vol. 50, no. 3, 1998, pp. 13–18.

define middle class in a way that applies to all countries, the range of values common to tourism and the middle classes is characteristic of modernity itself. They comprise the following:

- Secular education, to promote the understanding of the cultural, ethnic, historical, natural and moral diversities of the world.
- Conservation of the past for its own sake, and for the maintenance of continuities between the past and the present, often allied with nostalgia engendered by feelings of alienation.
- Status enhancement, both for tourists vis-à-vis their home reference group, and for museum personnel, seeing the museum as a marker of place, status, taste and enlightenment locally and in the larger world.
- Aesthetic appreciation of the awe-inspiring, that is, the sense of wonderment and discovery, directed particularly to places of historical and national importance.
- Entertainment and a relaxed social atmosphere, where the museum is a place where tourists can enjoy their time, often in the company of family and friends.

The latter two, and perhaps three, values are not exclusive to our twin modernities of museums and tourism, but could well apply to traditional places of religion and to pilgrimage. The connections between religious institutions, museums and tourist attractions and between the social organization of tourism and of pilgrimage are still very strong, especially in Japan, India, the Middle East and parts of Europe. But the same set of modern problems, overcrowding, physical degradation, the separation of the serious from the superficial are common to both pilgrimage and tourism.

Today's middle-class visitors thrust competing demands upon museum planners and curators. At the most general level a museum must be, in Claude Lévi-Strauss's sense,[3] a work of art: a museum must tread the line between being too strictly 'scientific or paradigmatic' in expressing basic principles and exactitudes which may be cold and boring to visitors, and too contingent in evoking fleeting mental associations which appeal superficially to the visitor's knowledge, but leave nothing of lasting value.

Museums are very important icons and tourist attractions in themselves. They are often among the main reasons to visit a city, such as the Louvre and the Beaubourg (the Pompidou Centre for contemporary art) in Paris, the National Anthropology Museum in Mexico City, or Catherine the Great's Hermitage Museum in St Petersburg: Richards stresses the crucial role of museums as icons and attractions in tourism circuits as a consequence of the meteoric rise of cultural tourism in Europe.[4]

In addition to their function as tourist attractions, museums may also be essential touristic guides to the history and geography of the cities or nations they represent. This is particularly true of the many smaller historical museums found all over the world, which, like guidebooks, serve as representations or condensations of the geography and history of an area or an era, such as the Santa Monica Heritage Museum in Los Angeles, the Unikkaarvik Interpretive Centre at Iqaluit on Baffin Island, or the Castle Museum in Guildford, United Kingdom. Such museums provide a means for the out-of-town tourist to quickly apprehend what the local authorities consider to be of historical value, worth knowing and visiting, as well as an educational introduction for children. A good example of this close relationship between a museum and associated tourist information is the display of pages from the guidebook *Malaysia: Land of Eternal Summer* on the wall beside the central Islamic exhibit in Malaysia's Muzium Negara (National Museum) in Kuala Lumpur.[5]

Museums and heritage: personal, social and global

It has often been said that museums are the great symbols of civilization, the storehouses of humanity's heritage. Great cities measure their 'symbolic capital' by the eminence of their museums and the array of the world's heritage that they have amassed. But between one's personal family heritage and world heritage are a variety of identities and heritages at the level of ethnicity, class and nation, which differ and may conflict with each other, complicating the efforts of museum planners and curators.

In the West, the idea of heritage is derived from the concept of personal inheritance or patrimony, that is, the materials, rights and obligations that we, as members of a family, except to inherit from our forebears. Material property is usually passed down in families at death through wills but, as members of a family, we also receive a constant non-material flow of knowledge, stories, status symbols, as well as names, relatives and acquaintances. We love to pass on those parts of our inheritance that we are proud of and may suppress others.

In addition, we are all members of larger social groups such as ethnic groups or social classes, and cities or nations. Each of these also passes on the symbols, stories, goods and personnel and even dialects, language and customs, to every generation. Thus, to each social group pertains a shared heritage. Though much of the cultural and spiritual heritage is passed on from person to person, by example or word of mouth, material aspects of heritage may be embodied in regalia, treasures, buildings or land.

One of the primary functions of a museum is to preserve and display the heritage of the specific social groups which form its clientèle. I often tell my university classes that the oldest museum in the world is the Shosoin building in Nara, Japan, which contains the paraphernalia and records from the death of the Emperor Shomu in A.D. 746. These are kept for the Japanese royal family, the ancient capital city of Nara and the nation, and are displayed to the general public for a few weeks every year. But by this measure, we should have also to consider every kind of container of a society's heritage as a museum, including the Pyramids in Egypt, the royal tombs in Osaka, Nara and Miyazaki-ken in Japan, and many of the Roman and Greek buildings of classical Mediterranean civilizations.

The concept of heritage is culturally constructed and historically contingent. Nowadays, in addition to our 'own' heritage – local, ethnic, class and national – all of us are aware of the heritage of other peoples and nations of the world, especially the symbolically important heritage of the great historical civilizations of East and West. The fact that many world-class museums contain materials from all the great civilizations of the world derives from the frenzy of collecting by the major

Western powers in the nineteenth century in the wake of their imperial and commercial expansion. Today, our knowledge of these cultural phenomena gives us a 'feeling of ownership' so that all of us, Asian, African and Western alike, might now feel that, for instance, the great monuments of China, Egypt, France or Italy are part of our own heritage.

Since the aftermath of the Second World War, UNESCO has institutionalized this expansive proprietorship by developing a long list of World Heritage sites, which we now regard as belonging to all humanity. Some of these sites are museums, and the contents of many museums would be included as world heritage. In some sense the local owners of these cultural and natural treasures are dispossessed of them, for their fate is monitored by international institutions. In fact Ames warns us how museums are possible sites for hegemonic class-based world views.[6]

Problems and pressures

The growth of tourism and museum visitorship that we expect to continue well into the next century will not be without serious problems. The problem of numbers will be aggravated as more of the world becomes wealthy and transportation relatively cheaper. There will be increased pressure to visit the world-renowned natural and cultural heritage sites, including museums. We can therefore expect rationing of access to famous institutions when their carrying capacities are reached. Two kinds of rationing can occur: rationing imposed on visitors on a first-come, first-served basis, as they arrive or when they try to make reservations, such as for the Gosho in Kyoto, the Imperial Palace that now serves as a museum. In museums, such limitations frequently occur when they house very popular exhibitions, especially travelling 'blockbuster' exhibits. But, if access and expansion are not possible, such limitations may occur more often, as has already happened in many places that preserve humanity's heritage. The other kind of rationing is by price. Again there are parallels between widely popular special exhibits which allow museums to raise their prices, and other desirable targets of tourism, which are now highly priced in order to limit numbers. For instance, in Kyoto, a city that attracts nearly 50 million tourists a year, Saihoji (Kokedera, the famous and fragile Moss Temple) charges a very high entrance fee (or donation) compared with other much cheaper or free temples, shrines and museums.

There is bound to be contention between those who think everything should be regulated by price, and those who think that everyone should have equal rights to visit and see examples of the world's cultural heritage. The world's museums are not only the target of larger numbers of tourists, but they receive more different kinds of people, often from classes, ethnic groups, regions or nations who used not to visit museums. As explained above, a people's heritage is something that they expect to see represented positively not only in dedicated museums such as the Judah L. Magnes Museum of Jewish history and culture, in Berkeley, California, and the La Raza Museum of Hispanic American culture, in San Francisco, but in general and national museums. Thus, museums are increasingly becoming arenas for contesting views of 'truth' about history and heritage, pitting the local against the metropolitan, one class against another, or different ethnic and nationalist views of value and ownership. Recent research in Israel, for instance, shows how different groups (for example, Jewish 'pioneers', urbanites and Palestinians) are included or excluded according to who controls the narrative of the particular museum.

Under the pressure of an ever greater proportion of the growing world population wanting to travel, not only must there arise new regulations on museum visits, but new attractions must constantly be found or constructed. As tourist attractions, museums overlap and compete with natural, cultural and ethnic interpretive centres and ecomuseums, with zoological and horticultural gardens, and with preserved landscapes such as archaeological sites, architectural monuments, and natural parks and reserves, as well as with places of entertainment such as wax museums, Disneyland or Universal Studios. Increasingly it is difficult to tell to which category an institution belongs, for instance the wonderful new Ring of Fire Museum and Aquarium (*kaiyukan*) in the port area of Osaka.

Next to museums and cultural centres, theme parks and other 'artificial' amusements are the most numerous and most profitable of new tourist attractions. Parks such as Disney World contain museum-like representations of exciting and famous places from all over the world. Just as the major international world fairs of the nineteenth century always included both serious exhibitions and amusement parks with rides and freak-shows, so modern museums are studying how to make themselves more fun-like and attractive. Major new museums, such as the National Museum of Civilization in Ottawa, Canada, are less confident of full government subsidy and are therefore consciously having to compete for tourist income to cover their costs.

In competition with the more commercial attractions, museums that are unique may draw visitors, both expanding the number of attractions within major destinations and dispersing tourists by taking them a little off the beaten track. Examples of the former include the Cartoon Art Museum and the Craft and Folk Art Museum, both in San Francisco, and of the latter the Insect Museum at Minoo City near Osaka, the Museum of the History of Japanese Lighting at Omachi near Nagano in Japan, or the French National Automobile Museum in Mulhouse near Strasbourg.

Dean MacCannell claims that modern humanity lives life like a tourist.[7] Increasingly dependent on representations of reality, we are turning to institutions such as museums to find authentic truths not only about the worlds of the past and the other, but to understand our own predicament. Thus even local museum visitors may be considered attractive to tourists bent on understanding life around them.

Notes

Nelson Graburn has been Professor of Anthropology at the University of California, Berkeley, since 1964 and, from 1972, curator of North American Ethnology at the Hearst Museum of Anthropology.

1   Greg Richards (ed.), *Cultural Tourism in Europe*, Wallingford, Oxon, CAB International, 1996.
2   Flora Kaplan (ed.), *Museums and the Making of 'Ourselves': The Role of Objects in National Identity*, London/New York, Leicester University Press, 1994.
3   Claude Lévi-Strauss, *La pensée sauvage*, Paris, Plon, 1962.

4   Richards, op. cit.
5   Laurie B. Kalb, 'Nation Building and Culture Display in Malaysian Museums', *Museum Anthropology*, Vol. 21, No. 1, 1997, pp. 69–81.
6   Michael M. Ames, *Cannibal Tours and Glass Boxes: The Anthropology of Museums*, Vancouver, University of British Columbia Press, 1992.
7   Dean MacCannell, *The Tourist: A New Theory of the Leisure Class*, 2nd ed., New York, Schocken Books, 1989.

Chapter 8

'A Place for All of Us'? Museums and Communities

Andrea Witcomb

'A place for all of us'?

O NE OF THE WAYS in which contemporary museums are attempting to
challenge dominant views of the museum as a site of power relations is
to invoke and encourage new relations between museum and communities. As a
movement, this phenomenon can be broadly defined as the 'New Museology'. It
has adherents across a variety of museums but is especially strong in contemporary
art galleries and in museums based in the disciplines of anthropology and history.
It also has supporters amongst museum critics writing from outside the museum.

New Museologists question a museology that focuses on museum processes and
ask instead for a focus on the political dimensions of museum work (Karp *et al.*
1992; Vergo 1989; Weil 1990). Quite often, this political dimension is encapsu-
lated in a call for a greater focus on the relation between museums and communities. The centrality of 'community' in these accounts of the purpose of museums
tends to associate the concept of community with radical democracy and resistance
to the dominant culture. Communities tend to be understood as existing outside
of government and even in opposition to it. By placing 'community' at the heart
of the museum enterprise, the argument runs, it will be possible to overcome the
role of museums as hegemonic institutions. In giving voice, to the powerless, a process of self-discovery and empowerment will take place in which the curator becomes
a facilitator rather than a figure of authority. It is a position which is succinctly summarized by Viv Szekeres (1995), Director of the Migration Museum in Adelaide,
who claims that her museum strives to make 'A place for all of us'.

This call to bring communities into the space of the museum is criticized by
Tony Bennett (1998) in his book, *Culture: A Reformer's Science*. Bennett's criticisms

Source: *Re-imagining the Museum: Beyond the Mausoleum*, London: Routledge, 2003, pp. 79–101,
172–3, 175–85.

are based on a questioning of the way in which this call relies on an opposition between the community and the museum. In querying whether 'museums should be transformed into instruments of community empowerment and dialogue', he is intent on suggesting that we recognize instead that museums shape and regulate the population in 'ways that reflect the genesis of cultural politics from within the processes of government' (Bennett 1998: 195).

In wanting to dislodge any hint of an opposition between the interests of the community and those of government, Bennett is aiming to remove the connotations of resistance which attach themselves to the notion of community. The intent is to offer a more positive reading of the cultural work of governmental institutions such as museums. For Bennett, the history of museums is one of civic reform. Museums are pedagogical institutions that play a role alongside the penitentiary, the police force and slum clearance in reforming newly formed populations into a modern citizenry. Whilst this role was developed in the nineteenth century, in the context of a rapid growth of industrial cities, it remains relevant today even if the specific aims of reform have changed. If, in the nineteenth century, the aim was to instil a sense of morality and good behaviour in the hearts and minds of citizens, the aim today is to foster an acceptance of cultural diversity.

There are two implications of Bennett's argument which need to be drawn out in the context of a discussion of the relations between museums and communities. The first is that it becomes impossible to maintain an opposition between cultural and governmental practices. Cultural workers, such as intellectuals and museum curators, can be seen, according to Bennett, as 'cultural technicians', as people who work within government rather than in opposition to it. Rather than 'seeing government and cultural politics as the *vis-à-vis* of one another', Bennett argues, we should 'locate the work of intellectuals within the field of government' seeing their political role as 'being committed to "modifying the functioning of culture by means of technical adjustments to its governmental deployment"' (1998: 195). The work of museums is to tinker with 'practical arrangements within the sphere of government – that is, the vast array of cultural institutions, public and private, that are involved in the cultural shaping and regulation of the population' (1998: 195).

The second implication is that museums need to be understood not as institutions which represent communities and cultures – which create a 'place for all of us' – but as institutions which actually *produce* the very notion of community and culture. This argument goes back to an earlier article 'The political rationality of the museum' (1990). Bennett argued in that article that the very aim of achieving equal representation is based on a faulty logic (Bennett 1990, 1995). The desire to achieve equal representation can only *remain* a desire, he argues, for there will always be some group who will find itself unrepresented. As a consequence, museums will always be open to the charge of being unrepresentative and therefore undemocratic. It would be better, he suggests, to understand their role as producing a culture that supports the political principles underpinning the very notion of representation.

Bennett's recent work on museums (1995, 1998) is part of a larger intellectual project within Australian cultural studies which, during the late 1980s and early 1990s, sought to transform cultural studies into *cultural policy* studies. Developed mainly out of the Key Centre for Cultural and Media Policy Studies at Griffith University in Queensland,[1] advocates of the cultural policy position sought to move the discipline of cultural studies away from what they considered to be a romantic legacy which emphasized a revolutionary rhetoric of opposition. Like others in this school (for example, Hunter 1988, 1994 and Cunningham 1992) Bennett opposes this legacy as reducing government to 'the interests of a ruling class or of patriarchy' (1998: 194). He proposes that it is possible to develop a critical perspective *within* institutions that are habitually perceived as representing power or cultural authority.

Bennett's refusal to demonize the museum is a breath of fresh air in a field in which many museum practitioners find themselves besieged by critics even when trying to change museum practices. His arguments are also valuable in recognizing that museum practices involve processes of cultural *production* as well as representation. They offer a more appropriate explanation of the context of relations between museums and communities (as well as a more accurate description of curatorial work), than that offered by the model of curator as facilitator. I will demonstrate this by applying Bennett's arguments to an exhibition I curated on the Portuguese community in Perth called *Travellers and Immigrants: Portuguêses em Perth* held in the Community Access Gallery of the Fremantle History Museum and to my work as a museum consultant with local museums in Queensland.

However, I will also point towards some serious limitations in Bennett's position. Bennett's determination to do away with romantic notions of community led him to ignore dialogue between actual communities and museum policy makers and curators. There is an increasing body of work that points to the need for museums to recognize their own cultural frameworks as well as those of their audiences. There have also been numerous attempts to address this need (Burton 1999; Hooper-Greenhill 1997, 2000; Karp and Lavine 1991; Karp *et al.* 1992). One notable example has been James Clifford's work on museums, particularly the latter's essay 'Museums as contact zones' (Clifford 1997: 188–219). It is a useful example as it is one with which Bennett has openly engaged. In the course of this engagement the limitations of Bennett's arguments become clear.

This section considers the issues raised by the Bennett–Clifford debate. I begin in sympathy with Bennett, using his arguments to explore how the community access gallery reflects a governmental desire to *construct*, rather than simply *represent*, a culturally diverse society. Then, I explore the limits of Bennett's arguments by discussing the actual process of developing the exhibition. Here I contrast his approach with Clifford's, utilizing their points of difference to explore some of the practical issues I have encountered in my own museological experiences. I suggest that one way of avoiding romantic notions of community, whilst also recognizing that museums are engaged in dialogue, would be to think of museums *themselves* as communities. Finally, I demonstrate how this perspective is useful in developing policy frameworks for museums as well as in curatorial work itself.

Teaching 'civic reform': the uses of community galleries

As the most explicit manifestation of the attempt by museums to allow communities to represent themselves, community access galleries are an excellent example for testing Bennett's general arguments. Within museological circles, the established understanding is that they offer a place within the museum building in which community groups can mount their own exhibitions rather than the usual practice of allowing the museum to represent them. In some cases, community groups use the museum collection, but they more often locate their own materials, particularly in history museums. The idea is to displace the authority of the museum and to foreground *people* rather than objects. In a roundtable discussion chaired by Margaret Anderson, a number of prominent Australian curators with responsibility for community access galleries defined such spaces as giving specific communities 'an opportunity to promote themselves' (Jane Scott in Anderson 1993: 4), and to 'run things themselves' (Kevin Wilson in Anderson 1993: 5). Community galleries, like the museums they are part of, are firmly understood within a framework of access to representation (see also GLLAM 2000; Hooper-Greenhill 1997).

As Bennett might argue, however, community galleries are as much about *producing* the notion of a culturally diverse community as they are about representing it. They have almost always been initiated by museums themselves, and can easily be used to illustrate that the notion of community is produced from within government rather than being something outside of, and in opposition to, it. This is sometimes quite explicit. The Western Australian Museum (1995) outlines the aim of their community gallery at the Fremantle History Museum as demonstrating a commitment 'to providing space and facilities . . . for community groups to mount their own exhibitions reflecting the social and cultural heritage of Western Australia' (Western Australian Museum 1995). In this way the Museum hopes to 'encourage a sense of community ownership of the Museum and to foster acceptance and understanding in Western Australia's culturally diverse society' (Western Australian Museum 1995).

Policy statements such as these are not purely a response to community pressure but spring from governmental discourses of access and equity. They reflect, in Bennett's terms, an agenda of civic reform. The call to 'foster acceptance and understanding in Western Australia's culturally diverse society' is both descriptive and proscriptive. The aim is not just to achieve equal representation in museums. It is also to instruct the community on the value of cultural diversity.

Access galleries also aim to teach the communities who use them. The Western Australian Museum attempts to facilitate equal access to representation by transferring professional skills to the communities concerned. The information sheets on the use of the gallery stress that 'Museum staff work co-operatively with community groups which have booked the Community Access Gallery to ensure that exhibitions are well planned and researched, that they focus on Western Australia's social cultural heritage, and that they are well presented' (Western Australian Museum 1995). It is not only the themes of the exhibitions with which the museum is concerned. The groups which have so far used the space also reflect the same interest in the project of civic reform, representing as they do various ethnic communities, women, the disabled and so on. As well as exhibitions which have focused on the Italian, Muslim, Irish and Portuguese communities, there have also been exhibitions on coping with breast cancer, on people with Down's Syndrome and on the Country Women's Association. Despite the rhetorical separation of the act of representation from the activity of producing that representation, the Museum and its client groups are co-producers in the imagining of community. The development of *Travellers and Immigrants* at the Fremantle History Museum's community access gallery provides an example of this process.

Representation versus production

The variety of audiences for *Travellers and Immigrants*, alone, makes it difficult to see the exhibition as simply about facilitating access to representation. It was required, from its conception, to serve a *number* of communities. There was the Portuguese community as a whole, the museum community, the university for which I worked at the time and of course the visitors to the museum including tourists, local residents and members of the Portuguese community. The exhibition had to serve the interests of all these groups, and also those of the sponsors – the Australia Foundation for Culture and the Humanities and the Western Australian Lotteries Commission.

For the Museum, as its explanatory notes on the access gallery make clear, the principal interest was to be seen to be relevant and accessible to diverse cultural communities as well as to educate the general public in the principles of cultural diversity. For the Portuguese Community Council, the exhibition was an opportunity to utilize the skills of a curator. Whilst not ethnically Portuguese, I was born in Portugal, speak the language, have contacts within the museum community and the ability to attract financial resources not available to them on their own. For the university, the exhibition was an opportunity to demonstrate the curatorial and research skills of its staff, to attract grants, provide training possibilities for students, and gain a higher public profile. For the visitors, the exhibition was an opportunity to learn something about the Portuguese in Western Australia and thereby undertake an act of ethical self-improvement called for by the project of civic reform.

All of these interests affected the way in which the exhibition was developed. Begun as a project that had, as its main aim, the representation of an ethnic minority in a public space, the exhibition became an exercise in producing a notion of community with which everyone could be satisfied. How and why did this change in orientation occur? The answer to this question lies both in the history of the Portuguese community and in the nature of the curatorial process itself – a process that challenged the idea that representation was a natural rather than a constructed process.

The role of history and its impact on the curatorial process

In starting with a group of people rather than a pre-existing museum collection, my first step was to get to know the community I was dealing with and to gain their confidence and interest in the project. This I did with the aid of the Portuguese Community Council who introduced me to the Portuguese Club, arranged interviews on Portuguese community radio, gave me lists of contacts and invited me to official community occasions. My ambiguous status as an insider/outsider – born in Portugal but of English-speaking parents – generated some interesting results. As I got to know various people and groups I began to notice a number of important characteristics in the Portuguese community. To begin with, there was little sense of a unified ethnic community. Rather, there were different interest groups, sometimes distrustful of each other but all with some claim to being Portuguese. Some of these distinctions would also be common to other migrant groups – distinctions of class, educational background and time of arrival. But there were also geographical distinctions which pointed to a larger history than simply that of nationality. For the patterns of immigration to Western Australia closely followed political and economic situations in Portugal and its overseas provinces. I was dealing with the history of an empire as well as with Portugal itself.

The first wave of Portuguese migrants to Western Australia began arriving in 1952. They were from the island of Madeira and almost exclusively involved in the fishing industry. The population of Madeira at the time was more than the island was able to support. With little in the way of industry, those who could not get jobs as fishermen or as farmers had to look for work elsewhere. In the 1960s, people began to arrive from Portugal itself, driven mainly by the desire for greater economic security. In April 1974 a revolution overthrew the right-wing dictatorship which had ruled Portugal since 1932. The aftermath was political upheaval, economic insecurity and general instability alongside a process of democratic reform. In the colonies, the 'Revolution of flowers' meant independence, followed shortly after by civil war. In Angola, Mozambique, Guinea Bissau, Cabo Verde and East Timor, thousands became homeless, lost their properties and savings and were politically persecuted. Many of them sought refuge in Portugal, or migrated elsewhere. The late 1970s and early 1980s, then, saw another wave of migration to Western Australia, of people who had very different experiences from those who had migrated earlier. Many of them were highly educated, having been involved in colonial administration.

It also emerged that all of these waves of migrants were people who had a long family history of migration – both internal to Portugal and its empire and to other countries. Portuguese people, as the title of the exhibition indicates, have a long history of travelling, of dwelling in places that they do not call home.

This history makes it very difficult to understand the Western Australian Portuguese community as a single ethnicity or unified cultural group – a difficulty that affected the nature of my curatorial task. Rather than providing a medium between the museum and the 'community', simply facilitating representation in a public space, my task became one of producing a notion of community. One which most people of Portuguese background could accept but which, at the same time, explained something of the historical context in which such a disparate group of people had come to Perth. I had to produce a notion of community for both the Portuguese and the Australian audiences while securing the confidence of all groups, assuring them that no one group was in control – a task that was only made possible by the fact that I was an outsider. The problem I faced was more than just recognizing that any given individual can belong to multiple communities at the same time, or that any community has differences of opinion within it. The problem was that I had to work within a notion of community that could be recognized by all but which was also attentive to the cultural work which it would do – to explain a group of people to outsiders as well as to themselves.

So far, then, my experiences support Bennett's arguments that the role of the museum is to provide a pedagogical space that supports the governmental aim of civic reform, in this case the recognition of cultural diversity. As Bennett suggests, part of this role is to produce the notion of community within a discursive space based on the principle of equal access to representation. If looked at in this way, this understanding of the role of 'community' in exhibitions also highlights the more general argument made by advocates of the cultural policy position that the role of public institutions is, in great part, about fashioning a framework in which different groups can get on with one another.

However, the steps I had to take to negotiate between the community and the wider public began to show the limits of Bennett's arguments. In wanting to reject oppositions between culture and policy, Bennett reduces culture to government. He then extends this argument to make the claim that communities and their sense of self are also an effect of government. For him, this means that the manner in which

> cultural forms and activities are politicised and the manner in which their politicisation is expressed and pursued – are matters which emerge from, and have their conditions of existence within, the ways in which those forms and activities have been instrumentally fashioned as a consequence of their governmental deployment for specific social, cultural or political ends. (Bennett 1998: 195)

The logical extension of this argument is that the interests of the community should coincide with those of government. Any resistance is in fact a playing out of a governmental rationality inscribed within the project of civic reform.

If this argument held, I would not have had a problem in producing a representation of the Portuguese community which served both the interests of the community and those of government. Those interests should have been the same. Both should have had a reformist or pedagogical agenda. That, however, was not the case. As I quickly learnt, there was a very different understanding about the purpose of the exhibition between myself as a representative of the museological/ governmental perspective and some members of the Portuguese community. These differences emerged over the way in which objects were understood. As I talked to various people in the community I became aware that some people could not understand the need for a contextual narrative which would interpret their experiences through the display of particular objects and images. As far as they were concerned there was no need to interpret the objects. They were not interested in coming to know themselves in order to demonstrate their difference from other ethnic groups or the dominant Anglo-Saxon majority. From my perspective, however, the narrative produced by such an interpretation was the means not only to give 'voice' to the community but also to offer an explanation of one community's experience to another. In other words, interpretation was the means to achieve the pedagogical aims of the museum as an institution for civic reform – an achievement which relied on an explicit articulation of the notion of community.

Community versus museum: empiricism versus abstraction

At the heart of my problem, I began to realize, was an assumption common to New Museologists that in order to develop a more democratic curatorial practice it is necessary to think of museums as 'ideas based' rather than as focused on objects (see, for example, Weil 1990). The basis of this claim is an argument that museums need to overcome the belief that because they work with *objects*, their knowledge claims are necessarily *objective*. The aim is to recognize the ideological basis of all museum work. The result has been a prioritizing of narrative. Objects are understood to be mute unless they are interpreted. Not to interpret has come to be seen as elitist and anti-democratic (Witcomb 1997).

As a curator who identifies with the New Museology, I wanted *Travellers and Immigrants* to be attentive to the problem of 'voice'. I wanted it to reflect the meanings Portuguese–Australian people themselves gave to the objects as symbols of their own migrant experience. My initial intention, therefore, had been to conduct oral history interviews with each person who offered to lend an object or a photograph for the exhibition. I felt that in this way, the exhibition would reflect a personal rather than an institutional viewpoint, the oral histories providing the narrative themes of the exhibition. The interviews would also provide an aural element in Portuguese for those who could not read the English labels based on the interviews.

Despite these intentions to be more democratic, to include the voice of different interests within the community, and to use oral history as the source of the exhibition's narratives and main ideas, I found that not everyone was comfortable with oral histories or even with having their experiences interpreted in a museum. This was not a question of language – most interviews were conducted in Portuguese. Nor was it a problem of reluctance to participate in the exhibition. I only spoke to those who either called me or whose names were given to me by their friends as people I should talk to. The problem appeared more to be one of trying to explain the purpose of story-telling in an exhibition. There was resistance, on the part of some, towards abstraction. In fact, some even said it was enough to have just the objects. What did I want stories for?

On a number of occasions I arrived in a home to do an oral history interview and discuss the possibility of lending objects, after making an appointment by phone and explaining the purpose of the exhibition, to find the entire family assembled to greet me, the television on, and a wish to talk to me within the family group. In these situations I never even got the tape recorder out. The expectations of the situation were just too different. I chose instead to be guided by them, allowing them to show me books, photographs and ornaments whilst sharing a coffee and cake. This provided them with an opportunity to reminisce, to remember their home, their village, family associations or even return trips. All the references were very specific to their immediate family or original neighbourhood. The strong preference was for concreteness – a preference that was reflected in the material culture of their homes, which were filled with memorabilia displayed on shelves and cabinets.

Any attempt to investigate further and get them to answer questions as to why they came, what the situation was in their home country, how they found Australia on arrival, what structures of support they had and so on were met with short, noncommittal answers. They were far more interested in reminiscing about their *terra* (birthplace), or in telling me about particular folkloric customs or ways of cooking food. Discussion of social conditions, politics or economics was resisted. In many ways their approach to the objects was an empirical one – the objects just *were*. They did not necessarily represent anything other than a sense of belonging.

Their response to my attempt to interpret their objects points towards the importance of recognizing what Eilean Hooper-Greenhill has called 'tacit' responses. As she defines it, 'tacit knowledge can be understood as all that is known by individuals, minus all that can be said' (Hooper-Greenhill 2000: 116). While tacit responses can be extremely influential in terms of people's behaviours, attitudes and values, Hooper-Greenhill suggests that their power is to some extent reliant on them remaining unexamined. To attempt to interpret the objects I was offered in terms of a more abstract narrative, then, would have been insensitive to the feelings of those who were lending them. It would have rendered those objects mundane and even, perhaps, profane.

Not to abstract, not to provide an explanatory framework would be, however, to turn my back on the culture of the museum. I had, therefore, to find a way to mediate not only between the museum and the community, but also between the needs of different sections of the community. I needed to provide a space in which this personal, concrete and familial approach to objects could be represented and at the same time explain, both to the community itself as well as a non-Portuguese audience, the different experiences of groups within the community and provide some sort of historical context. I needed to find a way in which the private nature of people's experiences and memories could be told and respected in a public space with a mission to educate – a mission which necessitated some level of abstraction and explanation.

The solution I developed was to provide an interpretative framework around the walls through the use of images, media and interpretative text. The objects were placed in the centre of the exhibition. For the most part, the only interpretation provided here was a short biography of the lenders rather than a formal interpretation of the objects themselves. This hopefully allowed the visitors to respond to the objects on display at the level of their tacit meanings rather than through a more abstract interpretative framework which situated those objects within public political, economic and social histories or within a more traditional stylistic interpretation.

Bennett's description of the relation between museums and communities did not offer an answer to my problem because his approach does not recognize that there can be a number of different interests. Bennett is so intent on erasing an oppositional politics in cultural analysis that he is unable to recognize a use of the notion of community which does not invoke a politics of resistance and opposition but which simply recognizes different interests and histories. The problem is that in throwing out the notion of community, Bennett loses the ability to recognize the co-existence of different cultures. This means that he is inattentive to the way in which museums are also sites for cross-cultural dialogues, for this requires the ability to recognize government as a community in its own right, with its own interests and cultural traditions.

It is the ability to relativize the museum (or in Bennett's terminology government) which, I shall argue, distinguishes James Clifford's (1997) essay 'Museums as contact zones' from the governmentalist position, offering an alternative understanding of the relations between museums and communities. Further, I shall argue that Clifford's approach does not involve a romantic notion of community, despite

Bennett's arguments to the contrary. Indeed, it is the ability to relativize the museum which allows Clifford to account for relations between communities and museums without invoking a revolutionary politics. There are ways in which Bennett and Clifford share a common dislike for binary oppositions and are working towards similar aims. Their difference is over their conclusion, not, as Bennett claims, over the identification of the problem.

Like Bennett, Clifford wishes to read museological practices sympathetically. Whilst his work engages with the difficult history of relations between museums and colonized peoples, he looks for moments within this history when the outcomes included positive experiences or the potential to change relations for those who came into contact with the museum. Clifford is careful to recognize the unequal power relations of such encounters, but he does not read the encounter within a simple binary system in which the imperial centre is always in a position of dominating power vis-à-vis the colonial periphery.

Clifford's arguments are also unusual within discussions about the relations between museums and communities because he attempts to describe those relations in ways which take the discussion beyond the question of parity in representation. His key concept here is that of a 'contact zone' which he borrows from Mary Louise Pratt (in Clifford 1997: 192). The term is developed by Pratt in the context of colonial history where she uses it to get away from understanding colonial encounters within a centre/periphery model. For Clifford, the term becomes a means of opening up the meanings of both colonial and post-colonial museological encounters from both sides so that both positive and negative implications can be explored. The focus is on cross-cultural experiences. Clifford also focuses on the temporal meaning of 'contact', pointing out how colonial experiences are ongoing ones with repercussions in the present.

In taking the term to the museum context, Clifford is interested in showing how it helps to shift analysis of the relations between museums and colonial peoples away from a binary system of meaning towards one which sees meaning as being shaped along a continuum of unequal power relations. The model of a contact zone is set in opposition to the model of the frontier. In the latter, the museum is a centre of accumulation, collecting from the frontiers of empire and controlling the process of making meaning. When seen from the perspective of 'contact zones', however, museums become 'an ongoing historical, political, moral *relationship* – a power-charged set of exchanges, of push and pull' (Clifford 1997: 192). The relationship is two way, involving two different cultures, two different communities. While the majority of Clifford's examples are from the present, he is careful to point out that even the nineteenth-century museum, while operating most of the time on a 'frontier' model, could and did at times become a contact zone.

The consequence of this approach is that Clifford is able to analyse specific instances of relations between museums and communities as cross-cultural encounters in which the museum, as much as the community, needs to make adjustments. Rather than understanding the museum as a static, monolithic institution at the centre of power, it is read as an unstable institution attempting to come to grips with the effects of the colonial encounter, an attempt which has both positive and negative affects on those involved. Whilst Bennett would also view museums as unstable institutions – any movement on the part of museums is seen as a reflection of small tinkering manoeuvres to enable the reform of the citizenry according to the requirements of government – Clifford's arguments interpret this instability, by contrast, as a result of an engagement between two different communities, two different cultures.

One of Clifford's strategies for exemplifying the shift from a centre/periphery or frontier model to a contact zone perspective is to point out the limits of 'consultation' as a concept to adequately describe the range of encounters between museums and communities in contemporary museum practices. Whilst consultation is the adjective currently used in describing attempts by museums to democratize, Clifford suggests that it belongs to the centre/periphery model in which museums collect information or advice from communities but are nevertheless relatively free to do as they wish with it. Actual experiences, however, indicate to Clifford that, quite often, something more is going on, that museums are being required to take into account community perspectives and radically alter their way of operating. Such a requirement is not, I would argue, simply a result of opposing interests, but is, if the notion of a contact zone is to be taken seriously, a result of contact history.

An example here is a process of 'consultation' undertaken by the Portland Museum of Art with Tlingit elders in reinterpreting its Rasmussen Collection of Northwest Coast Indian artefacts. When the Tlingit elders told their stories using the Rasmussen Collection of the Portland Museum, the museum became entangled not only in the past history of the colonial relationship but also in present relations:

> What transpired in the Portland Museum's basement was not reducible to a process of *collecting* advice or information. And something in excess of consultation was going on. A message was delivered, performed, within an ongoing contact history. As evoked in the museum's basement, Tlingit history did not primarily illuminate or contextualize the objects of the Rasmussen Collection. Rather, the objects provoked (called forth, brought to voice) ongoing voices of struggle. From the position of the collecting museum and the consulting curator, this was a disruptive history which could not be confined to providing past tribal *context* for the objects. The museum was called to a sense of its responsibility, its stewardship of the clan object. (Clifford 1997: 193)

What is remarkable about this passage and the discussion that accompanies it, is that both the museum and the Tlingit elders are treated as 'communities'.[2] The museum is also understood as having a tradition, a way of doing things, a culture, which came into contact with Tlingit culture and which has not recovered its former hegemonic status in that process. This is clear in Clifford's description of the encounter from the perspective of the curators (Clifford 1997: 188–92). The expectations of museum staff – namely that the objects in their collection of Northwest Coast Indian artefacts should be given their meanings by the elders of the tribe – is not fulfilled. In using the objects as their starting point and telling 'contact' stories in the presence of museum staff, the tribal elders challenged curatorial approaches to the collection and made it impossible for museum staff to ignore contemporary political struggles over land use. The result was a cross-cultural dilemma for the museum itself:

> Staff at the Portland Museum were genuinely concerned that their
> stewardship of the Rasmussen Collection include reciprocal commun-
> ication with the communities whose art, culture, and history were at
> stake. But could they reconcile the kinds of meanings evoked by the
> Tlingit elders with those imposed in the context of a museum of 'art'?
> How much could they decenter the physical objects in favor of narra-
> tive, history, and politics? Are there strategies that can display a mask
> as simultaneously a formal composition, an object with specific tradi-
> tional functions in clan/tribal life, and as something that evokes an ongo-
> ing history of struggle? Which meanings should be highlighted? And which
> community has the power to determine what emphasis the museum
> will choose? (Clifford 1997: 191–2)

For Clifford, then, the questioning the museum faced from the Tlingit community
was a product of a long history of contact between them. It was not simply that
the community came knocking on the museum's doors demanding change.

For Bennett, however, Clifford's account of the relation between museums
and communities suffers from a romantic understanding of community, seeing it
as outside of, and in opposition to, government. Bennett develops his criticisms by
making two moves. The first is to indicate that there were two frontiers in the
nineteenth century. The first one, as Clifford identifies, is that of the colony. The
second one, however, is internal to the nation and it involved both regional centres
and the working class. For Bennett, this second frontier means that museums were
centres of 'dispatch' as well as of accumulation and that they have a long history
of involvement with communities.

While he thus raises a question mark over Clifford's historical account which
only mentions relations between museums and national communities as a twentieth-
century phenomenon, the main point of his argument is that these relations were
and continue to be relations of government rather than of exchange. Bennett argues
his point by describing how, in the nineteenth century, museums used objects in
a governmental programme for the reform of populations. Such a programme, he
suggests, still continues today, although of course the actual reform agenda has changed
to encompass the principles of cultural diversity. The notion of a contact zone, he
argues, is only an effect of such a governmental programme. It is nothing more
than an expression of the governmental values of cultural diversity.

The effect of Bennett's criticisms is to negate the possibility of an open dialogue between two distinct communities. Any suggestion of different interests is
immediately suspected as invoking a binary system of meaning and an oppositional
politics. That differences do not have to be read in terms of oppositions, however,
can be demonstrated by using the very same set of historical facts that Bennett uses
against Clifford. It is possible to understand Bennett's account of nineteenth-
century relations between museums and communities as also a product of contact
history – only this time the contact was not between colonizers and colonized at
the fringes of empire but between agents and objects of domestic governmental
reforms. The effect of this reinterpretation would be to reverse Bennett's argument. Rather than his suggestion that the notion of a contact zone is an effect
of government, it might be possible to suggest that governmental relations with

communities are only one instance of a complex contact history between different communities.

Clifford's application of the notion of contact zones to museums provides an illuminating set of coordinates for the situation I faced in curating *Travellers and Immigrants*. The mutual incomprehension I observed over the communicative role of objects in exhibitions is similar to the problem faced by the curators at the Portland Museum discussed by Clifford. How could I reconcile the community's approach to the objects with a museological approach that prioritized ideas over objects? How could the culture of the community be reconciled with a curatorial culture?

The problem is also discussed by Hooper-Greenhill in her book *Museums and the Interpretation of Visual Culture* (2000). Hooper-Greenhill argues that in order to produce polysemic exhibitions curators need to recognize the existence of multiple 'interpretive communities'. The term is borrowed from work in Media Studies over the last twenty years. In borrowing it, Hooper-Greenhill wants to highlight that interpretation is socially based and the result of a two-way process – one that both produces and represents that which is being interpreted. The sociality of the process means that interpretation always takes place within a community: 'Individuals share interpretative strategies with others who share the same frame of reference, the same cultural references and the same positions within history' (Hooper-Greenhill 2000: 120). Such communities, Hooper-Greenhill argues, are recognizable through

> their common frameworks of intelligibility, interpretative repertoires, knowledge and intellectual skills. These will include specific uses of words and things, and particular textual and artefactual strategies. Attitudes, values and beliefs will become evident in those recurrently used systems of terms deployed to characterise and evaluate actions and events.
> (2000: 122)

In taking this idea to the museum, Hooper-Greenhill is arguing for the need to contextualize and relativize both the interpretative community of the museum itself and those of the audiences it hopes to attract. Only then, she argues, can exhibitions become sufficiently polysemic to attract the respect of multiple communities.

In the case of *Travellers and Immigrants* the solution was to develop a structure that catered for the various 'interpretive communities' that made up its audience. The role of explanation, which defines the community of the museum, was based not on objects but on oral histories and archival research. This was in line with the more abstract historical nature of themes such as reasons for migration, religious practices, working life and the history of Portugal and its empire. This explanatory role of the exhibition had to be portrayed mostly by photographs, use of media articles, interpretative labels and oral history recordings. The theme of continuity and cultural tradition, however, was based on objects and a personal perspective. As already argued, this enabled more tacit forms of interpretation to occur. The mix of the two modes helped to establish a bridge for those who did not belong either to the museum or to the Portuguese community.

That the exhibition worked on these different levels can be seen through some of the comments in the visitors' book:

We learnt a lot about ourselves.

It was nice to see so many objects from Madeira.

Fantastic!! We arrived in 1972 from Madera [sic] and we love Perth Western Australia. But we are proud of where we are from.

Being a child from a whole Portuguese family who has lost touch with their heritage, I have found this exhibition very informative as I have never been to Portugal but my mother and father are from Madeira. I also understand why for a Portuguese person living in Perth/Fremantle would not feel that this exhibition does their culture justice because a lot of history is lost and they are probably coming to this exhibition to be taken 'home' once again – perhaps some more photos and talk of other places in Madeira such as Paul de Mar. But congrats on the good effort, please do more like this in the future.

The entire time whilst perusing this exhibition, I had tears of joy and sadness in my eyes. Joy – being proud of my heritage. Sadness – knowing that my father Manuel B. Andrade, had passed away so tragically from this earth, but also knowing that he chose Perth as his home. To my dad (Para of meu Pai 1921–97, Fremantle 1957–97).

Such comments are an indication that such exhibitions are important for this group of people both because they can recognize themselves through the display of objects and photographs but also because they see themselves in a new light, as if from the outside. For quite a few, the exhibition also served as a memorial and a thank you to those who made the decision to come to Australia.

For those who did not belong to the Portuguese community, the exhibition provided a form of self-recognition in so far as it touched on experiences which all migrants have in coming to another country. But their comments also reveal the importance that such exhibitions have in providing some context within which to understand other cultural groups. This importance can be understood in terms of Bennett's role for museums as institutions which promote 'civic reform' as well as Clifford's notion that museums offer a space for cross-cultural dialogue:

A Western Australian: It's nice to learn about the background of all the Madeira women I worked with in the Sea Food Factories in Carnarvon in 1992. I always wondered how they ended up there.

An English tourist:

It's a fascinating display, very well laid out, clearly explained and interesting. I loved the old photographs.

A tourist from the eastern states of Australia:

As a migrant myself to Australia I appreciated your exhibition in order to gain knowledge and insight into your past as I too remember my own. It enables us all including our original settlers the Kooris to go on together to form a true Australia.

Dialogue, of course, cannot occur without some strategies for translation. Curatorial work is in many ways trying to develop appropriate strategies for the medium of exhibitions. In the example of *Travellers and Immigrants*, this translation work was achieved by allowing some objects to stand without an abstract interpretation but at the same time finding other media with which to provide the historical context and explanatory frameworks. Other strategies included the use of Portuguese in the titles for many of the labels, a catalogue which, whilst mainly in English, also included extracts from the oral histories in Portuguese, and a compact disc, with edited extracts from the oral histories which was played in the background on a continuous loop for those visitors who could not read English. The latter also had the effect of marking the space as 'foreign' to English speakers and putting them, even if only slightly, in the position of the stranger.

Dialogue and cultural policy

It is not only in the context of exhibition development that Bennett's arguments need to be tempered with a closer attention to the process of dialogue. The need is also there in the field of cultural policy. In some ways cultural policy is the ultimate test for Bennett's arguments. If culture is indeed a product of governmental strategies, there should be no problem with attempts to implement cultural policy. It should be possible, as Bennett plainly expects it to be, to reform society through the means of an effective deployment of cultural policies. Whilst Bennett recognizes that

> there is still a good way to go before satisfactory frameworks, customs and procedures will have been devised that will prove capable of managing complex and highly different forms of cultural diversity which characterise the relations between the Anglo-Celtic, multicultural and indigenous populations of Australia . . . (1998: 104)

. . . he fully expects that it is possible to design and implement them. For Bennett,

> culture still indefatigably tries not to make what each raw person may like, the rule by which they fashion themselves; but to draw ever nearer to a sense of what is indeed a liberal, plural, multicultural, non-sexist tolerance of diversity and to get the raw person to like this. (1998: 104–5)

Bennett's expectation that policy can achieve civic reform seems to be based on an understanding of the individual as formed entirely by governmental programmes. Hence his belief that people are 'raw', without culture until they come into contact with government. There seems to be no space for other formative experiences. That this position cannot be sustained, let alone supported, is the point of my next case study, based on my experiences working as a consultant with local museums in Queensland. Employed to teach local museum volunteers the values of the new museology through a grants programme devised as part of a raft of new museum policies at state government level, I found that my attempts to institutionalize the values of cultural diversity were not welcomed. As I shall argue, what I needed but did not realize at the time was an understanding of the need to dialogue and negotiate the values I was representing with the values of those I was working with. There was no such thing as a 'raw person' or group of people waiting for the imprint of government. For it is simply not the case that the imperatives of government can be easily matched with those of various communities. Policy will not, on its own, bring about a pluralistic society.

Like community galleries, local museums are another site in which a rhetoric of access and equity to representation is used by governments as a means to achieve civic and cultural reform. Excellent examples can be found in *Future Directions for Regional and Community Museums in NSW* produced for the NSW Ministry for the Arts and *Hidden Heritage* for Arts Queensland. Both reports illustrate Bennett's arguments that cultural policy makers use the rhetoric of community representation for purposes of cultural reform. Recommendations for funding are supported through a rhetoric of facilitating community self-representation. As *Future Directions for Regional and Community Museums* put it, local museums 'should be capable of truly reflecting the community back to itself in ways which illuminate complex, social, political and environmental issues' (NSW Ministry for the Arts Advisory Council 1994: 6). The Queensland version, *Hidden Heritage*, concludes with the statement: 'as we approach a new millennium and the Centenary of Federation, Queensland's Community Museums should be resourced to accept the challenge of promoting a distinctive sense of place and culturally diverse community' (Lennon 1995: 112).

The subtext of these reports is that representations in local museums should be brought into line with government policies on multiculturalism, gender equity and reconciliation. If read within the wider context of government policy, certain phrases become a code, meant to indicate the links to policies on multiculturalism and equity. For example, in return for a commitment to strengthening infrastructure, the NSW government hopes for 'strong museums [which will] create a strong sense of identity . . . foster awareness about an area's or a people's history of settlement, relationship with indigenous peoples and the land, technological and cultural achievements' (NSW Ministry for the Arts 1994: 6). Similarly, a 'culturally diverse community' in the *Hidden Heritage* report can be read as shorthand for multiculturalism. The policy objectives outlined by these reports are not only to support local museums – they are to extend governmental control of their representations. In short, cultural policy has become a pedagogical tool, a political intervention, in the process of redefining social and cultural values.

Hidden Heritage is particularly clever in furthering this agenda. Rather than just offer financial resources to local museums by means of small grants to buy equipment (such as storage shelves, a photocopier, or a computer) as in the past, such grants are tied to a pedagogical programme to improve conservation, documentation and interpretation. A rhetoric of crisis is used to support the recommendations in the report. Local museums 'are the protectors of our local, regional, state and national cultural and historical heritage' (Lennon 1995: 2).

> There is an urgent need to capitalise on the energy and dedication of volunteers who have established these museums for the benefit of all

peoples, not just those in their local community . . . the collections are
at a crisis point in management and assistance. (Lennon 1995: ii)

Instead of a grant system to support capital expenditure the report set in place a
programme under which professional training for the museum volunteers had
to be built into an application for funding. Under the Museum Development
Programme, then, the category of Individual Projects is available to 'assist in the
professional development of individuals working with Queensland collections' (Arts
Queensland 1996). The other major category, Organization Projects, is designed to
'support professional museological management of Queensland collections of move-
able cultural heritage and art. Priority will be given to projects which initiate
professional management and innovative interpretations of collections' (Arts
Queensland 1996).

The context for these changes in museum policy are not limited to those of
cultural reform. There are also important economic contexts that need to be considered. These reports were written at a time when rural and regional economies
were collapsing due to the impact of globalization, falling commodity prices and
changes in farming techniques such as increased mechanization which decreased labour
demand. In the case of Queensland the economic situation was exacerbated by
a major drought. The small example of Mitchell, a town of about 1,000 people in
south-west Queensland, provides a snapshot of the impact such changes can have
on communities.[3] Falling market prices for wheat, wool and beef, the drought and
changing farming practices all combined to create unemployment on the land. Young
men could not find work and left town. The major source of employment for women
– local business – also declined, as Roma, a larger town further east, expanded
and became the service centre for the area. There was no longer a supermarket in
Mitchell and banks were closing. Women who once worked as book-keepers and
secretaries were superseded by computers in those businesses which had survived.
This meant there was a dwindling source of off-farm income. It also meant that
women no longer met together in town as they once did. They had no reason to
come in to town – work or shopping – and many of them could not afford the
fuel. It also meant that the population of the town was ageing rapidly. All of these
changes impacted on the local community as memberships for various groups dwin-
dled. The local choir, for example, felt the effects of people leaving town as well
as the inability of those living in the district to come into town for rehearsals.

The story is similar throughout regional Australia, putting pressure on governments
to find alternative sources of economic development and to find ways of keeping
a growing number of unemployed people meaningfully busy. One of the strongest
possibilities is cultural tourism. The sites are already there – local museums and
heritage centres. They are run by a large army of volunteers which cost the government little. But to be attractive they need modernization – both in what they present and how they present it. This is the context for reports like *Hidden Heritage*,
which won government support for its recommendations by arguing that government should be interested in helping to establish a 'coordinated museums industry' in Queensland because, amongst other things, this would create jobs in regional
centres, diversify the economic base of regions, explain and reinforce regional and
local identity, and foster cultural and heritage tourism (Lennon 1995: i).

If we were to follow Bennett's arguments we would expect these policies to be welcomed by the communities they invoke, since they seek to implement necessary cultural reform, provide the structure for increased resources and affirm the value of local cultures. But my own experiences as one of the cultural technicians charged with 'professionalizing' local museums tells me that this is not always the case.

While living in Rockhampton, a regional city in Queensland, I was asked to act as a museum consultant to a small local museum, run by volunteers in Marlborough. The museum had just received a grant to improve their displays and catalogue their collection. They needed a museum professional to show them contemporary practices and techniques.

The history of the museum is not unusual. A committee of six people had inherited a museum from a private collector, who had entrusted its upkeep to them before he died. While realizing that the museum could not remain static, the committee was unsure what to do. Some thought it was enough to pay the rates, hold an annual fête and keep the doors open. Others thought they should be doing more with the collection and applied for a grant with the aim of cataloguing the collection and improving the display.

My job, then, was to give the museum some direction and introduce them to contemporary documentation and interpretation practices. As I quickly realized, this involved much more than teaching them a set of techniques – how to accession, collect information about an object, classification practices, legal responsibilities of managing a collection and so on. It involved a new way of looking at history and at their community. I began by showing the museum committee and the other volunteers that, if they knew a little more about the objects in their collection, they could use the objects to tell stories about the history of the local community. They could develop narratives based on the strengths of their collection, selecting some objects for display whilst storing others for 'changeover exhibitions'. This in turn would enable them to attract the local school to use the museum, something they had not been able to do. Changing the look of the museum would also attract town people in.

The group decided that they would take some of these ideas on board and began to develop thematic displays based on the existing collection. Those objects that did not contribute to the stories went into storage. The volunteers researched each object that went into an exhibition, setting up a manual collection management system so that they could accession the object and keep a file of information on it. Often this involved going back to the original donors, as the collection had grown since the death of the first collector, in order to get them to sign an official gift form as well as to find out further information about the object. The group developed three exhibitions in the space of two years – a remarkable effort. They divided into teams, some responsible for conservation, others for research and writing, others for accessioning. We thought that in turning standard museum tasks into part of an exhibition project everyone would feel part of the team and no one task would become boring. I took a number of workshops on preventive conservation, collection management, exhibition development and label writing.

Over time, however, cracks began to appear. I began getting phone calls from frustrated members of the committee: 'So and so is undermining the exhibition';

'They are not pulling their weight'; 'They don't see why we should be doing exhibitions'; 'They just want to run the annual fête'; 'They don't think we should be doing an exhibition on women's work'. Some members stopped attending the workshops, even though they signed the cheques which paid me. Open conflict between two different factions in the museum became entrenched. In the end, those who wanted to return to the old ways simply destroyed the exhibitions everyone had worked on. The result for the museum was catastrophic – half of the committee left and the other half did not have the skills or the willingness to look after the collection according to professional principles. Both the collection and the community suffered as a result.

How are we to understand what occurred here? And, more importantly, what might be the solutions?

At one level the conflict was a result of specific local contexts. For example, the committee of six was composed of people who lived in town as well as those whose properties were further out. Those who lived in town formed the executive because they could get to meetings more regularly and were 'on the premises'. However, their social and economic status was not as high as the 'out of towners'. They lacked tertiary education and sometimes even upper secondary. These issues probably led to a feeling of insecurity and eventually resentfulness on the part of the executive. They had formal power but were unable to play as full a role in the new processes of documentation and interpretation.

The executive group was also the group who wanted to limit the museum's activities to an annual fête and ensuring the door was open. This section of the committee regarded their role in the museum as a sign of their social status in town. The museum was one of their projects, much in the same way as they looked upon their membership of the Country Women's Association or their involvement in the Church. Their involvement was part of the way in which they established their social position and networks.

But I think the issues involved in this museum's conflict go much deeper than what could be described as issues of class or 'cultural capital' or even the role of museums as centres for social networking. The physical destruction of the exhibitions indicates, I think, a real discomfort with the kind of narratives, the kind of history, the museum was now involved in constructing. For a thematic approach to collecting and exhibiting had precisely the effect that the new cultural policies were designed for – to introduce principles of cultural diversity. It was these principles which were being resisted.

The first exhibition on Chrisoprase mining in the district was a challenge because it required the museum volunteers to recognize that museums did not only deal with the distant past. The display was an exercise in contemporary collecting as an attempt to bring more recent residents in the district to the museum. The strategy worked but in so doing it also brought people who were interested in developing thematic exhibitions which dealt with issues such as women's contribution to settling the district. The new volunteers were younger, had higher levels of education, an urban background and a different understanding of Australian history. The result was a group of women who were far more open to the possibility of extending the available narratives about the past. Supported by the collection, another two exhibitions were developed – one on an earlier dairying industry and the other simply entitled *Women's Work*. While not exactly revolutionary, these exhibitions did challenge conventional pioneer narratives by bringing in a gendered perspective on what is usually an implicit masculine narrative. Instead of the traditional themes of opening up the land, hard physical labour, technological and agricultural innovations, pastoralism and mateship between men, these exhibitions focused on domestic industries, the role of women on the farm and the difficulties of home life in a pioneer context. The introduction of other narratives into the conventional pioneer story also highlighted the fact that pioneer history was a form of narrative in itself, a narrative which could be told differently. This was a challenge to an older generation who assumed their version of history to be 'true'.

The negative response to these exhibitions on the part of the executive is not an isolated one. As the rapid rise of Pauline Hanson indicates, there is ample evidence that 'the bush' is in the midst of a revolt against the values of a mainly urban elite. As many media commentators keep reminding Australians, there is an increasing split between the urban and rural political landscapes. The cultural values each holds dear are increasingly poles apart. The division is, in part, over different perceptions of Australian history and cultural identity. Whilst urban elites tend to be more cosmopolitan, valuing the cultural experiences made possible by the increasing multicultural nature of Australian society and the effects of globalization on the flow of cultural goods, regional and rural Australians are mourning what they perceive as the loss of the dominant Anglo-Saxon culture. Much of this culture is expressed for them in the traditional pioneer narratives, particularly the notion of 'mateship' and its associations with other traditional Australian values such as a 'fair go'. These are values which are also central to the historical experiences of the urban industrial class, a class which is now disaffected, like those involved in primary industry, as a result of globalization. Both of these groups tend to express this disaffection with isolationist and racist discourses. The fact that the major conservative party feels the need to accommodate this revolt in order to neutralize the 'Hanson effect' is also an indication of its extent.

Where to now?

What, then, is the solution to this disjuncture between community and governmental responses to social change? Is it possible to develop a response which does not produce antagonisms? And is it possible to develop a notion of community which does not gain its meaning from an opposition to government?

For Bennett, the solution to such situations is merely to continue to work at refining the normative and reformative characteristics of cultural policy. Recognizing that 'the race debate unleashed in the aftermath of the 1996 election has shown there is a good deal further still to go before an acceptance of such goals will be firmly secured in "mainstream" Australia' (Bennett 1998: 104). Bennett has no qualms that a 'normative mechanism remains at the heart of what is still a reforming endeavour' (ibid.). True to his view that there is nothing outside of government, this is an answer which effectively takes the community out of the equation. Yet it seems to me that the root of the problem in reports like *Hidden Heritage* was an inability to think of cultural policy as an exercise in cross-cultural negotiation. Bennett worries about the tendency on the part of cultural critics to invoke a romantic notion of community which sets the latter in opposition to government. However, government technicians are themselves using a romantic notion of community as a naturally desiring community to erase the distinction between government and community. The problem here is not the assumption of *an opposition* between community and government but precisely the opposite – an assumption that they are one and the same. The result is a mismatch between the idealized governmental expectation that local museums 'should be capable of truly reflecting the community back to itself in ways which illuminate complex, social, political and environmental issues' (NSW Ministry for the Arts Advisory Council 1994: 6) and the reality that the values which communities want to represent may not be those associated with cultural diversity.

Clifford's focus on 'contact zones' as both a description and a prescription might offer a way out. There is, to put it simply, a need for more 'talk' which starts from a recognition that government is also a culture with a different set of interests from those of the communities it seeks to govern. A starting point, from this perspective, would be a recognition of the different interests involved. At one level, we have a variety of groups which have an interest in defining, preserving, documenting and interpreting their cultural heritage for themselves and others. At another level we have a governmental interest in cultural heritage – both as a means of shaping cultural values in the present and as an economic resource. And finally we have the interests of the heritage profession – with their values of the importance of preservation and the proper documentation and interpretation of collections. The differences between these 'communities of interests' or 'interpretive communities' need to be laid on the table for discussion.

For example, any attempt to professionalize the local museums sector needs to be explicit about the full agenda. Local museums need to be aware that in accepting grants they are also making a choice to 'reform' and to become part of a governmentalized public culture. This requires that cultural technicians argue the case for change. It involves discussing differences in cultural values, explaining professional attitudes as well as pointing out that public assistance comes with a system of accountability set by government. In some ways our task becomes that of explaining the options available and what the consequences of each may be. The downside of this approach is that we have to respect the right to choose *not* to learn professional ways of doing things or *not* to follow the values of cultural diversity. This means accepting that cultural diversity might need to include those who do not accept those very principles. We have to be more open to internal contradiction in our positions – we cannot use a rhetoric of community self-representation without accepting that many communities may have different ideas of history.

What are the implications of these case studies for thinking about the relations between museums and communities? Certainly we need to take on board Bennett's criticisms of current ways of thinking about this relation, particularly naive understandings of communities as outside of and opposed to the museum. The consequences of this are considerable. To begin with, curators can no longer be seen just as facilitators, enabling access to representation. Their role is a more demanding one which involves responsibility for actually defining the community being represented. This responsibility is not to be seen as a repressive exercise of power but as a positive one of civic reform, educating the public in the principles of cultural diversity. Such an understanding of the curatorial role does not assume that there is a community 'out there' that the museum can represent. This has a number of further consequences.

First, we need to reject the idea of an 'authentic' representation, including the belief that community groups must only represent themselves. Of course, the problems with these ideas are discussed by curators themselves. As many community gallery curators have argued, the representations that result in community galleries are those of particular *sections* of the community (Anderson 1993; Szekeres 1995). However, their answer has mostly been in terms of finding ways to achieve a 'truer' representation. Some curators advocate direct involvement in order to prevent 'inaccurate' or unbalanced representations, whilst others warn against interfering so that communities can decide how to represent themselves. The limits of understanding the situation in this way need to be better understood.

On the other hand, there is also a need to relativize the museum and avoid defining the representations purely as a result of governmental discourses and strategies. This does not mean that communities must be set in opposition to the museum but rather that the curatorial process is seen as the result of a set of exchanges between *different* communities.

This, I think, is the value of Clifford's work on museums. It tempers Bennett's exclusive focus on the effects of governmentality. Clifford's perspective enjoins us to engage also with the culture of the museum (and of government) and even to value some of its traditions. A dialogic perspective prevents a situation in which the only 'community' exhibitions which are valued are those which are perceived as having little or no input from the museum or 'curator'. By bringing the governmental and the dialogic perspectives together, it is possible to create a role for museums which focuses on their ability to translate between different groups without seeing this process as merely one of facilitation.

Notes

Andrea Witcomb was a curator at the Australian National Maritime Museum and at the Australian National Museum.

1   While cultural policy studies has also taken place elsewhere, most notably in Canada and in the UK, there is a generally recognized tradition within Australia centred at the Key Centre in Brisbane. For a discussion of cultural policy studies more generally, including the place of the Australian version, see Jim McGuigan (1992) *Culture and the Public Sphere*, London and New York, Routledge.

2   Clifford's efforts here are somewhat similar to Hooper-Greenhill's (2000) application of the notion of interpretive communities to the different interpretations of the Hinemihi – a Maori house whose history implicates it in just the kind of cross-cultural context Clifford is interested in exploring. Hooper-Greenhill looks at the various meanings of the house according to who is speaking (Maori, original collector, National Trust). Of interest to her is how all of these interpretations can/should affect the present day interpretation of the house.

3   My account of Mitchell is based on conversations I had with members of the local Progress Association whilst I undertook a small consultancy for the local museum/tourist information bureau.

References

Anderson, M. (1993) 'Roundtable – access: Commitment or containment?', *Museums National* 2(3): 4–7.

Bennett, T. (1988) 'Museums and "the people"', in R. Lumley (ed.) *The Museum Time Machine: Putting Cultures on Display*, London: Routledge: 63–86.

—— (1990) 'The political rationality of the museum', *Continuum* 3(1): 35–55.

—— (1995) *The Birth of the Museum: History, Theory, Politics*, London: Routledge.

—— (1998) *Culture: A Reformer's Science*, London: Routledge.

Burton, A. (1999) *Vision & Accident: The Story of the Victoria and Albert Museum*, London: V&A Publications.

Clifford, J. (1997) 'Museums as contact zones', in *Routes: Travel and Translation in the Late Twentieth Century*, Cambridge: Harvard University Press.

Cunningham, S. (1992) *Framing Culture: Criticism and Policy in Australia*, Sydney: Allen & Unwin.

GLLAM (Group for Large Local Authority Museums) (2000) *Museums and Social Inclusion: The GLLAM Report*, Leicester: Research Centre for Museums and Galleries (RCMG).

Hooper-Greenhill, E. (ed.) (1997) *Cultural Diversity: Developing Museum Audiences in Britain*, Contemporary Issues in Museum Culture Series, London: Leicester University Press.

—— (2000) *Museums and the Interpretation of Visual Culture*, Museum Meanings Series, London and New York: Routledge.

Hunter, I. (1988) *Culture and Government: The Emergence of Literary Education*, Basingstoke: Macmillan Press.

—— (1994) *Rethinking the School: Subjectivity, Bureaucracy, Criticism*, St Leonards, NSW: Allen & Unwin.

Karp, I. and Lavine, S.D. (eds) (1991) *Exhibiting Cultures: The Poetics and Politics of Museum Display*, Washington: Smithsonian Institution Press.

Karp, I., Mullen Kreamer, C. and Lavine, S.D. (eds) (1992) *Museums and Communities: The Politics of Public Culture*, Washington: Smithsonian Institution Press.

Lennon, J. (1995) *Hidden Heritage: A Development Plan for Museums in Queensland 1995–2001*, Brisbane: Arts Queensland.

New South Wales Ministry for the Arts, Museums Advisory Council (1994) *Future Directions for Regional and Community Museums in NSW*, Sydney.

Szekeres, V. (1995) 'A place for all of us', *Public History Review* 4: 59–64.

Vergo, P. (ed.) (1989) *The New Museology*, London: Reaktion Books.

Weil, S.E. (1990) 'The proper business of the museums: Ideas or things?' in *Rethinking the Museum and Other Meditations*, Washington: Smithsonian Institution Press.

Witcomb, A. (1997) 'On the side of the object: An alternative approach to debates about ideas, objects and museums', *Museum Management and Curatorship* 16(4): 383–99.

Primary sources

Arts Queensland (1996) Museum Development Program Brochure.
Western Australian Museum (1995) *Community Access Gallery: Policy and Guidelines*, Fremantle: Fremantle History Museum.

Chapter 9

From Treasure House to Museum . . . and Back

Moira Simpson

'The longer one thought about the idea of the museum the more the custom house seemed like one already.'

(Sidney Moko Mead, Professor of Maori Art at
Victoria University of Wellington, 1983)

IN DISCUSSIONS CONCERNING MUSEUM PROVISION for culturally diverse audiences, it is often stated that the museum is based upon western ideology; that the concept of visiting a museum – a collection of objects removed from their arena of active participation in cultural affairs, to a place in which they are put on public display to be preserved for future generations – is unique to western cultures. This argument then proposes that museums are therefore alien to many of the new audiences which curatorial staff are seeking to attract, making it difficult if not impossible to succeed in these endeavours. However, this impression of museums as a purely western concept is not entirely accurate. Museum-like models have existed traditionally in other cultures for many years, and some facets of conventional museum practice conform to these indigenous models.

Furthermore, western museum curators often argue that the museums and cultural centres recently established by indigenous communities are not museums and do not function as museums, but this is not the case. As the evidence presented here will show, many of these indigenous models do indeed function as museums and, in some instances, lead the way in developing methodologies which are relevant to the communities they serve, yet conform to the basic philosophies of the museum. Other cases provide examples of some of these philosophies being applied to the specific needs of a narrow group of people within the community to which the collection relates.

Source: *Making Representations: Museums in the Post-Colonial Era*, London: Routledge 1996, pp. 107–9, 112–15, 118, 119–22, 126–8, 133, 271–88.

The non-public role of such facilities may run counter to the aims of museums, which are intended to disseminate information to the public; however, these examples are evidence of the concepts of collection, storage and preservation being applied within a particular cultural framework as an extension of earlier traditions, but with the adoption, in some instances, of modern museological environmental, security and recording methods. This, then, is an example of museological methods being adapted to suit the demands of current social needs within a particular cultural context; such developments have featured throughout the history of museums and continue to effect change in museological methods today. Indeed, the issues surrounding the display and possible repatriation of human remains and sacred objects have begun to effect quite radical changes upon museum practices in the latter part of the twentieth century, resulting in restricted access, non-display of sensitive materials and repatriation. While such changes run counter to the most basic museological principles of collection, preservation and dissemination, they are gradually being accepted as necessary responses to concerns within contemporary society.

Various writers have documented the history of museums (Murray 1904; Shelley 1911; Wittlin 1949; Impey and MacGregor 1985; Krzysztof 1990) and, if we look at museum history, we find that the concept and philosophy has changed dramatically over the period of their development; various forms and functions of museums can be identified prior to the development of the classic European model. Henry C. Shelley, writing in 1911, argued that prior to the establishment of the public museum:

> the Englishman of the dark ages, however poor and comfortless his own dwelling, . . . lavished all his skill and much of his wealth on the house of prayer. The churches of his villages and the cathedrals of his cities provided him with objects for the exercise of such aesthetic taste as he possessed; and that fact should lessen the surprise which is sometimes expressed when those sacred buildings are found to contain such articles as the modern mind usually associates with a museum. The fact is, the parish church was not only the store-house and armoury of the fifteenth century, where corn and wool were deposited in unsettled days and weapons hoarded, but it was also the only museum. Its shrines were hung with the strange new things which English sailors had begun to bring across the great seas — with the 'horns of unicorns', ostrich eggs, or walrus tusks, or the rib of a whale given by Sebastian Cabot. (1911: 8)

In some non-western cultures there have been traditions of having buildings or sites in which were stored collections of objects of religious or ceremonial significance, which are in some respects analogous to the western concept of a museum. In Aboriginal Australian communities, although much of the material culture and imagery was of either an ephemeral nature or made from organic materials which were fragile and liable to degenerate, sacred objects and some everyday items were stored away in caches in caves or rock shelters. Such caches were vulnerable, however, to discovery and theft by non-Aboriginal people who might regard them as abandoned (Anderson 1990). Today many Aboriginal communities maintain Keeping Places in which to store securely their secret/sacred materials with access restricted to initiated individuals.

In addition, the European model of the publicly accessible museum and cultural centre is also being adopted. These function as educational facilities which enable Aboriginal communities to interpret their history and culture to non-Aboriginal communities, and may also provide display facilities and a sales outlet for Aboriginal arts. Although the Keeping Places serve to preserve secret/sacred material, their role is to maintain the secrecy of the objects and so restrict access rather than widening it. In this they differ fundamentally from the classic European model which has at its heart, public education and the dissemination of information. However, it is significant, perhaps, that, as anthropologist Chris Anderson notes, 'in some parts of Central Australia, Aboriginal people use the term "museum" for bush caches of restricted items' (Anderson 1988: 24). Evidently, the museum's function in the preservation of material culture has been focused upon and applied to the bush caches of secret/sacred objects.

An additional type of Keeping Place has been developed out of the debate over the holding of human remains in museum collections: that of a secure storage area to ensure community control over the remains without taking the more radical and damaging step of re-burial. According to Mulvaney, the process of storing human remains in a Keeping Place, 'a suitably designed underground vault, entry to which is controlled (or denied) by the community, simulates the burial process' (Mulvaney 1991: 19). Similar types of Keeping Places have been established in some of the state museums to provide a secure storage facility in which both human remains and cultural material can be stored with access limited and decisions concerning research made by the Aboriginal community concerned.

The carved meeting house of the Maori in New Zealand can also be compared to a museum in certain aspects, and in fact, those which are decorated are referred to by their owners as their museum or art gallery (Hakiwai 1993; Whiting 1994). Each Maori village has a *marae*, consisting of a ceremonial site (*marae atea*), in front of a meeting house (*whare whakairo*), and a dining hall (*whare kai*). The meeting houses are usually carved or painted, and inside display carvings of the ancestors, woven wall panels (*tukutuku*), and photographs of deceased relatives. In some meeting houses, *heitiki*, feather cloaks and books are also stored.

Sidney Moko Mead, Professor of Maori Art at Victoria University of Wellington, has noted that 'painted identifications of the ancestors on the wall indicate that the Maori housebuilders of the late nineteenth century were already moving towards the idea of a museum. In some houses the photographs are all labelled and identified' (Mead 1983: 98). Arapata Hakiwai, Curator of Maori Collections at Auckland Museum, has commented that:

> the whole concept of a meeting house is in essence a museum on its own. What a meeting house stands for, what it represents, the carvings, the *tukutuku* – they all tell stories, they are all meaningful. It is a living museum in the sense that it is an art gallery, it is a form of recalling past events, past history. It's everything, it's animate, it's inanimate, it's real, it's there. (Hakiwai 1993)

Here, then, are contained many of the finest art works and most important treasures of a Maori community. In this sense the *whare whakairo* is not dissimilar to the western model of a museum, although the actual functioning of each differs. The primary function of the *whare whakairo* is not display; rather it is a meeting house which is used by the community for formal gatherings and ceremonies. It is here that the community can gather for discussions, conduct wedding and funeral ceremonies, ceremonially greet visitors, and join together in a meal to mark important occasions or extend hospitality to guests. The *whare whakairo* serves the Maori community and is accessible only to villagers and to guests who are first greeted and invited in, usually for attendance at a formal meeting or ceremony. Hakiwai points out that even on *marae* where *Pakeha* are welcomed and shown around in order to give them insight into Maori cultural traditions, Maori protocol and Maori tradition will supersede any other function that might operate (Hakiwai 1993).

In contrast, the European museum is open to the general public as an institution which serves to instruct and entertain. The public display of the collections which the museum holds and conserves is a central focus of all other museum activities. There are, however, signs that the European model is also being adopted by Maori communities seeking to extend the function of the *marae* to include the interpretation of their culture to *Pakeha* or non-Maori through the preservation and exhibition of artefacts. Such developments will serve to reinforce cultural identity and also benefit the economic strength of the community.

According to Gavin Brookes, a Maori Anglican missionary involved in the development of a *marae* museum in Koriniti near Wanganui on New Zealand's North Island, the establishment of Maori *marae* museums reflects an enduring tradition within Maori culture in which Maori *taonga* were stored in caves. He believes that the adoption of the European museum model as the basis for the establishment of Maori *marae* museums is a modern development of this practice. Sidney Moko Mead (1983: 98–101) and Haare Williams (see Haldane 1984: 26) have suggested that the Maori carved meeting house, *whare whakairo*, fulfils much of the function of a museum in Maori society.

Professor Mead (1983: 100) also noted similarities between the custom houses found in the Eastern Solomon Islands and western museums when he visited Santa Ana Island in 1973:

> In the context of the village the custom house served a valuable purpose in presenting to the carvers fine examples of the local carving styles. Through the structure the men were able to examine art works done fifty years earlier. The large house posts lasted longer and so provided a greater sense of continuity with the past. There was a wide selection of objects to observe and study. In fact, the longer one thought about the idea of the museum the more the custom house seemed like one already.

In Papua New Guinea, the *haus tambaran* or spirit houses of the Abelam and Sepik River regions have traditionally served a similar function. Objects were stored and preserved in the *haus tambaran*, in so far as the climate would allow, for future generations. Meanwhile they were also being utilised in ceremonies, and for teaching history, beliefs and cultural practices to younger members of the community. Today, a *haus tambaran* serves a similar function but may also provide storage and display areas for artefacts made specifically for sale to dealers and tourists from the

Sepik Explorer, a tour boat which makes occasional journeys up the river. Often access to the *haus tambaran* is prohibited to women and to uninitiated males; however, outsiders are sometimes given entry privileges and female visitors from outside the community may be given honorary status as a man, so enabling them to enter. The *haus tambaran* and its contents then become a form of museum through which villagers guide visitors and explain the functions and stories of the artefacts, an appropriate means of interpretation in a society which has relied upon oral history for the recording and dissemination of its history and lore.

In their traditional forms, these types of building existed as an integral part of the village or community, in some ways akin to the church in medieval Europe, their function being inextricably linked to the religious and ceremonial use of the objects, and to the education of a non-literate society. Such cultural store-houses played a particularly important role in non-literate societies in which people relied upon oral traditions and the communicative powers of objects to educate the young and the uninitiated and to provide historical records.

Writing about Australian Aboriginal Keeping Places and museums, Margaret West (1981: 13) stated that 'the storage and contemplation of culturally removed objects is a peculiarly Western practice' and indeed it is true that these collections in the indigenous models tended primarily to represent only the community's own culture, a marked contrast to the encyclopaedic collections of exotica and natural history specimens gathered from throughout the world by European collectors in the eighteenth and nineteenth centuries. In the indigenous models, few objects from other cultural groups were displayed with the exception, in some cases, of trophies of war such as shrunken heads. Like many early European and American ethnographic collections, these were preserved and displayed to gain prestige or power for the owners, and demonstrate the successful domination of the enemy. They were a much more integral part of the daily and ceremonial life of the community than most European museums have been. In Europe museums tend to dwell on the past and cater for the cultural requirements of only a portion of society. Museums in Britain are, for example, frequently perceived by the public as a casual leisure facility, and by museum curatorial staff as a research facility for their own and other researchers' work, with the public services and education being secondary. The educational element is all too frequently centred upon schools, and left almost entirely in the hands of the education staff.

The traditional indigenous museum-like model differs most significantly in purpose; most of the objects continue to fulfil their original function, and indeed are frequently still in regular usage. Their positions in the Keeping Place or 'museum' provides accessible storage and enables the context, function and symbolism of the artefacts to be communicated to others within the community through oral traditions such as storytelling, song, dialogue, and through events such as dances, rituals and ceremonies, but only within traditional cultural parameters and subject to restrictions of ownership, initiation and so on. However, the extension of many of these activities to cultural centres that function as museums provides the opportunity for the community to take control over its own representation and to facilitate cultural awareness amongst a wider audience including outsiders.

The contemporary European model of a museum is more static in concept but is more active in terms of collecting, with a wider, research-based remit, constantly acquiring more material, and with clearly defined collecting policies determining the direction and scope of the collecting. The European model has tended to be used by a narrower section of the community, and is seen by many people to be élitist. Curatorial concerns such as preservation and research have tended to take precedence over public usage and education.

It could be argued then that the museum – a centre of cultural storage, pre-servation, education and activities – is not a purely European concept but can be compared with a number of related cultural models which take various forms, and therefore it is inappropriate to assume that an unassailable gulf exists between museums and non-European peoples. As traditional cultures have undergone a process of cultural revitalisation and have sought to establish and promote their cul-tural identity, European-style museums have proven to be a useful means of doing this. In contrast, European museums have played a much less integral role in society than the traditional types of cultural store-houses or spirit houses.

Perhaps it is for this reason that in some societies, modern museums are evolving as centres of cultural activity in which community involvement, public education and social issues are at the fore of the museum's aims, making them a focus for community activities. They provide a showcase for cultural representa-tion in a context which is neither insensitive to the host community nor alien to Europeans. They provide evidence of the community's ability to care for artefacts and therefore strengthen claims for the retention or return of cultural patrimony; and they present artefacts and information using formal interpretive methods and the written word, upon which so much emphasis is placed in western culture. The museum, then, is a useful and powerful tool for politicisation and promotion of culture.

In countries in which the European model of the museum was introduced by colonial powers, the museums have tended to adopt a slightly different role in the post-independence years, becoming more socially significant. They have grown with the newly independent nation in the post-colonial period as the people sought to preserve their cultural traditions and to develop a national identity, in some instances trying to draw together several different tribal, linguistic or religious groups. Their collections have concentrated mainly upon indigenous material and the active pro-motion of cultural traditions, education and the concept of the new nation. Kwasi Myles notes that, with regard to West Africa, museums were established by the British for purposes that were economic rather than educational, and that under the colonial administration, indigenous cultural activities were either ignored or discouraged. However, since independence, there has been a need to build up the national identity of these new nations, to make people aware of the variety of cultures which constitute the nation; and to rediscover and promote traditional cultural activities (Myles 1976: 196–202).

In Papua New Guinea, in the period since independence in 1975, the tradi-tional cultures of the many different ethnic groups living in the country have become expressions of the new national identity. The National Museums and Galleries of Papua New Guinea developed slowly from early origins under colonial rule, and have grown into a valuable mechanism for the preservation and display of the cul-tural heritage of the nation. As an Australian protectorate, efforts to create a national identity had threatened to subsume the individuality of the tribal communities. With independence came a new pride in the richness and diversity of the many traditional societies in the country; since then, the cultural expressions of the traditional societies have come to be the expressions of a new national identity.

Although the museum institution was introduced to Papua New Guinea by Europeans, G. Mosuwadoga, a former director of the Papua New Guinea Museum in Port Moresby, regards the modern museum as a continuation of traditional practices, noting that the concept of securing valuable cultural objects was a traditional one in Papua New Guinean societies:

> The necessity for building a communal type of house to secure and to house these objects is not a new or commonplace practice. Papua New Guinea was doing this long before the museum reached our country. The name and function of a museum can be looked upon in our society today as fitting into our basic ideals, which were with us long before any influence actually reached us. (cited by Smidt in Edwards and Stewart 1980: 157)

In 1973, the government launched the Cultural Development Programme to include the establishment of the National Museum, the National Arts School and the Institute of Papua New Guinea Studies. The Museum has been active in assisting village people to retain their valuable cultural artefacts in the face of great demand from dealers and private collectors from overseas. It has also been instrumental in slowing the illegal export of valuable and culturally significant artefacts which have been declared Proclaimed National Property by the government. At the Museums's opening ceremony, the Prime Minister spoke of the importance of ensuring that the older villagers pass on traditional knowledge and artistic skills to the younger men in order to preserve the past, but also emphasised the need for cultural development so that culture continues as a living, dynamic force.

Similar motivation lies behind the establishment of many museums and cultural centres by indigenous peoples in Canada, the USA, Australia and New Zealand, countries in which they now live as minority groups. Striving to reassert themselves politically and culturally, they must fight to retain their cultural identity against domination by the mass culture. Often the older generation is striving to preserve the old ways and pass the knowledge and traditions of the community on to the younger generation, who are more likely to have adopted all the trappings of popular, mainstream culture. Museums can assist in this process, providing a secure storage facility for the cultural material and community archives, and a focus for community activities. Such facilities enable them to interpret their own cultures and so educate visitors from other cultural backgrounds. They may also be seen as a possible source of financial income through the promotion of tourism, though this often proves to be an attractive but unrealistic proposition.

Aboriginal Keeping Places and museums

In Australia, Aboriginal peoples are also beginning to adopt the European museum model for their own uses and a substantial number of Aboriginal cultural centres and 'Keeping Places' have been established in recent years. Here, individual communities have adopted the aspects of museum provision that best suit their purposes and have developed two distinct entities: the Keeping Place, serving a traditional role, and the museum and cultural centre addressing contemporary educational and economic needs. In the central and western areas of the country, where Aboriginal communities live a more traditional lifestyle in remote locations, Keeping Places are specifically community-orientated and often embrace the traditional role of storehouse for sacred objects. Materials stored in traditional Keeping Places are of a sacred nature and access is restricted on the basis of gender and to those who have been initiated. In the south-east, in the states of Victoria and New South Wales, where Aboriginal peoples live primarily in urban areas, museums and cultural centres are seen essentially as educational facilities and tourist venues designed to generate jobs and income, to provide display facilities and retail outlets for artists, and to offer education about Aboriginal culture to non-Aboriginal people. Museums and cultural centres fulfilling both functions have been established amongst Aboriginal communities in the north where tourism plays a significant role.

Interest in the establishment of Aboriginal Keeping Places grew amongst Aboriginal communities in the 1960s and 1970s. Many of the earlier ones were simple, prefabricated stores for secret/sacred material continuing a tradition of storing caches of secret/sacred objects in caves and bush sites. The resettlement of Aboriginal communities on government reserves or missions far from their traditional sacred sites, and the increasing theft of secret/sacred objects, compelled the adoption of prefabricated store-houses in the vicinity of the settlement (Kimber 1980: 79; West 1981: 9–11). Paddy Roe, an elderly Aboriginal man, described the important role that museums could play for Aboriginal communities:

> to keep safe objects of great tribal significance; to show our young people that our cultural things are important to non-Aborigines – this in relation to things that can go on public display; for keeping tribal discipline, which keeps our culture alive; to preserve objects to be used in cultural ceremonies such as initiations. (Roe 1980: 53)

However, Chris Anderson of the South Australian Museum questions whether such centralised stores are indeed more secure (Anderson 1988: 25). Indeed, the practice of keeping certain items which in the past would have been destroyed after use, and the placement of a collection of sacred materials in one location, perhaps makes the risk of theft greater.

Support for Aboriginal Keeping Places

According to Margaret West, the first official Keeping Place in Western Australia was built at Twelve-Mile Reserve, Port Headland in North Western Australia. It was requested by ceremonial leaders who wished to obtain secure storage facilities for their ritual material. The earliest such Keeping Places were simple sheds which continued the traditional practice of storing secret/sacred materials. These sheds were originally supplied by the Western Australian Department of Native Welfare and, after the Department was disbanded, responsibility for this work was taken over by the Aboriginal Affairs Planning Authority and the Western Australian Museum (West 1981: 10).

At the UNESCO Regional Seminar *Preserving Indigenous Cultures: A New Role for Museums*, held in 1978, it was recommended that 'established museums and galleries . . . support the development of local cultural centres by provision of display items and records (including films, tapes and still photographs) and by the return, where requested, of sacred and ritual objects derived from that group or area'. They were asked to 'initiate training courses for indigenous peoples in all aspects of museum management'. It was also recommended that the Aboriginal Arts Board in Australia 'extends its resource of knowledge on cultural centres' in order to undertake an advisory role and provide to 'Aboriginal and Torres Strait Islander communities seeking to establish cultural centres, draft articles of association for the establishment of incorporated bodies to operate local community cultural centres' (Edwards and Stewart 1980: 13–15).

The Australian Archaeological Association (AAA) supported the establishment of Keeping Places as a means of safeguarding collections of human remains. A letter from the President of the AAA to the Victorian government in 1984 stated the AAA's support for the return of skeletal remains of known individuals, but argued that 'all other Aboriginal skeletal remains are of scientific importance and should not be destroyed by being re-buried or cremated'. In response to the growing threat of the repatriation and cremation or re-burial of human remains collections, the AAA gave its support to the development of Keeping Places. These would provide a means of returning the human remains to Aboriginal control while ensuring their continued preservation, thus keeping open the possibility of future research. The AAA urged the Victorian government 'to instigate a programme enabling the construction of Aboriginal Keeping Places and the training of Aboriginal people in the skills necessary for employment in these Keeping Places as well as in the State's museums' (cited in Mulvaney 1991: 16).

A paper presented to the Conference of Museum Anthropologists meeting in December 1986 by Cliff Samson of the Heritage Branch of the Department of Aboriginal Affairs (DAA), suggested that government involvement might be in the form of funding for training courses for Aboriginal people and sponsorship of individuals to attend the courses run by the Canberra College of Advanced Education. He also called for support of the establishment of positions for Aboriginal Liaison Officers in each State Museum.

While supporting and encouraging the establishment of Aboriginal Keeping Places, the DAA policy particularly noted that 'initiatives for the establishment of Keeping Places should come from Aboriginals. Care must be exercised that Eurocentric notions of what is desirable in the field of curation of Aboriginal material are not imposed on Aboriginals' (Sampson 1988: 22). However, Chris Anderson, in response to the paper, noted that the DAA had stated that government policy would give priority to the Keeping Places established to preserve the security of secret/sacred material, yet also promised financial support for training in museology. Such training, as Anderson explained, is less appropriate to those establishing Keeping Places as traditional secret/sacred stores than those establishing Keeping Places as cultural centres which have much wider remits involving public display and education. He argues instead for financial support from the government to fund qualified museum staff going to the communities in order to provide advice and aid appropriate to their individual needs.

The establishment of a Keeping Place, cultural centre or museum may also enable a community to negotiate loans or the return of cultural material from the collections of state and other museums. Tiwi Keeping Place on Bathurst Island in the Northern Territory was built in order to provide the Tiwi people with access to cultural artefacts which could inspire and renew the artistic traditions. While the main exhibition space is used for the display of contemporary works, a smaller environmentally controlled gallery space was also built with climatic conditions which would meet the stringent specifications of public galleries. It was hoped that this would enable them to receive important pre-contact material on extended loan or even permanent display (Myers 1980).

Arrangements with Australian museums for the return of material or the loan of material for display have normally been dependent upon the provision of suitable accommodation to house materials. Furthermore, the Australian government, in its efforts to facilitate repatriation of Aboriginal material from overseas collections, had made it clear that such returns were contingent upon material being professionally curated and this factor has led to the establishment of a number of Keeping Places. The government, while supporting the establishment of Keeping Places, therefore stated that 'priority should be given to projects primarily aimed at the return of cultural property to Aboriginal communities. Enterprises of a more overtly commercial nature should continue to seek funding from existing sources', such funding being from a variety of Commonwealth and State sources (Sampson 1988).

The Keeping Place in the Western, Northern and Central Australian Aboriginal communities continues to serve a community function as store-house for secret/ sacred material, although the necessity for such museums and their long-term viability has been questioned. Chris Anderson has expressed reservations about the need for and the success of European-style Keeping Places, noting that their presence in centralised communities can become the focus for power struggles amongst groups within the community and they may end up being relevant to only one group (1988: 25). Lissant Bolton has suggested that, where the repatriation of artefacts is contingent upon the provision of a secure storage facility and professional curation, 'once the museum is built and open, interest in continuing to curate the collection may fall away'. This is not because the material lacks importance to the Aboriginal community, but rather they do not place such importance upon the long-term preservation of the artefacts. As Bolton has noted 'it is the symbolism of the possession and control of the material, rather than the material itself, which is significant' (Bolton 1988: 27).

Museums

One of the most successful Aboriginal museums, in commercial and educational terms, is Brambuk Living Cultural Centre near *Budja Budja* (Hall's Gap) in the *Gariwerd*, or Grampian region of Victoria. Brambuk is named after the Bram brothers, two legendary figures believed to be responsible for the creation and naming of many of the landscape features in the region. Opened in December 1990, Brambuk is managed by a committee representing several Aboriginal organisations in the region under the umbrella of Brambuk Incorporated. The planning of the centre involved five communities who traditionally had used the Grampians as a spiritual base: the Kerrup-jmara, the Lake Condah people; the Gunditjmara (Dhauwurd Wurrung) from the cooperative in Warrnambool; the Framlingham Aboriginal community; the Goolum-Goolum from the Dimbula-Ebenezer-Horsham areas; and the Wergaia Jardwadjali.

The idea for Brambuk was conceived in the 1970s as a means of responding to the tourist interest in Aboriginal culture with some sort of museum or cultural centre run by Aboriginal people. Capital costs came from funding made available by the Victoria state government in order to promote the international tourist potential of the south-western region of Victoria. From the outset, the Aboriginal people involved insisted upon total control over the project, including the design, location and the function, and perceived it as substantially different from a museum. Geoff Clark, Chairman of the Framlingham Aboriginal Land Trust, described the concepts which the Aboriginal community wished to develop:

> We were familiar with the role of museums as they currently stood, and the way in which they interpreted Aboriginal culture as a dead culture, an ancient culture, in fact as something which needs to be protected rather than be maintained. We believed that, through the design of the building and its actual functions, we could achieve something closer to a display of living culture rather than a stagnant one that needs to be preserved. We wanted to include the political aspirations of people as well, because too often the image of Aboriginal people overseas is one of the Noble Savage standing on one leg with his spear, and 'you've got some nice dot paintings or some art work, and you can play your didgeridoo'. The image of what constitutes an indigenous person in this country needs to be changed, so hopefully Brambuk attempts to do all that and create understanding of the true history. (Clark 1993)

The centre consists of a permanent exhibition space, a shop, the Brambuk café and Gugidjéla restaurant, and a theatre. Outside, there is a ceremonial ground which is used for demonstrations of music, dancing and cooking, while the grounds around the building have been planted with native plants. The exhibition provides 'a journey through time'. An introductory audio-visual presentation describes how the people, the plants and animals were created by the legendary creator, Bunjil, who was also believed to have created the tools and weapons the people used for hunting and gathering food, and the religion and laws by which they lived. Inside, the small gallery begins with an area devoted to traditional Aboriginal life prior to European colonisation, particularly the hunting and gathering of plants and animals and their uses as food and medicine. It then proceeds to describe the processes of colonisation through video, photos and documents. It highlights the massacres of Aboriginal people and gives an insight into some aspects of the assimilation process, the establishment of missions, and the removal of children from their Aboriginal parents.

The first section, devoted to the Aboriginal uses of flora and fauna, includes photographs, as well as artefacts such as boomerangs, digging sticks and baskets. Text panels describe the wide range of uses to which the raw materials were put.

For example, kangaroos and wallabies provided meat; skins, used to make cloaks and rugs; sinew, which was dried and used as string or sewing thread; and bones, from which tools such as needles and fishing hooks were carved. From the grass tree, they obtained seeds which were crushed and ground to make flour, while the stem was used as a fire-stick, and the resin or sap provided an adhesive strong enough to attach a stone spearhead to a wooden shaft.

One of the most dramatic parts of the exhibition is the section highlighting the deaths of Aboriginal peoples following the arrival of European settlers in the Western Victorian region. A 'forest' of poles in a dimly lit corner of the gallery creates an impression of woodland. White text panels are pinned to the wooden poles like public notices pinned to trees. On each is a quotation taken from the journals of white settlers and travellers in the period 1836 to 1843 describing the killing of Aboriginal peoples as part of the efforts employed by some whites to obtain land for themselves and exterminate the Aboriginal population.

Following this are sections examining the establishment of missions, and the government assimilation policy, in which the text states: 'We became the innocent victims of an attempt to bring about cultural genocide.' It also highlights the bitter irony of Aboriginal (or Koori) servicemen's involvement in the Second World War: on their return all servicemen were promised land under the Soldier Settlement Scheme. 'Sadly the Koori soldiers were excluded from this. Even the very place they called home, the land around the Mission sites, was divided up and given to non-Kooris.'

The exhibition has drawn some criticism from visitors who are unaware of the more unpalatable aspects of Australian history and disbelieve what they read. As Geoff Clark (1993) explained: 'It's very difficult in this situation because we're walking a fine line between exposing the real history of this country and trying to please the taste buds, I suppose, or the curiosities of tourists, which is very difficult when you are trying to tell a history for its brutality.' Clark believes it is necessary to present an accurate, but balanced interpretation of history which will create awareness amongst visitors 'as opposed to making the guilt factor, or some of the other feelings that non-Aborigines might feel, and find themselves justifying, or having to rethink in terms of their perspective on how the place was settled or colonised'. He feels that many of the things they were saying in Brambuk have been reinforced by the Mabo decision, particularly the court's repudiation of the concept of *terra nullius* and the acknowledgement of Aboriginal resistance to white encroachment upon their lands.

The centre is not currently run purely as a commercial enterprise but as an educational centre. Clark believes that the centre is very important as a first point of contact for the many school children and international visitors who visit each year, many of whom are largely ignorant about Aboriginal people and culture, and the continuation and interaction of traditional life with modern-day society. He regards the education of the public as the primary function of Brambuk and believes that it offers a unique opportunity, 'through a very warm and open atmosphere', for visitors to view the artefacts and creative arts, and engage in various educational activities which provide an insight into traditional Aboriginal culture:

> What the centre attempts to do is provide . . . a holistic view, . . . a
> place where there is a window into Aboriginal lifestyle, philosophy, think-

ing, tradition, culture and heritage . . . rather than the stone implements that are normally seen in museums and also the skeletal remains that are sometimes used by museums to depict how our Aboriginal life was. . . . Those are aspects of culture you usually associate with a lost civilisation, with the 'Noble Savage'. (Clark 1993)

Interpretive programmes include the gathering, preparation and tasting of food, and provide examples of traditional methods used prior to European occupation, as well as showing how these same ingredients are being utilised today. In the Brambuk Café visitors can sample bush tucker: the modern presentation of native foods. Traditional ingredients, such as crocodile and kangaroo meat, wattle seed and bunya nuts, are prepared in a modern way to provide dishes such as crocodile and emu sausages, roo burgers and 'wattlechino' as an alternative to cappuccino. Three evenings a week, as the Gugidjéla restaurant, it is open for dinner for which dishes of a more 'cordon bleu' nature are served: *cumbungi djark gadjin cress* (hearts of reed and water cress), *gadjin yabidj* (garlic yabbies in bush tomato concasse and wild rice), and *midjun quandong* (kangaroo fillets pan-fried with wild peach and bush chutney relish).

Clark believes that the other important function of Brambuk is in teaching young Kooris. 'Aboriginal culture and indigenous cultures world-wide are continually under threat and we would like to use this place for the reintroduction of language, ceremonies, dance exchanges – an exchange place for cultures.' The centre provides an opportunity for Aboriginal people to practise their culture, to demonstrate some of their dances and to market their arts. The shop provides an outlet for good quality, Aboriginal products such as paintings, t-shirts, jewellery and toiletries. Visiting artists, dance performances and workshops are included in the centre's programme of events.

Such developments offer Aboriginal people the opportunity to develop commercial enterprises, bringing employment opportunities and cash into the community. They also enable Aboriginal communities to . . . safeguard their natural resources and artistic treasures. By combining Keeping Place and museum, the community is able to provide for the differing needs of its own people and visitors. In these instances, the western museum model and the traditional Keeping Place stand side by side to serve the community to the best advantage.

Note

Moira Simpson is based in the Department of English and Cultural Studies at Flinders University in Adelaide, South Australia.

References

Anderson, C. (1988) 'Comments on "Aboriginal Keeping Places" document from DAA', *COMA Bulletin of the Conference of Museum Anthropologists* 20: 24–6.
—— (1990) 'Repatriation, custodianship and the policies of the South Australian Museum', *COMA Bulletin of the Conference of Museum Anthropologists* 23: 112–15.

Bolton, L. (1988) 'Comments on Department of Aboriginal Affairs Policy Paper on Aboriginal Keeping Places', *COMA Bulletin of the Conference of Museum Anthropologists* 20: 27–8.

Clark, G. (1993) Interview with Geoff Clark, Chairman of the Framlingham Aboriginal Land Trust, July.

Edwards, R. and Stewart, J. (eds) (1980) *Preserving Indigenous Cultures: A New Role For Museums*, papers from a regional seminar held in Adelaide, Australia, 10–15 September 1978; Canberra, Australia: Australian Government Publishing Service.

Hakiwai, A. (1993) Interview with Arapata Hakiwai, Curator of Maori Collections, Auckland Museum, New Zealand.

Haldane, W. (1984) 'The museum and its relevance in a multicultural society', *Agmanz Journal* 15(4): 26–7.

Impey, O. and MacGregor, A. (1985) *The Origins of Museums: The Cabinet of Curiosities in 16th and 17th Century Europe*, Oxford: Clarendon Press.

Kimber, R.G. (1980) 'Desecration of Aboriginal sites and sacred objects in central Australia', *The Artifact* 5: 79–91.

Krzysztof, P. (1990) *Collectors and Curiosities: Paris and Vienna 1500–1800*, Cambridge: Polity Press.

Mead, S.M. (1983) 'Indigenous models of museums in Oceania', *Museum* 138, 23(2): 98–101.

Mulvaney, D.J. (1991) 'Past regained, future lost: the Kow Swamp Pleistocene burials', *Antiquity* 65(246): 12–21.

Murray, D. (1904) *Museums, Their History and Their Use*, Glasgow: MacLehose.

Myers, P. (1980) 'Tiwi Keeping Place, Ngaripuluwamigi Nguiu, Bathurst Island, Northern Territory', in R. Edwards and J. Stewart (eds) *Preserving Indigenous Cultures: A New Role For Museums*, papers from a regional seminar held in Adelaide, Australia, 10–15 September 1978, Canberra, Australia: Australian Government Publishing Service, pp. 63–6.

Myles, K. (1976) 'Museum development in African countries', *Museum* 28(4): 196–202.

Roe, P. (1980) 'How important are museum sites and buildings in preserving our culture?' in R. Edwards and J. Stewart (eds) *Preserving Indigenous Cultures: A New Role For Museums*, papers from a regional seminar held in Adelaide, Australia, 10–15 September 1978, Canberra, Australia: Australian Government Publishing Service, pp. 53–4.

Samson, C. (1988) 'Aboriginal Keeping Places', *COMA Bulletin of the Conference of Museum Anthropologists* 20: 20–1.

Shelley, H.C. (1911) *The British Museum: Its History and Treasures*, Boston, Mass.: L.C. Page.

West, M.K.C. (1981) 'Keeping Place vs. museum – the North Australian example', *COMA Bulletin of the Conference of Museum Anthropologists* 7: 9–14.

Whiting, C. (1994) Personal correspondence from Cliff Whiting, Director, Maori and Bicultural Museum of New Zealand *Te Papa Tongarewa* to author 31 July.

Wittlin, A.S. (1949) *The Museum – Its History and Its Tasks in Education*, London: Routledge Kegan Paul.

Who Controls the Museum?

Introduction to Part Two

MUSEUMS CAN BE PLACES of bitter contestation and all the chapters in this section deal with power struggles of one sort or another – some obvious but many hidden from view. Theories about knowledge and how museums exhibit certain ways of seeing the world as objective reality were considered in Part One. Here we explore some of these ideas further beginning with an article in which Macdonald examines issues of politics in science museums. This introductory chapter, from *The Politics of Display: Museums, Science, Culture*, traces the development of science exhibitions. For Macdonald museums in the nineteenth century were places where the 'imagined communities' of nations were represented (Anderson 1983). They were political constructs of the Western world, designed to allow Europeans to view and categorise other places. Science was an important part of this categorisation and the idea of scientific progress enabled countries to present themselves to their citizens and to tourists as advanced civilisations. At the same time, emphasis was placed on the way museums of all kinds could educate citizens.

She postulates that, during the twentieth century, science museums developed their educational role even further and, at the same time, established two particular forms: the industrial heritage museum and the science centre. The former sought to present the science of industrial production within the idea of a community; the latter reflects the national community within which the centre is based. For example, in Britain the use of interactivity in national museums of science tends to present the idea of the individual and choice-making consumer; in France, it stresses the notion of citizenship.

Macdonald thus reminds us that science, as exhibited in museums, is never objective and neutral, though it may appear to be so. It reflects power relationships and helps to construct community identity.

Certain groups and individuals occasionally overtly seek to use power to ensure that their version of the past, their concept of what is acceptable in museums or their vision for the future, is the one represented in museums. These disputes can place almost intolerable pressures on museum staff. Luke's account of the way the Smithsonian curatorial team attempted to consult with stakeholders and reconcile different views of the way the *Enola Gay* should be interpreted, and how museum staff inadvertently offended a range of communities of interest, such as the veterans, makes painful reading. To a certain extent this conflict exposed a generational divide, but it was also a battle over how Americans saw themselves and their role in the post-war world. The controversy called into question the purpose of the museum. Those who work in museums know how difficult it can be to reconcile groups who have a particular and exclusive version of their story to tell, whether this is a national or local narrative.

Dubin places the dispute over the *Enola Gay* within the context of some of the most controversial exhibitions in American museums, illustrating the impact that that public battle has had on subsequent displays. Demonstrating the ways in which powerful lobby groups seek to control museum exhibition policy he is led to consider the ways in which different individuals claim to speak for the community and he examines the validity of some of their claims.

Both Luke and Dubin illustrate what happens when powerful lobbies or communities of interest influence museum temporary exhibitions. Bordage presents a completely different case. His chapter is a moving account of his time in a German concentration camp, Sachsenhausen, and his disgust and dismay at the way in which the post-1945 story of the Nazi imprisonment (as a result of Stalinist policies) has been included within the space of the camp as part of the permanent display of the site. Bordage argues that this confuses the suffering of the concentration camp victims with that of their oppressors. He does not have power to change this so he writes this article instead. He represents those who have suffered in the camp but he has not yet mobilised others to support him. The unresolved questions remain – whose museum is this and who should control the stories it tells?

Bordage's hurt at what he sees as a betrayal of his own suffering and that of his fellow inmates is not unique. With the collapse of Communism in Europe in the early 1990s many historical narratives have been rethought. Stalinist regimes were oppressive and their victims look to museums to make public the terror they experienced during this period. Thus there sometimes arises, as in Sachsenhausen, an apparent conflict of interest. Which community owns a site when different groups suffered at different times, when different groups oppress others in the most disgusting and inhuman manner? There are several new museums in Europe that attempt to display the horrors of Nazism and Communism together, with subsequent resentments from different communities of interest. For example, the Terror Háza Museum or House of Terror, opened in 2002 in Budapest in Hungary, was both the home to the Hungarian Nazi Party and then to the Hungarian Communist Secret Police. Its critics argue that its Nazi past has been downplayed with the foregrounding of the Communist regime's cruelty (Morris 2004).

It is not clear whom, if anyone, the Sachsenhausen Museum and the Terror Háza, consulted when they developed their permanent displays. Szekeres, director of the Migration Museum in Australia, outlines what happened when the museum did consult communities and found them sometimes divided within themselves. Her chapter explores the difficulties of what exactly constitutes community. In the face of conflicting interests and complex ethical issues she argues for curatorial control as does Dubin.

The two chapters by Fforde and Watkins are concerned with the use of material culture and human remains (both their acquisition and confiscation) to dominate and colonise indigenous peoples, and the struggles of those peoples to regain control over collections, which originated with them. These examples illustrate Dubin's point that museums are becoming more democratised and more open to the different competing claims of groups. All three chapters illustrate that the struggle for control of material is inextricably linked to identity making.

Watkins and Fforde illustrate how contesting interests over the future of human remains, both within the indigenous population and outside it, and between different communities of interest, result in controversial decisions which polarise different sectors in society. These contests are not just over identities but increasingly over who has the right to be the guardian of those identities.

This theme, power within the museum and control over representation linked to identity, is one that is also considered in the next section.

References

Anderson, B. (1983) *Imagined Communities: Reflections on the Origins and Spread of Nationalism*, London: Verso.

Morris, J. (2004) 'State of fear', *Museum Practice*, Autumn, vol. 27, pp. 23–7.

Chapter 10

Exhibitions of Power and Powers of Exhibition

An introduction to the politics of display

Sharon Macdonald

IN RECENT YEARS POLITICS has erupted publicly into the imagined sanctity
of science and of museums on an increasing number of occasions. Two cases
which have caused world-wide ripples of concern are the controversy over the
representation of the *Enola Gay* – the aircraft which dropped the atomic bomb on
Hiroshima in World War II – and the *Science in American Life* exhibition, both at
the Smithsonian Institution in Washington. Although most science exhibitions have
not achieved the same notoriety, the questions that were raised in the controversies can be asked of other exhibitions too. Who decides what should be displayed?
How are notions of 'science' and 'objectivity' mobilized to justify particular representations? Who gets to speak in the name of 'science', 'the public' or 'the nation'?
What are the processes, interest groups and negotiations involved in constructing
an exhibition? What is ironed out or silenced? And how does the content and style
of an exhibition inform public understandings?

Here we explore the political nature, uses and consequences of representations
of science and technology for the public in exhibitions; and show that exhibitions
and science are productive arenas in which to investigate questions of cultural production and knowledge more generally. The focus is on museums and exhibitions that are identified as broadly scientific and are concerned with some aspect
of science and technology. This includes museums of science and industry, natural
history, geology, anthropology and medicine, as well as universal exhibitions (which
deal with industry, technology and their own peculiar anthropology) – all of which
are referred to here as either museums or exhibitions of science. . . . Science displays are never, and have never been, just representations of uncontestable facts.
They always involve the culturally, socially and politically saturated business of

Source: *The Politics of Display: Museums, Science, Culture*, Sharon Macdonald (ed.), London:
Routledge, 1998, pp. 1–24.

negotiation and value-judgment; and they always have cultural, social and political implications. This is the case not only for recent examples which have sparked such controversy, but also for other and earlier exhibitions which have not been publicly contested.

Exploring the politics of exhibitionary selections, styles and silences is not, however, an easy matter. Exhibitions tend to be presented to the public rather as do scientific facts: as unequivocal statements rather than as the outcome of particular processes and contexts. The assumptions, rationales, compromises and accidents that lead to a finished exhibition are generally hidden from public view: they are tidied away along with the cleaning equipment, the early drafts of text and the artefacts for which no place could be found. Likewise, exhibitions rarely seek to explain their contents in terms of a broader social and political context; and this may be something which even those involved in making exhibitions tend to overlook as they concentrate upon the intellectual, aesthetic and practical details of the task at hand. Generally invisible too, through paucity of research, are the understandings of exhibitions and science by those who visit. By analogy with the use of the term 'black box' (borrowed from cybernetics) in the sociology of science to describe those technical objects or scientific principles which are taken as given by scientists without any knowledge of their background or workings,[1] we might suggest that exhibitions tend to be presented as 'glass-cased' – that is, as objects there to be gazed upon, admired and understood only in relation to themselves. Research, however, must seek to move beyond this.[2]

In order to move towards a more thorough understanding of the potentials, difficulties and consequences of putting science on display we need to look analytically at the contents of exhibitions in relation to their production, contexts and reception. Clearly, it is rarely possible to do all of these within any one study (evidence of what visitors thought of historical exhibitions, for example, is scant) . . .

My aim is to set out some issues involved in the analysis of the politics of the public display of science . . . I do this partly through a schematic history of the exhibition of science and technology which seeks to highlight the changing relations between museums, science, publics and power.

Museums, knowledge and power

Here we bring museums and science together not just to explore the politics and cultural operations of each, but also to highlight the discursive inter-relationships between the two. Museums which deal with science are not simply putting science on display; they are also creating particular kinds of science for the public, and are lending to the science that is displayed their own legitimizing imprimatur. In other words, one effect of science museums is to pronounce certain practices and artefacts as belonging to the proper realm of 'science', and as being science that an educated public ought to know about. Moreover, some museums are sites of scientific research, and some collections have been formed as part of the development of particular scientific disciplines. In this way, they have played important roles in the constitution of scientific knowledge and have helped to define and perform scientific conceptions of 'truth' and 'objectivity'. At the same time, museums of science are widely conceived of as 'scientific' institutions in the sense that they are regarded as organized according to orderly and authoritative principles – principles conceived of as separate from power and politics.

Seeing 'truth' and 'values', 'science' and 'politics', and 'knowledge' and 'power' as divided off from one another is characteristic of ways of thinking which, in the Western tradition, have their roots in the seventeenth century, but which crystallized in the nineteenth century. From the late nineteenth century, however, with thinkers such as Nietzsche and Heidegger, and gathering pace dramatically since around the 1960s, there has been a growing number of cultural and historical analyses which have sought to subject these divisions to critical analysis rather than take them as given. Questions have been asked about their formation and effects: how did such separations come about and what are their consequences? This has opened up many fields of research exploring the workings of power in different domains of knowledge and practice, including modern science.[3]

Here, we are concerned with 'politics' in this broad sense of the workings of power. As Foucault has argued, power and knowledge are thoroughly mutually implicated: power is involved in the construction of truths, and knowledge has implications for power (see Foucault 1977, 1979). The production, distribution and consumption of knowledge are always political in this sense. 'Knowledge' here does not only mean that which is displayed in an exhibition as formal knowledge, of course. It also includes the knowledges (including unreflected-upon assumptions) of different parties involved in exhibition-making, their attempts to, for example, gather knowledge about visitors, and the understandings of visitors themselves.[4] These do not always work neatly with one another. Politics is, therefore, a matter of (often implicit) negotiation: a dynamic power-play of competing knowledges, intentions and interests. Moreover, if we view knowledge and power as intertwined, politics is not restricted to particular events or institutions; rather, it has ramifications throughout social life and cultural practice. Even where our concern is with what Foucault calls 'governmentality' – the administration of individuals and populations – we should look towards the detailed tactics, or 'semio-techniques', by which this may operate (Foucault 1977, 1991). Politics, in other words, lies not just in policy statements and intentions (though these are important) but also in apparently non-political and even 'minor' details, such as the architecture of buildings, the classification and juxtaposition of artefacts in an exhibition, the use of glass cases or interactives, and the presence or lack of a voice-over on a film. This is not to say that we will necessarily be able to detect the direct influence of, say, 'the State' in the design of such details; and it is likely in many cases that we will not even be able to say from where we draw our assumptions that particular display techniques are appropriate.[5] There will, however, be 'local' assumptions, claims and statements of intention – e.g. that exhibitions should 'speak to the eyes' or that labels should be designed for different 'levels' of reading skill and interest among the public. The task of the analyst is to explore these beliefs and rationales, and to see how they are associated with – perhaps reflecting or opposing – wider historically located cultural logics and political rationalities.

The task is also to explore the consequences of particular forms of representation in terms of the distribution of power: who is empowered or disempowered by certain modes of display? Within the cultural study of museums, one of the most productive theoretical developments has been the analysis of museums as 'texts' or as 'media'; and this is an approach that can usefully be harnessed to questions of the politics of display. While sometimes focused narrowly on content, in its more interesting forms this approach has sought to open up questions about production (encoding/writing) and consumption (decoding/reading), as well as content (text) and the inter-relationships between these.[6] It is an approach which leads to important questions about the determination of meaning and the distribution of the power to define in exhibitions. For example, who authors exhibitions? How much agency does an exhibition-maker have? What state political or economic interests impinge? How is the audience imagined? Who is excluded? To what extent do visitors to an exhibition define it in their own terms? And how do certain exhibitionary forms or techniques enable certain kinds of readings? More specifically, this is an approach which can lead to questions about inter-relationships between particular kinds of producers, exhibitions and audiences, and the different distributions of power these might entail and enable.

. . . That our focus is on museums of science is important, for it is by no means clear that the politics of production and reception necessarily work in the same ways for different media and genres of display. The strategies and techniques of, say, television, and the nature of the authority relationships that audiences have with it, are not the same as those of museums; likewise, the kinds of positioning of audiences through notions of taste, and the nature of appeals to authority, in art museums may well be different from those in museums of science. . . . A science museum trying to present an exhibition as 'art', or attempting to offer visitors choice, may easily be misunderstood. So, too, may understandings of science presented in the context of a museum differ from the understandings that the public may form in other contexts. Research into the public understanding of science has highlighted the importance to lay people of the perceived morality and trustworthiness of those who speak about science: judgments about the reliability of scientific knowledge and assessments of risk are made at least in part on the basis of estimations about the personal and institutional qualities of those providing the information (Irwin and Wynne 1996; Wynne 1996). Museums, . . . tend to be invested with cultural authority as trustworthy scientific witnesses – though increasingly, it seems, they have to work hard to maintain this status through rhetorical assertions of political impartiality and balance.

Of course, there are also variations between different types of science exhibition. Expectations of a national museum differ from those of smaller provincial museums or of universal exhibitions; assumptions about geology exhibitions may differ from those about modern technology or medical history. Likewise, certain exhibitionary styles – hands-on or hands-off, employing realism, hyperrealism, historical artefacts or reconstructions – also have consequences for the authority of producers, in relation to consumers, and for the types of meanings that it is possible to inscribe. Roger Silverstone has suggested that we might explore such specificities in relation to the ways in which different media articulate time and space (1992), and in terms of their thematic, poetic and rhetorical strategies (1989). An emphasis on time and space would direct us to consideration of such matters as the authority effects of the temporal stability of most museum exhibitions, many of which are in place for years; and to the implications of their spatial fixity and the fact that visitors literally must move through them. The interest here would be in how such features might limit or expand the definitional power of institutions and of audiences. Thematics concerns genre – what are the socio-political propulsions towards, and implications of, particular representational forms? Poetics focuses on the aesthetic strategies of display, those intended to bring pleasure; and rhetoric on the mechanisms of persuasion, those intended to instruct. Of course, these may well overlap in practice, and indeed such overlap – the blurring of the aesthetic and the rhetorical, say – itself has implications for the politics of representation . . . Nevertheless, such a framework is useful in helping analysis of museums move towards a more informed sense of the implications of particular display strategies. It will also help highlight the kinds of difficulties that might be encountered in trying to use exhibitions themselves to disrupt assumptions about, say, divisions between 'art' and 'science', and 'power' and 'knowledge'.

A schematic history of museums of science

Museums of science can be regarded as cultural technologies which define both certain kinds of 'knowledge' (and certain knowledges as 'Knowledge' or 'science') and certain kinds of publics. Museums of science have not, however, remained constant over time: the types of science displayed, the types of public enlisted, the representational strategies and the institutional contexts, political motivations and effects have all undergone transformation. The aim of the next part of this chapter is to provide a brief schematic account of some of these historical patterns and developments. There is, inevitably, much that is not touched on here, but my intention is to select examples in order to highlight some of the major continuities and shifts involved. In doing so, I divide the account into three unequal periods. The first deals with early modern museums of science, the growth of collecting during the Renaissance and the beginnings of 'scientific' ways of knowing in the seventeenth century. The next part considers the expansion of public museums of science and the development of world fairs, from the late eighteenth and more especially the nineteenth century; and the third part concerns a period, particularly since the 1960s, which has seen changing forms of display in science museums and the growth of industrial heritage and science centres.

Early modern museums of science: collecting, seeing and knowing

Histories of museums and, more specifically, of museums of science, generally trace their origins to the curiosity cabinets of Renaissance princes and scholars.[7] These were but one manifestation of a broader fascination with collecting which emerged in the fifteenth century out of 'an attempt to manage the empirical explosion of materials that wider dissemination of ancient texts, increased travel, voyages of discovery, and more systematic forms of communication and exchange had produced' (Findlen 1994: 3). Such an empirical profusion posed problems for ways of knowing that had centred upon the inscribed wisdom of the Bible and of the ancients: here was material that was neither contained within nor immediately accountable by them. In response to this, collecting developed as a 'way of maintaining some degree of control over the natural world and taking its measure. If knowledge of the world could no longer be contained in a set of canonical texts, then perhaps it could be displayed in a museum' (ibid.: 4).

Although these collections often contained fanciful artefacts, such as unicorns' horns and the remains of dragons, their attempt was to represent and comprehend 'nature' through the collection and interpretation of material culture, and to this extent it is useful to consider them in relation to the emergence of conceptions of science. However, as Findlen makes clear, there was at this time no identifiable category of 'science' congruent with that which we would today label as such: Renaissance natural philosophers' understanding of their activities was more 'expansive' and 'encyclopaedic' than this (ibid.: 9). Moreover, although their attempts to devise epistemologies based on observation of the natural world might be seen as a precursor of later scientific ideas, the ways in which they formed and ordered knowledge was also marked by major differences (ibid.; Hooper-Greenhill 1992). In the sixteenth century, according to Foucault (1970; see also Hooper-Greenhill 1992 and Prösler 1996), knowledge was based upon notions of 'similitude' and 'resemblance'. As Martin Prösler explains:

> Things as well as words were God's creation, bearing his signature at a 'deeper level'. These signs were laid down at the moment of the Creation, so that ultimately man might reveal its secrets. The form of knowing therefore corresponded to an *interpretation of signs* and of the resemblances that arose among them. Just as words and things meshed together seamlessly, so in the description of natural phenomena no distinction was made between observation, document and fable. The task of a natural historian like Aldrovandi, writing a natural history based upon his collection, was to represent this complex system – to draw together all that was known about an animal or plant and to present it in terms of the semantic relationships that connected it into the world. (Prösler 1996: 30; emphasis in original)

To later observers, cabinets often appeared haphazard, so unfamiliar are the principles according to which they are ordered. Moreover, by the seventeenth century natural philosophers were dismissing the principles of similitude and resemblance, and replacing them with ideas of *comparison*, of which, Foucault argues, there were two forms: measurement and order ('mathesis' and 'taxonomia') (Foucault 1970: 71). 'Henceforth, no longer did one search for signs of covert resemblance and affinity, but rather, through *observation*, isolated those characteristics whose comparison betrayed the identity, or diversity, of cosmic creations' (Prösler 1996: 30; emphasis in original). This was a 'project of a general science of order' (Foucault 1970: 71); and it was one in which *vision* became prioritized over other senses:

> Observation, from the seventeenth century onward, is a perceptible knowledge furnished with a series of systematically negative conditions. Hearsay is excluded . . . but so too are taste and smell, because their lack of certainty and their variability render impossible any analysis into

distinct elements that could be universally acceptable. The sense of touch is very narrowly limited to the designation of a few fairly evident distinctions . . . which leaves sight with an almost exclusive privilege, being the sense by which we perceive extent and establish proof, and, in consequence, the means to an analysis *partes extra partes* acceptable to everyone. (Foucault 1970: 132–3)

Museums and collections had a vital role in this new project of observation and comparison. Francis Bacon recommended that learned gentlemen should, as part of their scholarly endeavours, have at their disposal 'a goodly huge cabinet, wherein whatsoever the hand of man by exquisite art or engine has made rare in stuff, form or motion; whatsoever singularity, chance and the shuffle of things hath produced; whatsoever Nature has wrought in things that want life and may be kept; shall be sorted and included' (Bacon *Gesta Grayorum* (1594) quoted in Impey and MacGregor 1985: 1). Such a cabinet would provide 'in small compass a model of the universal nature made private' (ibid.); and on the basis of this 'world in micro-cosm' (Prösler 1996), the natural philosopher would be able to learn to 'read' the 'book of nature' (Findlen 1994: 55). It was to this end that early modern scientific collections, such as the Repository of the Royal Society, established in London in the 1660s, were set up. However, as Eilean Hooper-Greenhill describes, such collections mostly failed in their aim to provide a complete 'visual grammar of nature' (Hooper-Greenhill 1992: 157) because of the eclectic nature of collections (which were largely formed out of chance donations) and because 'The aim of cataloguing the whole of nature was too ambitious' (ibid.: 163).

The seventeenth century also saw the beginning of other changes in the criteria for authenticating and validating scientific findings. Prior to this period, the principal criterion of authenticity seems to have been the worthiness and gentle-manly status of the scientist (Shapin 1994). In other words, you could take a finding as true if it came from a noble fellow. During the seventeenth century, however, this was increasingly questioned and was partly replaced by the idea of authentica-tion in terms of particular *methods* carried out in defined spaces, notably laborator-ies. These were spaces of 'observation' in which 'truth' came to be defined as flowing not from worthy persons, but from specified procedures. In theory, any person (properly equipped) would be capable of replicating these truths. However, as Steven Shapin argues, the repudiation of personal testimony as the basis for truth did not mean that the association between personal identity and truth was severed; although publicly dismissed, it remained (and remains) influential within scientific know-ledge producing domains (ibid.: chapter 8).

Museums, which themselves had earlier validated their collections largely in terms of the worthiness of their donors, became important technologies for per-forming this new conception of truth. As Nélia Dias argues (1998), craniological collections assembled by nineteenth-century anthropological museums not only helped shape the craniological knowledge produced, they also helped to instantiate the new ideas about scientific method. In particular, what the museum offered was a site in which scientific findings were theoretically (and to a lesser extent practically) open to a general public as well as to a community of scientists: here, 'anybody' might come and survey the evidence of science.

The Repository of the Royal Society, like most other collections prior to the late eighteenth century, was not intended for the general public. It served primarily as a scientific research centre, a locus for gentlemanly scholars (Hooper-Greenhill 1992: 145). There were a few exceptions to the restricted access of scientific collections at this time: collections of natural and artificial curiosities in mid-sixteenth-century Florence and Bologna, and mid-seventeenth-century Copenhagen (the collections of Cesalpini, Aldrovandi and Worm, respectively) were 'public' collections according to Bedini (1965), though the majority of those who visited seem to have been of high social status and had usually been preceded by a letter of introduction.[8] Indeed, it seems that such visitors were also enlisted as part of the establishment of authoritative knowledge via personal nobility. As Findlen notes, seventeenth-century visitors' books 'immortalised the fame of a museum and its creator by recording their connection to the social, political and intellectual centers of power' (1994: 137); and, as such, they helped define the knowledge contained within the museum as authoritative knowledge.

The period between the Renaissance and the eighteenth century, then, sees considerable transformation in conceptions of knowledge and of museums. In the seventeenth century we see the beginnings of the growth of a particular kind of taxonomic knowledge based upon ideas of objective observation, visibility, mathematization and the ambitions of a science of order. While many of these ideas remain important, the period from the late eighteenth century sees further changes, in particular an 'opening up' of the museum to a much broader public, which is connected in part with changing conceptions of scientific authority. As we shall see in the next section, however, this is not the only impetus to the growth of the public museums, and the nineteenth century sees further changes in the nature of scientific knowledge – changes in which the museum again has an important formative role.

Modern museums of science: diagnosis, publics and progress

Particularly important to the shaping of the museum in this modern period are the following: the formation of nation-states – 'imagined communities' which sought to define and enlist a bounded citizenship (Anderson 1983); colonialist expansion – which both provided 'material' for display and territories requiring governance; the further development of 'scientific' and more specifically 'museological' ways of seeing the world, and the extension of these to other domains of life. The museum is not, however, merely a product of or a site for displaying the narratives of modern developments; it is also one of the technologies through which modernity – and the democratic ideals, social differences and exclusions, and other contradictions which this has produced – is constituted.[9]

Consequent particularly to the French Revolution, many previously private collections were claimed for the public, and numerous new museums – national and provincial – were established. It was during this period, as nation-states themselves emerged and sought to define their populations as citizens, that museums came to be conceived as symbols of national identity and progress, and as sites of civic education for the masses.[10] Not only was the previously private made public,

'exhibiting' also moved beyond the confines of museums with the remarkable flourishing of 'universal' exhibitions, of which the Great International Exposition held
at Crystal Palace in London in 1851 was the first.[11] At these the competitive dimension of 'national exhibitionism' was often made explicit, nations being awarded medals
and ranked in ceremonies modelled on the Olympic Games (Lindqvist 1993) . . .

While univeral exhibitions, which were largely concerned with industry and
technology, and most museums established in this period, with the exception of
art galleries, could be seen as broadly scientific (Forgan 1996: 47), the nineteenth
century is also characterized by the development of more specialized public museums
of science. Many of the earliest of these, some of which were established in the
late eighteenth century, were devoted to natural history, as was the Musée
d'Histoire Naturelle, which opened in Paris in 1793 or Charles Willson Peale's
Museum in Philadelphia (1784), though this also included some scientific and technological artefacts (Bedini 1965: 22).[12] So too were many of the first 'scientific'
museums to open in the New World (Sheets-Pyenson 1989). Anthropology collections were sometimes incorporated in the natural history museums, as in the case
of the Smithsonian's Museum of Natural History, the Chicago Field Museum or
the Dutch Museum of Natural History, or as part of national self-representations
as in the case of the National Museum of Denmark (1916), though from the 1830s
they also began to assume distinct identities in some cases, such as the ethnographic
museum of the Academy of Sciences in Petrograd (1836), the National Museum
of Ethnology, Leiden (1837) and the Pitt Rivers Museum, Oxford (1885).[13]
Museums specializing in machines and technical and scientific instruments also became
a distinct type in the nineteenth century, beginning with France's Conservatoire
National des Arts et Métiers, established in 1794. More specialist science museums
often developed out of more general collections, as did Britain's Museum of Natural
History (from the British Museum collections) and the Museum of the History of
Science, Oxford (from the Ashmolean collection) (Hackman 1992); or, as in the
case of the Science Museum (established 1857) or the Industrial Museum of Scotland
(1855), they were based on exhibits originally shown at international exhibitions
(Butler 1992). By the early decades of the twentieth century, most of the first wave
of nation-states, and many which were established later, could boast not simply
a national museum, but national museums of both natural history and of science
and technology, as well, perhaps, as national museums of art and other subjects.[14]

This flourishing of museums and exhibitions is bound up with the development
of distinctive modern ways of seeing the world. For modern cosmopolitan Europeans, Timothy Mitchell argues, representation – particularly 'rendering things up
to be viewed' (Mitchell 1991: 2) – became a key means of apprehending and 'colonizing' reality. The world was to be experienced as though it were a picture – a form
of apprehending that he calls, in a phrase borrowed from Heidegger, the 'world-
as-exhibition' (ibid.: 13). This entailed both a detachment of the viewer – '[t]he
person was now thought of as something set apart from the world, like the visitor
to an exhibition' (ibid.: 19) – and a depiction of the world as 'ordered and organised'
(ibid.). Even where Europeans were keen also to experience 'reality' as directly
as possible, as in their ventures into unknown places or, in a rather different way
through the development of highly accurate replicas (such as the 'Cairo street' at
the universal exhibition in Paris in 1889), the idea of detached representation

remained important. This is reflected in the desire of European travellers to photograph or paint the places they visited (preferably from a height which would set the site out as a panorama [ibid.: 24]); and in the proliferation of texts about exhibitions – 'catalogues, plans, signposts, guidebooks, instructions, educational talks and compilations of statistics' (ibid.: 20) – and the viewing platforms that were often built as part of them (Bennett 1995: 69). This capacity of exhibitionary representation to render the world as visible and ordered was part of the instantiation of wider senses of scientific and political certainty. As Mitchell emphasizes:

> Exhibitions, museums and other spectacles were not just reflections of this certainty, however, but the means of its production, by their technique of rendering history, progress, culture and empire in 'objective' form. They were occasions for making sure of such objective truths, in a world where truth had become a question of what Heidegger calls 'the certainty of representation'. (1991: 7)

Museums and exhibitions were thus sites in which political power could 'operate . . . so as to appear set apart from the real world' (ibid.: 160); they were a means of casting the newly realized nations, and cultural, racial and class differences, as fact. In this, museums and exhibitions were perhaps particularly effective in that they not only provided a 'picture' but also objects and other tangible 'evidences'.

The emphasis on gaining privileged vantage points from which order and objective truths might be discerned, as well as the disciplinary specialization of museums that occurred in the nineteenth century, can be seen as part of a broader epistemological development that the historian of science, John Pickstone, has called 'analytical', 'museological' or 'diagnostic' (Pickstone 1994). He is careful to emphasize that these new forms of knowing had earlier precursors and that some classical or savant forms of science, technology and medicine continue today. Nevertheless, he argues, it is useful to try to characterize a development which became much more widespread in the nineteenth century. Classical science, he suggests, tended to identify objects in terms of surface characteristics and to explain deductively according to particular natural philosophies (e.g. vitalism, mechanism) which in practice were 'rarely articulated with' the project of a general grammar of nature which the savants espoused (ibid.: 113, 117). Characteristic of the new 'analytical' or 'museological' sciences is 'that they presented their objects as *compounds*, analysable into *elements*', and that 'these elements were *domain specific*' (ibid.: 117; emphases in original). The aim was to be able, within specific types of science, to produce analytical classifications and to diagnose surface characteristics or the workings of compounds in terms of underlying *process*. This was different from the earlier idea of reading and cataloguing the 'book of nature', in that it sought to 'produce deeper, more specialized knowledge' (ibid.) – to delve beneath the surface – and thus to provide a means, ideally, of grasping 'deep structure' and process, which in turn would enable *explanation* and *prediction*. Museums, according to Pickstone, were a key site in which this new form of knowledge was articulated; and to this end universities often established museums or sought to associate themselves with existing museums (Forgan 1994, 1996), though at the same time it should be stressed that not all nineteenth-century exhibitions were 'museological' in Pickstone's sense (Pickstone 1994: 123). Nevertheless, museum collections were an important research source in the nineteenth century and displays were increasingly conceptualized as a manifestation of the analysis of objects into elements, and thus as a kind of diagnosis of an underlying reality. The attempt was to arrange objects and displays in ways which would reveal profound principles. Such profound principles might be evolutionary, though there were other possibilities too, such as the analysis into chemical elements and principles. As Sophie Forgan has described, this was a matter of a good deal of consideration in the planning of the layout of many nineteenth-century museums, including the Natural History Museum, London, and Jermyn Street Geological Museum (Forgan 1994).[15] Such exhibitions were conceptualized not just as containers of scientific facts, but as themselves integral to the scientific message. This had implications for, among other things, the expertise demanded of curators, links with universities, and museum visitors.

The layout of nineteenth-century museums also differed from earlier museums in that it was expected to speak not only to fellow savants and nobles, but to a general public, many members of which could not be expected to have much prior knowledge. It was often recognized, . . . that the kind of deep specialist knowledge that these classifications might divulge to scientists was not necessarily that which would be of most educative value and practical use for the lay person. Considerable effort, therefore, was directed towards making exhibitions educative for, and *legible* to, the new mass public. As Bennett argues,[16] this was also bound up with ideas about transforming the public, and producing citizens who would themselves take on the task of self-education and improving themselves.

Ideas of improvement and progress were integral to most nineteenth-century museums and exhibitions of science. These ideas operated at a number of levels, each of which provided mutual support for the others. At the most expansive level were evolutionary narratives about the progress of humankind and of scientific knowledge; at the national level, each country sought to represent its own story of self-betterment and of civilizing influence upon the rest of the world; and at the level of individual citizens, members of the public were invited to undertake their own personal journey towards greater knowledge and mastery. Museums were sites in which these parallel narratives could converge. Exhibitions could physically knit together the universal and national or racial, and visitors could embody the progressive narratives as they moved through the orderly museum space.

Much of the nineteenth-century museum achievement is still part of our physical and symbolic landscape. However, during the course of the nineteenth century museums were to become less important as sites of scientific activity, and 'museological science', while remaining central to many areas of scientific endeavour, was to become less prestigious and authoritative than 'experimental science', which entails 'control over phenomena in laboratories' (Pickstone 1994: 132, 113; emphasis in original). While museums have continued to have an important role in validating science for the public, the legitimization of research evidence itself has increasingly become a matter of specialized expert procedures and review, carried out largely in less public spaces. Moreover, with a continued specialization of scientific knowledge, with the increased use of sophisticated technologies and with scientific attention often turned to the infinitely small or large, science has developed a greater mystique of being beyond lay understanding. Yet, while this may signal a decline in the role of the museum as a site of scientific expertise and legitimization, it also heralds a renewed significance in its role in 'the public understanding of science'. Museums of science in the twentieth century have built on their earlier emphasis on public education to present themselves as experts in the *mediation* between the esoteric world of science and that of the public. This self-perception differs somewhat, I suggest, from that predominant in the nineteenth century, in that it seeks not so much to make science legible through making evident its underlying principles, as to *represent* science: not simply to *show* or *tell* but to *interpret* it. Moreover, such interpretations are increasingly framed primarily in terms of the public – e.g. through categories such as 'Your Body' or 'Shopping' – rather than science.

The distinction between nineteenth- and twentieth-century exhibitions should not be exaggerated, however, for as we have noted, nineteenth-century displays were often very much concerned with public education and with finding ways of displaying science that would appeal to a lay audience. Nevertheless, I suggest that what we see in the twentieth century are moves away from the dominant nineteenth-century institutional analogy of the museum as a library (Forgan 1994), and with this a greater sense that it is only possible to display fairly limited and partial accounts of science; and a growing conviction that science needs to be embedded in other kinds of stories – and in media which were not typically part of the museum-as-library – to make it attractive to a general public. The orderly visualism of reading, inherent in the library and book analogies, the desire to make *legible* and the obsession with labelling exhibits,[17] gives way to less directed and more multi-sensory approaches. Alongside these changes we also see further transformations in the conception of the public.

Recent museum transformations: contexts, interactivity and consumers

In the late twentieth century, many of the nineteenth-century triumphs – the nation-state, empire, racial and social hierarchies, progress and 'deep truth' – have come to seem much less inevitable. Particularly since the 1960s, we have seen challenges to all of these in the form of ethno-nationalist, liberationist and environmentalist movements, and the growth of interest in 'traditional' culture and heritage, 'minority', 'alternative' and 'New Age' beliefs and lifestyles. The acceleration of globalization and the transformations in capitalist production to more transnational, flexible, disorganized and consumer-led forms are also often seen both as a threat to the relevance of the nation-state and as factors involved in enabling new forms of identity and subjectivity.[18] While there has undoubtedly been a proliferation of different, particularly minority, 'voices' speaking in the public arena, the old political and cultural high ground has not simply been relinquished. On the contrary, what we have seen is an escalation of intellectual battles over the legitimacy of different kinds of representation. The 'Culture Wars' have focused especially on issues of 'political correctness' and 'intrinsic value' in relation to the literary and artistic canon;[19] the 'History Wars' on similar issues in relation to history, multiculturalism and national identity, focused partly on the *Enola Gay* episode;[20] and the 'Science Wars' have seen fierce debate over the epistemological status of science.[21]

It is in this same period that we see some marked changes in museums of science. Not only do existing museums of science come to adopt new technologies of display, new interpretive experiments and new concerns with their visitors and communities, there is also a massive expansion of two particular forms which could broadly be classified under the 'museum of science' label: industrial heritage and science centres. While there has been debate about whether these *should* be regarded as museums of science (e.g. Durant 1992), it is clear that they have posed challenges for more traditional science museums and that these have sometimes sought to borrow the strategies (and personnel) of industrial heritage developments and science centres. Intriguingly, some of the approaches that industrial heritage and science centres take to science are almost the inverse of one another. The former seek to present science entirely contextualized in a 'slice of history' in a specific community, whereas science centres are more concerned with universal laws and principles which transcend particular times and places.

Industrial heritage sites have a number of precursors, such as Skansen, a Swedish open-air museum which opened in 1891, and Henry Ford's Greenfield Village (1929).[22] Nevertheless, since the 1960s the number of these has vastly increased in an expansion which equals that of traditional museums of science and industry in the nineteenth century. In Britain, the Blists Hill development at Ironbridge Gorge (opened to the public in 1973) and the North of England Open Air Museum at Beamish (1972) are generally seen as particularly influential examples.[23] Unlike traditional science museums, these attempt to provide a 'total environment': artefacts are presented embedded in the worlds of which they were part and visitors are invited to enter, or at least get close to, those worlds and lives. In some cases, especially in France and Scandinavia, industrial heritage developments also go under the name of 'eco-museums' and are associated with community regeneration – linking past with present – and a much greater involvement of local populations in the development of displays than is typical of most museums.[24] The development of industrial heritage, as part of a more widespread discussion of what is sometimes called the 'heritage industry' (Hewison 1988), has already been subject to a good deal of debate about its political implications.[25] Questions have been asked about how far such representations provide accounts which are emancipatory for visitors and communities. Is the movement analogous to, and part of, a claiming of history by 'the people'? Or is it simply a way of commoditizing a past in the face of a lack of alternative sources of manufacturing? As with examples we discuss here, the answers are likely to be less clear cut when it comes to dealing with specific cases and the complexities of processes and different participants than the sometimes stark terms of the debate might imply. Nevertheless, these general arguments about the politics of industrial heritage and the extent to which presenting science as part of particular places, times and social relations may enable the public to better understand the importance and/or the dangers of science have clear links with debates taking place within many museums of science.

The very different strategies of science centres and the specialized hands-on galleries which have sprung up in many science museums also have pre-1960s precedents; in this case interactive exhibits in international exhibitions and museums of science (e.g. the Children's Gallery, established in the 1930s in the Science Museum, London). However, where the latter were often devoted to showing particular applications of science, the new science centres (especially the first to be developed) have concentrated more on relatively abstract scientific principles. The earliest example of a centre devoted to representing scientific principles through hands-on exhibits is the Exploratorium in San Francisco, which opened in 1969. In contrast to industrial heritage sites, science centres and their in-museum equivalents have been subject to rather scant commentary on their political motivations and effects. In many ways this is not surprising, given that such exhibits attempt to deal with 'pure' scientific principles which transcend cultural and social contexts. Yet, from the perspective of social and cultural disciplines, the emergence and rapid spread of this mode of representing science is surely also deserving of comment.

While we must certainly not assume that all science centres necessarily share identical motivations the Exploratorium is an interesting and prescient case to consider, both because it has been so influential and because its founder, Frank Oppenheimer, provided very clear statements of his intentions (Hein 1990). In the document which set out the rationale for establishing the Exploratorium, Oppenheimer expressed particular concern over the fact that 'For many people science is incomprehensible and technology frightening' (ibid.: 218). The aim of the Exploratorium, as the rationale concluded, was to 'convey the understanding that science and technology have a role which is deeply rooted in human values and aspirations' (ibid.: 221). In a century in which broadly triumphalist popular perspectives on science seemed, especially after World War II, increasingly to be discoloured by perceptions of the dangers of technology, there was a task, as scientists such as Oppenheimer saw it, to present positive visions of scientific potential and achievement. Indeed, the phrase which has been adopted by many science museums to describe their central activity in the late twentieth century – 'public understanding of science' – is often conceptualized in terms of 'public appreciation of science' (Lewenstein 1992; see also Irwin and Wynne 1996). It was to this, in part at least, that the Exploratorium was dedicated.

Oppenheimer had personal reasons for wanting to reclaim science as a worthy and positive endeavour, for, together with his brother Robert, he had worked on the production of the atomic bomb. He had, therefore, very direct involvement in the technology which, more than any this century, has created a sense of public fear of the potential of science.[26] Oppenheimer's attempt in the Exploratorium was to represent 'pure' scientific principles unsullied by the context of their production or of their applications. While, on the one hand, he claimed that an understanding of scientific principles was important for everyday life, he also fiercely resisted any suggestion that the Exploratorium should deal with areas of science that might readily be perceived as political (such as the environment) or even that it might include any directly 'how to' exhibits (Hein 1990). Instead, the Exploratorium was to represent scientific laws as transcendent, and scientific process as a formal art. Indeed, Oppenheimer was keen to draw analogies with art – the subtitle of the Exploratorium being 'Museum of Science, Art and Human Perception' – so pointing to the individual creative element of science rather than its social or political contexts.[27]

If science centres may have proved attractive partly because of their potential to provide positive and relatively politically 'safe' images of science, another source of their appeal clearly lies in their hands-on interactivity – a mode of display which is becoming increasingly common in contemporary exhibitions. This is sometimes embraced by those involved as a democratizing attempt to, as Oppenheimer put it, 'bridge the gap between the experts and the laymen' (in Hein 1990: 17). Whether this is how the 'hands-on' experience is seen by visitors remains however, an under-researched question, though . . . democratization is not *necessarily* an effect of such representations, and . . . in analysing interactive and electronic technologies of display, we need also to consider the politics of the way in which the visitor is imagined.

As Andrew Barry's comparison of the use of French and English use of inter-activity in national museums of science illustrates, we cannot simply infer the mean-ings of particular technologies of display without consideration of national cultural semantics (Barry 1998). In Britain in the late twentieth century, for example, visitors may be conceptualized more as individualized choice-making consumers and active learners than they are in France, where the notion of citizenship and the celebration of human–machine inter-relations appear more central. At the same time, however, there are also shared – though not universal – transnational conceptions of the meanings of new technologies of display . . .

In addition to the past-focused industrial heritage and the forward-looking inter-active and multimedia display technologies, the late twentieth century has also seen an increased number of exhibitions in museums of science which attempt to rela-tivize or question scientific authority, or to reflect upon the process of exhibiting itself. This may be seen as part of a growing questioning of previous certainties and an increased willingness of cultural institutions and academic disciplines to look reflexively at their own practices. There have been a number of such attempts in museums of science.[28] What is clear from these accounts is that such 'experiments' can certainly produce interesting and thought-provoking displays.[29] They may, how-ever, also provoke confusion and anger. That they do so is testament, in part at least, to the authority to sanctify science with which museums are still widely invested.

Notes

Sharon Macdonald is Professor of Social Anthropology in the School of Social Sciences at the University of Manchester, and was previously Professor of Cultural Anthropology at the University of Sheffield.

1   The use of the term 'black box' in the sociology of science was introduced by Bruno Latour in *Science in Action* to refer to 'a well-established fact or an unprob-lematic object' (Latour 1987: 131) or more specifically as 'an automaton . . . [involving] a large number of elements . . . made to act as one' (ibid.).

2   As is nicely implied in the title of Nick Merriman's analysis of museum visiting, *Beyond the Glass Case* (1991).

3   The sociology and anthropology of science in general, and particularly the social study of scientific knowledge and feminist analysis, have been concerned with such questions. For some overviews see Franklin (1995), Harding (1986), Law (1991), Nader (1996a), Star (1988), Traweek (1993), Woolgar (1988a).

4   A distinction is sometimes made in science studies and in the social sciences more generally between knowledge and practice. My characterization of knowledge here, however, is intended to incorporate both.

5   Foucault makes this point in a different context in *The History of Sexuality* (1979). This is not the same as saying that the State is not involved in the regulation of individuals and populations.

6   The 'encoding'/'decoding' vocabulary is from Hall's classic account of a textual approach to media (Hall 1980). For an account of a range of textual approaches to material culture see Tilley (1990); and for a brief discussion in relation to museums see Macdonald (1996).

7   See Bedini (1965); Findlen (1994); Impey and MacGregor (1985).

8   See Findlen (1994: 134–46), for a fascinating discussion of visitors to these museums, particularly that of Aldrovandi.

9   For an insightful theoretical account and illustration of museums 'rid[ing] the juggernaut of modernity's contradictions' see Fyfe (1996).

10   For discussion see Bennett (1995, especially ch. 3); Duncan (1995); Hooper-Greenhill (1992: ch. 7); Kaplan (1994).

11   For discussion of the Great Exhibition see Altick (1978); Bennett (1995 *passim.*); Greenhalgh (1988); and for more general discussions of universal exhibitions see Benedict (1983), Coombes (1994), Harvey (1996, 1998), and Rydell (1993).

12   It should be noted that dates of 'establishment' are not always clear cut and these should, therefore, be taken as approximations.

13   Anthropological collections during this period generally covered both cultural ('ethnological') and physical aspects of anthropology, though some collections focused more on one aspect than the other. For discussion of anthropological museums see Ames (1992), Clifford (1997), Haraway (1989), Jenkins (1994), Jones (1992), Jordanova (1989), Stocking (1985).

14   There are, however, national differences here which deserve further research. For example, neither Spain nor Italy established national museums of scientific or technological history (Begeron 1993).

15   For other discussions of the architecture of museums and related spaces in this period see Markus (1993); Outram (1996).

16   See Bennett (1998).

17   Ibid.

18   There is a large sociological literature discussing such transformations. See, for example, Giddens (1990), Lash and Urry (1994), Waters (1995).

19   For discussion see Bolton (1992), Hunter (1991) and McGuigan (1996: ch. 1).

20   See Linenthal and Engelhardt (1996).

21   Here the book by Gross and Levitt (1994) has been central in the 'backlash' against social perspectives on science. See Gieryn (1998), Nader (1996a) and *Social Text* (1996) for discussion.

22   For an analysis of Greenfield Village see Staudenmaier (1993).

23   For discussion of industrial heritage see, for example, Alfrey and Putnam (1992); Bennett (1995: ch. 4); Butler (1992: ch. 4); Fowler (1992); Walsh (1992).

24   For discussion of the eco-museum movement see Alfrey and Putnam (1992); Begeron (1993); Hoyau (1988); Poulot (1994).

25   For overviews see McGuigan (1996: ch. 6); Urry (1996); Walsh (1992).

26   He also knew first hand how political definitions could affect the course of a scientific career, having been made an outcast during the McCarthy era on account of a brief period of Communist Party membership.

27   See Barry (1998).

28   For examples see Ross (1995), and various examples in Karp, Kreamer and Lavine (1992), Karp and Lavine (1991) and Pearce (1996).

29   The term 'experiment' here is used to indicate the parallel with developments within anthropology to 'write culture' or present ethnographic research in new ways. For discussion see for example Clifford and Marcus (1986); James, Hockey and Dawson (1997); Rosaldo (1993). There has also been analogous critique in other disciplines, including the sociology of science. See for example Law (1993); Woolgar (1988b).

References

Alfrey, J. and T. Putnam (1992) *The Industrial Heritage*, London: Routledge.

Altick, R. (1978) *The Shows of London*, Cambridge, MA, and London: The Belknap Press of Harvard University Press.

Ames, M. (1992) *Cannibal Tours and Glass Boxes: The Anthropology of Museums* (2nd edition), Vancouver: University of British Columbia Press.

Anderson, B. (1983) *Imagined Communities: Reflections on the Origin and Spread of Nationalism*, London: Verso.

Barry, A. (1998) 'On interactivity: consumers, citizens and culture', in S. Macdonald (ed.) *The Politics of Display*, London: Routledge.

Bedini, S. (1965) 'The evolution of science museums', *Technology and Culture*, 6, pp. 1–29.

Begeron, L. (1993) 'The new generation of museums: technical, industrial and "eco-museums"', in B. Schroeder-Gudehus (ed.) *Industrial Society and its Museums, 1880–1990: Social Aspirations and Cultural Politics*, pp. 91–5, Chur, Switzerland: Harwood Academic/Paris: Cité des sciences et de l'industrie.

Benedict, B. (1983) *The Anthropology of World's Fairs*, London: Scolar Press.

Bennett, T. (1995) *The Birth of the Museum*, London: Routledge.

—— (1998) 'Speaking to the eyes: museums, legibility and the social order', in S. Macdonald (ed.) *The Politics of Display*, London: Routledge.

Bolton, R. (ed.) (1992) *Culture Wars: Documents from the Recent Controversies in the Arts*, New York: New Press.

Butler, S. (1992) *Science and Technology Museums*, Leicester, London and New York: Leicester University Press.

Clifford, J. (1997) *Routes*, Cambridge, MA: Harvard University Press.

Clifford, J. and G. Marcus (eds) (1986) *Writing Culture: The Poetics and Politics of Ethnography*, Berkeley, CA: University of California Press.

Coombes, A.E. (1994) *Reinventing Africa: Material Culture and Popular Imagination in Late Victorian and Edwardian England*, New Haven, CT: Yale University Press.

Dias, N. (1998) 'The visibility of difference: nineteenth-century French anthropological collections', in S. Macdonald (ed.) *The Politics of Display*, London: Routledge.

Duncan, C. (1995) *Civilizing Rituals*, London: Routledge.

Durant, J. (1992) 'Introduction', in J. Durant (ed.) *Museums and the Public Understanding of Science*, pp. 7–11, London: Science Museum in association with the Committee on the Public Understanding of Science.

Findlen, P. (1994) *Possessing Nature: Museums, Collecting, and Scientific Culture in Early Modern Italy*, Berkeley and Los Angeles, CA: California University Press.

Forgan, S. (1994) 'The architecture of display: museums, universities and objects in nineteenth-century Britain', *History of Science*, 32 (2), pp. 139–62.

—— (1996) ' "A nightmare of incomprehensible machines": science and technology museums in the 19th and 20th centuries', in M. Pointon (ed.) *Museums and Late Twentieth Century Culture*, pp. 46–68, Manchester: Manchester University Press.

Foucault, M. (1970) *The Order of Things: An Archaeology of the Human Sciences* (trans. A. Sheridan), London: Tavistock.

—— (1977) *Discipline and Punish: The Birth of the Prison* (trans. A. Sheridan), London: Allen Lane.

—— (1979) *The History of Sexuality, Volume 1: An Introduction* (trans. R. Hurley), London: Allen Lane.

—— (1991) 'Governmentality', in G. Burchill, C. Gordon and P. Miller (eds) *The Foucault Effect: Studies in Governmentality*, Hemel Hempstead: Harvester Wheatsheaf.

Fowler, P.J. (1992) *The Past in Contemporary Society: Then, Now*, London: Routledge.

Franklin, S. (1995) 'Science as culture, cultures of science', *Annual Review of Anthropology*, 24, pp. 163–84.

Fyfe, G. (1996) 'A Trojan Horse at the Tate: theorizing the museum as agency and structure', in S. Macdonald and G. Fyfe (eds) *Theorizing Museums*, pp. 203–28, Oxford: Blackwell.

Giddens, A. (1990) *The Consequences of Modernity*, Cambridge: Polity.

Gieryn, T.F. (1998) 'Balancing acts: science, *Enola Gay* and history wars at the Smithsonian', in S. Macdonald (ed.) *The Politics of Display*, London: Routledge.

Greenhalgh, P. (1988) *Ephemeral Vistas: The Expositions Universelles, Great Exhibitions and World's Fairs, 1851–1939*, Manchester: Manchester University Press.

Gross, P.R. and N. Levitt (1994) *Higher Superstition: The Academic Left and its Quarrel with Science*, Baltimore, MD: Johns Hopkins University Press.

Hackman, W. (1992) ' "Wonders in one closet shut": the educational potential of history of science museums', in J. Durant (ed.) *Museums and the Public Understanding of Science*, pp. 65–9, London: Science Museum in association with the Committee on the Public Understanding of Science.

Hall, S. (1980) 'Encoding/decoding', in S. Hall, D. Hobson, A. Lowe and P. Willis (eds) *Culture, Media, Language*, pp. 128–38, London: Hutchinson.

Haraway, D. (1989) *Private Visions*, London: Routledge.

Harding, S. (1986) *The Science Questions in Feminism*, Milton Keynes: Open University Press.

Harvey, P. (1996) *Hybrids of Modernity: Anthropology, the Nation-state and the Universal Exhibition*, London: Routledge.

—— (1998) 'Nations on display: technology and culture in Expo '92', in S. Macdonald (ed.) *The Politics of Display*, London: Routledge.

Hein, H. (1990) *The Exploratorium: The Museum as Laboratory*, Washington, DC: Smithsonian Institution.

Hewison, R. (1988) *The Heritage Industry*, London: Methuen.

Hooper-Greenhill, E. (1992) *Museums and the Shaping of Knowledge*, London: Routledge.

Hoyau, P. (1988) 'Heritage and "the conserver society": the French case' (trans. C. Turner), in R. Lumley (ed.) *The Museum Time-machine*, pp. 27–35, London: Comedia/Routledge.

Hunter, J.D. (1991) *Culture Wars: The Struggle to Define America*, New York: Basic Books.

Impey, O.R. and A.G. MacGregor (eds) (1985) *The Origins of Museums*, Oxford: Clarendon Press.

Irwin, A. and B. Wynne (1996) 'Introduction', in A. Irwin and B. Wynne (eds) *Misunderstanding Science? The Public Reconstruction of Science and Technology*, pp. 1–17, Cambridge: Cambridge University Press.

James, A., J. Hockey and A. Dawson (eds) (1997) *After Writing Culture*, London: Routledge.

Jenkins, D. (1994) 'Object lessons and ethnographic displays: museum exhibitions and the making of American anthropology', *Comparative Studies in Society and History*, 36 (2), pp. 242–70.

Jones, D. (1992) 'Dealing with the past', *Museum Journal* (January), pp. 24–7.

Jordanova, L. (1989) 'Objects of knowledge: a historical perspective on museums', in P. Vergo (ed.) *The New Museology*, pp. 22–40, London: Reaktion Books.

Kaplan, F.E.S. (ed.) (1994) *Museums and the Making of 'Ourselves': The Role of Objects in National Identity*, Leicester and London: Leicester University Press.

Karp, I. and S. Lavine (eds) (1991) *Exhibiting Cultures: The Poetics and Politics of Museum Display*, Washington, DC: Smithsonian Institution.

Karp, I., C.M. Kreamer and S. Lavine (eds) (1992) *Museums and Communities: The Politics of Public Culture*, Washington, DC: Smithsonian Institution.

Lash, S. and J. Urry (1994) *Economies of Signs and Space*, London: Sage.

Latour, B. (1987) *Science in Action*, Cambridge, MA: Harvard University Press.

Law, J. (1991) 'Introduction: monsters, machines and sociotechnical relations', in J. Law (ed.) *A Sociology of Monsters: Essays on Power, Technology and Domination* (*Sociological Review* monograph), pp. 1–23, London: Routledge.

—— (1993) *Organizing Modernity: Social Ordering and Social Theory*, Oxford: Blackwell.

Lewenstein, B.V. (1992) 'The meaning of "public understanding of science" in the United States after World War II', *Public Understanding of Science*, 1, pp. 45–68.

Lindqvist, T. (1993) 'An Olympic stadium of technology: Deutsches Museum and Sweden's Tekniska Museet', in B. Schroeder-Gudehus (ed.) *Industrial Society and its Museums, 1880–1990: Social Aspirations and Cultural Politics*, pp. 37–54, Chur, Switzerland: Harwood Academic/Paris: Cité des sciences et de l'industrie.

Linenthal, E.T. and T. Engelhardt (eds) (1996) *History Wars: The Enola Gay and Other Battles for the American Past*, New York: Metropolitan Books/Holt.

Macdonald, S. (1996) 'Theorizing museums: an introduction', in S. Macdonald and G. Fyfe (eds) *Theorizing Museums: Representing Identity and Diversity in a Changing World* (*Sociological Review* monograph), pp. 1–18, Oxford: Blackwell.

—— (ed.) (1998) *The Politics of Display*, London: Routledge.

McGuigan, J. (1996) *Culture and the Public Sphere*, London: Routledge.

Markus, T. (1993) *Buildings and Power: Freedom and Control in the Origin of Modern Building Types*, London: Routledge.

Merriman, N. (1991) *Beyond the Glass Case: The Past, the Heritage and the Public in Britain*, Leicester and London: Leicester University Press.

Mitchell, T. (1991) *Colonizing Egypt*, Berkeley and Los Angeles, CA: California University Press.

Nader, L. (ed.) (1996a) *Naked Science: Anthropological Inquiry into Boundaries, Power, and Knowledge*, London: Routledge.

—— (1996b) 'Preface', in L. Nader (ed.) *Naked Science: Anthropological Inquiry into Boundaries, Power, and Knowledge*, pp. xi–xv, London: Routledge.

Outram, D. (1996) 'New spaces in natural history', in N. Jardine, J. A. Secord and E.C. Spary (eds) *Cultures of Natural History*, pp. 249–65, Cambridge: Cambridge University Press.

Pearce, S. (ed.) (1996) *Exploring Science in Museums*, London and Atlantic Highlands, NJ: Athlone.

Pickstone, J. (1994) 'Museological science? The place of the analytical/comparative in nineteenth-century science, technology and medicine', *History of Science*, 32 (2), pp. 111–38.

Poulot, D. (1994) 'Identity as self-discovery: the ecomuseum in France', in D. Sherman and I. Rogoff (eds) *Museum Culture*, pp. 66–84, London: Routledge.

Prösler, M. (1996) 'Museums and globalization', in S. Macdonald and G. Fyfe (eds) *Theorizing Museums* (*Sociological Review* monograph), pp. 21–44, Oxford: Blackwell.

Rosaldo, R. (1993) *Culture and Truth: The Remaking of Social Analysis*, London: Routledge.

Ross, M. (1995) '"Passive smoking": controversy at the Science Museum?', *Science as Culture*, 5 (1), no. 22, pp. 147–51.

Rydell, R.W. (1984) *All the World's a Fair: Visions of Empire at American International Expositions, 1876–1916*, Chicago: Chicago University Press.

—— (1993) *World of Fairs: The Century-of-Progress Expositions*, Chicago: University of Chicago Press.

Shapin, S. (1994) *A Social History of Truth: Civility and Science in Seventeenth-century England*, Chicago: Chicago University Press.

Sheets-Pyenson, S. (1989) *Cathedrals of Science: The Development of Colonial Natural History Museums during the Late Nineteenth Century*, Montreal: McGill University Press.

Silverstone, R. (1989) 'Heritage as media: some implications for research', in D. Uzzell (ed.) *Heritage Interpretation, Volume 2: The Visitor Experience*, pp. 138–48, London: Frances Pinter.

—— (1992) 'The medium is the museum: on objects and logics in times and spaces', in J. Durant (ed.) *Museums and the Public Understanding of Science*, pp. 34–42, London: Science Museum in association with the Committee on the Public Understanding of Science.

Social Text (1996) (special issue on 'The Science Wars', ed. A. Ross) (Spring/Summer), 46–7.

Star, S.L. (1988) 'Introduction: the sociology of science and technology', *Social Problems*, 35, pp. 197–205.

Staudenmaier, J.M. (1993) 'Clean exhibits, messy exhibits: Henry Ford's technological aesthetic', in B. Schroeder-Gudehus (ed.) *Industrial Society and its Museums, 1880–1990: Social Aspirations and Cultural Politics*, pp. 55–65, Chur, Switzerland: Harwood Academic/Paris: Cité des sciences et de l'industrie.

Stocking, G.W. (ed.) (1985) *Objects and Others: Essays on Museums and Material Culture*, Madison, WI: Wisconsin University Press.

Tilley, C. (ed.) (1990) *Reading Material Culture*, Oxford: Blackwell.

Traweek, S. (1993) 'An introduction to cultural, gender, and social studies of science and technology', *Journal of Culture, Medicine and Psychiatry*, 17, pp. 3–25.

Urry, J. (1996) 'How societies remember the past', in S. Macdonald and G. Fyfe (eds) *Theorizing Museums*, pp. 45–65, Oxford: Blackwell.

Walsh, K. (1992) *The Representation of the Past: Museums and Heritage in the Post-modern World*, London: Routledge.

Waters, M. (1995) *Globalization*, London: Routledge.

Woolgar, S. (1988a) *Science: The Very Idea*, Chichester: Ellis Horwood/London: Tavistock.

—— (ed.) (1988b) *Knowledge and Reflexivity: New Frontiers in the Sociology of Knowledge*, London: Sage.

Wynne, B. (1996) 'Misunderstood misunderstandings: social identities and the public uptake of science', in A. Irwin and B. Wynne (eds) *Misunderstanding Science? The Public Reconstruction of Science and Technology*, pp. 19–46, Cambridge: Cambridge University Press.

Chapter 11

Nuclear Reactions

The (Re)Presentation of Hiroshima at the National Air and Space Museum

Timothy W. Luke

HERE WE RECONSIDER the controversy at the National Air and Space Museum in Washington, D.C., that arose in 1995 over the abrupt cancellation of the heavily criticized exhibition *The Crossroads: The End of World War II, the Atomic Bomb, and the Origins of the Cold War*. As the proposed title indicates, the show was to have examined the inter-connections between the atomic bomb, the bombing of Hiroshima and Nagasaki, and the atomic stalemate of the Cold War by commemorating the fifty years since V-J Day with a display of the partially restored *Enola Gay*. After the rhetorical brawling sparked by *The West as America* show, however, those broader educational goals were dropped in favor of a narrower patriotic fete for the airplane and her crew without any discussion of the atomic bomb or the Cold War.

While this event has been understood as a crass case of political censorship, I want to see it as symptomatic of far larger and more volatile ideological battles in America's culture wars.[1] James Davison Hunter argues that 'America is in the midst of a culture war that has and will continue to have reverberations not only within public policy but within the lives of ordinary Americans everywhere,' and this cultural conflict can be understood as 'political and social hostility rooted in different systems of moral understanding.'[2] Although he strangely ignores museums, Hunter argues that '*it is in the context of institutional structures that cultural conflict becomes crystallized*, because *cultural conflict is ultimately about the struggle for domination*.'[3] And domination always is well worth struggling to attain within any institutional structure in as much as it means getting power. Cultural forms of power are the most potent, because they carry a vital prerogative: 'the power to define reality . . . nothing less is at stake than a sense of justice and fair play, an assurance that life

Source: *Museum Politics: Power Plays at the Exhibition*, Minneapolis: University of Minnesota Press, 2002, pp. 19–36.

is as it should be, indeed, nothing less is at stake than a way of life.'[4] Most battles in these culture wars center on defining 'a way of life' with sufficient moral authority to assure everyone that 'life is as it should be.' These undercurrents pulled strongly on the body politic in the 2000 presidential election as Vice President Al Gore's cerebral understandings of the country's contemporary challenges were tested in the voting booth against Texas Governor George W. Bush's gut checks of America's more traditional heritage. Today in the United States many fights are triggered by museum exhibitions, as the nasty polemics about 'political correctness' in *The West as America* show at the National Museum of American Art . . . illustrates.[5]

Occurring in the fiftieth anniversary year of the end of World War II, the patriotic uproar over the exhibit's alleged 'political incorrectness' caused great consternation on both sides of the Pacific, but this chapter looks beyond and behind the international affair to examine how the Hiroshima bombing first was to be put on display, and then was moved off center stage, in the exhibition at the Air and Space Museum. Eager to counterattack any resistance to its conservative and nationalistic (re)imagination of America's exceptional moral mission and uncontestable global power after the USSR's defeat in the Cold War, cultural conservatives seized onto the meaning of historical artifacts and events, like the *Enola Gay*, the Little Boy A-bomb, or Hiroshima, to reaffirm them as instances of 'strategic necessity,' 'good decision making,' or 'world-class engineering.'

Even though these artifacts' dark magic as signs of nuclear credibility for the Cold War deterrence system of mutually assured thermonuclear destruction is no longer essential, any other commemorative assessments, which might attempt to recall their Cold War-era significance, are censored as politically incorrect. After World War II, America's nuclear monopoly was meant to keep the USSR in line. Stalin breached the monopoly in 1949, and Brezhnev brought the USSR up to nuclear parity with the United States by the early 1970s. The balance of terror lasted nearly three generations until the Soviet Union simply collapsed in 1991. Fifty years after Pearl Harbor, then, America's superpower once again became essentially a monopoly. While a few might question the nature of such superpower, many others stigmatize such questioning as left-wing 'political correctness.' Therefore, the cultural right as well as the seventy-somethings of the World War II generation would coalign to use the *Enola Gay* as a sign of celebration, victory, and deliverance from totalitarianism. As Speaker of the House Newt Gingrich declared, 'political correctness may be O.K. in some faculty lounge, but the Smithsonian is a treasure that belongs to the American people and it should not become a plaything for left-wing ideologies.'[6]

Recognizing this generational division is quite important. The Manhattan Project, B-29s, Hiroshima, and World War II Axis surrenders are one constellation of particular geopolitical icons, but they have a very specific historical meaning for most people over sixty. Moreover, a peculiar state formation – American superpower in World War II's Grand Alliance of United Nations as well as the victorious Cold War protagonist over the now vanquished USSR – has had a vested interest in associating these symbols in particular ideological contexts that attained stable canonical forms in many social/political/moral/economic/cultural networks from 1945 to 1995. Because these ideological frameworks anchored political debate and social alliances for nearly fifty years, publicly funded national museums, like the National Air and Space Museum, have always played a significant role in the 'history-making process' by associating heroic human beings, whether they were ordinary Americans at work in Manhattan Project labs, GIs at war in the U.S. Army Air Force, or Japanese victims in Hiroshima, with nonhuman objects, like B-29 aircraft or atomic bombs, in spectacular performances of American power during the Cold War.[7]

By memorializing various important linkages between war, technical innovation, peace, and organizational development in the technoscience practices of flight, the Air and Space Museum has always served explicitly on many levels as a high-visibility memorial to the fight that was World War II. It implicitly also has been a celebration of America's continuing nuclear strengths, providing a point of pride in the struggle against communism. After defeating fascism in the 1940s and communism in the 1990s, most Americans, as then-Speaker of the House Newt Gingrich claimed, are 'sick and tired of being told by some cultural elite that they ought to be ashamed of their country.'[8]

So the surviving flyboys of World War II imagined that the *Enola Gay* should serve, like the airplanes at the Pima Air and Space Museum, as a unique memorial to that war and America's triumphant superpower in 1945 *and* 1995: a purpose that the museum's curators openly acknowledged as legitimate.[9] Yet, in an effort to give some textured historical balance to a fiftieth-anniversary celebration of that power's costs and benefits, the curators wanted to append some memoranda of liabilities (the Cold War, nuclear terror, atomic tests, nuclear fuel cycle dangers, Japanese bomb victims, etc.) to the memorial, which clearly expressed another set of cultural associations with the *Enola Gay* for many people under the age of fifty. From these efforts to be objective, a firestorm erupted, mostly over the nature of these ideological associations and political subjectivity in America after the Cold War.

Factuality and fictiveness can become the objects of pitched rhetorical battles as history gets remade by museum displays, particularly if, as was the case with the *Enola Gay*, many of the original 'history makers' are still around to help refine and/or define what is fact and what is fiction. The display of artifacts, the discourse of historical authenticity, and the disposition of individual agency all must come together in history museums to show how 'this presentness' followed from 'that pastness.' The 1990s 'as a present' were made possible by events in the 1940s 'as a past,' but who should be, or will be, allowed now to remember then, and for whom, and in what fashion? These interpretative issues are unstable isotopes, and a critical mass of ideological contradictions inseparably chained to American superpower rapidly initiated many nuclear reactions to how the *Enola Gay* might be displayed at the Air and Space Museum. To discover the permissible political possibilities of 'who, whom' in these equations of intergenerational translation and ideological purification, one can reread the politics of complex cultural contradictions behind their aesthetic and rhetorical implementation in museum displays. Therefore, any museum's displays of meaningful divisions between the past and the present have a distinctly politicized character as founding writs of our reality. Indeed, relations of power and powerlessness in the world at large script such social ontologies unfolding at the core of museum exhibits.

Collision at 'The Crossroads'

The ferocious political combat over America's past at the National Air and Space Museum can be chalked up, in part, to the prestige of the venue itself. As a major institution receiving public monies to display cultural truths in the nation's capital city, this museum might be expected to appear 'objective' or 'nonpartisan,' because it is at these places that America, in some sense, tells its stories to itself in the broadest possible terms.[10] Hence, in an August 1994 *Washington Post* op-ed piece, The National Air and Space Museum's director, Martin Harwit, argued: 'This is our responsibility, as a national museum in a democracy predicated on an informed citizenry. We have found no way to exhibit the *Enola Gay* and satisfy everyone. But a comprehensive and thoughtful discussion can help us learn from history. And this is what we aim to offer our visitors.'[11] Yet it was precisely such rhetorical assumptions about objectivity or partisanship that the authors of *The Crossroads* script ended up contesting. If the terms of 'how' we learn from history and 'what' history we actually learn conflict, then the museum performance often must justify why it varies from what visitors expect.

As it was constructed by national media and the Smithsonian Institution from *The Crossroads* script, *The Last Act* exhibition, which was what the show came to be labeled after the media controversy, had fairly complex origins, because it was designed with the negative reactions to *The West as America* show at the National Museum of American Art during 1991 very much in mind.[12] To commemorate the fiftieth anniversary of the atomic bombings of Japan by the United States in 1945, the Smithsonian Institution's National Air and Space Museum drew up plans in 1993 and 1994 to stage a major display around a thorough renovation of the *Enola Gay*, which was the B-29 Superfortress that dropped the Little Boy U-238 fission bomb on Hiroshima. It sought to defuse public criticism by circulating the show's script among all interested groups as a strategy to vet the exhibit; indeed, it already had disassociated the *Enola Gay* from another exhibit on strategic bombing planned during the late 1980s.[13]

Harwit's sense of the *Enola Gay* exhibit, however, proved prophetic as he recalled the earliest discussions on the exhibition at the Smithsonian: 'There were two points everyone agreed on. One, this is a historically significant aircraft. Two, no matter what the museum did, we'd screw it up.'[14] Consequently, the Smithsonian sought to allay public criticism by circulating the script among any interested group to vet the exhibit.[15] Yet when the authors shipped their proposed script out to historians, military experts, and World War II servicemen, intense protests began almost immediately. Most importantly, the Air Force Association (an organization for retired and active personnel of the U.S. Air Force) and the American Legion (a national veteran's association) quickly mounted a massive lobbying offensive against the exhibition in the media and Congress to pressure the Smithsonian into excising its allegedly 'revisionist' representations of the atomic bombings of Hiroshima and Nagasaki from the 1945 commemoration.[16]

As originally conceived, the exhibition went well beyond already ideologically stabilized renditions of the Manhattan Project's technological heroics to ask why the bombs were dropped, who had been harmed when they exploded, and what has been the influence of nuclear weaponry in the post-1945 world.[17] As the newly inaugurated Secretary of the Smithsonian, I. Michael Heyman, claimed at his investiture in September 1994, this approach was legitimate. A former chancellor of the University of California, he asserted, 'The Smithsonian could have avoided controversy by ignoring the anniversary, simply displaying the *Enola Gay* without comment, setting forth only the justification for the use of atomic weapons without either reporting the contrary arguments or indicating the impact of the bombs on the ground. My view is that the Smithsonian has a broader role than simply displaying items in the so-called nation's attic or eschewing important topics because of the political difficulties created by an exhibition.'[18]

Consequently, the original script for *The Crossroads* exhibit was to have examined much of the post-1945 infighting over whether Washington should have dropped the bombs, the cultural significance of seeing all those burnt bodies of women and children from the blast zones in Japan, and the discursive elaboration of the nuclear mythos from the Cold War era that first arose out of the mushroom cloud over Hiroshima.[19] These historically valid associations, however, were impure ideological translations, which threatened existing forms of political detachment from nuclear war. Veteran's groups claimed these displays were both 'too soft' on Japanese aggression in World War II and 'too hard' on American servicemen who sacrificed their lives to defeat Imperial Japan. Responding to such protests, the Smithsonian removed material that some historians considered critical for understanding what happened when and why. Other historians then denounced the revised script as a 'historical cleansing' that substituted patriotic propaganda for careful commentary. After nine major rewrites, and in the face of threatened reductions in funding, the Smithsonian simply threw in the towel during January 1995.[20]

Rather than staging a major display about Hiroshima and atomic weapons, the National Air and Space Museum did exactly what Heyman promised it would not do a few months earlier. That is, it merely brought out pieces of the B-29 airplane itself, displaying a large section of the *Enola Gay* fuselage with bland news release copy about Hiroshima along with a celebratory short film about this B-29 and its crew to mark this major anniversary in world, American, and Japanese history. Even this was seen as blasphemous by many. The surviving members of the 509th Composite Group, which was the unit formed in September 1944 to deliver America's atomic bombs, had been angry for years that the *Enola Gay* was not already fully restored. Its pilot, Brigadier General Paul W. Tibbets Jr., described this display 'without wings, engines and propellers, landing gear and tail assembly' as a 'package of insults' that accentuates 'the aura of evil in which the airplane is being cast.'[21]

The *Enola Gay* has had a checkered history after being handpicked by then Lieutenant Colonel Tibbets from the Martin Aircraft factory line in Omaha, Nebraska, in May 1945. On 6 August 1945, Tibbets flew this B-29 over Hiroshima, while his crew delivered the first atomic bomb on any city in war. During the summer of 1946 the *Enola Gay* was retired from active service. It was put into storage at Davis-Monthan Air Force Base in Tucson, Arizona, until restored to operational condition and flown in 1948 to Chicago, where it was deeded into the Smithsonian's inventory. It sat out in the open on a parking apron at Andrews Air Force Base in Maryland from 1953 until 1960, when it was disassembled and moved to Silver Hill, Maryland. In 1984 a thorough mechanical renovation was begun on the *Enola Gay*, but after a million dollars and nearly eleven years of work, one engine and the forward section of the fuselage were all that was ready for display in June 1995.[22] This somewhat ambivalent treatment of the airplane over the past five decades perhaps reflected the division within the American public over its ultimate historical importance and cultural meaning. Is it the penultimate artifact of American victory in World War II or the first dark signifier of the Cold War's atomic stalemate? For those born after 1945, many of whom, ironically, could be born only because of Hiroshima, since their fathers might otherwise have been cut down on the beaches while invading Japan, the *Enola Gay* represented not deliverance from war but delivery to a world of mutually assured thermonuclear destruction. The *Enola Gay* is – like so many other sites in the 1990s – a flashback to the 1960s rather than the 1940s, reflecting an ongoing generational struggle for power and identity.

As Air and Space Museum Director Martin Harwit suggested, 'the commemoration the Museum has planned is designed largely for the benefit of those generations of Americans too young to remember how the war ended. It is they who will have the most to gain from the lessons to be learned.'[23] Particular political subjects, like any American too young to remember the 1940s or even the 1960s, would have much to gain or lose as political agents from the lessons to be museum-learned, not book-learned/school-learned/film-learned, from the curators of *The Crossroads*. In many ways, the exhibition was simply designed to show-case a collage of diverse perspectives on the atomic bombings, leaving it up to the viewer/visitor to conclude what the key messages were in its complex arrays of information.

Radical differences in historical perspective, such as those ignited by *The Last Act* controversy, typically are not taken as honest disagreements over either the raw facts or those various sets of individual and group assumptions that often let the same facts speak differently to assorted sets of listeners. As one negative analysis noted, the American veterans claimed the exhibition 'turned history upside down, casting Japan as a victim rather than the aggressor, and implying American servicemen were little more than war criminals. Moreover, *Enola Gay* was presented as an impure hybrid, symbolizing nuclear terror, rather than as a machine that brought a rapid end to an agonizing war. The veterans said the display failed to reflect the sentiments and realities that existed in 1945, but instead promoted the antinuclear leanings of the museum's curators 50 years later.'[24] As the *Washington Post* concluded, 'what's taking place is a tug-of-war for the perceptions of future generations between those whose political sensibilities remain anchored in the anti-government, anti-war sentiments of the Vietnam era and those whose perspectives include allowances for other times and all other circumstances.'[25] Once again, it was 'the 1960s generation' refusing to grow up or make sensitive allowances for other times and circumstances. As Major General Chuck Sweeney – the only man to fly on both the Hiroshima and Nagasaki missions – observed about the planned exhibit, 'I don't need some '60s-type professor poisoning the minds of our kids about how terrible America was.'[26] Ironically, it was an attempt to make allowances for other times and circumstances, including those of the Japanese victims and non-Japanese onlookers, that was in play in *The Last Act* exhibition.

Instead of *The Last Act* being the product of forty-something American New Left longmarchers through the institutions, refusing to countenance the times and circumstances of seventy-something ex-GIs, it actually was planned carefully by two foreign immigrants to America. Martin Harwit, the Air and Space Museum director, was born in Prague in 1931, raised in Istanbul, and educated at Oberlin and MIT after coming to the United States in 1946. His appraisal of nuclear weapons was cultivated at the Pacific atoll H-bomb test sites in the 1950s, when he served as a physicist for the U.S. Army to assess thermonuclear weapon effects. As the Smithsonian's project manager, Tom Crouch, noted, the *Enola Gay* exhibit 'was really Harwit's baby,' because 'he had seen himself what nuclear weapons can do and felt strongly about their danger.'[27] Harwit's other key aide, Michael Neufeld, is a Canadian citizen born in 1951. Educated at the University of Calgary in the 1970s (which the *Washington Post* took special pains to note is located in Canada, or that country where young Americans fled 'to escape the Vietnam War'), he is a historian, specializing in German aerospace technologies of the Nazi era.

Even so, Harwit and Neufeld's script shipwrecked on the reefs of the Smithsonian's higher managerial and outside advisory boards at the very beginning of its voyage through a public review process. In July 1993, Smithsonian Secretary Adams protested mightily against the preliminary plans, asserting there was a lack of 'what will be perceived by some as balance' in what 'should be an exhibit commemorating the end of World War II . . . I continue to be uneasy that later sections of the planning document treat fully the horrors of the bombing. . . . but do not present in adequate depth . . . the horrors experienced by the Americans during the island invasions culminating with Okinawa.'[28] However, it was former congressman and Smithsonian regent Barber Conable who put the sharpest point on the disagreement's general outlines at this juncture. An ex-marine who had been slated to hit the beach in Japan until the Hiroshima bomb fell on Honshu and the Nagasaki explosion visited Kyushu, he saw the curators' allowances for views from other (non-American) times and circumstances in these terms: 'I think it would be a big mistake to take that approach . . . Do you want . . . an exhibition intended to make veterans feel good, or do you want an exhibition that will lead our visitors to think about the consequences of the atomic bombing of Japan? Frankly, I don't think we can do both.'[29]

Here is the conflict *in nuce*. The curators wanted visitors to think about the consequences of bombing Japan with atomic weapons and their links to the Cold War, but in 1995 (during the fiftieth anniversary of the end of World War II) museum directors and regents also wanted veterans to feel good. The parameters for shaping political subjectivity through memory were at odds with the impulse to use this commemorative moment either to induce guilty introspection or to entertain strong national pride. As Conable sagely warned, the vantage points of retired American servicemen who had been close to contemplating Japanese beachheads from an LCI under heavy fire in March 1946 cannot mix with those of one-time Japanese bomb victims who had been floundering in rain gutters near ground zero at Hiroshima to cool their radiation burns in August 1945. In this environment, the veterans prevailed, particularly once the surviving *Enola Gay* crew members weighed in. Now eighty years old, but still 'hale and hearty,' General Tibbets asserted that Harwit and Neufeld's interpretations were little more than 'a package of insults' in which '*Enola Gay* has been miscast, and a group of valiant Americans have had their role in history treated shamefully.' Another World War II B-29 crewman noted, 'There is no need to glorify it, but there's no need to denigrate it, either.'[30]

As the *Wall Street Journal* put it, the Smithsonian Institution is 'the American museum whose business it is to tell the nation's story,' and in the case of *The Last Act* exhibition (as well as the earlier *The West as America* show) there is a sense that the Smithsonian 'now is in the hands of academics unable to view American history as anything other than a woeful catalogue of crimes and aggressions against the helpless peoples of the earth.'[31] John Correll, editor in chief of *Air Force Magazine*, saw no place for conflicted interpretations or ambivalent views in the nation's appraisal of Hiroshima. In his magazine, he argued that the decision to drop the two bombs was 'a legitimate military action taken to end the war and save lives'; hence, no one should be exposed to 'countercultural morality pageants put on by academic activists.'[32] The distinct possibility that questioning the decision could be part of the nation's story or that the story is, at least, contradictory, contestable, inflicted seemed utterly out of the question. Yet what is in dispute here?

Assertions in *The Crossroads* script, such as the following, are what the American Legion protested. Are they distorted or decontextualized? 'For most Americans, this . . . [World War II] was a war of vengeance. For most Japanese, it was a war to defend their unique culture against Western imperialism.'[33] For most Americans, World War II was a brutal war of vengeance to deliver retribution for Pearl Harbor, Bataan, and Corregidor. John Wayne, Humphrey Bogart, and Ronald Reagan attest to this truth over and over again every week, in old war movies on American Movie Classics or Turner Network Television. And from the Tokugawa shogunate's designation of Nagasaki as Japan's only open port in 1639 to Fat Man's descent from another B-29, *Bockscar*, over Nagasaki 1945, Japan's rulers did see themselves defending their unique culture against Western imperialism, first by closing the country to outsiders, and later (thanks to Commodore Matthew Perry's entreaties at Edo in 1854) by emulating Western-style imperialist methods against non-Western (China, Korea, Russia) foes and sites and then, later, Western (British, French, Dutch, American colonies) foes and sites. Japan under imperial war governments was not a helpless Third World victim, but plainly the West also had been an aggressor.[34] Two wrongs do not make a right, but two different rights seemed to have ended with a wrong.

In a less anti-intellectual time or in a more intellectual culture, such complexities in Japanese and American memories of World War II might be appreciated, even though they might not make us 'feel good.' Because American GIs in the years 1941–5 were almost totally ignorant about Japan and its history, and because they and their children learned little during the Cold War, these facts were seen as 'revisionist, unbalanced and offensive,' as Senator Nancy Kassenbaum (R-Kansas) dictated in her condemnatory Senate resolution against *The Last Act* exhibition.[35] Given this fact, it is no surprise that Tokyo now invests in blockbuster cultural exchanges to explain Japan's history to America's public. And because Japanese subjects were essentially ignorant about how America had been attacked by the Imperial war machine from 1941 to 1945, they could not comprehend the apparent operational necessity for staging atomic bombing strikes as a contextually warranted strategy, a blow of righteous retribution concocted by balanced democratic decision makers. Still, in sacrificing the possibilities of seeing how such contradictions always coexist uneasily in the specific context of struggle, in order to stage another sort of truly revisionist, unbalanced, offensive 'feel good' commemoration of World War II at the

Smithsonian, another vital opportunity for cultivating the faculties of such historical/ moral reasoning was lost.

The line taken by the American Legion ultimately set the tempo for the whole affair inasmuch as William M. Detweiler, the Legion's national commander, concluded that the National Air and Space Museum was badly damaged by 'its own mismanagement and zeal for revisionist history.'[36] After going through a line-by-line rewrite of the exhibit's 500-page script, spending nearly $300,000 to revise the display, and managing a firestorm of protest that led to eighty-two members of Congress demanding the removal of the Air and Space Museum's Director, Martin Harwit, and the exhibition's curator, Michael Neufeld, the Smithsonian Institution's Secretary, I. Michael Heyman, canceled the planned exhibition on 30 January 1995. Heyman thought it premature to dismiss Harwit in the midst of such a passionate public protest, but promised to 'look with great care at the management of [the] Air and Space [Museum] in an organized way.'[37] Sensing how volatile these museumological escapades of rhetorical reexamination were becoming, both houses of Congress planned separate hearings on the *Enola Gay* exhibition. Newly appointed Smithsonian regent Senator Thad Cochran (R-Mississippi) promised to recommend to the Senate Rules Committee, now chaired, strangely enough, by Senator Ted Stevens of Alaska, that the Senate would consider 'how the Smithsonian will be managed in the future and what standards will be developed for interpretive exhibits.'[38]

Acts of direct legislation from the halls of Congress, then, promised to recenter the actions of indirect legislation propounded by the Smithsonian Institution in its exhibition halls. Congress, of course, rarely does anything quickly or right, but in this case it moved with great dispatch far to the right by promising to investigate the ties behind art, history, and subjectivity. In the meantime, Smithsonian Secretary Heyman promised to stage the sort of exhibition that he thought Congress would be comfortable having all Americans visit. That is, 'the new exhibition should be a much simpler one, essentially a display, permitting the *Enola Gay* and its crew to speak for themselves . . . with labels that don't get into the wisdom, necessity and morality of using atomic weapons.'[39] Finally, in complete frustration, Harwit resigned in May 1995, leaving the museum's now heavily bowdlerized exhibition to celebrate the *Enola Gay* simply as an airplane.[40]

Revealing the first draft

Even though Heyman canceled Harwit and Neufeld's exhibition, parts and pieces of *The Last Act* were displayed in Washington during the summer of the fiftieth-anniversary of the end of World War II. They appeared, however, at two different venues. At the Air and Space Museum, a massive propeller and engine, the vertical tail fin, and two-thirds of the *Enola Gay* fuselage, which displayed the cockpit, bombardier's station, and bomb bay, were put on display for an indefinite run in late June.[41] The maximum daily capacity was 3,000 visitors, admitted by a timed-ticket system to the display, which revolved around a sixteen-minute film featuring the crew and their memories of the mission. Beyond the basic 'who, what, where, when, why' of the aircraft, its crew, and the Hiroshima bombing, the exhibition's wall captions said very little other than acknowledging the obvious: 'Something more than an airplane,' the *Enola Gay* now fifty years later 'seems almost larger than life; as much an icon, now, as an airplane. After all this time, it still evokes intense emotions from gratitude to grief, its polished surface reflecting the myriad feelings and meanings and memories we bring before it.'

Aptly reflecting the divisions in the nation over the exhibition, American University hosted a second, very low-profile display of artifacts and images from Hiroshima and Nagasaki that Harwit had planned to integrate into the Air and Space Museum show. Titled *Constructing a Peaceful World: Beyond Hiroshima and Nagasaki*, this show ran from 9 July through 27 July 1995 at the University's Butler Pavilion.[42] Nearly 20 percent of this exhibit's materials were to have completed the *Enola Gay* display, ranging from photographs of the blast damage at ground zero to a charred school lunchbox filled with the ashes of peas and rice left behind as its owner was burned to death by the blast. Facts, figures, and faces that are ignored at the Air and Space Museum were, however, named at the American University exhibit.

Indeed, this was its most telling difference from the Air and Space Museum show. The Hiroshima lunchbox's owner is named: Shigeru Orimen, a middle-school student. And the fact that it was his mother who found his unidentifiable body and the lunchbox also is recorded. Like the pieces and parts of the *Enola Gay*, these efforts to put another face on Hiroshima's inhabitants also tell a story from 6 August 1945 about other hybridizing associations of humans and machines. Unlike glorious war stories from the *Enola Gay's* crew, these exhibits, as the American University administrator overseeing the show noted, presented 'something people just don't want to think about.'[43] And while attendance was capped at 3,000 a day for the *Enola Gay* display, the paucity of visitors to the American University exhibition suggested a much more difficult subject matter; attendance there hit only 80 to 100 a day over its three-week run.

Here is where Harwit's and Neufeld's project violated all of the rules for the museum's discursive power play. In posing a moral conflict at the center of the Manhattan Project, and in exposing political contradictions in a liberal democratic state choosing to conduct nuclear warfare against civilian targets in a fascist empire, the original *Enola Gay* script remembered World War II in Strangelovian Cold War terms, associated Tibbets's 509th Composite Group with thousands of charred corpses in Hiroshima instead of millions of cheering citizens on V-J day, connected FDR's atomic bomb project with Hitler's atomic bomb project, and unified the *Enola Gay* with the start of a thermonuclearized cold war with the USSR instead of the end of conventionalized hot war with the Axis. The Cold War linkages between good humans (America's heroic B-29 flyers) and bad nonhumans (Japan's defeated militarists) shifted their ideological polarities to and fro, collectivizing good nonhumans (A-bomb artifacts) with bad humans (Hiroshima's and Nagasaki's dead women and children).

These more reflexive associations were taken as impure mistranslations, particularly when those aviators, who are now old veterans, sought a memorial to their acts rather than ambivalent post-Cold War introspection. Rather than simply presenting historic objects as authentic relics of the glorious past, which would respect the detachment of the visitors from the material as well as the separation of museum representations from external realities, *The Last Act* narrative openly crossed the road of apparent objectivity with its abstract universal point of view to follow its own concretely subjective path of antinuclear remembrance. The canonical collect- ivization of the *Enola Gay* with V-J Day parades, postwar prosperity, and American superpower was recoded in highly contradictive terms, confusing the *Enola Gay* with blast effects at Hiroshima's hypocenter, postwar radiation deaths, fifty years of nuclear proliferation. Furthermore, fifty years after the defeat of Nazi Germany and five years after the collapse of the USSR's empire in Eastern Europe, it was no longer as clear whether the bombings were worth the cost.

In the mid-1990s, America's military superpower often seemed almost irrelev- ant. Accordingly, the need felt by World War II veterans to memorialize America's once-vaunted military prowess taps into deeper fears about collective identity and purpose for the United States in the future. Many seventy-something members of the World War II generation wanted a second vindication for Hiroshima and Nagasaki in as much as these two atomic targets were the most tangible proof of America's nuclear credibility during the Cold War.[44] This American desire to cleave to the spirit of 1945 was seconded, ironically, in Japan. After failing to express much re- gret over World War II for fifty years, the Japanese Diet Issued a tepid declaration in June 1995, expressing 'remorse' for 'the unbearable pain' Japan had brought to people abroad. Unfortunately, the word chosen to express 'remorse,' *hansei*, also means 'reflection,' so that the remorse signaled was the kind meant when, for ex- ample, a pupil at school misses a homework assignment.[45] While then – Prime Minister Tomiichi Murayama and Emperor Akihito later bolstered their nation's sense of apparent contrition with more effusive apologies, it is clear that many Japanese do not see World War II in guilt-ridden terms. Consequently, a kind of balance binds Japan and America fifty years later. On the one hand, those few Japanese military men who were tried and executed by General MacArthur's war crimes tribunal now are worshiped as deities at one of Tokyo's major religious shrines where government leaders pay their respects every year during war commemoration rites. On the other hand, the surviving members of the 509th Composite Group and the U.S. Air Force resolutely maintain that Americans should not feel sorry for the atomic bombings of Japan, because, as Richard Hallion, the chief historian for the Air Force, claims, these nuclear attacks were America's answer to '15 years of aggres- sion, atrocities and brutality'[46] by Imperial Japan.

From the perspective of realist state power, the government should be able to instate its myths or restate its agendas at cultural venues, like the Smithsonian Institution, if nowhere else, for all persons living within its jurisdiction to access the proper codes for interpreting their own impersonations of American citizen- ship. Not celebrating Hiroshima at the end of World War II, because the atomic bombings shown in *The Last Act* were pictured as America's truly most lasting action, represented a major breach in the nation's state security to many citizens. Raising the spectre of anti-Americanism and antinuclearism in how some viewed a museum exhibition became a means of reaffirming this regime's circuits for gener- ating political subjectivity. Just as *The West as America* in 1991 never made it out West to contaminate America's heartlands in St. Louis and Denver, *The Last Act* was never performed, even in Washington, D.C., as it had been planned.[47] As it happened, 'the West' of brave cowboys and hardy pioneers civilizing Indian country 'as America' gained reauthorization from the cultural right's campaigns in

1991, allowing the *Enola Gay*'s dismembered fuselage in 1995 to stand starkly still as a totem of American superpower: the key signifier of the first and second-to-last delivery of a strategic nuclear weapon in wartime, which continues to be a sign to dangerous others across 'The Indian Country' in today's Third or Fourth Worlds that America possesses a violent will to sustain today's fragile nuclear peace.

The standard account of America's superpower defined Americans as humans and Japanese as nonhumans in clear, consistent myths that resurface in old World War II movies and Japan-bashing rhetoric every day. In the Cold War canon, the properties of Imperial Japan were those of a predatory feudal empire whose relations with America were sinister, untrustworthy, and antidemocratic. All of Imperial Japan's subjects rightly were grouped together as worthy targets of American air power, and the capabilities of Imperial Japanese objects working for those sinister subjects were ones of suicide, genocide, ethnocide. Harwit and Neufeld's apparently 'objective' reinterpretation of these canonical readings amounted to a series of radical amendments to the popular constitution of American superpower, which would have reread existing translations to propose some other impure possibilities. Furthermore, these pedagogical maneuvers also consciously moved against the objective detachment of museums to shake the subjective attachments of their visitors.[48] Thus, to begin the week leading into the fiftieth anniversary of the end of World War II, former U.S. Secretary of the Navy James Webb did a cover story interview in *Parade* magazine (the most widely distributed U.S. Sunday newspaper supplement) with Major General Chuck Sweeney. Their discussion entirely brushed over the Japanese A-bombing victims, concluding with Sweeney's succinct final assessment of the *Enola Gay* and *Bockscar* missions: 'We saved thousands of lives, we shortened the war, and we obviated an invasion.'[49]

Different generations with opposing identities exist along this divide. Is *Enola Gay* the penultimate artifact of American victory in World War II or the first dark signifier of the Cold War's atomic stalemate? Paul Fussell, who served in France as a GI during 1945 and had been put on notice for reassignment to the Pacific, summed up generational differences in his controversial 1988 book, *Thank God for the Atomic Bomb, and Other Essays*. Criticizing younger critics – like the political philosopher Michael Walzer or the revisionist historian Michael Sherry – of Truman's A-bomb decision, Fussell observed that Walzer was a ten-year-old kid and Sherry was not even ten months old in August 1945. For Fussell, 'the farther from the scene of horror, the easier the talk'[50] about its morality or immorality.[51]

History and political subjectivity

To a very real degree, the *Enola Gay* not only brought Imperial Japan to its knees; indeed, it also started the campaigns of atomic defense that kept the Soviet Union at bay until it collapsed from its own internal contradictions. Harwit and Neufeld tried to show this historical reality, but they felt that it was impossible to do so without addressing the dark side of the Cold War. In fact, the show's curators saw their exhibition fulfilling James Smithson's original intentions for the Smithsonian, namely, serving 'for the increase and diffusion of knowledge.'[52] In the aftermath of the 1994 elections, however, a new conservative Republican leadership in the

Congress successfully cast Harwit and Neufeld as having 'an ideological, narrow-minded, special interest – of dispensing opinion rather than fact.'[53]

The narratives guiding *The Last Act* exhibition fractured the objectivity of modern museum operations, because Harwit and Neufeld's text pointed out how, unlike Chernobyl in the 1980s, Hiroshima in 1945 is *not* everywhere. Instead of being out there in some stabilized material reality to be remembered, separate from us and today by being firmly fixed in the past (World War II) and elsewhere (Imperial Japan), the *Enola Gay* exhibition attached Hiroshima directly to bubbling anxieties from the present or uneasily repressed fears experienced here and now. And it did so in terms whose significance conveyed how this atomic bombing created a global nuclear contract whose underlying premise remains simple: nuclear war is only twenty minutes of any ICBM's flight away. The *Enola Gay* ended the war for GIs in the Pacific theater of operations – the fact that most seventy-somethings want to be memorialized. Yet it also transformed today's global theater of transnational Pacific relations into an unending skit of strategic deterrence stuck in a daily re-creation of that first B-29 atomic mission with each operational flight of SAC's B-52, B-2, and B-1B bombers today – the fiction of credible nuclear threat that others would recognize as topping the memoranda of liabilities still with us from the Manhattan Project.

Cultural conservatives prefer that visitors to the *Enola Gay* exhibition at the Air and Space Museum reconfirm their predictable patriotic orthodoxy. And the 'history wars' in the 1990s, like the culture wars, were being fought over the terms of political subjectivity to determine what is patriotic or who defines orthodoxy. Even with highly entertaining 'infotainment' at any museum, however, one must deal with the issues raised by these ideological struggles at the Smithsonian. The big problem for museums is simple: getting visitors to think beyond the diverting occupations of entertainmentality more often than not induces rage rather than cultivating reasoned reflection. The unwillingness to see Shigeru Orimen's lunchbox alongside General Tibbets's airplane in the same building in 1995 sadly illustrates this fact.

Notes

Timothy W. Luke is University Distinguished Professor in the Department of Political Science at Virginia Polytechnic Institute and State University.

1   Richard Bolton, ed., *Culture Wars: Documents from the Recent Controversies in the Arts* (New York: New Press, 1992).
2   James Davidson Hunter, *Culture Wars: The Struggle to Define America* (New York: Basic Books, 1991), 34, 42 (emphasis in the original).
3   Ibid., 173, 52.
4   Ibid., 52.
5   Paul Goldberger, 'Historical Shows on Trial: Who Judges,' *New York Times*, 11 February 1996, 21, 26.
6   Cited in Goldberger, 'Historical Shows,' 2, 26. A quite complete record of the entire controversy at the National Air and Space Museum, with all of its ideological dimensions, can be found in *Hiroshima's Shadow: Writings on the Denial*

of History and the Smithsonian Controversy, ed. Kai Bird and Lawrence Lifschultz (Stony Creek, Conn.: Pamphleteer's Press, 1998).

7   Bruno Latour, We Have Never Been Modern (London: Harvester Wheatsheaf, 1993), 1–5, 30. Also see his Science in Action (Cambridge: Harvard University Press, 1987). At the same time, Latour believes that hybrids always have existed as quasi-objective, quasi-subjective (con)fusions of nature/culture, human/nonhuman, object/subject, present/past, being/nonbeing, inside/outside elements. However, the discursive rules of museums conform to the three guarantees of the modern constitution. That is, first, 'even though we construct Nature, Nature is as if we did not construct it'; second, 'even though we do not construct Society, Society is as if we did construct it'; and, third, 'Nature and Society must remain absolutely distinct: the work of purification must remain absolutely distinct from the work of mediation' (1987: 93).

8   Martin Harwit, An Exhibit Denied: Lobbying the History of the Enola Gay (New York: Springer-Verlag, 1996), 427–8.

9   Ibid., 409–26.

10   Michael J. Hogan, Hiroshima in History and Memory (New York: Cambridge University Press, 1996), 200–31.

11   Cited in Philip Nobile, ed., Judgment at the Smithsonian: Smithsonian Script by the Curators at the National Air and Space Museum (New York: Marlowe and Company, 1995), xxxiii.

12   See William H. Truettner, ed., The West as America: Reinterpreting Images of the Frontier, 1820–1920 (Washington, D.C.: Smithsonian Institution Press, 1991).

13   Harwit, Exhibit Denied, 50–65.

14   Cited in Arthur Hirsch, 'Deadly Courier Retains Its Place in History,' Baltimore Sun, 9 June 1994, A1.

15   See Hogan, Hiroshima, 200–32.

16   Ibid.

17   New York Times, 5 February 1995, E5.

18   Cited in Nobile, Judgment at the Smithsonian, xliii.

19   For more discussion, see Gar Alperovitz, The Decision to Use the Atomic Bomb and the Architecture of an American Myth (New York: Knopf, 1995).

20   See Nobile, Judgment, xiii–xcvii, and Hogan, Hiroshima, 211–28. Harwit ultimately resigned as the National Air and Space Museum's director after the controversy; see New York Times, 3 May 1995, A9, 19.

21   Paul W. Tibbets, 'Our Job Was to Win,' American Legion 103 (November 1994): 28. The Enola Gay will be displayed in the National Air and Space Museum Center at Dulles International Airport, which should open in December 2003, with 15 million cubic feet of space and 177 other aircraft. Of its $238 million cost, $94 million was raised from private sources, including $60 million contributed from Steven Udvar-Hazy (See Jacqueline Trescott, 'Smithsonian "Too Shabby,"' Washington Post, 9 March 2000, C10, and, 'Reflections on an Institution,' Washington Post, 7 December 1999, C2). Nonetheless, as the Air and Space Museum's newest director, John Dailey, notes, the Smithsonian still needs to raise $95 million more for the Dulles Center. 'What I did not realize until I came here,' Dailey says, 'is that we have to raise our own money for almost every-thing we do.' Congressional appropriations pay for staff and maintenance, he says, but almost everything else – some 45 percent of the museum's funding – comes from nonfederal donors. Ken Ringle, 'With Feet Firmly Planted in the Air: For

Air and Space Museum Director John Dailey, the Sky's the Limit,' *Washington Post*, 25 May 2000, C7, C5.

22   William Garvey, 'The Shame of *Enola Gay*,' *Popular Mechanics*, August 1995, 45–9. Also see *New York Times*, 6 August 1995, 5–23; and *Washington Post*, 1 March 1995, A21. See Bird and Lifschultz, *Hiroshima's Shadow*, 377–409, for more op-ed treatments of the Smithsonian controversy. Much of the delay in this restoration could be attributed to shortfalls in funding during the 1980s. When Secretary I. Michael Heyman assumed office in late 1994, he found the Smithsonian Institution severely underfunded; then Congress shut down the government during November 1995 in a budget struggle with President Clinton. Heyman boosted the inflow of private donations to $92 million in 1999 from $51.8 million in 1995, but his successor, Lawrence Small, reported in March 2000 that the Smithsonian Institution's building and facilities still needed more than $250 million in repairs. See Jacqueline Trescott, 'Reflections of an Institution' C1, C2; and Smithsonian '"Too Shabby": Chief Seeks More Repair Funds,' C1, C10.

23   *Washington Post*, 26 September 1994, A11.

24   Garvey, 'The Shame of *Enola Gay*,' 49.

25   *Washington Post*, 26 September 1994, A10.

26   Cited in James Webb, 'Was It Necessary?,' *Parade*, 30 July 1995, 5.

27   Cited in *Washington Post*, 26 September 1994, A10.

28   Ibid.

29   Ibid.

30   Garvey, 'The Shame of *Enola Gay*,' 49.

31   Charles Krauthammer, 'World War II, Revised,' *Washington Post*, 19 August 1994, A27.

32   John Correll, 'Airplanes in the Mist,' *Air Force Magazine* 77 (December 1994): 2.

33   *Washington Post*, 26 September 1994, A10.

34   See Hogan, *Hiroshima*, 80–142.

35   *Washington Post*, 31 January 1995, A12.

36   Ibid.

37   Ibid.

38   Ibid.

39   Ibid.

40   See Garvey, 'The Shame of *Enola Gay*,' 49; and *Washington Post*, 9 July 1995, B2.

41   *Washington Post Weekend*, 14 July 1995, 30.

42   *Washington Post*, 9 July 1995, B2.

43   Ibid.

44   *The Wall Street Journal*, 29 August 1994, A10.

45   *The New York Times*, 7 June 1995, A1, 6. Also see *Washington Post*, 29 June 1995, A32.

46   Cited in Hogan, *Hiroshima*, 213.

47   See *Village Voice*, 25 June 1991, 99–100; and *Newsweek*, 27 May 1991, 70.

48   For more discussion, see Sharon Macdonald and Gordon Fyfe, eds., *Theorizing Museums: Representing Identity and Diversity in a Changing World* (Oxford: Blackwell, 1996). Lawrence M. Small, Secretary of the Smithsonian Institution, underscores this vital role played by the Smithsonian Institution's museums for the American people. More than 90 percent of the Smithsonian's visitors are

American citizens, and they travel great distances 'on a pilgrimage to the
nation's secular shrines . . . they're the physical manifestation of our shared sense
of national identity' *Washington Post*, 26 June 2000, A19.

49   Webb, 'Was It Necessary?,' 4. In contrast to the *Enola Gay*, the *Bockscar* B-29
has had a far less visible postwar presence. It too was put into storage during
1946 at Davis-Monthan Air Force Base in Tucson, Arizona, until the Air Force
refurbished it during 1961. On 26 September 1961, it was flown to Wright-
Patterson Air Force Base in Dayton, Ohio, where it was given a place of honor
at the United States Air Force Museum located there. Displayed next to SAC's
B-36, B-47, B-52, B-57, B-58, B-70, and B-1A bombers, it has engendered very
little controversy since 1945. See *New York Times*, 26 March 1995, 1–11.

50   See Paul Fussell, *Thank God for the Atomic Bomb, and Other Essays* (New York: Summit
Books, 1988), 23.

51   In my judgment, Fussell here is much too glib. One need not buy into this bazaar
of stereotypes. I was born in 1951 to a father who was drafted into the U.S.
Army in 1945 right out of high school. Having completed basic training in July
1945, he had been issued, as he recalls, tropical khakis for assignment to the Pacific
in preparation for the invasion of Japan. After the atomic bombs were dropped,
he returned that uniform to the quartermaster and was reissued woolen olive
drab kit for his reassignment to the Allied occupation forces in Berlin. Despite
what Paul Fussell or the *Wall Street Journal* claims about the implacability of '60s-
type professors,' I cannot help seeing both sides of the Hiroshima and Nagasaki
story. For more on patriotism and the generational divide, also see Edward T.
Linenthal and Tom Englehardt, *History Wars: The Enola Gay and Other Battles for
the American Past* (New York: Henry Holt, 1996), 97–114.

52   Harwit, *Exhibit Denied*, 428.

53   Ibid., 428–9.

Chapter 12

The Postmodern Exhibition
Cut on the bias, or is *Enola Gay* a verb?

Steven C. Dubin

M USEUMS are no longer dead zones or monuments to the past. Nor are they simply vanity sites, tributes to wealth, power, or the self-congratulations of mankind lording over other animal species, or of one race of humans reigning over another. Museums are now noisy, contentious, and extremely vital places.

. . . As we have seen time and again, displays of power represent both action and reaction. Displays of power have always been what museums do. But exhibitions today commonly reflect the interests of groups that are ideologically different from those previously in control – groups that are only recently flexing their muscle, having just elbowed their way into the cultural spotlight. To be sure, new viewpoints are being expressed in established institutions, channelled along disparate racial, ethnic, and doctrinal lines. But old voices are just as frequently being raised to fight back their challenge.

Yet remarkably, some observers view exhibition controversies simply as a slight arrhythmia in an otherwise healthy and vigorous museum world. To hear the *New York Times* tell it, for example, these are the 'glory days.' A feature story that sprawled across nearly two entire pages of one Sunday edition touts the boom, the blockbuster, the healthy bottom line for museums. Photos show hordes of visitors lolling on the steps of the Metropolitan Museum of Art, where nearly thirty years earlier crowds gathered to protest *Harlem on My Mind*. Vibrant banners overhead announce an exhibit of the work of the art world celebs Georgia O'Keefe and Alfred Stieglitz and the debut of the new Chinese Galleries. (In full color: the *New York Times*, like museums, is extremely market-savvy these days.) Or we see people queuing up to view the work of Picasso at the National Gallery of Art in Washington, D.C. He beat out all other competitors in the race for big numbers during the 1997

Source: *Display of Power: Memory and Amnesia in the American Museum*, NY and London: New York University Press, 1999, pp. 227–45, 281–2.

season. Still others dine, buy things, schmooze at corporate-sponsored events, or simply relax in the tranquility of museums throughout the country. Nowhere in this status report is any mention made of controversy.

The same author trumpets the prosperity awash in this world in another *New York Times* article. A box score of the top fifteen exhibitions of 1997 reports relative performance stats as if they were sports scores. Picasso, the champion, appears twice: Picasso: The Early Years packs in the crowds in both Washington and Boston. Other heavy hitters appear as well: Renoir and Monet; ancient cultures like Byzantium or Egypt; and even dazzling merchandise representing a more contemporary concept of civilization, courtesy of Cartier. Idea-driven exhibitions or any hint of trouble are noticeably absent in this roster.[1] The impression advanced instead is that museums are flush and self-satisfied – everything is copacetic.

Moreover, Joan Rosenbaum, the director of the Jewish Museum in New York City, concedes that conflictual episodes like the *Enola Gay*[2] and others don't really shape her thinking. Nor do they impact on how she does her job day-to-day. Her museum is a host site for *Sigmund Freud: Conflict and Culture*.[3] But the fierce debate it provoked in the planning stages doesn't concern her. She is primarily preoccupied with matters internal to the museum's operation: management issues, fund raising, dealing with her board of directors. She shares the mundane, unglamorous details of her job:

> The daily life of a director is sufficient to eclipse whatever you heard last week [about this or that controversy], I have to tell you. You deal with staff turnover. You deal with an emergency plumbing problem. The fact that something came in wildly over budget, that we're being offered a show that we had never planned for, and we'd have to move the whole schedule around. That someone very prominent and very wealthy is suddenly interested in the board, and how can we engage them? I mean, those are the things that have a certain urgency.

Only once or twice a year, when she attends conferences of her professional peers, can Rosenbaum find the time to focus on any larger political issues buffeting her world.[4]

William Truettner, the embattled curator of *The West as America*,[5] believes that the troubles over the past few years represent merely a tiny blip on the cultural radar screen: 'By and large, there are thousands of exhibitions that go on every year that are absolutely standard shows, and that haven't raised an eyebrow.'[6] Even so, the troublesome ones have attracted considerable attention; some people even argue that these disputes have commanded more notice than they deserve. David Lackey, for example, whose firm designed *Gaelic Gotham*,[7] was simultaneously working on a project in Chiapas, Mexico. From his perspective, 'I wish it [social conflict] were more in the streets, quite honestly. I call it the "taming of society." Museums are relatively safe places. Having traveled around the world a great deal, these controversies seem somewhat trivial.'[8]

Controversies over museum exhibitions vividly demonstrate that symbolic politics has displaced other political struggles over issues of race, representation, and inequality – struggles that could possibly alter the real conditions of people's lives. At the end of the day, we are still dealing with exhibitions, not natural disasters, revolutions, or even new public policies.

Even the most radical curator working in the most innovative museum is subject to many conservative pressures. There is the weight of institutional history, like the aristocratic legacy symbolized by the Museum of the City of New York's extensive silver collection. And fiscal constraints increasingly intrude on curatorial decision making. Although William Truettner of the National Museum of American Art believes that the number of museum controversies has not been significant, he concedes that their impact has. He states, 'I'm a bit depressed at the moment. Five years ago this institution was set to turn in a new direction. I think it had a great opportunity and lost it. And now it's more concerned with fund raising than what it presents to the public.'

Both Truettner and Harry R. Rubenstein of the Smithsonian's National Museum of American History note that their museums now must scramble more and more for the funds they require to present their shows. According to Rubenstein, 'Only the smallest shows don't require fund raising.' His museum is in keen competition with others for 'a pool of money that's getting smaller and smaller.' Michael S. Roth, who curated the Freud exhibition, notes that 'In a period of increased scarcity for cultural support, the nature of decision making by administrators changes. That's obvious. . . . What you get is a narrowing of the vision.'[9]

Finally, organizations like museums have a tremendous will to persist. Most museum officials will readily jettison a burdensome exhibition concept like ballast from an overloaded ship, should it seem essential to insure their future. Today they will likely consider what to bring aboard their program much more carefully in the first place. Legacy, finances, and endurance operate like the sturdy lines that tether a hot air balloon to guarantee that it not break loose and destroy itself.

Scholars subscribe to certain ideologies and myths, just as museum personnel, and the combatants in the various battles described here subscribe to theirs. My own credo includes a belief in the free exchange of ideas. It includes a belief in the right to present a distinct point of view, sustained by evidence, and yet acknowledging alternative explanations and points of view. It includes the right to make a fool of yourself, to be wrong, to be rebutted.

I strongly identified with the critics of exhibitions when I interviewed many of them: the general drift of their politics, their sense of exclusion, their keen desire to be heard, their support of ideals such as balance, fairness, and community participation, and especially their passion. Still and all, my allegiance to principles of authorship and open inquiry and my belief that you cannot and should not 'protect' people from making up their own minds about what they see trumped my other convictions and emotions. No matter how autocratic, bumbling, or acquiescent curators and museum officials have been – and granted, they have made many mistakes and many enemies – their right to proceed with their vision needs to be staunchly defended. Should opponents challenge what they present through spirited debate, written refutations, or even boisterous demonstrations – so be it. And so much the better. But attempts by various factions to radically reconstruct exhibitions to their own liking before they have gone up, to intimidate and threaten curators, museum employees, or supporters, or even to derail shows that they do not like are intolerable in a free society.

This chapter pushes beyond Matthew Arnold's concern with 'the best that has been thought and said in the world.'[10] It demonstrates that culture – and the struggles over it – can reveal us at our most unflattering, too, and that it is important to pay attention to such clashes. As is the case with all the partisans I've presented, my own preoccupations are intricately entangled with my sense of identity and my own particular preferences and convictions.

Some journalists and museum officials may deny that anything is amiss in the world of museums today. Even so, it is difficult to ignore the news of fresh controversies that surface regularly. For example, two controversies developed at the Ellis Island Immigration Museum within six months of one another in 1998. An exhibition about the massacre of Armenians by Ottoman Turks in 1915 became problematic when officials of the National Park Service (which administers the site) requested that the organizer of *Armenia: Memories from My Home* remove some photographs and text. The officials claimed that the images were 'gruesome and gory' and inappropriate for the many children who visit there. A compromise was reached after much hand-wringing, and some of the disputed images were restored.[11] Meanwhile, the legitimacy of classifying these events as genocide continues to be debated.

No sooner had that exhibition come down than another one became problematic. *America's Concentration Camps: Remembering the Japanese American Experience* addressed the imprisoning of Japanese Americans in internment camps during World War II. Along with visual documentation in the museum, curators reassembled a barracks, a guard tower, and barbed wire fence from Heart Mountain, Wyoming, outside on the grounds. The Smithsonian's Tom Crouch had used the term 'concentration camp' in *A More Perfect Union*, which he curated in 1987. It caused no problems at that time. But in the spring of 1998, some Jewish groups contested its applicability to this other group's experience (the executive director of the American Jewish Committee declared that the term 'deserves protection').

Ellis Island's superintendent feared that use of this label in this context could offend the metropolitan area's large Jewish population. She demanded a name change. That mobilized the intervention of Senator Daniel Inouye, which eventually resulted in a conciliation between Jewish and Japanese American groups. 'Concentration camp' was retained, while a detailed discussion of its origins and its applicability to various experiences was included. One commentator wisely observed that this was an example of a group sensing it was in danger of forfeiting something that has become central to its identity. He understood that for some Jews this curatorial decision posed the possibility that they might be 'losing their singular lexicon of anguish.'[12] This example points up once again the complexities of reception, and how it varies from time to time and place to place.

Just months before, the Smithsonian Institution became embroiled in a similar tussle. The Smithsonian was slated to host a lecture series as part of the fiftieth anniversary commemoration of the founding of the modern state of Israel. The roster included a wide range of voices: scholars, writers, Orthodox and conservative political Jewish spokespeople, as well as Arabs. But a plurality of voices can be threatening to certain people. Representative Michael P. Forbes (R-New York) wrote to Smithsonian secretary I. Michael Heyman that this was 'going to be an *Enola Gay* controversy,' and that the program represented a 'leftist approach' to Israel. Moreover, as if proceeding according to a dog-eared script, the media stirred up people's emotions. The *New York Post* editorially denounced the Smithsonian and accused it of bias. Later, the enraged author of a letter to the editor reiterated the major complaints veterans had directed against the *Enola Gay* exhibit, and once again invoked the passage from the first draft of the script regarding a Japanese 'war of vengeance.'

That preliminary National Air and Space Museum document had been written four years prior. As we know, curators subsequently edited it to avoid misinterpretation. Yet it was still being shamefully manipulated for ideological purposes rather than being put to rest. Heyman once again capitulated to political, media, and public pressure: he ordered the Smithsonian to disassociate itself from a group that had become defined as a controversial collaborator, and to produce a lecture series on its own.[13] The *Enola Gay* experience thus provides a benchmark against which many other exhibitions are subsequently measured.

The question arises, 'What *is* the Smithsonian – or any public institution – willing to do nowadays?' Are museum officials running scared? Playing it safe? Frank Rich of the *New York Times* answers in the affirmative. He opened his scathing review of *America's Smithsonian*, the Institution's 150th anniversary exhibition in 1996, with a dismissal that would make any curator cringe: 'There are some shows so dull they can't even give the tickets away.' When the traveling show reached Manhattan – one of twelve projected sites – it bombed with audiences; a behemoth 100,000-square-foot exhibition did a spectacular belly flop. But why?

The exhibition was a mishmash, an amorphous assortment of items from the Smithsonian's collections, much like a selection of musical greatest hits peddled on late-night television. It invited comparison with children's flip books, where a kid can construct new characters by randomly turning the selections of heads, torsos, and legs. You could imaginatively cluster Lincoln's top hat, Theodore Roosevelt's chaps, Franklin D. Roosevelt's lap robe, Eleanor Roosevelt's fur coat, and George Washington's battle sword and scabbard into a *fabulous* [a-]historical ensemble. You'd be dressed to take a fantasy voyage in a Mercury spacecraft or a 1948 Tucker automobile, or to view a smattering of artworks, gems and jewelry, manmade artifacts from around the world, and specimens from the natural world.

America's Smithsonian was the antithesis of *The West as America*. The one exhibition left it completely up to the viewer to furnish any interpretations. The other preached a party line, according to its harshest critics. Because the curators played it safe in this instance, it would be impossible to fault *America's Smithsonian* for theoretical heavy-handedness; no curatorial point of view was apparent. Objects appeared to have been chosen for their celebrity value or their sheer visual appeal. Like *People* magazine's 'fifty most beautiful people' of the year, these objects were all surface, no depth; thus they were accorded a shallow equivalency.

This sort of display is relatively immune from political attack, although it is not necessarily satisfying to the public or to experienced critics of exhibitions. To the exhibit designer David Lackey,

It was really disappointing. It's troublesome to see an exhibition that comes across almost like 'Ripley's Believe It or Not.'. . . . The Smithsonian did an exhibition on [founder] John Smithson in the 1980s that was absolutely splendid. It linked his travels around the world and understanding different cultures, and [demonstrated] how that collection was based. It was a link to an incredible human journey, an odyssey. And I never felt this exhibition had that depth. . . . For example, the beetles were like specimens of gems. They looked almost interchangeable.

Just as significant as the Smithsonian's choice of what to display and how to display it was the prominence of its 'proud partners,' corporate sponsors such as the Intel Corporation, MCI Communications Corporation, Discover® Card, and TWA. Each procured a huge space in the exhibit to pitch itself. MCI's 'cyber playground,' for example, offered Internet connections and free long-distance phone calls. These were infomercials, blatant self-promotions on a large scale. Their presence highlights both the increased dependence of museums upon corporate support and the blandness of many of the resulting exhibitions.

America's Smithsonian was conceived before the *Enola Gay* controversy had fully played out. It was the inaugural exhibition of a new regime. But the *Enola Gay* was connected to *America's Smithsonian* in a vital way. Martin Harwit insists that Secretary Heyman was charged with a new priority when he assumed office. It was up to him to secure financial stability for the Smithsonian, both from the private sector and from Congress, whose contributions have decreased over recent years. It took Harwit a long time to 'get it': the struggle over the *Enola Gay* was as much about money as it was about important principles. In fact, a *Washington Post* article disclosed that the controversy at the NASM over the proposed exhibit of the *Enola Gay* was thwarting the Smithsonian's efforts to convince corporate supporters to sign on to *America's Smithsonian*. *The Last Act* not only threatened the economic interests of the military and the aerospace industries. The debate it engendered also made it more difficult for the Smithsonian to raise funds on its own behalf.[14] When museums are forced to hustle more and more for their income, it is certain to have an impact on the decisions they make about what to present to the public.

Equally as troubling is what does *not* make it onto the walls — after *The West as America*, after the *Enola Gay* and all the other controversies of the past half dozen years, in a time when museums are no longer overlooked and undervalued by large segments of the public. The public, along with critics, can judge what appears within their range of vision. But the inchoate fears of controversy that can coalesce into self-censorship generally remain hidden from audiences and researchers alike. Robert Macdonald, the director of the Museum of the City of New York, reflects on the conflicts at other institutions:

Curators and officials at the Smithsonian and the Library of Congress were definitely afraid. They have jobs to protect, [and] the 'culture wars,' as they're called, had come down to where they were fearful of speaking what they believed to be true, because they would lose their jobs. . . . I was shocked, but I don't blame them at all. They have families to feed.

We have discovered how the controversy over *The West as America* caused the National Museum of American Art to beef up its internal regulations and carefully weigh in advance what it presents to the public. Moreover, the negative coverage of the Library of Congress after the conflict over *Back of the Big House*[15] sent that institution reeling too. For the LOC associate librarian Winston Tabb, the fallout served as a wake-up call:

> One of the things this uncovered for us was that we didn't have an adequate system in place for the planning of exhibitions and letting people in the Library know what was coming. We learned from this and have taken very active steps to remedy [the situation]. And that's the reason I'd say we've had no such difficulties since that time.

The LOC has, of course, faced controversy since then. But in the case of *Sigmund Freud: Conflict and Culture*, it was much more prepared to stand tough in the face of intense scrutiny and criticism. For Jill Brett, the LOC public affairs officer, 'The Library stood by the Freud exhibit, which was the right thing to do. And it's the same exhibit we were going to do, not a changed one because of the voices raised against it.'

What exactly has Winston Tabb instituted? A group of senior managers now oversees a double review process. First, they must approve the creation and scheduling of any exhibition. Second, closer to the projected opening date, the team reviews the images, objects, and anything else associated with the show, including educational and public programs and even the merchandise to be sold. This way, senior managers know exactly what's going on in every respect. According to Tabb, *Back of the Big House* likely 'accelerated' the development of an administrative structure he would have put into place anyway.[16]

The impact of controversies ripples out in circles far beyond their point of origin. For example, an exhibit of the work of the late-nineteenth- and early-twentieth-century western landscape artist Thomas Moran opened at the Gilcrease Museum in Tulsa, Oklahoma, in 1998. As a reviewer noted, it was the best opportunity to publicly examine this painter's work since *The West as America* in 1991. But the curatorial choices were strikingly different in this latter case. Rather than link artists like Moran to ideologies of nationalist expansion and exploitation of the land and its original inhabitants, this exhibition displayed a light interpretive touch. It opted for a 'noncontentious, "here-it-is" approach,' sidestepping the ideological minefield that the curators of *The West as America* hurtled through. The assistant to the museum director explained, 'People are becoming more gun-shy. I think we're being more contemplative and cautious.'[17] As with *Harlem on My Mind*,[18] when a daring curatorial leap forward is met with loud disapproval, a judicious institutional drawing back may follow in its wake. Certain subjects and certain treatments of them may simply prove to be not worth the headache.

I have continuously noted the pivotal role the media play in museum controversies. Journalists are always looking for a good angle. Controversy provides it. 'Censorship' is one such angle. 'Political correctness' is another. But at what point do angles become slants? How do they sharpen some details while they diminish others? That is, how do angles in fact round off the edges of a story, forcing it into a predetermined shape? Media coverage of museums has breathed life into disputes that might otherwise have remained arcane conflicts. It simplifies and packages these struggles for general public consumption. The intense hunger for a good story has generated a number of extreme illustrations of media professionals actively constructing their accounts.

In the case of *Gaelic Gotham*, for example, recall the political activist Brendan Fay's charge that 'fucking ethics of journalism were crossed' when a reporter initiated the call for a boycott of the exhibition. That exposed the slender lines between community newspapers, community membership, and journalistic advocacy. During the *Enola Gay* episode, a large number of special interest publications relentlessly hammered away at the National Air and Space Museum. This campaign was incited and supported in vital respects by the Air Force Association's exposés. The activities of this powerful lobbying organization, coupled with multiple channels to spread the message, helped generate a groundswell of dissent against the curators and their ideas. It is the most extreme example of a crusade waged against a museum and a proposed program. What is more, journalists working for more mainstream media also fed the fury by largely reproducing what the critics alleged, rather than thoroughly checking out the story for themselves or questioning how those ideas were filtered through certain lenses.

Museum directors such as Elizabeth Broun and Martin Harwit were simply out of their league in mounting public relations counterattacks. That wasn't an ordinary part of their duties. Recall Broun's sense of being unequal to the task: 'You don't want to go to war with people who buy their ink by the barrel.' Recall, too, that the LOC's Jill Brett described the media pouncing on the story of the Freud exhibition as if it were 'red meat.' That was the reaction of someone whose job it is to reach out to and interact with the media. Troubleshooting the debate over the Freud exhibition was a sobering professional experience for her, and it taught her colleague Irene Chambers something too: 'The story takes on a life of its own, and it's out there, and people are talking about something on the basis of one reporter's story. I guess I've known this all along, but this time brought it all home. And then people are talking on the basis of something that wasn't true, and they're responding to each other.'[19]

One additional key phrase surfaced in some of these controversies: 'the community,' or 'community participation.' But whose voices do you listen to? How can you be sure who they represent? How seriously do you take them? 'Community' became a particularly sensitive point in relation to *Harlem on My Mind*, *Back of the Big House*, and *Gaelic Gotham*. The Hunter College history professor Ed O'Donnell, one of the curators of *Gaelic Gotham*, pinpoints a fundamental problem with confronting individuals and coalitions who claim to speak for others. He argues that in communities based on ethnicity, religion, or sexual orientation, 'There's a segment that has a strong sense of itself, and begins to speak for the group. Those subgroups tend to be more motivated and more organized, while most [other] people are out there trying to put food on the table, and go through everyday life. [This privileging of identity] is not their burning passion.'

Jack Salzman, another member of the curatorial team for *Gaelic Gotham*, argues that

> Shows, like books, like everything else, get done by smart people. And those people are smart not because of their race, ethnicity, or gender. They're just smart. The real issue that has to do with race and gender and ethnicity is that too many people, too many women, too many people of color (to use a not-very-meaningful term), have been excluded from the realm of being smart.

But while Salzman is displeased that discrimination in the past has blocked opportunities for certain people, he voices doubts about the advisability of acceding to the demands of those whose credentials are based solely on group affiliation, not specific museum expertise:

> I know there are people who believe that these shows are to be done with the community. I just don't agree with that. It seems to me that you wind up just trying to cater to a community, and that the responsibility is to come up with the best and smartest show you can. . . . If communities were always involved, then how do you ever get anything done?

Robert Macdonald, the director of the Museum of the City of New York, stakes out an important philosophical and tactical response to various constituencies that are extremely vocal about expressing themselves and pressing their demands. Realistically, that sort of confrontational stance is not likely to wane in the near future. Macdonald asserts,

> We have to listen to as many voices as we can hear. But we have to select those voices that are going to be heard in our galleries, and that's the challenge. So you have to try to be as inclusive as you can in listening. But you have to have the intellectual courage to select what goes up on your walls. Then you have the responsibility to stand by it.

Macdonald made many enemies during the struggle to bring *Gaelic Gotham* to completion. Time and again, they remarked on his combativeness and what they perceived to be Macdonald's stubborn refusal to listen to opposing views. In other words, his personality may have prevented his ideas about curating a show from receiving their best test. But Macdonald's premise makes a great deal of sense and holds a great deal of promise. It requires that museum personnel clearly cordon off the preliminary, fact-finding stages from the exhibition-building stages. Community input would be welcomed in the first instance. Professional criteria would prevail in the second phase, where the curatorial vision could proceed without interference. All parties should be clear about what the ground rules are throughout the process.

Macdonald's ideas are echoed by Tom Crouch. As a curator of *The Last Act*, Crouch was drawn into a protracted struggle, largely not of his own making. He witnessed firsthand how repeated attempts to assimilate outside demands failed to quiet the critics. Once tinkering with the script was allowed, the outcome became less and less acceptable to *all* the parties. Looking back, Crouch now realizes, 'I think one of the lessons I learned is that fairly close to the beginning of the controversy, what you ought to do is find ground that you're comfortable on, dig your heels in, and see what happens. I think there's a lot of truth to that.'

The costs of not doing that in the case of the *Enola Gay* exhibition were that National Air and Space Museum personnel endured months and months of attacks and were forced to smooth critics' ruffled feathers continuously. The ultimate result, of course, was losing control over the show and being forced to settle for something entirely different from what they'd originally conceived. Not only that, but capitulation has led to repeated unpleasantness: NASM personnel are judged to be either ideologues or wimps. Moreover, new exhibitions proposed anywhere can become targets for fresh attacks by opponents emboldened by the collapse of *The Last Act*. Despite the denials of people like Joan Rosenbaum, exhibition controversies *do* have an impact.

One of the best examples is what happened when the Smithsonian's National Museum of American History was planning an exhibition on sweatshops in 1997. It was projected to have a sweep of almost two hundred years. The highlight would be the display of artifacts seized in the 1995 government raid of a sweatshop in El Monte, California, including sewing-machine workstations and sections of the razor wire that surrounded the building. Shockingly, this was in the United States itself, and it was now – not in some crowded, turn-of-the-century tenement eighty or a hundred years ago on New York City's Lower East Side, or in some developing country.[20]

But the executive director of the California Fashion Association (an apparel trade group) issued this chilling warning in 1997: 'We cannot stand idly by,' she cautioned. 'We want to turn this exhibit plan into another *Enola Gay*.' Wielding this earlier episode like a club, she appeared hellbent on halting *Between a Rock and a Hard Place: A History of American Sweatshops, 1820–Present* before it opened to public view. As the co-curator Harry Rubenstein ponders, 'All of a sudden it makes *Enola Gay* into a verb. Which is sort of an interesting creation.'[21]

Fashion designers cut fabric against its grain or bias so that it will hang in dramatically different ways. The co-curators Peter Liebhold and Harry Rubenstein did something similar with their material. Like Robert Macdonald, they work in a post-*Enola Gay* museum environment. But Liebhold and Rubenstein's achievement is probably a better test of how to pitch your camp under these changed conditions than *Gaelic Gotham* was. Their strategy for presenting a controversial topic such as sweatshops was to insist on 'different styles of conversation' or different voices within the exhibition. It too was 'cut on the bias.'

The historical section employed a curatorial voice. But they felt that using only this voice in the exhibition would be a mistake. Therefore, the El Monte section used the voices of the participants, be they workers or law enforcement agents. 'The Fashion Food Chain' (which addressed the range of manufacturing alternatives) had the dry, authoritative voice of a textbook. Furthermore, a video presented the industry voice, while a 'national leaders' section gave six individuals representing manufacturers, labor, government, community groups, and others the opportunity to offer their written comments.

Liebhold and Rubenstein cast a wide net to collect their information. But they carefully controlled the script. They subjected it to academic review, both within and outside the museum. Otherwise, it was 'very closely held,' explains Liebhold. 'We wanted to avoid one of the pitfalls that we saw from *Enola Gay*, which is where people were going to nitpick specific words, and not respond in a more general kind of fashion.' Did anyone actually request or demand a copy of this script? 'Only a couple of people had the courage to ask,' Liebhold explains. 'We made it clear that we were not going to [let it out].' And Harry Rubenstein adds,

> In this climate, we were just afraid. And in some ways it's a shame, because many times when we were developing the script we would wonder how a group would perceive something. They could be the best ones to find mistakes in your work. But people working in public history feel under attack, and therefore we can't share the material because this could jeopardize the project as a whole.

Once the story of the industry's displeasure broke in the media, the curators offered logical defenses of their approach. Yet had a political groundswell formed against *Between a Rock and a Hard Place*, these arguments would not have mattered much. In this instance, several key politicos rallied to support the exhibition. Representative George Miller (D-California) circulated a 'Dear Colleague' letter in Congress and initiated a letter to Smithsonian secretary I. Michael Heyman, signed by forty-five of his colleagues. At a regents' meeting, three of the nine members of the Smithsonian governing board spoke up in favor of the NMAH's plans. The Smithsonian administration stood firm this time.

These were demonstrations of support that never materialized for *The Last Act*. Veterans have a certified claim on American support and good will. Congress is one of the most important champions of their cause. Vets also boast a number of powerful lobbying groups, and they have the strength of numbers. When vets felt they were going to be presented unfairly in a Smithsonian exhibition, they could rally plenty of supporters to their side. But the topic of sweatshops does not activate claims of unfair representation that scores and scores of people will reflexively believe. For most of those who heard about the exhibition in advance, the stakes were not that high. They were willing to adopt a wait-and-see attitude.

Harry Rubenstein explains, 'We were under huge amounts of pressure, which is maybe different than [being] under fire,' as Martin Harwit, Tom Crouch, and Michael Neufeld were a few years earlier with the *Enola Gay*. Peter Liebhold reflects, 'Museums are a different place to work, post-*Enola Gay*. There were a number of exciting, interesting shows [before that] exploring the bounds of what type of material would be talked about in museums. And I think most people retreated from it.'

Liebhold and Rubenstein took care that a wide range of voices would come through in *Between a Rock and a Hard Place*. They represent a new wave of curatorship that is increasingly sensitive to the multiple voices connected to their subjects and the diversity of their audiences. For example, one of the much-denounced group of wall texts accompanying *The West as America* raised the question 'What's Wrong with the Language We Use?' The curators discussed the implications of employing either the generic 'Indian,' the racist 'Injun,' or a precise descriptor such as 'Oglala Sioux.' Moreover, these curators acknowledged that not everyone viewing *The West as America* would be like themselves. 'When these works were painted,' they wrote, 'their intended audience was almost certainly white. Many of us here today, however, are not white. Some of us, in fact, may be stubbornly unvanished Indians.'

In important respects, *The West as America* curators presaged the approach taken in the George Gustav Heye Center of the Smithsonian's National Museum of the American Indian, which opened in New York City in 1994. The *process* of curating the exhibitions in this museum has been brought to the surface, much as the design of the Centre Georges Pompidou in Paris brought that building's mechanical systems to the outside rather than burying them within. 'Selectors' of particular objects in Heye Center exhibitions are explicitly listed, along with their specific tribal affiliations. Three major interpretive approaches are emphasized: the anthropological, the art historical, and the native view. Every printed statement is identified by the person making it, as well as the perspective they represent.

The meaning of objects is magnified by native interpretations. The sensation of the objects themselves is enhanced by recorded voices and authentic music. The galleries are seen as places for dialogue. They are also seen as places where viewpoints may clash.

Other museums have followed this lead. A 1997 exhibition at the Yale University Art Gallery focused on objects produced by a tribe of people on Africa's Ivory Coast. *Baule: African Art/Western Eyes* sought to amplify the viewer's experience too. The four sections of the show corresponded to four native meanings of 'to see': private, public, sacred, or secular artifacts. Field photographs and sound-tracks helped reproduce natural settings. Documentary films further enlarged the context. Moreover, this art museum presented life-sized Baule environments, smudging the line between art and ethnography. It transcended conventional connoisseurship, offering an enhanced milieu where disconnected items customarily have been displayed instead.[22]

The West as America, the National Museum of the American Indian, and *Baule* have changed the way objects are presented and have enlarged the museum visitor's understanding of them. By doing so, museums are acknowledging that we live in an increasingly multicultural society and a multinational world. Because this recognition is relatively recent, it proceeds with fits and starts. It generates both profundities and follies. All too often, it involves a zero-sum game, where opponents see only victory or defeat — not the possibility of compromise. When one group fears that its power is slipping away, a visible way to stave the flow is to challenge various types of public representation. As we've seen, all too often that has meant that museums have been caught in the crossfire.

In New York, near the Brooklyn–Queens border, another multicultural vision unfolds quietly and unintentionally. Cypress Hills cemetery, the final resting place of Jackie Robinson and Mae West, has become a multiethnic neighborhood that has few counterparts in the world of the living. A Puerto Rican woman duplicates the Jewish ritual of leaving small stones at a gravesite. A Chinese mourner adapts an ancient tradition to the New World by leaving a plate of White Castle hamburgers for a loved one at another spot. Greeks, Lithuanians, and East Indians have found a home there too.

Like so many other features of New York City life, this mosaic is fabricated from need, not desire: with land so scarce and costly, it is not as simple as it once was to establish ethnically, racially, and religiously segregated burial grounds. The dead jostle one another over space in New York, just as the living do. But now their bodies could end up lying next to others whom they might never have had much opportunity (or desire) to associate with while they were alive. Moreover, the Museum of the City of New York presented a photo essay on such current burial practices in 1997, one additional example of the way contemporary museums have fixed on significant social phenomena.[23]

Museums have become places where conflicts over some of the most vital issues regarding national character and group identity – the struggle between universalism and particularism – regularly break out. These conflicts are displays of power, the result of groups flexing their muscles to express who they are or to beat back the claims of others. Even if such controversies were to cease immediately, they will remain an important artifact of an era of extraordinary social change and self-examination in America.

Notes

Steven C. Dubin was Director of the Media, Society, and Arts program at the State University of New York, Purchase.

1   See Judith H. Dobrzynski, 'Glory Days for the Art Museum,' *New York Times*, October 5, 1997, AR1; and *idem*, 'Museums Paint Prosperity by Numbers,' *New York Times*, February 26, 1998, E1. Idea-driven versus object-driven museums and exhibitions are a much-remarked-upon trend in museum literature today; see Amy Henderson and Adrienne L. Kaeppler, eds, *Exhibiting Dilemmas: Issues of Representation at the Smithsonian* (Washington, D.C.: Smithsonian Institution Press, 1997).

2   *Enola Gay* – this refers to the exhibition called *The Last Act: The Atomic Bomb and the End of World War II* about the dropping of the Atomic Bomb on Hiroshima by the aeroplane the *Enola Gay*. The proposed exhibition caused a great deal of controversy between veterans and curators. See Luke 2002 in this volume for details.

3   *Sigmund Freud: Conflict and Culture* opened in the Library of Congress in 1998 after considerable controversy over the interpretation of psychoanalysis.

4   Author's interview, October 9, 1997.

5   *The West as America: Reinterpreting Images of the Frontier, 1820–1920*, a temporary exhibition at the National Museum of American Art in 1991, courted controversy when it examined the American foundation myth of the settlement of the west of the United States.

6   Author's interview, February 9, 1998.

7   *Gaelic Gotham: A History of the Irish in New York City* opened in 1996 at the Museum of the City of New York. Some Irish Americans, who felt they had not been adequately consulted, criticized it, and resented the fact that the original curator, who had strong links with Irish community groups, had been replaced.

8   Author's interview, April 28, 1997. All subsequent unattributed quotes are from that interview.

9   Author's interviews, February 9, 1998, April 8, 1998, and September 26, 1997. All subsequent unattributed quotes are from those interviews.

10 Matthew Arnold, *Culture and Anarchy* (New Haven: Yale University Press, 1994 [1869]).

11 See Somini Sengupta, 'At Ellis Island Museum, Dispute on Armenia Show,' *New York Times*, September 11, 1997, B3; and *idem*, 'Ellis Island, Yielding, Permits Photos of Armenian Massacre,' *New York Times*, October 14, 1997, B2.

12 See Somini Sengupta, 'What Is a Concentration Camp? Exhibit Prompts a Debate,' *New York Times*, March 8, 1998, A35; *idem*, 'Accord on Term "Concentration Camp,"' *New York Times*, March 10, 1998, B4; and Clyde Haberman, 'Defending Jews' Lexicon of Anguish,' *New York Times*, March 13, 1998, B1.

13 See Lizette Alvarez, 'After Criticism, Smithsonian Revises Plan for Israel Event,' *New York Times*, January 7, 1998, A12; Michael Keller, 'Does the Smithsonian Hate Israel?' *New York Post*, January 2, 1998, 26; and Anthony Lewis, 'Silencing Other Ideas,' *New York Times*, January 12, 1998, A21.

14 *The Last Act* was the name given to the exhibition of the *Enola Gay*. See Luke (2002) in this reader for details. Author's interview, March 19, 1998; Martin Harwit, *An Exhibit Denied: Lobbying the History of the* Enola Gay (New York: Copernicus, 1996), 357, 379, 428; and Eugene L. Meyer, 'Smithsonian May Drop A-Bomb Exhibit,' *Washington Post*, January 27, 1995, A1. Days before *The Last Act* was canceled, Meyer reports that only one corporate sponsor had signed on to *America's Smithsonian*, with a requisite $10 million pledge. Moreover, it wished to remain anonymous because of the *Enola Gay* controversy. *America's Smithsonian* completed three-fourths of its proposed twelve-city tour. The Smithsonian public affairs office reports that corporate support ran out, and fund raising efforts in the three remaining cities were insufficient to continue the venture; telephone conversation, May 1, 1998. Martin Harwit reports that the Smithsonian suffered a major economic loss on *America's Smithsonian* – $20 million, perhaps much more; author's interview, March 19, 1998.

15 Back of the Big House: The Cultural Landscape of the Plantation was a traveling exhibition on slavery that reached the Library of Congress in December 1995. While it was well received elsewhere, a small number of employees at the Library complained about the exhibition and it was closed.

16 Author's interviews, December 15, 1997. All subsequent unattributed quotes are from those interviews.

17 Quoted in Alice Thorson, 'Natural Passion,' *Kansas City Star*, February 15, 1998, J3.

18 *Harlem on My Mind: The Cultural Capital of Black America 1900–1968* opened in 1969 at New York City's Metropolitan Museum of Art. It was severely criticized by some black Americans as being paternalistic.

19 Author's interviews, February 9, 1998, and December 15, 1997.

20 Sweatshops have been the subject of many recent investigations. Accusations have been made against Wal-Mart, Disney, Guess?, the signature clothing line of Kathie Lee Gifford, and others, for using exploitative labor conditions to manufacture their goods. A particularly sobering investigation 'followed the money' gained from the sale of baseball caps manufactured in the Dominican Republic, bearing the names of elite American universities. The caps retail for twenty dollars,

but workers receive approximately eight cents per item; see Bob Herbert, 'Sweatshop U.,' *New York Times*, April 12, 1998, WK13. For a similar global economic perspective on Barbie see Eyal Press, 'Barbie's Betrayal: The Toy Industry's Broken Workers,' *Nation*, September 30, 1996, 10.

21   Quoted in George White, 'Plan for a Sweatshop Exhibition Draws Fire,' *Los Angeles Times*, September 11, 1997, A1; and author's interview, April 8, 1998.

22   See the review by Holland Cotter, 'Beyond Beauty, Art That Takes Action,' *New York Times*, September 28, 1997, AR35.

23   See Celia W. Dugger, 'Outward Bound from the Mosaic,' *New York Times*, October 28, 1997, B1.

Chapter 13

Sachsenhausen: a flawed museum

Roger Bordage

UNLESS we want young people all over the world, and particularly in Europe, to become the orphans of history, cut adrift from the past, it is vital that we safeguard the historic sites of the Nazi deportations. The Nazi concentration and death camps, places of genocide and slaughter, left their mark on history, and the sites continue to bear witness to the crimes of the Hitler regime, to the suffering of millions of men, women and children and to the resistance put up by the peoples of Europe, with exemplary courage, to enslavement and oppression.

Just over forty-five years after the fall of a barbaric regime without precedent in history, these sites have lost none of their significance. Their terrible image is part of the 'heritage of humanity' and should be recognized and respected as such. The international committees composed of exprisoners of the Nazi concentration camps have accordingly urged all the governments concerned and all national and international social, political and ethical organizations to ensure that these historic sites be preserved. They must also be protected against the introduction of anything alien to the memory of the concentration camps. It is essential to preserve and maintain the museums and other institutions established on those sites, to open them to a respectful, interested public and to ensure that their contents are strictly confined to the Nazi era from 1933 to May 1945, to the exclusion of any other historical records. Here, no direct or indirect attempt to gloss over the responsibilities of the Nazis, or indeed to rehabilitate the executioners, can be tolerated; the reality of their crimes and genocides must be explicitly recalled, and the true value of respect for human rights, democracy and tolerance brought home to visitors.

At the Cracow symposium held from 28 May to 7 June 1991 on the European cultural heritage organized by the Conference on Security and Co-operation in Europe (CSCE) as part of its work on 'the human dimension', all the European delega-

Source: *Museum International*, 177, vol. XLV, no. 1, 1993, pp. 26–31.

tions (except for Albania, which had not yet become a participant) plus the United States and Canada adopted a text in favour of preserving and safeguarding the sites of the Nazi concentration camps as part of the European cultural heritage. Notwithstanding this memorable document the necessary action to save these sites from oblivion or desecration has not been taken by all the authorities geographically and administratively responsible for the museum-camps.

What is more, in our own day certain acts and events that have occurred on the sites of the camps – which I shall discuss further on with reference only to Oranienburg-Sachsenhausen where I was confined from May 1943 to May 1945 – appear to seek to muddle people's minds and mask the enormity of Nazism. How? For example, by lumping together the history of the Nazi concentration camps between 1933 and 1945 and the history of the imprisonment of Nazis and SS between 1945 and 1950 after the Potsdam agreements. It is, of course, easy to blur the distinction in the minds of the younger generation, as some parts of the camps were used by the Allies to imprison the Nazis and SS who were brought to justice and convicted. Yet millions of concentration camp prisoners were arrested but never brought to justice in accordance with due process of law, and their term of imprisonment was never fixed. The imprisonment of Nazis and SS never involved their systematic, long-drawn-out destruction by dehumanization, hunger (800 calories a day in the Nazi camps), exhausting work, beatings, physical ordeals, persecution, torture, pseudo-medico-scientific experiments, hanging, shooting or gassing, and finally the crematoria.

How it was

In the Oranienburg-Sachsenhausen camp alone, between 1933 and 1945, there were 200,000 prisoners, 100,000 of whom were systematically exterminated. In that camp, as in the Third Reich's other concentration and extermination camps, run by the SS Death's Head battalion (*Toten-kopfverbänder*) under the control of SS Reichsführer Heinrich Himmler, were imprisoned the 'enemies of national socialism' or those arbitrarily assumed to be political dissidents, including Germans themselves. The earliest victims were communists, socialists, social democrats, Protestants, Catholics, independents, Resistance fighters in the occupied countries, Soviet war prisoners (18,000 of whom were deliberately liquidated in that camp), members of the so-called 'inferior races' (Jews, gypsies and Slavs), 'beings considered inferior from the point of view of racial biology' and those regarded as 'asocial', and also criminals, used by the SS to police and ill-treat other prisoners.

The Oranienburg-Sachsenhausen concentration camp, established in July 1936 among the sandy plains and pines of the Brandenburg lowlands, started out as the Oranienburg camp, installed in March 1933 in a disused brewery in a village of the same name, some 24 km north of Berlin, on the right bank of the Havel River, a tributary of the Elbe. It originally covered 31 hectares and contained 78 huts (blocks). From 1936 to 1945 it increased in size to 388 hectares, becoming the Oranienburg-Sachsenhausen complex. The triangle formed by the surrounding wall of the actual prison camp was flanked by the installations of the SS central inspectorate responsible for all the Nazi concentration and death camps, the military workshops, stores and barracks of the SS, and the residential units of the families of SS officers.

In May 1943, after my arrest in France at the age of 18 for 'acts of resistance'. I was deported with other comrades in sealed goods trains and imprisoned in that camp for two long years. After a 48-hour journey with nothing to drink, the SS forced us off at Oranienburg station by beating us with clubs, and marched us to the Oranienburg-Sachsenhausen camp. As I passed 'A' tower, which housed the the SS command of 'KZ' and which was located at the base of the triangle formed by the camp walls, I was surprised to see emblazoned on the gate the maxim *'Arbeit macht frei'* (Work brings freedom). The walls marked the limits of the camp and were surmounted by eighteen watch-towers and electrified barbed wire. Its triangular shape made it possible for the SS to keep the entire camp within the sights of their firearms, usually machine guns. Each watch-tower was manned by three or four armed SS who beamed powerful searchlights over the camp throughout the night. The cynicism of the SS became even more cruelly apparent when a fellow prisoner pointed out to me the inscription on each hut around the semi-circle of the assembly yard in front of 'A' tower. They bore the following words, painted in white: 'There is a road to freedom: its stages are obedience, assiduity, honesty, order, cleanliness, sobriety, candour, sacrifice and patriotism.' Meanwhile the commander of 'KZ' had explained to us, translating into the various languages of the representatives of more than twenty nations imprisoned there, that the only path to freedom was 'up the chimney of the crematorium'.

The purpose of this article is not to recount in detail all the twists and turns of fortune to which my fellow prisoners and myself were exposed during the two years spent in that hell until the liberation in May 1945. I shall therefore do no more than touch briefly on a few facts which may convey something of the horror of the Nazi barbarity.

The executions quarter (gas chamber, crematorium and shooting-range or hanging area) was known as 'Z' station, after the last letter of the alphabet, which symbolized the end of the road for the prisoners. Over 100 *Kommandos* (subsidiary camps) were tacked on to the main camp between 1942 and 1944. These annexes used between 1,000 (sometimes fewer) and 7,000 prisoners for work connected with the construction of warplanes, the arms industry in general, chemistry, electrical installations and brick-making, forcing them to put in ten to twelve hours of exhausting work at a stretch, on 800 calories of food a day, and subjecting them to blows and beatings. The hiring out of prisoners to armament factories was a source of substantial profit to the SS. A prisoner's cost-effectiveness over a nine-month period, corresponding to his or her average life-span, was carefully calculated.

In 1945, when the Eastern front was no more than about 8 km away, the SS set fire to the camp records, and on 20 April, 30,000 men and women from Sachsenhausen were driven out by the SS in a terrible state of exhaustion on to the north-western road leading to Schwerin and Lübeck Bay. Kaindl, the former SS commander of 'KZ', had received orders from Hitler's government in February 1945 to exterminate the prisoners in the camp. Between February and March 1945, 5,000 prisoners were killed there. During the 'death march' (160 km on foot, which I personally was made to undergo) in April 1945 the SS shot dead 9,000 prisoners. On 22 April, the survivors who had been left behind in the camp because they were unable to walk were freed by a detachment of Polish and Soviet soldiers. According to statistics recorded in the camp documents saved from destruction,

204,537 prisoners entered the Oranienburg-Sachsenhausen 'KZ' between 12 July 1936 and 15 April 1945; 100,167 of them were deliberately exterminated there.

How it is now

In the 1970s and 1980s I went with others on pilgrimages to the camps – those places of remembrance – and particularly to Sachsenhausen. I went as a courier and guide to some young French people and also people of other nationalities, and I went to bear witness. I shall say nothing of the strength of feeling of those who return: that is not the point. The real purpose is, without hatred, to bear witness to the younger generation, lest people forget.

Since the unification of Germany – a welcome event – I have returned to the Oranienburg-Sachsenhausen 'KZ' and was extremely moved to set eyes again on that place where so many of my fellow prisoners, not only from France but from many other European countries, died in conditions of appalling suffering. I passed by the gate of 'A' tower. I saw again the assembly yard where, with shaven heads in the unbearable heat under the blazing sun, or in the bitter cold, in rain, wind or snow, thousands of prisoners would have to stand to attention three times a day for hours at a stretch, together with the dead who, if such was the pleasure of the SS, had to be carried out and held upright. I saw again the stone roller weighing several hundred kilograms that had to be dragged over the assembly yard for hours on end by members of the punishment gang to roll it flat. Looking around the yard in front of 'A' tower, I remembered the 'shoe-testing ground', which still exists – a track with 9 different surfaces where every day some 150 prisoners were forced to cover 30 km or so. On this track, overlaid with concrete, clinker, gravel, sand and loose chippings, a special Gestapo commando group had devised a terrible torture to extract confessions. The prisoners were forced to walk or run, depending on the mood of the torturers, in shoes one or two sizes too small for their feet while carrying a 20-kilo bag of sand on their backs, and all this with no more than the usual amount of camp food. As I made my way towards the apex of the triangle I passed by the place where the gallows was erected for the public hangings, which sometimes lasted a whole afternoon. The two iron sockets which held the posts are still there, as if time had stood still. At 'Z' station, where we laid wreaths in memory of our dead comrades, the remains of the crematorium furnaces which the SS blew up in April 1945 have been restored as museum pieces. In the autumn of 1943 the Nazis added a gas chamber. Many places were out of bounds to us during our term of imprisonment. In the course of these subsequent pilgrimages I discovered not only 'Z' station but also the execution trench, which amounted to a shooting-range with bulletproof wall, covered shelter and morgue, and in the same place a mechanical gallows for five people at a time, equipped with a trapdoor. I also saw for the first time such fixtures as the white-tiled pathology unit next to the infirmary. This was erected over a vault measuring 230 square metres and containing three large morgues that could take hundreds of corpses. The morgues were used by the SS doctors to dissect bodies and look for interesting cases so as to provide medical schools and anatomical institutes with skulls, skeletons and other items for demonstrations. Another part of the camp that is still preserved (which I had not seen before as it was isolated from the camp itself) comprised the bunker, the torture posts and the prison with its eighty cells where the German priest Niemöller was imprisoned and where, in absolute secrecy, ghastly crimes were committed. From the torture posts, prisoners were strung up for hours on end with their hands behind their backs. The bunker was just an underground vault used as an oubliette.

It is now possible, in a well-designed museum installed in the former kitchens, to retrace the history of the Nazi camp from 1936 to 1945. The visitor or pilgrim can also see documentary films about the camp, shown in the former laundry converted into a cinema. Unfortunately, on the occasion of my pilgrimage in April to May 1991, I learned that the staff who for years had been responsible for safeguarding and preserving the camp had been given notice, that the eighteen cleaners and caretakers had simply been dismissed, and that funds, too, had been cut off. An unofficial association now occupies the premises. As for this memorial to the 100,000 comrades who were killed by the Nazis between 1936 and 1945, the association claims to be using it to honour the memory of Germans known to be former Nazi SS who instigated or were accomplices in arrests and crimes universally regarded as war crimes and crimes against humanity, and who were legally tried, convicted and imprisoned from 1945 to 1950. It is just as surprising to hear the authorities responsible for historic monuments now state that the Memorial Museum Camp itself should be dedicated to the memory of the victims of both 'Nazism and Stalinist totalitarianism'.

More specifically, during my visit I saw that a new museum had been established, dedicated to the Nazi prisoners held in Camp No. 7 between 1945 and 1950. Camp No. 7 lay *outside* the triangular prison camp of the Sachsenhausen concentration camp transformed into a memorial. This new museum, however, has been established opposite the 1933–45 deportation museum and hence *within* the triangular perimeter of the Nazi concentration camp of Sachsenhausen. This attempt to blur distinctions has been compounded by the laying of a permanent memorial stone within the triangular walls of the Nazi 'KZ' of Oranienburg-Sachsenhausen. The memorial stone purports to be dedicated to the 'victims of arbitrary Stalinist offences in Special Camp No. 7–1945–50'.

It must be clearly understood that the imprisonment of former Nazis between 1945 and 1950 was decided by due process of law and did not end in wholesale and deliberate exterminations; it had nothing in common with the world of the Nazi concentration camps between 1933 and 1945. The memorial in question should therefore be located outside the triangular perimeter of the Sachsenhausen 'KZ'.

It should also be borne in mind that Sachsenhausen was the school of the Nazi concentration camp state and was used to train commissioned and non-commissioned SS officers who were required at different levels of command to run the 2,000 or so camps of the Third Reich. The Sachsenhausen SS supplied the prisoners whose corpses were dressed in Polish army uniforms so that, on 31 August 1939, the Gliwice Radio incident could be triggered by a simulated Polish attack. This gave Hitler the excuse to invade Poland.

In the outbuildings of Sachsenhausen, SS leader Skorzeny, chief of the shock troops put together by Himmler's secret services, trained the men who freed Mussolini. It was he who tried out poisoned bullets on prisoners. It was also at Sachsenhausen that Operation Andréa was launched at the instigation of SS chief Heydrich and became Operation Bernhard, involving the forging of pound notes which were intended to flood the United Kingdom and ruin its economy. Other, similar historical facts could be cited, but space does not permit. We must, then, accept the fact that the history of the Sachsenhausen concentration camp from 1933 to 1945 cannot be merged with that of the Nazi Special Camp No. 7 between 1945 and 1950.

In conclusion, a memorial museum of the importance of Sachsenhausen should help to convey the most accurate record possible of past events, and should not mislead or distort their historical context.

Note

Roger Bordage was arrested by the Gestapo for resistance activities in France in 1943. He survived for two years in Oranienburg-Sachsenhausen concentration camp and was freed in 1945 by the Allies.

Chapter 14

Representing Diversity and Challenging Racism: the Migration Museum

Viv Szekeres

THE MIGRATION MUSEUM IN ADELAIDE, South Australia opened in 1986 with the brief to document, collect, preserve and present the evidence of South Australia's immigration history. The museum also aims to create a greater aware-ness of the cultural traditions that survive and now contribute to the rich cultural diversity of the State.

These seemingly clear and simple aims do not perhaps immediately reveal the complexity that underlies them – unless of course questions are raised such as: Whose history? Told from which point(s) of view? Who is included and who left out? Whose voices are foregrounded and whose silenced – and is this typically the case? In fact, endless questions that are located in the arena of meaning-making and the construction and representation of reality.

It is these more difficult, though more interesting, questions that the twelve staff of the museum grapple with and debate. They do this not only from their own perspectives, but also from the perspective of operating within a State Govern-ment funded organisation, forming part of a larger South Australian History Trust that contains several divisions. The issues then, of voice, identity, and of who is speaking on whose behalf, surrounded the enterprise from the outset.

It is interesting that images and understandings about Australia from overseas often focus on the bizarre and exotic. There are the sharks, the cuddly koalas, the nasty snakes and spiders and some dubious cultural ambassadors, such as Dame Edna, Rolf Harris and Crocodile Dundee. Not to mention of course, the images and misinformation that surround Indigenous Australians. Given this picture alone it is difficult to contemplate what social inclusion might look like, so a brief demographic history providing some sense of a social and cultural framework is a useful backdrop.

Source: *Museums, Society, Inequality*, Richard Sandell (ed.), London: Routledge, 2002, pp. 142–52.

Australian demography: an overview

Australia sits on the edge of the Pacific Rim. It is a somewhat ambivalent position because while this logically fits, at least in geographic and economic terms, with Asia, Australia has in fact been aligned, since 1788, by strong cultural bonds to what is still referred to in some circles as 'The Mother Country'. Approximately 75 per cent of Australia's population claim Anglo-Celtic origin.

A map of Indigenous Australia before colonisation demonstrates the existence of hundreds of Aboriginal groups. This may help to explain the continuing indignation of Aboriginal peoples at the assumption that was made by the British Crown when, in 1788, they declared Australia to be *terra nullius*, the land of no one. This fiction was only recently and reluctantly acknowledged by the Australian Government and is still by no means resolved. Invasion, as it was for the Aboriginal people, or colonisation as it is called in European history books, began with a penal colony in New South Wales and continued as a gradual process across the continent. It wasn't until 1836 that South Australia was proclaimed a colony, where the sale of land to wealthy businessmen raised sufficient funds to ship out free settlers, who it was hoped would work the land. To give some sense of attitudes about who belonged and who did not at this time, from the point of view of white settlers, one example (and there are hundreds) is some evidence presented to the House of Commons in 1837 by the Reverend E. Yates who reported:

> I have heard again and again people say that they [Aboriginal people] are nothing better than dogs, and that it was not more harm to shoot them, than it would be to shoot a dog when he barked to you. (cited in McConnochie *et al.* 1988: 59)

The Migration Museum

The Migration Museum itself houses its own history of several groups of outsiders who have been and continue to be treated as pariahs – Indigenous peoples, unemployed men, dispossessed women and the elderly poor. In the 1850s the first Aboriginal school was built on the museum's site. Aboriginal children were removed from their parents to be taught the ways of the whites. It took another 150 years before a Royal Commission was to investigate this practice and document the effects of the removal of Aboriginal children from their parents. The museum acknowledges this early Aboriginal history with a plaque in the courtyard, exhibitions and education programmes. Following the closure of the Aboriginal school, the site became a Destitute Asylum and was surrounded by a high wall, topped with tumble brick and broken glass, which effectively separated the poor inmates from the 'good citizens' of nineteenth-century Adelaide.

By the late 1850s the combination of economic recession and the discovery of gold in Victoria had created huge social problems for the early colony. There was a mass exodus of men seeking their fortunes in Victoria and leaving behind hundreds of destitute women, many pregnant. The residue of this history still clings to buildings known as the Lying-in Hospital and the Mothers' Wards. The stories of these women and their children are told in a display and publication called *Behind the Wall* (Geyer 1994).

The Migration Museum then, deals by definition with concepts of belonging, of inclusivity and with meanings surrounding the notion of 'home'. For the staff of the museum the task was understood to be that of representing the immigrant experience. Such stories would include those of early settlers, immigrants and refugees, not to mention the devastating impact that colonisation had on Indigenous peoples.

One of the first questions to be addressed was a basic one – which groups to represent? Some of the larger and more established community groups also began to lobby the museum, as they wished to be represented under their national banner. Had this model been adopted, the museum would have had for example a Polish section, Italian section, Greek section and so on. There are more than 150 groups who identify themselves by their ethnic origin, Australia being one of the most culturally diverse nations in the world. The model that was finally adopted followed a chronological story of immigration to, and settlement in, Australia, which enabled the museum to include different stories and different voices representing diverse moments in history. Another issue, which took longer to resolve, was how we should establish a collection. Within the first year it became clear that the museum was not going to acquire a collection through donated objects for many years. Analysis of why individuals and community groups were reluctant to donate objects revealed that many immigrant groups were cautious about dealing with government agencies. Furthermore, many had come to Australia as refugees with few possessions. Over the years these possessions had acquired great cultural significance to their owners and, understandably, they were not about to hand them over to anyone. The museum then introduced a policy of borrowing objects for display and it adopted a passive collecting policy. Currently the museum has a small collection of approximately 6,000 artefacts and 11,000 copy photographs. About 70 per cent of all objects on display at any time will be on loan from individuals and communities.

Planning of programmes emerged as a very sensitive area to navigate. On the one hand the museum was representing and even promoting cultural difference, but on the other hand it was desperately trying to avoid reinforcing stereotypical images and the potentially divisive aspects of difference. These tensions are, I believe, intrinsic for anyone involved in the work of representing diversity, and they are not easy to resolve.

A concrete example of such tension is provided in a description of early meetings held in my office. The curator and myself are negotiating between two groups from the same country with different religious beliefs. The several meetings with each group are held on separate occasions. The two groups do not wish to meet together. Each group has quite definite ideas of which bits of information are relevant and, even more clearly, which bits are to be left out. The discussion is confusing. It lacks logic until we intuit that we are negotiating around some very real but unspoken fears. Information that could be used in the programme in Australia has dangerous consequences for those who still live in the country of origin. Now this becomes not only a question of different points of view but also an unspoken ethical dilemma. The challenge is to find a way to present the information in ways that have integrity and meaning and reflect their experiences, while at the same time protect their rights to privacy.

In representing people's real experiences, histories and identities the museum not only had problems between what is public and what is private, but also between competing versions of history amongst communities, particularly if they had been enemies for centuries. Of course, as in the previous example, there was and is, also, the problem of competing versions of the past from within the same community and across the generations.

What made it possible to proceed at all was that the nation was enjoying a period of buoyant optimism in the first flush of exploring the relatively new concept of multiculturalism. For the many who had lived through decades of a previous policy known as assimilation, there was a great sense of relief. The policy of assimilation is just as it sounds. Throughout the late 1940s, the 1950s and 1960s it had promoted the idea that to become a 'Good Australian' it would be wise to abandon all vestiges of personal cultural origin, customs and language and adopt cultural norms of Australian English, Australian dress and behaviour codes.

In contrast, multiculturalism appeared to accept ethnic, racial and cultural difference and promote ideas of self-esteem, respect and tolerance. This enthusiasm for the concept of multiculturalism enabled the museum to navigate around some of the internal politics within community groups and organisations. It enabled a critical analysis of previous policies that had impacted on immigrants and also, importantly, it allowed representation of a history of racism and intolerance.

Challenging racism

An example, which is featured in *The Immigration Story*, is a display about the Immigration Restriction Act. The legislation was more commonly known as the White Australia Policy and is central to the immigration story because it had a huge impact on the demography of Australia. Another probable legacy was that it encouraged a distrust and fear of immigrants, especially those from Asia. It was also the first piece of legislation to be enacted by the new Federal Government of Australia in 1901.

Although changes were made to the White Australia Policy during its seventy years of operation, it effectively prevented non-white immigrants from entering the country. For more than fifty years a dictation test was used as one of the mechanisms for judging eligibility. The dictation test was not always administered in English and one of the more notorious and absurd examples was the case of Egon Kirsch. He was a Jewish political activist from Czechoslovakia who spoke at least six languages fluently. When he tried to enter Australia in 1934 to warn people about what was happening in Nazi Germany he was given the test in Scottish Gaelic. Naturally he failed. The Act was designed to keep out anyone who was judged by the immigration authorities to be an 'undesirable'. Egon Kirsch was considered to be from the dangerous political 'left'. One of the reasons we know of his case is that he actually jumped ship and his supporters took the government to court. Scottish Gaelic was found not to be a language but a dialect.

This is just one of the stories that is told in the museum, along with others that do not reflect well on either the nineteenth-century colonial government or on the twentieth-century Federal Government. Given that most of the Museum's funding comes from government sources, visitors from countries such as China, Indonesia and even America find it unusual that many of the displays are openly critical of government policies. It is interesting here to reflect about whether there is more freedom to be outspoken when funding comes from a democratic government than when it comes from business or industry sponsorship, particularly given the economic stringencies that most museums face.

When the museum was established, a deliberate decision was made to take an ideological position which would be clearly stated. Exhibitions were, and are, sympathetic to the experience of the immigrant. There is an acknowledgement that immigrants have been used as cheap labour; policies have discriminated against them for much of the century; and throughout this history there is the continuing presence of racism. For the individuals and communities whose stories were presented, and for many museum visitors, this position was welcomed. For others, fortunately only ever a small minority, the museum was viewed as a 'lefty' sort of place and as such, of course, could be relegated to the margins of what is taken seriously.

Under the banner of the newly embraced multiculturalism, the museum embarked on the process of mapping how to represent all migrant groups. Though well intentioned, the production team would probably agree that we were fairly unsophisticated in our approach. The museum's first two changing exhibitions, one about costume from the Balkans and one about lace, did little to investigate cultural difference or to explore different histories. They simply displayed pretty things from different cultures. They were more ethnographic in content, rather thin on social history and certainly lacked any political analysis. Later a much more rigorous historical interpretation was introduced. Exhibitions were developed that focused on particular communities – for example, in 1988 a display about early German settlers called *Passenger from Hamburg*. Later one called *Il Cammino Continua* charted the continuing journey of South Australian Italians. The complexities involved in such stories opened possibilities to represent issues with more subtlety, to explore multiple meanings, and allow voices to speak about previously silent areas.

This style of working led also to an interest in highlighting specific themes in terms of their social and cultural impact. Exhibitions on themes such as sport or childhood were developed, for example. This enabled the inclusion of many groups and analysis of cross-cultural connections. Interestingly, these topic-based exhibitions had enormous popular appeal. For example, *Strictly Black*, which explored the many different cultural reasons and meanings behind why people have worn and still wear black clothes; an exhibition about sport, called *Fair Game*, which took gender and discrimination as its main theme; and recently a travelling exhibition about food, called *Chops and Changes*, which showed that the ubiquitous lamb chop was now off the menu, displaced by foods from all over the world, brought in by immigrants after the Second World War.

Dozens of members from the communities whose stories we were representing were actively involved and participated in the process of developing programmes. But in the final analysis, or exhibition, it was essentially our version of their story that was displayed. Of course community members were interviewed, their stories recorded and their objects borrowed for display. But it was the museum staff who interpreted what was of significance within this range of material. Our brief, as we saw it, was to focus on ethnicity and difference – which would of course affect what we saw as important. Perhaps one of the key points here is that history museums cannot pretend to be objective. Historical interpretation and objectivity are contradictory ideas. Given that we cannot be objective, then at least let us honestly own our own bias and author displays. Let us also ask the public for their opinion and include these responses – as we frequently do with pin boards, which allow the visitor's interpretation as well as their opinion of displays.

Multiple voices

To balance the voice of the museum, a Community Access Gallery called *The Forum* was established. In *The Forum* for a period of three months, a community group presents their own display, telling their history from their own perspective. It is an ongoing programme with four *Forum* displays a year. In the mid-1980s this was a very novel concept. By now there are few history museums in Australia that do not have a community access space. From the perspective of community groups *The Forum* is a resounding success.

From the museum's perspective it enables us to meet and work with a range of people who become involved and interested in the museum's programmes and usually stay in contact. Each *Forum* launch brings notable community leaders, politicians and media to the museum, all of which helps build the profile. At another level the success and vibrancy of *Forum* activities depends significantly on the skills, cultural awareness and commitment of the curator who manages it.

The Forum raises the really big question of who exactly constitutes community. Who is it that the museum works with when we say we are working with the Slovenian, Indian or Cornish community? The answer is not straightforward. It would be possible to choose from dozens of different models to describe the protocols, procedures and levels of interaction that take place before even one of these displays can open.

For example, there was one community where power and control was administered entirely through the religious patriarchal leaders but where it was women who did all the work. Or the group where the organising committee was ruled with an iron rod by a quite formidable woman in her late seventies who made all the decisions and had the committee members running around in a frenzy trying to be helpful. Or the organising committee of twenty who were representing a relatively small community, but where every member of the committee had a different opinion about everything. Or a committee who represented just one of the regions of Italy and who managed to involve and represent a huge range of interests and who included the young and the very old, the religious and the secular.

To return briefly to the production process, which involves curators, designer, educator, and front of house staff, operations manager and myself as programme coordinator, decisions are made by consensus. As many of the staff have worked together for many years, their shared history is full of important moments of change and new directions based on emerging understandings. These have come sometimes as small incremental changes in approach, perception or presentation. At other times, a change of direction can represent a significant shift in thinking.

Exploring identities

One such moment was when a conclusion was reached that the way the museum was interpreting multiculturalism was much too narrow. It was decided to expand the definition to include not just ethnicity but other elements of identity such as class, race, gender, age and religion. It would have been good to say that our definition also included sexual preference, but it didn't. Perhaps at some stage the museum will include issues about sexual preference in its programmes. The reason this has not happened thus far indicates not only a lack of courage, but also the fact that most of the communities who work with us prefer not to think about, and certainly do not want to talk about, the gays and lesbians who are amongst them.

However, in spite of such limitations, our thinking represented a major shift, for it meant that ethnicity became only one of a number of aspects of identity. Visitors could now be introduced to some of the complexities that surround the concept of identity. Elsewhere I have described these as being like layers of an onion. A more poetic analogy is the petals of a tea rose. Under each layer of petals is another, which under the right circumstances of light and sun unfurls to reveal itself. So it is with identity – each of us has several identities, some of us have many, and different aspects of identity are relevant in different contexts.

An example, which might illustrate the point, happened a few years ago. The Hellenic Women's Cultural Group of the Pan Macedonian Society asked one of the museum's curators to attend a discussion that they were having about their past and their lives. They showed her household items and personal treasures, which they had brought with them when they emigrated. Each item triggered a memory and a story. The result of this meeting was a display, which they called *Cycles of Life, Our Family, Our Home, Our Church*. Although this group identifies strongly as Macedonian Greek, the story they wished to tell, and which ended up being in the display, was not about themselves as Macedonian Greeks. It was about themselves as women, as daughters, granddaughters, wives and mothers. It also highlighted another major feature of identity and of cultural difference, that of age. As they grew older they knew their story to be grounded in their times. With immense clarity they set out to communicate to later generations because they knew that their memories had begun to fade. They also realised that, as members of their group died, much of their history died with them.

The matter of who is included in museum displays starts with perceptions about identity – exactly which aspects of identity will be the subject matter represented in the display. The second issue is the question of why a particular subject matter has been chosen. Perhaps this is best understood in the context of another example from the museum's experience.

In the early 1990s Australia reluctantly began to prosecute some of those accused as war criminals from the Second World War. The first case in Adelaide involved a man accused of being a member of the Ukrainian Special Police. He was accused of commanding a troop who had massacred a large number of Jews. Public opinion was divided about whether this man was a monster or, as the right-wing press described him, a gentle, 70-year-old grandfather. Nevertheless, in spite of the ambivalence that surrounded his trial, South Australia's Ukrainian community became nervous and concerned that they could be labelled as war criminals. At about this time the

President of the Ukrainian community contacted the museum, as the community wanted to mount an exhibition about their history, culture, religious practice and the traditions they brought with them to Australia. The museum agreed to assist them to mount their display, which opened with a lively festival over a weekend. Neither the President nor members of the Ukrainian organising committee talked to staff about their motives for wanting to mount this exhibition at that particular time – not, that is, until after the display was finished and the war criminal prosecution had failed for lack of evidence.

How staff at the museum feel when we are clearly involved, wittingly or unwittingly, in matters of legitimising and promoting certain aspects of a past, whilst keeping silent about other aspects, is a matter of ongoing discomfort and debate amongst us. Every time a decision is taken about which exhibition is included in the programme, the museum faces the same kind of dilemmas. Every decision will include some individuals and groups but will exclude others. Long-term strategic planning has become an absolute necessity for us.

A feeling of belonging

Another story from the Second World War illustrates a slightly different point, which is about the importance of belonging. The vast majority of the museum's constituents or stakeholders want to tell their stories and want recognition for their contributions to the development of Australia. Furthermore, they want to feel that they now belong somewhere. This need to belong is especially true for those who came as refugees.

This particular story began on the nights of the 13 and 14 of June 1941; the Soviet armies made hundreds of lightning strikes against the people, in particular against the intelligentsia of Estonia, Latvia and Lithuania. As a result thousands were arrested and deported to Siberia and were never seen again. Those who escaped this round-up fled west into Germany. After 1947 they were amongst 170,000 Displaced Persons who came to Australia as refugees. The Baltic Communities Council who represented some of these refugees wanted to find a way to tell Australians why they had come here and, for the first time in fifty years, to remember and commemorate those who had not made it. The museum's response was to establish a Remembrance Wall called *Reasons to Remember*, and currently we have eight plaques, which include one from the Vietnamese, Jewish, Serbian, Slovenian, Ukrainian, Polish, Tatar Bashkurt and Baltic communities. What has emerged quite spontaneously, and I doubt that the museum could have planned it even if it had tried, are the annual commemorative 'services' arranged by the communities represented on the wall. Several of these groups come each year and lay a wreath and enact a small ceremony of remembrance. The wall, and in this sense the museum, has become a sacred site as a symbolic resting place for the dead and a tangible example of belonging. In fact, at the launch for the Vietnamese Plaque last year, which was attended by several hundred members of the Vietnamese Community, they performed the Blessing of their Ancestors – a ceremony never performed in Adelaide before. One of the museum's curators was told that this event and the plaque had extraordinary significance for them and represented a feeling of belonging, of acceptance and of finally being at home, in ways that they had not felt before.

The idea of belonging raises another highly complex issue, which surrounds the concept of inclusion. It assumes, albeit loosely, a sense of ownership. Put bluntly, it implies that some have the defining power to include or not to include – to define as important or not so important in the broad picture.

This issue has come to the fore in the museum recently when immigrants who came from Britain have felt that they should feature more prominently in exhibitions. A visitor who went through a *Forum* display mounted by the Tatar Bashkurts, who are a refugee community oppressed for many years by the USSR, left a comment in the visitors' book. She said: 'As the English in Australia are now an abused and oppressed minority, should they be represented here?' Numerically, Anglo-Celts are by far the largest group in Australia and they are, of course, represented in museum displays. Reality is not the issue here but, rather, perceptions or misconceptions that the museum must deal with.

At the same time that the exhibition production team is finding ways to address such problems, Australia is also dealing with a change in Australian politics, which has impacted on concepts of multiculturalism. For the current Federal Government, multiculturalism is off the agenda, which has repercussions for museum programmes. The current Conservative Government is critical of former multicultural policies and in the political climate that they have created, parties such as Pauline Hanson's One Nation Party gained enormous public support. Her main message was that Australia was at risk of being overtaken by Asians – and that the real 'battlers' (working-class Anglo-Celts) were being overrun. Although the One Nation Party is thankfully disintegrating, there is no doubt, especially in economically difficult times, that the sentiments still exist. The facts are that the 1996 census estimated that 8 per cent of Australia's population are from Asia, the Middle East and North Africa.

A similar backlash against the stance taken by the museum is the notion that any analysis that is critical, or that raises problems from the past, is suspect. So when the museum recently mounted a very confronting exhibition about the plight of refugees, called *A Twist of Fate*, it was attacked from some quarters for being 'too politically correct', this phrase now being used as a term of abuse.

When the museum launched a plaque in the courtyard, which acknowledged the existence of the Aboriginal school on the museum's site, and we also made a public statement of 'Sorry' for previous wrongs done to Aboriginal people, some accused the curators and myself of peddling a 'black armband history'. This phrase has become that which is used to refer to any analysis of colonisation that is not celebratory and is a concept that is having a huge and detrimental impact on the process of Aboriginal Reconciliation.

A couple of years ago a Conservative Federal politician, a member of the Prime Minister's Cabinet, from a family who were prominent in South Australia during the nineteenth century, told me that in his opinion the Migration Museum was nothing but a museum of misery. Why couldn't the museum proudly tell the 'Happy Migrant' story, the many stories of success? Given that there is no doubt that in more ways than not Australia's immigration history has been an extremely successful experiment, why does the museum not follow his advice? The answer is because the story he would like us to tell is less than half the story. It would only include a fraction of the people whose stories are currently included. Even if the museum restricted displays only to those of the majority who came from England, Ireland, Scotland and Wales, or the early pioneering settlers, the process of immigration, of leaving one place and settling in another, is never easy even if the story may have a happy ending.

One of the museum's curators has just completed a photographic history of 100 years of immigration to mark the Centenary of Federation. Amongst the 500 photographs that she chose are some smiling faces, but the stories behind even those photographs often contradict that happy image. Alienation, isolation, struggle and deprivation are much more common themes. And then there are the gaps in the photographic record, the people who were rarely included in the life of the Nation, out of sight and out of mind.

For the moment, with projects like this photographic one, *The Forum* and the changing exhibition programme, the Migration Museum is attempting to tell a larger story. It will never be the whole story, or the whole truth. It will always be our version or someone else's version of the truth. But perhaps over the years, the museum can create a mosaic of different interpretations, which will contribute to shaping the picture of our country. The picture needs to include Indigenous people, immigrants, settlers and refugees, and they need to be placed very firmly in the centre of the picture rather than in the margins or just outside the frame.

Note

Viv Szekeres began work in the Migration Museum in Adelaide, South Australia, in 1984 and was appointed director in 1987.

References

Geyer, M. (1994) *Behind The Wall: The Women of the Destitute Asylum, Adelaide, 1852–1918*, South Australia: Axiom.

McConnochie, K., Hollinsworth, D. and Pettman, J. (1988) *Race and Racism in Australia*, Australia: Social Science Press.

Chapter 15

Collection, Repatriation and Identity

Cressida Fforde

Repatriation and reburial

IN THE LATE EIGHTEENTH, nineteenth and early twentieth centuries, perceptions of identity and identity construction suffused the history of the collecting and interpretation of human remains. At the end of the twentieh century, identity can also be identified as one of the fundamental issues of the reburial debate. The perception and construction of Aboriginal identity play a significant role in both repatriation requests and arguments put forward by those who have opposed them.

In Australia, the beginnings of the reburial campaign can be traced to the late 1960s. At the start of a decade in which Aborigines first held Australian citizenship and which witnessed the emergence of the Land Rights movement, Australian museums, archaeologists and physical anthropologists began to consider Aboriginal concerns regarding the curation and scientific use of sensitive cultural material. In separate campaigns, yet part of a general drive for the restitution of Aboriginal cultural heritage, museums were approached by Aborigines to discuss the future of secret/sacred objects and the Aboriginal human remains housed in their collections (see Lampert 1983; Hemming 1985; Anderson 1986). The 1970s and early 1980s witnessed some changes in museum policies and the return to communities, particularly in Tasmania, of human remains of named individuals (such as Truganini) or those collected in what was widely viewed as unethical circumstances (such as the Crowther Collection).[1] These developments demonstrated that, by the early 1980s in Australia, in general the scientific community would no longer contest Aboriginal ownership of the remains of named individuals, individuals whose cultural or biological descendants could be traced, or those which had been obtained

Source: *The Dead and their Possessions: Repatriation in Principle, Policy and Practice*, C. Fforde, J. Hubert and P. Turnbull (eds), London: Routledge, 2002, pp. 34–46.

by what was now considered to be unethical means. When Aboriginal bodies (two adults, a young child and a stillborn baby) preserved in fluid in a box at the South Australian Museum came to light in August 1983, there was little question that, after a coroner's inquiry, they would be given to the appropriate Aboriginal community for disposition.[2]

However, in 1984 many scientists in both Australia and overseas began publicly and forcefully to oppose Aboriginal claims when it became clear that all Aboriginal human remains, including ancient and fossil remains, might be returned to Aboriginal communities. Such material, they argued, was of great scientific significance and too old to be legitimately claimed by one group of people to the detriment of the world community (see *The Bulletin* 4.9.1984, Kennedy to the editor, *The Bulletin* 9.10.1984). Aboriginal people, on the other hand, argued that such remains were also, by definition, their ancestors, and required appropriate treatment. Despite the return of a significant number of human remains to Aboriginal communities in the previous decade, it was not until the mid-1980s that the debate surrounding reburial and the scientific use of Aboriginal human remains escalated to become a major national and international issue.

Repatriation requests

In the mid-1980s, at a time in which the reburial issue had already caused considerable antagonism between various Aboriginal groups and many archaeologists and physical anthropologists, a consultancy was carried out by Steven Webb on behalf of the Australian Archaeological Association. The results afford a good indication of Aboriginal attitudes at the community level towards the reburial issue at that time. The project aimed to open communication with Aboriginal groups, by consulting with communities, and particularly those with a direct interest in a collection housed at Melbourne University that was contested at that time (the Murray Black Collection).[3] Webb found that because archaeologists had rarely, if ever, consulted with Aborigines about the removal or study of skeletal remains, communities were highly suspicious and held the general opinion that researchers 'had little regard for Aborigines, either as the living descendants of the populations whose remains were studied or as people' (Webb 1987: 294). Aboriginal people, shocked at the quantity of remains in collections, the length of time they had been kept in a 'seemingly secretive manner' (Webb 1987: 294), and the way in which they had been collected, frequently pointed out the double-standards in operation, noting that such practices would not have been tolerated if Aborigines had dug up European cemeteries. Some people were disgusted that scientists should even wish to interfere with the dead, and little distinction was made between researchers who analysed remains today and those who had studied and collected the bones in the past. Webb also discovered that some Aboriginal people were genuinely surprised that the majority of anthropologists would not support the campaign for reburial. Coupled with the recent use of the media by scientists and their canvassing of international scholars for support, Aboriginal people were angered by the unsympathetic attitude accorded to the very people 'archaeologists and anthropologists purported to understand and professed to help' (Webb 1987: 294).

Nonetheless, despite the anger and concern which he encountered, Webb also realized that many Aboriginal people acknowledged the importance of archaeological research and were willing to discuss compromises regarding the future of skeletal collections. Primarily, Aboriginal people desired control over the remains, communication with the potential researchers and involvement in future projects (Webb 1987: 295). Webb concluded that the reburial issue could only be overcome with continued and considerable discussion between scientists and Aborigines.

The opinions held by the communities consulted by Webb are also voiced by those who have been at the forefront of the reburial campaign. In addition, central to many arguments for the repatriation of remains has been the contribution made by past scientific research on remains to the construction of an inferior identity for Aboriginal people, and the role that this played in the justification of their oppression by settlers and the Government (e.g. Mansell 1990). As Turnbull (1993: 14) has pointed out, 'in demanding control of remains Aboriginal people were articulating a politics which stressed the degree to which their identity had been forged through the historical experiences of colonialism'. Moreover, the aims and results of modern scientific enquiry have also been questioned by Aboriginal people, who argue that such research can negate Aboriginal concepts of their own history and in doing so continues to prescribe identities for, and thus to disempower, Aboriginal people (e.g. Weatherall 1989: 12). The campaign for Aboriginal control of their ancestors' remains can therefore also be seen to be part of the wider criticism and refutation of the scientific monopoly over 'valid' interpretations of the indigenous past (Langford 1980; Pardoe 1992: 135–6; and see McGuire 1992).

The tension inherent in, and exemplified by, the reburial debate between archaeological and indigenous views about the past, and who should have the authority to interpret it, is shown in the following exchange of letters. These appeared in a leading British newspaper at a time in which the issue of returning ancient and fossil remains was being strongly opposed by members of the scientific community. Don Brothwell, a British physical anthropologist then at the Institute of Archaeology, University College London, wrote:

> While we would all wish to honour the thoughts the Aborigines have for their ancestors, it is important to remember that ancient remains, from whatever world site, have international scientific importance and this should take precedent over local issues. Secondly, ancestor claims are more than likely to be based on ignorance of history or pre-history, a state of affairs which archaeological investigation attempts to rectify. (Brothwell to the Editor, *The Times* 29.8.1990)

And Mandawuy Yunupingu of the Northern Land Council responded:

> I am a Yolngu (Aboriginal) person from Australia and I know where my ancestry starts from. We have a living history that we practice, which provides us with information, just like your archaeological investigations. Our history is alive to us. We do not need archaeological investigations to tell us where we came from or from who we are descended. The

remains of Aboriginal people must be returned to their rightful people
and country. It's only just to do so. (Yunupingu to the Editor, *The Times*
10.9.1990)

Many of those who opposed repatriation simply could not accept that Aboriginal
people were articulating strongly held spiritual beliefs and expressing a deep
concern for their ancestors, however ancient the remains were. Instead, some believed
such claims to be formulated only to achieve political objectives (Brown to Jones
29.6.1984, reproduced in Meehan 1984: 139; *The Herald* 23.7.1984; see also
Hiatt to the Editor, *The Australian* 2.8.1990). A British archaeologist, Stuart
Piggott, wrote expressing a similar standpoint to that held by Brothwell (see above)
which rejected the validity of Aboriginal beliefs, claimed that requests were
politically motivated, and upheld the primacy of scientific authority. His letter protested
at claims by the Echuca Aboriginal community for the return of the Kow Swamp
fossils:[4]

> . . . when emotion mixed with political objectives takes over from
> common sense and reason, the results can be disastrous. If we are to
> ignore great men of science such as Emeritus Professor John Mulvaney
> and Dr Alan Thorne, and act on the radical recommendations of those
> less knowledgeable, we throw archaeology to the winds in Australia.
> (*The Times* 18.8.1990)

Not all Australian archaeologists who opposed the reburial of all remains questioned the validity of Aboriginal beliefs or the motivation of governments which
acceded to Aboriginal requests (see Meehan 1984). The fact that some changes had
taken place throughout the 1980s was demonstrated by the fact that at the time
of the Kow Swamp issue some archaeologists and anthropologists had become
sympathetic to Aboriginal opinion and highly critical of the views expressed by their
colleagues (e.g. Bowdler to the Editor, *The Australian* 3.8.1990; O'Brien and Tompkins
to the Editor, *The Australian* 5.8.1990; McBryde to the Editor, *Melbourne Age* 1.9.1990).
For example, Webb's consultation with communities had convinced him that although
the reburial issue was sometimes used as a political platform, the argument that it
was entirely politically inspired by individuals or organizations 'opposed to "white"
science' (Webb 1987: 295) was facile and simplistic.

Many of the Aborigines who have been the most visible in the requesting and
receiving of ancestral remains from institutions in the 1980s and 1990s have been
those who are perceived as 'non-traditional' or 'urban' people. This is, of course,
not to say that such people are not indigenous (Aboriginal or Koori, Murri, Noongah,
etc.), but only that they may not conform to common outside perceptions of the
culturally 'pristine' Australian Aborigine. Accusations that requests for the return
of remains were solely political in nature were commonly, explicitly or implicitly,
conjoined with the assertion that such requests were invalid because they had
no basis in 'traditional' beliefs and were being made by 'non-traditional' people.
Given that spiritual concerns have been the overriding grounds for requesting the
repatriation of ancestors, it is perhaps unsurprising that arguments employed to oppose
these requests have sought to deny their authenticity.

The reburial campaign is clearly saturated with political issues and is in itself a modern development. However over and above the testimony heard from a broad cross-section of Australia's indigenous community (as, for example, described by Webb 1987), there is ample historical evidence of Aboriginal opposition to the removal of their ancestors' remains (see p. 245, this volume and Turnbull 2002). Furthermore, particularly in the context of the issues raised in this chapter, discussions about the legitimacy or otherwise of Aboriginal claims are deceptive, as they mask what has been a significant sub-text in the reburial issue: a widely held common distinction made between 'traditional' and 'non-traditional' Aboriginal people, and the frequent denial of legitimacy to the latter.

Although Australian legislation no longer employs definitions of Aboriginal people based on genetic inheritance, it has been argued that an assumed association between biology and culture continues to exist. There is a frequent popular and academic (and not exclusively non-Aboriginal [see Myers 1994: 690]) division made between 'traditional' and 'non-traditional' or 'urban' Aborigines, and the perception that only the former are somehow 'real' Aborigines. Such perceptions deny Aboriginality to those who do not exhibit what is perceived to be a 'pristine' (i.e. pre-contact) Aboriginal culture (see Gilbert 1977: 5–31; Chase 1981; Langton 1981, 1993; Cowlishaw 1986, 1987, 1988, 1992; Beckett 1988; Eckermann 1988; Jacobs 1988; Hollinsworth 1992; Attwood and Arnold 1992). Modern anthropological discourse has frequently been at least complicit with the accordance of greater legitimacy to 'traditional' Aborigines. Chase (1981: 24) and Cowlishaw (1986, 1987, 1988, 1992) argue, amongst others, that this stance can be partly attributed to the implicit retention by modern social anthropology of some of the fundamental tenets of nineteenth-century physical anthropology. Cowlishaw, for example, has shown how, even after social anthropology began to disassociate itself from theories of racial classification in the 1920s, and finally rejected them in the 1940s and 1950s, a 'submerged or implied definition of Aborigines as a race was retained' (Cowlishaw 1992: 23) and the Aboriginal 'race' came to be equated with 'traditional' Aborigines. The almost exclusive interest of early physical anthropologists in the remains of 'full-bloods' was therefore perhaps echoed in the concentration by social anthropologists on the study of 'traditional' groups. So-called 'non-traditional' groups have often found themselves in a catch-22 situation: while (and because) they are the most dispossessed they are the least able to claim the return of their heritage on 'traditional' grounds, as is often required by the wider Australian community.

The questioning of the legitimacy of Aboriginal claims for remains which are made by people that are not perceived as living 'traditional' lifestyles can be seen as an expression of a continuing denial of an 'equal' Aboriginality to 'non-traditional' groups. Such perspectives not only deny the very real spiritual concerns of many Aboriginal people today but disempower those who are not seen to follow a 'traditional' lifestyle, regardless of how they perceive themselves. Arguments opposed to repatriation on these grounds presume an authoritative knowledge about Aboriginal culture, past and present, and consequently impose identities upon Aboriginal people. They also illustrate what appears to be a continuing manifestation of the ossification of 'true' Aboriginal culture in a static and timeless past, and thus the denial of truly authentic Aboriginality to many people living today.

In his analysis of the reburial debate in the US, McGuire (1989) identified a similar relegation of American Indians to 'the pages of history books'. He noted that one reason why there was a distinctly different attitude held by the white population towards disturbing white burials and those of indigenes was that only the former were perceived to be part of an ongoing culture. Such a stance appears to contend that authenticity is static, that mutability and tradition are mutually exclusive. However, one thing that the reburial debate demonstrates is that 'tradition' can and does change. Indeed, in the case of reburial, science can be said to have been instrumental in the development of new cultural practices: the many reburial ceremonies that have occurred since the late 1970s would never have taken place without the acquisitive practices of scientific scholarship in the first place.

Repatriation and reburial are loci for processes which both construct and reaffirm Aboriginality, empowering its participants by enabling them to assert, define (and thus take control over) their own identity – often in a very public manner. One way in which this occurs is through their focus on persisting pan-Aboriginal spiritual concerns to accord the dead appropriate treatment. The use of traditional elements in most reburial ceremonies also articulates Aboriginality and at the same time is felt to be appropriate for the individuals interred. Moreover, the identification of collected remains as ancestors confirms the descent of modern 'urban' communities from individuals from the traditional past, thus confirming their Aboriginal identity by virtue of descent. Nowhere has the 'descent' factor perhaps been more apparent and more significant than in Tasmania, a state with a history of denying Aboriginal status to its indigenous population, usually on the promulgated fiction that Truganini . . . had indeed been the 'last Tasmanian' (Cove 1995: 86, 102– 39). As Cove observes, by demanding the return of Truganini's remains in 1970 'for her descendants', the Aboriginal Information Centre effectively challenged the State Government's grounds for denying Tasmanian Aboriginality at a time when establishing an outwardly 'acceptable' basis for such an identity was crucial for the advance of Aboriginal rights in Tasmania:

> Truganini provided a basis for self-identification as stipulated in the Common-wealth's definition of Aboriginality. Individuals of Aboriginal descent had probably experienced discrimination which could be readily linked to the dehumanised treatment of Truganini's remains and continued denial of her deathbed request for dignity. Not only was the Tasmanian Aboriginal rights movement based on individual self-identification, there was a need for concrete issues around which mobilisation could occur and acquire external validity. The issue of Truganini's remains spoke to all these dimensions. (Cove 1995: 150)

The skeletal remains of other nineteenth-century Tasmanian Aborigines have a similar significance for some of today's Tasmanians. As one member of the Flinders Island community reportedly commented about the importance of the discovery of the exact location of Tasmanian Aboriginal graves in the cemetery at Wyballena, 'it's also about our identity – that we are here, that we exist' (*Hobart Mercury* 29.11.1990).

Reburial is one facet of what has been termed Aboriginal 'cultural revival' (e.g. Creamer 1988) that has occurred throughout Australia since the 1970s, but particularly within communities living in more settled areas. Creamer (1988: 57) observes that cultural revival frequently employs knowledge about the traditional past in conjunction with traditional material items and the use of sites of traditional significance to make a 'powerfully symbolic statement about the distinctiveness of modern Aboriginal identity'. Reburial (sometimes comprising parts or all of a traditional burial ceremony), ancestral remains and the reuse of Aboriginal burial grounds can be viewed as a fusion of many of the factors which contribute to cultural revival. They not only articulate, strengthen and construct local Aboriginal identity but also Aboriginality as a pan-Australian commonality. Reburial, while using elements from the past specific and significant to one local group, also clearly differentiates between those who are Aboriginal and those who are not.

However, while not to deny the occurrence of the phenomenon it describes nor the vital importance of tradition in the construction of modern Aboriginal identity, 'cultural revival', at least in the case of reburial, may be a misleading term. The term 'revival' ignores the frequent conjunction of modern and traditional concerns that occurs in reburial ceremonies, as well as the fact that reburial has more to do with the shared history of Aboriginal and European society than it does with pre-contact Australia. The contribution that repatriation and reburial make towards the construction of modern Aboriginal identity (locally and/or nationally defined) does not derive only from the revitalization of pre-contact tradition, but rather from the way in which various elements from both the pre- and post-contact past *and* the present are conjoined in the active development of contemporary Aboriginal customs.

Conclusion

Throughout the history of their collection and interpretation, and the development of the reburial debate, human remains have accrued a variety of meanings – ancestors, commodities, scientific specimens, fossils, symbols of oppression, data, etc. – which have not always been mutually exclusive. The reburial debate has often revolved around control of definitions of these categories, as it has about the control of the remains themselves. As the definition of remains as 'ancestors' may be seen as central to Aboriginal identity, so too was the definition of remains as 'scientific data' central to the identity of those whose research was threatened by the loss of their primary data. For many scientists remains were primarily viewed as important specimens, the collecting and study of which affirmed and authenticated their own group identity as the authority which produced knowledge about the past. For Aborigines who wished for the same remains to be returned they were ancestors, whose presence and proper disposal were often viewed as essential components of Aboriginal self-identity. Michael Mansell of the Tasmanian Aboriginal Centre, the organization which played a prominent role in the repatriation campaign in Tasmania, asked in the mid-1980s, 'if we can't control and protect our own dead, then what is there to being Aboriginal?' (*Melbourne Age* 5.10.1985). However, because some scientists have viewed repatriation as a symbol of the extinction of physical anthropology as a discipline (e.g. Lewin 1984: 393), they could also have asked, 'if we can't control and study human remains, then what is there to being a physical anthropologist?'

From the way that physical anthropologists once 'constructed' the Aboriginal body as inferior to that of the European, to the dismissal by some of modern demands for the repatriation of remains made by 'non-traditional' Aborigines, Aboriginal remains have been situated within a discourse made hegemonic in part by its imposition of identities upon Aboriginal people. In repatriation campaigns and reburial events, Aboriginal human remains have continued to be a locus for processes that have constructed and articulated Aboriginal identity (whether locally or nationally defined), but the defining has been under Aboriginal control and has been instrumental in the empowerment of Aboriginal people. Repatriation and reburial have challenged concepts that restrict tradition to the practices of a pre-contact past, and demonstrate that tradition is a vital and constantly developing theme within modern Aboriginality.

Notes

Cressida Fforde completed her PhD at the University of Southampton in 1997 on 'Controlling the Dead: an analysis of the collecting and repatriation of Aboriginal human remains'. She is currently an independent researcher and consultant.

1   In 1909, William Crowther (Grandson of Dr W.L.H. Crowther, who had removed the skull of William Lanne in 1869 (see Ryan 1981; Fforde 1992)), accompanied by other medical students, had dug up a number of graves in the Christian cemetery at Oyster Cove, a settlement on the D'Entrecasteaux Channel which, from 1847 to 1868, had been the final home for many of the so-called 'last' Tasmanian Aborigines (Ryan 1981: 182–221).

2   In August 1985, the adults were buried at Ooldea by the Kokotha people and the child and still-born baby interred at Raukkan (Point McLeay) by the Ngarrindjeri (*AAP* News Report 3.8.1985).

3   The Department of Anatomy, University of Melbourne housed over 800 remains, most of which had been collected from Aboriginal cemeteries along the Murray river by George Murray Black between 1931 and 1951. This included late Pleistocene remains of some 70 individuals discovered at Coobool Creek, widely considered to be 'one of the most important collections of this type in the world' (Brown, University of New England, to Jones, Federal Minister for Science and Technology, 29.6.1984, reproduced in Meehan 1984: 139). The Australian Archaeological Association and the Australian Vice-Chancellor's Committee both expressed deep concern that the Victorian collections might be lost to science (Meehan 1984; *Canberra ANU Reporter* 12.10.1984).

4   The Kow Swamp fossils comprised the remains of some 40 individuals dated to between 9000 and 15000 BP. Some were rediscovered by Alan Thorne in store at the Museum of Victoria in 1967, and the rest were uncovered during his later excavations at Kow Swamp in northern Victoria between 1968 and 1972. The fossils represented the world's largest collection of late Pleistocene/early Holocene human remains from a single site, and contributed unique information

to the debate about human evolution in Australia (Thorne 1971; Thorne and Macumber 1972).

References

Anderson, C. (1986) 'Research and Return of Objects as a Social Process', *COMA Bulletin* 19, 2–10.

Attwood, B. and Arnold, J. (eds) (1992) *Power, Knowledge and Aborigines*. Special Edition of the *Journal of Australian Studies* 35.

Beckett, J.R. (1988) 'The Past in the Present; the Present in the Past: Constructing a National Aboriginality', in J.R. Beckett (ed.), *Past and Present. The Construction of Aboriginality*, 191–217. Canberra: Aboriginal Studies Press.

Chase, A. (1981) 'Empty Vessels and Loud Noises. Views about Aboriginal people today', *Social Alternatives* 2(2), 23–7.

Cove, J. (1995) *What the Bones Say. Tasmanian Aborigines, Science and Domination*. Ottawa: Carleton University Press.

Cowlishaw, G. (1986) 'Aborigines and Anthropologists', *Australian Aboriginal Studies* 1, 2–12.

—— (1987) 'Colour, Culture and the Aboriginalists', MAN n.s. (22), 221–37.

—— (1988) 'The Materials for Identity Construction', in J. Beckett, (ed.), *Past and Present. The Construction of Aboriginality*, 87–107. Canberra: Aboriginal Studies Press.

—— (1992) 'Studying Aborigines: Changing Canons in Anthropology and History', in B. Attwood and J. Arnold (eds), *Power Knowledge and Aborigines*. Special Edition of the *Journal of Australian Studies* 35, 20–31.

Creamer, H. (1988) 'Aboriginality in New South Wales: Beyond the Image of Cultureless Outcasts', in J.R. Beckett (ed.), *Past and Present. The Construction of Aboriginality*, 45–62. Canberra: Aboriginal Studies Press.

Eckermann, A. (1988) 'Cultural Vacuum or Cultural Vitality?' *Australian Aboriginal Studies* 1, 31–9.

Fforde, C. (1992) 'The Posthumous History of William Lanne', *World Archaeological Bulletin* 6, 63–9.

Gilbert, K. (1977) *Living Black. Blacks Talk to Kevin Gilbert*. London: Allen Lane.

Hemming, S. (1985) 'Development of the Issue', *COMA Bulletin* 16, 22–31.

Hollinsworth, D. (1992) 'Discourses on Aboriginality and the Politics of Identity in Urban Australia', *Oceania* 63(2), 137–55.

Jacobs, J.M. (1988) 'The Construction of Identity', in J. Beckett (ed.), *Past and Present. The Construction of Aboriginality*, 31–43. Canberra: Aboriginal Studies Press.

Lampert, R. (1983) 'Aboriginal Remains and the Australian Museum', *COMA Bulletin* 12, 19–20.

Langford, R. (1980) 'Our Heritage – Your Playground', *Australian Archaeology* 16, 1–6.

Langton, M. (1981) 'Urbanising Aborigines. The Social Scientists' Great Deception', *Social Alternatives* 2(2), 16–22.

—— (1993) 'Rum, Seduction and Death: "Aboriginality" and Alcohol', *Oceania* 63(3), 195–206.

Lewin, R. (1984) 'Extinction Threatens Australian Anthropology', *Science* 225, 393–4.

Mansell, M. (1990) 'The Case for Bringing Shiney Home', *Australian Financial Review* 28.6.1990.

McGuire, R.H. (1989) 'The Sanctity of the Grave: White concepts and American Indian burials', in R. Layton (ed.), *Conflict in the Archaeology of Living Traditions*, 167–84. London: Routledge.

—— (1992) 'Archaeology and the First Americans', *American Anthropologist* 94 (4), 816–36.

Meehan, B. (1984) 'Aboriginal Skeletal Remains', *Australian Archaeology* 19, 122–47.

Myers, F. (1994) 'Culture-Making: Performing Aboriginality at the Asia Society Gallery', *American Ethnologist* 21 (4), 679–99.

Pardoe, C. (1992) 'Arches of Radii, Corridors of Power: Reflections on Current Archaeological Practice', in B. Attwood and J. Arnold (eds), *Power, Knowledge and Aborigines*, 45–62. Special Edition of the *Journal of Australian Studies* 35.

Ryan, L. (1981) *The Aboriginal Tasmanians*, St Lucia: University of Queensland Press.

Thorne, A.G. (1971) 'Mungo and Kow Swamp: Morphological Variation in Pleistocene Australians', *Mankind* 8, 85–9.

Thorne, A.G. and Macumber, P.G. (1972) 'Discoveries of Late Pleistocene Man at Kow Swamp, Australia', *Nature* 238, 316–19.

Turnbull, P. (1993) 'Ancestors not Specimens: Reflections on the Controversy over the Remains of Aboriginal People in European Scientific Collections', *Contemporary Issues in Aboriginal and Torres Strait Islander Studies* 4, 10–35.

—— (2002) 'Indigenous Australian people, their defence of the dead and native title', in C. Fforde, J. Hubert, P. Turnbull (eds), *The Dead and Their Possessions*, London and New York: Routledge, 63–86.

Weatherall, R. (1989) 'Aborigines, Archaeologists and the Rights of the Dead', unpublished paper presented at WAC Inter-Congress, Vermillion, South Dakota.

Webb, S. (1987) 'Reburying Australian Skeletons', *Antiquity* 61: 292–6.

Chapter 16

Yours, Mine, or Ours?

Conflicts between archaeologists and ethnic groups

Joe Watkins

'Bones represent many things today: political domination, subculture identification, cheap thrills in horror movies, and religious iconography. Bones also represent science and history. Past patterns of human social behavior are carved on the skeleton as holes, bony bridges, accessory bones, and suture lines, and as shape and size.' (Pardoe 1994: 182)

Introduction

THE 1996 DISCOVERY of an ancient skeleton washing out of the banks of the Columbia River in Washington state, and the various public reactions to its discovery, have exposed once again the conflict between archaeologists and Native groups regarding the cultural material of the earliest inhabitants of any recently colonized area. This conflict is nothing new, nor is it limited only to the United States. The struggle of Native groups to obtain, tell, or protect their past in the United States (Ferguson 1996; Green 1984; Klesert and Downer 1990; McGuire 1992; Messenger 1989; Swidler et al. 1997; Trigger 1986, 1989) and Australia (Anderson 1985; Archer 1991; Davidson 1991; Mulvaney 1991; Pardoe 1992; Thiele 1991) has frequently been discussed during this past decade. But most of these discussions center around the issues in one particular country or the other. While Hubert (1989: 131–166) offers a good overview of repatriation in both the United States and Australia, a comparison of the conflict between archaeologists and Native peoples regarding attitudes toward the disposition of the remains of founder populations (which may be considered ancestral to entire continental populations) suggests that the concerns of Native peoples in these two industrialized countries are quite similar.

Source: *The Future of the Past: Archaeologists, Native Americans and Repatriation*, T.L. Bray (ed.), New York: Garland Pub Inc., 2001, pp. 57–68.

The politics of repatriation, the politics of the past

Bray (1996) is one of the more recent authors to discuss the various political implications of working with another people's past and there have been many other writings on this subject. Anyone in the field of archaeology anywhere in the world realizes the extent to which archaeological material and human remains have been politicized by Native populations, scientists, and elected officials.

Handler (1991: 67) divides the various groups competing for ownership of cultural materials into two camps: retentionists and restitutionists. Retentionists argue that museums have possessory rights over cultural items they have safe-guarded for years, while restitutionists believe that such things should be returned to their places of origin. Such places of origin, however, now often have different bound-aries and different occupants than the ones in place at the time the cultural items were initially removed. How would one define the ancient boundaries of the 'Sioux Nation,' for instance, when such a 'nation' did not exist as a political unit until the Indian Reorganization Act of 1934?

In *The Plundered Past*, Karl Meyer (1973: 203) writes that 'the nationalist, the collector, and the curator . . . each look upon the past as a piece of property. Another approach is possible – to see our collective cultural remains as a resource whose title is vested in all humanity.' Is there a point in time at which cultural material may actually cease belonging to any one group or individual and become the uni-versal property of every one? Warren (1989: 22) feels that we should '. . . rethink the dispute as one of preservation (not, or not simply, as one of ownership) of the past.' In this way, she argues, the importance rests more on the preservation of an object for the sake of cultural heritage rather than on which individual or institu-tion retains or regains the physical object in question.

Handler (1991: 71) notes that those who wish to retain the cultural property of others '. . . are quick to condemn the parochial nationalism of their opponents, but rarely question their own more imperial nationalisms, which they mask in the name of internationalism.' Pardoe (1992: 140) suggests that archaeologists have '. . . legitimized our curiosity by appealing to the noble view of world history, a demo-cracy of knowledge for all . . . (which) no one person could own . . .'

The situation becomes increasingly volatile when human bones are involved. As the epigraph to this chapter suggests, bones hold a different meaning for each group that regards them as important. While archaeologists may be more amen-able to returning human skeletal materials, physical and forensic anthropologists argue that to rebury these remains leads to a significant loss of information on past cultures and civilizations (Landau and Steele 1996; Rose *et al.* 1996). Ubelaker and Grant's (1989) article 'Human Skeletal Remains: Preservation or Reburial?' offers a concise overview of the issues from the perspective of physical anthropology and a rationale for continued study. Providing a list of reasons for the scientific analysis and long-term curation of skeletal remains, a review of Native American concerns, and a discussion of institutional responses to the reburial issue, these authors offer a strong argument for the scientific value of all human remains.

Archaeologists have generally been united in calling for the return of human remains to ethnic groups who can demonstrate 'cultural affiliation' with the remains (c.f. Ferguson 1996; McManamon and Nordby 1992; Zimmerman 1989,

1996). There is also some support for the return of remains that may not be demonstrably affiliated with any specific group but which are known to have come from a specific region and may be more generally affiliated with a larger culture group. Repatriation is even taught as a likely outcome in some introductory archaeology text books (Ashmore and Sharer 1996).

However, extremely old skeletal material that is difficult to link with any existing ethnic groups becomes a philosophical sticking point for many archaeologists. In the following discussion I offer three 'case studies' regarding the ways that American and Australian archaeologists have reconciled the issue of returning 'founder population' material (greater than 7,500 years old) to modern groups who can claim only a generalized descent from those populations.

Kennewick Man

On Sunday, July 28, 1996, Will Thomas and Dave Deacy came upon a human skull eroding out of the banks of the Columbia River near Kennewick, Washington. A brief article in the July 29 edition of the *Tri-City Herald* by John Stang gave little indication of the impact the skull would have on archaeology and physical anthropology in North America. The nearly complete skeleton of the so-called Kennewick Man set into motion a court case that has involved several Native American tribes, individual anthropologists, and the U.S. government in a legal conflict over the control of heritage and human remains.

Shortly after its discovery, the skull was examined by archaeologist James Chatters, acting as agent for the Benton County coroner's office. The physical features of the cranium led Dr. Chatters to conclude that it belonged to a Caucasian male. Two other physical anthropologists, Dr. Catherine J. MacMillan and Grover S. Krantz, also agreed that skeletal characteristics suggested Caucasian origin. The controversy started when a CAT scan ordered by Chatters revealed a projectile point fragment embedded in the hip of the individual. After the projectile point fragment's discovery, the left fifth metacarpal was sent to the University of California at Riverside for radiocarbon testing. The sample returned dates between 9,200 and 9,600 years ago, and Chatters' opinion of 'a white guy with a stone point in him' (as quoted in Slayman 1997: 16) fell to the wayside. Once the antiquity of the bones was tentatively determined, the Corps took possession of them, citing the Native American Graves Protection and Repatriation Act (P.L.101–601) as authority for its actions.

The Native American Graves Protection and Repatriation Act (NAGPRA), passed in 1990, constitutes human rights legislation. The Act protects Native American burials (Hutt 1992) and requires the repatriation of human remains, burial goods, and cultural patrimony housed in federally funded museums and institutions to culturally affiliated tribes (Trope and Echo-Hawk 1992). As custodian of the property on which the Kennewick remains were found, the Corps was obliged to follow the procedures established under NAGPRA regulations for the inadvertent discovery of human remains (43CFR Part 10.4). Consequently, the Corps halted analysis of the bones and had them transferred to their facility.

As per the clause pertaining to inadvertent discoveries [45CFR Part 10.4(d)(iii)], the Corps was required to notify Native American tribes that were 'likely to be culturally affiliated with' the remains, that had 'aborginally occupied the area', or that were 'reasonably known to have a cultural relationship to' the human remains. As a result, five tribes, the Umatilla, the Yakama, the Nez Perce, the Colville, and the Wanapum were contacted and subsequently filed a joint claim for the return of the Kennewick remains. The Corps published a 'Notice of Intent to Repatriate' in the September 17 and 24, 1996, editions of a local newspaper, the *Tri-City Herald*. But on October 16, before the mandatory 30-day waiting period after the second publication of the 'Notice' expired, eight anthropologists filed suit in District Court to block the repatriation.

The names of the eight anthropologists read like a 'Who's Who' of North American archaeology and physical anthropology. They included Robson Bonnichsen, C. Loring Brace, George W. Gill, C. Vance Haynes Jr., Richard Jantz, Douglas Owsley, Dennis Stanford, and D. Gentry Steele. The law suit forced the Corps to halt plans to repatriate the skeletal material until the Court could decide on the merits of the plaintiffs' intervention.

The anthropologists' complaint alleged that the Corps determined the remains were culturally affiliated without sufficient evidence. At issue was the assumption that the skeleton's age automatically meant the individual was Native American. Secondly, since NAGPRA allows the study of remains when the outcome of the study would be 'of major benefit to the United States' [45CFR Part 10.10(c)(1)], the anthropologists asserted that the Corps' intent to repatriate would prevent such a study. Thirdly, the scientists asserted that their civil rights were being denied by the Corps' action, claiming that they were being denied the right to study the remains simply because they were not Native American (*Bonnichsen* v. *United States*, USDC CV No. 96–1481-JE, filed October 16, 1996).

To further complicate matters, a third party entered the fray prior to the expiration of the 30-day notification period. The Asatru Folk Assembly, a pre-Christian, indigenous European religious organization, filed a similar complaint against the Corps alleging they also might be culturally affiliated with Kennewick Man (Horn 1997: 511).

On June 27, 1997, United States Magistrate Judge John Jelderks issued a written opinion 'to supplement and amplify . . . bench rulings, and to provide additional guidance to the defendants so that this controversy may be resolved in a timely and orderly manner' (Jelderks 1997: 3). The opinion provided 17 issues which it felt the Corps should consider, several of which go to the very heart of the NAGPRA legislation (Jelderks 1997: 45–51). First and foremost among these was whether the remains in question were actually subject to NAGPRA (Jelderks 1997: 45).

Subsequent to the legal proceedings, Congressman Doc Hastings of Washington State, had introduced a bill to amend NAGPRA to allow for scientific access to important, culturally unaffiliated human remains such as in the case of Kennewick Man. The bill, H.R. 2893, was introduced in Congress on November 7, 1997. According to Richard Jantz, one of the plaintiffs in the suit against the U.S. Army Corps, the proposed bill would 'make it much easier for [scientists] to gain access to study unaffiliated material, and it would require that [cultural] affiliation be documented to a much greater extent' (as quoted in Lee 1997). The general counsel of the National Congress of American Indians, John Dossett, disagreed with this interpretation. He felt that the proposed amendment would 'put scientific study in a place of greater importance than the protection of the graves of Indian ancestors' (quoted in Lee 1997). Though introduced, the amendment never reached the floor of the House for a vote and has since died.

The conflict over Kennewick Man is still far from over. The plaintiffs won the right to have the remains scientifically examined for the purpose of obtaining additional information on cultural affiliation. The analysis is being conducted under tight security at a neutral location. The outcome of this dispute will ultimately have major and far-reaching consequences for the practice of archaeology within the United States.

The East Wenatchee Clovis cache

The second case study involves another archaeological site in Washington state where just the possibility of happening upon human remains was enough to create problems between archaeologists and the local Native population. In 1987, an irrigation project in an apple orchard on a terrace above the Columbia River uncovered the a cache of the largest Clovis points ever recorded in North America. Robert Mierendorf, an archaeologist for the National Park Service, and Russell Congdon, a local amateur archaeologist, subsequently performed test excavations at the site that confirmed the existence of *in situ* cultural deposits of Clovis age.

In April of 1988, additional testing was undertaken by professional archaeologists, paleo-Indian specialists, and representatives of the Colville Confederated Tribes. The purpose of this work was to obtain additional data to be used in planning for more extensive excavations in the future. Soil samples from immediately below the artifact level were found to contain an abundance of fine sand and silt-sized Glacier Peak pumice, which dates to about 11,250 B.P. (Mehringer *et al.* 1984). But excavations were suspended when 'apparent bone fragments and associated artifacts – *suggesting* a possible burial – appeared in the floor of one of the excavation units . . .' (Mehringer 1989: 54, emphasis added). The testing operation was closed after one week; all the units were backfilled and the area protected by covering the surface with over 30 tons of concrete slabs.

In March of 1990, the Buffalo Museum of Science, with Dr. Richard M. Gramly as the Principal Investigator, applied for a permit to conduct archaeological excavations at the East Wenatchee Clovis site. On May 14, 1990, the state issued a permit which allowed for the excavation of 35 square meters to be undertaken between October 15 and December 7, 1990.

Excavations were initiated by Dr. Gramly over the protest of the Colville and Yakama tribes. Because of the political pressure brought to bear by the tribal demonstrations, however, only ten square meters – the units previously opened by Mehringer plus an L-shaped geological trench along the north and east edges of the artifact concentration area – were excavated.

The Colville and the Yakama both claimed cultural ties to the area. Colville Acting Police Chief John Dick was quoted as saying that the excavation of any Clovis remains 'would be like somebody trying to dig up the bones of my father' and that '. . . no matter who or where they're at, they're still my people . . . nobody should disturb them' (Wren 1990). The Yakama agreed with the Colville. Yakama Indian

Nation Councilman Harry Smiskin said the Yakama feel that '. . . there's a strong probability that Clovis man was ancestral to all local bands' (Wren 1990).

Gramly viewed things differently. He told reporters that he felt the issue was the right to conduct science and that it was pointless to try to connect any modern people, such as the Colville, to remains more than 4,000 years old. 'I took that as gospel. Obviously it's not gospel to the Colville' (*Spokane Chronicle* 1990). His application for the archaeological permit further explicates this view:

> It cannot be assumed, a priori, that human skeletal remains from the East Wenatchee Clovis site, if any are found, are American Indian, however defined. East Asia is home to a variety of genetically-distinct populations. Any or all of these groups could have participated in the peopling of the Americas. Some of these initial immigrants may have left no descendants who survived in the present era. (Gramly 1990: 9–10)

This topic is open to debate. Meltzer (1989), for instance, writes about the '. . . possibility that the earliest migration was not a single episode, but a multiple series, and that some of those in the multiple series may have failed . . .' (ibid.: 482). He also feels that '. . . we lose sight of the fact that Clovis may represent a composite of migratory "dribbles" . . .' and that '. . . by virtue of the success of the Clovis groups, we miss the possibility that others . . . (pre-Clovis groups) simply disappeared without issue' (ibid.: 484). Meltzer does believe, however, that the ancestral Clovis group to which the eastern Washington tribes might belong represent a successful cultural group in the Americas, and that the Colville and Yakama probably represent descendant groups. An alternative interpretation, proposed by Greenberg, Turner and Zegura (1986), suggests that the North American continent was settled by three migrations – the first occurring around 11,000 years B.P., and the other two sometime after 5,000 years B.P. (Greenberg *et al.* 1986: 479–480).

Ultimately, an agreement was reached for the purchase of the East Wenatchee Clovis site by the Pacific Northwest Archaeological Society for an amount believed to be around $500,000, with the state of Washington paying $250,000 for the artifacts recovered during excavations (Wheat 1991a). Gramly was pleased at the acquisition, stating that '[w]e were in it for the science; we don't want to keep [the artifacts] permanently in Buffalo and never have' (Wheat 1991a: 2).

In conjunction with this purchase, an agreement was drawn up between the Pacific Northwest Archaeological Society and the Colville Confederated Tribes regarding archaeological work undertaken on tribal and aboriginal lands. Upon finalizing this contract, the president of the Society noted that he was 'glad to sign what hopefully will become a landmark agreement,' and that he felt 'it was time to codify a system of ethics for digs' (Wheat 1991b). A complete text of this agreement was published in 1991 in the British journal *Antiquity* (65: 917–920). The Colville people also acknowledge that:

> (A)rchaeology on tribal lands can be beneficial both to the public domain and to the tribes insofar as such research may serve to substantiate, or in some cases add new dimensions to, the tribes' oral tradition. (Wheat 1991c)

The East Wenatchee Clovis cache is one of the largest, earliest, and best documented in the country. Because no human remains were discovered during excavations, the protests and concerns of local tribes proved to be a moot point. Even so, many of the local archaeologists were quick to side with the tribes against someone they perceived as callous toward Native American concerns.

Kow Swamp

In 1967, Alan Thorne discovered a large number of burials along the edge of a reservoir named Kow Swamp. These were subsequently excavated between 1968 and 1972. The salvage operation recovered approximately 40 individuals. The burials exhibited a variety of mortuary treatments and contained both artifacts and pigments. According to one of the archaeologists, the remains represented 'a crucial statistical assemblage for any investigation of Aboriginal origins' (Mulvaney 1991: 14).

While the Commonwealth government of Australia had assumed responsibility for Aboriginal affairs in 1967, administration was generally left to the separate states. The Australian Archaeological and Aboriginal Relics Preservation Act of 1972 (Victoria Act No. 8273/1972, since amended) was the first legislation aimed at protecting the heritage of Aboriginal people in Victoria. A subsequent law, the Aboriginal and Torres Strait Islander Heritage Protection Amendment Act of 1987, later proclaimed that 'the Aboriginal people of Victoria are the rightful owners of their heritage and should be given responsibility for its future control and management' (as quoted in Mulvaney 1991: 14).

In August 1990, the Museum of Victoria presented the Kow Swamp Collection of human remains and associated grave goods to the Echuca Aboriginal Co-operative on the Murray River in central Victoria, a community that wished to accord those 9,000 to 15,000-year-old human remains a mass reburial. Mulvaney decried the reburial of this collection noting that 'the case merits record for its implications for intellectual freedom. . . . It is not simply the Kow Swamp relics which are at stake, but the future of past Aboriginal culture and the freedom of all peoples of any race to study it' (1991: 12).

Pardoe (1992) however, feels that scientists have no right to determine the ultimate disposition of human remains. 'Some have distinguished between more recent remains, which Aborigines may control, and the older remains, which belong to the world. This denies the concept of full and unfettered Aboriginal ownership of the past' (Pardoe 1992: 133).

In *The Australian Journal of Anthropology*, Special Issue 2, entitled 'Reconsidering Aboriginality' (1991, 2: 2), the authors provide a collection of articles reflecting on the status of 'Aboriginal Studies' in Australia. Archer (ibid.: 163), for instance, notes that 'Aboriginality as a construction for purposes of political action has all the characteristic contradictions of nationalism,' while Lewins states that 'it is not possible to keep "aboriginality" and politics apart' (ibid.: 177). Thiele (ibid.: 80) argues that 'aboriginality' involves 'descentism' based solely on the grounds of biological parentage. Another author deconstructs the stereotypical belief that 'aboriginal values and practices are somehow more "ecologically sound" than those of non-Aborigines'

(Sackett 1991: 235); while still another observes that, in the ever changing relationships between archaeologists and Aborigines, 'the motives of Aboriginal and non-Aboriginal peoples have not always been the same' (Davidson 1991: 256).

'Aboriginality' in Australia, is thus construed by these scholars as a political, descent-based construction. North American authors involved with Native American issues could easily produce a similar set of papers on the aboriginal peoples of North America. The current state of relations between scholars and indigenous peoples in these two countries is remarkably similar.

Conclusions

The question has been raised as to whether it is reasonable to assume that a single Native American group or individual, by virtue of their 'Indianness' or 'Aboriginality', or some genetic relationship, should have rights to control cultural material which may be equally related to an entire population. Should any one of us have the right to determine the fate of the biblical Adam were he to be excavated?

Winter (1980: 126) asks whether we should always respond positively to Native Americans, just because they are 'Indians.' Another anthropologist questions: 'who has the right to excavate, or prevent the excavation of, a recent or ancient burial site, and on what authority is that right to be based?' (Rosen 1980: 6). While Pardoe (1992: 133) notes that 'aboriginal demands for ownership and control of their heritage has been consistent for over a decade,' he also notes the tension level between archaeologists and Aborigines rises when it is Pleistocene remains (over 10,000 years old) that are slated for reburial.

In the United States, Meighan (1984, 1992) is one of the most outspoken opponents of wholesale repatriation and reburial of human remains that cannot be directly linked with specific modern day groups. He argues that current repatriation agreements 'assume all Indian remains of whatever age are the property of contemporary claimants and that it doesn't matter how old things are' (Meighan 1992: 39). Though not alone in his belief that cultural material from extremely old sites is not the property of any particular group of Native Americans, he was, by far, the most vocal in his dissent.

Even the NAGPRA Review Committee, mandated to decide the status of claims by Native American tribes regarding 'culturally unidentifiable human remains,' is having difficulty establishing a proper process for determining the repatriation of human skeletal material that cannot be assigned to specific cultural groups. Indeed, the Review Committee at its March 1997 meeting proposed a 'seminar' to address this topic with hopes that interested parties, including archaeologists, anthropologists, and traditional Native peoples, could together devise a workable solution to this dilemma.

Much like Clement Meighan in America, David Mulvaney in Australia feels that, while 'archaeologists support the return of remains from recent generations to local communities for reburial, because social and spiritual considerations outweigh other factors,' for older remains, 'their kin cannot be presumed to have shared the same cultural values or religious concepts of this generation' (1991: 16).

As suggested in the title of this chapter, there seems to exist a point in time where the relationship to the cultural material from an archaeological site might accurately be described as 'ours' (which denotes ownership by the entire world) as opposed to 'yours' (which denotes ownership by a specific, bounded cultural group). While the latter portion of this chapter contains a plethora of rhetorical questions for which there are no ready answers, archaeology today is immersed in trying to find answers to such questions. As archaeological practitioners like Pardoe, who argues that 'a scientific view of the world is not corrupted by advocacy, or by an interest in the wishes of Aboriginal people' (1992: 138), and Zimmerman, who openly describes himself as 'a radical spokesman for reburial' (1989: 66) become more prominent, members of the discipline are as likely to find themselves at odds with one another as with Native people when it comes to Native rights and cultural heritage.

During the conflict over the archaeological excavations at the East Wenatchee Clovis cache, Matthew Dick of the Colville tribe noted that:

> The Colville tribe has said that for many years it has watched the desecration of its grave sites in the name of progress and thirst for knowledge. I still believe there has to be a balance between the thirst for knowledge of our past and the sacredness of our burial grounds. (quoted in Wheat 1991d)

Such a balance would ideally be worked out directly by the indigenous populations and the scholarly community. But it appears that it may be up to the courts to decide the fate of human remains in the two former colonial states of America and Australia. The case brought by Bonnichsen *et al.*, ultimately may decide at what point 'founder populations' become 'aboriginal populations,' at least in the United States. It will also help to establish the right of science to pursue answers in opposition to the religious concerns of certain groups. If it must be up to the courts to decide such issues, however, anthropology will come out the loser regardless of the verdict, because it will have demonstrated a failure to understand the cultures about which it endeavors to learn and to prove its worth to the world of which it is a part.

Note

Joe Watkins (part Choctaw Indian) has worked as Agency Archaeologist for the Bureau of Indian Affairs in Oklahoma.

References

Anderson, Christopher. 1985. 'On the notion of aboriginality: A discussion.' *Mankind* 15(1): 41–43.

Archer, Jeff. 1991. 'Ambiguity in political ideology: Aboriginality as nationalism.' In 'Reconsidering Aboriginality', Steven Thiele (ed.), pp. 161–170. *The Australian Journal of Anthropology*, Special Issue 2.

Ashmore, Wendy and Robert Sharer. 1996. *Discovering our Past: A Brief Introduction to Archaeology*. Mountain View, California: Mayfield Publishing.

Bonnichsen v. United States. 1996. USDC CV No. 96–1481 JE; filed October 16, 1996.

Bray, Tamara. 1996. 'Repatriation, power relations and the politics of the past.' *Antiquity* 70(268): 440–444.

Davidson, Iain. 1991. 'Archaeologists and Aborigines.' In 'Reconsidering Aboriginality,' S. Thiele (ed.), pp. 247–258. *The Australian Journal of Anthropology*, Special Issue 2.

Ferguson, T.J. 1996. 'Native Americans and the Practice of Archaeology.' *Annual Review of Anthropology* 25: 63–80.

Gramly, R.M. 1990. *Archaeological Excavation Permit Application*. Document on file at the State Historic Preservation Office, Pullman, Washington.

Green, Ernestine L. (ed.) 1984. *Ethics and Values in Archaeology*. London: The Free Press.

Greenberg, Joseph, Christy Turner, and Stephen Zegura. 1986. 'The settlement of the Americas: A comparison of the linguistic, dental, and genetic evidence.' *Current Anthropology* 27(5): 477–497.

Handler, Richard. 1991. 'Who owns the past? History, cultural property, and the logic of possessive individualism.' In *The Politics of Culture*, Brett Williams (ed.), pp. 63–74. Washington, D.C.: Smithsonian Institution Press.

Horn, Amanda. 1997. 'The Kennewick man loses sleep over NAGPRA: Native Americans and scientists wrestle over cultural remains.' Sovereignty Symposium X: Circles of Life, pp. 503–524.

Hubert, Jane. 1989. 'A proper place for the dead: A critical review of the "reburial" issue.' In *Conflict in the Archaeology of Living Traditions*, R. Layton (ed.), pp. 131–166. London: Unwin Hyman.

Hutt, Sherry. 1992. 'Illegal trafficking in Native American human remains and cultural items: A new protection tool.' *Arizona State Law Journal* 24(1): 135–150.

Jelderks, John. 1997. Opinion, Bonnichsen v. United States, USDC CV No. 96–1481-JE. *Online version available at: http://www.goonline.com/science/kennewic/court/opinion.htm.*

Klesert, Anthony L. and Alan S. Downer. (eds) 1990. *Preservation on the Reservation: Native Americans, Native American Lands and Archeology*. Navajo Nation Papers in Anthropology Number 26. Navajo Nation Archeology Department and the Navajo Nation Historic Preservation Department.

Landau, Patricia and D. Gentry Steele. 1996. 'Why anthropologists study human remains.' *American Indian Quarterly* 20(2): 209–228.

Lee, Mike. 1997. 'Doc pushes bill to study old bones.' *Tri-City Herald*, November 14.

McGuire, Randall H. 1992. 'Archaeology and the First Americans.' *American Anthropologist* 94(4): 816–836.

McManamon, Francis and Larry Nordby. 1992. 'Implementing the Native American Graves Protection and Repatriation Act.' *Arizona State Law Journal* 24(1): 217–252.

Mehringer, Peter J. 1989. *Age of the Clovis Cache at East Wenatchee, Washington*. Report presented to the Washington State Historic Preservation Office, Pullman, Washington.

Mehringer, Peter J., Jr. and F.F. Foit. 1990. 'Volcanic ash dating of the Clovis cache at East Wenatchee, Washington.' *National Geographic Research* 6(4): 495–503.

Mehringer, Peter J., J.C. Sheppard, and F.F. Foit. 1984. 'The age of Glacier Peak tephra in west-central Montana.' *Quaternary Research* 21(1): 36–41.

Meighan, Clement. 1984. 'Archaeology: Science or sacrilege?' In *Ethics and Values in Archaeology*. E. Green (ed.), pp. 208–223. London: The Free Press.

—— 1992. 'Some scholars' views on reburial.' *American Antiquity* 57(4): 704–710.

Meltzer, David J. 1989. 'Why don't we know when the first people came to North America?' *American Antiquity* 54(3): 471–490.

Messenger, Phyllis Mauch. (ed.) 1989. *The Ethics of Collecting Cultural Property: Whose Culture? Whose Property?* Albuquerque: University of New Mexico Press.

Meyer, Karl E. 1973. *The Plundered Past.* New York: Athenium Press.

Mulvaney, D.J. 1991. 'Past regained, future lost: The Kow Swamp Pleistocene burials.' *Antiquity* 65(246): 12–21.

Pardoe, Colin. 1992. 'Arches of Radii, corridors of power: Reflections on current archaeological practice.' In *Power, Knowledge and Aborigines*, M. Attwood and D. Arnold (eds), pp. 132–141. La Trobe University Press: Melbourne, Australia.

—— 1994. 'Bioscapes: The evolutionary landscape of Australia.' *Archaeology in Oceania* 29: 182–190.

Rose, Jerome, Thomas Green, and Victoria Green. 1996. 'NAGPRA is forever: The future of osteology and the repatriation of skeletons.' *Annual Review of Anthropology* 25: 81–103.

Rosen, Lawrence. 1980. 'The excavation of American Indian burial sites: A problem in law and professional responsibility.' *American Anthropologist* 82(1): 5–27.

Slayman, Andrew. 1997. 'A battle over bones.' *Antiquity* 50(1): 16–23.

Spokane Chronicle. 1990. History, controversy both buried at Clovis site. December 3.

Swidler, Nina, Kurt Dongoske, Roger Anyon, and Alan Downer. (eds) 1997. *Native Americans and Archaeologists: Stepping Stones to Common Ground.* Walnut Creek, California: AltaMira Press.

Thiele, Steven. 1991. 'Taking a sociological approach to Europeanness (Whiteness) and Aboriginality (Blackness).' In 'Reconsidering Aboriginality,' Steven Thiele (ed.), pp. 179–201. *The Australian Journal of Anthropology*, Special Issue 2. Vol 2(2).

Trigger, Bruce. 1986. 'Prehistoric archaeology and American society: An historical perspective.' In *American Archaeology Past and Future*, D.J. Meltzer, D.D. Fowler, and J.A. Sabloff (eds), pp. 187–215. Washington, D.C.: Smithsonian Institution Press.

—— 1989. *A History of Archaeological Thought.* Cambridge: Cambridge University Press.

Trope, Jack and Walter Echo-Hawk. 1992. 'The Native Graves Protection and Repatriation Act.' *Arizona State Law Journal* 24(1): 35–78.

Ubelaker, Douglas H. and Lauryn Guttenplan Grant. 1989. 'Human Skeletal Remains: Preservation or Reburial?' *Yearbook of Physical Anthropology* 32: 249–287.

Warren, Karen J. 1989. 'A philosophical perspective on the ethics and resolution of cultural properties issues.' In *The Ethics of Collecting Cultural Property: Whose Culture? Whose Property?*, P. Messenger (ed.), pp. 1–25. Albuquerque: University of New Mexico Press.

Wheat, Dan. 1991a. 'Gramly applauds Clovis purchase.' *Wenatchee World*, August 1.

—— 1991b. 'Colvilles to be consulted on digs in future.' *Wenatchee World*, May 2.

—— 1991c. 'Archaeologists, tribe set forth dig principles.' *Wenatchee World*, May 1.

—— 1991d. 'Buffalo museum offers $485,000.' *Wenatchee World*, April 29.

Winter, Joseph C. 1980. 'Indian heritage preservation and archaeologists.' *American Antiquity* 45(1): 121–131.

Wren, Patricia. 1990. 'Tribes want Clovis dig stopped.' *Wenatchee World*, July 20.

Zimmerman, Larry. 1989. 'Made radical by my own: An archaeologist learns to accept reburial.' *Conflict in the Archaeology of Living Traditions*. R. Layton (ed.), pp. 60–67, London: Unwin Hyman.

——— 1996. 'Epilogue: A new and different archaeology?' *American Indian Quarterly* 20(2): 297–307.

PART THREE

Museum and Identities

Introduction to Part Three

Identity

HERE WE EXPLORE the roles museums play in the validation and making of community identities. Identity is a complex concept. Within the Western framework of thinking it is understood that each of us possesses an individual identity. At the same time it is accepted that we express and experience our identities by demonstrating loyalty to groups that share common characteristics such as nationality, gender, socio-economic factors, sexual orientation, interests, family loyalties, religion, ethnicity or culture. Identities are temporal. In constructing them we consider not only the past but also some sense of shared future. Identities are relational. We understand what we are by what we are not. Thus an essential element of identity is the idea of 'the other' (Woodward 2002).

Identity is produced by representational systems and includes 'the signifying practices and the symbolic systems through which meanings are produced' (Woodward 2002: 14). Few doubt the importance of museums' role in identity making. Jones asserts that they 'are the edifices through which communities of all sizes and types represent themselves, both to themselves and to others' (2000: 4). They are also places where identities can be challenged, explored and rethought. As Macdonald points out 'museums . . . are significant sites in which to examine some of the claims of identity transformation' (2003: 6).

Museums, however, are places where two different concepts of identity are made manifest and sometimes compete: essentialist and non-essentialist. Where identity is perceived to be essentialist it is immutable. For example, national identity can be conceptualised as being rooted in a version of an uncontested past. Similarly, national characteristics are understood to have been forged and reenforced over time by historical circumstances and these are then drawn together to express a sense of unchanging, essential identity. In contrast non-essential perspectives conceive of identity as fluid, changing in response to political, social, religious, economic and personal factors (Woodward 2002: 11). Museums, as the chapters here illustrate, have become more aware of the need to include multiple perspectives in the national story but at the same time some continue to present history and archaeology in a way that suggests there is one uncontested narrative.

National identity

Traditionally museums have been deliberately constructed to represent the national community. 'National museums are implicit in the construction of national identities, and the ways in which they voice or silence difference can reflect and influence contemporary perceptions of identities within the national frame' (McLean 2005: 1). Currently throughout the world, nationalism is a contentious and debated concept. For example, within Europe disputes about the role of the European Union and its constitution, the breakup of the Soviet Empire and the emergence of small nation states from within it, and consequent military conflicts and tensions, international migration and the adoption of multiculturalism and devolution within the United Kingdom, all result in confusion about what it is to belong to a nation and what the nation can expect from its citizens. For some these changes threaten their identity. For others change offers new opportunities to rethink how they conceptualise themselves and the national community to which they belong.

The role of museums in supporting and defining national identities has been examined by Carol Duncan. She argues that the art gallery as epitomised by the Louvre, was 'able to convert signs of luxury, status, or splendour into repositories of spiritual treasure – the heritage and pride of a whole nation' (Duncan 2000: 27). Within the walls of this national gallery a ritual was re-enacted by visitors, as they literally progressed through the story of the artistic genius of the nation state made explicit on the walls of the galleries (ibid.). Although the National Gallery was not founded until 1824 nevertheless in eighteenth-century England 'art was understood to be a source of valuable moral and spiritual experience. In this sense it was cultural property, something to be shared by a whole community' (Duncan 2000: 36). 'High culture' was seen as a method of civilising the general populace (Bennett 1995: 19). In this sense museums fulfil the national role expected of them according to the theories of Gellner (1983). He saw nationalism as the imposition of high culture on society, which then 'imagined' common bonds (Anderson 1983). Indeed when social inclusion issues are debated within the United Kingdom, access to 'high culture' is seen as an important part of the government's agenda (Mason 2004). In addition historical and archaeological narratives are used to demonstrate a specific national history and, at the same time, to illustrate the progress of civilisation and the nation state's role within it (Bennett 1995: 76–7).

Yet as Mason has pointed out, attitudes towards culture have changed. There is a move away from the idea of high culture as all that is the best towards the idea of culture as 'a way of life' (Jordan and Weedon, cited in Mason 2004: 58) 'and a collective term for aesthetic products and everyday practices' (ibid: 58). This has seen a shift towards questioning implicit value systems. What is excellent and of quality is now contested. Bourdieu (1984) has demonstrated that concepts of social class, identity and control are implicit in judgements of taste. 'Tastes demonstrate the advantage for the privileged of being able to draw on greater volumes of social, economic and cultural capital' (Knell 2004: 1). At the same time, historical narratives and ideas of progress are contested. National myths and heroes are debunked. Multiculturalism is promoted as a national model in countries such as the United Kingdom (though recently challenges to this have found their way into the political mainstream). Museums find themselves in the centre of a debate about the way nations see themselves, what is symbolic of the nation's culture and who is included in the national community and who is deliberately or unintentionally excluded.

In some respects the resurgence of nationalism has taken place at a time when globalism appears to threaten such separatist developments. The rise of globalism as well as the resurgence of nationalism in the old Soviet Union have led to a re-examination of the role of local culture and its relationship to nationalism and identity. Hall postulates that the rise of 'capitalist globalism . . . has not necessarily resulted in the destruction of these specific structures and particularistic attachments and identifications which go with the more localized communities which a homogenizing modernity was supposed to replace' (Hall 1999: 36).

The chapters in this section all explore the complexities of the making of identities within museum frameworks, and debate some of the issues considered above. The first two chapters MacDonald and Alsford, and Casey focus specifically on national identity.

MacDonald and Alsford (1995, this volume p. 276) examine 'the changing relationship between human history museums and aboriginal and ethnic communities within the context of Canadian multiculturalism'. Placing their article within the context of the development of museums as tools of the 'dominant cultural group' in society (MacDonald and Alsford 1995: 18, this volume p. 279), the authors look at two controversial exhibitions in Canada, *The Spirit Sings* at Calgary's Glenbow Museum, and *Into the Heart of Africa*, at the Royal Ontario Museum, and the objections made by ethnic community groups at the way they were depicted by professional curators from outside their communities. These examples raise similar issues to those considered in Part Two by Dubin, in particular anxieties that museum professionals face censorship and will lose their ability as 'caretakers of society's collective heritage' (MacDonald and Alsford 1995: 27, this volume p. 286).

However, the chapter is optimistic in its view of the future. The Canadian Museum of Civilization, focussing on defining national identity, adopts a variety of ways of including in this identity the diverse cultures within Canadian society. Co-curatorship, consultation and cooperation with community groups are all methods of sharing some of the power. Museums and material culture are seen to be important elements of community identity, and many ethnic groups created their own museums between the 1950s and 1970s to express this. The slowdown in the growth of such museums is seen, in part, to be a result of the improved relationships between minority cultural groups and the majority culture (MacDonald and Alsford 1995: 25, this volume p. 284). The authors consider different models that allow communities more control and ownership of the way they are represented.

An Australian case study, by Casey, illustrates just how controversial museums can be when they attempt to present a particular view of a national story within their walls. The new National Museum of Australia in Canberra opened in March 2001 and was immediately the focus of intense debate. Its director, Dawn Casey, presented a spirited defence of the museum but she did not have her contract renewed. Controversy surrounding the museum was so intense that there was a public review of its exhibitions (Dean and Rider 2005). One of the museum's own councillors, David Barnett said 'there is nothing in the museum to engender pride in being Australian' (Safe 2004: 7). Luke's account of the *Enola Gay* episode in the previous section provides another example of the way museums question national myths at their peril.

While the National Museum of Australia aroused the anger and disappoint-ment of some Anglo-Celtic Australians, people from a powerful political and economic dominant group in that society, MacDonald and Alsford examine the reactions of the minority and relatively powerless indigenous groups to the way they are presented within a national story (MacDonald and Alsford 1995). They also consider the ways in which museums until recently regarded the indigenous people as 'part of their subject-matter rather than as a component of their audience' (ibid: 19, this volume p. 279). Indigenous peoples, they argue, have been harmed by the way in which part of their culture has been absorbed by a museum and fossilised. At the same time Canadian museums are increasingly recognising that the way they have previously represented indigenous peoples has denied them an active role in the nation's story. The authors also consider the challenges facing national museums confronted with diversity. They con-sider the way in which cultural pluralism can be seen as inimical to the nation state and how Canadian museums are dealing with a range of issues. To some extent the solution has been the creation of separate museums for different com-munities such as Ukranian Canadians and Jewish Canadians. However, at the same time the Canadian Museum of Civilization has recognised the need for consulta-tion and dialogue with all the different communities in order to help find 'a workable expression of multi-culturalism while at the same time preserving national unity' (ibid: 28, this volume p. 287). It is interesting to compare this chapter written in 1995 with Ashley's in Part Five on Canadian museums and identity in 2005. The latter provides an interesting example of an attempt to share power with an African Canadian group to try and create a site of 'public identity discourse' (Ashley 2005: 5) about the concept of nation and belonging.

Crooke's chapter on Northern Ireland provides an interesting analysis of the role of museums and community heritage initiatives in supporting personal and local as well as national identities. As she points out there is no single national group 'rather, collectively we form a myriad of sometimes shifting communities' (Crooke 2005: 71, this volume p. 302). Her research illustrates the non-essentialist view of identity and gives some interesting examples of museums tentatively exploring different views of a historical past that is hotly contested. She places museum activities within the context of a range of community heritage initiatives to illustrate that public representation of the histories of a place is not the prerogative of museums. She also considers how difficult it is for museums to facilitate the personal past and, at the same time, remain 'neutral'.

Community identity

People symbolise and express their identities with objects whose importance remains integral to the way individuals and communities articulate their sense of themselves, even when meanings of objects change over time. Some of the issues facing museums in the twenty-first century relate to the way in which they treat indigenous groups whose material culture they currently own when this material culture is part of the groups' identity. In Part Two Fforde and Watkins illustrate the emotional and legal minefields that surround issues relating to human remains and how important these human remains are for indigenous human identity. For many of these groups this material is integral to an understanding of who they are. As MacDonald and Alsford comment, once 'heritage artefacts are removed from the original owners and put into a museum, there are adverse effects on Native cultures' (MacDonald and Alsford 1995: 19, this volume p. 280). However, cultures are not static. Repatriation of the artefacts can be seen as a means of a community regaining a sense of itself. Hill points out that this can be seen as a new beginning of a relationship between museums and source communities, not an end (Hill 2001). Hill writes as a member of the Iroquois nation, and his is a rare indigenous voice among museum studies literature (see also Watkins this volume Part Two). He places the struggles for the restitution of cultural material, here Wampum beads, from museums to indigenous groups within a historical social and political framework, as part of the latter's growing sense of their separate and proud identities and argues that museums are not just about preventing objects from decaying but also 'about keeping ideas, values, and beliefs viable for many generations to come' (Hill 2001: 137).

'Ethnicity and race are social structures which influence the identities people can adopt' (Woodward 2000: 156, this volume p. 322). There are, perhaps, two issues here for museums to acknowledge. The first is the way in which a white European perspective dominates the idea of national identity in many countries. Ashley's chapter in Part Five considers this in relation to Canada, and in the United Kingdom Hall has challenged the way in which British institutions promote a type of 'heritage' that marginalises or excludes a range of experiences of identity linked to race (Hall 2005). The second issue is the way in which people define themselves by their ethnicity, but this identification is complex. In an increasingly multicultural world many individuals now claim allegiance and feel affinity with more than one ethnic group. Nevertheless some communities define themselves and are defined by others through ethnicity. One of the ways in which these groups assert and confirm their identities is through the foundation and maintenance of museums. These museums usually operate through outreach programmes as well as exhibitions, and their supporters are very anxious that they are for everyone, not just the ethnic community they represent. It is as important for the museum to represent the ethnic group's culture to the rest of the world as it is for the museum to engage with the group itself (Zamora 2002). At the same time tensions can arise between different subgroups within an ethnic group and over whether the museum should become mainstream or not (ibid: 41, this volume p. 329). A complementary article on minority art in an established art museum considers the way in which art is categorised and can be marginalised. Marzio's chapter from the museum director's point of view illustrates the economic pressures on museums to concentrate on mainstream exhibitions. It also raises interesting issues about how art from minority communities is exhibited. Merriman's chapter illustrates some of the issues raised when exhibiting different communities in London, and explores the way in which the Museum of London tackled institutional attitudes to ethnicity and belonging. Merriman also provides useful practical examples of ways of working with different community groups and considers all the processes that go towards making a successful community exhibition from consultation, an events programme, marketing and evaluation.

Finally, is there a risk that celebration of difference will lead to a fragmentation of society? Golding's chapter on the Horniman Museum's 'Inspiration Africa!' provides an interesting analysis of the way in which complex individual and community identities can be supported and developed by programmes in museums that encourage tolerance and understanding using tangible and intangible resources.

References

Anderson, B. (1983) *Imagined Communities: Reflections on the Origin and Spread of Nationalism*, London: Verso.

Ashley, S. (2005) 'State authority and the public sphere', *Museum and Society*, vol. 3, no. 1, March, 5–17.

Bennett, T. (1995) *The Birth of the Museum: History, Theory, Politics*, London: Routledge.

Bourdieu, P. (1984) *Distinction: A Social Critique of the Judgement of Taste*, Cambridge: Harvard University Press.

Crooke, E. (2005) 'Museum, communities and the politics of heritage in Northern Ireland', in J. Littler and R. Naidoo (eds) *The Politics of Heritage: The Legacies of Race*, London: Routledge, 69–81.

Dean, D. and Rider, P.E. (2005) 'Museums, nation and political history in the Australian National Museum and the Canadian Museum of Civilization', *Museum and Society*, vol. 3, no. 1, March, 35–50.

Duncan, C. (2000) *Civilizing Rituals: Inside Public Art Museums*, London: Routledge.

Gellner, E. (1983) *Nations and Nationalism*, Oxford: Blackwell.

Hall, S. (1999) 'Culture, community, nation', in D. Boswell and J. Evans (eds) *Representing the Nation: A Reader: Histories, Heritage, Museums*, London and New York: Routledge, 33–44.

Hall, S. (2005) 'Whose heritage? Unsettling "the heritage," re-imagining the post-nation', in J. Littler and R. Naidoo (eds) *The Politics of Heritage: The Legacies of 'Race'*, London: Routledge, 23–35.

Hastings, A. (1997) *The Construction of Nationhood: Ethnicity, Religion, and Nationalism*, Cambridge: Cambridge University Press.

Hill, R.W. (2001) 'Regenerating identity', in T. Bray (ed.) *The Future of the Past: Archaeologists, Native Americans and Repatriation*, New York: Garland Pub Inc.

Jones, M. (2000) 'Why a museum of Scotland?' in J.M. Fladmark (ed.) *Heritage and Museums: Shaping National Identity*, Shaftsbury: Donhead Publishing Ltd, 3–15.

Jordan, G. and Weedon, C. (1995) *Cultural Politics: Class, Gender, Race and the Postmodern World*, Oxford, Blackwell.

Knell, S. (2004) 'Identity and the marketplace', unpublished teaching paper, University of Leicester.

MacDonald, G.F. and Alsford, S. (1995) 'Canadian museums and the representation of culture in a multicultural nation', *Cultural Dynamics*, vol. 7, no. 1, 15–36.

Macdonald, S. (2003) 'Museums, national, postnational and transcultural identities', *Museum and Society*, vol. 1, no. 1, 1–16.

Macdonald, S. (2005) 'Commemorating the Holocaust', J. Littler and R. Naidoo (eds) *The Politics of Heritage: The Legacies of 'Race'*, London: Routledge, 49–68.

McLean, F. (2005) 'Museums and national identity', *Museum and Society*, vol. 3, no. 1, March, 1–4.

Mason, R. (2004) 'Conflict and complement: An exploration of the discourses informing the concept of the socially inclusive museum in contemporary Britain', *International Journal of Heritage Studies*, vol. 10, no. 1, March, 49–73.

Safe, G. (2004) 'New phase for museum', *The Australian*, 19 July, 7.

Smith, A.D. (1999) 'History and modernity: Reflections of the theory of nationalism' in D. Boswell and J. Evans (eds) *Representing the Nation: A Reader: Histories, Heritage, Museums*, London and New York: Routledge, 45–60.

Woodward, K. (2000) 'Afterword', in K. Woodward (ed.) *Questioning Identity: Gender, Class, Nation*, London: Routledge, 155–8.

Woodward, K. (2002) 'Concepts of identity and difference', in K. Woodward (ed.) *Identity and Difference*, London: Open University Press, Sage, 7–50.

Zamora, H. (2002) 'Identity and community', *Museum News*, vol. 81, no. 3, 36–41.

Chapter 17

Canadian Museums and the Representation of Culture in a Multicultural Nation

George F. MacDonald and Stephen Alsford

USEUMS ARE ONE OF SOCIETY'S principal agencies for defining culture, largely through their determination of which elements of the past are of value, memorable and worthy of preservation. This activity defines the present as much as it does the past. The significance of this task, not least for social stability, might itself suffice to explain why governments have played leading roles in establishing and maintaining museums. It has long been believed that museums, partly through their image as purveyors of objective truth, have great potential to influence public attitudes and perceptions. In the context of postmodernism, however, this authority is under challenge, as is the whole issue of who defines culture. Indigenous, ethnic and women's groups are paying increasing attention to how museums represent culture, and are acquiring sufficient influence to oblige museums to address their concerns. One of Canada's most respected museum professionals has suggested that 'what we are seeing is the most significant revolution in cultural institutions in this century' (Cameron 1990: 14).

The dynamics of this situation go beyond simply museum reform. Conventionally, culture is seen as a definable and delimitable set of values, beliefs, traditions and experiences shared by a people and providing some kind of yardstick against which membership in a culture may be measured. In a postmodern and culturally pluralistic society it is harder to perceive culture as a coherent whole. Instead, it is more like a jigsaw puzzle whose parts are rearranged into variant pictures, each suiting the eye of the particular beholder, and to which new parts are constantly being added as the composition of society alters. That culture is in constant process of recreation ultimately defeats attempts to 'museumize' it.

This chapter proposes to address aspects of cultural redefinition through an examination of the changing relationship between human history museums and aboriginal and ethnic communities in the context of Canadian multiculturalism. Recent

Source: *Cultural Dynamics*, vol. 7, no. 1, 1995, pp. 15–36.

examples of conflict and cooperation will provide a basis for exploring the politics of representation, concluding with a brief look at the new course that the national museum of human history is pursuing in a changing Canada.

Canadian cultural identity

All viable cultures continually reinvent themselves, to adapt to changing circumstances and the pressure of often competing forces. Many nations are now trying to come to terms with growing cultural diversity within their borders. Canada was described in 1968, by celebrated British economist and writer Barbara Ward, as the world's first international nation (Ward 1970); for 23 years it has been officially multicultural (a term originally coined in Canada). This apparently modern development ignores the historical reality that Canada has always been ethnically heterogeneous. The aboriginal peoples constituted dozens of cultures and several distinct linguistic groups, while Norse, Acadians, French, Métis, English, Irish, Scots, Welsh, Germans and Dutch all were among resident groups prior to Canada's achievement of nationhood in 1867. In recent decades Asian countries have outstripped Europe as the main source of immigrants.

Immigration is one of the factors – alongside democratization, tourism, industrialization, mass production and consumerism, international business and telecommunications – pointed at to predict the emergence of a global culture, although this cultural homogenization tends to be thought of as predominantly western and technological in character. Perhaps ironically, the cultural proselytism is undertaken not by the bearers of high culture (with which group traditional museums are intimately linked) but those of pop culture (Huey 1990), such as television, films and rock music: images and sounds that transcend language barriers and communicate at emotional levels. It is no concidence that the western world is seeing growing numbers of museums (or quasi-museums) dedicated to stars of the entertainment industry, to the film and mass media industries, and to commercial products such as Coca-Cola.

Cultural homogenization has given rise to fears that ethnic peoples, in the process of conforming, will have to abandon traditional cultures (for example, Kurin 1990: 13–14). These concerns are justified to an extent; for instance, all but a handful of languages of Canada's indigenous peoples have virtually disappeared. Much attention is paid today to the preservation of natural environments and zoological species, but there is less public consciousness of the need to protect traditional cultures – not least on the understanding that diversity here, as elsewhere, is an evolutionary survival mechanism. Tourism is a major factor in creating awareness and demand for preserving wildlife and habitats. Cultural tourism, although a two-edged sword, is likely to be as important in protecting traditional cultures; museums, as motivators of cultural tourism, feel themselves to have some responsibility here. However, cultures cannot be conserved as museum pieces. Museums' preoccupation with material heritage has sometimes engendered the false belief that some cultures can be consigned to temporal/spatial tombs within the graveyard of the past.

The emergence of a homogeneous global culture may be contributing to the erosion of traditional cultures, but is not directly displacing them. It is best conceptualized as a parallel culture, a macro-culture that in some respects helps sustain micro-cultures (Moore 1989: 28; Minkin 1990). Witness, for example, the combination of western and Third World musical forms in World Beat, the continuing use of folk music to create political consciousness of the need to protect the rights of cultural minorities (Seeger 1990), or cultural tourism's stimulation of demand for authentic traditional crafts (Nicks 1990; Thompson 1991: 39).

In the same way, although cultural homogenization may to an extent be counteractive to cultural pluralism, it is not an either/or situation. The two processes operate concurrently. If cultural pluralism is inimical to anything, it is more likely the concept of nation-state, rather than a global supra-culture (Moore 1989: 27–30). Efforts at creating culturally homogeneous nation-states produce emigrants and refugees, whose influx into existing states (characterized by centralized political authority sponsoring a monolithic cultural identity dominated by the high culture of the power-holders) may eventually create pressures for pluralization there. This is the case in North America today.

It has become commonplace in Canada to distinguish citizens by using ethnic qualifiers (for example Chinese-Canadian) and the same trend is predicted for the United States in the next century. Demographic changes are expected to make those of European heritage a minority group in North America, one of several factors prompting the search for a new model of national unity. Canada certainly appears to be facing a cultural perestroika. Roughly 10 percent of the population is wholly or partly of Native ancestry, and there are well over 100 ethnic groups represented in Canadian society, 18 of them with more than 100,000 members. Perhaps half the population is either first or second generation immigrants. It is in fact difficult to categorize the population ethnically, because so many individuals trace their ancestry to more than one cultural group. Canada's present cultural turmoil is partly the consequence of the government policy of multiculturalism being, at present, more a matter of principle than a practical way to democratize power and define national identity. Many doubt the possibility of reconciling cultural democracy with national unity. Yet Canada is not really an amalgam of cultures, for no ethnic group brings a total culture to its new home, or maintains intact that which it does import. The issue is rather how to account for diversity of ethnic *identity* within the formulation of national culture.

A country in transition is a country under stress, a country seeking guidance. Museums ought to be capable of providing such guidance. But the museum establishment is itself uncertain how to respond to social changes in Canada. At the root of their dilemma lies the question: whom should museums serve?

The politics of representation

Museums justify their presence in society by the services they perform for their audiences. The assumption is that those audiences make up the total public, at least potentially. Hence, in culturally pluralistic societies, growing numbers of human history museums are expressing the desire to identify and meet the diverse needs of their diversified constituencies (for example, Adams 1990). It is coming to be recognized that groups whose cultures are portrayed in museum presentations should have their perspectives accounted for in those portrayals. The reality, however, is that most museums were created to represent the values and attitudes of the dominant cultural group within society, and that their actual core audiences (those who visit repeatedly and regularly) are still drawn largely from that group; those two facts are causally interdependent. As studies constantly reconfirm, the profile of the typical visitor to Canadian museums includes a university-level education and a value-system that is European and middle class. Traditional museum presentation technologies and techniques are designed to suit the learning styles of this audience. Museums are torn between their responsibility to this actual source of their support and their desire to broaden the reservoir from which visitors are drawn – or else face becoming institutions catering to an increasingly minority segment of society. But cultural democratization requires sharing of decision-making and museums are finding it hard to surrender their view of self as authoritative interpreters of history.

Museums' own history reveals the barriers that hinder their adaptation to social change. The public museum (as opposed to private cabinets of curiosities, or for-profit fairground shows) of the nineteenth century is sometimes seen as an expression of democracy: an attempt to educate the working classes. But it can also be seen as a tool of the dominant socio-economic group, controllers of the state, seeking to reinforce their values by promulgating them among the ruled (Cameron 1990: 14; Stapp 1990: 8). The perceptual biases thus embodied in museums (as in academic scholarship generally) are well enough understood. The aesthetic standards of high culture were extolled over those of popular/folk culture. History (and its heroes) was celebrated and portrayed as the story of Progress. Progress was, in turn, equated with technological advance and the subordination of nature to humanity. Technologized societies were considered superior to non-European cultures, seen as 'primitive' and 'static'. Colonialism – a source of wealth for the dominant social group – was justified as spreading this supposedly superior form of civilization and its values. Museums' architecture, collections classification systems and exhibition styles have all reiterated colonial and capitalist values.

Hardly surprising, then, that museums in colonial nations, as validations of the monocultural world-view and the power-base of the colonizing conquerors, have been described by members of cultural minorities as tools of western imperialism (T. Hill 1988; Conaty 1989: 407; Kurin 1990: 14; Tawadros 1990). Nor that Native peoples in North America are scarce among museum visitors. Until recently, most Canadian museums considered the country's indigenous peoples as part of their subject-matter, rather than a component of their audience. Canada's national museums evolved out of an institution which obtained legislated permanence just ten years after the nation was founded, and which was charged with surveying the natural resources of the country. That this came to include also the aboriginal cultures reflects one model of the nineteenth-century museum in which supposedly primitive cultures were seen as specimens of nature rather than strands in the tapestry of history. That linkage (in Canada) was severed only in relatively recent times. The whole western scientific approach, of which museums are one institutionalization, has also had an excluding effect. Classification of knowledge within a rigid framework and conceptual separation of past and present do not correspond with the way in which Native peoples perceive the world. Thus the very 'capture' of heritage artifacts and their isolation in display cases is in contradiction to the Native belief that such objects have no value or meaning except when employed in traditional expressions of a living culture.

Native cultures are founded more on spiritual and oral than on material heritage. The building of large museum collections of Native artifacts, mostly between the mid-nineteenth and early twentieth centuries, had adverse effects on Native cultures. Although collecting was often done under the belief that those cultures were facing extinction and a record of them needed to be saved, the very removal of the objects contributed to cultural decline. Once in museums, the objects were adapted into western classification frameworks or judged according to western aesthetic standards. Interpreting them from a foreign viewpoint often obscured or distorted their original significance. At the same time, western legalistic and scientific biases devalued Native oral tradition, equating it with opinion or hearsay evidence lacking the weight of historical fact. Through what they selected for preservation and display – and what they ignored – museums defined 'Indianness' for the mainstream population (Doxtator 1988: 26; Harrison et al. 1988: 13–14; Sullivan 1989; Edgar 1990: 43–4).

Perhaps what Natives feel to have been most damaging was that museum interpretations focused on the state of their cultures prior to the European settlement of Canada, representing any subsequent change as a loss of culture. Since they were 'presumed dead', Native cultures have been excluded from past efforts to define Canadian identity. Now that those cultures are experiencing some resurgence, a legacy of resentment is finding expression, as in the declaration of Native leader Georges Erasmus that:

> We do not want to be depicted the way we were, when we were first discovered in our homeland in North America. We do not want museums to continue to present us as something from the past. We believe we are very, very much here now, and we are going to be very important in the future. (Preserving Our Heritage 1988)

At a time when Natives are voicing their objections to their cultures being interpreted, as they believe unsympathetically, by a museum profession infused with European cultural ideology, museums are fortunately beginning to acknowledge the unavoidably subjective nature of interpretation, never independent of the interpreter's ethnocentric biases; there is growing acceptance of the idea that no subject can really be understood unless explored from different perspectives (Conaty 1989: 407; Huston 1990: 338). In a multicultural nation with a colonial history, such as Canada, interpretation can be a minefield. An object that symbolizes law and order to one group, for instance, may speak of repression to another.

Nonetheless, the relationship between Canada's museums and its indigenous and ethnic communities has been relatively peaceful until fairly recently. The question of the right of museums to interpret Native cultures or own their ceremonial objects was really only brought to the full attention of the Canadian public in 1988, with the exhibition The Spirit Sings at Calgary's Glenbow Museum, part of the Winter Olympics Arts Festival. Tom Hill, a Native and a museum director, described the case as the straw that broke the camel's back (Portman 1990).

The Spirit Sings was a fairly conventional exhibition of Native artifacts — most from non-Canadian collections — whose aim was to enhance public awareness of the cultural and artistic traditions of Canada's First Peoples. The exhibition developers were of European heritage, although provision was made for consultation of Native organizations. The Lubicon Lake Cree, to draw attention to their land claim dispute with the government, mounted an international media campaign urging boycott of the Olympics, and focused their efforts on *The Spirit Sings* — whose principal sponsor happened to be an oil company with drilling leases on land claimed by the Lubicons. The protest, which continued in the national capital when the exhibition was subsequently hosted by the Canadian Museum of Civilization, had little impact on the exhibition besides a few museums refusing to lend artifacts. Nor is it clear that there was any significant influence on political attitudes. But it did bring Native grievances into an international forum. And, despite the exhibition's defenders' claim that there was no objection to exhibition content, the protest demonstrated Natives' dislike of their cultural heritage being controlled by non-Natives. It also resulted in the initiation of a process of dialogue between Native groups and the museum profession that has now taken the form of a Task Force on Museums and the First Peoples (Harrison *et al.* 1988; T. Hill 1988; Cameron 1990: 15; Graburn and Lee 1988: 13).

Similarly, the more recent exhibition by the Royal Ontario Museum (ROM), *Into the Heart of Africa*, became a political forum for the expression of discontent over museum representation of the cultural heritage of ethnic groups established in Canada. The exhibition's curator, a well-respected anthropologist who was well aware that a museum collection can tell more about the culture of the collectors than that of the society from which collected, hoped to communicate this reality to the public. But the plan backfired badly.

As with *The Spirit Sings*, the intent of *Into the Heart of Africa* was to stimulate public appreciation of African artistry and aesthetics, as well as to provide an opportunity to display the ROM's African collection. As this collection is primarily historical, and so inadequate for depicting modern cultural developments, it was decided to use the exhibition to reveal the cultural values and racist attitudes of European colonists and missionaries, as well as their motivations for collecting the objects on display. Unfortunately, where it was hoped to counteract Eurocentric misconceptions of the African past, for a number of visitors the exhibition appeared to endorse cultural stereotypes.

The ROM is a long-established and scholarly institution that places great confidence in the expertise of its scientists. Although the exhibition development process included consultation with members of the Black (not just African) communities in Toronto, doubt lingers that concerns expressed, from early on, with the tone of the exhibition were treated as seriously as they might have been. Among these concerns were that some of the images for use in the exhibition were stereotypical and emotionally charged, from an African perspective; that images might be misconstrued by the public as representative of Africa today; and that community consultation was, for the ROM, aimed simply at rubber-stamping a 'fait accompli' (Crawford *et al.* 1990: 11).

The exhibition opened in November 1989, to generally favourable reviews. It was not until four months later that the Coalition For the Truth About Africa (CFTA), which claimed to represent over 15 Black community groups, began a protest by picketing the museum. Media coverage now started to reflect the objections of the CFTA to the exhibition. At times tempers ran high, demonstrators tried to enter the museum, the police were called in, and the ROM sought a legal injunction. The exhibition survived for its planned duration at the ROM, despite growing adverse public opinion – including the prohibition by the Toronto Board of Education of field trips to the exhibition by younger schoolchildren – but never travelled to booked locations. In September 1990 the Canadian Museum of Civilization and the Vancouver Museum, each after consultations with representatives of their cities' Black communities, cancelled the show; and in November the Natural History Museum of Los Angeles County and the Albuquerque Museum followed suit.

To an extent *Into the Heart of Africa* was simply a convenient political platform for expressing broader frustrations. The CFTA protest cannot entirely be dissociated from general inter-racial tensions then peaking in Toronto. And it is also worth noting that while Blacks were complaining about the portrayal of *their* ancestors, a smaller number of voices objected to the exhibition's portrayal of Christian missionaries as ethnocentric, bigoted and insensitive. Nonetheless, the protesters' concerns were, in this case, primarily with the exhibition's content (or, rather, its perceived content). They expressed opposition to the interpretation of their culture through European eyes; they took exception to such interpretation occurring in an institution credited with the power to shape public attitudes; and they complained that for the exhibition not to tell the whole truth was tantamount to condoning a lie (Crawford *et al.* 1990: 14–17). The principal sources of offence were a wall-sized depiction of a Zulu warrior being killed by a sword-thrust from a mounted British officer, and a photograph of a missionary 'teaching' African women how to do laundry.

Elicited visitor comments suggest that the exhibition's message was adequately understood by many – perhaps most – visitors; bearing in mind that these were, again, predominantly from the traditional museum-visiting audience. But it is equally clear that the message was too subtle for other visitors, and therefore amenable to misunderstanding. Even defenders of the exhibition conceded that the anti-racist message should have been presented more prominently and unequivocally (Baele 1990; Freedman 1990). The exhibition was, strictly speaking, curatorially correct. But it failed to account satisfactorily for the sensitivities of the Black community or to communicate well with the spectrum of the public beyond traditional museum audiences. In particular, it made evident the potency of images, the character of exhibits as primarily visual media, and the ambiguity of both images and artifacts: their ability to hold different meanings for different beholders. The anti-racist message of the show was carried principally in its text. But museum visitors in North America are notorious for reading exhibition text only partially, or not at all. A survey showed that perhaps half the visitors to the exhibition did not read the introductory text panel, nor see the opening of the introductory audiovisual presentation that would have oriented them to the intentions of the exhibition. Some of the grammatical conventions, such as the use of ironic quotation marks (for example, 'teaching') were likely lost on non-traditional visitors. And the danger of visuals showing Black subjugation overpowering text speaking of racism was particularly real in the case of young children seeing the exhibits. Indeed, one of critics' fears was that the exhibition would reinforce an inferiority complex in

Black children, instead of providing a positive self-image. Cancelling institutions felt the exhibition unsalvageable without changes so significant they would destroy its curatorial integrity. In the final resort, the opponents of *Into the Heart of Africa* simply wanted a different kind of exhibition.

The controversies surrounding *The Spirit Sings* and *Into the Heart of Africa* demonstrate the objections of minority cultural groups to being depicted from the perspective of Euro-Canadians rather than from their own; and to being portrayed as historical entities without reference to their status in the 1990s. These events have sounded warning bells throughout the Canadian museum community, inspiring a fresh consideration of the need for close consultation and cooperation with cultural groups represented in museum exhibitions, while at the same time giving rise to fears that any surrender to interest group pressure may set a precedent leaving all exhibitions vulnerable.

The same aversion to establishing dangerous precedents has also influenced museums' handling of issues such as repatriation of Native artifacts or display of sacred objects. Again, for Native peoples these matters are tied in to their cultural resurgence, their self-image as a people with a present, not just a past; they consider control of their sacred objects as vital to preserving and defining their culture (Doxtator 1988: 27; R. Hill 1988: 32). A subsidiary concern is that museums treat Native sacred materials differently to such materials associated with the dominant culture in society (Washburn 1990: 16), so that museum ownership of Native objects becomes seen as an expression of cultural domination.

Although it can hardly be said that the floodgates have opened, North American museums have seen, since the 1970s, growing demands for return of wampum, medicine bundles, potlatch pieces and human remains. There is as yet no consistent response by museums to these problems, although the Repatriation Act passed in November 1990 in the United States has forced museums' hands there (Thompson 1991: 37). How to reconcile Native rights with the needs of science and the concept of the museum as a public trust is still under discussion. In essence, the issue of repatriation highlights the clash of cultural value systems (Sullivan 1989). Some museums steadfastly refuse to entertain repatriation requests; some will satisfy any well-substantiated claims. Most take a more pragmatic and careful approach to dealing with claims on a case-by-case basis. The last is the position of the Canadian Museum of Civilization, which has repatriated a number of Native artifacts in the last few years, and is now exploring the feasibility of a more general decentralization of parts of its collections that would return control of interpretation to Canada's indigenous peoples.

Museums' commitment to democratic access to heritage dictates the desirability of repatriation in contexts where at least some of the repatriated materials will continue to be used to advance scientific knowledge and to inform the public. In 1974 the Canadian Museum of Civilization (then the National Museum of Man) arranged to repatriate elements of its Northwest Coast ceremonial collection, confiscated after the 1922 potlatch trials, on condition that Native-run museums be built to house them. The result of this, the first major repatriation in Canada, was the Kwagiulth Museum and Cultural Centre at Cape Mudge and the U'Mista Cultural Centre at Alert Bay. Other of the seized potlatch materials were recovered from the Royal Ontario Museum – although only after federal government pressure was brought to bear – while a third portion has been sought from an American museum and was just recently returned to Canada (Webster 1988: 44; MacDonald 1993).

The Native-operated museum is one of the newer forms of museum to emerge in Canada. Some, as in the cases noted above, or such as the Secwepemc Museum of the Shuswap people, are founded on collections repatriated from other institutions (Jules 1988). As yet there are barely a dozen such museums, almost all of which were created during the last two decades; this lack means that aboriginal culture has only a small voice directly within the museum community. It is significant that several of these institutions prefer the name cultural centre to museum, reflecting their mission to teach cultural tradition – a role that Natives do not perceive museums to have (Conaty 1989: 410). The Secwepemc Museum, for instance, is run by the band's Cultural Education Society which also operates an archive, a language retention programme, a newspaper, and develops curricula for schools. Also notable is that several recent proposals for new Native-controlled museums have been for tourist-targeted open air museums in which Native culture can be portrayed holistically and with emphasis on performative and oral, rather than material, aspects of culture.

More numerous in Canada are ethnic museums that focus on one particular cultural group within the population. The increase in ethnic and aboriginal museums reflects both the growing legitimization of cultural diversity in Canada and the democratization of interpretation of cultural identity (Ames et al. 1988: 49; Bloom and Mintz 1990: 14). The 1990/91 edition of the Canadian Museums Association Directory lists no fewer than 24 museums representing (exclusively) Ukrainian-Canadian heritage; the great majority were created and are run by community-based organizations. Although the first appeared in 1936, most were created between the 1950s and 1970s. No other ethnic group within Canada is so well served, although Mennonite and Jewish cultures are each the focus of several museums. In providing an outlet for the voice of minority cultural groups the development of ethnic museums must be considered healthy for the museum community as a whole. No single museum has a monopoly on truth, or the ability to present an authoritative interpretation of Canadian cultural identity. The proliferation of museums aids the diversification of perspectives needed to represent a subject.

The 1980s saw a slowdown in the appearance of ethnic and aboriginal museums. This was perhaps partly due to economic circumstances, but also to the increasing attention given to minority cultural groups by the dominant culture. For instance, Alberta's provincial government is behind both the Ukrainian Cultural Heritage Village, the major museum development relating to that cultural group during the 1980s, and the Head-Smashed-In Buffalo Jump Interpretive Centre (opened 1987), which employs only Natives in interpretive roles. The Canadian Museum of Civilization opened a major exhibition on Ukrainian-Canadian culture in 1991 (and plans to incorporate a full-scale reproduction of a Ukrainian church in its developing Canada Hall), which it followed with an exhibition on German-Canadian culture in 1993.

Museums and cultural minorities: models for cooperation

For mainstream museums to pay more attention to Canada's cultural minorities makes good business sense, in terms of audience development. But the ethical issues related to closer museum–community cooperation have yet to be resolved. Museums are experimenting with different models of working relationships. The extent of museum–community cooperation – which is to say, the degree to which museums are prepared to surrender some of their authority and control – will be influenced by the philosophy underlying each museum. The Royal Ontario Museum, for example, despite its experience with *Into the Heart of Africa* prompting it to establish a committee to consider future involvement of special interest groups in exhibition development, is unlikely to relinquish the central role of its own curatorial staff in that process. A position that will be supported by reference to the practical problems of consultation: disunity within a cultural community and the difficulty of determining which individual members accurately represent community perspectives. Such doubts certainly affected the ROM's handling of the *Into the Heart of Africa* affair (Baele 1990; Crawford *et al.* 1990: 12, 59; see also Conaty 1989: 410).

One model for cooperation is a project-by-project approach. This may involve, for example, arranging with community groups to present aspects of their culture as special interpretive events – such as craft demonstrations, storytelling or traditional dance. The University of British Columbia's Museum of Anthropology went slightly further in its Native Youth Project (begun 1979) in which Natives were engaged as interpreters in a continuing programme. Or it may involve consultation with community members during the process of exhibition development, including the possibility of a community member participating on the development team. This has been the case with the creation of Native peoples galleries at the Saskatchewan Museum of Natural History and the New York State Museum (Conaty 1989; Sullivan 1989). Such consultation was found useful in identifying objects to whose display Native sensitivities objected, in furnishing the interpretive perspective of the represented cultural group, and in thereby (it was hoped) authenticating exhibit interpretation and avoiding unnecessary confrontation with the Native community. Similar involvement is evidenced at Head-Smashed-In Buffalo Jump Interpretive Centre (Sponholz 1988). There, Blackfoot elders were consulted on exhibition themes, on artifacts suitable for display and on interpretive bias; they participated in the installation of sacred objects and conduct periodic purification ceremonies.

Another option is co-curatorship, a partnership characterized by the degree of control relinquished to community representatives in the process of exhibition development, and by the existence of a (written or unwritten) policy of addressing community concerns and interests on an ongoing basis. The Royal British Columbia Museum provides Canada's principal example of a museum that has cooperated with the Native community for decades, as a matter of course (Hoover and Inglis 1990). True partnership, by providing for polyphony in the curatorial voice, is more empowering than the consultation model (Fisher 1990: 26). *The Living Arctic*, a collaborative production by Britain's Museum of Mankind and Indigenous Survival International, is an excellent example of a partnership through which the perspective of the Inuit – presenting the case in favour of hunting and trapping – was enabled to emerge.

The Living Arctic, by focusing on one side of the argument, was perceived as playing an advocacy role (Cruikshank 1988; Graburn and Lee 1988: 12). In similar vein was *Trapline/Lifeline* produced by the Prince of Wales Northern Heritage Centre, and exhibited at the Canadian Museum of Civilization in 1989. Again the exhibition argued the importance of trapping and hunting to northern peoples. It was the product of wide consultation with residents and municipal councils of the Northwest Territories, hunters' and trappers' associations, and other Native political and cultural organizations, and it employs extensive use of quotations from northern residents (Irving and Harper 1988). These two exhibitions approach the third model of cooperation, in which the museum simply provides a forum, database and technical support for exhibitions of which cultural community representatives are the sole curators. Such exhibitions might be initiated through invitation of the museum to the community, or through a proposal from the community. As yet this model of community authorship is largely theoretical, although the University of British Columbia Museum of Anthropology did mount a photographic exhibition, *Proud to Be Musqueam*, in which all curatorial decisions were made by two Natives (Hoover and Inglis 1990: 274).

Ethnic and aboriginal museums remain, at this time, the main outlet for the interpretive perspectives of cultural minorities in Canada. Most mainstream museums are wary of the ramifications of cooperative relationships with cultural communities. As Michael Ames, director of the Museum of Anthropology, put it: 'how wide should consultation be, to whom does one listen, when does seeking advice mean taking orders?' (Harrison *et al.* 1988: 16). To many museum professionals, the protests surrounding *The Spirit Sings* and *Into the Heart of Africa* gave rise to the spectre of censorship and the threat of external political interference in the process of free enquiry and expression. And, from the museum standpoint, the issue of repatriation challenges the role of museums as caretakers of society's collective heritage. However, it is becoming recognized that museums' legal title to artifacts they hold (putting aside the question of whether those objects were acquired through legitimate process), and their legislated responsibilities as public repositories of heritage objects, are now counter-balanced by growing societal support for the moral and sacred rights of Canada's indigenous peoples (Ames *et al.* 1988: 48–9; Conaty 1989: 413). Consequently, efforts are being made by the museum community to formulate guidelines that will accommodate the concerns both of museums and the communities whose cultures they portray.

What is called the New Museology views these changing political circumstances as an opportunity rather than an obstacle. The interest of indigenous (and, by extension, ethnic) communities in having a voice in how their cultures are represented in museums is considered legitimate. The forging of constructively cooperative relationships between museums and communities is seen as a way to reverse the alienation of cultural minorities from mainstream museums; as a way for museums to come to understand how those groups perceive themselves and wish themselves to be portrayed to others; and as a way to bring together different cultural components of society to educate them about each other.

It would not be unnatural to assume that Canada's national museum of human history would be part of the state machinery to support cultural domination and centralized definition of cultural identity. However, the country's official multiculturalism and an entire overhaul of the Canadian Museum of Civilization's (CMC) exhibitions, programmes and policies during the last decade – in preparation for the move to a new building (opened in 1989) – have facilitated that museum's adoption of principles of the New Museology, with its emphasis on democratization and empowerment.

While its focus is on defining *national* identity, CMC recognizes that this process must arise out of a dialogue between the cultural components of Canadian society. Finding a workable expression of multiculturalism while at the same time preserving national unity must be premised on intercultural understanding: the ability to entertain diverse alternate viewpoints, to tolerate difference and dissonance, to accept that all cultures are valid expressions of their temporal and spatial contexts, none inherently superior. At the same time, acquiring a multicultural perspective has implications for Canadians' participative competence in the emerging global supra-culture. Consequently, CMC's aim is to help its audiences become familiar with different cultural grammars, for the acquisition of cultural literacy is the key to the ability to act in multiple cultures.

Cultural grammars cannot be taught through the medium of material objects alone, especially not when those objects are decontextualized and adapted to a western epistemological framework. Therefore CMC's exhibitions have a multimedia nature, with emphasis on visual communication as opposed to heavy use of textual language which is a major carrier of cultural bias. And, since the meaning of cultural elements derives from their context, CMC's permanent exhibitions try to reconstruct environmental contexts. Although any museum presentation has boundaries to its recontextualization, and any reconstruction has the essence of hypothesis, it is felt that environmental reconstructions will be more meaningful for the general public than seeing isolated objects in display cases. To give a concrete example of CMC's approach, its Grand Hall contains a full-scale reconstruction of a Pacific Coast Native village. Included are: historical artifacts such as totem poles; replicas of historically documented houses, recreated through the traditional skills of Native artists and craftsmen from the cultural groups of each house's origins; and simulated environmental elements such as tidal pools and a life-size photograph of the coastal rainforest towering behind the villagescape. Audiovisual and special effects enhance the environmental ambiance. An optional audiotour (scripted by a Native), together with conventional exhibits and audiovisual presentations inside the houses, broaden the interpretive scope. A similar approach is used in the museum's Canada Hall.

As use is one of the most meaningful contexts for material objects, and because culture resides in process at least as much as product, CMC places much emphasis on live interpretation and cultural performance programmes. It employs an in-house theatre company that performs vignettes for interpretive enrichment of Grand Hall and Canada Hall exhibits (for further information see Alsford and Parry 1991); one, for instance, examines the significance of masks in contemporary Native society. A Native Youth Cultural Programme employs students to give demonstrations and talks about aspects of Native culture. And thousands of performances have been given, since the new museum opened, by guest individuals or groups. At the museum's opening, for instance, there were presentations of traditional dances by Plains, Abinaki and Nisga'a Native groups, recounting or dramatizing of Cree, Ojibway and Mohawk legends, Inuit throat-singing, and a totem pole dedication by Nuuchahnulth representatives, as well as performances by numerous Canadian ethnic groups. Off-duty performers mixed with visiting crowds, providing opportunities for intercultural conversation. The role of the live agent in cultural transmission cannot be overvalued – a principle expected to be central also to the Smithsonian's planned National Museum of the American Indian (Garfield 1991: 55).

Through multimedia, multisensory and occasionally interactive presentations, CMC is trying to create opportunities for experiential learning of cultural grammars. To date it has focused on presentations of a celebratory character, in the belief that an individual's first experience of his or her cultural heritage in a museum should be a positive one that fosters cultural self-esteem, confidence in the institution and motivation for further learning. Two major temporary exhibitions produced for the new museum – *A Coat of Many Colours* (on Jewish-Canadian culture) and *Beyond the Golden Mountain* (Chinese-Canadian culture) have been in this vein. Each involved heavy community participation through both consultation during exhibition development and interpretive programmes featuring community members. However, it has also pursued the 'museum as forum' model, notably through its exhibition *Indigena*, which gave Native Canadian artists a chance to respond to the Columbus quincentenary by creating new works embodying Native perspectives on what the European arrival meant for their cultures.

As *Into the Heart of Africa* showed, examinations of colonial history can still serve to open old wounds and animosities, and may therefore be counter-effective to the promotion of intercultural understanding. Museum exploration of sensitive issues is both valid and necessary, but evidently must proceed from an existing foundation of trust and mutual respect that museums have yet to establish with cultural minorities. CMC certainly wishes to build a firmer relationship with its cultural constituencies before venturing too far into the area of controversial issues. This challenge will be faced during the development of its First Peoples Hall, in the second phase of gallery completion later this decade. Consultation with Native communities, both directly and through the intermediation of the University of British Columbia Museum of Anthropology, was an integral element in developing exhibits in the Grand Hall village. One consequence, for example, was arriving at a special way to exhibit Kwakwaka'wakw masks that satisfied Native concerns related to display of sacred objects, yet still allowed the public some visual access. Another was that interpretive information accompanying exhibits in the Nuxalk house is given in the voice of the Native peoples: a narrative-anecdotal, rather than objective-analytical, style, with heavy use of the present tense to affirm the contemporary relevance of the subject matter; both here and in an introductory audiovisual presentation in the Kwakwaka'wakw house the story is told from Native perspective. What was learned from the development of the Grand Hall exhibits will be more formalized when the First Peoples Hall exhibits are produced. It is now CMC's policy that all exhibitions be developed in close consultation with communities depicted therein, and it is planned to establish from Native representatives a national reference committee and regional sub-committees. Co-curatorship will be the order of the day, with provision for showing different points of view in cases where conflicting interpretations arise. It is intended to design into the gallery large open spaces for live cultural interpretation, where control over content will be in the hands of Native peoples. Co-curatorship is also expected increasingly to become one criterion for judging whether CMC will host travelling exhibitions produced by other institutions.

CMC's intent to be a museum for *all* Canadians is symbolized in its architecture. Designed by part-Native Douglas Cardinal, it avoids European architectural forms, preferring a humanist, post-industrial style that harks back to the Canadian landscape, the foundation of culture. It is also symbolized in the museum's coat of arms, whose elements include: the beaver crest of a Haida chief; a fan of eagle feathers, a traditional Plains Native symbol of honour; Inuit and Algonquian underwater spirits; an astrolabe, to represent the arrival of Europeans and subsequent immigrant groups; maple leaves, a nationalist symbol; and the motto 'Multae Culturae Una Patria'.

The museums of a culturally pluralistic Canada are faced with the challenge of becoming a model for intercultural respect and cooperation. The tightrope they must walk is to examine the past without revisionism and yet in a way that responds to the sensibilities of those whose cultures they represent – which will, at least on occasion, mean learning to deal with values in conflict (Cameron 1990: 15). If museums are now beginning to acknowledge the right of cultural minorities to participate in the interpretation of their own cultures, this stems from a deeper appreciation of the diversity within the society they exist to serve, and recognition that the gradual empowerment now under way of those minorities makes it impossible to ignore their interests any longer. One option is to give special emphasis to ensuring that the voices of minority groups have a forum in which they may contribute to the defining of cultural identity. Another is for mainstream museums to dig in and defend the status quo, with the likely consequence of further cultural separatism in the form of museums created by and for cultural minorities. The decisions that museums make will have repercussions on the framing of the attitudes of society as a whole. One way or the other, it can be expected that the 1990s will not be restful years for the Canadian museum community, as it struggles to come to terms with a new perception of its role in a multicultural society.

Note

George F. MacDonald is Director Emeritus of the Canadian Museum of Civilization having begun his career there in 1960. He became Museum Director in 1983. **Stephen Alsford** is website manager for the Canadian Museum of Civilization Corporation.

References

Adams, Robert McCormick (1990) 'Cultural Pluralism: A Smithsonian Commitment', in *1990 Festival of American Folklife*, pp. 5–6. Washington, DC: Smithsonian Institution/National Park Service.

Alsford, Stephen and Parry, David (1991) 'Interpretive Theatre: A Role in Museums?', *Museum Management and Curatorship* 10: 8–23.

Ames, Michael, Harrison, Julia and Nicks, Trudy (1988) 'Proposed Museum Policies for Ethnological Collections and the Peoples they Represent', *Muse* 6 (October): 47–52.

Baele, Nancy (1990) 'Exhibit Protest Proves Need for More Dialogue', *Ottawa Citizen*, 20 November: G3.

Bloom, Joel N. and Mintz, Ann (1990) 'Museums and the Future of Education', *Journal of Museum Education* 15(3): 12–15.

Cameron, Duncan (1990) 'Values in Conflict and Social Redefinition', *Muse* 8 (November): 14–16.

Conaty, Gerald T. (1989) 'Canada's First Nations and Museums: A Saskatchewan Experience', *International Journal of Museum Management and Curatorship* 8: 407–13.

Crawford, Belinda, Hankel, Lillian and Rowse, Gloria (1990) ' "Into the Heart of Africa": An Evaluation'. Toronto: Royal Ontario Museum (unpublished).

Cruikshank, Julie (1988) 'Living Arctic: Hunters of the Canadian North', *Muse* 6 (October): 74–5.

Doxtator, Deborah (1988) 'The Home of Indian Culture and Other Stories in the Museum', *Muse* 6 (October): 26–8.

Edgar, Darcy (1990) 'Silence the Teller, Silence the Tale: Evidence Gathering in Law and Museums', *Muse* 8 (November): 43–5.

Fisher, Jennifer (1990) 'Foundations of Vision: Constructing Culture at the Canadian Museum of Civilization', *Parachute* 59: 22–8.

Freedman, Jim (1990) 'Bringing It All Back Home: A Commentary on *Into the Heart of Africa*', *Museum Quarterly* 18 (February): 39–43.

Garfield, Donald (1991) 'Cultural Chronology', *Museum News* 70 (January–February): 55–6.

Graburn, Nelson H.H. and Lee, Molly (1988) '*The Living Arctic*, Doing What *The Spirit Sings* Didn't', *Inuit Art Quarterly* 3(4): 10–13.

Harrison, Julia, Trigger, Bruce and Ames, Michael (1988) 'Museums and Politics: *The Spirit Sings* and the Lubicon Boycott', *Muse* 6 (October): 12–16.

Heron, R. Peter (1990) 'Museums: Cultural Institutions and Islands of Hope', *Muse* 8 (November): 49–52.

Hill, Rick (1988) 'Sacred Trust: Cultural Obligations of Museums to Native People', *Muse* 6 (October): 32–3.

Hill, Tom (1988) 'First Nations and Museums', *Muse* 6 (October): 2.

Hoover, Alan and Inglis, Richard (1990) 'Acquiring and Exhibiting a Nuu-chah-nulth Ceremonial Curtain', *Curator* 33 (December): 272–88.

Huey, John (1990) 'America's Hottest Export: Pop Culture', *Fortune* 122(16): 50–60.

Huston, Mary M. (1990) 'New Media, New Messages: Innovation through Adoption of Hypertext and Hypermedia Technologies', *The Electronic Library* 8 (October): 336–42.

Irving, Sue and Harper, Lynette (1988) 'Not Another Fur Trade Exhibit? An Inside Look at *Trapline/Lifeline*', *Muse* 6 (October): 38–40.

Jules, Linda (1988) 'The Secwepemc Museum', *Muse* 6 (October): 6–7.

Kurin, Richard (1990) 'Folklife in Contemporary Multicultural Society', in *1990 Festival of American Folklife*, pp. 8–17. Washington, DC: Smithsonian Institution/ National Park Service.

Lumley, Robert (1987) 'Museums in a Post Modern World', *Museums Journal* 87(2): 81–3.

MacDonald, George F. (1991) 'What is Culture? How is it Transmitted and Learned?', *Journal of Museum Education* 16(1): 9–12.

MacDonald, George F. (1993) 'Changing Relations between Canada's Museums and First Peoples', *Museum National* 16(1): 9–12.

Minkin, Mark J. (1990) 'Indigenous Cultures on the Altar of Technology', *Global* 1 (October–December): 1.

Moore, Sally Falk (1989) 'The Production of Cultural Pluralism as a Process', *Public Culture* 1(2): 26–48.

Nicks, Trudy (1990) 'Marketing of an Image', *Artscraft* 2(3): 4–8.

Phillips, Ruth B. (1988) 'Indian Art: Where do You Put It?', *Muse* 6 (October): 64–7.

Podger, Andrew, Martin, Ross and Crossfields, Len (1989) *What Price Heritage? The Museums Review and the Measurement of Museum Performance*. Canberra: Department of Finance Discussion Paper (unpublished).

Portman, Jamie (1990) 'Museums Giving up Native Treasures – But Slowly', *Ottawa Citizen*, 10 March: C10.

Preserving Our Heritage, A Working Conference for Museums and First Peoples: Outcomes and Recommendations (1988) Unpublished transcript of conference at Carleton University, Ottawa, Canada, 3–5 November.

Seeger, Anthony (1990) 'Musics of Struggle', in *1990 Festival of American Folklife*, pp. 56–9. Washington, DC: Smithsonian Institution/National Park Service.

Sponholz, Edward (1988) 'Head-Smashed-In Buffalo Jump Interpretive Centre', *Muse* 6 (October): 8–9.

Stapp, Carol B. (1990) 'The "Public" Museum: A Review of the Literature', *Journal of Museum Education* 15(3): 4–11.

Sullivan, Robert (1989) 'Museums, Artifacts and Multi-cultural Education', paper presented at International Symposium: Museums for the Global Village, Hull, Quebec, 5–10 June.

Tawadros, Giliane (1990) 'Is the Past a Foreign Country?', *Museums Journal* 90 (September): 30–1.

Thompson, Raymond H. (1991) 'Dealing with the Past and Looking to the Future', *Museum News* 70 (January–February): 36–40.

Ward, Barbara (1970) 'The First International Nation', in W. Kilbourn (ed.) *A Guide to the Peaceable Kingdom*, pp. 45–8. Toronto: Macmillan.

Washburn, Wilcomb (1990) 'Museums and the Repatriation of Objects in their Collection', in *The Hall of the North American Indian: Change and Continuity*, pp. 15–18. Cambridge, MA: Peabody Museum Press.

Webster, Gloria Cranmer (1988) 'The "R" Word', *Muse* 6 (October): 43–4.

Chapter 18

Museums as Agents for Social and Political Change[1]

Dawn Casey

T HE NATIONAL MUSEUM was a birthday gift to Australia for the Centenary of Federation. Has it been a welcome gift? Is it just what you always wanted? Has it made a useful contribution to public life?

And from the museum professional's point of view, is it worthy to join the ranks of the great twenty-first-century museums? These are the museums breaking new ground in redefining their national history, becoming more inclusive and accessible, and establishing themselves quite consciously as a forum for the debate of contemporary issues.

I'm also going to consider how you, the press, have responded to Australia's new museum, and whether you've got it right. Some critics have called us 'a profound intellectual mistake' or accused us of belittling white history, so we are sometimes referred to as the 'controversial' National Museum. How fair is that, and how do we feel about it?

Well, let's get back to basics. Let's put the whole discussion in context and remember that Australian public life is being shaken by a number of fierce debates. They're about issues that run a lot deeper than current events or party politics, and they include:

- Who are we exactly, and how did we get to be this way?
- What sort of people should we allow to join us in this nation continent, and why?
- How many of us should there be?
- What is the proper place of Indigenous Australians, and do we owe them special consideration?
- Does what happened to them in the past matter today?
- Is the way we have developed the land a matter for pride in achievement, or is it a slowly emerging environmental catastrophe?

Source: *Curator*, vol. 44. no. 3, July 2001, 230–6.

If any of you have well-considered, fair, and just answers to these questions you shouldn't be lunching here today, you should be over at Parliament House advising the Prime Minister. Because they're enormous questions, they're complex and confronting. They're also about the kind of place we want Australia to be in future, and they're the reason the National Museum of Australia will *always* be 'controversial.'

Our subject matter places us right in the front line of public debate. But let me say we didn't get there by accident. Tackling the tough issues, and providing a physical and intellectual space in which such debate could take place, was part of our planning from the early stages.

I wonder if any of you recognize these words?

> A new national museum will illuminate new fields of knowledge and also link traditional fields in revealing ways. It will chart a course quite different to that followed by those earlier Australian museums which were founded during a different educational and scientific climate.[2]

> The museum, where appropriate, should display controversial issues. In our view, too many museums concentrate on certainty and dogma, thereby forsaking the function of stimulating legitimate doubt and thoughtful discussion.[3]

That vision for an entirely new kind of Australian museum comes not from the trendy postmodernists of the 1990s, but the Pigott Report back in 1975. It's a good idea which seems to have stood the test of time. However, it also ensured that we would find ourselves in plenty of trouble.

Let me summarize what our critics have said.

First, there's the outraged traditionalist. People convinced that museums should be dignified classical structures, temples, if you like, inside which Truth with a capital T is handed down to the people. They are upset by what they see as our eccentric and contemporary architecture – and even more by our inclusive approach to history.

What bothers them most is that the Museum refuses to provide a 'master narrative' – a strong, authoritative voice with a simple chronology of civilization and progress. But, as most of us accept, the truth is never simple, and Australian history has no one valid viewpoint. The national story we attempt to tell is complex, and emerges not from a neat timeline, nor from a list of simple facts, but from the interplay of many stories and points of view. These can range from the profoundly tragic, through the ironic or quirky, to the absurd or the joyful. They are the sum of us.

One outraged traditionalist was Miranda Devine, who complained in the Sydney *Daily Telegraph* about what she called our 'sneering ridicule at white history.'[4] Others called us 'tangled,' or 'trivial.'[5] Peter Ward in the *Australian* was unhappy with the unusual architecture and the sinister messages he thought it must contain. Others have called us a 'theme park.' They seem to be afraid that visitors might actually enjoy themselves. Well, perish the thought!

What unites these critics, apart from the need to generate startling headlines, is a reluctance to concede that museums have changed. The world's newest museums inhabit bold contemporary buildings, and they take a similarly bold, many-stranded approach to national history. They entertain, as well as inform. Well, we are one of those. We accept that there are few absolute truths in history. We admit many voices to the debate. We use many media to tell the stories.

Another kind of critic is the one who objects to a perceived bias in our subject matter. Most commonly they would say: '*Where are all the heroic explorers and pioneers?*' or '*There's far too much about Aborigines,*' or even '*The whole thing is pro-Aboriginal*' – whatever that means.

This raises the interesting question of how much our Indigenous people should be included in national history, and how much is 'too much' – to which there is, of course, no satisfactory answer. I invite you to pick your own, on a spectrum ranging all the way from '*All of it, they are the true Australians,*' to '*None at all, perhaps a footnote at best.*'

But the National Museum was guided by the eminent historian Geoffrey Blainey, who together with Emeritus Professor John Mulvaney contributed to the original Pigott Report with the following words:

> The argument for a major display of Aboriginal history is overwhelming. The chronology of the human occupation on Australia is dominated by Aboriginals. If the human history of Australia were to be marked on a twelve-hour clock face, the era of the white man would run for only the last three or four minutes.[6]

Our approach is not, in fact, chronological, but we took the point that Indigenous people must have a substantial place in the Museum. The Indigenous narrative is blended in with the other great Australian stories – you will find it not just in the Aboriginal gallery, but in amongst the stories of settlement and exploration, and our evolving relationship with the land. Most importantly, many of these stories are told from the Indigenous perspective.

However this deeply offends critics like Keith Windschuttle, who has denounced us in *Quadrant*[7] and elsewhere for alleged offences against truth and objectivity. These include the mention of a massacre at Bells Falls Gorge, near Bathurst, in the 1820s, which he claims did not take place. How does he know this? There is no official, written record. The oral tradition of the Wiradjuri people he discounts – after all, it is long ago and they weren't there.

Many incidents from Australia's land wars have been forgotten – or even suppressed – by white Australians. But you have my word for it that they live on in the hearts and minds of Aboriginal Australians descended from the people who fought in those wars. A proper telling of history must consider *all* available sources – including theirs, as oral history. They are not the only voices, but they must have a place.

Can you imagine the comments by Keith Windschuttle, Angela Shanahan, and others linked to *Quadrant* if I were to write my story – of how my grandmother was sent to Palm Island because she was 'cheeky' to the cattle owner's wife and had to leave my mother and her four other children in Croydon never to be seen again for some 30 years, and how my father was placed on a cattle station at the age of seven because he was 'half-caste'? Both of these stories were verbally told to me by my mother and father.

My story would include me being told at high school that I couldn't go into a French class because Aboriginal kids leave school to work on the cane fields or become domestics, being told by a potential landlord she wouldn't rent her flat out because she didn't rent to Aborigines or Yugoslavs, and, overhearing a nurse telling a doctor in the outpatients section of a hospital that there are no other patients – only a black baby (who happened to be my son) – therefore he could go off to dinner.

As these stories are not 'officially' recorded should they therefore be regarded as myths and never be told in the National Museum?

Even more curiously, Mr. Windschuttle tells us that *'feminists, ethnics, indigines and gays'*[8] – and I quote his words – have no place in a national museum because, as he says, none of them were major players in national history. Well, this is news to all of us. It's news that the suffragist Mary Lee, the spiritual pioneer Mary MacKillop, the Eora man Bennelong, the song-writer Archie Roach, or Ron Muncaster of the Gay and Lesbian Mardi Gras are not a proper part of history. While it may be true that the nation's *political* leadership has been dominated by 'Anglo-Celts of the male sex,'[9] the nation's history is a different matter. That story is about all Australians and – as a social history museum – we tell it for all Australians.

By the way, don't imagine that the National Museum is alone in drawing fire because it includes alternative views of national history. Remember the Smithsonian's dilemma over the *Enola Gay* – the Hiroshima bomber – in 1995? There was an outcry from veterans' groups, complaining that the exhibition was unpatriotic and politically biased. There were similar controversies in Germany when a 1995 exhibition exhibited new evidence of the role of the German army in wartime. It was bitterly attacked by some former soldiers, while others agreed that it was factual and were glad to see the story told at last.[10] Stories like this are common wherever alternative perspectives of national history are given. Being honest, and admitting the existence of multiple viewpoints, can be a dangerous business for any museum.

So far I have quoted some journalists and commentators who were fiercely critical of the National Museum's approach. But we should remember that they are in the minority. Most have praised the Museum.

An independent survey we commissioned last year found that 83 percent of all our media coverage – both at home and overseas – was favourable. That is, 83 percent of all media responses deemed the Museum to be interesting or worthwhile.

Michael Fitzgerald from *Time Magazine*[11] said he enjoyed the . . .

> sense of a history moving towards the future, not trapped in the past
> . . . They've come up with a museum in motion, small in scale but big
> in ideas, supple and sexy where museums can often be solemn monu-
> ments to nationhood. The National Museum of Australia is an open book.

Susan McCulloch-Uehlin in *The Australian*[12] identified our Indigenous gallery as *'rich in material culture, but also ripe with ideas.'*

But I have called this address 'Museums as agents for social and political change.' Assuming that they should be – is it in fact true? How can dusty old museums act as agents of social change?

Essentially, we provide a forum for debate, by offering a reflective space in which people can consider issues in context – against their historic background. We offer comfortable spaces and a stimulus for thought – '*a safe place for unsafe ideas,*' as museum consultant Elaine Gurian says.

In the terrible days following September 11, many museums proved their worth as civic spaces. The museums of New York did more than offer a physical haven. The Brooklyn, Manhattan, and Staten Island children's museums opened their doors free of charge to families, and offered special programs which enabled children to reflect and express their feelings. Parents and teachers found ways to encourage cultural understanding at a time when children wanted to know, 'Who did it?' 'Who were the bad people?' They needed someone to explain the terrible instances of blame and hatred they were seeing, directed against other kids at school, or Middle Eastern shop owners.[13]

At the National Museum we responded simply by switching our Optiwave screen in the main Hall to live TV coverage. But the story played out in other ways. From September there was a marked change in the tone of people's own stories, which they record themselves in our *Eternity* gallery. Suddenly they were all about 'hope' and 'fear' – especially the fear that Australia would once again find itself at war.

A contemporary issue even closer to home of course involves refugees. But there's little in the *Tampa* story which Australia hasn't seen before. I refer you to our *Horizons* Gallery for a fairly offensive National Action poster of some years ago, calling for the Vietnamese boat people to be . . . 'sunk in the water.' And we've had Afghani settlers before. Remember the cameleers of South Australia? Their descendants today are proud of that contribution to our history.

What makes the National Museum different from a newspaper or a pub when it comes to the discussion of hot issues is our contribution to *informed* debate. Our foundation in scholarship and research enables us to give background information in a way not available to the front page or the soapbox orator. We provide a venue which is 'safe' in the sense of calm and comfortable, where the rules of engagement encourage respect for multiple viewpoints. Museums are the new civic space – the place where you can gather to talk over the news of the day. Has this ever happened before? What are the newspapers not telling us? Does anybody else think like me?

And in museums, there's a crucial interplay between intellectual and emotional knowledge. Our visitors often say, 'Sure I knew it happened, but I didn't realize what it was actually like.' Take the visitor who was moved to tears, because she'd heard about the removal of Aboriginal children, but only understood its human impact when she encountered the personal stories in our museum. The same is true about stories of Australians at war, or arriving in migrant ships, or finding ways to survive the Great Depression. Emotional connection, founded on scholarship, is what we do best.

But is the Museum biased? Of course we are – take your pick. It all depends on your point of view. Republicans object to our display of the monarchist Tee-shirt. Christians object to the images of Australian Jews and Muslims at prayer. We've got far too much about women, if you're a man, and not nearly enough about migrants, if you or your parents are recent arrivals. But if you're a citizen from Struggle Street you probably appreciate the stories of humble Australians, and enjoy hearing ordinary people tell extraordinary stories. Every visitor is different. But for nearly all of them, a museum visit includes the pleasure of recognizing the familiar, as well as the shock of encountering something new. Always, there is the challenge of understanding that there are many different ways of looking at the world.

But they cope. Australia has a well-rehearsed democratic tradition, and the election process teaches us to assert our own views. But in order to live with one another, we understand that tolerance of opposing views is also necessary. The average visitor to the National Museum feels the same way.

Some elements of the media are doing the Australian people a very great disservice if they assume that a museum exhibition could dupe them or mislead them. How condescending! People are well able to think for themselves. As Angela Shanahan said in yesterday's *Australian*,[14] the 'Mr. and Mrs. Average' who walk into a museum don't belong to any particular 'side' in the historical debate. But we don't insult their intelligence, either, by giving them nothing more than a simplistic set of dot points about 'what happened when.'

If people find material in our exhibitions which startles or disturbs them – and they should, if they are paying attention – it becomes something to take away and think over. Discuss, perhaps reject, perhaps even take on board as part of a broader perspective. Our debate here should be everybody's debate – it's about Australian history and identity, and that's a very useful debate to have right now.

Prominent citizens helping us to carry on the debate have included the Prime Minister and the Foreign Minister – who made themselves available to school-children in 'Talkback Classroom,' a program transmitted like many others from our Broadcast Studio. We've also had space scientists, cartoonists, historians of frontier conflict or experts on prehistory – all talking at the Museum, mostly to full houses.

This shows that we are successfully fulfilling our role – to be a forum for national discussion and reflection, to be a real agent for change. And there are other signs. Take visitor numbers – coming up to a million this week, which is, in fact, twice our original estimate – the Australian public are voting with their feet.

The vast majority of our visitors tell us that they appreciate the democratic approach, the mixture of famous and ordinary people, the fact that we don't condescend to our visitors but give them something they can relate to – and their kids love it, too.

But I have to say that the small number of visitors who are dissatisfied are really outraged. They want their comfortable conception of Australian history confirmed – and we let them down. We present them with complexity and debate, a whole lot of black faces, and one or two unpleasant facts. Frankly I think their problem may not be with the Museum, but with real life.

In fact, hundreds of thousands of Australians are going on their way better informed, a bit more thoughtful, and better equipped to deal with the claims and counter-claims of national public life. The way we do it risks the disapproval of some, but without risk there is no opportunity. Some people may well prefer a world without risk, where everything is fully guaranteed, pleasant, inoffensive, bland. But that's not a world in which you could hope to learn – or to change.

How do we feel about being 'controversial?' Well, it would be hard to avoid. Remember that the Museum of Australia Act obliges us to exhibit historical material, conduct research and disseminate information relating to Australian history. And you can't talk seriously about Australian history without treading on somebody's prejudices. Blame Geoffrey Blainey if you must, or Peter Pigott or John Mulvaney, for insisting back in 1975 that Australia's national museum should embrace controversy.

Let me assure you that I'm only human. I don't enjoy being attacked. But it's a whole lot better than being irrelevant. One of our advisers, the historian, Professor Graeme Davison, said that if the National Museum offended nobody, it would be hopelessly bland. So if we tread on a few toes, or upset a few preconceptions, we're obviously doing our job properly.

Australia should be proud of its museums. They are places of entertainment, discovery and debate. They help us to get to grips with the big questions about our country and ourselves. In museum exhibitions today you can find dry facts and emotional insights – both intended to help you learn. Australia desperately needs places for intelligent dissent and debate. Museums can encourage people to understand the limits of their own experience, to cross the imagination boundary and gain insight into the view-points of other people, or other times.

You *do* have to challenge or surprise people. You *must* push them beyond the comfortable or the familiar. You have to keep on reminding them that their kind of person, or their experience of life, is not the only one. We can't hope to grow and mature as a nation without doing that. And from my personal perspective as an Indigenous Australian, I can assure you that Australia needs change. The National Museum has been working at it for a year so far, and we still have a way to go. Watch this space.

Thank you.

DAWN CASEY
Director, National Museum of Australia

Notes

Dawn Casey was appointed Director of the National Museum of Australia in 1999. She left the museum in December 2003.

1   First anniversary address from the Director of the National Museum of Australia, National Press Club, Canberra. 13 March 2002. Ms. Casey began her address by acknowledging the Ngunnawal people, traditional owners of Australia, and welcoming members of the National Press Club, and other assembled dignitaries.

2   *Museums in Australia 1975: Report of the Committee of Inquiry on Museums and National Collections*, Australian Government Publishing Service Canberra 1975, section 12.2.

3   Ibid., section 12.16.

4   Devine, M., *Daily Telegraph*, 12 March 2001, Sydney Edition.

5   'Museum offers tangled vision of Australia,' *The Age*, 10 March 2001. 'New museum, same old trivia,' *Sunday Telegraph*, 11 March 2001.

6   *Museums in Australia 1975*, section 12.8.

7   Windschuttle, K., 'How not to run a museum,' *Quadrant*, September 2001.

8   Ibid., p. 15.
9   Ibid., p. 16.
10 'War of extermination – crimes of the Wehrmacht 1941–1944,' mounted by the Hamburg Institute for Social Research.
11 Fitzgerald, M., *Time Magazine*, 12 March 2001.
12 McCulloch-Uehlin, S., *The Australian*, 24 March 2001.
13 Personal e-mail from Carol Enseki of the Brooklyn Children's Museum.
14 'More edification, less of the gee-whiz factor,' *The Australian*, 12 March 2002.

Chapter 19

Museums, Communities and the Politics of Heritage in Northern Ireland

Elizabeth Crooke

Introduction

THE PUBLIC REPRESENTATION of the past in Northern Ireland has never been the single domain of the 'official' museum and heritage sector. The traditions of marching, murals and street painting has ensured that a sense of history is omnipresent in particular urban and, sometimes, rural spaces. A form of political stability has begun to emerge since the 1998 Belfast Agreement and now military fortifications, ephemera of legal and illegal organisations, as well as oral histories of the Troubles are emerging as 'political heritage' in the landscape of reconciliation. Alongside this, Northern Ireland has three national museums, which together form part of the National Museums and Galleries of Northern Ireland, a number of county museums, and several museums specialising in aspects of local heritage, such as the linen industry or the Battle of the Somme. In addition to this, new museums are currently in planning. As we review heritage provision in Northern Ireland, it can be considered in two ways. The most predominant includes the official representations offered by local and national museums; that preserved by the sites and monuments record; and that provided by other heritage organisations such as the National Trust. An alternative form of heritage in Northern Ireland, which is beginning to come to the fore, is the unofficial, unsafe, contested history of the conflict, which is seeking recognition.

This chapter is a consideration of the presentation of heritage in Northern Ireland, with particular reference to the work of museums and the creation of community exhibitions. Its main interest is two-fold: how museums in Northern Ireland are attempting to engage more successfully with a broader audience by embracing

Source: *The Politics of Heritage: The Legacies of 'Race'*, J. Littler and R. Naidoo (eds), London: Routledge, 2005, pp. 69–81.

new histories; and how communities are undertaking 'museum-like' activities to communicate their own histories. In order to investigate these themes, this chapter will first consider the redevelopment of the museum idea as a community space. This has encouraged museums to be more aware of the diversity of their local communities. This is followed by a discussion of the development of a community focus in Northern Ireland's museums and how this has been linked to the ideas of inclusion and fostering good community relations. The community sector is considered in the following section, through a discussion of two oral history projects and local exhibition initiatives. This chapter will conclude with a discussion of how this activity relates to the themes of heritage, identity and nationality.

Museums as a community space

Museums are a contested terrain where the public representation of place, the past and identity is always the subject of debate and sometimes dispute. Once the place of privilege, where state leaders would display the booty of war, travel and exploitation, by the nineteenth century museums were also being established to forge national identities and open to a wider public. In the national museums of Europe, museums were often places where the idea of an ancient and superior national community was presented unchallenged (Bennett 1995). In Ireland, the museum founded in Dublin in 1877 was established as a branch of the Museum of Science and Art in South Kensington and reflected its London counterpart. Although the Irish character of the Dublin institution was still strongly felt, the museum was reinvented in the early twentieth century to reflect more closely the desires of an independent Ireland (Crooke 2000). The history of the National Museum of Ireland in Dublin reveals that museums continually reinvent themselves to reflect the context of changing times. The space of the museum is continually revisited and represented to meet new needs and desires. Increasingly, too, the idea of the museum is being rethought consciously to introduce new hierarchies of power, responsibility and accountability. Today, the move to democratise museums is associated with the issues of community representation and inclusion. One of the most powerful example of this is the 'People's Movement' in Australia, which aims to recognise past injustices and foster reconciliation among indigenous groups and descendants of European settlers in order to lessen racism and marginalisation suffered by indigenous peoples. The impact of this on the Australian museum sector is illustrated by the ways in which established museums are finding new methods of engaging with indigenous groups. In addition, indigenous groups have established new community museums, expressed as 'Keeping Places' and 'Cultural Centres'. In both cases, the new forms of engagement with museums have developed understanding between indigenous and European communities and raised esteem among indigenous groups (Kelly and Gordon 2002).

The example of Australia is a good demonstration of the two-fold method by which 'the museum' is moving from being a state space, where the winners told their story, to the community space, in which history is told from alternative positions. On the one hand, established museums are beginning to reach out to groups previously excluded from museums, both because of an internal desire to do so and because of pressure from external bodies. On the other, the groups themselves are representing their own histories and identities in self-appointed community spaces. Many of the perspectives presented in *Including Museums* discuss the slow introduction of such changes in UK museums (Dodd and Sandell 2001). The South East Asian Arts Officer at the Victoria and Albert Museum (V&A), for instance, illustrates how the V&A is attempting to represent a multi-ethnic Britain better through improved collecting and appropriate interpretation of existing collections (Shaikh 2001). Within South Africa the political changes brought in with the end of apartheid have been expressed in the rise of community-based museums. In the District Six Museum in Cape Town, for instance, former residents who were forced out of the District during land clearances are using the museum as part of the political campaign to bolster support for reclaiming that land. In this example the idea of being a museum is paramount as public display of personal stories develops self-esteem and community confidence (Rassool and Prosalendis 2001).

Museums are now establishing themselves as community spaces, as places where the personal and the local are of equal importance as the state or national story. Lost or hidden histories are now coming to the fore – histories of slavery associated with a painting in the National Gallery in London (Hooper-Greenhill 2000: 147) or with silver candlesticks in Nottingham Museum and Art Gallery (Wallace 2001: 84) have now been brought out in the open. Women's history, as well as the experiences of ethnic groups, disabled and children are gaining prominence in museum spaces. In a bid to increase their relevance, museums are improving links with local groups – be it through the health, social and educational sectors, or by working with leaders of neighbourhood groups. There are diverse stories to be told, more ways of telling those stories, and a wider range of people prepared to share their experiences in public spaces. Memory work in history museums, through oral history and reminiscence, has revealed the value of telling and sharing stories (Kavanagh 2000). Reminiscence work, responsibly handled, has been shown to have numerous positive benefits. It becomes a means to preserve and transmit cultural and community history; promote effective communication between groups of people; enhance self-esteem; aid the preservation of unique individual identity; enable life-review; promote self-development; and is an activity that many find enjoyable (Gibson 2000: 26). It is the recognition of these new stories and the mutual benefits of learning about them that is encouraging museums to diversify.

The concern for museums attempting to become relevant to more diverse audiences is to understand the communities outside the museum. Together we need to realise there is no single national group; rather, collectively we form a myriad of sometimes shifting communities. Communities can be identified by activity, gender, interest, ability and economics; we move between these communities and sometimes feel uncomfortable in the categories we are placed. Nevertheless, we need communities in order to build our experiences and forge our identities. Together these experiences produce 'communities of practice' in which knowledge and relationships are socially constructed (Falk and Dierking 2000: 46).

In Northern Ireland the identification of communities of practice is intertwined with the political environment. The politics of the region has not only ruined lives, it has also formed our understanding of identity, history and culture – both our own and that of others. When the Community Relations Council was founded in

1990, its aim was to promote better relations between the two communities in Northern Ireland; in other words, among Republican and Loyalist groups; or, Nationalists and Unionists; or, Protestants and Catholics. The 'two traditions' model never really worked in Northern Ireland; the conflict may often be reduced to this binary but the reality is more complex. In order to investigate the creation of identities, the Community Relations Council embraced cultural traditions work that encouraged the affirmation of personal histories, reflection on beliefs, the sharing of information between groups and the legitimisation and sharing of different cultural traditions (Fitzduff 1993). The practice of inclusion policies in Northern Ireland's museums reflects this political context. While the region's museums attempt to embrace the ideology of inclusion, as they aim to incorporate diverse histories and new audiences, they are continually brought back to the question of how to represent the Troubles in museum spaces (Crooke 2001). Questions being asked include: how do you tell the history of the conflict in museums; what is the material heritage of the Troubles that could be displayed in exhibitions: should we preserve the built remains of the Troubles; whose story should we tell, and what if that story causes offence? Of course, there are 'communities of practice' that need not reflect on the Troubles but, for now, one of the most significant issues facing the heritage sector in Northern Ireland is the method and purpose of the public representation of the history of the past 30 years.

The official community heritage sector

There are numerous reasons why Northern Ireland's museums are being nudged into asking both how and why they should represent the Troubles. In the first place, national and international debate on museum definition and purpose is encouraging the sector at large to make exhibitions and collections more representative of different people's histories, rather than one grand narrative. Second, and as a consequence of the previous point, museums are exploring local stories, identities, and the means to express these in collections representative of the way most people live. In Northern Ireland, this interest links to the activity of community groups that increasingly are engaged with the public expression of their histories. The region's museums are recognising that they must involve themselves with local groups and their histories in order to maintain relevance and not to lose core, or potential, audiences to these alternative initiatives. A third reason for the museum sector taking part in the representation of the Troubles might also be the potential positive impact of working together on interpreting the conflict. Community-relations work in Northern Ireland has long used history and heritage as the basis for exploring identities and division. Finally, underpinning all of these considerations is the more subtle point that representing the Troubles in museums and as part of our 'heritage' is a confident move for Northern Ireland. Through display, this process can present a changed place and suggests for us and to our visitors that the Troubles have ended.

In Northern Ireland, museums are linking with new communities principally through outreach and the development of new more challenging exhibitions. The county museum services have small numbers of staff and often a low budget.

Frequently, the key concerns of dealing with documentation backlog, collections care, funding applications and staff training can dominate everyday work, and for some it is difficult to see where the museum fits into the wider community agenda. There is still innovative work in the local museums – an exhibition entitled *Local Identities* that toured in 2000 is an example. This exhibition explored the construction of identity in Northern Ireland and the diversity of faith, leisure and politics (Pollock 2000). Such work is often achieved in collaboration with other local museums or through the support of the Community Relations Council or the Northern Ireland Museums Council. The contact between museum work and community relations varies from place to place. In some museums it is minimal or low-key while in others it is very apparent. Community-relations work at a local level is supported by the district councils, of which there are 26 in Northern Ireland. Although each council has a community relations officer, Down District Council is unusual in placing its officer within the Department of Museum Services. In the Down County Museum Plan the rationale for this was expressed thus:

> The community-relations section of the department is an expression of Down District Council's commitment to improving and supporting good community relations in its area. Its work is concerned with bringing about equality, promoting reconciliation and mutual respect for the various traditions which exist within Northern Ireland, and creating a community which accommodates people's differing beliefs, aspirations and traditions. This brings it very close to the cultural concerns of the museum and arts functions. (Down District Council 1997)

The 'Community Education Officer' in Down County Museum has developed a programme focused on developing a sense of community identity, civic pride, the appreciation of the diversity of cultural traditions and museum staff believe they have created a shared and safe museum space (McKenna 2003 personal communication). The museum has attempted to broaden its audience through a diverse range of activities: events in association with the bicentenary of the 1803 Rebellion, for instance, include lectures, living history, mock trials and a play hosted by the drama department of a local school (Down County Museum 2003).

In the Ulster Museum, part of the National Museums and Galleries of Northern Ireland group, the European Union's Special Support Programme for Peace and Reconciliation has funded an outreach officer working in the history department. The post is closely associated with the Community Relations Council – the council administers its funding and monitors activity through regular reports. The outreach activity has taken the form of working on new exhibitions linked to exploring identity in Northern Ireland (some of these are referred to below), identity workshops based around a CD-Rom on the Troubles, and community history projects based in areas that have had high rates of violence or polarisation as a result of the Troubles. Through this post, the museum has made a number of new links with cross-community and single interest groups in Northern Ireland (Leonard 2001 personal communication).

The Ulster Museum has often been criticised for giving scant consideration to the events of the past three decades in its permanent history displays (O'Toole 2000).

A more holistic view of the museum gives a better picture – often the events of the recent past can be linked to temporary exhibitions and less high-profile outreach work. In 1998 the exhibition *Up in Arms! The 1798 Rebellion in Ireland* got considerable press attention for providing the opportunity for a cross-community contact. In search for a venue in which both sides would feel at ease, cross-community groups from a village outside Belfast visited the 1798 exhibition in the Ulster Museum. Led by a member of the Orange Order and a Catholic priest the visit was considered as something they could do together that would not compromise each other's principles (Sheridan 1998). The exhibition was well attended by community groups; of the 22,500 visits the museum recorded approximately 1,500 from members of community groups; in addition 7,000 members participated in linked activities and resources developed specifically for such groups (Parkhill 2003).

Opportunities for further cross-community impact were provided in 2000 with the *Icons of Identity* exhibition, also at the Ulster Museum. In Northern Ireland, symbols are widely used to bind communities, represent allegiances and mark territory. In this exhibition nine symbols of life in Northern Ireland were selected: the mythical warrior Cu Chulainn; the Virgin Mary; Christ crucified; Saint Patrick; Erin, the female embodiment of Ireland; King William III; Sir Edward Carson (1854–1935), leader of the Ulster Unionists and one of the creators of Northern Ireland; the Somme and the contribution of the 36th (Ulster) Division to this battle on 1 July 1916; and the republican revolutionary leader Michael Collins (1890–1922). Some symbols are predominantly Protestant (King William, Carson and the Somme); others are used manly by the Catholic community (such as Collins and Erin); and, the remaining icons are used by both, but often in very different ways. Interpretation of the icons acknowledged associated myths, contradictory interpretations and the various ways the icons were understood in different communities, and how some have been used to fuel sectarianism. The introductory essay in the exhibition catalogue provides a record of some of the questions the exhibition team faced and the approach they took to their subject. To begin, they quoted from Carlo Gebler to convey the purpose of interpreting a troubled history: 'you cannot change the past, but with understanding you can sometimes draw the poison out of it' (Gebler cited in Warner 2000). The purpose of a museum in such a context was defined as: 'to preserve and present for discussion and information the cultural heritage of its community . . . [It should include] objects that illustrate the history, warts and all, of *all* the members of that community'. Finally, the essay concludes on the most significant question for Northern Ireland: 'why do we want to learn about the past, when it seems to be responsible for the Troubles of today?' The answer provided is: 'a community without a sense of past is a community in denial' (Warner 2000: 2). People in Northern Ireland have a very keen sense of the past: it is how the past is used to inform the present that is the issue.

Although the introductory booklet gives a sense of the aims of the exhibition team it is almost impossible to tell if such an impact was achieved. One of the methods employed to collect visitor reactions was the provision of blank postcards and the invitation to provide feedback. The exhibition ran for six months and got feedback from about 1,400 visitors, approximately half of which were from children. The exhibition seems to have received a generally positive response – it brought many requests for peace to be brought to the region and a fairly equal number saying that it was either too nationalistic or unionist. For some it emphasised a void in their own understanding, one visitor wrote: 'Excellent exhibition. Very evocative for me of good feeling for my own identity and growing appreciation of other folk'. Another visitor wrote: 'as a 37 year old brought up in the north of Ireland. I never once seen a photo of Michael Collins – so I think this exhibition is long overdue'. A number of visitors commented on evidence of bias; one visitor wrote: 'I thought it was a very good exhibition, but slightly biased. I found the amount of information noted to the Orange Order and Carson quite intimidating'; however, on the other hand, another wrote: 'as a prod, I notice a few attempts to debunk Protestant myths, the commentators should resist the urge to write judgments'. One visitor questioned the very approach of the exhibition: 'Surely Northern Ireland gets enough exposure by media etc what about real art we're very disappointed that the more orthodox viewing has been closed due to Icons which should remain in the past' (Ulster Museum, Icons visitor cards).

The outreach work undertaken in the history department at the Ulster Museum has a deliberate community-relations agenda; much of it has been achieved through funding administered by the Community Relations Council. The actual impact of museum outreach on community-relations is almost impossible to quantify; as noted by one commentator 'if reports, conferences, exhibitions, think-tanks and books were enough, the Northern Ireland question would have been solved long ago' (Longley 2001: 41). However, some indication of the success of the outreach work must be taken from the fact that the Ulster Museum has continued to secure support for outreach from the EU Special Support Programme for Peace and Reconciliation. When considered together, the museum exhibitions and outreach described above do have resonance. Histories that were previously taboo and symbols that were misunderstood are now beginning to be discussed in public and secure spaces. However, the true impact of these museum initiatives can only be measured through forms of evaluation. The creation of an appropriate methodology for measuring the real impact of museum initiatives on behaviour and attitudes is a growing area of concern in museum studies (Hooper-Greenhill 2002). The Northern Ireland example helps to complicate such investigations: are museums being visited by those most closely involved in sustaining division; if they do visit, what do they gain from their experience; and, can a museum visit have a long-term impact on deeply held views? Research has shown that it is often the visitor who has the most influence over what is learnt from an exhibition, rather than the curator or designer. Instead visitors bring their own personal experiences, histories and beliefs to the exhibition and it is through these that he or she will interpret the exhibitions.

The unofficial community-heritage sector

Away from museum debate and government policy, rural and urban groups are coming together to explore their history and heritage and forming their own exhibitions and collections. These community groups are not interested in the concerns of the museum profession, yet they are engaging with the past in ways to which museums aspire. As regards representing the recent past in Northern Ireland, a gap seems to be growing between the official museum sector, which is trying to find its direction, and the unofficial heritage sector, which is more confident about how to engage with notions of political heritage. In Northern Ireland numerous groups of people are engaging in local history work, in the way that museums are being encouraged to in various recent 'inclusion' publications published in Britain. Over the past decade, with the increasing availability of peace, community-relations, and sometimes National Lottery funding, there has been an increase in people coming together in groups to engage in heritage-based activity.

One of the trends likely to have the greatest impact on creating an archive of the Troubles is the growing interest in collecting oral histories of the conflict. In both Belfast and Londonderry, local groups have gained government and European funding to support such initiatives. In Derry a proposal has been put forward to establish 'The Bogside History Centre', located in an intensely republican part of the city. Acknowledgement seems to be key – the centre seeks 'recognition' of the history of the area of the city known as 'the Bogside'. The stated aim of the group is to contribute to 'the process of community regeneration through increased community confidence and esteem'; and, to aid 'the process of reconciliation and healing between our divided communities, by increasing knowledge of our troubled past'. They acknowledge their use of cultural identity as a tool with which to 'tackle social and economic marginalisation'. The proposed centre will have an exhibition area, research room, collect experiences of the Bogside community and provide tours for school groups and tourists. The main subjects to be investigated are civil rights and the events of Bloody Sunday, 30 January 1972 (Bloody Sunday Trust 2003). The Derry initiative seems to follow the format of that developed by the Falls Community Council in Belfast, which is well underway. The Falls Community Council was established in the 1970s to represent people in the mostly nationalist Falls Road area. In the mid-1990s the group developed the idea of a community oral history archive and a living history centre. The project, known as Duchas, which means 'heritage' in Irish, was made possible through the availability of funds associated with the peace process. At the moment the Duchas project takes the form of a drop-in centre where people can access the archives of interviews, and where they can go to gather advice and support for groups interested in gathering oral histories. Again, the long-term objective is the creation of what has been described as a 'living history centre' with open access to a listening archive and, possibly, exhibition panels and objects to support the oral history (Hackett 2002 personal communication).

These two examples of urban oral history projects are closely associated with experiences linked with the Troubles, and the characteristics of the projects have important implications for our understanding of the role of public history-making in societies emerging from conflict. The themes chosen by the Duchas project to shape the oral archive are intensely political. Oral testimonies of internment and hunger strikes have been collected – selected because they are of greatest relevance to the local community (Hackett 2002 personal communication). Internment, in this case, refers to the Special Powers Act of 1922, an emergency law in Northern Ireland, which was, in 1971, used to legalise detention without trial. Between 1971 and 1975, over 2,000 republicans and about 100 loyalists were detained until the power was withdrawn in 1975 (Arthur 1980: 107–14). The hunger strikes were a protest tactic used by IRA prisoners for six months in 1981, leading eventually to the death of ten of the strikers. Both of these themes, internment and the hunger strikes, are intensely emotive. These are histories that do not want to be forgotten; in the case of both the Duchas and Bogside initiatives the most contested aspects of the history of Northern Ireland in the past 30 years have been selected for representation. These histories are ideal for creating a sense of community because they are histories that still have a lot at stake. The events shaped lives, are highly emotive and already in the public domain. When captured in a living history centre the stories will take on a new dimension; this new representation defines them as central to understanding the place in which they are exhibited. The local accounts, once handed down through story-telling, can now be made tangible in exhibition displays. Recognition of these local experiences, and how they are part of the national or state history is central for community empowerment. The authority brought by self-representation binds the community. An essential characteristic of this work also seems to be that it is independent of the 'official' heritage sector. Duchas is not interested, for instance, in liaising with the local or national museums in the creation and preservation of its oral archive; it does not want a state institution to be put in charge of its story (Hackett 2002 personal communication).

Both the Duchas and the Bogside initiatives claim a community-relations agenda, and the nature of this invites consideration. In Northern Ireland community-relations work has taken various forms. In some cases it has been learning about the 'other' tradition, in the hope that myths can be expelled and common experiences valued. Other forms are based around learning about one's own history, on the premise that only when we are secure in our own identity can we be expected to understand difference. Certainly, the oral history projects described above are centred on the experiences and interpretations of one community. However, irresponsibly managed, the risk with such an approach is that the work will fall into the old stereotypes and prejudices and only serve to isolate and divide the communities further. Such local stories have the potential for both a positive and negative impact. In a divided society, this experience can be used to bind one community against the other. It is important to allow people to be in control of their own history and therefore 'outside' interference in the collection of those stories would be anathema. However, when those individual stories become a collective heritage and when they move from the realm of the personal to the public, their purpose changes. There is a difference between stories shared privately between groups of people and the public display of those stories in history, community or heritage centres. The public dimension adds a new significance, is a form of recognition, and provides endorsement. We must, therefore, consider the impact of displaying oral testimonies that are largely partial in public spaces.

The Derry and Belfast initiatives are just two examples of projects that hope to become a permanent contribution to the Northern Ireland heritage landscape. In addition to these there are numerous other heritage initiatives that complete their life cycle more quickly. If it is possible to keep up to date with the numerous community exhibitions reported in local papers and developed in local community centres or parish halls, one would get a sense of the high level of local heritage activity and awareness. Many of these initiatives have modest, but nevertheless highly significant, aims. One example is the exhibitionary enthusiasm generated by the recent Royal Jubilee. Numerous local history societies and groups used the jubilee as an opportunity to create exhibitions on their local area – the *Diary of Events for the Jubilee Year* provides a list of these (Golden Jubilee Unit 2002). One such exhibition held in a village church hall in County Fermanagh was an opportunity for the local community to develop an exhibition on life in the area. During the jubilee weekend, visitors in a packed hall were treated to 50 years of local news, awards and achievements. The contribution to local cohesiveness and community memory-making was undoubted. This rural example can be compared with the work of the People's History Initiative, a course hosted by the Ulster People's College in Belfast. The college was formed in 1982 with the aim to 'support people tackling social and economic problems as well as overcoming cultural, educational and political divisions' (Ulster People's College 2002). The People's History Initiative, funded by the Community Relations Council, takes the form of an adult education class with the main aim to explore how 'local people have shaped the story of our common past'. Participants are both student and teacher: they learn about the history of Belfast and share their own expertise of their area of the city. By researching and eventually creating an exhibition or CD-Rom of an aspect of their history, the process aims to allow participants to take control of the interpretation and presentation of their own community. Belfast community groups have produced exhibitions that have covered subjects such as shopping; life, work and entertainment; boxing; history of women; housing, dock life; the Troubles; and, the Second World War.

In the examples of community exhibitions discussed above both the processes and the product are important. In the example from County Fermanagh and those of Belfast, the exhibitions were part of a process of celebration and remembrance. Not only were the exhibitions ends in themselves, they were also a means to an end. The exhibitions were the by-product of processes based on needs of the local community. In the People's History Initiative, for example, the process was a regular meeting of groups, within which they discussed the history of their community and area. Meeting, discussing, sharing experiences, and developing a historical record aided the development of friendships, community pride and good self-esteem. The final product is also significant – public display and acceptance brings with it a sense of value and importance. In both the smaller initiatives and those developed for a national and international audience, such as the Duchas project, recognition is key. The most significant benefits of this recognition are the likely political outcomes: community confidence, empowerment and cohesion.

Conclusion: heritages, identities and nationality

This chapter has considered two forms of heritage production in Northern Ireland: that undertaken by the county and national museum services; and the local initiatives generated from within the communities themselves. Each of these initiatives contributes to our understanding of the interlinked notions of heritage, identity and nationality in Northern Ireland.

The initiatives discussed in this chapter illustrate a key characteristic of heritage: its fluidity. In Northern Ireland the interpretation of the past is changing, who is doing that interpretation is broadening, and the past remembered in public spaces is more wide-ranging. The creation of history, and its presentation as heritage, is an ongoing and live process. History is continually being written and rewritten, and the definition of heritage shifts according to current need. Public display, in books, exhibitions and monuments is not limited to the official academic, museum or heritage sectors. As well as the revision of well-known events, who is included in the process of creating history is becoming more diverse: wider ranges of people are both telling their histories and are being listened to. Some histories are being told for the first time, such as that emerging from the People's History Initiative, and other histories are being retold, such as that of the Bogside and Duchas projects. There is little permanence in Northern Ireland history, and the established museum sector is approaching these histories with caution. This point is demonstrated by the Ulster Museum, which in 2001 removed its permanent history gallery; instead, they will use the space for a series of temporary exhibitions, before attempting another permanent exhibition. The presentation of history in the museum is being tested, sampled and evaluated. The museum realises they have to tread carefully on the Northern Ireland story. One of the reasons for this sensitivity stems from the interest local and national museums have in establishing themselves as neutral venues for the presentation and negotiation of history. Museums often hope to achieve 'neutrality' through the creation of safe and open spaces where all personal experiences are valued. The notion of neutrality is, of course, highly problematic, as is the view that all versions of history command equal respect. Similarly, diversity of involvement does not always bring with it the benefits associated with a policy of inclusion. Just because more diverse histories are being made known, it does not mean they are being told in a less exclusive or partial manner.

Together, the heritage initiatives discussed in this chapter are an important contribution to the creation of identity in Northern Ireland. Analysis of the move to record the events of the Troubles in public spaces reveals the complexity of identity in Northern Ireland. For many, the experiences of the Troubles are personal and only shared with a limited group within well-defined boundaries. The impact of the Troubles may have been very public, but individual experiences were often kept private. Now, with the collection of oral experiences of the Troubles, the creation of history centres and other proposed memorials to the Troubles people are choosing to place their private story in the public domain. A high-profile example is the proposal to preserve part of the Maze Prison site as a museum, which is being forwarded by a Republican ex-prisoner group. With these new initiatives accounts of the Troubles that were previously concealed are now being disclosed. People and events that may have only been commemorated in private are now entering the public domain in the form of archives and exhibitions. It is important to evaluate the consequences of the shift from the private to the public domain. We must ask what is being recorded, why is it being shared, and for whom are these initiatives being created? Such moves to create a heritage out of the Troubles also challenge us to reassess the contribution of the Troubles to identity formation and re-formation in Northern Ireland. Rather than wishing to believe that the Troubles only impacted on certain people or places, with public display we are invited to consider the broader influence of the Troubles in shaping the identity of everyone in Northern Ireland. Furthermore, these initiatives will have an impact on the perceived national identity of Northern Ireland, whether that is Irish or British. It is likely that as the heritage sector becomes more confident in telling the history of the past 30 years, the identity of the six counties as a unique place will gain prominence. Within both the United Kingdom and Ireland, the history of the Troubles is essentially a local story – together many of these heritage initiatives tell the 'Troubles experience'. No one in Northern Ireland is outside the Troubles; to a greater or lesser extent it has impacted on everyone. This is an aspect of the past in Northern Ireland that everyone shares, even if they experienced it, and remember it, in different ways.

Note

Elizabeth Crooke is a senior lecturer in Museum and Heritage Studies at the University of Ulster.

References

Arthur, P. (1980) *Political Realities: Government and Politics of Northern Ireland*, London: Longman.

Bennett, T. (1995) *The Birth of the Museum: History, Theory, Politics*, London and New York: Routledge.

Bloody Sunday Trust (2003) www.bloodysundaytrust.org/historycentre (accessed 1 April 2003).

Crooke, E. (2000) *Politics, Archaeology and the Creation of a National Museum in Ireland: An Expression of National Life*, Dublin: Irish Academic Press.

Crooke, E. (2001) 'Confronting a Troubled History: Which Past in Northern Ireland's Museums', *International Journal of Heritage Studies*, vol. 7, no. 2, pp. 119–36.

Dodd, J. and R. Sandell (eds) (2001) *Including Museums*, University of Leicester: Research Centre for Museums and Galleries.

Down County Museum. (2003) *The Bicentenary of the 1803 Rebellion: Events Pamphlet*, Down County Museum.

Down District Council. (1997) *Down County Museum Plan 1997–2001*, Down District Council.

Falk, J.H. and L. Dierking. (2000) *Learning from Museums: Visitor Experiences and the Making of Meaning*, California: Altamira Press.

Fitzduff, M. (1993) *Approaches to Community Relations Work*, Belfast: CRC Pamphlet no. 1 (3rd edition).

Gibson, F. (2000) 'Reminiscence and Museums', *Museum Ireland*, no. 10, pp. 26–35.

Golden Jubilee Unit. (2002) *Celebrations*, Belfast: Golden Jubilee Unit.

Hooper-Greenhill, E. (2000) *Museums and the Interpretation of Visual Culture*, London: Routledge.

Hooper-Greenhill, E. (2002) 'Evaluating the Impact on Learning of the Museum Visit', paper delivered at Museums and Audiences Seminar, Tate Liverpool, Museum and Society Study Group, 31 October 2002.

Kavanagh, G. (2000) *Memory and the Museum*, Leicester: Leicester University Press.

Kelly, L. and P. Gordon. (2002) 'Developing a Community of Practice: Museums and Reconciliation in Australia', in R. Sandell (ed.) *Museums, Society and Inequality*, London: Routledge.

Longley E. (2001) 'Multiculturalism and Northern Ireland: Making Differences Fruitful', in *Multi-culturalism: The View from the Two Irelands*, Cork: Cork University Press.

O'Toole, F. (2000) 'Art has not reflected our grief', *Irish Times*, 1 August 2000.

Parkhill, T. (2003) '"That's Their History": Can a Museum's Historical Presentation Inform the Reconciliation Process in a Divided Society?', paper delivered at the *Heritages Seminar Series, Academy for Irish Cultural Heritages*, University of Ulster, 7 February.

Pollock, V. (2000) 'Local Identities at Armagh and Fermanagh County Museums', *Museum Ireland*, no. 10, pp. 68–74.

Rassool, C. and S. Prosalendis. (eds) (2001) *Recalling Community in Cape Town: Creating and Curating the District Six Museum*, Cape Town: District Six Museum.

Shaikh, H. (2001) 'Exploring Cultural Diversity', in J. Dodd and R. Sandell (eds) *Including Museums*, University of Leicester: Research Centre for Museums and Galleries.

Sheridan, K. (1998) 'A Farewell to Arms', *Irish Times*, 13 June 1998.

Ulster People's College. (2002) *Prospectus*, Belfast: Ulster People's College.

Wallace, A. (2001) 'Collections Management and Inclusion', in J. Dodd and R. Sandell (eds) *Including Museums*, University of Leicester: Research Centre for Museums and Galleries.

Warner, M. (2000) 'Sorry: the present state of apology', www.opendemocracy, 7 November.

Chapter 20

Regenerating Identity
Repatriation and the Indian frame of mind

Richard W. Hill, Sr.

ABOUT FORTY GENERATIONS AGO, the Iroquois of upstate New York received a message of peace, power, and unity that formed the basis of what is called The Great Law of Peace. This Great Law served as the founding constitution for the Six Nations Iroquois confederacy. The oral tradition surrounding the formation of this confederacy and its procedural requirements were encoded in a series of sacred belts and strings of tubular shell wampum beads assembled about 1,000 years ago. Messages, beliefs, and hopes were spoken into these belts as a way to preserve their power for future generations. Through this wampum, the Iroquois were connected to previous generations and acted as a cultural bridge to future ones.

Unfortunately, this continuity was ruptured through the coercive sale, theft, and removal of many of these belts during the nineteenth century. The wampum documents have since become the center of strained relations between the 45,000-strong Iroquois nation and several major museums that hold these sacred items. In this chapter, I focus on the struggle of the Iroquois to recover these wampum belts as a way of illustrating the cultural issues behind the politics of repatriation.

It has been twenty-five years since I first heard of the sacred wampum. Even growing up as an Iroquois though, I never saw any of these pieces in our communities. Most of the known wampum belts were locked away in museums. As a young man, I learned of their fate and was part of a movement to recover the wampums. It seemed to many Native people that the glorious beauty of the past, as well as the spiritual legacy of the future, was imprisoned in museums. I felt strongly that if we were to survive as a people, we needed to hear the messages from the past and be empowered to carry this knowledge forward.

Culture is, indeed, more than objects, but for many Native American nations, there are certain objects that are essential to manifesting that culture. Most Native

Source: *The Future of the Past: Archaeologists, Native Americans and Repatriation*, T.L. Bray (ed.), New York: Garland Pub Inc., 2001, pp. 127–38.

American children were growing up without ever having seen the treasures of their cultural heritage. To me and many Native Americans of my generation, it seemed that the sanctioned institutions of culture in our society were actually contributing to our cultural decline, and this became intolerable.

The changing political landscape

It is important to remember that the Native American Graves Protection and Repatriation Act (NAGPRA) was preceded by decades of confrontations between museums and Native Americans over the issues of cultural patrimony, representation, religious rights, and human rights. During the 1960s, a period of intense political unrest, the federal government had begun to redefine its relationship to Native Americans. An era of forced relocation and assimilation was coming to an end and a new age of self-determination loomed on the horizon. Native Americans were growing stronger in their own sense of identity, and consequently became more vocal and aggressive in addressing social inequities. Museums were just one sector of American society to come under scrutiny as part of the associated spiritual revitalization movements, and repatriation needs to be understood as one component of these larger social reforms.

It is difficult to explain how deeply these movements affected Native Americans. Generations of poverty, oppression, and self-doubt had to be overcome. Leaders came to see the restoration of traditional cultural values as one of the most important avenues for enabling change. A stronger cultural base, it was thought, would provide Native people with a stronger sense of self, a stronger sense of place, and a stronger sense of destiny. But as more college-aged Native Americans began to seek out their spiritual heritage in order to reconnect with traditional values, they found many of the paths blocked because the objects needed to perform necessary ceremonies and rites were in the possession of museums. When those same Indian students began to visit these institutions, they found the material component of their cultural heritage behind glass and strangely silent, the objects of non-Native's gawking stares. Freeing the objects from their ethnological fate came to be equated with the struggle for the liberation of the Native American mind and spirit.

Around this same time, museums and the field of anthropology were undergoing their own kind of reformation. Various policies, programs, and practices were being questioned with regard to standards of fairness and equity. African Americans, Asian Americans, Hispanic Americans, women, and the alternative arts were all demanding more attention from museums. Museum trustees were just beginning to address inconsistencies in standards of conduct on issues of accessioning and deaccessioning. The mishandling and outright illegal activities of some museums caused administrators to take a hard look at their practices and critically examine whether they were in fact upholding the public trust with which they were charged.

With demands for the reburial of human remains, the removal of sacred objects from public display and the repatriation of cultural patrimony, Native Americans forced standard museum policies and practices onto the public stage. I cannot say which museum was the first to return human remains or which was the first to formally recognize the rights of Native Americans to their own cultural patrimony. Some museums, mainly smaller ones, responded immediately to the claims of Native peoples without requiring the force of law to compel them. But the Native American Graves Protection and Repatriation Act came about because many of the major museums would not address our concerns. While NAGPRA was the final resort for Native Americans at the time, we now see it as a new beginning.

The Iroquois wampum case

In 1970, the New York State Assembly Subcommittee on Indian Affairs recommended that the century-old Wampum Law be amended to allow the return of five wampum belts to the Onondaga Nation. The amendment was proposed in recognition of the Onondaga's traditional role as the wampum keepers of the Iroquois Confederacy, an alliance which also includes the Seneca, Cayuga, Oneida, Mohawk, and Tuscarora Nations. When we learned of the proposed amendment, it came as a surprise to many of us that the Wampum Law even existed. How had New York State become the wampum keeper for the Iroquois? How had wampum, one of the Iroquois' most sacred objects of cultural patrimony, ever left our possession?

In many ways, the Iroquois experience is similar to that of other Native nations. Many Native Americans of my generation were born into communities rent asunder by the divergent beliefs of their own members. Differing views of religion, governance, education, economy, and culture tore at the very fabric of our common identities. We had become confused about who we were, what we were supposed to do, and how well our traditional culture served our needs in Cold War America.

Visits to museums exacerbated this cultural disorientation. Museums were painful because Native bones, as well as objects we believed to be sources of power for our communities, were on display. Many of these items were trophies collected by soldiers, priests, teachers, and government bureaucrats which had once belonged to our ancestors. Native Americans felt profoundly disconnected from those sources of power. Repatriation became the process through which we sought to reconnect with the ideals represented in those objects and reclaim authority over them.

Like many young Indians in the 1970s, I was able to learn of the significance of these objects from two sources: the scholarly literature produced by non-Natives and the stories that were still known by the old people in our communities. As the Iroquois pushed an agenda of cultural and political renewal, museums, anthropologists, educators, and movie-makers were targeted as obstacles to Iroquois progress. My own search for information lead me to the campus of the State University of New York at Buffalo, where I now teach, and the place where I first met the leading proponent of repatriation, Oren Lyons, an Onondaga artist, college professor, and representative on the Onondaga Council of Chiefs. It was a meeting that changed my life.

Lyons and several other chiefs, together with the New York State Council on the Arts, had convinced the State of New York to pass legislation to return the major belts from the State Museum to the Iroquois Confederacy. However, an aggressive campaign to block that move was launched by the Committee on Anthropological Research in Museums under the aegis of the American Anthropological

Association (Sturtevant *et al.* 1970). The scholars on this committee were able to convince then-Governor Nelson Rockefeller to veto the proposed legislation. The 'Iroquoianists' subsequently became embroiled in a very public controversy with the traditional Iroquois chiefs over the primacy of cultural and religious rights versus scientific and academic rights (e.g., Henry 1970). The wampum case set the general tone for negotiations over repatriation that eventually would affect all museums with Indian materials in their collections. In many ways, the issues raised in New York are still at the forefront of the debate over repatriation.

During this battle, the Iroquois used the media effectively to create public sympathy for their cause and public opinion came to favor the return of the wampums. In addition, the Iroquois challenged the anthropologists and historians at every turn. Essays written by scholars were critiqued by the Native press. Confrontations with scholars became standard operating procedure. Academic conferences could no longer just be about Native Americans; they had to include Native Americans.

Relationships between the Iroquois and scholars reached an all-time low in 1976 as America turned its attention to the celebration of its two-hundredth birthday. To the Iroquois, the dispute over the wampum was symbolic of racist policies that continued to subject Native peoples to cultural oppression. The Iroquois argued that the belts were illegally removed without the consent of the traditional chiefs, and that they were essential to the cultural and spiritual continuity of the Iroquois. They argued that for one culture group to assert that its scientific interests took precedence over the religious rights of another was itself evidence of how deeply entrenched racial bias was in the social sciences.

The scholars responded that museums 'owned' the sacred objects and that these items were essential for future studies of the Iroquois. They felt that by studying Native people, American society at large could learn more about human cultures in general. Their position hinged on the argument that the public had a right to know the cultural heritage of their homeland and a right to view and enjoy these objects. To the scholars, it was an issue of academic freedom, which, for them, entailed the right to study anything, secular or religious, in the pursuit of truth. They might have won more support if they had stuck to that argument.

Instead they turned to character assassination and this lost support for their cause among many museum professionals. The anthropologists argued that the contemporary Iroquois were acculturated and no longer understood their own traditions. The scholars reasoned that they knew more about Iroquois traditions than the Iroquois themselves and that the wampums would be best left in the care of the non-Native professionals (Fenton 1971; Sturtevant *et al.* 1970). They tried to discredit the Iroquois by labelling them as 'Red Power militants.' In a letter written in 1970 to the Governor, the scholars argued that 'state property should not be legislated away lightly in the illusion of religiosity or as capital in the civil rights movement' (Sturtevant *et al.* 1970: 14).

Not to be outdone, the Iroquois painted the scholars as egomaniacal racists who were more concerned with their research, grants, and publications than the cultural preservation of their 'subjects.' They made it difficult for archaeologists to continue excavating Native American grave sites without publicly justifying their actions. They also forced museums to address the issue of repatriation and obliged them to publicly refute accusations of racism and political sabotage. The situation reached a boiling point in 1979 when the New York State Senate, for the ninth year in a row, failed to amend the Indian Law relating to the custody of the wampums. The scholars thought they had defeated the Iroquois once and for all, but this was not to be the end.

The function of wampum

Wampum undergirds the entire cultural worldview of the Iroquois. It is sacred by virtue of the shell from which it is made and because it was chosen by the Creator as the medium through which the Iroquois would retain and transmit information from generation to generation (cf., Hewitt 1892; Noon 1948; Tooker 1978). This is why the Iroquois felt so strongly about the need to have the wampum returned. Turmoil had become a way of life in the thirteen Iroquois communities spread across New York, Ontario, and Quebec. Elective governments had replaced the traditional systems in all but three of the communities. Most of the Iroquois people, who now attended Christian churches, no longer visited the longhouses where traditional ceremonies took place. The legendary Grand Council, once respected and feared by Dutch, French, English, and colonial American leaders, was but a shadow of its former self. The Great Law was suffering and the hope was that it could be revitalized with the return of the wampum belts, the repositories of the original messages.

The term 'wampum' refers to the small, tubular beads that are drilled through their long axis and range in color from white to blue to purple (Abrams 1994; Beauchamp 1901). The word derives from the Algonquian 'wampumpeag' which, during the fur trade era, came to refer to any type of shell bead and took on specifically monetary connotations. But originally, among Native American cultures of the Northeast, wampum had numerous meanings, functioning, as it did, within the social, cultural, political, and spiritual realms of the Iroquois, Huron, Ojibwa, and Algonquian nations (Hewitt 1912). In the Iroquoian language, the word for wampum is *gatgoa*, while the word for a string of wampum is *sgadgoad*. Each different wampum belt originally would have had its own specific name. For instance, the wampum belt used in the Iroquois condolence ceremony was called *henodosetha gatgoa*.

Wampum had been used in many ways in the past. Wampum beads could be offered to a grieving family to atone for the death of a loved one. They could be used to ransom a captive relative. In 1622, for instance, a Dutch trader received 140 six-foot-long strings of wampum in exchange for a Chief who he was holding hostage. Wampum strings were given to Chiefs and Clan Mothers as confirmation of their title and oath of office, the strands of tiny shell beads representing their pledge to uphold the Great Law. Wampum strings with notched sticks attached were used to announce upcoming council meetings, the wampum serving both as the credentials for the messenger and to prove that the delegates attending would be the official representatives of their community. The symbolic designs woven into wampum belts recorded the terms of treaties between nations. Wampum strings also recorded the order of ceremonial speeches. As an item of ritual exchange between different groups, wampum served to confirm agreements or requests. It was, for instance, the appropriate gift to offer a bride's family, and newly married couples were given wampum to verify their marriage oath. The beads also functioned as articles of personal adornment among the Iroquois and were worn as headbands, necklaces, armbands, belts, shoulder sashes, earrings, chokers, cuffs, or kilts (Abrams 1994; Tooker 1978).

The importance of wampum among Native American nations was quickly recognized by Euroamerican officials and settlers. In one account of a Native conference in Montreal in 1756, the significance of the shell beads is reported as follows:

> These belts and strings of wampum are a universal agent among Indians, serving as money, jewelry, ornaments, annals, and registers; [they are] the bond of nations and individuals, [recognized as] an inviolable and sacred pledge which guarantees messages, promises and treaties. As writing is not in use among them [the Indians], they make a local memoir by means of these belts, each of which signifies a particular affair or circumstance of affairs. The chiefs of the village are the depositories of [these belts], and communicate them to the young people, who thus learn the history and engagements of their nation. (O'Callaghan 1968 [1756]: 556)

It is also interesting to note how quickly wampum came to figure in intercultural protocols. Both the French and the English adopted aspects of the Native system to convince the Iroquois of the earnestness of their intentions. The French, who referred to wampum as 'porcelain collars,' recognized its importance as an element of ritual protocol early on. In 1636, for example, Father Le Jeune noted that '. . . as the Porcelain that takes the place of gold and silver in this country is all-powerful, I presented in this Assembly a collar of twelve hundred beads of Porcelain, telling them [the Iroquois] that it was given to smooth the difficulties of the road to Paradise.' George Washington, as a military officer and later as president, used wampum both to petition the Iroquois and to confirm agreements made between his government and the Iroquois Confederacy. Wampum was regularly exchanged at treaty councils and nearly every other official function.

The loss of the wampum

Once Native Americans were no longer considered a military threat, the era of treaty making was over. Iroquois were isolated on small reservations, and wampum lost its political significance. But the belts, which verified the original treaties, remained a visible and problematic reminder of promises unkept as the federal government attempted to discontinue its relations with the Confederacy. As the Iroquois became objects of study in the emerging field of ethnology in the mid-nineteenth century, scholars began to report on the cultural and spiritual significance of wampum in the past tense. While some wampum remained actively in use within the internal spheres of Iroquoian life, many belts began to slip away.

By the late nineteenth-century, the Iroquois were embroiled in great debates about modernization. Reformers wanted the Iroquois to give up their old ways, including the Council of Chiefs. As a result of these conflicts, the Onondaga came to have two political bodies, the traditional chiefs who sat in council in the longhouse and a dissident government that had been elected under the terms of the Bureau of Indian Affairs. The old wampums, descended from the time of the founding of the Iroquois Confederacy, symbolized the ongoing power of the Council of Chiefs. Many modern-day Iroquois believe that the removal of the wampum that ensued was an attempt to destroy the traditional form of government.

In 1891, Onondaga Chief Thomas Webster, a member of the rival BIA-backed government, sold all the wampums in his possession to Major Carrington, a U.S. Indian Census Agent (Carrington 1892). Webster may have felt that by dislocating the wampums, the traditional chiefs would lose their source of power and authority. But many Iroquois leaders of today believe that he was coerced into selling the belts. It was well known among members of Iroquoian society that no individual had the authority to give, trade, or sell the wampum belts. These items were only held in trust by the Onondaga for the member nations of the Confederacy. The belts were understood to belong to all Iroquois people and were recognized as part of the cultural patrimony of the Iroquois Nation. It is this idea of shared communal property that lies behind much of the repatriation movement. If a collector or a museum were to have purchased wampum from individuals without the sanction of the collective, the sale would, by definition, be invalid.

Between 1900 and 1940, many of the old wampums were obtained by scholars (Fenton 1989). It is hard to understand why some Iroquois, many of them traditionalists gave up the wampum to anthropologists, but the results were devastating. Some Iroquois feel that the scholars tricked the people into giving up their sacred materials. Some say that times were hard financially and ritualists sold the only possessions they had in order to feed their families. Other say that some longhouse people truly believed that their traditions were coming to an end and wanted museums to preserve the sacred wampums. Whatever the motivation, the modern generation of Iroquois wanted their wampum back.

The first wampum comes home

In 1963, a wampum belt in the collections of the Buffalo Historical Society turned up missing after becoming a primary object of interest in a lawsuit. This wampum belt had been given by the Tuscarora nation to the Holland Land company in 1799 to document the transfer of one-square mile of land to the Tuscarora people. This land today constitutes the core of the Tuscarora reservation. This particular wampum belt subsequently became the focus of a legal battle between the Tuscarora Nation and the New York State Power Authority, which was seeking to condemn part of the Tuscarora reservation to build a giant hydro-electric plant at Niagara Falls. The belt was removed from the Historical Society and supposedly sent to a laboratory for authentication. It disappeared at this point and was never seen again. Many Iroquois suspected foul play on the part of the State. The Tuscarora lost their case and one-third of their reservation (cf., Landy 1978: 523–524).

In 1975, as a research assistant at the Buffalo and Erie County Historical Society, I helped to arrange the return of several thousand wampum beads to the Onondaga Nation. It was an important occasion because the traditional leaders had to develop unified statements on cultural patrimony and the way in which the repatriation of the sacred objects was to proceed. They were also meeting to negotiate the display and handling of human remains with the museum officials. Dr. Walter Dunn, then-director of the Historical Society, was open-minded and committed to a respect-ful resolution of the Iroquois' concerns. He and I subsequently travelled to the Onondaga reservation to return the wampum beads. For the first time in nearly a century, wampum flowed back into Iroquois hands.

The Iroquois who resided on the Canadian side of the border were also pursuing wampum missing from their territory. Their story is similar to that of the Onondaga. One of their longhouse leaders, unbeknownst to the Council of Chiefs, had sold several belts to a collector. In 1975, the Council officially declared that the belts, which were now housed in the Heye Foundation's Museum of the American Indian in New York City, had been improperly sold. The Chiefs hired Paul Williams, a young lawyer and the Director of Treaty Research for the Union of Ontario Indians, to pursue their case in 1977. The Onondaga on the American side also put pres-sure on the Museum. But the Museum's Board of Trustees, which included both William Fenton and William Sturtevant, two scholars who had strenuously fought the repatriation of the wampum in the New York State Museum, resisted the Onondaga claims.

The Iroquois consequently changed their tactics. Rather than pressing the Heye Foundation to respect the religious rights of the traditional people, they sought to show that the wampums had been illegally removed and that the Museum was in the possession of stolen property. Museum records clearly show that George Heye, the founder of the Museum of the American Indian, was aware of the questionable legal status of these items, and that one of the trustees actually suggested the Museum sell the wampums before the Iroquois could recover them.

In the end, the Iroquois lawyers and the traditional chiefs were able to con-vince then-President of the Board of Trustees, Barber Conable, of the integrity of their position, and the Trustees subsequently moved to return the belts that could be shown to have been illegally removed. In 1988, the Museum of the American Indian returned eleven wampum belts to the Council of Chiefs at the Grand River Reserve near Brantford, Ontario. It was one of the first examples of the repatri-ation of sacred objects from an American institution to a Native nation in Canada. The return involved only the belts that could be shown to have been unethically acquired, however. There are still a number of sacred wampums that remain part of the Museum's collections.

The Onondaga wampum repatriation

On the American side of the border, a similar effort was underway to recover the wampum belts of the Onondaga Nation, by the traditional 'Wampum Keepers' of the Iroquois Confederacy. Late in the nineteenth-century, Onondaga Chief Thomas Webster had sold four of these belts to Henry B. Carrington, U.S. Indian Census Agent, for $75. Carrington subsequently offered them to a Dr. Oliver Crane, who sold them in 1893 to the mayor of Albany, John B. Thatcher, for $500. Thatcher wanted the belts to be displayed as unique cultural treasures of great antiquity. In 1893, they were shown at the World's Columbian Exposition in Chicago where they were included in a larger display on American Indians. The following year the belts were loaned to the Onondaga Historical Association for display during the Onondaga County Centennial celebration. People displayed a genuine respect for what the wampum belts represented, but they were construed as relics of the glorious Iroquoian past. The Iroquois themselves were generally understood to be a 'vanishing race' with little hope of surviving through the next century.

Chief Webster was removed from office in 1897 by the traditional chiefs for his actions. The Iroquois wanted their wampums back even then, but the collectors, who had a bill of sale, ignored the Chiefs. To strengthen their position, the Chiefs sought the assistance of anthropologists. The scholars convinced them that they needed the State University of New York to help them recover the wampum from the private collectors. In one of the strangest events in Iroquois history, the Regents of the State University of New York were appointed the Keepers of the Wampum in 1898 by a group of Onondaga. In the past, a traditional Onondaga Chief had always been the holder of that title. The University, with the implied endorsement of the Onondaga, began to acquire most of the remaining wampums in order to make a case for the cultural integrity of the belts.

Section 27 of the New York State Indian Law, passed in 1899, conferred the title of Wampum Keeper upon the University of the State of New York. The State then took possession of several wampums they had acquired from private collectors on behalf of the Iroquois. The University held that by virtue of its title of Wampum Keeper, all wampums fell under its authority. In 1900, the Onondaga Nation and the University of the State of New York combined forces to file suit against John Thatcher, the 'owner' of the wampums sold by Chief Webster, seeking their return. In this important early legal case for repatriation, the Iroquois lost. Judge Frank Hiscock ruled that the wampums 'are curiosities and relics of time, a condition, and a confederation that has ceased to exist,' and that the Onondaga claim could not be upheld. Thatcher was allowed to keep the wampum. Ironically, the University of the State of New York later decided to bequeath the wampum it had collected to the New York State Museum, rather than return it to the Onondaga.

The Chiefs were not ready to give up. In 1907 another lawsuit was filed to obtain the return of the four wampum belts held by Thatcher. But this suit, too, was dismissed by a New York State judge who ruled, in effect, that the Confederacy no longer existed, that Thomas Webster did not hold the wampum in trust, and that he had a legal right to sell the belts. In 1909, the New York State Legislature passed another Wampum Law that bestowed upon itself the title of Wampum Keeper and claimed rights over any wampum in the possession of any Iroquois, past, present, or future. Having legislated away the rights of the Iroquois, the rush was on to collect wampum with anthropologists leading the charge.

Years later, Thatcher's widow decided to end the unwanted attention that had plagued her family by donating the four wampum belts originally obtained from Chief Webster to the New York State Museum. There they rested quietly from 1927 until the 1970s when the Onondaga raised the issue of return again. Deeming repatriation one of their highest priorities, the Iroquois began to track down the museums holding wampum. They knew that the old Heye Foundation, since re-named the Museum of the American Indian, and the Smithsonian Institution had wampum in their collections, but a survey conducted between 1978 and 1982 uncovered over 200 additional wampum belts and dozens of wampum strings in numerous other museums around the country.

In the mid-1980s, Martin Sullivan, Director of the New York State Museum, and Ray Gonyea, cultural specialist for the Onondaga Nation, crafted a plan to circumvent the racist and unethical Wampum Laws of New York State. It involved transferring control of the wampum in the Museum's collection to the State Board of Regents, a body independent of the State Legislature. Previous attempts to have the wampum repatriated had been repeatedly voted down by the State Legislature. Once control over the belts was transferred to the Regents, the consent of the State Legislature was no longer required and the Regents were free to return these important items of Iroquoian cultural patrimony. The principal wampum belts in the State Museum's collection were returned to the Onondaga Nation on October 21, 1989.

Wampum and the seventh generation

What will the return of the wampums mean to the coming generations of Iroquois? Will the reading of the wampum affect the way the Iroquois live in the future? Will the current generation be able to interpret and transmit the messages contained in the ancient wampums? These questions remain unanswered at present. The fact is that the wampums carry a significant part of our cultural history. It remains to be seen just how much of an impact they will have on the functioning of the Great Law and in dealing with the issues faced by this generation of Iroquois. The long delay in the recovery of the wampums has taken its toll. There are only two or three people left who have enough cultural memory and linguistic fluency to interpret the meaning of these belts for the next generation. Hundreds of long-house elders have passed away as museums and scholars argued over their rights to our heritage. With the passing of each elder, some knowledge is lost. It is as if we are burying a cultural library in the ground at each funeral.

As Iroquois, we are told to think of the seventh generation to come when we deliberate on our future. In making our decisions and choosing our paths, we are to consider not our needs or the needs of our own children but the welfare of the generations to come. If Thomas Webster and the other Iroquois who sold the wampum entrusted to them had thought about the seventh generation, we might not be in the mess we find ourselves in today.

Many of my museum colleagues question the sincerity of the repatriation requests coming from Native tribes. They ask whether Native Americans might not simply turn around and resell the objects that they are recovering from the museums. I cannot speak for other Native nations, but the Iroquois have learned an expensive lesson. It has taken us one hundred years to undo a cultural crime committed against our people. As long as we remember our cultural mandate, to consider the seventh generation to come, those wampums will never leave our possession again. Our very future as a people rests within those tiny shell beads.

But if the promise of repatriation is to be achieved, all museums need to cooperate. We need to recover all the wampum, as well as our other sacred objects. Museums need to consider new kinds of partnerships with Natives, ones that go beyond the object. Museums can help insure that cultural and religious beliefs continue and thrive. They can share their archival information, their photographs, and their recordings. They can play an important role in the Native American future.

Repatriation is not an end, it is, in many ways, a new beginning. Through the processes and relations it engenders, museums will come to understand that cultural preservation is not only about keeping objects from decaying but also about keeping ideas, values, and beliefs viable for the many generations to come.

Note

Richard W. Hill, Sr., is the former Director of the North American Indian Museum Association and has been involved with repatriation issues for nearly three decades.

References

Abrams, George. 1994. 'The case for wampum: Repatriation from the Museum of the American Indian to the Six Nations Confederacy, Brantford, Ontario.' In *Museums and the Making of 'Ourselves,'* edited by F. Kaplan, pp. 351–384. London: Leicester University Press.

Beauchamp, William. 1901. 'Wampum and shell articles used by the New York Indians.' *New York State Museum Bulletin* 41: 321–480.

Carrington, Henry. 1892. 'Report on the condition of the Six Nations of New York.' In *Extra Census Bulletin: Indians*, edited by T. Donaldson, pp. 19–83. Washington, D.C.: Bureau of the Census.

Fenton, William. 1971. 'The New York State wampum collection: The case for the integrity of cultural treasures.' *Proceedings of the American Philosophical Society* 115(6): 437–461.

—— 1989. 'Return of eleven wampum belts to the Six Nations Iroquois Confederacy on Grand River, Canada.' *Ethnohistory* 36(4): 392–410.

Henry, Jeannette. 1970. 'A rebuttal to the five anthropologists on the issue of the wampum belts.' *Indian Historian* 3(2): 15–17.

Hewitt, John. 1892. 'Legend of the founding of the Iroquois League.' *American Anthropologist* 5: 131–148.

—— 1912. 'Wampum.' *Handbook of American Indians North of Mexico*, edited by E.W. Hodge, 2: 904–909. Washington, D.C.: Smithsonian Institution.

Landy, David. 1978. 'Tuscarora among the Iroquois.' *Handbook of North American Indians: Northeast*, edited by W. Sturtevant, pp. 518–534. Washington, D.C.: Smithsonian Institution Press.

Noon, John. 1949. *Law and Government of the Grand River Iroquois*. Viking Fund Publications in Anthropology, No. 12. New York.

O'Callaghan, E.B. 1968. 'Historical Manuscripts in the Office of the Secretary of State, Albany, State of New York, 1664–1776.' Ridgewood, New Jersey: Gregg Press.

Sturtevant, William, *et al.* 1970. 'An "illusion of religiosity".' *Indian Historian* 3(2): 13–14.

Tooker, Elizabeth. 1978. 'The League of Iroquois: Its history, politics and ritual.' *Handbook of North American Indians: Northeast*, edited by W. Sturtevant, pp. 418–441. Washington, D.C.: Smithsonian Institution Press.

Chapter 21

Identity and Community
A look at four Latino museums

Herlinda Zamora

Latinos are a culturally, demographically, and geographically diverse population. According to the 2000 census, persons of Mexican origin form the largest Latino population in the United States, numbering more than 20 million, followed by Puerto Ricans at 3.4 million, and Cuban-Americans at more than 1.2 million. The latest U.S. Census figures show that Latinos are the second-largest minority in the country, with 35.3 million people, about 13 percent of the total population. By 2010 Latinos will be the largest single ethnic group, accounting for nearly one in seven Americans. . . .

After World War II, Latinos in the United States became aware of their growing numbers and potential political power, and sought to develop different aspects of their socio-economical, political, and cultural life. The Chicano and Puerto Rican movements that began in the 1960s were rooted in American history. Like the Civil Rights Movement, they evolved from a struggle for self-determination and self-definition as well as a growing awareness of the contributions of Latino Americans in the United States. These movements brought about change for the Latino community through political activism, creative outlets, and a renewed sense of identity.

During this time and the years that followed, four Latino museums were founded with the goal of engaging and supporting their communities. El Museo del Barrio was founded in New York City in 1969 by artist and teacher Rafael Montañez Ortiz. The Mexican Museum in San Francisco was founded in 1975 by artist Peter Rodrìguez. Chicago's Mexican Fine Arts Center Museum was founded in 1982 by a high school history teacher named Carlos Tortolero and a group of educators. And the Mexic-Arte Museum, Austin, Tex., was founded in 1983 by artists and activists Sylvia Orozco, Pio Pulido, and Sam Coronado. These four museums were among the first to show-case the works of Latinos and collect, promote, and exhibit the works of Chicano/a,

Source: *Museum News*, vol. 81, no. 3, 2002, pp. 36–41.

Mexican, and Puerto Rican art and culture. Their founders strove to provide positive resources at a time when there was a serious lack of outreach to Latinos from
mainstream institutions, many of which historically had excluded Latino artists.

As institutions that grew out of their communities with historically strong ties
to the people and the cultures they continue to serve today, these Latino museums
can offer some valuable lessons to mainstream museums about what it means to
engage and reflect the values and aspirations of a community.

El Museo del Barrio

Susana Torruella Leval, director of El Museo del Barrio, describes the museum's
founders as 'Puerto Rican educators, artists, and community activists who got together
here in *El Barrio* . . . [and] wanted to establish an institution that would survive
and last.' Born of the legacy of cultural activism, El Museo del Barrio was founded
in 1969 by a group of Puerto Rican parents, educators, artists, and community activists
in New York's East Harlem. The context surrounding its founding was the national
Civil Rights Movement and the campaign to diversify New York's art world,
during which major art institutions in New York were urged to decentralize their
collections and represent a variety of non-European cultures in their collections
and programs.

In the late 1960s, Martin W. Frey, superintendent of New York's School District
4 in Central and East Harlem, was under pressure from parents and community
activists to implement cultural enrichment programs for Puerto Rican children. Frey
appointed artist-educator Rafael Montañez Ortiz to create educational materials for
district schools on Puerto Rican history, culture, folklore, and art. Montañez Ortiz
was hired primarily to serve the population of East Harlem, known as *el barrio*,
where the majority of the Puerto Rican population lived. As an artist, activist, and
teacher, he was aware of the urgent need to create cultural resources for Puerto
Ricans of all ages.

In 1971, El Museo del Barrio became a nonprofit institution dedicated to Puerto
Rican heritage. In the years that followed, the museum established itself as a leader
among institutions devoted to interpreting Puerto Rican and Latino culture. It also
became a vital and central part of the local community. Leval was appointed director of El Museo del Barrio in 1994, a position she holds today.

The museum's educational programs and public activities are drawn from the
permanent collection, and are presented to the public through exhibitions and related
lectures, forums, workshops, and seminars. One of El Museo's more notable
exhibitions was *Voices from Our Communities: Perspectives on a Decade of Collecting at
El Museo del Barrio*, which ran June 12–Sept. 16, 2001. It accomplished two
important objectives, raising awareness of the richness of El Museo's permanent
collection and showing the depth and diversity of El Museo's constituency and audiences. *Taino: Ancient Voyagers of the Caribbean*, now on permanent exhibition, is comprised of selected works from the Taino culture that flourished from 1200 to 1500
A.D. on several Caribbean islands. It is the most comprehensive exhibit of its kind
in a U.S. museum, and provides visitors with an overall view of the history, cosmology, art, and culture of the Taino.

The Mexican Museum

In 1975, artist Peter Rodrìguez founded the Mexican Museum, located in the heart of San Francisco's Latino community, the Mission District. The Mexican Museum is acknowledged by many as the first American institution devoted to Chicano and Mexican art and culture. Rodrìguez became its first director and remained in the position until 1984. Similar to Sylvia Orozco, the director of Mexic-Arte Museum, Rodrìguez was inspired by his early visits to Mexico. He came back to the United States eager to tell about and exhibit the treasures of Mexican culture and with a dream of creating a center for the purpose of educating various communities about the richness of Mexican culture.

In 1982, the Mexican Museum moved into the Fort Mason Center and was led by different directors until 1997, when Lorraine García-Nakata was appointed executive director. Citing health problems, she resigned in April 2002. 'In retrospect,' says García-Nakata, 'the 1990s at the museum very much mirrored what was happening in the United States. It was a time of losing and gaining important ground, a period when the community had to ask itself a fundamental question: how important is the museum, and what are we each willing to contribute in order that it may continue? The fact that the museum received an affirmative answer from enough people in the community to bring it to its current state was its greatest and most important accomplishment in the 1990s.'

The Mexican Museum has been described as a first-voice institution; that is, it communicates the primacy of Latino self-definition and interpretation. As the museum's website notes, 'It utilizes Latino cultural expression as a lens for examining parallel experiences shared by the many cultural communities that constitute the Americas. This philosophy grows from the understanding that a community consists of many influences, histories, and experiences simultaneously.'

The museum's permanent collection grew from Rodrìguez's own personal collection of Mexican art and now includes more than 14,000 objects consisting of Pre-conquest, Colonial, Popular, Mexican, Latino contemporary, and Chicano art. *Street SmArt*, one of the museum's best-known programs, was developed in partnership with Mission Housing and Development Corporation, an organization that develops and manages low- to moderate-income housing in San Francisco. According to museum staff, *Street SmArt* serves as a direct response to the scarcity of after-school programming in the primarily Latino Mission District. Its workshops, offered to participants free of charge, address the needs of young people ages 5 to 18 who live at the corporation's housing sites. The Mexican Museum also has a free Family Sunday series designed to strengthen family ties; and exhibition and curriculum guides that enable teachers to interpret the museum's exhibitions to their students.

The Mexican Fine Arts Center Museum

Founded in 1982, the Mexican Fine Arts Center Museum (MFACM) evolved out of a commitment to awaken the city of Chicago to the wealth and breadth of Mexican culture, and to stimulate and preserve an appreciation of the arts of Mexico in the city's large Mexican community.

Its expanded space, which opened in April 2001, allows for 6,000 extra square feet of exhibition space, an education center, a new gift store, a new main entrance, a library, an interactive computer gallery, classrooms, and a climate-controlled art vault. The museum also is planning to create a National Memorial Plaza for Mexican-American veterans, the first national memorial to honor all Mexican-American servicemen and women. According to MFACM staff, numerous individuals and organizations in the community overwhelmingly support the idea, and acclaimed Chicano artist Luis Jimènez has been selected to create the memorial.

Throughout the museum field and among members of the public, MFACM is recognized as the first Mexican cultural center-museum in the Midwest and the largest in the nation. 'The museum is for every Mexican in the world,' says Director Tortolero. 'Our honor is at stake. We want both the local community and the mainstream world to visit . . . so that we can break down some of the barriers. . . . If only our own people come here, we will have failed in our mission. We really believe that this is a place for everyone.'

MFACM is located in the heart of the Pilsen community in Chicago, the largest Mexican community in the Midwest. A primary goal is to stimulate and preserve the knowledge and appreciation of Mexican culture as a culture *sin fronteras* ('without borders') that includes traditional and contemporary artistic expressions of Mexico and of the Mexican communities in the United States.

As a leading community-based arts organization, MFACM has accepted the responsibility and welcomes the opportunity to address critical contemporary topics such as cultural diversity, freedom of expression, first-voice issues, public funding in the arts, and arts and community development. The museum currently participates in three important partnerships. MAPS – the acronym for Museums and Public Schools: A New Direction for Teaching Chicago's Children (see *Museum News*, March/April 2000, page 60) – is an innovative, collaborative program between museums and the city's parks and the Chicago Public Schools that seeks to integrate the rich and varied resources of nine great museums into the local classroom curriculum. Park Voyagers, a collaboration with the Chicago Park District, is designed to provide Chicago youth with educational and experiential enrichment in an informal setting; children and parents are invited to participate in after-school programs and evening sessions, as well as guided visits to the museum. Furthermore, MFACM is proud of its ongoing relationship with Mexico's El Museo del Templo Mayor (The Aztec Main Temple Museum). In 1992, a sister-museum agreement was signed to further the bonds of friendship between MFACM and El Museo del Templo Mayor. The Mexican Fine Arts Center Museum is also the first and only Latino museum accredited by the American Association of Museums.

Tortolero believes that the museum's success is due to its location and that his museum and the community share a reciprocal experience. Without the community the museum would not have such a strong presence, but without the museum the community would not take such pride in its culture. That is why MFACM does not charge admission, creating a sense of ownership among the community residents.

The Mexican Fine Arts Center Museum's permanent collection is featured in *Mexicanidad*, a comprehensive cultural exhibition that explores aspects of ancient Mexico, colonial Mexico, modern Mexico, contemporary Mexico, and the Mexican experience in the United States. The exhibition concept derives from the

Mexican Revolution (1910–20) and identifies the shared aesthetics, beliefs, and customs that characterize Mexican culture today. More than 60 percent of the exhibition consists of artwork from the permanent collection. The museum supplements its permanent collection with works from other U.S. museums, museums in Mexico, and individual collectors.

The most intriguing examples of the museum's youth initiative are its radio station and youth museum, which target the primarily Mexican-American community of Pilsen. Radio Arte-WRTE 90.5 FM and the Yollocalli Youth Museum serve to provide positive resources for young people in the Pilsen neighborhood and 'confirm the museum's commitment to the young people of our community,' says Tortolero.

Mexic-Arte Museum

Mexic-Arte Museum's mission states that the institution is dedicated to cultural enrichment and education through the presentation and promotion of traditional and contemporary Mexican, Latino, and Latin American art and culture.

Artist, co-founder, and current director Sylvia Orozco was a student at the University of Texas at Austin during the late 1970s. At that time, she joined the Austin-based League of United Chicano Artists (LUCHA) and the Mujeres Artistas de Sudoeste (Women Artists from the Southwest), a group of Chicanas who organized programs and exhibitions dealing with women's issues.

Orozco longed to study the masters of Mexican art first-hand; she accepted a scholarship from the Mexican government and the Committee for Rural Democracy, co-sponsored by Raza Unida, a Chicano/a activist group, to study at the National Autonomous University of Mexico in the San Carlos Academy, the oldest art school in the Americas. There she met Pio Pulido, a painter who later teamed up with her for more than a decade at Mexic-Arte Museum. Together they catalogued exhibits and collected reference works on Mexican art. In 1983, Orozco returned to Austin, expressing a need to share Mexico's rich culture with the community.

In July 1984, Orozco, Pulido, and artist Sam Coronado (who later founded Coronado Studios, a silkscreen printing workshop located in Austin's Latino community) officially established Mexic-Arte Museum at Galeria Mexico. That year Orozco and her colleagues acquired some city funding for Austin's first Day of the Dead Parade and Celebration. 'People were nervous about it,' Orozco says of the first *Dia de los Muertos* parade. 'Latinos and Anglos had never really met on the street that way. It was fear of the unknown.' In 1988, Mexic-Arte moved to downtown Austin where it continued its commitment to serving as a multicultural center that includes rather than excludes artists, actors, and musicians of different races.

In 1993, the museum established a sister-city relationship with the Diego Rivera and Frida Kahlo Studio Museum in Mexico City, connecting Texas and Mexico through cultural exchanges. The partnership has enabled Mexic-Arte to showcase important exhibitions of Mexican art throughout the state of Texas, including works by Adolfo Mexiac, Rosario Cabrera, Jean Charlot, and others. For Orozco, it always has been important to include the Mexican influence in her efforts to make Mexic-Arte Museum a quality institution, equal to those found in Mexico. She strongly believes that one day the museum will be a world-class art museum that will display the full richness of Mexican culture. Linking today's artists to Mexico's past is her goal.

'We reach out to everyone,' Orozco says. 'We are not elitists. We want the community to feel a sense of ownership, and provide a welcoming environment.'

As these museums expand their missions, facilities, and outreach efforts and continue to add to their credibility and approval within the community, they are experiencing growing pains. The Mexican Museum and Mexic-Arte Museum are each in the middle of a struggle to build larger and more Latino-diverse institutions. The Mexican Fine Arts Center Museum recently expanded its space, and El Museo del Barrio is looking into relocating. Relocation and growth add a serious burden to these grass-roots organizations. They were all created, in a sense, by the community itself, which they helped to define even as the community defined the museums.

In the Latino community, there is often concern that when new development occurs for museums such as these, they might 'sell out' and become mainstream institutions. El Museo del Barrio, for example, was criticized by some in its Puerto Rican community for concentrating too much on other Latino communities as it expanded its mission, according to a January 2001 *New York Times* article. In defense of El Museo del Barrio, however, other members of the Latino community have praised the museum for recognizing that 'El Barrio' of East Harlem has undergone huge demographic changes as it has welcomed diverse Latino communities in the last decade.

But these problems of identity were also familiar to mainstream museums at similar stages of their own development. As critic Michael Kimmelman points out ('Museums in a Quandary: Where Are the Ideals?' *New York Times*, August 2001), mainstream art museums 'were conceived in the 19th century as places to improve public taste, to educate the middle classes. Self-improvement and commerce went hand in hand in the early history of museums, especially in the United States and Britain. But they were never places of consensus.'

'Let's face it,' says Tortolero of the Mexican Fine Arts Center Museum, 'museums are very conservative institutions and are reluctant and afraid to take on the issue of the "culture" of mainstream museums. Many of these institutions were created for the elite and never saw themselves as serving society as a whole. Now museums are reacting to the pressure to change. Unfortunately, this pressure usually comes from the outside, rather than inside, the institution, especially where funding sources are concerned. Many mainstream institutions have placed the issue of inclusiveness on the back burner.'

The challenges of Latino museums were and continue to be external and internal in nature, just as they are for mainstream museums. Those who use Latino museums as a resource for academic research, cultural activity, and personal identity are looking forward to their continuous growth. These museums should be applauded for their vision and willingness to focus on a historically rich and diverse culture. Their presentation of the full range of Latino art and cultural performances is something that everyone can enjoy and appreciate, Latinos and non-Latinos alike.

Note

Herlinda Zamora is a graduate student in Museum Studies at the University of Texas.

Chapter 22

Minorities and Fine-Arts Museums in the United States

Peter C. Marzio

. . . I WOULD LIKE TO COMMENT on the 'silent criticism' from professionals within the art establishment.[1] The lesson that is clearest in my mind
is that those of us who care about making the minority arts a vital part of mainstream museum programs must work together. When curators, art critics, college
professors, and museum directors debate about exhibition format or style, we must
remember that we are trying to improve our efforts, raise our standards, and make
our message clearer to a larger audience. The enemy is not within our group but
beyond the debating arena. Apathy and disregard among the general public and professionals toward minority art, particularly when that art is placed in the general-
art-museum environment, must be changed to cooperation and understanding. We
must keep that ultimate goal in mind as we explore this complex subject.

My duty here is to give the museum director's point of view. As director of
the Museum of Fine Arts, Houston, which organized *Hispanic Art in the United States*,
assumed financial risks, and raised the funds, I was impressed by how difficult this
project was. When I gave the curators a mandate to find the best art, I had no idea
of the problems that would follow.

Despite the fact that many people 'know' about contemporary Hispanic art,
we found not a single individual who had both strong curatorial credentials and a
catholic viewpoint on the subject. This meant that the curators – Livingston and
Beardsley – had to carry out in-depth, primary research on a national scale; and
they had to do it quickly enough so that the word *contemporary* in the exhibition's
title retained its meaning. If the ARCO Foundation and the Rockefeller Foundation had not stepped in at the research stage of this project, the exhibition would
not have been possible. The reason: basic research is expensive. Since contemporary

Source: *Exhibiting Cultures: The Poetics and Politics of Museum Display*, I. Karp and S.D. Lavine
(eds), Washington: Smithsonian Institution Press, 1991, pp. 121–7.

Hispanic art is not studied in many universities or reviewed in professional or mass-circulation periodicals, information about the artists and their works is not coherent or easy to locate. The curators had to spend enormous amounts of time assembling the kind of fundamental information that is readily available for the traditional art-historical disciplines in any library. Because contemporary minority art, by virtue of its recency and subject, has not been researched, one must prepare to undertake a massive effort if one wants to do the job well.

Gathering the information and putting it in a narrative form may be sufficient for the art historican, but it is only the start for a curator. These curators were looking for the 'best.' There were few art dealers who could advise and guide them in this process; many Hispanic arts organizations had local or regional missions, and their recommendations had to be translated to a national level. A process as simple as gathering slides for comparison became a complex project. Every step along the path that led to selecting the artists and the artworks was difficult. There were no well-illustrated catalogues *raisonnés* or university slide libraries of Hispanic art. The curators often went back two or three times to view an artist's work. Comparing and sorting art for an exhibition of contemporary minority art is expensive and time-consuming.

Within the contexts of basic research and looking for great works of art, this project, like all large contemporary exhibitions, was the topic of endless discussion and debate. In the field of contemporary art, everyone has an expert opinion. Add to this the ethnic element. Some people debated that non-Hispanics had no right to curate a Hispanic exhibition, others complained that one Hispanic group was being favored over another, and some leaders in Hispanic arts organizations fought against the exhibition because they felt that the art and artists were being taken from the Hispanic organization's sphere of influence. In organizing this kind of exhibition, an enormous amount of time must be spent in communication with the minority establishments. Silence can be misinterpreted and can lead to fear, mistrust, and malicious, destructive rumors. An efficient communication system will not eliminate all these evils, but it helps to create a foundation of understanding that is essential in an exhibition of this kind. This is a significant difference from most of the art exhibitions that I have worked on during my twenty-year museum career.

My goal in directing this project was to help broaden the programming in mainstream art museums and to begin a long-term commitment to bringing the Museum of Fine Arts, Houston, closer to the diverse Hispanic communities that make up the city's population. This latter goal is in concert with the belief broadly shared among art museums that they must provide educational and community service to all constituents. During the time that the exhibition was in Houston, there were approximately 150,000 visitors. Approximately thirty percent were Hispanic, based on sample audience surveys. There were major symposia, film festivals, artists' and writers' book festivals, concerts, family days, tours in Spanish and English, and a host of other activities in Houston during the run of the exhibition. A special committee of fifty Hispanic community leaders helped the museum with outreach and publicity. When the exhibition closed in Houston this committee remained with the museum, helping the Education Department to recruit Hispanic docents and to bring general art education into the Hispanic communities via church groups, schools, and other organizations. Moreover, the museum was introduced to numerous Hispanic businesses and organizations that now work with and for the museum on a regular basis. In short, the exhibition was a small but important step forward in bringing the general art museum and the Hispanic peoples of Houston closer together.

In another sense, the exhibition went against the tide of today's art museums. Most directors I know believe that great museums must specialize. In this sense, adding a new kind of exhibition to the program can be seen as confusing an institution's identity and taking funds away from an older, dedicated purpose. This exhibition is a good example. Approximately one-half of the cost of the exhibition was paid out of the operating budgets of the Museum of Fine Arts, Houston, and the other five museums on the tour. The other half came from grants from the Rockefeller Foundation, the ARCO Foundation, the AT&T Foundation, and the National Endowment for the Arts (NEA).

In the long run, the barrier to placing minority arts in the general art museum may be part of a much larger issue. Despite the enormous success of art museums in the United States during the last two decades, the fact remains that among the 150 top museums all but a handful are undercapitalized. Look closely at their budgets and you will see that few of our museums have the funds needed to carry out basic research or to expand into new program areas. For more and more institutions an overwhelming effort is being put into raising funds and earning income – not to create massive expansion programs, but to remain effective at present levels. Also, the traditional funding mechanisms for eleemosynary institutions are being altered gradually, making program innovation and expansion even more difficult. First, the budgets of the NEA and the National Endowment for the Humanities have remained relatively flat in the last eight years, losing ground to inflation. The incentives for philanthropy in the private, corporate, and foundation sectors have been reduced and in some cases eliminated by changes in the Internal Revenue Code. By reducing federal funding for the arts and eliminating incentives, the federal government has forced, and even encouraged, art museums to earn a higher percentage of their incomes. I have argued elsewhere that this pressure has tended to make art museums and other nonprofit institutions act like commercial or profit-oriented entities. This pressure to earn revenue has many ramifications for minority arts. Whether anyone is willing to say it or not, the question museum directors must ask themselves is simple: Can the large, established art museum afford minority-art exhibitions? Can the cost be offset by income? If a director does not ask that question, then he or she should look for another job.

The challenge for those of us who are dedicated to placing high-quality minority exhibitions in the broad context of general art museums is to find a way to make these projects a part of 'normal' operations. In Houston there was concern that attendance would be low for an exhibition of Hispanic art. As I have said, the result was nearly 150,000 visitors, which is considered very good by Houston standards. A special public-relations plan, aimed at the major Hispanic neighborhoods and carried out by a Hispanic firm, was a huge success. In addition, while the exhibition was open in Houston, two other popular exhibitions were on view: *Drawings by Holbein from the Court of Henry VIII* and *The Quest for Eternity*, a major exhibition of Chinese tomb sculptures including life-size soldiers and horses from Xian. Hispanic Art in the United States benefited from the cross-over attendance stimulated by these two great exhibitions. In addition, the visitors attracted by *Hispanic Art in the United States* were treated to great works of art from other cultures that may not have interested them initially.

I feel strongly about the role of general art museums in the presentation of minority exhibitions because in my experience, while minorities appreciate exhibitions dedicated to their unique art forms, people do not want a steady diet of their own work. The message that the Museum of Fine Arts received was loud and clear: make the broad range of fine art understandable and accessible to minorities.

The general art museum is uniquely suited to achieve these goals. By intelligent scheduling of exhibitions, the 'high-risk' exhibitions can be placed in a favorable position, thus hedging the risks of low attendance and low income. This allows these innovative programs to become gradually better known and more readily accepted, and thus supported by the community at large.

Placing minority exhibitions in general art museums also makes important statements about quality. A recent survey in Houston showed an overwhelming preference for European Old Masters over all other art forms, including American Western art. Our museum is fortunate to own great works by artists such as Rogier van der Weyden, Fra Angelico, Chardin, Monet, van Gogh, and many others. Important works by these artists were on view while *Hispanic Art in the United States* was open. Many of the artists in the exhibition expressed to me a tremendous sense of satisfaction that they were under the same roof with such hallowed colleagues. In short, we organized the *Hispanic Art in the United States* exhibition because many artists we showed met and sometimes exceeded the standards of past masters. The unique contribution of the general art museum is that it can demonstrate this by exhibiting concurrently these different works.

In exhibiting minority artists in the same manner as Italian Renaissance artists or French Impressionists, the Museum of Fine Arts, Houston, also addressed another controversial issue: how much interpretive information should be provided and how should it be presented? In our ongoing programs related to the permanent collection, we follow a fairly rigid philosophy. Exhibition labels are kept to a minimal size to encourage visitors to focus on the works of art themselves. We do not believe in installations that try to place art in context by installing large reproductions or long labels that 'explain' the art. This approach is balanced by our Education Department, which aggressively provides visitors with tours, pamphlets, catalogues, films, teacher-student packets, and other pedagogical tools. This translates into the belief that a minority artwork should be able to stand alone – apart from its cultural context, if you will – just the way a panel painting from a Renaissance predella, for example, may hang alone, out of context, in a museum. In our philosophy, the context is supplied in educational materials.

I mention this because in doing this exhibition I found an attitude that puzzles me to this day: the belief that contemporary minority art needs a kind of anthropological or sociological interpretation. I am not against museums that follow this attitude, but I – as director of the Museum of Fine Arts, Houston – want the right to exhibit contemporary artists the way I exhibit Old Masters.

In emphasizing the general art museum's role in presenting minority art, I am not in any way denigrating the institutions that specialize in African American, Hispanic, or any other minority art. On the contrary, the general art museum cannot function in this area without the specialized museum. Unfortunately, in my experience I have not seen much of an established network between the mainstream and minority spheres. The fault lies on both sides. The director of the general art museum is racing full speed ahead just to keep his or her institution operating at its current level. The directors of minority-oriented institutions, on the other hand, are sometimes fearful that cooperation will somehow hurt their identity and their unique role in their communities. And when it comes to the funding formulas of various government agencies – city, county, state, and federal – I have seen too much confrontation: too often battle lines are being drawn between big and little, general and specialized, minority and establishment. When art museums fight among themselves, everyone who cares about art loses. Our goals must be to enlarge audiences, to increase funding, to work together to rise above the status quo, and to make innovation a popular cause. I say this because my experiences with the *Hispanic Art in the United States* exhibition as well as other exhibitions of minority art tell me that while bigotry is, to a certain extent, ingrained in our society, the real obstacle to overcome is the lack of exposure and, therefore, the lack of experience of the general public and art-history professionals. This simple fact is not sufficiently understood by those of us who want to expand the aesthetic boundaries and definitions of fine art. We expect too much from any single exhibition or book on minority art. These high expectations are the products of frustration and hype. Artists who finally get a chance to be seen by the general public and professionals might have expectations that are unrealistic. Curators who work for years on a minority exhibition find out that it is received like any other exhibition. And that is just the point. Moreover, as museums strive to fund an exhibition and stimulate attendance, they can easily overemphasize the words *first* or *new* and create expectations that are not met. I see each exhibition and book as building blocks, parts of a large edifice that includes academic, critical, and commercial elements as well. All are needed to establish and sustain any vital art form in our society. I hope we will arrive at a point where the minority exhibition will be received with the same thoughtful review process that serious Old Master exhibitions receive, with the same potential commercialism, and with the same in-depth study. Those will be the ultimate signs of acceptance.

Notes

Peter C. Marzio is Director of the Museum of Fine Arts in Houston, Texas.

1   The 'silent criticism' referred to here was of the exhibition *Hispanic Art in the United States: Thirty Contemporary Painters and Sculptors*, described by Jane Livingston and John Beardsley in 'The poetics and politics of Hispanic art: a new perspective' in I. Karp and S.D. Lavine (eds) *Exhibiting Cultures: The Poetics and Politics of Museum Display*, Washington: Smithsonian Institution Press, 1991, pp. 104–20. They commented that this criticism 'was, perhaps, to be expected: the exhibition posed a challenge to customary ways of looking at art. . . . Our exhibition suggested that curators can and should look for demonstrations of achievement outside the establishment to which they are bound and which they help sustain.' (119).

Chapter 23

The Peopling of London Project

Nick Merriman

Introduction and background

IT IS AN UNDENIABLE FACT that Britain today is a culturally diverse nation. What is not often recognized is the long presence that many communities have actually had in this country. The acknowledgement of both of these facts is slowly having an impact on museums. First, museums are realizing that, in order to maintain their claims to be responsive to the needs of their communities, they must make themselves relevant to the diversity of populations that make up their constituency. Second, some museums are beginning to realize that, in the interests of historical balance, they must begin to represent the previously neglected presence and contribution of minority ethnic communities in their areas.

London is a cosmopolitan city on a global scale. Some 20 per cent of its citizens identify themselves as belonging to a major ethnic group of non-European origin, and a much larger percentage belong to Irish, Jewish, Italian, Spanish, Cypriot, Polish and other groups. Some 200 languages other than English are spoken in London homes.[1]

This chapter describes a project, The Peopling of London: 15,000 years of Settlement from Overseas, which has been undertaken by the museum of London in an attempt to embrace the concept of cultural diversity within the museum's work. It is presented as an evaluated case study of some of the issues, pitfalls and rewards of undertaking a project that attempts to present a long history of population diversity to a pluralistic audience. It tries to put into practice some approaches advanced in previous work (Merriman 1991) to wider museum audiences by dismantling some of the barriers that deter people from visiting.

The idea for the Peopling of London project evolved over the course of 1990 in response to a number of different ideas and developments both within and

Source: *Cultural Diversity: Developing Museum Audiences in Britain*, E. Hooper-Greenhill (ed.), London: Leicester University Press, 1997, pp. 119–48.

outside the museum. One of the catalysts was the adoption by the museum in that year of a comprehensive and regular programme of market research surveys which established for the first time the characteristics of the museum's visitors. One of the most telling findings was that seemingly only around 4 per cent[2] of the museum's visitors were from 'ethnic minority'[3] groups, compared to the 20 per cent in London's overall population mentioned above.[4] There was rightly a concern that the museum's programmes and displays were not appealing to around a fifth of the museum's constituency in the Greater London area.

Some of the reasons for this lack of interest amongst many of London's communities have been investigated in a survey by the London Museums Service (Trevelyan 1991) on the attitudes of non-visitors to London's museums. For many members of 'ethnic minority' groups, it is clearly shown that museums are perceived as irrelevant in their content, intimidating in their architecture and unwelcoming in their attendant staff. In the case of the Museum of London, this is borne out by the fact that the permanent galleries (currently) finish at 1945, with the result that the histories of people who have settled in London since then receive no mention. Unconsciously, the museum was giving recent settlers the impression that they were not part of the continuum of London's history. In addition, at the time the project was being formulated, it was extremely difficult to gain any sense of London's long history of cultural diversity when visiting the museum's galleries. There was a small section on the Huguenots, a panel put up in 1989 on eighteenth-century immigration and a small panel on the nineteenth-century Jewish community, but little else. There was no mention of the medieval Jewish community, the continuous black presence since the sixteenth century, the establishment of Asian communities from the seventeenth century, the Chinese, Italians and Germans of the nineteenth century, nor anything on the early twentieth-century communities with origins overseas.

At the same time, work on the redevelopment of the museum's prehistoric gallery was focusing on the need to draw out a theme linking prehistoric times with the present. It was decided that population movement from overseas would be a suitable theme. This sprang from the observation that there was a period around 15,000 BC when Britain was devoid of population because of the severity of Ice Age climatic conditions. When the climate improved, people colonized the empty land again, since which time Britain has been permanently occupied. Settlement from abroad therefore presented itself as a theme which is of contemporary relevance, and which could be placed in a truly long-term historical context by a museum display.

These observations coalesced around the idea of developing a project which aimed at highlighting the neglected history of London's diverse populations by placing contemporary communities in a long-term historical context. The starting point would be the colonization of an empty landscape in the Ice Age, progressing through the varied population of Roman times, and on through London's history to the present. The fundamental aim of the project was to demonstrate that London – or the London area – has always had a culturally diverse population originating from various parts of the globe. Far from being a recent 'problem', immigration from overseas would be presented in the project as a fundamental characteristic of the city since earliest times, and something of which London could be proud. By treating this topic in this way, the aim of the project would be both to inform the museum's existing audience about a neglected aspect of London's history, and to open up the museum to a new audience which up until now had tended not to visit.

A final development made the project even more relevant. While some of the above ideas were being developed, xenophobia and racism were becoming more prevalent across Europe (including Britain) as the fall of the Berlin Wall and the collapse of communism led to large-scale movements of people and the unleashing of long-standing hatreds previously held in check. This was combined with the onset of deep recession amongst the Western industrialized countries, which in turn led to unemployment, increased poverty and the perennial selection of immigrants as scapegoats. Perusal of the rhetoric of racist groups made it clear that much of their message was predicted on the notion that – in Britain at least – there had been a homogeneous white population prior to 1945, bound together by a common history and set of values, and that after 1945 this homogeneity had been overlain by the introduction of – in their terms – alien non-white populations with different histories, values and cultural backgrounds who did not belong to Britain and were the source of many of the nation's current woes.

As museums play a fundamental role as interpreters of public history, the team working on the project felt that they must be able to challenge such abuses of history, and offer an alternative to the myth of pre-war population homogeneity. This would be a significant departure for the Museum of London in that it would be taking a view of a particular issue (i.e. that racism should be challenged), rather than maintaining its usual position of apparent neutrality. Given the growing critical understanding within museums of the impossibility of value-free objectivity in historical discourse, this departure was viewed primarily as a useful and explicit recognition of an existing state of affairs. A fundamental objective of the project therefore became to challenge the view that post-war immigration in London was a recent 'problem', by turning this argument on its head and celebrating the diversity of London's people since prehistoric times.

The formulation of the project

Having established these basic parameters, a small internal team began to examine the different elements of the project in more detail. It was important to be explicit about the objectives of the project, because it was intended that it should be thoroughly evaluated, particularly in terms of the target audiences. After some discussion the following aims were agreed:

- to widen the focus of the museum by presenting the histories of communities not previously represented in the museum's galleries;
- to make contact with, involve and attract to the museum a new audience who had little or no previous contact with it;
- to make the museum more accessible, both physically and intellectually, to the different people of London;
- to challenge traditional views of what it is to be a Londoner;
- to stimulate discussion of, and interest in, the history of London;
- to encourage new thinking and practice within the museum.

Five target audiences were also identified:

- existing museum visitors;
- people who do not normally visit the museum, especially members of London's ethnic minorities;
- school pupils and teachers;
- tourists, especially those from the countries of origin of some of London's communities;
- museum professionals.

The aim of the project was to challenge the 'them' and 'us' mentality by showing that all communities come ultimately from overseas. As a result, the most important aspect of the project was to give an indication of the great time-depth to the history of London's cultural diversity. It was also clear that if the museum were to develop a broader approach to representing history in this way, the project would have to have long-term aims beyond the production of a temporary exhibition. In a sense, the Peopling of London project was to be a 'pilot study' to establish the parameters of a new approach to London's history, the ultimate aim of which was to incorporate the previously hidden history of cultural diversity into the museum's permanent galleries. The new approach was also to emphasize the importance for museums of putting a human face on the past. While original objects were still to be at the heart of the enterprise, they were not to remain ends in themselves. Where possible, it was intended to relate objects to individual people and, in the more recent periods, use oral history and photography to provide a personal dimension to the process being described.

In taking on this subject the museum was confronting head-on some of the more contentious issues in the public representation of history, and needed to develop the project in a manner that was sensitive to the feelings of London's communities, whose histories had hitherto been largely ignored by the museum world. In particular, the issue of community involvement was fundamental to the success of the project. Museum staff felt neither comfortable nor qualified in presenting the history of, for example, the Chinese or Cypriot communities, so a key feature of the project had to be consultation and collaboration. On the other hand, with so many communities in London, this had to be managed in a way that did not over-inflate expectations, given the constraints of the museum's resources and the size of the exhibition space. As relative novices in this area, the team began investigating their approach by holding two brainstorming sessions with museum professionals who had experience of community history projects in London and with academics with an interest in community history or immigration. The experience of those who had worked on the Museum in Docklands project was also invaluable. This was a Museum of London initiative to establish a museum of the Port of London and had pioneered community history at the museum. Through its use of oral history, its outreach work amongst schools and local communities, and its use of a mobile museum, it provided a model for the approach of the Peopling of London project. One of the 'Docklands' staff, Andy Topping, was later seconded to the Peopling project to develop the public events programme, and his experience proved decisive in shaping the project.

Following these discussions a basic programme for the project was established: it should involve extensive consultation and liaison work; it should conduct synthetic research in libraries and archives, review sources of objects and images; and develop a package of activities for the public. The different elements of the project underwent considerable revision as a result of discussion and as the research and collecting process revealed what would, or would not, be possible. The final elements consisted of the following:

- a programme of outreach and consultation, including use of a mobile museum;
- a programme of research amongst archives and public collections;
- a temporary exhibition;
- an accompanying publication;
- a resource pack;
- a programme of activities for schools;
- a programme of events for adults and family groups;
- a related film season;
- a programme of collecting (including oral history recordings) to ensure that the museum's holdings reflected something of London's cultural diversity;
- an archive of information generated by the project to be permanently available in the museum library;
- an evaluation exercise with a final report on the success of the project.

The research phase

Following this, the team began an extensive research phase. This was particularly important because there were few syntheses of the histories of different community groups available, and in a number of cases – notably amongst recent immigrant groups – there was almost no information at all. Crucial to this process – and to the success of the overall project – was the appointment of Rozina Visram as the project researcher and advisor. A respected historian, teacher, author of *Ayahs, Lascars and Princes. The History of Indians in Britain 1700–1947* (Visram 1986) and co-author of the Geffrye Museum's report into the *Black Contribution to History* (Fraser and Visram 1988), she already had experience of working in the field of anti-racist and equal opportunities teaching and had a wide network of contacts amongst academics and community groups.

Her role in the first instance was to scrutinize the archives of the Museum of London and to visit the archives of local history libraries and national repositories to search for material concerning settlers from overseas. Each visit resulted in notes on the archives' holdings, which were then incorporated into a synthesis outlining the history of each major community in London, the location and content of historical records and illustrative material, and bibliographical references. This then assisted in the reappraisal of the museum's own object holdings. For example, the discovery that nineteenth-century German settlers specialized in, amongst other things, the sugar-baking industry, led to the use of sugar loaf moulds in the display on the German community in London. A photograph of Italian ice-cream sellers similarly led to the display of a glass ice-cream 'lick' identical to the one in the picture.

Just as important was her role in discussing the project with members of community groups. At an early stage in the project it was decided that community liaison should be done not by a formal committee with nominated representatives, which would be unwieldy given the large number of communities being studied, but on an informal basis using a whole variety of contacts. In this way it was hoped to gather a broad range of views from different age groups, genders and social classes within each community, and from academics as well as non-academics.

Rozina Visram's existing contacts, for example, with the Black Cultural Archives and the India Office Library, led to further contacts within the communities, both for advice and for historical information. It had become clear at an early stage that much of the history of recent settlers resided principally in the memories of first and second generation migrants, and that therefore oral history would form an important component of the project. One of Rozina Visram's initial tasks was to identify potential contributors to a programme of oral history recording. This was then followed up by the museum's recently appointed Curator of Oral History, Rory O'Connell.

Rozina Visram's other principal role, together with the leader of the project, Nick Merriman, was in publicizing the project amongst community groups, and in gauging reactions to different approaches. The attitude of the project team[5] was to be as open as possible about its existence and objectives, on the basis that early initial contact and discussion was the best way to generate support and to avoid misunderstandings and antipathy. Partly because of Rozina Visram's credibility as researcher and advisor, and the circumstances of the project's inception (against a background of increasing racism), to the satisfaction of team members the basic concept of the project met with strong approval amongst almost everyone consulted, from community leaders and academics to social workers and oral history contributors. Although many commented that it was 'about time' that the Museum of London remedied its neglect of their history, they were glad that an effort was finally being made, at a particularly appropriate time. In turn, they too passed on many of their network of contacts.

At the same time as this archival research and community consultation was being undertaken, the project team were carrying out research on suitable two- and three-dimensional material for the exhibition, which was envisaged as the centrepiece of the project. One of the first things that had to be demonstrated was that the subject of the project would make a viable exhibition. While many themes make excellent books, videos and lecture series, it is not always easy to translate them into an exhibition where visitors move physically through a space absorbing and being stimulated by ideas and information. As a museum is fundamentally concerned with material culture, it was essential that the exhibition was not simply a 'book on the wall', consisting of text panels and flat photographic images. Initial reactions amongst museum staff were that the museum did not have much material relevant to this theme. In particular it became clear that the museum records were largely silent on the cultural background of the people from whom objects had been collected, no doubt because this information had not been deemed worthy of recording at the time of collection.

Further investigation of the museum's collections, however, revealed material that could be used to illuminate the theme of the exhibition in a number of different ways. First, there was material that was without doubt associated with certain communities, being demonstrably made, used or in some other way associated with the group. This material included Roman tombstones showing the place of birth of the deceased, a tombstone with a Norse inscription, a medieval Italian merchant's seal, Huguenot silverware, an eighteenth-century gravestone from the Dutch Church, various nineteenth-century Jewish items, including a charitable lottery wheel, and nineteenth-century dock labour cards relating to three Irish brothers. Paintings, prints and photographs showing early African-Caribbean, Asian and Chinese inhabitants helped to fill in some of the gaps. The second category of material was that which was typically associated with certain processes of certain communities, even though the documentation did not explicitly state that there was a direct association. In the prehistoric period, for example, certain stone tools stood as icons for the earliest settlers. In later periods documentary records showed that some communities specialized in certain crafts and industries. Items typical of these crafts could therefore be used to illustrate that fact, even though the particular item exhibited had no definite link (impossible to prove in the case of excavated artefacts). This type of material included leather shoes to illustrate 'Doche' inhabitants in the medieval period, Delft ceramics to highlight the Dutch-inspired development of the industry in London, and nineteenth-century tools used in railway construction to symbolize the impact of the rebuilding of London by a predominantly Irish labour force. This second way of using objects, in a generic rather than a specific way, represents a departure from the traditional practice of developing exhibitions that are driven primarily by objects, in favour of one where objects are used as typical illustrations of a theme. This approach has been discussed in detail by Spencer Crew and James Sims (1991) in their account of the National Museum of American History's exhibition *Field to Factory*. There they encountered the familiar problem that the material culture of disadvantaged ('invisible') communities has rarely if ever been collected by museums, with the result that programmes designed to make such communities visible in the museum must necessarily develop a different way of looking at objects as evidence.

The Peopling of London team was relatively fortunate in that the museum's archaeological collections were extensive, allowing a reasonably full treatment of the earliest periods using both directly and typically associated material. Some later communities were relatively well-represented, because their craft products fell within the traditional decorative arts field of museum collecting. The prime examples of this sort of material was that relating to the Huguenot and Dutch communities. Jewish material of a religious nature had also been collected, possibly because of its easy identification with that community through the Hebrew script on the objects. Other communities had been barely, if at all, collected. Three-dimensional material culture relating to the African-Caribbean, South Asian and Chinese communities was absent, and, surprisingly, apart from the one group already mentioned there was almost no material relating to the large and long-established Irish community.

Some of these deficiencies could be remedied through loans from existing institutional collections. Having reviewed the Museum of London's collections, the second task of the project team was to investigate material held elsewhere. Some institutions were obvious sources: the Black Cultural Archives, the Jewish Museum, the London Museum of Jewish Life, the India Office Library, the British

Museum (particularly the Prints and Drawings Collection) and the National Portrait Gallery. Other important material came from less obvious sources. The Royal Albert Memorial Museum in Exeter, for example, had a portrait of the eighteenth-century British black campaigner and writer Olaudah Equiano. The Science Museum had a barometer made by the famous Italian-London firm of Negretti & Zambra and the British Library had copies of books written by eighteenth-century black Londoners. A particularly large source of exhibits was the Public Record Office, which lent documents ranging from a bill of sale of around 1220 for a Jew's house in West Cheap to Karl Marx's unsuccessful application for British naturalization.

Despite this extensive trawl amongst public collections, a review of the material available on communities from overseas showed that there were still a large number of gaps, particularly in the more recent periods. It was clearly necessary to embark on a programme to collect or borrow additional material. Before this could commence, we had to be clear about the themes that the exhibition would cover. This involved an extensive review of the evidence available and a consideration of the different approaches that could be explored.

Exhibition themes

The fundamental question that the exhibition team had to confront was whether the topic should be covered thematically or chronologically. It would be possible to take, for example, 20 of the largest overseas communities in London's history and devote a section to each one, showing its history and impact on the development of London. This would have had the advantage of explicitly recognizing the importance of the history of these communities in the museum context. However, it would also have carried with it several disadvantages. A large number of communities would have been excluded; there would have been a large degree of repetition in the historical information and processes exhibited in each section; and it would have presented each community as a hermetically sealed unit, and not allowed an exploration of the important aspects of interactions between different communities. It is rare in London for any community to live its life insulated from the rest of London's population, so this method of presentation would have produced a false impression of the way in which the city's populations conduct their lives. Finally, it would have been difficult to establish a clear sense of chronology with such a thematic treatment. As the ultimate aim of the project was to demonstrate the great time-depth to cultural diversity in London, this would have been a grave disadvantage. The team therefore decided that the exhibition, like the Museum of London itself, should follow a chronological path, and focus on London and its diversity of populations rather than on specific communities. However, realizing that many first-time visitors would be wishing to see displays specifically on their own communities, the team attempted to develop thematic sections within defined chronological periods which allowed the histories of certain communities to be explored. The broad chronological sections, together with their sub-themes, were eventually as follows:

1.   Before London (15,000 BC–AD 50)
2.   Roman London (50–410)

3. The Age of Migrations (419–1066)
   a. Germanic Soldiers and Settlers
   b. Britons, Saxons, Norsemen and Normans
4. Medieval Europeans (1066–1500)
   a. Christian Migrants
   b. The Jewish Presence
   c. Craftworkers (focusing on settlers from the Low Countries)
   d. Merchants and Traders (concentrating on Italian, French and German merchants)
5. London and the Wider World (1500–1837)
   a. Patrons, Artists and Craftworkers (the role of the court in bringing in overseas artists and craftworkers to London; rulers from overseas such as William of Orange, the House of Hanover)
   b. The Early Black and Asian Presence
   c. The Jewish Resettlement
   d. Refugees and Migrants: the Dutch, Germans and Italians
   e. Refugees and Migrants: The Huguenots
6. The Heart of the Empire (1837–1945)
   a. Building London: the Irish Connection
   b. Living and Working in the Port (including Chinese, South Asian and African settlers)
   c. Imperial Citizens (with sections on African, African-Caribbean, Indian and Cypriot settlers)
   d. In Search of a Better Life (with sections of the late nineteenth and early twentieth-century Jewish settlers, Italians, Germans and Americans)
7. After the Empire (1945–present)
   a. Invited to Work (1945–1962)
   b. Through the Closing Door (1962–present)

Predictably the post-war section caused the greatest degree of debate amongst the project team and the network of advisors. Again, it would have been extremely difficult (particularly given the restricted space available) to have a separate section on each of the communities of overseas origin living in post-war London. On the other hand, treating the post-war period chronologically would be difficult, given its relative brevity in comparison with the other major sections of the exhibition.

The final decision was to treat the post-war period thematically in an introductory section, to set the scene, before visitors began with the prehistoric section (see below). The *chronological* changes within the last 50 years were then covered briefly in the 'After the Empire' section, above. The subjects of the themes themselves were naturally of crucial importance because they would determine the contemporary collecting and oral history programme. They – and the way in which the earlier sections were treated – would fundamentally determine the stance and credibility of the exhibition, both with existing visitors and the new audiences we hoped to attract. The exhibition team and academic advisors were determined that a critical stance should be taken which would not fight shy of tackling issues such as racism, unemployment and discrimination. Consultation with non-academic members of various communities, however, produced a different reaction. The general feeling was that such issues were frequently tackled in the media and would be well-understood by most people visiting the museum. They instead wanted the exhibition to concentrate primarily on showing the long presence and positive contribution of communities from overseas to London's economic and social life. From their point of view the exhibition should be celebratory rather than pessimistic or depressing. This disparity between the critically distanced academic view and the non-academic view has also been noted by Jane Peirson Jones in her analysis of Birmingham Museum's Gallery 33 project. As she notes 'Experience suggests that displays focusing on discord and social conflict will not necessarily be the chosen goal of a community's museum programme' (Peirson Jones 1992: 229).

The museum is itself a culturally high status artefact, and an exhibition in a museum conveys a hidden message of recognition by mainstream society (hence the desire of many 'minority' groups to see their history represented in museums). Understandably there is a desire on the part of many community members to be presented in a positive light in such an institution, which museum workers must be sensitive to. Similarly, some advisors expected a fairly traditional treatment of their history, avoiding – to their minds – gimmicks such as electronic 'games' or cartoons, so that it achieved parity with other mainstream accounts of history in museums. Even though the uncritical and traditional approaches to display technology may be against the instincts of curators themselves, they must be sensitive to these responses. In turn, this raises issues about the degree of influence that community consultation has over the final product in the museum. A range of different attitudes are possible, depending on the nature of the project. In the case of the 'Peopling of London' dealing as it did with a large number of communities and a huge time-span, a reasonably strong degree of direction and central editorial control was required to co-ordinate the many different aspects of the project. As the fundamental aim of the project was to tackle racist beliefs and mythical history, the exhibition team felt that it was important to examine racism in the exhibition, as well as stressing the positive aspects of the peopling of London. We chose, in the light of communities' advice, not to dwell on negative issues such as crime and social dislocation.

The post-war section 'World in a City' was therefore finally displayed along thematic lines which included the following:

The World in a City

a. Coming to London (examining the processes both of leaving the homeland and arriving in London)
b. A Liberal City? (noting the existence of racist beliefs and the search for scapegoats on whom to blame economic ills, and the existence of anti-racist movements amongst both the black and white communities)
c. A Place of Work (stressing the economic contribution made by post-war settlers from overseas)
d. London Lives (a largely photographic section showing the diversity of communities through depictions of children and schools, adulthood and old age)
e. Celebration Time (presenting an impression of the diversity of festivals, from the *mela* to the Notting Hill Carnival)

f.   Leisure (showing the contribution of overseas settlers to London's music, and other leisure activities)
g.   Religion (giving an impression of the range of religions existing in London)
h.   A Taste of London (a montage highlighting the revolutionary impact that the presence of overseas settlers has had on London's food)
i.   Fashion (a market stall displaying a selection of the mixture of dress styles that can be seen in the city which are influenced by traditional clothes from different communities)
j.   Shopping (a mock-up of a local store, with typical food associated with different communities and a range of community newspapers).

The contemporary collecting programme

Having decided on the themes of the exhibition, it was then possible to assess those areas where additional collecting was needed. The most obvious gap in the museum's collections was the virtual absence of oral history recordings relating to immigrants. With first generation post-war immigrants now mostly in their sixties and older, it was becoming increasingly important that a record be made of their experiences. The other major gap was a great dearth in the museum's collections of most kinds of material relating to post-war settlers. Thanks to the recent acquisition of a large photographic archive, some communities were relatively well-covered photographically, although many were not. There was some paper ephemera relating to racist and anti-racist groups of the 1970s, but otherwise no original two- or three-dimensional material. Clearly a process of collecting a range of post-war material would have to accompany the oral history campaign. The collecting exercise took the form of several inter-related strands.

The museum on the move

As part of the desire of the project team to consult widely and publicize the Peopling of London project as extensively as possible, it was decided to mount a series of outreach events using a mobile trailer called 'Museum on the Move'. The 20ft trailer, and the Range Rover used to pull it, were borrowed from the Museum in Docklands project, where they were used primarily for outreach work amongst schools. A small panel-based exhibition was mounted inside the trailer detailing the aims of the Peopling of London project. One wall included 20 questions about little-known aspects of London's cultural diversity (such as a picture of the first known black person living in London in 1511) with lift-up flaps revealing the answer, to give a taster of the kind of information that would be available in the final exhibition. The exhibition in the trailer concluded with a request for visitors to come forward to help with the project by sharing their memories with the team, or by lending some items for the exhibition. Leaflets were also produced giving further information and a voucher giving free admission to the museum. Staff were also on hand to talk to visitors and there was a small display on the sort of material that we were looking for, such as passports, letters and diaries.

In selecting venues for the 'Museum on the Move' to travel to, the team targeted areas that market research had shown did not generate many visitors to the museum. These also tended to be areas with a wide variety of ethnic minority groups. In total, 10 venues were visited between October 1992 and May 1993. The locales chosen were ones where people already congregated, such as markets, parks and supermarket car parks, so that a ready-made audience was available. These included Ridley Road Market in Dalston, the car parks at the Asda supermarket in Lavender Hill and Tescos in Brixton, Lampton Park in Hounslow, Surrey Quays Shopping Centre in Southwark and a public space near the Westway in North Kensington. Each visit was accompanied by a substantial publicity campaign, with its own press release, targeted particularly at raising local awareness of the project and of the visit of 'Museum on the Move'. This resulted each time in good coverage in the local press, on local and/or ethnic radio stations, and on London television. Over a thousand people visited the trailer on its visits, a good deal of publicity and support for the project was generated, and many people came forward with offers of loans of objects or offers to help by sharing with us their memories of settling in London.

Oral history collecting

The museum's Curator of Oral History, Rory O'Connell, took up many of the contacts made by Rozina Visram in her discussions with members of different communities and generated his own additional contacts for possible oral history interviewees. Through this, the 'Museum on the Move' campaign, and other people coming forward as a result of general publicity about the project, some 65 individuals were eventually interviewed and some 100 hours of recordings generated. Each individual was given a copy of their own recording, and was allowed to decide him or herself the extent to which the recording would be available to the public. While it was only possible to make brief segments of the interviews available in the exhibition, all of the tapes are deposited in the museum's archive and transcripts of all of the interviews are currently being prepared.

Collecting of objects, ephemera and images

In order to supplement the photographic material available for communities underrepresented in the museum's collections, three principal approaches were followed. The first of these involved a trawl of existing photographers' work conducted both by contacting photographic libraries and agencies and by publicizing our need for supplementary pictures amongst the photographic press. Our aim was, where possible, to use photographers from the communities themselves. This resulted in the identification of a large number of existing bodies of work amongst, for example, the Vietnamese, Somali, Chinese, Greek-Cypriot and Italian communities, that we were able to draw on in the exhibition and publications. The second strand consisted of commissioning a freelance photographer who had experience of photographing a number of communities, and good contacts within them, to photograph certain themes for inclusion in the post-war section of the exhibition. These included images of the Chinese Saturday School in Euston and the Chinese community centre in Gerrard Street, arranged through contacts with community leaders, and photographs of Turkish families at home. The third gap-filling exercise was for members of the museum's photography section to photograph buildings such as synagogues, mosques and restaurants, and general street scenes, to produce images for the photo-montages on the wall of the post-war section. Extensive collections were also made of ephemera around the themes outlined above for the post-war section. These included copies of current immigration documents, posters advertising training courses, racist and anti-racist material, business cards, menus and posters of festivals, plays, con-certs and clubs. A large range of newspapers was also collected to represent London's role as a centre for the ethnic press. It was decided that all of this material should be disposable, as it was to be displayed and stuck directly on the walls of the post-war section. It was therefore collected without being accessioned. Frequently, two examples of each item were collected so that the one not used in the exhibition could be incorporated formally into the collections in due course.

Collections of three-dimensional objects were a bigger challenge. On the one hand, the museum did not feel it possible to collect 'typical' objects associated with even a range of communities, given that space restrictions meant that any such attempt would inevitably tend towards the stereotypical. On the other hand the material with the greatest symbolic and emotional significance is that intimately associated with the lives of given individuals. Understandably they are usually unwilling to part with the objects, which would anyway tend to lose some of their significance on transfer to a museum.

The project team's policy was therefore to cover most of the themes photo-graphically or with ephemera, and to request the loan of objects from oral history interviewees when these would further illustrate themes that were covered by their oral history testimony. In this way material such as a suitcase brought by a woman from Trinidad and an identification badge worn by a child refugee from the Spanish Civil War were loaned to the exhibition, to illuminate highly personal stories in a concrete way.

The one exception to this policy was in the area of clothing and accessories. The museum's costume section had for some while felt the lack of material illus-trating contemporary cultural diversity and was anxious to use the project as an opportunity to enhance its collections. A small project was therefore set up which involved photographing people in the streets wearing clothes that summarized the mixture of ethnic fashions found in London, including combinations such as saris worn with anoraks and training shoes, or white people wearing Rastafarian-influenced clothes. Clothes and accessories similar to those in the photographs were then bought from retail outlets (with their provenance, price and other details documented). In the final exhibition the photographs were made into a montage which formed a backdrop to the mock street market stall on which the clothing was displayed.

The elements of the project

From all of this huge investment in research and collecting, the details of the indi-vidual elements of the project began to come together.

The exhibition

Always planned as the centrepiece of the project, the temporary exhibition was scheduled to run from 16 November 1993 to 15 May 1994. The six months' duration was dictated by the fact that this was the maximum period for which a number of major lenders were prepared to lend. There was no additional charge for entry to the exhibition, although there is an admission charge to the museum as a whole.

The basic format of the exhibition (the chrono-thematic approach) had already been formulated, and most of the objects and images chosen, by the time that the designer, John Redman of Redman Design Associates, was appointed. The rather awkward configuration of the space led to the decision to begin the exhibition (in the former shop area) with the most recent section, the survey of London's post-war cultural diversity. Visitors then moved down a corridor with a sound track of different languages spoken in London, compiled by multimedia students for a course project, to a small video area where a five-minute introduction to the main themes of the exhibition was played. It was felt important, given the didactic nature of the exhibition, that visitors were primed at an early stage with the basic concepts behind the exhibition which it was hoped would inform their subsequent viewing of the exhibits. The visitor then passed through the main body of the exhibition (divided into the sections described above), with the visit ending with the brief chronological overview of the post-war period 'After the Empire'. After passing a comments book and a panel giving details of further elements of the project, visitors found themselves back where they started, at the entrance to the exhibition. We hoped that, in completing the circle in such an obvious way, we would encourage visitors to look again on contemporary London in a new way, informed by the historical context provided by the exhibition.

The overall feel of the exhibition was intended to be informal, but serious. Generous use was made of bright colours, photographs and ephemera were stuck haphazardly on the wall, a good deal of material was on open display, and music could be heard in most parts of the exhibition. Specially commissioned set paintings above many of the cases gave a flavour of London of the period, while other elements, such as a giant suitcase, provided visual focus. There were four oral history points consisting of pairs of telephone handsets, each with a choice of four different two-minute extracts held on a digital sound store. An upright board provided a picture of each informant, some brief biographical details and an indication of the subject they were talking about.

Graphic panels were designed to be as attractive as possible, with liberal use of colour and illustrations, and text limited to a hundred words. Realizing the power of text to be interpreted in a variety of unintended ways, and of its ability to reinforce rather than challenge stereotypes, the exhibition team consulted extensively over the content and means of expression. All text was written by one person (Nick Merriman) to provide coherence of narrative. It was circulated to all team members, all curators whose periods were covered in the exhibition, education staff and senior management. It was then circulated to the informal networks of advisors who were asked to comment on it from the point of view of their community. This exercise led to some substantial revisions.

The selection of objects and images for the exhibition had largely been carried out in collaboration with advisors and other community members. Where particular images were felt to be contentious, further advice was taken specifically. For example, it was difficult to find images of the nineteenth-century Jewish community which did not have elements of caricature. Discussing possible images with the curator of the London Museum of Jewish Life helped to ensure that appropriate selections were made which would not offend or reinforce prejudices.

The final issue that had to be debated was that of language. Clearly it was impossible to translate all captions and panels into all languages spoken in London, or even the largest language groups. Audio guides would have been too expensive to provide and administer. On the other hand, the project's aim of inclusiveness and expanding audiences would not be assisted by the production of a solely English text. Eventually the decision was taken to provide a free leaflet summarizing the main chronological sections of the exhibition in the eight languages most spoken in London (as well as English): Urdu, Hindi, Gujarati, Arabic, Chinese, Greek, Polish and Spanish.

The publication

Given that the exhibition was of limited duration, it had been agreed from the outset that an important component of the project would be the production of an accompanying book. After discussion, the project team decided that the publication should not be a traditional catalogue of the material in the exhibition, but instead a series of historical essays on some of the major communities that are, or have been, distinctive in London. This particular approach was adopted because advisors felt that many people would wish to have convenient summaries of the history of their own community, which was something that was less easy to pick out in the more thematic approach in the exhibition.

In selecting authors for the volume, our first concern was with historical knowledge of individual communities. We also wished, where possible, to use historians who were members of the communities about which they were writing, to give the contributions something of an insider's point of view. It turned out that a good proportion of the academics we were using as advisors on the project in general were willing and able to contribute to the book, so we were able to recruit authors relatively easily. The book is introduced by a chapter, 'World in a City', drawing out themes from the long history of London's cultural diversity, followed by a chapter, 'Invisible Settlers', on overseas settlers from prehistoric times to the Huguenots, who are now absorbed into the general population (indeed they *constitute* the general population) and who are not culturally distinctive. The bulk of the book consists of 17 chapters on the larger contemporary communities, each illustrated, with occasional features called 'Voices of Experience' presenting more of the oral history testimony gathered for the project. The final section consists of a listing of all of the institutions in London, national and local, that were found during Rozina Visram's research to have material relevant to the 'Peopling of London' theme. Each entry has a brief summary of the kind of material available, and details about the institution. The book ends with an extensive bibliography. This final section, it is hoped, will prove a useful resource in itself and stimulate further research.

Resource pack

Discussions with advisory teachers and inspectors at an early stage of the project revealed a great deal of enthusiasm for the theme and a clear desire for teaching materials. A resource pack for the exhibition was developed by education department staff in consultation with advisors. It provides basic source materials for use in the classroom, and gives examples of how a visit to the exhibition could be tied into various aspects of the National Curriculum – not only history, but also English, geography, religious education, art, technology, music and mathematics. Four case studies, with illustrative material, are provided. The first concerns Elizabeth Lindsay, a black woman who became a companion and servant of Lady Elizabeth Murray, and lived at Kenwood House in London in the eighteenth century. The second is a study of the building on the corner of Fournier Street and Brick Lane in Spitalfields, which started out as a Huguenot church, was a synagogue for 80 years, and is currently a mosque. The third concerns Haji Mohammad Abdul Rahman, a Bengali sailor who served with the British merchant navy earlier this century and settled in London in 1965, and the fourth outlines the life story of Suzanne Samson, who came to England in 1939 as a child fleeing Nazi persecution because of her Jewish parentage. Her story is accompanied by a cassette. Some of the production costs were offset by sponsorship from Carlton Television.

The events programme

One of the key elements of the project was to be the programme of public events for adults and family groups. This, it was planned, would animate the static exhibition, attract new audiences, allow for participation, debate and comment, and enable certain issues to be treated in greater depth and with more subtlety than an exhibition permits. In choosing the different elements of the project, the team tried as much as possible to select the appropriate medium for each particular topic. Thus, while an exhibition is an excellent vehicle for a historical overview using objects, images, music and small amounts of text, it is not a good medium for a sensitive treatment of, for example, racism and anti-racism, which may be better served by a film, play or debate (although these issues were raised in outline form in the exhibition).

The public events programme was itself divided into a number of different elements. Alongside several one-off events such as the 'World Music in London' weekend held to mark the opening of the exhibition, poetry readings and drama performances, the principal strands consisted of a series of lectures designed to highlight the themes 'Women in a Multicultural Capital' and 'Images, Myths and Realities', and a series of 'focus weeks' which highlighted particular communities.

The two lecture series were put on by the museum's education department because it was felt that there were certain important themes relating to anti-racist education that warranted serious exposition using a traditional lecture format followed by discussion. The first theme was aimed at highlighting the often neglected experience of women in minority communities, while the second theme examined how stereotypical views of certain communities had become historically constituted, and how these contrasted with contemporary reality.

The focus weeks formed the core of the public programme. The principle behind these was that community groups were invited to use any or all of the museum's public spaces (entrance hall, galleries, temporary exhibition areas, lecture theatre and corridor, classroom and refectory) to represent, in their own terms, something of the community's historical presence and cultural distinctiveness in London, to other Londoners. The community groups were to have complete editorial control, with museum staff acting as facilitators and providing publicity. No suggestion was turned down unless it was financially or logistically unrealistic.

A total of seven focus weeks were arranged by groups from the Cypriot, Jewish, Chinese, Arab, Irish, African-Caribbean and South Asian Communities. In addition there was a refugee focus week co-ordinated by the Refugee Council, a Spitalfields focus week and a shorter programme examining the Soho area. The different groups organizing the focus weeks put on a huge variety of activities. These included formal lectures, discussion workshops, films, videos, dance, music, exhibitions, poetry readings, food tastings, drama, craft workshops and even a fashion show. Publicity was undertaken both by the museum and by the community groups themselves.

The museum also organized a number of programmes itself, such as the three-month residency of an artist, Timo Lehtonen. He produced works of art in response to the exhibition in a studio adjacent to the display space, which visitors could walk through. At Christmas the museum departed from tradition by, for example, organizing a Caribbean Christmas festivity, and displaying a 'Celebration Tree' which drew on the end-of-year celebrations of various cultures. The museum's season of films, 'Made in London', incorporated films that reflected London's cosmopolitanism.

The schools programme

The Peopling of London gave the museum's education department an opportunity to develop a programme for schools which targeted a much wider variety of curriculum areas and involved a broader range of interpretive strategies than had previously been possible.

In consultation with advisory teachers, the department organized a full programme of curricular teaching for ages 5–18, using methods such as exhibition trails, gallery drama presentations and creative art workshops, as well as more formal teaching sessions. The gallery drama sessions were also aimed at families, and included a dramatization of the life of Olaudah Equiano and a play called *The Amazing Arnos*, about a family of Italian settlers. Teachers' courses were held to show how the exhibition and resource pack might be used to cover aspects of various curricula.

The project also enabled education department staff to develop new links with schools, teachers and other educational organizations or projects. One of the most valuable of these links was with the group Artists and Craftspersons in Education (ACE). Museum staff worked with ACE members to develop a project which involved children from two London schools working with artists to produce their own creative responses to the exhibition theme. The project was a new departure for the education department in that it involved the same pupils working for a sustained period (five days) in the museum towards a specific outcome, which was the display of their work in a well-received temporary exhibition in the museum.

With encouragement from the museum a number of London primary schools used the exhibition to generate class research projects into pupils' own families to discover patterns of recent immigration and settlement. Elements of these projects were incorporated into the introductory 'World in a City' part of the exhibition, including video footage of a primary school pupil discussing his own family history, and a montage of photos, creative writing, pictures and transcripts of interviews with their parents by pupils from Lucas Vale School in Lewisham.

More explicitly anti-racist strategies were followed in a wide variety of school activities. For example, in the Refugee Focus Week, which was co-ordinated by the Refugee Council, there were two programmes for schools. One, for primary schools, 'Learning about Refugees', consisted of an interactive puppet show about refugees supported by the Save the Children Fund. Another, for secondary schools, 'Who are Refugees?' consisted of workshops about refugees coming to London, past and present. Both programmes invited pupils to question their attitudes and assumptions about refugee settlers.

Fundraising

Despite a great deal of effort, it was found to be very difficult to raise commercial sponsorship for the project. This was presumably because of the combined effect of the economic recession and the potentially controversial nature of the subject matter. In the event the only sponsorship forthcoming was £3,000 from Carlton Television towards the production of the resource packs.

However, the subject matter was fortunately one that matched the policies of a number of charitable funding bodies. The largest grant to the project came from the Baring Foundation, followed by the City Parochial Fund. Smaller donations from other charitable foundations and City livery companies brought the total raised to around £40,000. It is clear, though, that commercial sponsors are generally not willing to take risks on exhibitions dealing with potentially difficult subjects, whereas charitable and educational foundations may be, although they may not be able to cover all costs.

Marketing campaign

In attempting to generate a wider audience for the museum, an extensive marketing campaign was essential. The five audiences identified at the beginning of the project (existing audiences; current non-users, especially ethnic minorities; school groups; tourists; and museum professionals) were targeted by a combination of intensifying existing approaches and exploring new avenues.

General publicity coverage was intensified by targeting greater numbers of newspapers and radio stations than ever before. These included building up a press list of 250 contacts catering for minority community interests. Particularly useful was

Spectrum Radio, a station entirely devoted to specialist ethnic minority programming. For the first time, interviews were secured with satellite and cable TV stations. The education department sent information about the education programme and the exhibition to all primary and secondary schools in Greater London. All members of visiting school parties were given vouchers entitling children to come back free if they bought a paying parent with them.

Given the small budget available for marketing, it was decided to target much of the publicity campaign on London Underground poster sites. These were chosen because the tube is used both by a high proportion of Londoners, including those who do not visit museums, and a high proportion of tourists. A series of posters were designed, each targeting one of the three major communities in London today: South Asian, Chinese and African-Caribbean. The posters showed members of these groups dressed in the costume of pearly kings and queens – the traditional cockney Londoners – accompanied by a slogan pointing out the long period of time these communities have actually been in London. These were also sent to community centres in an attempt to target communities directly.

A second, more traditional, poster showing the oil portrait of Olaudah Equiano, was produced to target existing audiences and sent to local libraries and museums. The leaflets summarizing the content of the exhibition, which were made available in nine different languages, were also used as promotional material. Over 36,000 were sent directly to community centres and local libraries. As already mentioned, those communities more closely involved in the project, either in providing oral history interviewees, or organizing focus week activities, also generated their own publicity about the project, which greatly added to the coverage already provided by the museum.

Evaluation of the project: was it successful?

Measurement of the success or failure of a project is always relatively subjective and dependent on the approach taken. What follows is an attempt to assess some of the qualitative and quantitative information that was gathered as part of the evaluation programme. Quantitative research was undertaken by the museum's marketing department, while the qualitative evaluation was facilitated by the New Ethnicities Unit at the University of East London and carried out by Sara Selwood and Diana Irving for Art and Society. A fuller summary of the evaluation is available in Selwood (1996).

Some of the exhibition aims, such as widening the focus of the museum by presenting different community histories, or challenging views of what it is to be a Londoner, were achieved to a certain extent simply by implementing the project itself. Others, such as attracting and including new audiences, required more detailed assessment.

The exhibition

Over the course of its six-month run, the exhibition attracted 94,250 people. This compares favourably with the museum's previous exhibition *The Purple, White and*

Green on the women's suffrage movement, which attracted 62,547 over a nine-month period. Of visitors to the museum over the duration of the *Peopling of London* exhibition, 64 per cent actually visited the exhibition itself, and 10 per cent said they had come specifically to see it. This also compares favourably with the previous exhibition.

In terms of broadening the museum's audience, the exhibition can be deemed a success. From a pre-exhibition baseline of 4 per cent ethnic minority visitors, market research showed that the proportion of ethnic minority visitors to the museum during the exhibition rose to 20 per cent (but see note 2).

This did at least demonstrate unequivocally that, with extensive community liaison and a relevant theme, it is perfectly possible to attract people who do not normally visit museums. The challenge then becomes to persuade one-off visitors to become regular visitors (see below).

In order to assess the extent to which the exhibition achieved its other aims, it was necessary to undertake a qualitative evaluation exercise using focus groups. Four focus groups took part, including regular museum visitors and first-time visitors from minority communities. Reactions to the exhibition were also gauged from the comment books, from press reviews and from letters received.

From these it was clear that the fundamental aim of the exhibition – to demonstrate London's long heritage of cultural diversity – had been achieved. Typical comments were 'An important reminder that we are all immigrants, and that diversity has been part of life since well before 1950' and 'Made me realize that our history lessons at school were often biased'. Both press and visitors commented on the timeliness of the exhibition with respect to growing public concern about the activities of the British National Party in London (Selwood 1996).

Within this overall positive response there was a great deal of varied comment. While much was favourable, a significant proportion was critical in some way or other, showing that the exhibition theme provoked debate and raised thoughts about ways in which the theme could have been treated more satisfactorily. As with most such exercises, there was little consensus. For example, some visitors felt that there had been too much text in the exhibition. Others, however, wished there had been more information on their particular area of interest. Others complained that the exhibition was rather cramped or that there was not enough for younger children to do. Some felt that the lower quality of the finishes in the design compared with the main permanent exhibition implied a disparagement of the subject.

In terms of the content of the exhibition, the commonest criticism from the focus groups was that there was not sufficient information on their own particular community. This was particularly acute in instances where, due to the thematic approach, some contemporary communities did not have an explicit section devoted to them, but were subsumed in, for example, a section on 'Living and Working in the Port', as the Chinese were. This highlights the tension between separatist and inclusivist approaches outlined in an earlier section. The strongest criticism, almost inevitably, was voiced concerning the most recent section 'The World in a City', which many group members felt was unfocused and difficult to follow. Again, the decision not to concentrate on specific communities was criticized by community members themselves.

This aspect of the evaluation showed that, in tackling a subject such as the history of immigration and trying to attract a new audience, a museum creates a new constituency of expectation, even if its overall aims are successfully achieved. It is also clear that very broad-brush treatments may be unsatisfactory to those who have a detailed stake in one particular aspect of the broad theme. Nevertheless, the exhibition's aim to bring together the histories of diverse communities in an account of London's population, does seem to have been achieved. There was a noticeably strong call amongst visitors' comments and focus group members for the exhibition to be made a permanent feature of the museum.

Other elements of the project

The focus weeks, as predicted, were the most successful element of the public programme, and possibly of the whole project. The fact that they were co-ordinated by community groups themselves meant that each community added its own publicity to that of the museum, and brought its own audience. The majority of people coming for many of the focus week events were first-time visitors to the museum. The programme of events had the additional advantage of providing a further impetus to visit the museum, alongside the temporary exhibition. The focus weeks seem generally to have achieved their aim of adding another, deeper dimension to the necessarily relatively superficial treatment of an exhibition. In one instance, though, there was criticism that the museum had marginalized some of the community panel exhibitions brought in for the focus weeks by mounting them in non-prominent areas. In total, 135 activities or events were put on during the six months of the exhibition, generating 8,400 visits.

From the museum's point of view the publicity for the exhibition and events was successful. The wider press campaign, coupled with the television and radio coverage, as well as word of mouth, seems to have helped generate a wider audience. The column inches devoted to the exhibition were calculated to be the equivalent of £244,000 worth of advertising. Research showed that 7 per cent of visitors came to the exhibition purely because of the tube poster campaign, while 25 per cent recognized the posters once shown them. The downside of this was that some people felt that the exhibition did not deliver what the posters promised, as they could be read to imply an exhibition mostly concentrating on the Chinese, South Asian and African-Caribbean communities.

The *Peopling of London* book has sold over 3,500 copies to date and has been reprinted. The resource pack, however, has sold less than 500, possibly because the (cheaper) book may have been perceived as a competing, rather than a complementary item. At £14.95 it was unusually expensive for museum materials. Despite this, all education programmes and workshops were fully booked by school groups for the duration of the exhibition.

Conclusion and future prospects

The Peopling of London project was a new departure for the Museum of London, and one that was successful in achieving most of its aims. It showed that a museum can tackle supposedly difficult topics of contemporary relevance and place them in long-term historical context in such a way as to interest a new audience. Through the extensive campaign of outreach and consultation, the museum achieved a much higher profile amongst communities with whom it had previously had little or no contact. We also gained practical experience of the different forms that 'community involvement' can take. Given the complexity of the Peopling of London project, especially the number of communities represented, it was not practicable to 'hand over control' to a range of communities. In practice, museum staff had to develop the confidence to direct the project themselves and take full responsibility for the content of the project, while *consulting* closely with communities. The museum also learned that this approach is extremely time-consuming and resource-intensive. Altogether almost all of the museum's staff were involved in some aspect of the project, however briefly. An estimate of the amount of staff time spent on the project is around 1,000 person weeks. At the same time, we learned that concentrating our resources on a single project comprising a number of different elements was extremely beneficial both because of economies of scale and because of the resulting highly focused and high profile project. As a result, the Peopling of London was probably the most prominent project the museum has undertaken. Well over a year after its closure visitors continue to ask if the exhibition is still on, and a steady stream of requests for further information are received.

This in turn results in much higher expectations from London's communities. The task for the museum now is to ensure that those expectations are not dashed in the future. Accordingly, since the exhibition closed, a number of initiatives have been taking place to keep up its momentum. The first of these is the gradual refurbishment of the museum's permanent galleries, which will include explicit recognition of London's diverse communities from earliest times. An important element of this will be a display on post-war London that will be installed in 1996. The museum is also in the process of appointing a Community Access Officer with funding from the London's Docklands Development Corporation, Midland Bank and from Museum of London income. His or her role will be to continue some of the relationships already established with community groups, and work with them on community history projects resulting in exhibitions that will be shown at community venues and the Museum of London. This is part of a plan by the museum to use some of its spaces, such as the entrance hall, for community exhibitions. The Community Access Officer will also help formulate a long-term policy on community access. In the meantime, the museum has been adopting some of the approaches and lessons learned in the Peopling of London project to the rest of its activities. We hope and intend that from now on cultural diversity is no longer something dealt with in separate projects, but at the heart of everything we do.

Notes

Nick Merriman is director of the Manchester Museum and was formerly reader in Museum Studies at the University College London.

1   Figure taken from a 1993 survey by the Association of London Authorities, quoted in *The Runnymede Bulletin*, No. 266, June 1993, p. 6.

2   It is difficult to be precise about the absolute proportion of ethnic minority visitors to the museum before the *Peopling of London* exhibition because the

sample of visitors surveyed on this question was too small to be entirely reliable. The size of sample was increased during the exhibition.

3   The term 'ethnic minority' is an unsatisfactory one, both because of the difficulties of defining ethnicity and the implied marginalization of the term 'minority'. In the absence of a better alternative, however, the term is used here as a shorthand for non-dominant cultural groups self-defined through their ethnicity and/or religion.

4   Strictly speaking one needs to compare statistics of ethnic minority museum visitors *from London* against statistics of ethnic minorities in London overall. The former figures are unfortunately not available. It was nevertheless clear to museum staff that we were not attracting members of ethnic minority communities in anything like their proportions in London's overall population.

5   The project involved most of the museum's staff at some stage. The initiators of the project were Nick Merriman and Nichola Johnson, with help from Peter Stott. When the latter two moved to new posts, the basic project team developing the project consisted of Nick Merriman, Rozina Visram, Rory O'Connell, Sophia Pegers, Andy Topping, Geoffrey Toms, Emma Webb and Russell Clark, with contributions from Suzie Burt and William Tayleur. Other colleagues, too numerous to mention here, were involved at later stages.

References

Crew, S.R. and Sims, J.E. (1991) 'Locating authenticity: fragments of a dialogue', in I. Karp and S.D. Lavine (eds), *Exhibiting Cultures. The Poetics and Politics of Museum Display*, pp. 159–175, Smithsonian Institution Press, Washington, DC.

Fraser, P. and Visram, R. (1988) *Black Contribution to History*, CUES Community Division and Geffrye Museum, London.

Merriman, N. (1991) *Beyond the Glass Case. The Past, the Heritage and the Public in Britain*, Leicester University Press, Leicester.

Peirson Jones, J. (1992) 'The colonial legacy and the community: the Gallery 33 project', in I. Karp, C.M. Kreamer and S.D. Lavine (eds), *Museums and Communities. The Politics of Public Culture*, pp. 221–241, Smithsonian Institution Press, Washington, DC.

Selwood, S. (1996) *The Peopling of London: an Evaluation of the Exhibition*, Museum of London/New Ethnicities Unit, University of East London joint publication, London.

Trevelyan, V. (ed.) (1991) *'Dingy Places with Different Kinds of Bits'. An Attitudes Survey of London Museums amongst Non-visitors*, London Museums Service, London.

Visram, R. (1986) *Ayahs, Lascars and Princes. The Story of Indians in Britain 1700–1947*, Pluto Press, London.

Chapter 24

Inspiration Africa!

Using tangible and intangible heritage to promote social inclusion amongst young people with disabilities

Viv Golding

Introduction: aims and structure

IN THE SOCIO-CULTURAL LANDSCAPE of the twenty-first century the museum has power. The museum has the power of sanctuary, shrine, place of knowledge, forum and a vital role in democracy. This chapter will focus on the power of the anthropology museum, the tangible and intangible collections, as a forum for democratic exchange to promote social inclusion and community cohesion amongst young people with disabilities. The museum, as it will show, has the potential to function as a 'frontier': a zone where learning is created, new identities are forged; new connections are made between disparate groups and their own histories. In some cases, tangible and intangible collections will be shown to have a new and more positive power: to help disadvantaged groups of young people with disabilities to raise self-esteem.

The chapter is structured into two main sections. First, a definition of key terminology and the theoretical underpinnings of the Inspiration Africa! project at the Horniman Museum, South London, are provided. Then the creative work of young people involved, from two of the twelve schools, illustrates the value of constructivism informing museum/school partnerships. Finally some concluding remarks and recommendations for future project work at other locations are made.

Source: Paper presented for ICME at Museums and Intangible Heritage ICOM 2004 general conference, Seoul, Korea, October 2–8, 2004, facilitated by a British Academy travel grant.

Terminology

Intangible heritage and tangible heritage

In October 2003, at its 32nd General Conference, UNESCO produced a working definition of intangible cultural heritage, which highlighted:

> . . . the practices, representations, *expressions*, knowledge, skills – *as well as* the instruments, *objects*, artifacts and *cultural spaces* associated therewith – that communities, groups and in some cases individuals recognize as part of their cultural heritage. This intangible cultural heritage, transmitted from generation to generation, is *constantly recreated* by communities and groups in response to their environment, their interaction with nature and their history, and it provides them with a *sense of identity* and continuity, thus *promoting respect for cultural diversity and human creativity*. (UNESCO 2003: 4) [my emphasis]

I emphasise three main points from this definition. First, the importance of tangible objects *as well as* the practices associated with their production and use. An idea, which seems to mark a 'both and' feminist approach, as distinct from the 'either or' of dualist thought (Golding 2000). Second, the notion of *constantly recreating* is vital, as creativity and creating something new is central to this paper. The chapter does not speak of the sterile processes involved in any simple reproduction of cultural objects and echoes Fanon's warning against the desire of colonised societies to preserve 'mummified fragments' of culture (Fanon 1993: 41). Finally, it is argued that embedding both tangible and intangible aspects in a complex peopled domain strengthens an individual and community *identity*, while pointing to a wider shared humanity, which promotes *respect for cultural diversity* or intercultural understanding at a global level.

My thesis here also leans on Giovanni Pinna's paper for ICOM News (Pinna 2004). Pinna notes the 'indefinite boundaries between': expressive objects, the language and the oral tradition from which they emerge, as well as the symbolic and metaphorical meanings attached to objects that derive from their histories and the interpretations to which the museum contributes through the exhibition process prompting the visitor's individual interpretation. Pinna's comments helpfully raise the perspective of the museum visitor and their personal meaning-making alongside curatorial intentions. While the visitors' initial interpretations, according to constructivism, are based on prior knowledge, personal background and the socio-cultural group they belong to, Pinna reminds us that the museums' strategies of display and operational practices are also inevitably influenced by wider socio-philosophical factors (Hein 1999; Macdonald 1996). Since the 1970s, motivated in part by the postcolonial demands of previously subjugated people, museums in the West seem to be moving from their traditional position of temple of cultural authority to a more dynamic forum of dialogical exchange and debate. In this new location museums are increasingly engaged in self-reflexivity and raising 'questions about knowledge and power, about identity and difference, and about permanence and transience' (Macdonald 1996: 1–2).

In the light of Macdonald's questions this chapter will explore a creative zone between tangible and intangible cultural heritage. Specifically the personal responses of learning disabled pupils, to a new framing of knowledge on African objects, Horniman's *African Worlds* exhibition, which privileged perspectives from Africa and the Diaspora.

Special educational needs. Medical and social models

Four of the twelve schools involved in the 'Inspiration Africa!' project were exclusively for pupils with learning disabilities and two of the mainstream secondary schools were located in Educational Action Zones (EAZ) where almost one third of the pupils had learning disabilities. 'Inspiration Africa!' pupils had a range of learning disabilities and throughout the projects team leaders worked in 'effective partnership' to facilitate activities disabled pupils might 'do with support', rather than focus on 'what they can't do' (Valuing People 2004: 14). As team leaders we developed educational programmes for disabled pupils that were characterised by high expectations for all. We recognised that pupils with disabilities may take longer to learn new skills and grasp complex information but were determined that as much choice and control over their project work as possible should be enabled.

The Horniman partnership worked with the social model of disability, which points to the social construction of disability and false ideas of normality within the creation of capitalism (Barnes *et al.* 2002). The social model highlights social barriers and environmental issues, and locates problems and prejudices within the minds of able-bodied people, individually or collectively (Oliver 1996). This model is distinct from the medical or individual model, which is influenced by biological determinism and focuses on medically orientated control, 'care and cure' agendas (Oliver 1996).

Employing an appropriate model and terminology was regarded as crucial to the success of the project. Since language work was central to many project activities disabling labels were interrogated and terms such as 'handicap', derived from earlier periods of history when disabled people went begging 'cap in hand', were avoided as denoting passivity.

The language activities were enjoyed by the pupils who simply wanted to be included in ordinary activities and not always seen as 'special' (Valuing People 2001: 11).

In the UK 1 in 4 families have a disabled member and 8.7 million disabled people or 15% of the population, are covered by the Disability Discrimination Act (DDA). The DDA was passed in 1995 to enshrine the rights of disabled people to social inclusion and highlight the responsibilities of employers as service providers. By October 2004 the DDA requires 'reasonable access' to buildings, and institutions such as museums will need to ensure their policies, procedures and practices enable access for all members of society. Horniman was concerned to offer a range of auxiliary aids and services including ramps, loops and braille labels as far as possible throughout the 10-year period of my work there from 1992, including 'Inspiration Africa!' Therefore Horniman was reasonably well prepared to address the new Labour Government agenda based on 'social inclusion, civil rights, choice and independence' (Valuing People 2001: 14).

Social inclusion, social exclusion and community cohesion

In 1997 the Social Exclusion Unit established by the New Labour Government defined social exclusion in holistic terms. The 'shorthand term' Social Exclusion was intended to replace the concept of 'poverty' to encompass holistically 'what can happen when people or areas suffer from a combination of linked problems such as unemployment, poor skills, low incomes, poor housing, high crime, bad health and family breakdown' (www.socialexclusionunit.gov.uk/, 17 September 2003). At the time of writing, the latest government report 'Tackling Social Exclusion' importantly returns the discussion to the earlier emphasis on the economic basis of social exclusion, as passed through families from one low income generation to the next and effects certain high risk groups, including people from 'ethnic minorities' and people with 'disabilities', which the 'Inspiration Africa!' project targeted (www.socialexclusionunit.gov.uk/tackling, 10 October 2004: 4).

While 'Inspiration Africa!' cannot claim to have alleviated the wider problems of economic deprivation the participants certainly developed a range of skills, which is one key factor highlighted by the government documents. Horniman also became the sort of location that David Fleming helpfully attached to the government definition of social inclusion in the museum context, one 'that inspires and uplifts people, that confronts them with ideas, that helps them understand a little more about themselves and their surroundings' (Fleming 2002: 224).

I further argue that 'Inspiration Africa!' enabled Horniman to utilise cultural objects, 'things of quality', to progress social cohesion (Smith 1998: 37). Social Cohesion, according to Chris Smith, New Labour Minister for Culture's recommendation is dependent upon two factors. First making available '. . . cultural experience and activity . . . to the many not just the few' (ibid.). Second, linking these cultural experiences to an understanding that certain aspects, which determine identity construction, are shared in common across cultural divides. As Smith noted.

> . . . developing our own individual sense of identity through cultural experience, and touching *a sense of shared identity* through shared cultural emotion, must be achievable by everyone, no matter what their circumstances or class background or location may be. (Smith 1998: 37) [my emphasis]

Smith later contends it is exclusion from a *sense of shared identity* that weakens communal bonds and leads to a fragmentation of society. During 'Inspiration Africa!' Horniman was able to illustrate British society as a 'community of communities' through creatively connecting its African cultural artefacts and the intangible oral traditions with the lived experience of UK pupils (Parekh Report 2002: 3). 'Inspiration Africa!' was a proactive project that emphasised the responsibility and role of the museum as agency on the Government's inclusion and cohesion agenda.

Learning disabled pupils access the National Curriculum

In reaching out to excluded audiences and developing innovative ways of progressing intercultural understanding, it was crucial to work within the access guidelines of the National Curriculum for England. The guidelines state three principles that are essential to developing an inclusive curriculum. 'Setting suitable learning challenges, responding to pupils' diverse learning needs and overcoming potential barriers to learning and assessment for individuals and groups of pupils'. Imaginatively adhering to these guidelines enabled the key aim of the National Curriculum, to 'provide opportunities for all children to learn and to achieve' a high degree of 'success', by offering 'varied teaching approaches' that build on 'diverse interests and experiences', matching 'challenges of work to the pupils' skills' and ensuring a degree of 'success' (National Curriculum 2000).

'Inspiration Africa!' project work aimed to promote four key skills. First, 'communication: speaking and listening, reading and writing a range texts'. Second, 'working with others, contributing to discussion, valuing different perspectives, co-operating and meeting challenges together'. Third, 'creative thinking, extending ideas and using imagination'. Finally, 'evaluation, valuing, have confidence in judgments'. The project work outlined in the next section will clarify the relationship of communication in the English curriculum to the museum context.

Stories, histories and a Benin plaque

The 'Inspiration Africa!' team-leaders at Marjorie McClure School (SEN) included Sola Oyelele (writer/storyteller), Tony Minion (artist), Jacqui Callis (ICT specialist), and myself (museum educator). I had deliberately selected a multiracial team, who all felt a strong resonance or personal affinity with the museum objects, as well as a determination to employ them as part of an educational agenda, to challenge racism in contemporary multicultural Britain. The composition of my team follows research findings, which demonstrate that if the curriculum and the people who deliver it positively reflect multiracial society this has a positive effect even on the most disaffected audiences, who are too often African Caribbean boys (Golding 2000).

Marjorie McClure School is situated in the London Borough of Bromley and the school population is predominantly white working class. Research shows there is an even more urgent need for antiracist-multicultural education in areas such as this, where media stereotypes and misunderstandings persist partly because diverse communities never actually meet. Working in partnership a Benin plaque from Nigeria was selected as the key object for the creative work with Marjorie McClure pupils in Year 7, who are aged between 11 and 12 years old, and the word 'Stories' was chosen as their key theme.

Throughout the *African Worlds* exhibition at Horniman and on a website link, there is an excellent text accompanying the objects and providing valuable new research information, which was written by the four-person Anthropology Advisory Panel (AAP). The AAP comprised African, Caribbean and UK scholars: Emanuel Arinze, Joseph Eboreime, Catherine Chan and Anthony Shelton. In their Benin text the AAP highlight positive features of the socio-cultural background in which the object was made. For example Benin is described as 'a powerful and sophisticated West African Kingdom, founded in the 11th century by the Edo people', which 'commanded great respect from the early Portuguese visitors in the late 15th and early 16th centuries'. The text also traces the purchase of the plaque to events in 'the late 19th century when British soldiers destroyed its capital' and 'looted the city of its rich art traditions' . . . which, 'tragically and ironically, first alerted Europe to the level and range of achievement of Benin artists'. This text, written at a reading age of 16+ years was not immediately accessible to our pupils with learning disabilities and so the 'Inspiration Africa!' team-leaders developed achievable language activities to build on the pupils 'diverse interests and experiences' (National Curriculum 2000).

At Marjorie McClure 'Inspiration Africa!' team-leaders introduced the project on day one through the concept of naming. At the outset, just under the header the museum text explains the plaque was made by an 'unknown' craftsperson, but later in the third paragraph of the text panel a 'Chief' is mentioned by name, 'Uwangue'. Using this information the pupils began to learn about the importance of naming for all cultural groups, including the Edo speaking people of Benin City in Nigeria who made the plaques. They were able to draw similarities between the histories of the UK and Nigeria, which record the most powerful people and the events of their lives. Then Sola spoke about her recent visit to Benin City where the oral tradition of storytelling with musical performance is still strong and she led a name game where name sounds were invented.

Sola started the game by using her own name 'Sola' and asked the group to imagine wind whistling through the trees calling her name, shhhhhooooollllllaaaa. Everyone enjoyed practising wind talk around Sola's name and soon felt confident to try experimenting with their own names, which included: Chris – biting apple, Sarah – ssssnake, Thomas – steam train and Viv – vruuuuuu vacuuuum cleaner! This initial work established a fun framework for the project and set all the participants at their ease, since enjoyment and feeling comfortable are vital factors necessary to promote learning (Hein 1999).

Next the group mind-mapped the name of the project 'Inspiration Africa!' and decided inspiration means excitement or being interested in something. Then individuals and small groups of pupils played musical instruments, part of the *African Worlds* 'hands on' collection, which always arouses 'minds on' interest (Hein 1999).

Minds on activities with museum objects are designed to extend quality looking and promote critical thinking on the contextual information attached to the object and the wider socio-political world of past and present times from which the object emerged. For all pupils, including those with learning disabilities, understanding of the past is never complete but always partial and never instantaneous but takes time. During 'Inspiration Africa!' work at Marjorie McClure the team-leaders developed creative work that would enable pupils to extend the period looking, thinking and connecting their increasing understanding of objects originating from the ancient Benin Kingdom, Nigeria with their everyday life experiences in London, UK. Creative writing consistently proves a fruitful means of achieving this.

For example, working from musical instruments Sola encouraged the pupils to think of words that expressed music and they wrote acrostic poems. To write an acrostic poem, a word is written lengthways down a page and each letter is used to start the first line of the poem. This simple structure is a helpful way of working on language activities with all pupils in the museum context and is especially productive with learning disabled groups. The pupils wrote a joint acrostic poem on the whiteboard before writing their own poems. They used their names to describe favourite things in their own lives, to begin making personal present day connections with objects, which aids understanding of the past. Two examples of Majorie McClure's 'name' and 'things I like' poems illustrate this work.

> Charli likes football
> Harry Potter is my favourite book
> Arsenal is my team
> Riding my bike is fun
> Lots of toys are great to play with
> I like my friends in G3B and G3A
> Nigel
> Is twelve, he
> Goes to school, he
> Eats fish and chips and ketchup at
> Lunchtime

In the afternoon of day one the pupils used the school's excellent Internet facilities to look at their Key Object, the Benin plaque, which they would be seeing at the museum on day two of the project. According to the museum text the plaque shows Chief Uwangue 'wearing ceremonial dress of coral headdress and necklace, pea bell anklets and highly decorated skirt'. At this time the pupils also explored a modern museum plaque made especially for the handling collection, which represented Oba Ohen with similar ceremonial dress and mudfish legs. Mudfish, commonly denoting the supreme power of the Oba, over the land as well as the watery sea realms of the God Olokun, was employed by Ohen to explain his stroke and the need to be supported in movement. This plaque enabled everyone to feel the textures and discuss the features of a possibly 'tall story', which prompted their own imaginative writing and was vital for one blind pupil to access the curriculum (Picton 1995: 399).

The museum object and the text prompted the team leaders to provide original African garments, specially purchased from Markets in Brixton London, Lagos, Nigeria and Kumasi Ghana, which permitted the pupils to literally 'try on' aspects of another culture. While the children were dressed up Sola gave them parts and told the story of 'How music came to the world'. This story, from the Yoruba people of Nigeria, is about a talented young man who was the drummer for his village and whose family name is prefixed by Ayan, which Sola explained means he comes from a drumming family. The story ended with the whole class playing music together again.

After break Year 7 looked at the materials and technologies of Benin plaque production, the complex 'lost-wax method', which the pupils saw illustrated in a video. The pupils drew the musical instruments and representations of the sounds that they made. Hands were waved to form the shapes made by the instruments before they were drawn. Then Tony demonstrated the screen-printing process and the pupils worked from their drawings simplifying, enlarging, cutting out shapes and placing them onto fabric to create their own banner. Raffia and wool were also used to create patterns that represented the sounds from the instruments. The screens were placed over the images and pupils painted freely through the screen. The banner was printed twice with the first print using cold colours and the second print using warm colour, work which offered an opportunity to discuss the colour of the metal that the Benin plaques are made from, a warm 'red', the colour of life-blood that the Edo people specially prize. This dialogue was prompted again by part of the museum text on the plaque material, 'brass', a material 'reserved for royalty . . . enduring and permanent, and its "red" and shiny qualities were believed to be protective of the king and the kingdom'. At the end of the session the class posed in front of their banner.

When Jaqui documented this day she asked the class to suggest some captions for the photographic record that the team-leaders were in the habit of making, since images of individuals and groups with the handling objects are seen to prompt memories and further creative activity. The pupils made some lively comments that Jaqui recorded on tape. The following are taken as illustrating the variety of feelings.

> In this picture I am playing the drum – it is called a talking drum. On my head I am wearing a brightly coloured hat. Sola put the cloth on my head. It felt BAD! playing the drum.

> It sounds like music boom, boom, boom, boom, boom. Nice. Noise. The stick moves bam! The strings moving boonder! boonder! boonder! la, la, la, la, la, la. I WAS EXCITED, LOOK AT ME!!!!!

> I like the African hat from the Horniman museum. In this picture I look pretty and I'm enjoying myself. I think I will enjoy the project.

> My friend dressed up as a Queen and wore some very colourful clothes. Then we played the instruments after, I played the shaker.

> Tony is holding the screen-printing. We printed a shaker – blue, red, orange, yellow. I like Tony – because I JUST DO.

There was a strong sense of irritation in this last remark, which shows a pupil, at the end of a long tiring day, exasperated by the effort of extended dialogue and the work of evaluation demanded by the National Curriculum. This provided a salutary lesson for team-leaders, who reminded themselves that, just as museum text can be too long and prevent successful communication, so can museum activities.

On day two of the project the school visited Horniman Museum and the pupils talked about the 'stories' on the Benin plaques as illustrations of important events from the history of the Benin people. 'Stories' was their key word and Sola talked about where you can find them. She also asked about their favourite stories and things to draw and write about, reinforcing the work on favourite things started on the introduction day. Taking every opportunity to reinforce learning has proved especially important for pupils with learning disabilities and the desire to repeat the pleasurable experiences triggered by the object handling made this a simple task.

At the museum Sola told two stories from memories of her family life in Nigeria, called 'Pepper Soup' and 'The Bike Ride', which led the class to discuss: where stories can come from (Africa, around the world, Bromley, home, brain or imagination and memories); where you can find stories (in books, comics, magazines, from parents, grandparents, other family members, artists and teachers); favourite stories (Cinderella, Goldilocks, Pokemon, Lion, Matilda, Witch and Wardrobe); favourite things, buildings, pets (cats, dogs – dalmation, beadle) and people. At the end of the session the pupils were asked to bring in a funny story from home to work on in the project.

These stories were developed throughout the week and read out at the beginning of day four. Some were written and some recorded onto audio tape. The stories were later illustrated and transferred onto screens to be printed and also scanned into computers to be worked on digitally. Two stories are provided below as representative of this work.

Mrs Doubtfire

One day it was my brother's anniversary and my nan had some curlers in her hair and I said 'I got a nickname for you nan, Mrs. Doubtfire!' My brother had a camera and he sneaked round the door and he took a picture of her and her face dropped down to the floooooooorrrrrrr . . .

The Flower

About four years ago I was a bridesmaid for Mrs Cox. I had to wear a nice dress that was cream and light green. I also wore cream shoes. I got dressed and ready at my home, and then I went to Mrs Cox's home to meet her and the other bridesmaid.

I had really long shiny curly hair, they put a big fresh flower in my hair. When we were all ready we got into the very posh car and drove to the church. On our way there Mrs Cox had to keep placing my flower back into my hair, because it kept slipping down as my hair was so shiny. In the end as it did not want to stay in my hair, Mrs Cox tucked it into my waistband.

On day four of the project Sola also did a 'too big for' frame poem. A frame poem provides a structure for pupils to complete their ideas, in this case 'I'm too big for . . .' First Sola asked: 'What are we too big for?' The class answered: too big for chocolate, too big for sitting on the potty, too big for sucking dummies. Then the team-leaders pointed out that we are never too big for museums, just to amuse the group and everyone made up a line for Sola. Finally Sola talked about language and how we say things like 'you know what I mean' at the end of sentences. From this Sola made a poem song/game up and all of the class did a round.

> Person 1 says 'I'm too big for sucking my thumb.'
> Person 2 says 'I'm too big for Bob the Builder.'
> Person 3 says 'I'm too big for lower school.'
> Then all together say:
> 'You know yeah, you know yeah,
> I'm too big for that yeah.'
> 'I'm too big for that you know,
> I'm too big for that yeah.'

All pupils involved in 'Inspiration Africa!' had the opportunity to evaluate each day of their project work through interview or specially designed forms provided on the Internet. Some worksheet forms gave pupils the opportunity to choose a photograph, write a caption for it and send it to Cloth of Gold. The following comments tell about their favourite part of the project and something they would like to have been different.

> The screen-printing was good and the writing was good. It was hard writing the poem because I had to do something personal and I only tell people that I trust.

> My favourite part was doing the drawings and screen-printing with Tony. I have really enjoyed this project, I wish it didn't have to end but mum says all good things come to an end.

This pupil's family, along with the families of her classmates in Year 7, became regular visitors to Horniman, despite living at a considerable distance in Bromley. It could therefore be argued that while one project ended for one school group, the positive project experiences were a motivating factor in cultural inclusion for their wider family groups. Motivation, with reference to another school project will be considered in the next section.

Facing fears with artefacts: inclusion and motivation

A Midnight Robber Carnival Mask was selected as the key object by the 'Inspiration Africa!' team-leaders, for a project on the key word theme of Bravado, with Year 9 boys from Mallory Secondary School. Mallory is situated in an Education Action Zone (EAZ) in Lewisham. EAZs are a geographical focus of special effort to improve achievement in the UK and at Mallory the underachievement of African Caribbean boys was a particular cause of concern for the schoolteacher, Mary Mabey, which determined her decision to work exclusively with these boys on 'Inspiration Africa!' I offer some student voices to describe their project.

> We used the Midnight Robber's hats [in Horniman] to inspire an exploration of bravado. We looked at the use of metaphors and similes. Then we developed our own boasting poems and raps. We worked in two groups developing our own Midnight Robber character, looking at the alter ego of the Robber – the face behind the mask.

In dialogue with the team-leaders at the planning stage of this project, bravado emerged as an appropriate key word, since it accurately described the aggressive and disruptive face that the boys presented to the school world. Before 'Inspiration Africa!' the boy's bravado behaviour was destructive. It often led to exclusion from school, which resulted in a downward spiral of poor academic performance, uncontrollable bravado, exclusion and worse academic performance.

The 'Inspiration Africa!' team-leaders decided to explore the root causes of the boy's negative school attitude with them as a group, rather than simply treat the symptom with exclusion. In 2000 the Office for Standards in Education (Ofsted) report attributed the multiple levels of deprivation, which the boys suffered as at least partly responsible for the poor performance in the Standard Attainment Test (SATs). The school role also showed a higher than average number of newly arrived students who were learning to speak English as an additional language. Mallory's Midnight Robber project therefore aimed to present a range of new learning opportunities at the museum/school frontiers, for the students to creatively express bravado in ways that were not destructive and did not depend on Standard English for successful expression.

Csikszentmihalyi's and Hermanson's thought on motivation can be employed to support praxis on this point. In devising innovative learning opportunities, the team-leaders vitally based project work on the key object in the museum, the Midnight Robber Carnival Mask. Looking at this spectacular mask powerfully engaged the sense of sight and provided a fundamental 'hook' to arouse the student curiosity and provoke 'situational interest' (Csikszentmihalyi and Hermanson 2000: 149). Situational interest describes the sense of wonder, which is aroused in the visitor by the 'novelty, surprisingness, complexity and ambiguity' inherent in an object, but this may have been of short-term significance unless some connection was made with the visitors 'individual interest' (ibid.). Individual interests are characterised by Csikszentmihalyi and Hermanson as 'relatively enduring preferences for certain topics, subject areas, or activities' (ibid.).

The individual interests of the Mallory students revolved around music, especially rap music, and the Inspiration Africa! work harnessed this interest in the literacy, ICT and artwork. A useful strategy, which Horniman educators often employ to improve literacy is the use of a simple frame format for the students to organise their ideas around. Midnight Robber characters in Trinidad provide a rich source of poetic rap frames, which use imaginative metaphors to shock and to amuse their audience. The Mallory students particularly admired the examples they found during ICT work on the web with Jaqui, such as this extract from the Satellite Robber album.

I am the Agent of Death Valley. From the day my mother gave birth to me the sun refused to shine, the earth began to tremble! Terror hit the city streets! At the age of one my toys were cannons and machine guns. At the age of two I had met and slain all mockmen like you.

This notion of boasting about origins impressed the Mallory students who were inspired to create their own bravado rap poems around a simple frame, 'at the age of . . . I . . .' The rap frame can continue until imagination is depleted, but the team-leaders were mindful of the boys limited attention span and restricted the length of the poem to six lines, beginning with the creation of a name for the character, spoken in the Robber persona 'I am . . .' This example of a rap frame poem illustrates this work.

I am The Angel of Darkness

From the day my mother gave birth to me I . . . could kill people with my acid tongue and the foul breath coming from my lung.

The sky became dark, the stars became black.

At the age of 1 I . . . was as fast as a bullet flying through a gun, I was as hot as the sun, I became master of all evil, firing machine guns, cannons and missiles with lots of style.

At the age of five I . . . ate five bears alive, I took a dive, the earth split into four pieces and I created a new species.

At the age of eight I . . . had robbed and assassinated everyone in Tony Blair's government, because they wouldn't pay the rent.

At the age of twelve I . . . could dig and delve my way out of any difficulty. I was ruler of my country and brought terror to the streets by trampling my enemies with my feet.

Now I . . . am thirteen I look very mean and clean. Now I am killing other Midnight Robbers who try to control the city, for them I have no pity.

In this way the team-leaders ensured that the 'challenges' of the task matched and extended the person's 'skills' and one condition for 'flow' learning was satisfied (Csikszentmihalyi and Hermanson 2000: 150). Flow is characterised as a state of 'intrinsic' motivation, which denotes deep pleasurable engagement in a task undertaken entirely for its own sake and no external reward (ibid.). Csikszentmihalyi and Hermanson usefully distinguish between intrinsic motivation and extrinsic motivation, which is marked by an external reward of some sort, such as good examination results. Artistic activity, chess, mountaineering are cited as examples of activities that induce flow in the participants questioned by Csikszentmihalyi and Hermanson and the strong desire to continue art, language and ICT activities during 'Inspiration Africa!' confirm their findings. Following the rap work Mallory pupils readily developed a series of metaphors around the printing experience and I offer a selection here as evidence of this claim.

When I print I am as powerful as a lion and as talented as Michael Jackson.

When I print I am as proud as punch and I thought *it was the best*.

When I was printing I was as nervous as a fox in the middle of speeding traffic.

But *my print came out brilliant*. I was very relieved.

[My emphasis]

These metaphors also highlight a mixture of powerfulness and nervousness, which is probably part of our shared human experience. No one is really all-powerful and it seems important for young people to develop a repertoire of appropriate character tools to lead fulfilling lives. Developing techniques of dialogical exchange permit a range of feelings and fears to be acknowledged and verbalised. On this point I extend the remaining conditions necessary for the state of flow. In addition to skills meeting tasks, Csikszentmihalyi states that individuals need to feel free from anxiety, fear and other 'negative' states to experience flow learning (Csikszentmihalyi and Hermanson 2000: 151).

My Horniman experience demonstrates that a supportive environment can be nurtured at the museum frontiers and in this safe space individuals might share certain fears and anxieties. Before 'Inspiration Africa!' the Mallory boys were trapped in limiting self-defeating modes of interaction at school, constantly playing the role of hard man and ignoring the softer sides of their personalities. The project vitally enabled them to explore this softer side and ultimately to engage with the school community as more rounded individuals, who were willing to return to learning tasks, again and again. According to Csikzentmihalyi's thesis, the desire to return to the learning situation is attributed to the flow learning process. Flow learning is of long term benefit since the pleasurable feelings encountered during flow incur a desire to repeat the learning experience.

Another frame rap task will demonstrate these points. The following example of the Robber's Alter Ego task is selected as typical.

> I am HARD LIKE metal . . . I am *soft like* water in a kettle
> I am HARD LIKE steel . . . I am *soft like* orange peel
> I am HARD LIKE iron . . . I am *soft like* Diane
> I am HARD LIKE wood . . . I am *soft like* a coat hood
> I am HARD LIKE a chair . . . I am *soft like* hair

For the Alter Ego task the boys were divided into two groups, HARD and soft. They worked in pairs with one HARD lad working with a *soft* lad. The partners were encouraged by the rap poet/musician Andrew Ward to use their bodies and especially their voice to enhance the words of their poems and really enter into the Robber characters. Because the writing skills of the students were weak Horniman volunteers were enlisted to act as scribes. The scribes were importantly able to assist the movement of suppressed feeling into speech and then into a written form. This experience provided evidence that even the most 'troublesome' [school phrase] boys could be motivated and could achieve a degree of success, if they were offered the opportunity to engage at a more personal one to one level with a mature person. Perhaps Horniman staff could be said to act as listening guides, facilitating a student 'apprenticeship in thinking' here (Rogoff 1990).

Conclusion

In this chapter I made a strong case for the museum to facilitate the use of tangible museum objects *and* intangible oral tradition as triggers to creative dialogue for pupils with learning disabilities, who are amongst the most socially excluded groups in the UK (Valuing People 2001). This *both/and* approach to the curriculum was viewed as an appropriate learning pathway for everyone regardless of age or ability levels to access culture and promote intercultural understanding, although the chapter demonstrated that an object-centred dialogical work was particularly motivating for pupils who were underachieving academically or in danger of becoming disaffected since it offered a high degree of academic success.

Success was achieved during 'Inspiration Africa!' through the social experience of opening pupil's minds to critical thinking based on an idea of learning that included: close multisensory work with African objects; discussing ideas alongside feelings to interrogate what is considered 'fact' about Africa in the contemporary museum and the media; and most importantly making creative connections between the communities the objects emerged from and the daily lives of the pupils. Overall 'Inspiration Africa!' work at the museum and school frontiers provided a symbolic forum space to affirm positive new identities for individuals, as well as a notion that aspects of cultural identity and values are shared in common amongst people of the world.

In practical terms, other museum sites concerned with extending socially excluded pupil's communication skills and literacy levels are recommended to use the key word, acrostic poem and sentence frame techniques outlined here. These simple, low cost and effective techniques have been developed in a creative partnership, which opened the museum to a range of alternative voices and positively affected cultural inclusion in South London. Other museums at other locations are advised to engage in museum/school partnerships, to develop other ideas and to disseminate them via their museum websites, their local universities or the professional journals. We all benefit by pooling good resources.

Finally, this short article was only able to outline some main points but further information can be found in three sources. First the independent qualitative evaluation, which confirmed the success of the project work in terms of raising the students self-esteem and achievement (Clarke *et al.* 2001). Second at the website clothofgold.org.uk/archive, where a wealth of images and details of all 12 projects can be found. I would be very pleased to share ideas and enthusiasms by email at vmg4@le.ac.uk since I believe the museums of the world have a role in increasing democracy and progressing social equality amongst global citizens. Let the pupil's comment, 'all good things come to an end', actually mark a series of fertile new beginnings. I thank you.

Note

Viv Golding is lecturer in Museum Studies and Education at the University of Leicester.

References

Barnes, C., G. Mercer & T. Shakespeare (2002) *Exploring Disability: A Sociological Introduction*, Polity Press, Cambridge.

Clarke, A. *et al.* (eds) (2001) *Inspiring Learning*, Research Centre for Museums and Galleries (RCMG), Leicester.

Csikszentmihalyi, M. and K. Hermanson (2000) 'Intrinsic motivation in museums: why does one want to learn', in Hooper-Greenhill (ed.) *The Educational Role of the Museum*, Routledge, London: 146–160.

Department of Health, *Valuing People: A New Strategy for Learning Disability for the 21st Century, A White Paper* (2001) The Stationery Office, London.

Fanon, F. (1993) *Black Skin, White Masks*, Pluto Press, London.

Fleming, D. (2000) 'Positioning the Museum for Social Inclusion', in Sandell, R. (ed.) *Museums, Society, Inequality*, Routledge, London.

Golding, V. (2000) 'New Voices and Visibilities at the Museum Frontiers', unpublished PhD thesis, University of Leicester.

Hein, G. (1999) *Learning in Museums*, Routledge, London.

Macdonald, S. (1996) 'Theorising Museums: Introduction', in Macdonald, S. and Fyfe, G. *Theorising Museums*, Blackwell, Oxford.

National Curriculum (2000) www.curriculumonline.gov.uk/.

Oliver, M. (1996) *Understanding Disability: From Theory to Practice*, Macmillan, Basingstoke.

Parekh, B. (2002) *The Future of a Multi-Ethnic Britain, The Parekh Report*, Profile Books, London.

Picton, J. (1995) 'West Africa and the Guinea Coast', in Philips, T. (ed.) *Africa Art of a Continent*, Prestel, Munich and New York.

Pinna, G. (2004) 'Intangible Heritage and Museums', *ICOM News*, no. 4.

RCMG (2000) *Learning Through Culture*, University of Leicester.

Rogoff, B. (1990) *Apprenticeship in Thinking: Cognitive development in social context*, Oxford University Press, New York.

Smith, C. (1998) *Creative Britain*, Faber and Faber, London.

UNESCO (2003) www.unesco.org/education.

Valuing People (2001) http://www.valuingpeople.gov.uk/ Valuing People: A New Strategy for Learning Disability for the 21st century, A White Paper, Department of Health.

Valuing People (2004) http://www.whssb.n-j-nhs-uk/partner/cd_stategy_2006, 'DHSS valuing people 2004'.

Websites

http://www.clothofgold.org.uk/archive
http://www.curriculumonline.gov.uk/, National Curriculum 2000.
http://www.ofsted.gov.uk/reports
http://www.re:source.gov.uk
http://www.socialexclusionu.gov.uk/ Tackling Social Exclusion: Taking stock and looking to the future, 2004, Office of the Deputy Prime Minister.
www.unesco.org/education, 2003.

Communities Remembering and Forgetting

Introduction to Part Four

THE RELATIONSHIP BETWEEN MUSEUMS AND MEMORY is a complex one and Misztal helps us understand the roles museums play in memory making within the context of a range of other institutions such as textbooks, legal systems and the mass media. For many museums the objects they curate appear to be beyond personal memory yet the process of collecting and exhibiting organises memory around material culture (Misztal 2003: 21, this volume p. 389). Those who determine collecting policies and design exhibitions are keepers of a collective memory and what they choose not to collect is a kind of forgetting. Misztal explores the ideas of collective memory and cultural memory, analysing theories of memory as a social and cultural process (Ray 2003: x). Misztal defines collective memory as 'the representation of the past, both that shared by a group and that which is collectively commemorated, that enacts and gives substance to the group's identity, its present conditions and its vision of the future' (2003: 7). This definition provides us with a useful starting point when we consider the role of the museum as an institution in the business of making memory and thus helping to develop and sustain communities. She identifies three main mnemonic communities of memory that socialise us into what we should remember: the nation, the ethnic group and the family. However, she argues that we are witnessing the fragmentation of national memory as cultures become more diverse and, as a result, 'the episodic narrative of groups' (2003: 18, this volume p. 387) becomes more important. Such group narratives may well produce contested memories, and museums sometimes find themselves offending those whose collective memory does not coincide with the interpretive narrative of the museum. Disputes over the National Museum of Australia (Casey 2001) illustrate this point. Nevertheless, more usually, these narratives are uncontested and thus 'museums anchor official memory' (Davison 2000: 145).

Misztal recognises that memory is an individual act so that, despite being constrained by social context (2003: 11, this volume p. 380), individuals remember subjectively and emotionally, and this idea has been explored more fully by Kavanagh (2000) who, drawing on the ideas of Sheldon Annis (1987), conceives of the museum as a 'dream space' where museum objects interact with the subconscious of the viewer. If we recognise that memory is individual, emotional and irrational can we accept that museums do anything more than facilitate private and personal remembrances? Lubar's analysis of the *World War II: Sharing Memories* exhibition at the National Museum of American History is useful here. He examines the way individuals, many of whom had been born after the hostilities ended, wrote about their memories of their relatives who fought in the war in a 'Share Your Memories' section. They wrote about the suffering and sacrifice of their loved ones and this elicited national pride. Thus the personal became mediated by the museum into part of a collective memory of the Second World War, placed within the context of national memory and identity. Beresford, in contrast, reminds us that there are people whose memories are excluded from museums. His is a strongly worded protest at the way that mental health service users/survivors' memories are usually ignored and how members of this community, united by their experiences, have been marginalised.

It has long been recognised that memory is transient, inaccurate and fallible. Individuals use memory to support their sense of who they are. Painful episodes are suppressed both deliberately and unconsciously or exaggerated and used to justify certain actions. What we forget tells us as much about ourselves as what we remember. In a similar way nations and smaller communities are selective in what they choose to remember and forget (Misztal 2003: 18, this volume pp. 386–7; introduction to Part Two, pp. 173–5 this volume).

Museums and their visitors often work on the premise that there is one accepted public memory of events. While individual stories may be woven into a display, either in the form of oral history through quotations in text panels or audio wands, these testimonies are usually there as illustrations to support the curators' chosen themes, even when oral histories are themselves the focus of the exhibition (Green 2006, this volume pp. 412–13). Changes in technology now mean that museums can provide such recordings through a variety of media both inside the museum and outside, such as in the Linked project by the Museum of London that allowed pedestrians to hear the stories of a community alongside the motorway that destroyed it (Butler and Miller 2006). Oral history can thus become both a means of confirming a community identity and a record of a lost community.

Museums can attempt to reflect changing memories and national and local stories in a variety of ways. Muzaini and Yeoh examine how the Changi Chapel and War Museum in Singapore has become a place where commemoration and memories are relocated within a sense of local, national and international constructs. Walsh's chapter on France and the Second World War illustrates the way in which collective memory is reshaped to support a changing sense of the past and national identity.

Over the last two decades there has been a rapid growth in the politics of oppression. Nations or specific communities within nation states use the memory of past acts of atrocity, suffering and suppression to articulate national or

community identity (Crooke 2001). There are some memorial museums that
have been specifically created to commemorate and memorialise certain events.
These museums, according to Young (1993), are seen 'as places where communities can localise memories and build identity around stories' (Young, quoted in
Jenkins 2005: 22, this volume p. 448). It has been claimed that 'more memorial museums have been opened in the last 10 years than in the past 100' (Anon:
22). For example, in 2005 the Holocaust Memorial opened in Berlin, where
Germans sought yet again to come to terms with Jewish suffering during the Second
World War by constructing a place to remember the dead. Holocaust memorials
and exhibitions recognise mainly Jewish suffering but there are many other
victim memorial museums such as the Museum of Genocide Victims, Vilnius,
Lithuania, and the Tuol Sleng Genocide Museum, Phnom Penh, Cambodia. The
expansion of these types of museums is undertheorised at present and much of
what is written relates specifically to the Holocaust (for example, Young 1993;
Macdonald 2005). The memorial museum is not without its critics (Jenkins 2005).
Duffy's chapter looks at the way in which the Holocaust museum type has been
a way of 'transposing concern with the memories of the Holocaust into a
broader platform of human rights issues' (Duffy 1997: 57, this volume p. 454).
McEachern's chapter (1998, this volume ch. 33) on the District Six Museum in
Cape Town, South Africa, provides an analysis of the way in which a museum can
support the remembering of a painful past and the creation of a new way of thinking about it which provides a community with a sense of identity and pride.

Museums, like historians, place objects and displays into context. They select
the stories that the nation or the community wishes to remember when it appears
that these might be lost if there is no form of formal commemoration. Museums
are in the business of both forgetting and remembering and are thus powerful agents
of community identity.

References

Anon (2005) 'Introduction to Jenkins', *Museums Journal*, no. 5, 22.
Annis, S. (1987) 'The museum as a staging ground for symbolic action', *Museum*, 151,
        168–71.
Bordage, R. (1993) 'Sachsenhausen: a flawed museum', *Museum International*, 177,
        vol. XLV, no. 1, 26–31.
Butler, T. and Miller, G. (2006) 'Linked: a landmark in sound, a public work of art',
        in R. Perks and A. Thomson (eds) *The Oral History Reader*, second edition,
        London: Routledge, 425–33.
Casey, D. (2001) 'Museums as agents for social and political change', *Curator*, vol. 44,
        no. 3, Walnut Creek: Altamira Press, 230–6.
Crooke, E. (2001) 'Confronting a troubled history: which past in Northern Ireland's
        museums?' *International Journal of Heritage Studies*, vol. 7, no. 2, 2001, 119–36.
Davison, P. (2000) 'Museums and the reshaping of memory', in S. Nuttall and C. Coetzee
        (eds) *Negotiating the Past: The Making of Memory in South Africa*, Oxford: Oxford
        University Press, 143–60.

Duffy, T. (1997) 'The Holocaust museum concept', *Museum International*, vol. 4, no. 1, 54–8.

Green, A. (2006) 'The exhibition that speaks for itself: oral history and museums', in R. Perks and A. Thomson (eds) *The Oral History Reader*, London: Routledge, 416–24.

Jenkins, T. (2005) 'Victims remembered', *Museums Journal*, vol. 105, no. 5, 22–5.

Kavanagh, G. (2000) *Dream Spaces: Memory and the Museum*, London and New York: Leicester University Press.

Lubar, S. (1997) 'Exhibiting Memories', in A. Anderson and A.L. Kaeppler (eds) *Exhibiting Dilemmas: Issues of Representation at the Smithsonian, Washington DC*, Washington and London: Smithsonian Institution Press, 15–27.

Macdonald, S. (2005) 'Commemorating the holocaust: re-configuring national identity in the twenty-first century', in J. Littler and R. Naidoo (eds) *The Politics of Heritage: The Legacies of 'Race'*, London: Routledge, 49–68.

McEachern, C. (1998) 'Mapping the Memories: politics, place and identity in the District Six Museum, Cape Town', *Social Identities*, vol. 4, no. 3, 499–521.

Misztal, B. (2003) 'Memory experience', in B. Misztal *Theories of Social Remembering*, Maidenhead Open University Press, 9–26.

Muzaini, H. and Yeoh, B. (2005) 'Contesting "local", commemoration of the Second World War: the case of the Changi Chapel and Museum in Singapore', *Australian Geographer*, March, vol. 36, no. 1, 1–17.

Ray, L. (2003) 'Series editor's foreword', in B. Misztal *Theories of Social Remembering*, Maidenhead: Open University Press, ix–xi.

Young, J. (1993) *The Texture of Memory: Holocaust Memorials and Meaning*, New Haven, London: Yale University Press.

Chapter 25

Memory Experience
The forms and functions of memory

Barbara Misztal

'. . . whatever takes place has meaning because it changes into memory'

(Milosz 2001)

Hᴜᴍᴀɴ ᴀʙɪʟɪᴛʏ to retain and recollect a fact, event, or person from memory has been a topic of considerable interest to both scientists and artists for a long time. Yet, taking into account varieties of personal remembering (ranging from remembering an emotional feeling, through remembering where I left my car keys, or how to run the spelling check on my computer, or the date of the Battle of Hastings or how my daughter looks), it seems almost impossible to find a common underlying conceptualization of the process. Moreover, as its task involves summarizing, condensing or rewriting past events, memory is a complex but fallible system of storing information (Baddeley 1989: 51). Because of this difficulty in analysing memory we should view this faculty as some kind of active orientation towards the past, as an act of 'thinking of things in their absence' (Warnock 1987: 12). By referring to the process of remembering as 'memory experience' (Warnock 1987), we focus on the uniqueness of memory as a 'dialogue with the past' (Benjamin quoted in Lash 1999).

Memory has many forms and operates on many different levels, and the things that we remember are of many different kinds and are remembered for many different reasons. For example, there is the memory of how to ride a bicycle, which has been defined as a *procedural* memory; there is also the memory of such facts as that bicycles have two wheels and sometimes a bell, which has been defined as a *declarative* or *semantic* memory (Baddeley 1989: 35–46). Another type of memory is personal memory or *autobiographical* memory, which is the way we tell others

Source: *Theories of Social Remembering*, Maidenhead: Open University Press, 2003, pp. 9–26, 162–80.

and ourselves the story of our lives. Although autobiographical memories are not necessarily accurate, they are 'mostly congruent with one's self knowledge, life themes, or sense of self' (Barclay and DeCooke 1988: 92). When talking about *cognitive* memory, we refer to remembering the meaning of words and lines of verse: 'What this type of remembering requires is, not that the object of memory be something that is past, but that the person who remembers that thing must have met, experienced or learned of it in the past' (Connerton 1989: 23). Yet another kind of memory is *habit* memory, which refers to our capacity to reproduce a certain performance and which is an essential ingredient in the successful and convincing performance of codes and rules. Habit is the mode of inscribing the past in the present, *as* present. In this case, memory denotes a habitual knowing that allows us to recall the signs and skills we use in everyday life. This kind of memory, like all habits, is sedimented in bodily postures, activities, techniques and gestures. Such conceptualization of the process of remembering, where memory 'gets passed on in non-textual and non-cognitive ways' (Connerton 1989: 102), allows us to study social remembrance by focusing on the performance of commemorative rituals.

Habit-memory differs from other types of memory because it brings the past into the present by acting, while other kinds of memory retrieve the past to the present by summoning the past *as past* – that is, by remembering it. Remembering submits the past to a reflective awareness and it permits, by highlighting the past's difference to the present, the emergence of a form of critical reflection and the formation of meaningful narrative sequences. Although remembering, like habit, can be seen as a constant effort to maintain and reconstruct societal stability it, unlike habit, is also a 'highly active, effortful process' (Young 1988: 97). While remembering, we deliberately and consciously recover the past, so whatever memories 'route into consciousness, they need to be organized into patterns so that they make some kind of continuing sense in an ever-changing present' (Young 1988: 97–8). Hence, memory, as the knowing ordering or the narrative organization of the past, observes rules and conventions of narrative. For example, successful narratives about the past must have a beginning and an end, an interesting storyline and impressive heroes. The fact that memorizing is not free of social constraints and influences suggests the importance of another type of memory – namely, *collective* or *social* memory, which is our main concern here.

Here I focus on similarities between the ways in which people assign meanings to their common memories, while adopting the intersubjectivist approach which allows us to avoid both theories rooted in social determinism (which subordinate individuals totally to a collectivity) and visions of an individualistic, atomized social order (which deny the importance of communicative relations between people and their social embeddedness). My main assumption is that remembering, while being constructed from cultural forms and constrained by our social context, is an individual mental act. Therefore, our intersubjectivist explanation of how we remember also acknowledges that – despite the fact memory is socially organized and mediated – individual memory is never totally conventionalized and standardized. The memories of people who have experienced a common event are never identical because in each of them a concrete memory evokes different associations and feelings. The relation between collective and individual memory can be compared to the relation between language (*langue*) and speech (*parole*), as formulated by Saussure

(Funkenstein 1993: 5–9). Language, as a collective product, is separated from the variety of uses to which particular speech acts may be put; thus it is, like collective memory, an idealized system. Variations in individual memories, which can be compared to the scope of freedom with which we use language in particular speech, reflect the degree to which a given culture permits conscious changes and variations of the narrator in the contents, symbols and structures of collective memory.

Underscoring the intersubjectivity of memory, the sociology of memory asserts that the collective memory of a group is 'quite different from the sum total of the personal recollections of its various individual members, as it includes only those that are *commonly shared* by all of them' (Zerubavel 1997: 96). The collective memory, as the integration of various different personal pasts into a single common past that all members of a community come to remember collectively, can be illustrated by America's collective memory of the Vietnam War, that is more 'than just an aggregate of all the war-related recollections of individual Americans' (Zerubavel 1997: 96). Moreover, the prominent place of the Vietnam War (rather than, for example, the Korean War) in the memories of Americans also suggests that the division of the past into 'memorable' and 'forgettable' is a social convention, as it is society that ensures what we remember, and how and when we member it.

Memory is social because every memory exists through its relation with what has been shared with others: language, symbols, events, and social and cultural contexts. Much research illustrates that memory is intersubjectively constituted because it is based on language and on an external or internal linguistic communication with significant others (Paez *et al.* 1997: 155). The way we remember is determined through the supra-individual cultural construction of language, which in itself is the condition of the sharing of memory, as a memory 'can be social only if it is capable of being transmitted and to be transmitted, a memory must first be articulated' (Fentress and Wickham 1992: 47). As the past is made into story, memories are simplified and 'prepared, planned and rehearsed socially and individually' (Schudson 1995: 359). Any retrospective narratives' chance of entering the public domain is socially structured: 'Within the public domain, not only the recording of the past but active re-working of the past is more likely to be transmitted if it happens in high-prestige, socially consensual institutions than if it happens at or beyond the edges of conventional organization' (Schudson 1995: 359). That remembering is social in origin and influenced by the dominant discourses is well illustrated by Zerubavel's (1997: 12) example of cognitive battles over memory, which are typically between social 'camps' rather than simply between individuals. The fact that major changes in the way we view the past usually correspond to major social transformations that affect entire mnemonic communities, as shown in many studies of changes in attitudes to the past in postcommunist countries after the collapse of communism (Szacka 1997), also provides the evidence that remembering is more than just a personal act and the nature of political power can influence the content of our memories.

Memory is also social because remembering does not take place in a social vacuum. We remember as members of social groups, and this means assuming and internalizing the common traditions and social representation shared by our collectivities. Memory cannot be removed from its social context, since whenever we remember something – for example, our first day at university – we also recall the social circumstances in which the event took place: the city, the university, friends and so on. Moreover, collective memory constitutes shared social frameworks of individual recollections as we share our memories with some people and not others, and – in turn – with whom, for what purpose and when we remember, all of which contributes to what we remember. Furthermore, memory is social because the act of remembering is itself interactive, promoted by cultural artefacts and cues employed for social purposes and even enacted by cooperative activity (Schudson 1997).

In today's societies, which 'are no longer societies of memory' (Hervieu-Leger 2000: 123), social memory refers not so much to living memory but to organized cultural practices supplying ways of understanding the world, and providing people with beliefs and opinions which guide their actions. As modern societies suffer from amnesia, we witness the transformation of living memory into institutionally shaped and sustained memory (Assmann 1995). *Cultural memory*, memory institutionalized through cultural means, is 'embodied in objectivations that store meaning in a concentrated manner' (Heller 2001: 1031). As 'memory that is shared outside the avenues of formal historical discourse yet . . . is entangled with cultural products and imbued with cultural meaning' (Sturken 1997: 3), cultural memory refers to people's memories constructed from the cultural forms and to cultural forms available for use by people to construct their relations to the past (Schudson 1995: 348). These cultural forms are distributed across social institutions and cultural artefacts such as films, monuments, statues, souvenirs and so on. Cultural memory is also embodied in regularly repeated practices, commemorations, ceremonies, festivals and rites. Since the individual 'piggybacks on the social and cultural practices of memory', cultural memory can exist independently of its carriers (Schudson 1995: 347). Cultural memory, as memory constituted through cultural means, comes close to Warburg's concept of the 'social memory' as communicated in visual imageries (Assmann 1995) – a notion which is popular mainly in the vast literature concerning museums, monuments, sculpture and festival culture in art and cultural history.

This approach, therefore, suggests that collective memory is not limited to the past that is shared together but also includes a representation of the past embodied in various cultural practices, especially in commemorative symbolism. Collective memory is not only what people really remember through their own experience, it also incorporates the constructed past which is constitutive of the collectivity. For instance, although citizens of Quebec, whose licence plates proudly state 'I remember', do not really remember the French colonial state, this past is a crucial element of the national memory of Quebec. Thus, the notion of collective memory refers both to a past that is *commonly shared* and a past that is *collectively commemorated*. As the word 'commemorate' derives from Latin *com* (together) and *momorare* (to remember), it can be said that the past that is jointly remembered and the past that is commonly shared are the crucial elements of collective memory (Schwartz 2000: 9). The fact that a commemorated event is one invested with extraordinary significance and assigned a qualitatively distinct place in a groups' conception of the past prompts some writers to assert that if 'there is such a thing as social memory . . . we are likely to find it in commemorative ceremonies' (Connerton 1989: 4).

Memory's essential role in social life is connected with the fact that 'collective memory is part of culture's meaning-making apparatus' (Schwartz 2000: 17). Our need for meaning, or, in other words, for being incorporated into something that transfigures individual existence, grants enormous importance to collective memory since it 'establishes an image of the world so compelling as to render meaningful its deepest perplexities' (Schwartz 2000: 17). In this way, collective memory not only reflects the past but also shapes present reality by providing people with understandings and symbolic frameworks that enable them to make sense of the world. Because the past is frequently used as the mirror in which we search for an explanation and remedy to our present-day problems, memory, is seen 'as [a] cure to the pathologies of modern life' (Huyssen 1995: 6). By mediating and paring the past and the present, as well as providing analogies to events of the present in past events, collective memory is strategic in character and capable of influencing the present. In other words, as we search for a means to impose a meaningful order upon reality, we rely on memory for the provision of symbolic representations and frames which can influence and organize both our actions and our conception of ourselves. Thus 'memory at once reflects programs, and frames the present' (Schwartz 2000: 18).

Furthermore, the importance of memory lies in the identity that it shapes. The content of memory is subject to time as it changes with every new identity and every new present, so memory and temporality cannot be detached from each other. As self-identity presumes memory and because perception hinges upon remembered meanings, two processes are at work here. On the one hand, collective memory allows people to have a certain social identification, both on an individual and a societal level. On the other, following the old sociological assertion that the present influences the past, it can be said that the reconstruction of the past always depends on present-day identities and contexts. Memory can also play an important role as a source of truth. This happens where political power heavily censors national history and where oppressed nations have a profound deficit of truth. Therefore, they tend to look towards memory for authentic stories about their past. This inseparability of the content and form of memory and the issue of power is well illustrated by the situation in Soviet Latvia from 1940 to 1991, where people's memories conflicted with the official version of history and therefore they acquired 'a central importance of the preservation of authenticity and truth' (Skultans 1998: 28).

Social memory is also the crucial condition of people relations, since both conflict and cooperation hinge upon it. Groups' cooperative attitudes are the result of their ability to critically evaluate their respective pasts in a way that secures tolerance and removes barriers to mutual understanding. On the other hand, memory which is used to close boundaries of ethnic, national or other identities and which accepts some versions of the past as 'the truth' can aggravate conflicts. For example, the central memory of the Serbs, the lost Battle of Kosovo in 1389, symbolizes the permanent Muslim intention to colonize them and therefore is one of the obstacles to harmonious relations between Serbs and Muslims (Ray 1999). Another very important function of social remembering, which is best expressed in Karl Deutsch's remark that 'memory is essential for any extended functioning of autonomy' (quoted in Hosking 1989: 119), emphasizes the role of memory as helping us to ensure and improve the conditions of freedom by mastering our democratic institutions. Without memory – that is, without the checking of, and reflection upon, past records of institutions and public activities – we will have no warnings about potential dangers to democratic structures and no opportunity to gain a richer awareness of the repertoire of possible remedies. Memory, understood as a set of complex practices which contribute to our self-awareness, allows us to assess our potentialities and limits. 'Without memory', writes Deutsch, 'would-be self-steering organizations are apt to drift with their environment' because they are unable to reassess and reformulate their rules and aims in the light of experience. This statement is supported by many empirical studies which show that the lack of interest *in* the past and the lack of knowledge *of* the past tend to be accompanied by authoritarianism and utopian thinking, and that 'the root of oppression is loss of memory' (Gunn Allen 1999: 589). However, we need also to remember that since the nineteenth century, 'memory has seemed the mechanism by which ideology materializes itself' (Terdiman 1993: 33).

Memory, functioning as organized practices designed to ensure the reproduction of social and political order, is a source of 'factual' material for propaganda. Its task is to provide social groups or societies with identities and a set of unifying beliefs and values from which objectives are derived for political programmes and actions. Memory, when employed as a reservoir of officially sanctioned heroes and myths, can be seen as a broad and always (to some degree) invented tradition that explains and justifies the ends and means of organized social action and provides people with beliefs and opinions. This role of memory has been important since the end of the eighteenth century, when the new nation states started to construct their citizens' national identities with commemoration rituals, marches, ceremonies, festivals and the help of teachers, poets and painters (Hobsbawm and Ranger 1983). Thus, collective memory is not *just* historical knowledge, because it is experience, mediated by representation of the past, that enacts and gives substance to a group's identity. In order to understand the production of social memory we need to examine how a group maintains and cultivates a common memory. One way to start studying the social promotion of memory is to analyse social contexts in which memories are embedded – groups that socialize us to what should be remembered and what should be forgotten; so-called *mnemonic communities*.

The communities of memory

In many languages 'memory stands, originally, not only for the mental act of remembering but also for the objective continuity of one's name – the name of a person, a family, a tribe or a nation' (Funkenstein 1993: 30). These groups – the family, the ethnic group and the nation – are examples of the main mnemonic communities which socialize us to what should be remembered and what should be forgotten. They affect the 'depth' of our memory; they regulate how far back we should remember, which part of the past should be remembered, which events mark the beginning and which should be forced out of our story. The process of our mnemonic socialization is an important part of all groups' general effort to incorporate new members. As such it is 'a subtle process that usually happens rather tacitly; listening to a family member recount a shared experience, for example, implicitly teaches one what is considered memorable and what one can actually forget' (Zerubavel 1997: 87). Mnemonic communities, through introducing and familiarizing new arrivals to their collective past, ensure that new members, by identifying with the groups' past, attain a required social identity. Since we tend to remember what is familiar – because familiar facts fit easily into our mental structures, and therefore make sense to us – groups' identities and collective memory are continuously reinforced. Due to a group's mnemonic tradition, a particular cognitive bias marks every group's remembering. Typically, such a bias expresses some essential truth about the group and its identity and equips the group with the emotional tone and style of its remembering. For instance, the partition of Poland in the eighteenth century gave that country an essential identity as 'the Christ among nations: crucified and recrucified by foreign oppression', and through this established prism of victimhood many Poles still interpret their national fate.

Furthermore, a group's memory is linked to places, ruins, landscapes, monuments and urban architecture, which – as they are overlain with symbolic associations to past events – play an important role in helping to preserve group memory. Such sites, and also locations where a significant event is regularly celebrated and replayed, remain 'concrete and distinct regardless of whether they are mythological or historical' (Heller 2001: 1031). The fact that memories are often organized around places and objects suggests that remembering is something that occurs in the world of things and involves our senses. This was well understood by the ancient Greeks. Halbwachs, on the other hand, brings to our attention the fact that there are as many ways of representing space as there are groups and that each group leaves its imprint on its place. Arguing that our recollections are located with the help of landmarks that we always carry within ourselves, Halbwachs observes that space is 'a reality that endures', thus we can understand how we recapture the past only by understanding how it is preserved by our physical surroundings ([1926] 1950: 84–8). In *The Legendary Topography of the Gospels in the Holy Land*, Halbwachs (1941) demonstrates the working of memory. He shows how Jews, Romans, Christians and Muslims rewrote the history of Jerusalem by remodelling the space according to their religious beliefs. Hence, 'When one looks at the physiognomy of the holy places in successive times, one finds the character of these groups inscribed' (Halbwachs [1941]: 235). The discovery of several strata of memory superimposed on the Holy Land leads Halbwachs to argue that memory imprints its effect on the topography and that each group cuts up space in order to compose a fixed framework within which to enclose and retrieve its remembrance.

The link between landscape and memory is also present in Benjamin's (1968) viewing of the city as a repository of people's memories. Seeing the urban landscape as the battleground for the past, where the past remains open and contestable, he argues that the city can be read as the topography of a collective memory in which buildings are mnemonic symbols which can reveal hidden and forgotten pasts. Although the city offers us 'an illusionary and deceptive vision of the past' as many real histories are buried and covered (Gilloch 1996: 13), new events or new encounters can help us to uncover the city's true memories. So, memory and the metropolis are interwoven as memory shapes and is in turn shaped by the urban setting.

The nation is the main mnemonic community, for its continuity relies on the vision of a suitable past and a believable future. In order to create a required community's history and destiny, which in turn can be used to form the representation of the nation, the nation requires a usable past. Typically the creation of such a past is the task of nationalist movements, which propagate an ideology affirming identification with the nation state by invoking shared memories (Gellner 1993). Such movements owe their success, therefore, to memory, which they effectively employ to establish a sense of continuity between generations. The main way to shape societal aspiration for a shared destiny is by the rediscovery of memories of the 'golden age' and a heroic past (Smith 1997). In addition, appeals 'to the earliest individual memories of childhood – turns of phrase, catches of song, sights and smells – and [linking] them to the idea of the historical continuity of people, its culture and land' (Wrong 1994: 237), contributes significantly to the success of nationalist movements. However, as nations need to establish their representation in the past, their memories are created in tandem with forgetting; to remember everything could bring a threat to national cohesion and self-image. Forgetting is a necessary component in the construction of memory just as the writing of a historical narrative necessarily involves the elimination of certain elements. The role of forgetting in the construction of national identities has been noticed by Ernst Renan, who, in 1882, insisted that the creation of a nation requires the creative use of past events. He pointed out that, although nations could be characterized by 'the possession in common of a rich legacy of memories', the essence of a nation is not only that its members have many things in common, but also 'that they have forgotten some things' (Renan [1882] 1990: 11). In order to ensure national cohesion there is a need to forget events that represent a threat to unity and remember heroes and glory days. Renan's interpretation of collective memory continues to exert considerable influence on the way in which nations articulate themselves in the twentieth and twenty-first centuries. Anderson (1983) argues that being reminded of what one has already forgotten is a normal mechanism by which nations are constructed. He demonstrates how national memories, themselves underscored by selective forgetting, constitute one of the most important mechanisms by which a nation constructs a collective identity or become an 'imagined community'. Hobsbawn and Ranger (1983: 14) show that states engaged in historical construction of modern nations claim nations 'to be the opposite of novel, namely rooted in the remote antiquity'.

It has also been argued that our relation to the national past can be better described not so much as remembering but as forgetting. Billig (1995) suggests that established nations depend for their continued existence upon a collective amnesia. In such societies, not only is 'the past forgotten, but also there is a parallel forgetting of the present' (Billig 1995: 38). Forgetting, however, can also be highly organized and strategic, as examples from less open and democratic societies illustrate. Forced forgetting (Burke 1989) was of particular importance in communist countries, where people understood that 'the struggle against power is the struggle against forgetting' (Kundera 1980: 3). As the majority of communist regimes were also nation-building regimes, they 'went to great lengths to create new myths and to instill these in society through . . . political socialization mechanisms' (Cohen 1999: 27). They, like all new states, were busy constructing the national self-consciousness and used official ceremonies, education and socialization to create and foster a single, national, Marxist-Leninist class-based interpretation of the national history (Wingfield 2000). Politically and culturally oppressive states impose forgetting not only by rewriting and censorship of national history, but also by the destruction of places of memory. The Chinese communist government, for example, aimed to destroy all places of memory, such as temples and monasteries, after the occupation of Tibet in 1951.

In today's societies, with their diversity of cultures, ethnicities, religions and traditions, we are witnessing the fragmentation of national memory. The processes of globalization, diversification and fragmentation of social interests further enhance the transformation of memory from the master narrative of nations to the episodic narrative of groups. The denationalization of memory, on the one hand, and an arrival of ailing and dispersed memories, on the other, in the context of the growing cultural and ethnic pluralization of societies, have provided a new importance to ethnic identities, whose formation is based on traditional memory narratives. Among all the groups in need of memory, 'ethnic groups have had the easiest task, for they have never entirely lost their cultural memory' (Heller 2001). Moreover, many forgotten elements can be brought to light, 'fused with new myths and stories of repression and suffering, or combined with heterogeneous cultural memorabilia such as music, crafts, and religious lore' (Heller 2001). As we witness the emergence of small, surrogate ethnic memories and a growing reliance on the specific content of a group memory to legitimize the group's political claims, battles 'for minorities' rights are increasingly organized around questions of cultural memory, its exclusions and taboo zones' (Huyssen 1995: 5). With ethnic memories surfacing in affiliation with the politics of identity, which itself is a result of the increasing importance of discourses of human rights in the global and postcolonial world, memories of past injustices are a critical source of empowerment. Today's fascination with ethnic memory, in the context of the declining of authoritative memories (traditional religious and national memories), poses new challenges for democratic systems.

The family is another group that plays a crucial role in the construction of our memories. As long as the family jointly produces and maintains its memory, its cohesion and continuity is ensured. The content of the shared family's narrative, symbolic of family unity across generations, reproduces family traditions, secrets and particular sentiments. These memories, objectified in old letters, photographs and family lore, are sustained through family conversations, as past events are jointly recalled or co-memorized (Billig 1990). Middleton and Edwards (1988) illustrated this process by researching how families collectively remembered past events by talking about photographs. As much research shows, children learn to remember in the family environment, guided by parental intervention and shared reminiscence. We do not remember ourselves as very young kids very clearly, so we rely on the memories of older members of our family, with the result that many of our earliest memories are actually recollections of stories we heard from adults about our childhood. Our memory is more accurately described as a collection of overlapping testimonies from our narrative environments, which influence our memory's emotional tone, style and content.

Presently we witness two processes: on the one hand, the growing impact of what might be described as the quest for family roots; and on the other the decline in the family's capability to maintain a living chain of memory. Family history was one of the most striking discoveries of the 1960s and has given rise to the most remarkable 'do-it-yourself archive-based scholarship of our time' (Samuel 1999: 169). This trend has been popularized by the mass media, with many books and films blending private and public memories. The growing interest in telling a family story has been recently assisted by new technologies such as the internet, where the numbers of family websites devoted to the construction of families' memory increases daily. At the same time there is a trend that suggests that families are less and less capable of maintaining their traditions due to changes in their structures and memberships, and this reflects the wider fate of memory in modern society. The decline of the extended, multi-generational family is leading to the destruction of a social framework that ensured the transmission of collective memories from one generation to the next. As family size and stability declines, the depth of family memory also suffers.

All three communities of memory (nation, ethnic group and family) are affected by the growing differentiation of society, the globalization of the world and by the development of new means of communication. These factors have also caused changes in the functioning of the institutions of memory.

The institutions of memory

In today's society, collective memory is increasingly shaped by specialized institutions: schools, courts, museums and the mass media. The growing number of 'ideas, assumptions, and knowledges that structure the relationship of individuals and groups to the immediate as well as the more distant past' (Sherman 1999: 2) is formed, interpreted and preserved by public institutions. The ideological themes that pervade the rhetoric of public authorities and the educational curricula, with history classes in school being the main example, 'tutor' public memory and promote a specific version of the past. Schools and textbooks are important vehicles through which societies transmit the idealized past and promote ideas of a national identity and unity. Textbooks have always been updated and rewritten to present the acceptable vision of the past, and although now, due to international pressures and national voices, textbooks are frequently the subject of external and domestic scrutiny, in many national narratives past events that could harm social cohesion and the authority of the state are still underplayed. Where the state controls the educational and media system, collective memory is fragmented, full of 'black holes', dominated by ideological values and used to produce legitimacy for the ruling élite. For example, in Tito's Yugoslavia, the official sanctioned memory of World War II, around which textbook narratives were structured, was a crucial element in the creation of legitimacy, myth and identity for the new communist state (Hoepken 1999). In such a situation, where the legitimization of social and political order depends upon official censorship, socially organized forgetting and the suppression of those elements that do not fit the regime's image of past events, unofficial and informal institutions as well an oral memory transmitted informally, frequently with the help of jokes, gossip, double-speak and anecdotes, are essential to the preservation of collective memory.

Another institution which increasingly shapes our collective memory is the legal system. The relationship between public memory and the law is at the foundation of many countries' original conceptions of themselves. For example, such legal documents as the Magna Carta (UK) or the Declaration of Independence (USA) are essential for understanding these societies' origins and values. Not only is the legal system itself an enormously influential institution of collective memory, but in many countries changes in collective memory are legally induced. In all societies, to a considerable extent, courts, through their input in deciding historical questions, form collective memory. Postwar Europe saw many criminal prosecutions which aimed to influence national collective memories, the Nuremberg trials being the main example. Despite controversies and debates surrounding attempts to punish state-sponsored mass murder and readdress national memories, the trials' achievements for constructing the basis for new memories and a new order cannot be overlooked. Today, due to the proliferation of the language of human rights and the new strength of the politics of identity, we see an increase in demands for governments to address historical injustices committed in their name. Consequently, many nations, and not only those emerging from their authoritarian past, use the legal system to bring justice and to teach a particular interpretation of the country's history. Legal attempts to construct collective memory are not without tensions and difficulties (Misztal 2001) but because they allow for confrontation of various memories, they can serve the periodic need to reawaken and strengthen the public's feelings of moral outrage.

A further important institution of memory is the museum. Museums originated in the late eighteenth century as monuments to wealth and civic patrimony, in the form of collections of material objects in courts and churches. From the nineteenth century it was an educational imperative of the emerging nation state to form national identity and 'to elevate the working class' that was responsible for the opening of exhibitions to a national public. Although museums have much in common with other institutions of memory, their authoritative and legitimizing status and their role as symbols of community constitute them as a distinctive cultural complex (Macdonald 1996). Museums are unusual not only because their development is connected to the formation and honouring of the nation state, but also because of their role in the social objectification of the past and organized memory around diverse artefacts.

Until recently, museums were mainly devoted to the preservation of a memory that constituted one of the high points of a national history, and therefore they were collecting 'objects to which the observer no longer has a vital relationship and which are in the process of dying' (Adorno 1967: 175). 'Museum and mausoleum', in Adorno's famous phrase, were associated by more than phonetics. Today, however, their authority as the curators of national treasures and the dictators of distinction and taste is challenged. This is a result of several factors, such as the availability of new technologies the fragmentation and denationalization of memory and the development of a popular passion for heritage – that is, for 'the interpretation of the past through an artefactual history' (Urry 1996: 53) – resulting in an interest in old places, crafts, houses, countryside, old railways and so on.

With many museums fundamentally transforming their practice of collecting and exhibiting, their function now bears a strong relationship to memory production (Crane 2000). Thus, 'the museum is no longer simply the guardian of treasures and artefacts from the past discreetly exhibited for the select group of experts', but has moved closer to 'the world of spectacle, of popular fair and mass entertainment' (Huyssen 1995: 19). In this process of transformation from the position of traditional cultural authority to a new role as cultural mediators in a more multicultural environment, museums redefine their strategies of representation of the past and find spaces for marginalized memories. This new opportunity for excluded memories, in the context of the decline of the management of public memory by the state, has resulted in the increased articulation of memory by various agencies from civil society and the enormous explosion of heritage and conservation organizations and movements.

Today, the most important role in the construction of collective memories is played by the mass media (McLuhan 1962). Before the development of the mass media, most people's sense of the past and the world beyond their immediate milieu was constituted by oral traditions that were produced and reproduced in the social context of everyday life. The shift from relying only on face-to-face exchanges to depending on mediated interaction has profoundly affected the ways in which people organize material for recall as well as their modes of reconstructing the past (Thompson 1996: 95). Rapid technological advancements in the field of communication in the late nineteenth and twentieth centuries and the creation of the mass audience have ensured that the media is an extremely powerful instrument of ordering our knowledge of the past. In the nineteenth century it was the press that was the central means of communication and that provided people with images of groups that they could identify with. The press helped the transition from the local to the national by turning existing societies, through highlighting the common past and a constant repetition of images and words, into national communities (Anderson 1983). Now, the function of memory-keeping and presentation is 'increasingly assigned to the electronic media' (Samuel 1994: 25). The nature of this media and their interest in meeting public demands for instant entertainment are not without impact on the content and form of representations of the past. Thus, the input of media into how and what we remember is a crucial factor influencing the status of memory in contemporary societies.

The shift from oral culture, through writing and print, to electronic processing of the word has induced changes in the experience of time, brought about a new conception of the past and created growing possibilities for abstract thought. Thus, it can be said that the evolution of the role and form of social memory has been shaped by technological changes in the means of communication, and this is one of the most important factors structuring the status of memory in modern society.

The status of memory

Our discussion so far suggests that we rely on many social frameworks, institutions, places and objects to help us remember. The relationship between memory and objects is rather complicated because material objects, operating as vehicles of memory, can be of various types (e.g., dynamic or stable). Moreover, they provide us either with images and words, or both, while at the same time memory does not reside specifically in any image or word. Not only does our ability to remember depend on images and/or words, but how images work depends largely on their complex linkage with words, since images have in part always depended on words for direct interpretation, although images also function differently from words. If words and images offer two different kinds of representation, we can expect that as 'modes of representation change, both the relationship between words and images changes as well as how we understand images and words independently of each other' (Zelizer 1998: 5). Thus, the dependence on either words or images results in contrasting cultural values and also in contesting roles of memory. In order to throw light on changes in the status and meaning of memory, it is useful to have a quick look at discussions of the cultural consequences of the shift from oral culture to literacy.

When discussing the role of memory it is often assumed that in an 'oral' society – that is, in a society where communication occurs in forms other than written documents – culture depends upon memory and hence memory is highly valued. A further argument is that the 'rise of literacy' threatens memory. The assertion that technological change means the devalourization of memory has been a permanent element of the history of memory since ancient times. Starting with Plato's argument that the development of writing itself is a threat to individual memory, the idea that memory is in crisis has become the focus point of the centuries-long debate about memory. However, many writers protest against misconceptions about the value of memory in oral cultures and against the notion of memory crisis with the rise of literacy (Ong 1983; Carruthers 1990; Le Goff 1992; Goody 1998).

These scholars argue that the distinction between oral and literary societies is misleading because, as the continuation of the oral component in literary societies illustrates, the possession of writing does not mean that a society has ceased to be an oral culture as well. The majority of researchers agree that the rise of literacy does not necessarily bring the devalourization of memory and that learning by hearing material and reciting it does not necessarily imply an ignorance of reading. The reliance on living memories, associated with the oral transmission of a living past persisted long after the advent of print, and indeed continues to the present day (Ong 1983). In all cultures, not only in those without writing, memorizing is a part of everyday life (Goody 1977: 35). Moreover, basing the distinction between preliterate and literate cultures on a difference in levels of rationality embedded in those cultures needs to be rejected, as the extent to which a society is capable of transmitting its social memory in a logical and articulate form is not dependent upon the possession of writing but is rather connected with that society's representation of language and its perception of knowledge (Fentress and Wickham 1992: 45). Many studies illustrating a continuity between the mnemonic habits of preliterate and literary cultures argue that the privileged cultural role of memory depends 'on the role which rhetoric has in a culture rather than on whether its texts are presented in oral or written forms' – so in societies where literature is valued for its social function, rhetoric and interpretation works to provide the sources of a group's memory (Carruthers 1990: 10, 12). In similar vein, Assmann (1997) stresses the importance of oral transmission in cultures which, despite the possession of written means for preserving the past, keep their main texts alive through commentary.

Nevertheless, although preliterate cultures do not necessarily differ in terms of tasks and the value they assign to memory, the content of memory and the principal domain in which memory crystallizes have been affected by various processes such as the transformation of the technical means of preserving the past, changes in the experience of time, the increased interest in the past and the occurrence of dramatic events. For example, writing, because it generates cultural innovation by promoting economization and scepticism, encourages 'the production of unfamiliar statements and the thinking of novel thoughts' (Connerton 1989: 76). Furthermore, while speech can preserve memories over long intervals of time, it is too fleeting to permit any listener to pause for recollection; thus a sense of the past 'that is primarily based on hearing tales from others is different from one that is primarily based on reading oneself' (Eisenstein 1966: 49). As the 'pastness' of the past depends upon a historical sensibility, this can hardly begin to operate without permanent written records. Hence, literate societies, where records reveal the past is unlike the present, differ from oral cultures in their attitudes to the past. The repetitive regularity of most orally transmitted history means that most knowledge of the past is in fact shared, while in literate societies 'printed historical texts are widely disseminated but most knowledge of the past is fragmented into segments exclusive to small clusters of specialists and the consensually shared past shrinks to a thin media-dominated veneer' (Lowenthal 1998: 238). In literary cultures, past events, removed from living memories and fixed to printed pages, lose their vividness and immediacy. Moreover, as nobody could be expected to remember the content of continuously expanded libraries, the past is not entirely known. However, printed texts facilitate critical approaches and open inquiry into the past (Ong 1983). The new awareness of historicity came into being 'when it became possible to set one fixed account of the world beside another so that the contradictions within and between them could literally be seen' (Connerton 1989: 76). In contrast, oral societies live very much in the present and only with memories which have present relevance and which articulate inconsistent cultural inheritance.

The 'electronification' of memory provides a new dimension to the role memory plays in our image-fed society (Urry 1996: 63). Digital technology, interactive media and information systems have greatly changed the facets of memory practices in our time, and as a result today's memory is 'composed of bits and pieces' (Hervieu-Leger 2000: 129). The immediacy of communication, information overload, the speed of changing images, the growing hybridity of media, all further expand and problematize the status of memory. We have unlimited access to facts, sources and information, which we can store, freeze and replay. At the same time, visual images can interfere with and confuse our memories. For example, computer-generated graphics can fake the truth about the past (as they do in films like *Forrest Gump* and *Zoolander*). This decline of the credibility of photographic images and other visual evidence, together with the overabundance of flickering and changing narratives and images, is a threat to the status of memory as it raises the question of whose vision of the past and whose memories should be trusted. In the same vein, just as in print culture, readers' assessment of trust in the book underwrote the stability of knowledge and society (Johns 1998), trust in media (in other words, institutional trust) is crucial in making narratives of memory and identity into dominant cultural representations of reality.

The importance of institutional trust means that technological change is not the sole factor responsible for the status of memory. Both the shift in means of communication and the changes in modes of social organization, including changes in the practice of power, influence the nature of mnemonic practices. In other words, the structuring of memory in society is shaped by technological changes in the means of communication and the transformation of the dominant institutions of society. Memory, as the main source of collective identity, has always been employed by various social forces to boost their control and standing. When the main social authority was religious institutions, for example (as in ancient Israel), religious memory was called upon to sustain followers' allegiance; thus the biblical continuous appeal to 'Zakhor' ('remember') that ensured that remembering was 'felt as religious imperative to an entire people' (Yerushalmi 1982: 9). Similarly, the emergence of the nation state was accompanied by inventions of new memories to enhance national identities. Today, memory is more distant from traditional sources of power, while at the same time it becomes increasingly shaped by mass media . . .

Note

Barbara Misztal is Professor of Sociology at the University of Leicester.

Further reading

Baddley, A. (1989) The psychology of remembering and forgetting, in T. Butler (ed.) *Memory: History, Culture and the Mind*, pp. 33–60. Oxford: Basil Blackwell.
Goody, J. (1998) Memory in oral tradition, in P. Fara and K. Patterson (eds) *Memory*, pp. 73–94. Cambridge: Cambridge University Press.
Renan, E. ([1882] 1990) What is a nation?, in H.K. Bhabha (ed.) *Nation and Narration*. London: Routledge.
Schudson, M. (1995) Distortion in collective memory, in D.L. Schacter (ed.) *Memory Distortion*, pp. 346–63. Cambridge, MA: Harvard University Press.
Sennett, R. (1998) Disturbing memories, in P. Fara and K. Patterson (eds) *Memory*, pp. 10–46. Cambridge: Cambridge University Press.

References

Adorno, T.W. (1967) *Prisms*, trans. S. and S. Weber. London: Neville Spearman.
Anderson, B. (1983) *Imagined Communities*. London: Verso.
Assmann, J. (1995) Collective memory and cultural identity, *New German Critique*, 65 (Spring–Summer): 125–35.
Assmann, J. (1997) *Moses the Egyptian*. Cambridge, MA: Harvard University Press.
Baddeley, A. (1989) The psychology of remembering and forgetting, in T. Butler (ed.) *Memory: History, Culture and the Mind*, pp. 33–60. Oxford: Basil Blackwell.
Barclay, C.R. and DeCooke, P.A. (1988) Ordinary everyday memories: some of the things of which selves are made, in U. Neisser and E. Winograd (eds) *Remembering Reconsidered: Ecological and Traditional Approaches to the Study of Memory*, pp. 91–126. Cambridge: Cambridge University Press.
Benjamin, W. (1968) *Illuminations: Essays and Reflections*, trans. H. Zohn, ed. H. Arendt. New York: Schocken Books.

Billig, M. (1990) Collective memory, ideology and the British royal family, in D. Middleton and D. Edwards (eds) *Collective Remembering*, pp. 60–80. London: Sage.

Billig, M. (1995) *Banal Nationalism*. London: Sage.

Burke, P. (1989) History as social memory, in T. Butler (ed.) *Memory: Culture and the Mind*, pp. 1–32. Cambridge: Blackwell.

Carruthers, M. (1990) *The Book of Memory: A Study of Medieval Culture*. Cambridge: Cambridge University Press.

Cohen, S.J. (1999) *Politics Without Past*. Durham, NC: Duke University Press.

Connerton, P. (1989) *How Societies Remember*. Cambridge: Cambridge University Press.

Crane, S.A. (ed.) (2000) *Museum and Memory*. Stanford, CA: Stanford University Press.

Eisenstein, E. (1966) Clio and chronosm, *History and Theory*, 6: 36–64.

Fentress, J. and Wickham, C. (1992) *Social Memory*. Oxford: Blackwell.

Funkenstein, A. (1993) *Perception of Jewish History*. Berkeley, CA: University of California Press.

Gellner, E. (1993) *Nations and Nationalism*. Oxford: Blackwell.

Gilloch, G. (1996) *Myth and Metropolis: Walter Benjamin and the City*. Oxford: Polity Press.

Goody, J. (1977) *The Domestication of the Savage Mind*. Cambridge: Cambridge University Press.

Goody, J. (1998) Memory in oral tradition, in P. Fara and K. Patterson (eds) *Memory*, pp. 73–94. Cambridge: Cambridge University Press.

Gunn Allen, P. (1999) Who is your mother? Red roots of white feminism, in C. Lemert (ed.) *Social Theory: The Multicultural and Classic Readings*, pp. 585–594. Boulder, CO: Westview.

Halbwachs, M. ([1926] 1950) *The Collective Memory*, trans. F.J. and V.Y. Ditter. London: Harper Colophon Books.

Halbwachs, M. (1941) *La Topographie Legendarie de Evangiles en Teore Sainte*. Paris: Presses de Universitaires de France.

Heller, A. (2001) A tentative answer of the question: has civil society cultural memory?, *Social Research*, 68(4): 103–42.

Hervieu-Leger, D. (2000) *Religion as a Chain of Memory*. Oxford: Polity Press.

Hobsbawm, E. and Ranger, T. (eds) (1983) *The Invention of Tradition*. New York: Cambridge University Press.

Hoepken, W. (1999) War, memory and education in a fragmented society: the case of Yugoslavia, *East European Politics and Societies*, 13(1): 190–227.

Hosking, G.A. (1989) Memory in a totalitarian society, in T. Butler (ed.) *Memory, History, Culture and the Mind*, pp. 97–114. Oxford: Blackwell.

Huyssen, A. (1995) *Twilight Memories*. London: Routledge.

Johns, A. (1998) *The Nature of the Book: The Print Knowledge in the Making*. Chicago: Chicago University Press.

Kundera, M. (1980) *The Book of Laughter and Forgetting*. New York: King Penguin.

Lash, S. (1999) *Another Modernity: A Different Rationality*. Oxford: Blackwell.

Le Goff, J. (1992) *History and Memory*, trans. S. Rendall and E. Claman. New York: Columbia University Press.

Lowenthal, D. (1998) *The Heritage Crusade and the Spoils of History*. Cambridge: Cambridge University Press.

Lyotard, J.F. (1988) *The Postmodern Condition: A Report on Knowledge*, trans. G. Bennington. Manchester: Manchester University Press.

Macdonald, S. (1996) Theorizing museums: an introduction, in S. Macdonald and G. Fyfe (eds) *Theorizing Memory*, pp. 1–20. Oxford: Blackwell.

McLuhan, M. (1962) *Gutenberg Galaxy: The Making of Typographic Man*. Toronto: Toronto University Press.

Middleton, D. and Edwards, D. (1988) Conversation, remembering and family relationships: how children learn to remember, *Journal of Social and Personal Relationships*, 5: 3–25.

Milosz, C. (2001) *New and Collected Poems*. New York: Penguin.

Misztal, B.A. (2001) Legal attempts to construct collective memory, *Polish Sociological Review*, 133(1): 61–76.

Ong, W. (1983) *Ramus: Methods and the Decay of Dialogue: from the Art of Discourse to the Art of Reason*. Cambridge, MA: Harvard University Press.

Paez, D., Basabe, N. and Gonzales, J.L. (1997) A cross-cultural approach to remembering, in J.W. Pennebaker, D. Paez and B. Rime (eds) *Collective Memory of Political Events*, pp. 147–74. Mahwah, NJ: Lawrence Erlbaum.

Ray, L.J. (1999) Memory, trauma and genocidal nationalism, *Sociological Research Online*, 4(2), www.socresonline.org.uk.

Renan, E. ([1882] 1990) What is a nation? in H.K. Bhabha (ed.) *Nation and Narration*. London: Routledge.

Samuel, R. (1994) *Theatres of Memory*, vol. 1: *Past and Present in Contemporary Culture*. London: Verso.

Samuel, R. (1999) Resurrectionism, in D. Bowell and J. Evans (eds) *Representing the Nation: A Reader*, pp. 163–84. London: Routledge.

Schudson, M. (1995) Distortion in collective memory, in D.L. Schacter (ed.) *Memory Distortion*, pp. 346–63. Cambridge MA: Harvard University Press.

Schudson, M. (1997) Lives, laws and language: commemorative versus non-commemorative forms of effective public memory, *The Communication Review*, 2(1): 3–17.

Schwartz, B. (2000) *Abraham Lincoln and the Forge of National Memory*. Chicago: Chicago University Press.

Sherman, D.J. (1999) *The Construction of Memory in Interwar France*. Chicago: Chicago University Press.

Skultans, V. (1998) *The Testimony of Lives*. London: Routledge.

Smith, A.D. (1997) The 'Golden Age' and national renewal, in G.A. Hosking and G. Schopflin (eds) *Myths and Nationhood*, pp. 36–59. London: Hurst & Company.

Sturken, M. (1997) *Tangled Memories: The Vietnam War, the AIDS Epidemic, and the Politics of Remembering*. Berkeley, CA: University of California.

Szacka, B. (1997) Systematic transformation and memory of the past, *Polish Sociological Review*, 118(2): 119–32.

Terdiman, R. (1993) *Present Past: Modernity and the Memory Crisis*. Ithaca, NY: Cornell University Press.

Thompson, J.B. (1996) Tradition and self in a mediated world, in P. Heelas, S. Lash and P. Morris (eds) *Detraditionalization: Critical Reflections on Authority and Identity*, pp. 89–108. Oxford: Blackwell.

Urry, J. (1996) How societies remember the past, in S. Macdonald and G. Fyfe (eds) *Theorizing Memory*, pp. 45–68. Oxford: Blackwell.

Warnock, M. (1987) *Memory*. London: Faber & Faber.

Wingfield, N.M. (2000) The politics of memory: constructing national identity in the Czech land, *East European Politics and Societies*, 14(2): 246–60.

Wrong, D. (1994) *The Problem of Order*. Cambridge, MA: Harvard University Press.

Yerushalmi, Y. (1982) *Zakhor: Jewish History and Jewish Memory*. Seattle, WA: University of Washington Press.

Young, M. (1988) *The Metronomic Society: Natural Rhythms and Human Timetables*. London: Thames & Hudson.

Zelizer, B. (1998) *Remembering to Forget: Holocaust Memory Through the Camera's Eye*. Chicago: Chicago University Press.

Zerubavel, E. (1997) *Social Mindscape: An Invitation to Cognitive Sociology*. Cambridge, MA: Harvard University Press.

Chapter 26

Exhibiting Memories

Steven Lubar

'WE ALL REMEMBER WORLD WAR II.' That's the way a recent exhibit at the National Museum of American History welcomed visitors.

At first reading, this seems absurd. Only those over fifty can remember the war. But in another, deeper, sense, we all do remember the war. We remember it in family stories, national mythology, the history we learned in school, and the movies we saw on television. *World War II: Sharing Memories*, a temporary exhibit open from June through November 1995, was about the war — but its true subject was memory and history. We wanted our visitors to think not only about the war but also about how we know the past, about the ways that memory and tradition relate to history and historic artifacts. I think we succeeded. In this essay, after reflecting on the ways in which memory and history intersect in museums and describing the exhibit, I will look at some of the memories our visitors shared with us, considering especially the ways in which they thought about the past.

Memory and history

Memory is how we connect with our individual past. It serves our own purposes: writer Stefan Zweig called it 'a power that deliberately arranges and wisely excludes.' History, too, partakes of this rearrangement of the past, but it must aim for a less personal point of view. Historians, Eric Hobsbawm wrote, are 'the professional remembrancers of what their fellow-citizens wish to forget.' How to combine memory and history in an exhibit? How to recognize and honor memories

Source: *Exhibiting Dilemmas: Issues of Representation at the Smithsonian*, Amy Henderson & Adrienne L. Kaeppler (eds), Washington: Smithsonian Institution Press, 1997, pp. 15–27.

while at the same time moving beyond them? These were the problems I faced as curator of *Sharing Memories*.

One difference between historians and the general public is the extent of critical distance we put between ourselves and our subjects. We share an interest in history, but the approach we take is different. Our sources are different also; historians want to use archives and objects, the public more often turns to memory, personal connections, and family stories. We use those sources in different ways; historians are careful to assess the bias of their sources, to question the evidence. And we consider different contexts; historians must cast a broader net. These factors help to determine our critical distance. Historians have no end of words to describe the degree of critical distance. Our stories of the past can be com- memoration, remembrance, reminiscence, explanation, interpretation, or analysis. Objects move from keepsake to memento to souvenir to reminder to evidence. Our presentations move from celebration to memorial to exhibition.

All of these means of explaining the past have a place in our understanding of it. One can walk around Washington and find history presented in every one of these ways. Arlington Cemetery is properly the home of monuments. The Holocaust Memorial Museum has both an exhibition and, carefully separate, a Hall of Memories, a memorial. The Smithsonian encompasses a wide range of his- toric presentations. The National Air and Space Museum is, for the most part, a temple to technological progress. The National Portrait Gallery is a hall of heroes. Art museums show aesthetic masterpieces.

History museums have a different and, I think, more difficult task. The goal of a history exhibit is to move people from the ideas and information that they bring with them to the exhibit to a more complex, problematized, and nuanced view of the past. Exhibits should not be limited to reminiscence or commemoration; they should add perspective by aspiring to a greater critical distance and by putting the artifacts in context. Consider the exhibits at the National Museum of American History that examined aspects of World War II. The least successful, in my view, was *World War II GI*, which told the public about the soldier's life by presenting objects and images without much context. Much more successful were *Women War Workers* and *A More Perfect Union*, which told the stories, respectively, of women on the home front and Japanese Americans at home and on the battlefield, situating their stories in the context of changing American ideas about gender and race. An exhibit on wartime production posters explained the way they fit into the history of adver- tising and patriotism, analyzing the intentions and effects of the posters, which had often been presented in merely aesthetic terms. These exhibits are about history, mostly ignoring whatever memories visitors might bring with them to the museum or using those memories only as a hook to attract audience interest.

This disjunction between memory and history was the problem faced by the curators of the controversial *Enola Gay* exhibition at the National Air and Space Museum. Their first script moved too far for comfort from the veterans' memor- ies, and the veterans had enough political clout to let the curators know it. The *Enola Gay* exhibition that finally opened has exactly the opposite problem: It focuses almost solely on the object, the airplane, with little context to allow it to move the visitor's understanding beyond memory. Its technological and restoration history is given in loving detail. Technological details are safe; they do not assume any responsibility for moving visitors beyond where they were when they came to the museum. Indeed, they seem, as presented here, to be beyond questioning, and they add the weight of their seeming inevitability to that of the actions that made use of the technology. (My guess is that the visual and technological authority of the airplane would have overcome even the strong message of the early script – something that readers of the script would have found difficult to judge.)

The authority of the artifact is reinforced by allowing the voices in the show to be only those of the plane's designers, builders, restorers, and, most important, crew. The crew's point of view is interesting and important, of course, but why it should be more privileged than, say, that of the residents of Hiroshima, or the atom bomb's makers, or, for that matter, the millions of Americans who grew up in the shadow of Hiroshima – that's a political issue. Each era – each community – nowadays, each political pressure group – emphasizes the history it thinks important. Each listens to the history that speaks to its concerns. The *Enola Gay* exhibit speaks in the veterans' voice.

World War II: Sharing Memories

The *Enola Gay* exhibit was very much in our minds as we thought about *World War II: Sharing Memories*. It was clear, in the political environment that the *Enola Gay* controversy had brought to the Smithsonian, that we needed to move beyond the usual museum exercise of presenting history from a historian's perspective, beyond our usual techniques of displaying objects and providing explanations and interpretations; these techniques privileged historical analysis and depreciated the value of memory. We simply couldn't do that after the *Enola Gay* fiasco; we had to find a way to allow both memory and history to play a role. And so, in *Sharing Memories*, we experimented with the ways in which memory and history allow us to comprehend the past. Memories are personal and specific; exhibits are general. Memories are incorporeal, exhibits show things. Memories stand on their own; a good history exhibit provides context. We had to somehow join the two. Just as important, from my point of view, we needed to allow thoughtful visitors to reflect on the very nature of memory and history. To allow our visitors to understand the value of both approaches to the past would be an important contribution to the ongoing history wars.

The way to do this was to share the job of interpretation, of creating meaning, with our visitors. To that end, we selected our artifacts to elicit a wide range of memories. We set aside a memorial area, a distinctive design indicating that it was intended for commemoration. And, most important, we asked our visitors to participate. We encouraged them to write down their memories of the war, and we displayed their contributions prominently, so that other visitors could share them.

Choosing artifacts was the first step. The objects selected for display were, mostly, everyday objects without a specific history. This is unusual; most recently mounted history exhibits aim for the specific, to tell a particular tale, surrounding an object with labels and photographs to provide the context that explains it both specifically and more generally. But in *Sharing Memories* we chose another approach. We wanted our visitors' stories, not ours. We wanted the visitors to supply their own context.

The objects were to serve as aide-mémoire, not history lessons. We let them speak for themselves, allowing them to whisper something different to every visitor.

The exhibit started with 'The Home Front.' The objects here were the everyday things that touched American life in the 1940s. The symbolic object used to introduce the section was the most mundane artifact, but one that spoke to the all-encompassing nature of the war: a matchbook printed with a *V* for Victory. There were ration coupons and steel pennies and *Life* magazines and movie posters. Of course, there was selection here. There was a curatorial voice, but a quiet one, in a conversation with the visitors, not lecturing them. And so a few of the objects had a bit of a spin to them: the application for gas rations was signed 'Mrs. Harry Truman,' suggesting a level of equality in sharing the burdens of the war that might surprise some visitors. The *Life* magazine was open to an article titled 'Negro Soldiers,' reminding visitors that in the segregated 1940s equality went only so far. The section on production included union badges, suggesting that even during the war there was not unity in all things.

The curatorial voice was loudest in 'The Things They Carried,' part of 'The Battlefield' section of the exhibit. The title was borrowed from a collection of short stories by novelist Tim O'Brien about soldiers in Vietnam, and the things the soldiers carried were, of course, symbolic of their thoughts. (Another title might have been 'For Which They Fought.') And the things they carried, physically and metaphorically, were not the politicians' hoary clichés of patriotism. Rather, they were much more down-to-earth: candy bars and gum and pinup pictures and a picture of the girl back home. They fought for the everyday pleasures of American life. It would have been easy to simply drape this area with the flag, both literally and metaphorically – politicians, fifty years later, might suggest this – but there's good historical scholarship to suggest that what the GIs were fighting for was not God and country but mom, apple pie, and the girl next door. We chose objects that evoked those memories. These quiet objects suggested – but did not insist on – that historical truth. Historical analysis can bring to the fore some of the memories that individuals might forget.

How to deal with the front lines of the war? Here, I think, objects have less utility. In the 'Tools of War' section of the exhibit, we displayed basic military equipment – an M-1 rifle, hats and helmets, a mess kit. Though they evoked memories for those who used them, these objects seemed to me insufficiently time-specific to evoke memories of World War II. For those who were not there, guns and helmets speak simply to the idea of 'war,' not specifically World War II. These objects, like those displayed in another exhibit at the museum, *World War II GI*, had special meaning to those who were in the military during the war, but not to most of our visitors. Weapons, like other technologies, might be too specialized to allow visitors to see themselves or their pasts in them.

We might have used photographs of the war; there are wonderful images available. But most of them seem either too specific or too general. That is, some are pictures of specific scenes that mean everything to those who were there but little to those who were not. Others (the flag-raising on Iwo Jima, say) have a meaning that has become so enmeshed in our national memory that it's hard for people to see beyond the 'official' story. Instead, we used wartime art – paintings from the collections of the army, navy, and air force. Visitors had not seen this art before, and so they had to figure it out for themselves. More than that, the paintings were in some sense generic. The artists were drawing specific individuals and situations, but paintings are more removed from the actual event than are photographs. They are therefore better at evoking memories than photographs would be.

Accompanying the paintings was a series of quotes taken from Bill Mauldin's *Up Front*. Mauldin, a cartoonist and writer who accompanied the infantry in Europe, captured the feel of the front lines. His words evoked for our visitors the boredom and fear of war and served to bring back memories for those who were there – but they also added some real-life complexity to the triumphal combat images of so many bad World War II movies, the list-of-battles sort of history that textbooks present, or the clichés in which politicians speak. Like so many of the other objects, Mauldin's words grounded our visitors in the day-to-day historical details. Perhaps they will shape future memories.

The section of the exhibition devoted to commemoration was set apart from the other sections by its design and by the tone of the words used. The area was carpeted, the structure was modeled loosely on the Tomb of the Unknown Soldier. There is a photograph of a Normandy cemetery. But here too, we did not go for the easy emotional tug on the heartstrings. To have done so would have moved the exhibit too far into the realm of memorial. On exhibit, in a window setting, was not a gold-star flag, symbolizing that a family member had died in the war, but rather a blue-star flag, symbolizing that a family member was in the armed forces. The symbol for this section was not the Congressional Medal of Honor but rather the Purple Heart – awarded to anyone who was injured in the line of duty.

The final element of the experience, and one that I think is essential, was music. We played, at a low background level, a Smithsonian Collection of Recordings CD, *We'll Meet Again: The Love Songs of World War II*. The love songs of the 1940s, the liner notes suggested, were 'songs of love, loneliness, parting, and yearning.' They were songs of memory – memory of better times, of lovers and love lost. Popular songs are both personal and general; they provide a structure for specific memories, yet at the same time they tell universal stories. That is exactly what we hoped the exhibit would do.

Visitors' memories

The most interesting part of the exhibit was neither the objects nor the stories we told around them, but rather the visitors' own contributions. There were tables and chairs in the home front and memorial sections of the exhibit, and on the tables were spiral-bound books with Share Your Memories written on the cover. Our visitors responded enthusiastically, filling page after page of those books with personal and family stories of the war. These were available for everyone to read – some were mounted on a bulletin board – and it was these handwritten stories, a few paragraphs at most, that were the hit of the show.

I've read many of the several hundred memories that we collected. These stories suggested a fascinating complexity of memory and history and mythology that would delight anyone interested in the war, family traditions, and the process of remembering. In many of the stories visitors conveyed, in the space of a page, what the war meant to them, what was important, what they remember, or the stories that have been passed down in their families. They wrote down the stories to honor family in the war, to preserve memories, to let others know just how proud they were. The memories revealed a personal history that wasn't in the textbooks. Our visitors were fascinated too. They spent a long time paging through our 'memory books,' reading each other's stories.

Most of the men who were soldiers during the war told straightforward stories, a listing of assignments, bases, battles. Perhaps their deeper memories were too difficult to put down in a few words. But when their children or, especially, grandchildren told the tales, we get the purified essence of memory.

Consider one story, typical both in that it was a family story – probably 80 percent of the stories we collected come from children or grandchildren of those who lived through the war – and in that it nicely situated its hero in both the family and the war. 'My grandfather was in the Canal Zone during the War,' it began. It went on to describe the injury he received, the story he told the family about it – capturing saboteurs – and then the real story, admitted only years later – a car accident. The story was a gem. Like so many of the stories, it suggested the personal dimension to the war, and the family dimensions of memories. It was an everyday story, not a heroic one.

> My grandpa fought in WWII. He was in the navy. His weapon was a 5 inch anti-aircraft destroyer. The name of the ship is U.S.S. Luce and the ship was sunk.

There were some fine stories tied to objects. Sometimes it was an object of memory:

> My Grandfather . . . He was a great man. I have his Bible which he carried in World War II.

> My grandfather was an officer in the Pacific during the war and brought a string of pearls back for my mother. Years later I heard my father say that they were very special, expensive pearls . . . I imagine a desperate Japanese family had to sell them cheaply to get themselves through the war. I never thought such a strange, disturbing detail of the war would touch me personally.

Sometimes it was an object left behind:

> My father . . . served in Europe in the army's 3rd armored, Reconnaissance. In December of 1944 they were trapped in the Belgian village of Marcouray. Attempted supply drops all fell short. On Christmas they decided to leave under cover of darkness. He was a magician, specializing in slight-of-hand tricks involving thimbles. When they left, he left the thimbles behind. I have often thought about the possibility of a Belgian housewife sewing using those thimbles.

But most of the family stories were stories of humble heroism. You can almost imagine the stories being told over and over, passed down from father to son to daughter, sometimes expanding, sometime contracting. The big picture might be forgotten, but the details never are.

> My Grandfather was one of those people who decode messages. He was stationed in a jungle somewhere and was attacked by a jungle cat. I am proud of him.

> All I want to do is thank all the men and women who helped us win the war.

> All I know about it is my grandfather was in it and I saw him in a picture with his uniform on. He helped the court reconsider about sending a man to death for falling asleep on his shift. For that person and all of us he's a hero. Thanks.

> My daddy was shot down on his first bombing mission . . . He was the only man from 2 bomber crews who was not captured. He hid out for 6 months in Czechoslovakia being helped by partisans. After the war was over he had been declared legally dead and hitchhiked 1800 miles across Europe to be declared alive. This week he will be celebrating his 70th birthday with his family.

My favorite hero story, short and to the point:

> My grandpa fought in WWII. He's awesome!

Some of these family memories were bittersweet:

> My grandpa was a medic in the army. He helped save many peoples lives. I was very proud of him. He had a lot of nightmares at night. I pray that there is no more wars.

> I am a late 'Baby Boomer.' My father went in to the service as the war was ending and was stationed in Italy. He is still, thankfully, alive today but continues to carry many of the emotional scars that have been too many years in the healing. My husband is a Viet Nam vet who has physical and mental scars — they are quite the pair — the men in my life.

And some proceeded from the family stories, moving or angry or bittersweet, to a moral:

> My father was a Marine Raider
> Has Three Purple Hearts, Should Have
> Had Four, Worked Two Full
> Time Jobs, Chicago
> Policeman 26 yrs. And I am
> Damn Proud He Is My Father.
>> I am finally spending time with him now.
>> You only have 1 father and 1 mother.

My grandfather fought in the Pacific in WWII. He was a ranger for the marines. He sat me down one day and told me stories of how it was his job (as he was in a field artillery unit) to direct the mortar shells. He told me, with a pained look on his face, how he saw people being blown apart. Very moving. He also told me how he had to jump into a fox-hole and slice a man's throat. He then saw a picture of the man's girl. 'She was might pretty,' he said. My God, war is sick. God bless all of the soldiers who fought for us.

Those who were on the home front remembered jobs, and rationing, and worry:

We remember the lonely times, the joy of letters, the rationing and the *pleasure* of our small sacrifices.

Those who were children during the war remembered mostly the small changes in their lives:

My vivid memories include selling Victory Garden seeds as students, riding the bus everywhere because of rationing, and having a milk horse named 'Queeny' (dappled gray) because there was no gas for the milk delivery truck . . . I thought black-outs were exciting – not realizing what they really meant.

But most of all, children seemed to remember the end of the war – specific events, images, stories:

In my memory V-J Day was a rush downtown where everyone was throwing torn up newspapers, hugging, kissing, yelling – and I could see only *knees*.

The whole family except me had ptomaine poisoning from bad (and rationed) hamburger. In the middle of the afternoon guns started shooting across the lake and my uncle drove down the lane honking the horn of his truck and yelling 'The war is over!' My mother raised her head and said good! and then threw up.

I was born in 1939 and when the war ended I remember asking my father what would be on the news. As a child I thought news was only about the war. I also remember decorating my tricycle with red, white and blue crepe paper to celebrate. VJ Day – August 14, 1945 – Bklyn, N.Y. Party! Party! Party! Parents didn't care what time we got home. We passed a house on Ave. U and Brown St. 3! Three! Blue stars in the window. There was a bust out party of tears and joy, the mother of the house ran out grabbed us three 12 year old boys – hugged and kissed us and cried, 'My 3 sons are coming home *and* you kids won't have to go in!!' That night we had our first beer in the crowded kitchen from a cold wooden barrel. 'Yuk! How can they drink this stuff!'

We cried with that happy mother!

We went in 7 years later (Korea).

The fiftieth anniversary celebrations of World War II are over now. Memories remain. Reading these many memories gave me — and, I hope, our visitors — a new appreciation of the complex relationship between memory and history. Memories fill out the complicated story of the war. They make it personal, real. Indeed, in their own way, they are more real, because more strongly and emotionally held, than any well-researched history. But just as fascinating as what the stories tell about the war is what they tell us about the way we remember history. History is a personal story, a family story. Personal stories become family legend, a way of connecting to parents and grandparents. There are as many histories as there are memories.

In the post-*Enola Gay* world of history museums, curators must think increasingly carefully about the tone of exhibitions. Once we did not much worry about what the public brought with them to exhibits, but that is not the case anymore. The public is demanding to be considered a partner in the creation of meaning. This is good, but the trick is how to share authority with our public while not simply abandoning the job of the curator and the historian to those who have the political clout to demand that their own historical truths — their point of view — be given the museum's endorsement. I suggest that one way to accomplish this is to pay careful attention to the interplay of memory and history, reminiscence, and research. The past holds many truths. There are many ways to understand it. Looking through the prism of memory as well as the prism of history gives us a fuller, more honest, and more interesting picture.

Note

Steven Lubar is Professor of American Civilization and History and director, John Nicholas Brown Center for the Study of American Civilization.

Chapter 27

Past Tense

Peter Beresford

IF MENTAL HEALTH SERVICE USERS/SURVIVORS are to take charge of our future, then we must also regain control of our past. That past, at both individual and collective levels, has largely been appropriated, denied, controlled and reinterpreted by other powerful interests, notably medical professionals, the state, politicians, charitable organizations and the media. This has been destructive to all our futures. In recent years, the survivors' movement has begun to challenge this rewriting of our history. In this article I want to explore one particular way of giving this challenge further concrete expression: creating a survivor-controlled museum of madness and the psychiatric system.

Now is a crucial time in our history to reclaim our past. I am focusing here on two recent events which highlight the paramount importance of recording our side of the story before it becomes too late. The first is the announcement of the sudden death of community care in the UK. Since Frank Dobson's (the then Health Secretary) reported reversal of policy ('Care in the community' is scrapped *Daily Telegraph*, 19 January 1998), confusion and uncertainty have surrounded future policy. Best guesses point to a reinforcement of failed medical solutions, without adequate financing, as the likely way forward.

For service users, community care has been the most chequered and ambiguous of policies. The efforts of individual survivors, survivor organizations, allies and supportive practitioners have meant the winning of some genuine gains in policy and provision. Rights, involvement and empowerment have been forced onto the agenda. But, crucially for mental health service users, community care has been a public relations disaster. Its inadequate implementation and under-resourcing have set back by a generation both public perceptions of madness and distress, and how many service users may see themselves. The most appalling Victorian stereotypes

Source: *Openmind*, vol. 91, May/June, 1998, pp. 12–13.

of subhumanity, dangerousness and axe-wielding murder have been reinforced with all the power and subtlety of the modern media. It is probably difficult to over-estimate the destructive effects that this has, both for current mental health service users and for anyone facing madness or mental distress for the first time.

The rather more specific event which highlights the need for a user-created history has been the celebration of the 750th anniversary of Bedlam. We might have expected that a history that from its earliest days reveals a familiar catalogue of inquiries, scandals, abuse and inhumanity would be approached with the same sadness and solemnity as any other past inhumanity or oppression. Instead it has become an opportunity, complete with commemorative mug, keyring, paper clip and teeshirt, for reinforcing professional pride and the brand identity of a medical product which by its users' accounts has more to correct than to be proud of. Perhaps most disturbing of all has been its associated exhibition. This is presented in classic modernist terms of centuries of progress, culminating in modern psychiatry and the Maudsley Hospital.

It is made all the worse because it is given the respectability of being housed in the Museum of London, which generally shows a sensitivity to issues of differ-ence and discrimination. The current psychiatric orthodoxy that 'genes contribute to most mental illness' is presented as fact. The experience of thousands of inmates is reduced to a handful of indecipherable photographs posed in hospital wards and grounds, and select biographies of the famous and curious few.

The commemoration and exhibition are disturbing snapshots of how powerful dominant versions of psychiatry remain, despite the emergence of survivors' organ-izations and movements. They offer a warning, but it is one which survivors and mental health service users' organizations are heeding. One of the good things that has come out of the commemoration has been the direct action by survivors, and the news coverage that it has sparked. This is just one expression of a much bigger survivors' culture which has flowered in recent years, reflected in our own poetry, art, photography and creative writing, our own accounts and biographies, our own analyses, evaluations and training materials and our own histories of ourselves and our movement. But the Bedlam revival, like the current shift in government policy, is a reminder of just how much more survivors still have to do, with less power, credibility and money than the psychiatric system.

There is also another cause for concern. When the psychiatric hospitals and asylums have gone and the last of the thousands who spent decades in them are dead, how will people know what life was really like for their inmates? How will the scale of suffering and physical, mental and sexual abuse within them be remembered? What sanitized accounts of the aims and regimes of these institutions will be offered? Many of them have already been demolished. Others are being recycled as indus-trial units and private housing. The biggest psychiatric hospital in the world was recently advertised in the *Sunday Times* as 'a rare and unique opportunity to acquire luxury apartments in a period listed building, set within 30 acres of woodland, with no mention of its original function – its history deliberately hidden'.[1]

One of these institutions should be preserved as living testimony of the experi-ence of the generations who lived and died within their walls. There have already been some attempts to create institutional museums, for example, at the Stanley Royd Hospital, the old 'West Yorkshire Pauper Lunatic Asylum' and at Calderstones

Hospital. But what, crucially, should distinguish this initiative is that it is planned, established and run under the control of psychiatric system survivors and our organizations. Then the possibility of perpetuating professional accounts or becoming another peep show is minimized. It could also build on work that survivors have already done, putting together our accounts in exhibitions, books, news and broadcast media. Such a memorial could collect and house:

> 1. the accounts and testimony of psychiatric system survivors over the years;

- a developing archive of survivor material;
- survivors' mementoes; and
- artefacts of psychiatry and its institutions.

It could reflect the different periods in the history of psychiatry, from the insane asylums of the last century, to the chemical-based warehouse psychiatric hospitals of the second half of the twentieth century. It could make a strong case for lottery funding – unusual in being strong on heritage and 'user involvement'!

For some survivors, the idea of retaining the bricks and mortar of even one psychiatric hospital may be too painful and they want them all razed to the ground. This view demands respect, but will future generations be able to conceive of what these grim institutions were really like, without any presence to remind them? Could survivors, if they had not experienced them? Wouldn't it have been easier to deny the holocaust if the remains of the extermination camps had been destroyed, as the Nazis intended? Such institutions are the embodiment of both the failure and the cruelty of the medical model of madness. Reclaiming one as a home for our history gives us an opportunity to tell our truths; to show how badly psychiatry failed, and to ensure that there can be no going back.

Notes

Peter Beresford is professor of Social Policy and Director of the Centre for Citizen Participation at Brunel University. He describes himself as a mental health service user, having experience of using statutory mental health services over a period of 12 years.

1   Partridge, C. 'Taking over the Asylum', *Sunday Times* 15 February 1998, p. 5.13.

Chapter 28

The Exhibition that Speaks for Itself
Oral history and museums

Anna Green

IS IT POSSIBLE TO CONSTRUCT a museum exhibition structured around sound and storytelling? This is the question we faced early in 1995, following the completion of a large oral history project on the community of Frankton Junction, New Zealand. Over the previous eighteen months my graduate oral history class recorded about two hundred life histories with men and women who had lived and worked in this railway community, once the largest railway junction in New Zealand. In addition to the interviews, we had sought permission to borrow and copy photographs of everyday life from family photograph albums. Despite the gradual dispersion of the railway workforce over previous decades, the response was overwhelming, and the oral testimonies and photographs combined to create a rich account of life in a working-class railway community from the 1920s to 1970s. A grant from the Environment and Heritage Fund of the New Zealand Lottery Board then made it possible to return the history to the community in the form of an exhibition.

Determined to make the oral history the central focus for the exhibition, but having no previous experience in museums, I began research with a small team of graduate students, exploring the journals and handbooks on social history in museums. Was it possible to construct an exhibition around oral testimonies presented in audio, not transcript, form? There was virtually nothing to be found on this subject. Stuart Davies's comment in 1994 that 'oral history occupies an ambivalent, uncomfortable and vulnerable position in museums' seemed to be an understatement.[1] For example, a handbook for museum professionals, frequently cited in the British and New Zealand literature, contains one short chapter on oral history. Two-thirds of this chapter is devoted to the inherent unreliability and flawed nature of memory,

Source: *The Oral History Reader*, R. Perks and A. Thomson (eds), London: Routledge, 2006, pp. 416–24.

and the author finally concludes that oral history has limited value and may best be presented, heavily contextualised, in a separate 'library' space.[2]

The journal articles indicated that most social history museum curators continue to perceive oral history as, at best, a useful adjunct to the material object collections. 'History provision without objects would be and usually is something else . . . objects make museums', wrote one museum curator in 1993.[3] The role of objects in stimulating reminiscence among visitors has received favourable comment.[4] But when oral history was incorporated into exhibitions, the spoken word was usually transformed into text on walls, and consequently lost the multi-layered complexities and entrancing vigour of oral narration. On those occasions when oral history remained in its original form, it frequently accompanied a recreation of social or working life and as a consequence sound was defeated by the busy visual panorama and became little more than background noise. None of this does justice to oral history, nor the importance of memory as a living, active engagement between past and present. Memories should not be regarded like shards of pots, inert fragments from a long-dead past. As Michael Frisch has suggested, we need to 'involve people in exploring what it means to remember, and what to do with memories to make them active and alive, as opposed to mere objects of collection'.[5]

To achieve this, the memories must become the central focus of an exhibition or display. The Frankton exhibition team decided to try and construct a museum exhibition using oral testimonies as an oral source: in other words sound and listening would take precedence over sight and looking. We shared the conviction that creating a highly detailed stage-setting can distract visitors from listening to the oral testimonies. Furthermore, we did not wish to allow surviving material objects, or photographs, to determine the direction and content of the exhibition. The oral testimonies focussed upon human relationships at home and at work, drawing upon the whole range of human experience. The photographs, in contrast, primarily recorded special and happy family occasions, or masculine work or sporting culture. Only one set of photographs, taken by a professional photographer of his wife, recorded the experience of married women engaged in household work, in contrast to the strength of these memories in the oral histories. While there were many photographs of children at play, there were none, of course, of corporal punishment, or the ritual exchange of insults on the way to school between Catholics and Protestants. Consequently the themes for the exhibition were derived from the oral histories, and the lack of correspondence between the audio and visual aspects of the exhibition, apparent in nearly every section, was briefly discussed in the accompanying written guide.

The oral history exhibition

The exhibition was a co-operative venture with the staff at the Waikato Museum of Art and History, whose design, photographic and technical expertise were invaluable.[6] A special graduate class also worked with me on the exhibition, and the individual and collective contribution to the project is gratefully acknowledged.[7]

The shape of the gallery space, and the desire to create five separate sections to the exhibition, determined the final plan, which is shown in Figure 28.1.

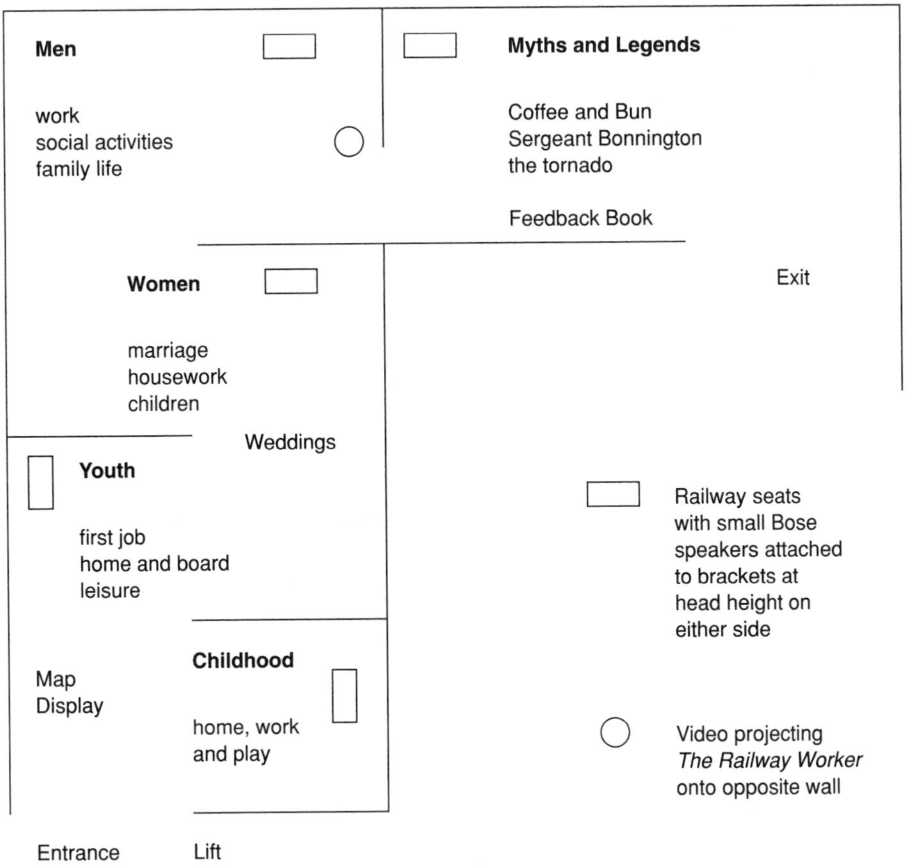

Figure 28.1   Final plan of the exhibition

Technical problems

The principal technical problem we had to overcome was that of making the oral history accessible and audible, while minimising sound bleeding in a relatively open-plan exhibition. We did not want any barrier, such as the requirement to use earphones, to stand between the visitor and the oral history. Furthermore, it was essential that the visitor was comfortable while listening, and this indicated the need to use seating. We were fortunate to be loaned old red railway seats, temporarily removed from carriages undergoing renovation, by the Waikato Branch of the New Zealand Railway and Locomotive Society. Each seat became an independent sound unit, with the CD player hidden underneath. The oral histories were transmitted through robust bookshelf-sized speakers, with internal amplifiers, attached to brackets at ear-level on either side of the seat. Placing the speakers in this way reduced the volume necessary for comfortable listening, and sound bleeding between sections was negligible. To further emphasise the oral history, the lighting was deliberately subdued. The walls were painted a dark green, and both the railway seats and the surrounding photographs were illuminated by spotlights.

Exhibition goals

We began with three goals for the oral history exhibition:

* to represent as fully as possible the diverse range of oral testimony;
* to encourage visitors to reflect upon their own memories;
* to enable visitors to contribute their own responses and memories.

The extent to which we were able to achieve these goals was dependent upon a number of factors, including the principles of selection, editing and sequencing developed as we worked our way through the tapes. Following advice from the curatorial staff we agreed that the whole exhibition should only be approximately one hour in length, therefore each of the five sections could only use ten minutes of recordings. This entailed selecting, in total, under sixty minutes of oral history from the three hundred hours or more recorded! For the first four sections on children, youth, men and women, we decided to include material on the three broad themes of family life, work and leisure. With ten minutes' playing time, only two or three quotations could be included on each particular topic. The childhood section, for example, finally consisted of twenty oral history extracts, roughly half a minute each in length.

Selection

To represent the diverse range of experience within the oral testimonies with an oral history cohort of this size was going to be an immense problem from the start. Our first decision was to include only firsthand experience as far as possible. This reduced the pool of information on any one theme to more manageable proportions. Sound quality also eliminated some recordings, and played a far greater role in the selection process than we would have liked. We found that it took very little extraneous noise to render a recording unusable for exhibition purposes. A panting fox terrier, chiming clock and intrusive interviewer rendered some oral histories unusable.

But we were still left with many more stories than we could include. Two criteria in particular became central to the choices we subsequently made. The first related to the context – an exhibition – and the need to interest a wide range of people. We tried to choose topics within the themes that would have most appeal to a contemporary audience. Although we agreed that the broad themes of work, family life, and play/community activities should form the internal skeleton for the first four sections, there were of course many different aspects to these themes from which we could have chosen. Stories which appeared to offer the most interesting options for engaging with the present-day audience through lively narration, humour or emotion tended to survive the radical selection process in which we were constantly engaged.

The second criterion was based upon the weight of evidence within the oral testimonies themselves. We decided to make representativeness the major criterion for inclusion. Subjects and perspectives dominant within the testimonies were selected (linked by a minimalist narrative smoothing the transition from one subject to another). This may seem, on the face of it, rather indefensible, particularly in a postmodern world. There were, however, positive aspects to this approach. The choice of representative stories did enable us to strengthen the focus of the exhibition. An example of this is evident in the childhood section. Nearly every interview described incidents of severe corporal punishment, either at school or at home. These accounts are profoundly moving, indicating that experiences of physical violence can remain a source of mental anguish throughout life:

> People always hammered their kids in those days, I mean, God, my mother used to take to me with the bloody stock whip actually and she used to beat the living hell out of me, I mean, . . . just because I bloody well annoyed her, you know. But it was the thing that was done.[8]

> I was the one who always got the hidings, I think, only because I used to answer him back . . . I can remember one occasion when I was up the road where I used to play at the end of Lake Road, which was only just up round the corner, and I was coming home, it was dark, my father yelled out to me, 'hurry up', I said, 'I'm coming', when I got to the back door he was waiting behind the back door and let me have it. I was bruised all over.[9]

The disadvantage of selecting representative stories lay in the risk of stereotyping experience. This was most problematic in the section on women, where housework and motherhood dominated the accounts almost to the exclusion of all else. Gaby Porter has rightly warned us about the risks of representing women's lives with a narrow domestic focus.[10] We had no desire to reinforce a conservative popular belief that a married woman's place is in the home. But it was important that we remained faithful to the experiences repeatedly described in the oral testimonies. These were dominated by descriptions of the hard physical work involved in looking after a house and family of five or six children, prior to the widespread ownership of refrigerators, gas or electric ovens and washing machines. Such accounts make the indispensable contribution of working-class women to the household economy transparently obvious. Heating the copper and washing everything by hand, scrubbing the floors and cooking meals on a wood- or coal-fired stove at irregular times for family members on shiftwork showed that household labour was time-consuming and physically arduous in the middle decades of the century.[11] The contrast with housework in contemporary society is implicit within the testimonies, and challenges facile comparisons with the present.

Editing

Editing the tapes for inclusion within the exhibition involved both technical and ethical considerations. We were fortunate in having access to the Pro-Tools computer software on which to edit the tapes, but the process took far longer, and was far more expensive, than had been anticipated. To transfer the recordings from analogue to digital audiotape, and edit every oral history extract, took approximately five days. I had budgeted for five hours. The interviews were conducted in the homes of the interviewees, and consequently while the quality of sound was generally quite good, individual voice levels fluctuated enormously. We tried to make the sound levels more consistent, so that listeners would not have difficulty adjusting between loud and quiet voices, but this was only possible to a limited extent. However, we were able to remove interjections, irritating laughter and extraneous noises, when they did not overlap with the voice of the interviewee. While students record-ing the interviews had been asked to confine themselves to non-verbal responses (smiling, nodding), many did not. Yet those students who engaged actively with the interviewee, through humour and shared interests, created a rapport and envir-onment that appeared to elicit much more lively and extended storytelling. Although these stories required more extensive editing, they became the backbone of the exhibition.

While constructing the exhibition tapes, we were also aware of the need to protect the personal authenticity of people's memories. It is important not to distort the intentions of the interviewee, or alter the tenor of their testimony. Edit-ing the extracts for inclusion on the exhibition tape became a matter of balancing the desire for short, dramatic or effective extracts with the narrator's provision of an explanatory or ambivalent conclusion to these stories. The following exam-ple of this dilemma is taken from the section on men, where Matt Andrew discovered that while some celebrated the male work culture, others were less sure:

> but, again, it was wrapped up with the job you were doing, and as an indication of how you became isolated from your family, I was work-ing in the lounge one night on some papers and an argument developed at the kitchen sink with the son and the daughter and my wife, and I could hear it of course. I thought, now, the next thing that's going to happen is that we'll get Dad. The discussion and the argument went on and it was resolved, and I was still sitting there. I suddenly realized that I had become an extension of the family, and that I was no longer involved in the decision-making process. I was no longer involved in the discip-line of it.

The first version of the tape extract ended at this point, and the focus of the story is sharp and clear. However, the interviewee goes on to say:

> And whilst that may be comforting to some people, it was disturbing to the extent that I resolved that I would resign, I would not stand at the next election for national counsellor.[12]

The inclusion of the final statement may have detracted slightly from the impact of the story. But it helps to explain why the narrator chose to retell this particular experience, for it was the catalyst that made him resolve to give up his position within the railway union. In so doing, the attention of the listener is drawn to the narrative purpose which often underlies our stories about the past.

Sequencing

The sequencing of the recordings may also enable the curator to illustrate other aspects of storytelling in oral history. This was of particular relevance in the final exhibition section – on Frankton myths and legends – which drew upon the imaginative and collective dimensions of memory. One of the legends concerned the 1948 tornado, which caused considerable damage, and was responsible for the deaths of three people. It was remembered by virtually everyone, and the stories were a combination of direct experience, hearsay and imagination. Jane Moodie wished to illustrate the evolution of community myth, through which accounts of the tornado acquired the patina of repeated narration and were characterised by humour and exaggeration. From the wide range of possible stories, she chose examples which gradually moved from the prosaic to the much more imaginative:

> When the tornado struck we were right in the middle of it and of course the whole roof went off the house, but the ceiling was left and it was just full of about four or five inches of this greasy railway soot. And of course then there was a really heavy rain came after the passing of the tornado, and it just washed all this sticky, dirty, greasy soot just came down the walls and on to everything in the house. It was unbelievable.[13]

> But Mrs Hill down the road actually, they had a rotary clothesline, and her husband was a guard on the railway, and she heard this terrible roaring, you see, and she went outside to see what it was. And here was the clothesline about fifty feet up in the air, going round and round, and round and round, and round, and she had Johnny's railway overalls pinned to the line – and it was going round and round and round, and the overalls were standing straight out.[14]

> Yeah, I was there, right in it. We were playing up in Seddon Park and we went down to Frankton and watched the house where the railway line crossing Lake Road is, my sister and me, and we actually saw the house get picked up and taken across the railway, and the people sitting at the table having their tea.[15]

Interaction

Finally, we hoped that the exhibition as a whole would encourage visitors to reflect upon their own lives and memories, and make comparisons with their experiences in the present. In particular, we wondered whether a younger generation would compare the memories of the earlier generation with their own experience and current orthodoxies about family and working life. The recollections of shift-work, and the havoc it played upon the ability of men to play an active role in family life, have as much relevance now as in the past. Questions such as these were raised within the printed exhibition guide. This provided a brief summary of each section, concluding with a couple of questions intended to elicit comparisons with visitors' own experiences. The section on men, for example, read:

Shiftwork dominated the daily experience of those men who worked for New Zealand Railways. The long, irregular hours adversely affected their family lives. Jobs on the railways were keenly sought after, however, for these offered both security of employment and opportunities for advancement. A hierarchy based upon skill divided the workforce, while a powerful camaraderie existed among workmates.

• How would you define the roles of the husband and father today? Do they differ from the roles apparent in the memories recounted here?
• Do irregular working hours have an impact upon your family?

We thought that questions such as these might encourage people to contribute their ideas to the exhibition. Limited resources meant that we could not record oral histories in the museum, and so we opted for a book with written comments at the end of the exhibition.

The book contains pages and pages of comments and memories, from both older and younger visitors. Virtually none directly address the questions posed in the exhibition guide, a lesson perhaps for the didactic curator! Many entries begin, 'I remember', which suggests that the exhibition did encourage the audience to reflect on their own memories or those of their parents or grandparents. Some visitors described encounters they observed within the exhibition space: men and women sharing memories, or sitting on the railway seats and engaging in one-sided arguments with the oral history! Others found the exhibition profoundly moving, with one visitor writing simply, 'I cried, memories of feelings.' Very few entries indicate discomfort with the absence of objects, while many expressed satisfaction with the focus of the exhibition along the lines of the following entires: 'Real history – good to hear people giving their own version of what happened', and 'Wonderfully interesting exhibition, more should be made of oral histories.'

Conclusion

Is it possible to construct an exhibition around oral history in an audio form? The Franklin Junction exhibition suggests that the answer is a resounding yes. The oral testimonies communicated directly with each visitor, and conveyed a richness of experience and imagination which was sufficient to capture their interest. The subjects, family life, childhood and work, have resonance for us all. People will sit and listen, if the stories interest them and the environment is comfortable and inviting. There is no need to banish oral history to the walls, listening posts, booths, earphones or, worse still, libraries!

For the museum itself, the exhibition significantly increased attendance and attracted many who had never visited before. However, the human resource devoted to this exhibition far exceeded those normally available to museum staff. Combining the project with my graduate teaching programme, and acquiring external funding, made it possible to record large numbers of people, work our way through the tapes, and construct the exhibition within the space of two and a half years.

Returning the history to the community has to be done within a reasonably short time-frame, if most of the contributors are to live to hear it. *Love, Labour and Legend* was the result of a rewarding collaboration between academic historians and museum staff in the sphere of public history. I hope that there will be many more exhibitions that speak for themselves in the future.

Notes

Anna Green is head of the School of Social Sciences at Auckland University of Technology, New Zealand.

1   S. Davies, 'Falling on deaf ears? Oral history and strategy in museums', *Oral History*, Autumn 1994, vol. 22, no. 2, p. 74.
2   G. Griffiths, 'Oral history', in D. Fleming, C. Paine and J. Rhodes (eds), *Social History in Museums: A Handbook for Professionals*, London: HMSO, 1993, pp. 111–116.
3   G. Kavanagh, 'The future of museum social history collecting', *Social History in Museums*, 1993, vol. 20, p. 61.
4   J. Urry, 'How societies remember the past', in S. Macdonald and G. Fyfe (eds), *Theorizing Museums*, Oxford: Blackwell/The Sociological Review, 1996, p. 50.
5   M. Frisch, *A Shared Authority: Essays on the Craft and Meaning of Oral and Public History*, New York: State University of New York Press, 1990, p. 27.
6   In particular, Sally Parker (Senior Curator), Michele Orgad (Exhibitions Manager), Max Riksen (Designer), Stephanie Leeves (Photographer), Kent Eriksen (Exhibition Preparator).
7   The members of the exhibition graduate class were Matt Andrew, Chanel Clarke, Sue Garmonsway and Jane Moodie.
8   Frankton Oral History Project (FOHP), interview 172, tape 1, side B, 39.4 m.
9   FOHP, interview 157, tape 1, side B, 18.6 m.
10 G. Porter, 'Putting your house in order: representations of women and domestic life', in R. Lumley (ed.), *The Museum Time Machine*, London: Routledge, 1988, pp. 102–27.
11 See S. Garmonsway, 'Just a wife and mother: the domestic experiences of Frankton women, 1940–1960', unpublished MA thesis, University of Waikato, 1996.
12 FOHP, interview 022, tape 1, side B, 7.1 m.
13 FOHP, interview 014, tape 1, side B, 17.6 m.
14 FOHP, interview 172, tape 1, side B, 28.2 m.
15 FOHP, interview 187, tape 1, side B, 6.0 m.

Chapter 29

Contesting 'Local' Commemoration of the Second World War

The case of the Changi Chapel and Museum in Singapore

Hamzah Muzaini and Brenda S.A. Yeoh

Introduction

IN AN ERA OF RAPID GLOBALISATION, one might argue that nations are increasingly coming under siege, perpetually struggling to hold their own against the emergence of global cultures eviscerating the particularity of single nations. The counterpoint to this is that nations are not mere passive receivers of the exogenous processes of globalisation, and to say that nations would be rendered passé when faced by these global forces does not necessarily hold up (Kong & Yeoh 2003). This is because nations, too, may react against the similarising tendencies of global trends by greasing the wheels of what Sack (1992) refers to as 'localisation' in a bid to stress the unique quirks of the nation in the light of foreign invasions prone to render it 'the same' as other nations. It is too simplistic, however, to stress 'globalisation' and 'localisation' as mutually exclusive processes, or that where one prevails the other automatically recedes. Often, they subsist (uncomfortably) together, feeding off – and at times, antagonistic towards – one another; with one never really succeeding in completely obliterating the other.

In this chapter, we seek to demonstrate the 'global-local' dialectic by examining how the Singapore state has sought to 'nationalise' its memories of the Second World War by extracting the 'local' out of what was essentially a 'global' war. The case study draws upon the Changi Chapel and Museum (hereafter, the Museum), a memoryscape devoted to honouring the scores of (predominantly foreign) POWs who fought for the Allies and were interned in Singapore during the Japanese Occupation (1942–45). Given the global nature of the war and the cast of what has been referred to as the 'story of Changi' (Nelson 2001), and the initial impetus for its *in situ* memorialisation as a largely transnational enterprise,

Source: *Australian Geographer*, vol. 36, no. 1, March 2005, pp. 1–17.

driven by demands from foreign war pilgrims for the sacrifices made by the POWs to be remembered, we seek to highlight how the state has sought to 'localise' the site so as to make it relevant to both foreigners (as a site of pilgrimage) as well as Singaporeans (as a site of national reflection). We then explore the ambivalent attitudes of Singaporean visitors towards the site and their views about its reconfiguration as a 'national' icon. In doing so, we intend to illustrate how the state's task to make the Museum 'local' (in the sense of 'national') is highly vexed and deeply mired in multifarious complexities, especially since the term 'local' can in itself be fluid and contextually defined in a myriad of ways. On a broader note, we also demonstrate how the act of 'localising' war memoryscapes as national iconography is often a fraught terrain involving constant (re)negotiations of intersecting (f)actors emanating from within as well outside the nation.

This chapter is based on data collected through a textual analysis of the Museum (and its predecessor), and interviews, conducted on-site between 2002 and 2003, with its key personnel and 20 of its Singaporean visitors. This is further supplemented with information acquired from newspaper reports, press releases and comments made in the Museum's visitor books and notes left at the chapel walls. From these sources, it is possible to reconstruct the background of the Museum and extract public reactions and viewpoints to the way the Museum has, over time, been (re)fashioned as a national trope. In addition, this chapter also benefits from personal observations made by the first author who was the curator of the Changi Chapel and Museum from 2001 to 2002. This is an important strategy, allowing insights that could only be acquired by being part of the routine operations of the Museum (see Delyser 1999 for a similar strategy). However, care has also been exercised to ensure that research integrity has not been compromised. Specifically, where possible, any data accumulated via the first author's own experiences are also corroborated by other sources.

Memoryscapes as (contested) national iconography

In recent years, the spatialisation of war memory as national iconography, and the accompanying politics of inclusion (remembering) and exclusion (forgetting), have received critical attention from geographers. One of the key themes focuses on how dominant war memories are embedded in public space – via the physical and symbolic appropriation of memoryscapes – as a platter serving the much-needed fodder to nourish national citizens with a sense of a 'shared history', hence uniting the populace as one (see Johnson 1995). At the same time, geographers are also widely appreciative of the fact that such hegemonic acts of anointing a vision/version of collective memory as national history – often by downplaying, if not exorcising, other variations of the same event – may not necessarily gain acceptance by all the different segments of the citizenry. The way a state chooses to manifestly remember the war, and fashion it to the demands of its nation-building processes, is therefore charged with tension and constantly thrown open to complex dialogues between the state and its people (see, for example, Jeans 1988; Charlesworth 1994; Raivo 2000; Azaryahu 2003).

According to Ashplant et al. (2000: 15), however, 'studies of memoryscapes have not been analytical enough of the fact that contentions over the way in which wars are remembered nationally may also emerge from "external" pressures of transnational power relations brought to bear on the nation-state'. In the context of the Second World War within the Asia-Pacific region, this is a crucial oversight. As an event that transgressed national boundaries, and where its (Allied) combatants comprised men from diverse corners of the world fighting a common Japanese enemy alongside each other, a transnational dimension to its war memoryscapes is inevitable. Indeed, how the war is remembered today has become somewhat transnational, as evidenced by intrigues spawned by tactless forms of national war remembrance (e.g. the spat over Japan's Prime Minister visiting a shrine honouring Japanese war criminals; Hack & Blackburn 2004), controversies among nations over how events of the war are to be publicly represented (Yoneyama 2001) and the presence of supranational entities that regularly organise trips to overseas war memorials for their members. As a result, a nation-state no longer has free rein over how it recalls the war and cannot be immune to how the international public may perceive it; the way one nation manipulates the war is also scrutinised by potent forces that lie beyond its geobody (see also Zolberg 1996; Gough 2000).

In the light of these potentially destabilising threats, nation-states have resorted to manufacturing memoryscapes in a way that makes them 'locally' appealing to their citizens as national sites but without drawing any negative impressions from other nations (see Raivo 2000). In this chapter, 'localisation' is understood to be the act of 'de-stressing' the 'globality' of the Second World War by omitting aspects of the event that are sensitive to 'local' conditions, and concocting a more representative version of a nation's experience of the war. Conceptually, we problematise the production of the 'local' in three ways. Internally, we argue that, in conjuring up the 'local' for nation building, there is the need to create a sense that its people are all 'the same' by virtue of being in the same nation. The problem, though, arises if one accepts that members of most states 'include people who do not belong to its core culture or feel themselves to be part of a nation so defined' (Hastings 1997: 3). Sub-national affiliations may thus fracture the 'local' collectivity that is the state's desired formation (Appadurai 1995). Externally, what is 'local' is seen as fluid and may be shared among nations if the subject in question appeals to the national imaginaries of more than one nation, as is the case with the Second World War (Ashplant et al. 2000).

Historically, the way a global event is tagged as 'local' in the contemporary present is also bounded by prevailing sources of historical data and material realities that may themselves be unevenly available and/or constructed. As such, this chapter seeks to demonstrate two things. First, we exemplify Yoneyama's (2001: 340) thesis against seeing the nation as being 'a noncontradictory and undivided subject with containable boundaries'. This is done by elucidating how the Singapore state – and its attempts to craft a national theme out of the war – is constantly subjected to penetrative counter-forces emerging not only from within but also from beyond its territorial margins. Second, we extricate the many complex ways in which the construction of a 'local' (national) memory is frequently debated and almost always constantly manipulated, suggesting how these memoryscapes to the Second World War may actually benefit from a more 'postnationalist' treatment of its historiography (Yoneyama 2001: 341).

The historical background to the Changi Chapel and Museum

During the Occupation of Singapore, the Changi Peninsula, an area on the eastern coast of the island, became part of the Japanese incarceration camp networks in the region. As there were already military and civilian installations – set up by the British – spread over Changi at the time, the Japanese set these buildings aside, and their immediate environs (where makeshift huts were put up), as the main internment complex for more than 7,000 Allied POWs who surrendered (Probert 1988). Given the intensity of the POW suffering, where many of them died under the Japanese, the Changi area soon became almost legendary in the minds of returning war pilgrims. It is hence not surprising that, when these pilgrims visited Singapore in the 1980s and saw that nothing specific had been done to remember their fallen comrades, many lobbied for the Changi POWs to be honoured *in situ*. In the face of such pressure, the Changi Prison Chapel was launched by the Singapore Tourist Promotion Board (now Singapore Tourism Board, STB) in 1988 (*Straits Times* 1987). For the war pilgrims, this site, located outside Changi Prison – once a site accommodating many of the POWs, but now an operational prison – soon became a fitting tribute to those whose lives were dramatically altered during the war (Blackburn 2000). As the name suggests, the central frame of remembrance was a replica of a POW-built chapel (made of wood and thatch), where visitors can come to honour the war dead. A modest museum was also set up, displaying POW mementos to recreate their lives.

In 2000 came news that the Changi Prison was to be demolished and rebuilt to incorporate the minor prisons littered around the island into one huge prison complex. As part of the process, the Changi Prison Chapel was to be shifted so that land could be freed for the prison's new extensions (STB 2001a). According to one historian who was involved in setting up the Museum, while there was initial scepticism as to the need to set up another memorial because 'the war generation was passing away', the decision was carried as 'there were still a few who felt the site is too well-known to be erased'. As such, a team of people from the STB, the National Heritage Board (NHB) and appointed historians (hereafter, the Committee) was put together to design the Museum (*Straits Times* 1999). This task of relocating a place that has become a prominent site for foreign visitors (Blackburn 2000) also followed a change in the mindset of the state. From an initial disavowal of the war as nationally pertinent in the early post-independent era, in the 1990s the state began to inscribe the event as an integral part of its nationhood (Muzaini & Yeoh 2005). The main narrative emerging from the war is that it released Singapore from the British grip and set the colony on a path to eventual independence in 1965 (Wong 2001). This narrative has since been expanded to include the celebration of 'local' spirit under adversity, and the remembrance of Singapore's war heroes (Hong & Huang 2003).

In the face of the turnaround, the state began to initiate the task of bringing the war into the public domain by setting up more memorials as a means of reshaping war memory into national history. Aside from leading new projects centred on more 'local' aspects of the war, such as the Reflections at Bukit Chandu, a site honouring the 'local' Malay Regiment (Brunero 2002), the state also sought to 'replace memory' (Azaryahu 2003) at existing war sites to make them more 'localised'. The Museum was one such site. Given that the Changi Prison Chapel has been the fruit of largely foreign support since its inception, it has not been particularly popular with Singaporeans owing to its 'foreignness'. To amend this, according to a historian involved in the project, the Committee set to 'make the new site [i.e. the Museum] from one just for foreign war pilgrims to one which Singaporeans too could relate to'. Beyond existing as mere discourse, this desire for the Museum to be 'national' as well as 'global', in character as well as in its appeal, was also translated into a series of spatial strategies that were implemented on the ground.

The performance of the 'local' within the Museum

On 15 February 2001, in conjunction with the 59th year of Singapore's fall, the Museum was inaugurated. Like its predecessor, the new site 'pays tribute to the . . . civilians and soldiers [who were] interned in Changi'. The chapel replica was brought over, and a new museum was built around it, which captures the internees' stories through storyboards, paintings and other displays of POW memorabilia. The Museum generally follows a thematic approach with sections on various aspects of the POWs' lives. According to one brochure (undated), the Museum 'fulfils many roles: an important educational site, and for POWs and families, a site that allows closure of the many emotional scars of the war years'. Concomitantly, the new site has also been underscored as 'a powerful link to the past to stand as a reminder of our shared [Singaporean] history' (STB 2001a). According to the then Minister for Information and the Arts (2001), '[through this site], the war shows that it is important we do not take peace for granted, that we do not assume there will be no more war; that there's no need to defend ourselves'. The inclusion of the NHB – the stewards of the nation's history and cultural memory – on the Committee also suggests an overall desire to check the 'outwardlooking' visions of the STB, and ensure that the Museum becomes relevant not only to foreigners but also to Singaporeans.

Given that the whole Peninsula was used as an internment camp, the Museum still draws upon the historical essences of the area as the place 'where the POWs were', despite being further away from Changi Prison. Set amidst 'remote and tranquil environs, with no factories or estates nearby', attention was focused on 'preserv[ing] the idea behind the chapel, to create a place of peace and worship for the prisoners' (*Straits Times* 1999). In architectural terms, the Museum is modelled on a prison: high ceilings, a metal *ala* prison gate and barred windows to simulate the experience of being a prisoner. The flora of those days such as tapioca and coconut – representative of the POWs' diets then – was planted near the Museum to help visitors get an idea of what the area used to look like. There is also a section that displays items from Changi Prison such as old locks, the cat's tail whip and an old artillery shell transformed into a bell. Outside, there is a 'kampong' (village) setting composed of a wooden longhouse-inspired structure and walkway to re-create Changi as it was before the war.[1]

These tactics, we argue, are meant to transport visitors back to the past where they can indirectly witness the experiences of the POWs, and make the site, in the words of the Senior Director of the STB, who headed the Committee, relevant to 'all visitors, foreign or local'. Generally, the sense was that 'place memory' – or the use of place triggers to convey the past by association – was generic enough to appeal to anybody. The 'kampong' motifs also helped to 'localise' the site by giving an idea of what the area looked like before the time of the British. Changi therefore became a site not only where foreign POWs were interned but also where 'locals' had a 'place' in its historical (and geographical) imaginations. The emphasis on locale was also instrumental in insisting that the POW experience *did take place* in Singapore, regardless of the 'foreignness' of the Museum displays. Hence, the salience of the site's location was reoriented from a site where POWs suffered to include the visible presence of the 'local'.

Within the Museum displays, there is now more emphasis on 'local' war experiences to overtly show that 'local' people – as well as foreign POWs – also suffered during the war. These stories include heroic tales, such as that of Elizabeth Choy, a canteen operator tortured by the Japanese for helping the POWs; accounts of mass tortures, such as of the Sook Ching incident where many Chinese men suspected of being anti-Japanese were massacred; and recollections of the routine everyday lives of 'local' civilians under the Japanese. These devices, we argue, also serve to de-centre the previous emphasis on the foreign POWs by adding more 'localised' narrations of what happened to the 'locals' during the war. In-house guided tours, some conducted by local military retirees, also provide visitors with more stories of the 'locals', while planned group tours link the Museum to other nearby 'local' war sites such as Changi Beach (one of the sites of the Sook Ching massacres of the 'local' Chinese civilians) (Museum brochure). For a small donation, visitors are also allowed to pay tribute to the many 'locals' who died during the massacres at Changi Beach by lighting candles within a small box filled with Changi beach sand. Signboards and docents also encourage visitors to paste notes on the chapel walls, pluck hibiscus flowers to place at the altar, or lay wreaths and paper poppies at the chapel, a practice that has considerable popularity, judging from the quantity of this commemorative paraphernalia placed on the altar.

Even memorial services in honour of the internees who went through Changi during the war have been the subject of some degree of localisation. Unlike the ceremonies previously organised at the Changi Prison Chapel, which were attended mainly by ex-POWs and their respective families, those at the Museum – usually including the observance of a minute's silence, sermons and the laying of wreaths – are, as the Museum director puts it, promoted and 'open to all, including Singaporeans'. Further, while services at the old site were held only upon request, the new site now has annual services to mark dates such as 15 February (signifying when Singapore fell to the Japanese), when Singaporeans are encouraged to attend. To entice more locals to visit the Museum, the Committee has also promoted the chapel and Museum as quotidian spaces where visitors can arrange to hold their weddings and other special events.

The Committee's subscription to the more implicitly 'localised teleology' (Appadurai 1995) is also accomplished by the tactic of 'universalising' the narratives within the Museum to make it relevant to Singaporeans without compromising its appeal to visitors from abroad. For example, visitors are very much encouraged to extract and learn from 'universal' POW qualities rather than focus on the (foreign) POWs themselves. That way, it becomes immaterial whether those interned were mainly foreigners; Singaporeans would still be able to relate to – and be inspired by – what the POWs did. In the words of the Museum director:

> There is a desire to have people, Singaporean or tourists, leave the Museum with hope rather than despair, to focus on what good man can do and other noble attributes that the POWs exhibited under such harrowing circumstances. We then make the site relevant to locals as well even though we are in actual fact representing the foreign POW experience.

Another way in which the Museum has been 'universalised' is in how, according to the Museum director, the chapel should not be interpreted specifically as a Christian entity but a more generic emblem of religious devotion, symbolic of the POWs' affiliation to God (rather than to Christ alone), and hence something that all Singaporeans, even non-Christians, can identify with. The extent to which the Museum was able to transcend its Christian associations is, however, limited (see below). Still, such a move to 'universalise' the Museum's narratives – while maintaining the core stories of the foreign ex-POWs – is significant in that it allows the memoryscape to remain deeply relevant to other foreign visitors (especially war pilgrims) despite the discursive espousal – and material approbation – of the Museum as now being more 'national' or 'local'.

Ambivalent attitudes: the Museum as a 'local' landscape?

Generally, Singaporeans have responded warmly to the way the Museum has been reconfigured as a 'landscape of nationhood' where an important aspect of their 'local' history can now be reflected upon. Despite its location further away from Changi Prison, most of these visitors tend to be of the view that the Museum is able to trigger memory of the Changi internees by virtue of its location within the historically rich Changi area. In terms of the Museum's narratives, Singaporeans also broadly concur with the state that the site can now be used to raise public awareness of a 'shared history' among Singaporeans. As one guide mentioned, '[the Museum] ponders over how the war signified the turning point for Singapore; seeing how the British failed to defend us makes me realise the importance of never being colonised again'. There is also an appreciation on their part of the newly added inclusion of how the 'local' people then suffered in their everyday worlds, as opposed to just stories related to the fighting. As a visitor to the site remarked:

> The new Museum has allowed us a way to appreciate sacrifices of those civilians who were involved in the war; and I am talking about the life of the 'local' people; it is a more humanistic stance of war compared to the ultra-militaristic nature of the old site.

More saliently, Singaporeans have also identified with the Museum's attempts to include the stories of the 'local' encounters during the war years as a means of rectifying the misconception that the war involved only foreigners. As another visitor observed:

> The 'local' people were there too. It was not just about the soldiers or the POWs who were there. 'We' were there amidst the foreign forces albeit in the background. Life was bad for the 'local' civilians as well, and I appreciate the Museum showing that fact.

As such, Singaporeans do identify with the Museum as a metaphor of the nation. However, opinions about the Museum have not been completely unequivocal. For example, in terms of visitorship, there has not been a major leap in Singaporean visitors. While official figures are unavailable, after a year of its opening, the Museum director lamented that, like its predecessor:

> Most of the site's visitors, about 60 per cent, are still foreigners. While the 'locals' do come, they are usually part of requisite school excursions, making up the rest of the visitors. So we have not really seen a big jump in the number of 'locals' to the Museum.

It is thus clear that foreigners still predominate over the 'locals' numerically. This fact is also observed during the services, where the attendees tend to be foreign as well.

It is also instructive to observe the behaviour of these 'locals' while at the Museum. Compared with the foreign visitors who tend to treat the site with the utmost respect and a sombre attitude, Singaporean visitors tend to be indifferent to the sacred nature of the site as a place honouring the men and women who suffered or died during the war. As one foreign visitor exclaimed:

> It is outrageous when you see these 'locals' and they are just running around the Museum and talking so loudly within it without any sense that the place is a solemn and sacred place. They just do not see why they should be paying more due respect to the place.

A few visitors have also observed that 'while foreigners spend a long time at the Museum, Singaporeans sometimes do not attempt to spend more than half an hour at the site'. One explanation for this might be attributed to the fact that the exhibits within the Museum are in English, and hence inaccessible to some locals, such as senior citizens on tours, who are not conversant in the language. Yet it might just be a reflection of the lack of any commemorative culture among Singaporeans who are just not too bothered about a war fought by foreigners.

There are also Singaporeans who clearly resist the adoption of the Museum as a national symbol. Three main reasons for this have been cited. First, despite the state's conscious insertion of more 'local' stories as part of the site's content, it is felt that there is still too little coverage of the experiences of the 'locals' during the war. As a Singaporean's entry in the visitors' book testifies: 'I find this museum disgusting as it pays no tribute to the thousands of Asians; it romanticises the Europeans; where are the local histories?' This reinforces the idea that, despite state efforts, there are those who still argue that the site is too foreign, elevating Europeans at the expense of the 'locals' who also suffered. For example, while the coverage of the foreign POWs' stories is extensive, hardly anything is said of how the area was also

> where about 15,000 local soldiers, including men from the *Singapore Volunteer Corp*, the *Malay Regiment* and *Delta Force Volunteer Corp*, and 3,000 civilians were also imprisoned . . . among whom was the late David Marshall who went on to become Singapore's chief minister. (*Straits Times* 2003)

Second, it was also felt that the 'Christian' focus of the Museum, as suggested by the presence of the chapel and the site's toponymy, is another critical reason why some locals, particular non-Christians, have refrained from visiting the site.[2] As one Malay visitor mentioned when asked if he thought the Museum could be considered 'national' in any way:

> When you hear Changi Chapel, the word chapel is linked to Christianity. So when the Malays hear it, for example, they don't want to go because they feel the site will be slanted more towards promoting the Christians who suffered and died at Changi.

It is also telling that memorial services held on-site invariably tend to assume a 'Christian' hue. For example, one service had a program that was heavily spiced with 'Christian'-related elements such as 'The Lord's Prayer', 'Prayer of Thanksgiving' and the 'Reading of Romans 12'. Such religious undertones were responsible for marginalising – if not outright offending – non-Christians visitors. Recalling one instance when the first author was the curator of the site, students from an Islamic school refused to enter the chapel due to its 'Christian' associations. It was only after they were told that the chapel is an important relic from history despite its holy underpinnings that some felt comfortable enough to go in. Still, quite a number chose to stay away, reflecting how non-Christian visitors occasionally do feel excluded from what is perceived to be a 'Christian' mode of commemoration. This is an issue even with the Museum's nomenclature. As the Museum director put it: 'if we had our way, the Museum would be called *Changi Museum* so as to remove the element of religion', indicating that the misconception of the site as a religious one is all too real. The main barrier to the name change, he continued, was that the 'STB wanted to keep within the name the element that had led to the setting up of the first memorial'. This might be perceived as a fear on the part of the STB that if the name were changed foreign visitors may no longer identify with the site, reflecting the fact that, though the site has been revalorised as a 'national' site, keeping the site relevant for foreigners still ranks high on the STB's agenda.

Third, there are those who complained that the site cannot be considered 'locally Singaporean' because it does not cover the experiences of all the different ethnic groups during the war. As one note in the visitors' books says: 'I must mention that the Muslims who suffered are hardly mentioned; the Malays are truly invisible in Singapore.' Essentially, this oversight is verified by the Museum director who was stumped when asked if there were any representations of the Malay war experience within the site: 'We have the stories of the Chinese as well as a little of the Indians though, unfortunately, the accounts of the Malays who went through the war are still something we are trying to work on.' This lack of coverage of certain races within the site has in turn been perceived by some who saw the site as ethnically biased in its 'national' portrayal of the war. As a Malay visitor pointedly asked, 'why is it there is the *Sook Ching* story of the Chinese here? I doubt there were Chinese POWs in Changi.' The criticism extends also to the ethnicity of Singapore's 'national heroes'; as the same visitor reiterated: 'You have Elizabeth Choy and Lim Bo Seng represented, but nothing is said about Adnan Saidi', the officer with the Malay Regiment who led his men against the Japanese during one of the last battles to take place before Singapore's fall (see Brunero 2002). This again feeds into the perception that the Malays are being progressively sidelined in Singapore, and seen as becoming increasingly sinicised.

The main root of the three contentions, we propose, lies in how the term 'local' is itself understood. According to those who feel that the site cannot be perceived as 'national', it is by virtue of the fact that, in their minds, the term 'local' can be – and is – defined using a number of different indices: 'local' as in *all* Singaporeans, 'local' as in *all* faiths, or 'local' as in *all* ethnic groups, which have translated into perceptions of the Museum as being 'too foreign', 'too Christian' or 'too sinicised' to be 'national', respectively. While the Museum's producers may have felt that they were creating a specifically 'local' landscape by adopting various tactics of 'producing locality' (Appadurai 1995), it was not something that was similarly perceived by Singaporeans who have visited the site. As such, what is seen as 'local' in the manufacturing of a 'national' memoryscape is indeed poly-vocal (Rodman 1992), and may be defined differently not only between the state and the people but also among the nation's citizens.

The task of making the Museum 'national' is also made difficult by the fact that much of the writing that has culminated in the telling of 'the Changi story' has been largely uneven, favouring the experiences of foreigners who went through Changi (particularly that of the ex-POWs). This may be because, unlike the many accounts of war and internment experiences by Westerners in print, their Asian counterparts have not been as forthcoming in penning their own stories about Changi, resulting in a distinct absence of material centred on the 'locals' who lived at Changi during the war (see Lim 1995). This paucity of literature is further compounded by the lack of any attempts to conduct additional research, given the practical exigency of the Committee's timetable to coincide the site's opening with the actual date when Singapore fell into the hands of the Japanese. As one historian pointed out:

> As much as we wanted to, it was not possible to focus more on the 'locals' because not much is known. Research on them has been superficial at best. We were also rushing for time to meet the date of completion which was the 15th of February 2001.

In an effort to save time, the Committee also resorted to relying on information already available at the Changi Prison Chapel. Since the latter was already

Western-centric (as it was a product of specific requests by foreign war pilgrims for *in situ* remembrance to take shape within the nation) the Museum, too, also inherited its Western-oriented legacy. The selection of the chapel – vis-à-vis other religious sites that were also built in Changi at the time – as the Museum's centre of attraction may also simply be due to its being the most prominent icon at Changi, where substantive information about what it looked like was more easily available. Hence, the task of 'localising' the war within the site becomes especially difficult because of the biased nature of available historiography on Changi itself.

Transnational inflections to producing the 'local'

> The *Changi Chapel* is a symbol of the enduring faith and courage of our [Australian] soldiers who fought in Singapore during WWII. Like many of our national memorials in Canberra, the chapel recognises those who sacrificed so much for our country. Its place here in the National Capital will guarantee that future generations will have the opportunity to better understand the bravery of those POWs. (Canberra Newsroom 2003)

Apart from challenges that are more internally provoked, the task of 'localising' the Museum is also inflected by issues emerging externally. While the Singapore state has sought to promulgate a more 'localised' version of the Changi narrative, it is not, as the above quote by the chairman of the National Capital Authority of Australia implies, exclusive in doing so. Indeed, as much as 'the Changi story' did take place *in* Singapore, many of the internees were Australians (among other nationalities), such that the POW episode has become a much more 'global' manifestation of the war. In Australia, there is even a mini-series, entitled *Changi*, 'about the Australian experience in World War II and about the individuals who went through Changi' (*Sunday Times* 2001). The criticisms that came from Australians over 'glaring inaccuracies' of the Changi story as depicted in the program (*New Paper* 2001; Garton 2002) also attest to the eminence of the event, as part of its ANZAC (Australian and New Zealand Army Corps) tradition, in the psyche of not only the state but the Australian people as well (Jeans 1988; Baker 2003).

The salience of the Changi story within Australian national imagining is strongly tied to the Museum's chapel. In fact, the original Changi Chapel (after which the Museum partially derives its name) was one that was first constructed in 1944 within the Changi Prison mainly by Australian POWs. It is therefore not surprising that, after the war, the original chapel was dismantled by the Australian War Graves Registration Unit, and shipped back down under. Since almost all of the POW-built chapels within Changi have been destroyed since the war, the one in Australia retains the enviable status of being one of a few such authentic POW chapels in existence today (Canberra Newsroom 2003). In 1998, the chapel was reassembled, no less as an *Australian* memorial, at the Royal Military College in Canberra to honour the courage of the Australian internees. As a means of 'localising' the chapel in Australia, emphasis was shifted from its geographical origins to how it represents the experiences of Australians who went through the war. A plaque on-site reiterates the importance of the memorial as a symbol of the sacrifices made by 'the 35,000 Australian servicemen and women [who were] taken prisoner of war', not only in Singapore but also in other wars such as the Boer and the Korean Wars. As reflected in its official brochure (undated), the site is now known as the 'National Prisoner of War Memorial' rather than 'The Changi Chapel', again de-centring the geographical salience of the site.

Planting a piece of the (POWs') history on Australian soil serves to make the chapel more relevant – and inspirational – for the Australians. As it could not bank on the *real* (Changi) landscape to derive a sense of historical aura for its people, authenticated relics (i.e. the chapel) thus become suitable replacements to stir the imagination of Australians who throng the site, especially during special occasions. In this way, the Australian state is able to cast its commemorative net wider and more effectively to include a larger proportion of its citizenry who will not need to leave their own country to honour their POW forebears.

Given that the Australians, too, use the Changi Chapel as part of their own commemorative gesture, there have been a few instances where visitors – especially the 'locals' – to the Museum become confused over the existence of the two chapels in different continents. According to one visitor:

> I just found out the [Museum] chapel is not the original, it is a replica. If it is a replica, why was it not designed exactly after the original one then? If the one here is supposed to be different from the one in Australia, why do they then share the same name?

Aside from the confusion that it triggers, the presence of the chapel in Australia has also discounted the efficacy of the Museum as 'Singaporean' in two other ways. First, it has made it difficult for visitors to reconcile the fact that a 'local' Singaporean 'national' icon is also one that is celebrated as 'national' by the Australians as well. According to one visitor, 'the Changi chapel here cannot be national, simply because Australia has one too'. Second, upon learning that the original chapel was built by Australian POWs, many seemed even more convinced that Singaporeans do not have the right to use the Changi Chapel as part of their national apparatus. As another visitor said, 'how can we call the chapel our own national symbol? We did not build it!' Hence, it is apparent that parallel commemoration of the Changi story – in the form of an 'authentic' chapel on a 'relocated' site vis-à-vis a 'replica' on an 'original' site – does chisel away at the stability of the Changi Chapel as Singapore's own 'national' memorial.[3]

The perception of the Museum as 'national' is also eroded by the presence of transnational commemorators in Singapore. As mentioned above, visitorship to the Museum is still predominantly foreign (particularly the war pilgrims). Despite attempts to make the site more 'localised', the Museum producers also had to contend with the expectations of foreign commemorators who view the Museum as a site remembering *all* the POWs incarcerated in Singapore during the war. In that regard, the Museum has not been completely spared controversy with respect to its 'national' representations. In one incident, an Australian visitor who came to the Museum reflected in the visitors' book (2001) that 'the picture of the Australian about to be executed is very disturbing and should be removed; God bless Australia.' To date, the picture of the Australian is still part of the display within the Museum, but the incident does reflect that the Museum is not entirely free from criticism that may arise from its international audience. In another example, in 2002, the Museum was censured by a few American visitors for not telling the stories of the Americans who were stationed in Singapore during the war. To correct this, the Museum, in conjunction with the American Association of Singapore (AAS), held a special service on 7 December 2002 to mark the significance of the date for both nations – for the Americans, the day Pearl Harbor was attacked; and for Singaporeans, the day the island was first bombed by the Japanese. A section of the Museum has also, since then, been devoted to displaying a collection of war memorabilia that were generously donated by surviving American POWs and their families. Essentially, these collaborative tactics are meant to remind us of the 'shared sacrifices and friendships between Americans and Singaporeans [which] is indelibly written in the history of our two nations' (STB 2001b).

As such, controversies may not necessarily end negatively. In fact, as the American case has shown above, it might even become a platform on which diplomatic ties between nations can be forged, especially between those who went through the experience together. In addition, the Museum also receives artefacts from other countries as gestures of goodwill. In February 2003, the Museum received an honorary plaque from the New Zealand High Commission dedicated to the ANZAC soldiers who died, and in 2002, it received from the Australian Commando Association a picture of the trawler *Krait*, used in one of the war's successful small-scale raids in Singapore (*Straits Times* 2002), a symbol of the close friendship between the two countries given their shared common history. As such, apart from the Museum potentially becoming a site of transnational friction, it also has the ability to become a landscape of co-operation where inter-nation commemoration leads to 'trans-border' sites to remember their respective war dead as well as to promote peaceful causes between nations involved in the war (Gough 2000).

Conclusions

This chapter has examined how the Singapore state has sought to 'localise' (or 'nation-alise') – through the Museum – the Second World War. This was attempted through various 'localisation' tactics to narrate, represent and perform the memory of the war as closely to how the local people (as opposed to foreigners) experienced, and were impacted by, the conflict. By doing so, the state wove a compelling (but con-troversial) web of signs to make the war one to which Singaporeans, too, may relate. However, the task was inflected by a number of challenges. First, it was marred by the fact that what the state had positioned within the site as 'locally' Singaporean is not necessarily what different factions of the citizenry could unanimously agree to. In fact, by valorising the Museum as reflecting upon *how 'local' the war was*, visitors began also to reflect upon *what 'local' really means*, even raising critical questions about the state's commitment to its policy of multiracialism, opening a floodgate of multiple nuanced opinions which may not at all cohere with the state's nation-building aims. In addition, the task of 'localising' the Museum is also inflected by the foreign-centricity of its predecessor, as well as the paucity of literature on the 'locals' of Changi which the Committee had not been able to interrogate fully.

Since 'the Changi story' is an aspect of the nation's experience of the war that is also remembered internationally, the Museum has also become a passionately contested landscape shaped simultaneously by global forces as much as local pressures. In that regard, how memories of the Second World War are 'nationally' remembered is deflected not only by 'national differences' but also by the 'transnational penetration' of 'factors that cross the boundaries of a nation's official remembering' (Yoneyama 2001: 332, 324). In exploring the Australian remembrance of the POW experience, we have shown how the production of the 'local' in a national framework is highly contextual, subjected to how the term is defined. Inasmuch as the Changi story can be deemed 'locally Singaporean' when viewed through a geographical lens, it was also 'local' for the Australians since many of the Changi internees were Australians. How the Changi experience has been represented and narrated within the Museum has also been critically scrutinised by its foreign visitors. Hence, in 'localising' the Changi story though the Museum, complex contestations, especially in relation to what the term means within the context of the nation, as well as on a more transnational terrain, have emerged.

To be sure, the Changi episode is a celebration not only of how specific nations – and their citizens – went through the period of Japanese Occupation of Singapore but more of how it embodies the spirit and strength of many men and women from different corners of the world who had to learn to live together regardless of their nationalities. Instead of specifically 'nationalising' the story, a more useful strategy might be to position it as a site remembering a time when many (Allied) nations had put aside their differences to focus on that most basic of needs: survival. Positioned as such, rather than pitting it as either 'locally' Singaporean or Australian, the Museum might be better seen as 'a facet of our own national character and a reflection of the depth of the bond between Australians and Singaporeans through the most powerful shared moment [i.e. Changi]' (Scourfield 2003). Perhaps the best way to commemorate the Changi experience is not for one nation to justify how 'local' a site is for it but to herald the Museum more as an 'international memoryscape' where *all* nations involved in its 'making' also come together in its 'telling'. Only then may we fashion, in Yoneyama's (2001: 341) words, 'postnationalist public spheres in which diverse historical understandings can overlap in multiple ways and be shared coalitionally'.

Notes

Hamzah Muzaini is a research associate in the Department of Geography, Durham University, UK. Brenda S.A. Yeoh is a senior lecturer in the Department of Geography, National University of Singapore.

1   There were also discussions to construct life-sized Malay and Chinese 'kampong' houses (representing the multicultural complexion and physical landscapes of Singapore even then) within the vicinity of the Museum to better associate the memoryscape with its pre-colonial history, but this was scrapped because of logistical problems.

2   The major ethnic groups in Singapore are: Chinese (76.8 per cent), Malays (13.9 per cent), Indians (7.9 per cent) and Others (1.4 per cent). Apart from

being multiracial, Singaporean society is also divided by a diversity of religions: Buddhism (42.5 per cent), Taoism/Chinese Traditional Beliefs (8.5 per cent), Islam (14.9 per cent), Christianity (14.6 per cent), Hinduism (4.0 per cent), Others (0.6 per cent) and No Religion (14.9 per cent) (Singapore Department of Statistics 2000).

3   The toponymic similarity of the Changi Chapel in both Singapore and Australia has often meant that differences between the two tend to be overlooked. For example, rather than a copy of the Australian equivalent, the chapel in Singapore is meant to be a replica of a more characteristic model of the many chapels that used to be in Changi then, a more rudimentary wooden and thatched hut compared to the aesthetically elaborate design of the original namesake. The chapel replica within the Museum also houses actual war relics not only of the original chapel but also from other chapels that were built, such as the candle-stands from St George's Chapel, hence reinforcing the chapel as representative of not only the one built by the Australians but also others as well. The decision not to copy the original chapel, and the tactic of amalgamating various chapels into one, may perhaps be a way to differentiate the chapel in Singapore from the one in Australia. By making the chapel generic for all Changi chapels, it would also be easier to deflect any claim that it represents any one chapel which, independently, might have been built by specific nationalities.

References

Appadurai, A. (1995) 'The production of locality', in Fardon, R. (ed.) *Counterworks: managing the diversity of knowledge*, Routledge, London.

Ashplant, T., Dawson, G. & Roper, M. (2000) 'The politics of war memory and commemoration: contexts, structures and dynamics', in Ashplant, T., Dawson, G. & Roper, M. (eds) *The politics of war memory and commemoration: contexts, structures and dynamics*, Routledge, London, pp. 1–86.

Azaryahu, M. (2003) 'RePlacing memory: the orientation of Buchenwald', *Cultural Geographies*, 10, pp. 1–20.

Baker, M. (2003) 'Veterans rally to save a prison that became a legend', *The Age (Melbourne)*, 14 June.

Blackburn, K. (2000) 'Commemorating and commodifying the prisoner-of-war experience in Southeast Asia: the creation of Changi Prison Museum', *Journal of the Australian War Memorial*, 33, pp. 1–18.

Brunero, D. (2002) 'Heritage and nationalism: a critique of reflections at Bukit Chandu, a World War II interpretive centre', paper presented at the Singapore-Malaysia conference, National University of Singapore, Singapore.

Canberra Newsroom (2003) '58th anniversary of victory in the Pacific Day sees RSL National Trustees hand over historic Changi Chapel to National Capital Authority' (available online at: www.nationalcapital.gov.au), 15 August 2003, accessed 16 April 2004.

Charlesworth, A. (1994) 'Contesting places of memory: the case of Auschwitz', *Environment and Planning D: Society and Space*, 12, pp. 579–593.

Delyser, D. (1999) 'Authenticity on the ground: engaging the past in a California Ghost Town', *Annals of the Association of American Geographers*, 89, pp. 602–632.

Garton, A. (2002) 'Changi: narratives of imprisonment and identity', paper presented at the Frontlines: Gender, Identity and War conference, Melbourne.

Gough, P. (2000) 'From heroes' groves to parks of peace: landscapes of remembrance, protest and peace', *Landscape Research*, 25, pp. 213–228.

Hack, K. & Blackburn, K. (2004) *Did Singapore have to fall? Churchill and the impregnable fortress* RoutledgeCurzon, London.

Hastings, A. (1997) *The construction of nationhood: ethnicity, religion and nationalism*, Cambridge University Press, London.

Hong, L. & Huang, J.L. (2003) 'The scripting of Singapore's national heroes: toying with Pandora's box', in Ahmad, A.T. & Tan, L.E. (eds) *New terrains in Southeast Asian history*, Singapore University Press, Singapore, pp. 219–248.

Jeans, D.N. (1988) 'The First World War memorials in New South Wales: centres of meaning in the landscape', *Australian Geographer*, 19, pp. 259–267.

Johnson, N. (1995) 'Cast in stone: monuments, geography and nationalism', *Environment and Planning D: Society and Space*, 13, pp. 51–65.

Kong, L. & Yeoh, B. (2003) *The politics of landscapes in Singapore: constructions of nation*, Syracuse University Press, New York.

Lim, P. (1995) 'Memoirs of war in Malaya', in Kratoska, P. (ed.) *Malaya and Singapore during the Japanese Occupation*, Journal of Southeast Asian Studies, Singapore, pp. 121–147.

Muzaini, H. & Yeoh, B.S.A. (2005) 'Reading representations of women's war experiences in the Changi Chapel and Museum', *Geoforum*, 36, pp. 465–476.

Nelson, D. (2001) *The story of Changi Singapore*, Changi Museum Private Limited, Singapore.

New Paper (2001) 'Upset over Changi: Australian TV series is a "big joke"', 15 October.

Probert, H.A. (1988) *History of Changi*, SCORE, Singapore.

Raivo, P. (2000) '"This is where they fought": Finnish war landscapes as a national heritage', in Ashplant, T., Dawson, G. & Roper, M. (eds) *The politics of war memory and commemoration*, Routledge, London, pp. 145–164.

Rodman, M. (1992) 'Empowering place: multilocality and multivocality', *American Anthropologist*, 94, pp. 640–656.

Sack, D. (1992) *Place, modernity and the consumers' world: a relational framework for geographical analysis*, Johns Hopkins University Press, London.

Scourfield, S. (2003) *West Australian Weekend Extra*, 22 March.

Singapore Department of Statistics (2000) *Singapore census of population*, Singapore Department of Statistics, Singapore.

Singapore Tourism Board (STB) (2001a) 'Changi Chapel and Museum officially opens today', press release, 15 February.

Singapore Tourism Board (STB) (2001b) 'American WWII prisoners-of-war honoured at Changi Chapel', press release, 7 December.

Straits Times (1987) 'Replica of Changi Chapel built', 9 September.

Straits Times (1999) 'New home for Prison Chapel, Museum', 27 September.

Straits Times (2002) 'Museum exhibit recalls daring raid', 6 July.

Straits Times (2003) 'Changi Prison may be spared', 29 March.

Sunday Times (2001) 'Soldiers' story: pitting wit against barbed wire', 15 July.

Wong, D. (2001) 'Memory suppression and memory production: the Japanese Occupation of Singapore', in Fujitani, T., White, G. & Yoneyama, L. (eds) *Perilous memories: the Asia-Pacific wars*, Duke University Press, London, pp. 218–238.

Yoneyama, L. (2001) 'For transformative knowledge and postnationalist public spheres: the Smithsonian Enola Gay controversy', in Fujitani, T., White, G. & Yoneyama, L. (eds) *Perilous memories: the Asia-Pacific wars*, Duke University Press, London, pp. 323–346.

Zolberg, V. (1996) 'Museums as contested sites of remembrance: the Enola Gay affair', in Macdonald, S. & Fyfe, G. (eds) *Theorizing museums: representing identity and diversity in a changing world*, Blackwell Publishers/The Sociological Review, USA, pp. 69–82.

Chapter 30

Collective Amnesia and the Mediation of Painful Pasts

The representation of France in the Second World War

Kevin Walsh

T HE ANALYSIS OF THE RELATIONSHIP between museums and the need
to promote certain types of memory within various societies is one element
in an approach to the history of museums. We can consider that museums, along
with archaeology and history, were important tools in the construction of national
identities during the nineteenth century. Museums have had, and will always have,
a role in the creation and maintenance of memories and identities.

This is not the place to outline a history of the development of museums; such
accounts are more than plentiful.[1] Most authors quite naturally promote a particular explanation for the evolution of what is undoubtedly one of the most successful,
and globally prolific, Western institutions. There can be no single definitive
account explaining the success of museums. However, we can confidently assert
that museums do emerge within quite a specific spatial and temporal context – Europe
and North America during the eighteenth and nineteenth centuries. The origins of
each museum system and, indeed, each museum, are related to a set of specific
circumstances and influences. We can try to identify a series of general processes
that give rise to these institutions, but such an enterprise can only aspire to limited success. Rather, we should attempt specific studies of particular cases or trends
within this web of processes.

In this contribution, a fluid model is proposed (see figure 30.1), that offers
one very generalised approach to the understanding of the development of museums and the control of memory and identity. This is followed by a specific case
study that analyses the selection and representation of one particular theme of the
recent past in a specific region – that of the role of France and, in particular, the
resistance during the Second World War.

Source: *International Journal of Heritage Studies*, vol. 7, no. 1, 2001, pp. 83–98.

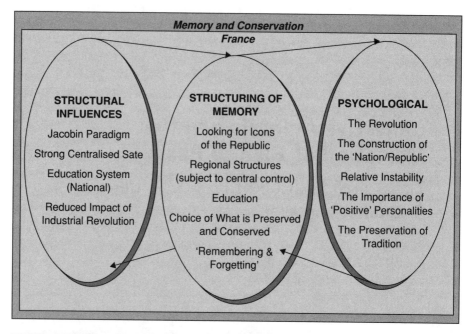

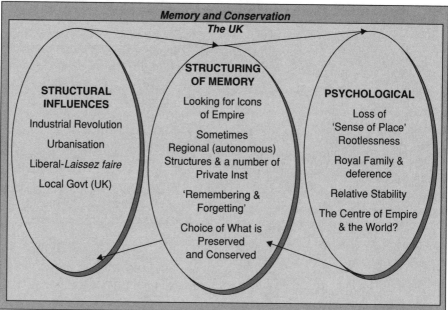

Figure 30.1   Simplified hypothetical model that illustrates some of the processes that have influenced the development of museums

Memory, museums and modernisation

The dramatic changes caused by the Industrial Revolution during the eighteenth and nineteenth centuries had profound consequences on the ways in which many people in the industrialising world perceived the past and their sense of place.

We can argue that a sense of rootlessness took hold during this period. However, once the second and third generations of industrial workers and urban dwellers appeared, we cannot necessarily argue for rootlessness as such, but rather the evolution of different ways of perceiving the past. As Bowler argues, despite the fact that the Victorian period was dominated by industrial and scientific progress, it '. . . was also an age dominated by a fascination with the past'.[2] We can suppose that pre-industrial societies had a more profound attachment to their immediate locality, and contact with other places (through people and objects) was relatively limited. In the rural or pre-industrial context, there seems to have been an appreciation of the processes that had shaped, and still did affect, daily life. The past was something that was present in the construction of the sense of place. This may be considered as a more organic form of memory, one that recognised the crucial contingency of past processes on present places. Places, natural and human-made features, acted as 'time-marks', physical phenomena which exist in the present but possess, for those who know them, a temporal depth which gives them a special meaning.

For the UK, the origins of museums have been well documented elsewhere, but here a model that attempts to identify some of the principal processes that influenced, and still influence, the development of museums (see figure 30.1) is introduced before moving on to consider a similar model for France. Museums developed at a time when Britain and France were the two major imperial powers; the great national museums such as the Louvre and the British Museum were repositories for collections pillaged from around the respective empires and elsewhere. These national museums were an articulation of imperial power – the world perceived, represented and owned by these two nations. In France there was also a need to construct a new national identity based around the Republic. Schaer argues that the Republic needed to create a neutral space where national achievements in the fields of architecture could be celebrated and that such a space should ensure that these achievements had their religious, monarchical and feudal connotations removed.[3] Consequently, the museum, through its appropriation of royal and ecclesiastical belongings, represented the Revolution and the Republic.

When looking at the proposed models for museum development it should be borne in mind that the structuring, or restructuring, of the collective memory can be affected by a number of processes, none of which is really divisible or which operates in isolation. Broadly speaking, there are psychological and structural influences. The order in which these phenomena appear is almost impossible to define; they are part of structuration and have a mutually enhancing effect.[4]

In the French model, the Revolution is obviously the most important element both in terms of structuring institutions in society, and also in terms of psychological influence. The Jacobin paradigm was, and still is, the primary influence on the development of government and quasi-governmental institutions, such as the education system and the curation and presentation of culture. The strong centralised state that embodies the Republic and protects and guarantees citizens' rights through its institutions undoubtedly promotes a certain form of republican psychology and collective memory. Within these new contexts, identity and memories were mediated by new institutions including museums and education systems.

After the Revolution, the creation of the notion of the 'nation/republic' was imperative. The need to create an identity was important during the period of post-Revolutionary instability, and has been vital during several periods of France's recent history due to the instability caused by three German invasions, the collapse of empire, and then finally the need to come to terms with a post-war world dominated by *les anglo-saxons*. On the other hand, despite this, France in some ways benefited from the limited impact of the Industrial Revolution and the maintenance of a large rural population with its traditions, thus maintaining a certain level of cultural stability.

All of these historical and psychological factors have had an influence on the development of French museology, and also the structuration of the collective memory. After the Revolution, the state obtained many religious and bourgeois buildings and ultimately established the Musée des Monuments français in 1796. The appropriation of bourgeois and ecclesiastical property was evidently a crucial tactic within an overall strategy designed to create a republican identity. The Louvre was established as a part of la Convention Nationale (1792–1795) along with the Muséum Nationale (which became the Muséum central des arts), the Muséum d'Histoire Naturelle (developed under Napoléon III), and finally, the Conservatoire Nationale des Arts et Métiers (1794). In some ways the Louvre played a role similar to that played by the British Museum in London as a collector of world antiquities. The Louvre also fulfilled a role as an icon for the Republic, representing its success and its power; plus, the appropriated classical and Egyptian material allowed the state to enhance the Republic's historical pedigree through direct reference to the great civilisations.

The prominent French museologist Georges-Henri Rivière considered that towards the end of the nineteenth century there was a trend towards the regionalisation of museums in France.[5] Prior to this, regional museums in France were essentially imposed on the principal French towns by the state. Jean-Antoine Chaptal instructed certain towns, such as Marseille, Dijon, Nantes, Lyon, to take collections that were imposed on them by Paris.[6] However, even at the turn of the nineteenth and twentieth centuries, regionalisation of museums was still an element within a national agenda. And even during the second half of the twentieth century, these national agendas still had a profound influence on the types of museum that were officially sanctioned, and consequently on the memories that were curated.

The representation of France and her role in the Second World War

The struggle over the curation of memories associated with the role of France during the Second World War has been a long, and sometimes bitter, experience for some people. Such a process reveals how the role of museums in any situation has a profound and lasting effect on what societies choose to remember and choose to forget.

This is obviously not the place to detail the role of France in the Second World War and the reader should consult the wide range of publications that deal with this.[7] However, what does require development here is an account of the evolution of the memory of the role of the French resistance during the war and, by default, the nature and level of collaboration, not just within Vichy, but throughout France as a whole.

The memory and the representation: resistance and deportation

The fact that there is a large number of museums that deal with the Second World War and, especially, resistance and deportation, is important in itself. Traditionally, museums of history or archaeology have attempted a totalising, event-based approach to the presentation of the past; the fact that a relatively large number of museums dealing with a specific topic (i.e. resistance etc.) reflects a need to mediate this difficult period in French history. If we compare this with the representation of the war in Britain, there are some obvious differences. The British have the Imperial War Museum with its *Blitz Experience*, and museums up and down the country will often have a section that represents the role of that place in the war effort, often with some emphasis on the Blitz and the subsequent bombing campaigns. The underlying themes of such representations often revolve around 'typical' British characteristics – stoicism and strength in the face of absolute adversity. Obviously, these displays also merit a certain level of critique, but our principal aim here is to consider the French experience in particular.

A geographical analysis can help us understand the evolution of museums that deal with resistance. Geography in this instance means the study of phenomena across time and space; therefore, we must consider both the chronology and the spatial distribution of these representations. Also, such an analysis includes the study of landscapes of memory which, in the French context, must include the assessment of the importance of *Lieux de Mémoire* as defined, for example, in the multi-volume work edited by Nora.[8]

On the face of it, one of the most surprising characteristics of the 25 or so museums in France that have 'resistance' or 'deportation' in their title, is the fact that the majority opened after the mid-1980s. There are, of course, exceptions, and these are essentially comprised of the small private museums that were set up by individuals who had usually been in the resistance. More recently, we have witnessed the creation of museums established by regional, communal, as well as private bodies. The state, through its national museums, appears to be reluctant for one reason or another to involve itself in such representations, although its presence and role in the development of a certain type of memory of the war is important.

Two major institutions that deal with the resistance, both as museums, or display centres, as well as acting as documentation centres and research sources, are located in Lyon and Grenoble, the first having opened in 1992 and the latter in 1996. Another major museum that opened during the late 1990s is that at Venissieux, in the Vercors (an area of the pre-Alps to the south-east of Lyon) not far from a private museum that also deals with the resistance at Vassieux-en-Vercors, which has been open for about 20 years. These examples are representative of the general chronological development of museums and display centres which represent resistance. Apparently for some time after the war the need or desire to discuss and represent this subject was either not required by society or, rather, the state felt that judicious amnesia might be the order of the day. This desire to forget, or to omit certain elements of the nation's past, should be seen in the light of the guilt associated with collaboration and the mechanism developed for mediating this guilt. De Gaulle seems to have created a myth that France as a whole resisted and, therefore, it was expedient to leave the story of the real resistance untold. Such a strategy was in fact quite logical, as any investigation into, or representation of, the role of genuine resistance may by default have revealed the true level of collaboration.[9] De Gaulle was also obliged, for practical reasons, to include a large number of high-level civil servants who had collaborated during the war, in his own post-war administration – Maurice Papon being the most infamous of these. Unsurprisingly, those who had been active in the resistance were upset by the notion that their behaviour during the war was placed on a par with millions of compatriots who had either collaborated passively, or actively. The refusal of the state to recognise both the true level of collaboration, or the real nature of resistance was reflected by the virtual absence of historians or state museums that honestly dealt with these issues. For this reason the earliest museums representing the resistance tended to be those owned and run by private individuals who had been active in the resistance. Ultimately, their struggle to inform the collective memory received its greatest boost not from a Frenchman, but from an American – R.O. Paxton, who in 1972 published *Vichy France* with the French translation appearing in 1973.[10] The impact of this book, which for the first time revealed the truth about the level of collaboration in France, is almost unquantifiable, although even today there are many French people who are blissfully ignorant of the role played by their country during the war. Within France the establishment of the Institut d'histoire de temps présent (CNRS) in 1979 was the next important step towards a more open and honest analysis of France's recent past.

By the 1980s, the resuscitation of the collective memory was underway, with new museums dealing with the role of the resistance opening every year. However, the spatial distribution of these museums (the second element of our geographical analysis) across France was not even.

A study of the distribution of museums and interpretation centres (see figure 30.2) that deal directly with resistance and deportation reveals how the majority of these institutions fall within the area that was known as Vichy or 'Free France'. This distribution can be interpreted in a number of ways. First, we can argue that the distribution is stronger in Vichy as this is the region that would most like to forget its real role during the war. This was the region that directly collaborated with the Nazis and, therefore, the over-emphasis on the role and relative importance of the resistance allows the development of an alternative memory. The second interpretation of this distribution might consider that this is the region where genuine resistance, especially in the Vercors, was in fact quite strong, and there is, therefore, a natural desire to maintain and develop an accurate memory. What such an analysis reveals is that it is very difficult to discuss national memories, and in fact a regional approach to the study of identity is the only valid and useful approach.

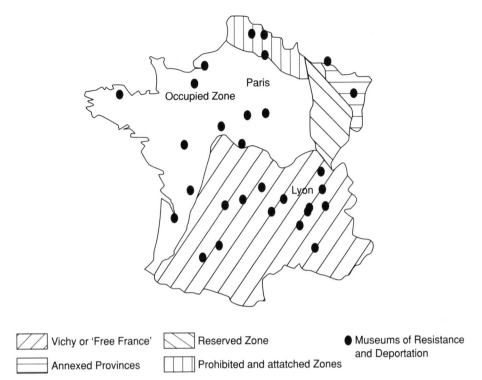

Figure 30.2   Map of France (during the Second World War) with the distribution of museums and interpretation centres that have 'resistance' and/or 'deportation' in their title

The representations

Le Centre d'Historie de la Résistance et de la Déportation: un lieu d'Histoire et de Mémoire, Lyon

One of the most important representations to deal with resistance is Le Centre d'Histoire de la Résistance et de la Déportation. This centre, as with most of the others around France, was not established with direct funding from the state. In this instance, the centre in Lyon is a Local Authority initiative (Ville de Lyon). The state's interest in this project is indirect, but we can argue that it does exist, as the deputy-mayor of Lyon is the ex-prime-minister, Raymond Barre.

Le Centre d'Histoire de la Résistance et de la Déportation is located in the building used by the Gestapo in Lyon, Klaus Barbie being the most infamous agent based here. The choice of locality is important for the preservation of memory. This building is undeniably a *Lieu de Mémoire*.

The centre at Lyon is not just a museum or representation; it also serves as an archive, and possesses conference/audio-visual facilities and an area for young people to come and study. In this chapter we are essentially concerned with a description and discussion of the permanent displays, as it is through these that the development of popular memory is often most profoundly influenced.

Table 30.1   A list of museums that deal with resistance and deportation in France

Town/village	Name of museum
Auch	Musée de la Résistance
Auvers	Musée de la Résistance du Mont Mouchet
Besançon	Musée de la Résistance et de la déportation
Bonneville	Musée Haut-savoyard de la Résistance
Bordeaux	Centre National Jean Moulin
Brive-la-Gaillarde	Centre Nationale d'Études de la Résistance et de la Déportation Edmond Michelet
Champigny sur Marne	Musée de la Résistance Nationale
Denain	Musée de la Résistance en Zone Interdite
Estivareilles	Musée de l'Armée Secrète et de la Résistance
Fargniers	Musée de la Résistance et de la Déportation en Picardie
Forge les Eaux	Musée de la Faïence et Musée de la Résistance et de la Déportation
Grenoble	Musée de la Résistance et de la Déportation de l'Isère
Hennezel	Musée du Verre, du Fer, du Bois et de la Résistance
Izieu	Maison des Enfants d'Izieu
Lorris	Musée de la Résistance et de la Déportation
Lyon	Centre d'Histoire de la Résistance et de la Déportation
Manneville-sur-Risle	Musée de la Résistance et de la Déportation
Nantua	Musée d'Histoire de la Résistance et de la Déportation (1986)
Natzwiller	Musée de la Résistance et de la Déportation
Neuvic	Musée de la Résistance Henri Queuille (family home)
Saint Brisson	Musée de la Résistance en Morvan
Saint Marcel	Musée de la Résistance Bretonne
La Teil	Musée de la Résistance
Thionville	Musée de la Résistance et de la Déportation
Thones	Musée de la Résistance et de la Déportation
Vassieux-en-Vercours	Mémorial de la Résistance du Vercors
Venissieux	Musée de la Résistance et de la Déportation

A theme present in the representation at Lyon, and also in many of the other similar institutions around France, is that of deportation; many of the representations around France (see table 30.1) include the word 'deportation' in the title. Here we can consider that the development of the theme of deportation is useful for the redefinition of memory, it allows the promotion of the idea that the French were victims in the same way as were Jews and other persecuted groups. The choice of the ex-Gestapo headquarters as the building within which the centre is located clearly perpetuates this theme, as it was here that resistants were tortured and murdered.

The first noteworthy element of the display is the decor itself. The display is centred around reconstructed streets from wartime Lyon, with sombre lighting and anti-Nazi graffiti that is designed to represent oppression and the darkest period of French history. Here we see how an emotion can be successfully engendered by a careful choice of museographic format.

Obviously, metaphor is important in any museum, and one of the first displays that we come across uses the speech made by de Gaulle after the liberation where he refers to 'Lyon Capitale Gauloise'. This imagery is quite important, the image of the Gallic warrior and resistant, in the form of Vercingetorix who resisted the Romans, has been and still is important to the French. Today, this image still exists, not just through Vercingetorix but also represented through Asterix, and has become an important symbol for the construction of French identity, especially within nationalist milieus. This historic thread of French freedom fighters continues through to the Second World War where the most obvious candidate is Jean Moulin.[11] No museum display that represents France in the Second World War is considered complete without some kind of reference to Jean Moulin.

Unsurprisingly, one of the most important sections within the museum is that which deals with civil resistance and military resistance. Obviously a lot is made of the French role in fighting the Nazis, both in terms of resistance within France, and the role of the Free French forces around the world, especially in North Africa and in the invasions of Normandy and the Côte d'Azur. Even today, the role of the French is exaggerated; we are sometimes told how Paris was liberated by the French with the 'help' of the Americans.[12] For the representations concerning D-Day, there is little or no mention of the role of the French militia (French who actually fought alongside the Nazis), whereas the role of the resistance is highlighted.

Other themes that are pursued in this museum include, *engagement*, where we learn how people joined the resistance and how they carried out their struggle against the Nazis. This is followed by a chronology of the resistance in which the evolution of the various groups is detailed. In another section we learn about the Jews who were saved by the French, but this is balanced by another section (which is in smaller print) on how the Vichy authorities, plus members of the French public, helped send 70,000 French Jews to the death camps. However, all these subjects fall within the rubric of France as a victim and the fact that many French people were deported. These deportations were essentially related to forced labour, where French workers were sent to Germany in exchange for French soldiers captured and held by the Germans.

An obvious reaction to the occupation and collaboration is to distance one's self by creating the myth that those who collaborated were part of a system that was not really France or French; part of the creation of memories includes the rejection of truths through the use of scapegoats. Vichy is often portrayed as being an aberration, and other non-republican structures are blamed, including the Catholic Church.

Other themes covered in the display include the role of women in the resistance, then a section on the extent and nature of collaboration. Here, at least, there is some attempt to strike a balance – a balance almost entirely absent even 10 years ago. Understandably we want to see the liberation for all of its positive aspects; however, this museum, and others like it, does tend to gloss over the blood-letting and the internecine struggles that occurred subsequent to liberation.

The Vercors: a landscape of commemoration

The Vercors is recognised as being one of the few regions where the resistance was genuinely active and supported by the majority of the population within the area. During the summer of 1944 there was an impressive mobilisation of the resistance

within the Vercors, but for a number of reasons the Nazis quickly and effectively rendered this military action ineffective. The German army not only defeated the military elements within the Vercors, but also murdered and tortured a large number of civilians. For this reason the Vercors holds an important place in the construction of memories both regionally and nationally.

Even from the *autoroute*, which does not directly cross the Vercors, the exit to this area is signalled by a brown, 'heritage' panel composed of a simple image of faces of 'resistants' with the title 'Le Vercors, Haut-Lieu de la Resistance'. In order to appreciate the importance of this area for the collective memory, one needs actually to visit. The history and importance of the Vercors in the maintenance of memories becomes all the more meaningful when one encounters the physical geography of this hidden and naturally protected region. This topography, as much as anything else, explains the relative strength of the resistance in the Vercors. In many ways the Vercors is a landscape of memory. The collective memory is conserved and mediated by several types of representation. There are two museums, but there is also the cemetery, numerous plaques commemorating particular events and people, there are the villages themselves with their monuments to the different groups of victims. All of this is set within a very particular landscape that itself represents for many people the essence of resistance.

The two museums that deal with the resistance in the Vercors include a private museum, established by an ex-member of the resistance, at Venissieux, and is called the 'Musée de la Résistance'. This museum was originally established in 1973, much earlier than many of the other museums of this genre that have sprung up over France since the 1980s. The museum is dedicated to the fighters of the resistance of the Vercors and comprises displays of photographs, paintings plus various objects. This museum is clearly a very personal attempt by someone who was directly involved in the struggle to ensure that people do not forget. There was genuine fear amongst some French people that the desire to forget about the war also meant not only forgetting Vichy, the collaboration and occupation, but also forgetting the role played by the small proportion of French citizens who did directly resist the Nazis.

The second museum, which is in fact referred to as a 'memorial', is the recently opened 'Mémorial de la Résistance du Vercors' at Vassieux-en-Vercors. This centre is representative of the relatively recent trend of establishing commemorative centres that discuss the Second World War. These establishments are sometimes funded directly or indirectly by government or local government; for example, the memorial museum at Vassieux is jointly funded by the Parc naturel régional du Vercors, the Conseil Général de l'Isère, Conseil Générale de la Drôme and the Région, Rhône-Alpes.

First, we should appreciate its geographical situation; set high on a steep hill overlooking the plateau, this centre possesses an architecture that is clearly designed to reflect a military presence. In the form of a large bunker, this building shocks us with its stark concrete aspect, and its dowdy grey colour. Its physical appearance alone seems to be effective in creating a sober and oppressive ambience. This is quite different from the converted farmhouse with its mural at the private museum at Venissieux.

As with the museum at Lyon, there is an attempt to create a sombre and depressing ambience with low lighting; however, the display media are not as homogeneous as in the Lyon display. At Venissieux we enter a large room with a series of displays, one of the introductory elements being a series of signposts that point to the various displays and themes dealt with in the museum. These include the following: artistic collaboration (the role of actors etc. in the collaboration), represented by theatre seats, a Nazi cap plus other objects all within a cage. Gestapo interrogation is represented by a desk with a swastika flag, a lamp, and a chair with handcuffs attached. Deportation is, as with many other similar displays across France, one of the principal themes in the display; a house door with the yellow Star of David represents this.

One of the most effective elements within this museum is the section where personal accounts of actions and events during the struggle in the Vercors can be listened to. This section is dominated by a bunker-type structure, the openings of which look out on to the final part of the museum where large panels and videos detail the battle for the Vercors that took place during the summer of 1944. This section includes sculptures that represent the personalities from the resistance.

On the whole this museum attempts a balanced and critical representation, detailing the specificity of the struggle within a particular area rather than attempting a totalising narrative which attempts to represent the French experience during the war at a national level.

Collective amnesia and the resuscitation of memory . . .

One question that we do need to ask is why most of these museums are recent undertakings. Does this mean that the events represented therein are now far enough back in time that they are no longer directly contingent on the present? Can we argue that such displays mediate and relegate past events to a completed past, i.e. a problem that is dealt with and finished – the objectification of historical processes and the truncation of the past from the present?

We often talk about the preservation of memory, keeping alive an identity that has never died, but with this example of the representation of France during the war, we are almost dealing with the resuscitation of memory. The collective French memory of the war (beyond those who had actually witnessed the events) was somewhat blighted by a collective amnesia, an amnesia that the nation (through the state, through historians and the media) had sanctioned. For those who do not directly witness the past, forgetting is often easier than remembering. One of the reasons for 'forgetting' is that the French had a long and serious debate surrounding the problem of collective responsibility and the idea of guilt as relating to both German and French roles in the Second World War. We also have to consider the impact on the collective memory of the French atrocities in Algeria not so long after the war and, in one case, during the war.[13] Obviously it was expedient for French society to support and promote the idea of non-collective responsibility and emphasise the guilt and faults of individuals rather than groups or collective bodies. This attitude is reflected within the French legal system, where the principle of vicarious liability is almost entirely absent and where overt critique of the Republic seems to be unacceptable, as it is the Republic that guarantees and protects its citizens. Vichy, as de Gaulle argued, was a digression in France's history, it was not the real France. However, some have argued that 'national amnesia' is a French speciality.[14]

Part of the construction of any national memory includes the use of certain 'important' individuals as heroes or role models. What is interesting is how the category of hero or role model varies from country to country, and also how the list of popularity of these figures from the past changes over time. A recent survey in the popular French history magazine *L'Histoire*[15] is discussed under the heading 'Le palmarès de la mémoire nationale'. The poll suggests that the French feel more attached to political and military figures from the past (Charles de Gaulle and Napoléon occupying the first two positions in the list) than other nationalities. For example, the British place Shakespeare at the top of their list, and the Italians give Leonardo da Vinci their vote. What is interesting in the French example is that the popularity of Charles de Gaulle and Napoléon has risen since the 1980s. In fact, in 1948 de Gaulle received only 1% of the vote, whilst in the new poll the figure stood at 29%. What is most interesting in the context of the discussion surrounding the 'resuscitation' of the collective memory and the role of France during the war is the fact that Jean Moulin, one of the key figures in the French resistance, has entered the list for the first time. This entry was within the category where the following question was asked: 'who is the person for whom you have the greatest sympathy?' In 1980 Moulin did not figure in this list at all. This category is still headed by Marie Curie. Moulin has jumped straight to second place, having displaced Jeanne d'Arc from this position and relegating her to number 3. This reflects the continued rationalisation of the memory of the war and the need for the French to retrieve a positive memory from this difficult period in their past. The presence of Jeanne d'Arc and Vercingetorix in the list, two figures who also represent resistance against foreign occupation, is also noteworthy. Philippe Pétain makes an appearance at number 12 in this poll. As the two authors note, the appearance of Jean Moulin in this poll shows how he is 'participating in the reorganisation of the history of France during the Second World War'.[16]

Conclusion

This brief study of the evolution of the memory and the representation of the role of France during the Second World War shows us how all memories are contingent upon an infinite number of factors. These include the media, education systems, museums and popular memory passed down from one generation to another. No matter how hard the state tries, popular memory at the local or regional level cannot always be subsumed by a crafted national memory, constructed through national ideology. In particular, the example of the Vercours shows us how regional identity and memory can be preserved, and can evolve to the point where it is sanctioned by the establishment of a public, or semi-public, funded museum. Memories are not static; they develop and change with each generation and museums and other forms of representation must respond to and nurture this process.

> L'objectivité n'existe pas. Surtout quand il s'agit de souffrance et de mort, de victimes et de coupables.

Notes

Kevin Walsh co-directs the MA in Archaeological Heritage Management at the University of York, UK.

1 See for example: T. Bennett, *The Birth of the Museum*, London: Routledge, 1995; E. Hooper-Greenhill, *Museums and the shaping of knowledge*, London: Routledge, 1992; S. Pearce, *Museums Objects and Collections: A Cultural Study*, Leicester: Leicester UP, 1992; K. Walsh, *The Representation of the Past*, London: Routledge, 1992.

2 P.J. Bowler, *The invention of progress: the Victorians and the past*, Oxford: Blackwell, 1989, p. 1.

3 R. Shaer, *L'Invention des musées*, Paris: Gallimard, 1993.

4 A. Giddens, *The constitution of society*, Cambridge: Polity, 1984.

5 G.-H. Rivière, *La muséologie*, Paris: Bordas, 1989, p. 53.

6 Shaer, op. cit. (note 3), p. 72.

7 Most notably, Ousby's recent and most readable and balanced account of the occupation, I. Ousby, *Occupation: the ordeal of France 1940–1944*, London: Pimlico, 1999.

8 P. Nora (ed.) *Les lieux de mémoire* (Vols 1, 2, 3), Paris: Gallimard, 1997.

9 Ousby, op. cit. (note 7), p. 310.

10 R.O. Paxton, *Vichy France*, New York: Columbia University Press, 1972.

11 One of the most important figures in the French resistance who was caught, and then identified by Klaus Barbie, and ultimately died in the hands of the Gestapo in July 1943.

12 French troops under Leclerc did march in to Paris, largely because the allies realised that this was important for French morale and national unity.

13 In 1945 French forces put down a demonstration in the Algerian town of Sétif, killing 5,000 civilians.

14 D. Nicolaïdis (ed.) *Oublier nos crimes: l'amnésie nationale, une spécificité française?*, Paris: Autrement, 1994.

15 Ph. Joutard & J. Lecuir, 'Les palmarès de la mémoire nationale', *L'Histoire*, No. 242, April 2000, pp. 32–39.

16 Ibid., p. 35.

Chapter 31

Victims Remembered

Tiffany Jenkins

B EFORE THE ELECTIONS IN IRAQ, before any talk of withdrawing troops
and amid continued fighting, the Americans proposed building a memorial museum
in Baghdad documenting the atrocities of Saddam Hussein's regime. While the plan
was rejected by other countries (it was not a decision the Iraqi people were to make),
the speed of the suggestion shows how popular memorial museums have become.

Museums that document trauma and conflict are important. Israel's national
Holocaust memorial Yad Vashem (which inagurated its New Museum in March)
has, since its 1953 foundation, provided both authoritative exhibition and research
facilities. In the last 20 years, other memorial museums have proliferated across
the globe. The list includes the Nanjing Massacre Memorial Museum in eastern China,
Robben Island Museum in South Africa and the genocide museums outside Kigali
in Rwanda. In the United States, the Washington Holocaust Memorial Museum
is one of many in that country.

James Young, the author of *The Texture of Memory: Holocaust Memorials and Their
Meanings*, puts the growth of memorial museums down to different trends that
came together around the idea of global suffering: 'Some were stimulated by the
passing and near-passing of survivors and changing regimes in Eastern Europe.'

He points to a change in the role museums play in society: 'There was also a
tendency to see museums as places where communities can localise memories and
build identity around stories.' Young says other factors are the decline of national
institutions, the crumbling of the church and the family. 'Everyone feels they have
the right to tell their own stories and this is often done today through the identification
with martyrdom and suffering.'

While the unique events memorialised and the specific circumstances of each
mean that every museum is different, the increase in the number of memorial

Source: *Museums Journal*, May 2005, pp. 22–3, 25.

museums and the claims that are made for them is something that requires examination. Not everyone is comfortable with the trend. Of course, due to the nature of their subjects, they will disrupt and disturb, but is this always good for those they claim to help, the dominated?

And is the proliferation of such institutions a sign of a healthy society trying to understand and make amends, or one with an unhealthy obsession with the past and the worst aspects of man?

A common criticism is that the purpose – to stop such events happening again – fails. John Lennon, the co-author of *Dark Tourism: The Attraction of Death and Disaster*, complains: 'Never again does not work.'

For Lennon, erecting and visiting memorial museums can be a get-out clause for those not wanting to examine the real and present problems: 'It's easier to look at the dark heart of other nations and times than our own. What about discussing the state of immigration centres here today? That's more significant than the Imperial War Museum talking about the Holocaust.'

Lennon has a point: there are more Holocaust museums in America than any country, despite a tenuous relationship to the event, and they were created during periods when the country's leaders waged war on others. To date, the Holocaust Memorial Museum in Washington has been visited by 76 heads of state and government, many of who were engaged in unfriendly fire elsewhere.

But museum directors cannot be held responsible for this – although they should refrain from claiming their institutions can achieve so much. Presidents and prime ministers use memorial museums to make them look good, so the criticism should be directed at them, not curators and education departments that examine the past.

Indeed when these museums do try to discuss the present they can run into problems. The Anne Frank Museum in Amsterdam raises the threat of the far right in Europe today and racism in football; the Beit Hashoah Museum of Tolerance in Los Angeles transports the concern with the Holocaust into a discussion about intolerance today. Museum texts compare 'cursing and shoving your sister' to war and all audiences are lectured that 'the potential of violence is within us all'.

While intolerance exists today, it is not helpful to compare the Holocaust to a squabble between siblings: it distorts our understanding of the power relationships that built up in Europe and the state organisation of the attempted elimination of a population. The comparison of the horrific events that led to the murder of Anne Frank to the reactionary, but far less powerful impact of the far right today, is an insult to her experience. It is possible that some institutions are too interested in comparisons to the present at the expense of understanding the gravity and specificity of the past.

Susan Jacoby, the author of *Half-Jew: A Daughter's Search for Her Family's Buried Past* has other concerns. She argues that visits are a temporary trip in people's happier lives making them feel morally right-on: 'These museums are problematic because they leave tourists with a self-satisfied glow at having given up a day of ordinary sightseeing and shopping for an exhibit of Hell on Earth.' Other critics have questioned the use of multimedia in these museums, which are often full of interactive exhibits, sound effects and films.

But these complaints can underestimate the intentions of the audiences. Visitors are not on jaunts to ace cafes with good museums attached: high levels of emotion are induced and contemplation takes place. In fact most of these museums aim to relate to the individual through their emotions. It is this aspect of them that is especially interesting, suggests Edward T. Linenthal, author of *Preserving Memory: The Struggle to Create America's Holocaust Museum*. 'What is new', he says, 'is the individual focus with the emphasis on the emotions. This therapeutic turn is different to the previous civic ideas at the heart of museums.'

For example, at the Apartheid Museum in Johannesburg, South Africa, visitors receive a card arbitrarily assigning them a racial classification: white or non-white. It encourages them to personally relate to the story they are told.

Many of these museums have been architecturally designed to manipulate. Daniel Libeskind's design for Berlin's Jewish Museum has passages cambered at slight angles, the ensuing destabilisation only hinting at disorientation of the Nazis' victims. At the Washington Holocaust Memorial Museum, the entrance to the permanent exhibition reminds people of a concentration camp: the elevators are claustrophobic, with stark lighting, exposed metal, and low ceilings. A video monitor plays a clip of liberators arriving at the camp. A voice says: 'We don't know what it is; some sort of prison.' As it stops, the doors open and people walk into the elevator. While they are not cattle cars, there is no doubt that they recall them. It is a brutal experience.

The audience is treated as if its empathy can only be triggered by turning the experience of others into versions of what is happening to them. A gallery space that forces the visitor to bend down and uses harsh lighting is nasty but radically different from the places it is supposed to represent. The visitor is encouraged to think about 'me', not them, now, not then. This may trivialise what happened, reducing the understanding of the conflict to a bad 'reality museum' experience.

But, for sociologists Nicola Lisus and Richard Ericson, the spectacle of multimedia turns the Beit Hashoah Museum of Tolerance into an 'emotions factory'. 'It is not clear whether people will feel the need to translate their emotions into knowledge useful for the prevention of genocide', they write.

Alternatively, many think that relating to others through emotion creates a connection with the victims. Some go so far as to argue that the concept of suffering provides a way for a fragmented world to create meaning.

Jeffrey Alexander, a sociologist at Yale University, has written about this. He asks: 'Is the suffering of others also our own?' He continues: 'In thinking that it might in fact be, societies expand the circle of the we . . . By refusing to participate in what I will describe as the process of trauma creation, social groups restrict solidarity leaving others to suffer alone.' In Alexander's view, suffering can help provide meaning and understanding with others today.

Edward T. Linenthal says: 'When I was writing about the Holocaust Museum it became clear that there was recognition as prestige in being a victim. All sorts of groups who were previously uninterested in saying they were part of the experience now want to be defined as such.'

According to Linenthal, we have to be careful of this trend and cautious of elevating the value of trauma. Sometimes closure or forgetting is appropriate. 'Promoting the line that my ancestors were slaves as a crutch or a weapon would not be good. Competing over how hurt your people were is not constructive. At times it is good for people to move on. Sometimes forgetting is good.' However,

Linethanal does thinks that the memorial museum message can be a good one. '[If it] . . . makes us more humble, exposes the distance between reality and ideals, then it is remembering in a constructive way', he believes.

In the past, national myths presented in traditional museums promoted the idea of the unique greatness of peoples. It was a one-sided history that reinforced the position of the powerful at the expense of the trodden-on. In this respect it is right that the kings and the generals have been knocked off their pedestals. But it is not necessarily right that this version of history has been replaced by so many stories of suffering.

This is not to deny suffering; it happens, and will continue to do so. But how we understand it matters to our understanding of the past and our attitude towards the future. First, we should steer clear of promoting suffering as a way to connect to others. It is not a hopeful vision for the future or what makes us human. One problem is that it suggests the past defines the future; but the past does not have to determine what happens. Another problem is that it misrepresents the hope and struggle of those who fought for freedom and equality.

Paul Robeson, the black American singer and activist, often changed the lyrics of songs. He altered 'Old Man River', from the musical *Show Boat*, in way that is relevant here. Instead of 'Git a little drunk and you land in jail. Ah gits weary, an' sick of tryin' ah'm tired of livin' and scared of dying', Robeson sang, 'You show a little grit and you land in jail. But I keeps laughin' instead of cryin' I must keep fighting until I'm dying.' The attitude in the rewritten lyrics is dramatically different. His spirit is tough and strong.

Of course we need museums that show us the brutal past – because it happened and we need to understand it. But we should be careful not to elevate the suffering of people over their struggle in the search for meaning today.

Note

Tiffany Jenkins is the arts and society Director at the London-based Institute of Ideas.

Chapter 32

The Holocaust Museum Concept

Terence Duffy

IN THE PAST FEW YEARS, inspired equally by the impact of Steven Spielberg's sensitive filmography and the serenity of wartime commemoration, the European Holocaust has become a truly 'popular' concept. The international media have transformed the Holocaust event so that its resonance for world society is universally understood. The suffering endured during the years 1933–45 has inspired research by all who oppose the abrogation of human values. Among museum curators, the increasing treatment of Holocaust materials alongside other human rights issues marks the transformation of the Holocaust concept in museum programming.

The European memory of the Holocaust is enshrined in the series of interpretative centres in the former concentration camps. One thinks, in particular, of Dachau, Buchenwald, Bergen-Belsen, Auschwitz-Birkenau, Natzweiler, Treblinka, Terezin, and also of the remnants of Jewish communities across Russia and Eastern Europe. The ruins of the crematoria and gas chambers constitute fragments of a physical heritage of suffering. In the same tradition is the Anne Frank Museum in Amsterdam, which explores the daily life of a Jewish family entrapped by the Nazi occupation. However, it is encouraging that this museum is increasingly concerned with contemporary intolerance, focusing on Europe's extreme right-wing political movements.

As museums, the former concentration camps offer a primarily descriptive approach to the Holocaust. The staff often include survivors, but visitors complain that nothing is said about the relevance of the camps to contemporary human rights. One hopes that with growing interest in tracing the Holocaust through the concentration camps of Europe, the connections between this horrific experience and the question of global human rights may be reinforced.

Source: *Museum International*, vol. 49, no. 1, 1997, pp. 54–8.

A lasting memorial and a tribute to the Diaspora

For the world Jewish community, Jerusalem's Yad Vashem commemorates the greatest tragedy in their history. It was felt that only Israel could discharge this historic task and in 1953 Yad Vashem was established to preserve the memory of 6 million Jews annihilated by Nazi Germany. At the museum entrance, the massive bas-relief by the Israeli artist Naftali Besem symbolizes Yad Vashem's preoccupations, for its panels depict the Holocaust juxtaposed against the Israeli homeland. Yad Vashem exhibits the artwork of victims and survivors while its Hall of Names records more than 3 million victims. The Wall of Remembrance and the Monument to the Victims of the Death Camps evoke Holocaust suffering. The help of Gentiles is acknowledged in the Avenue of the Righteous. Yad Vashem is a powerful symbol of the importance of the Holocaust in Jewish life and of its overwhelming centrality in Israel. The memorial staff organize the national day of remembrance conducted throughout Israel and among Diaspora communities across the world.

Yad Vashem represents the self-conscious perpetuation of the Holocaust memory in the psyche of the entire Jewish community. It offers a critique of the historical roots of anti-Semitism, and it seeks to transmit this information to future generations. The combination of commemoration, education and research makes it a unique institution. The impulses that it articulates are still the dominant ones in Jewish thinking about the Holocaust, and have substantially influenced the image of the Jewish community in the international world.

Israel's Beth Hatefutsoth (Nahum Goldmann) Museum of the Jewish Diaspora opened in Tel Aviv in 1978. It is still the only museum devoted to the Jewish Diaspora and a radical departure from the accepted notion of a historical museum. Beth Hatefutsoth drastically alters the view of museums as custodians of authentic objects. The underlying principle of its permanent exhibition is 'reconstruction'. This approach evolved out of a realization that it was impossible adequately to assemble the physical heritage of the Diaspora. Instead, it sought a 'visual re-creation' using audio-visual and electronic techniques. The museum thus adopted a historiographic approach then unique among Jewish historical museums. All historical museums have a natural prejudice towards the national past and in Jewish museums the history of the Diaspora and Jewry is often described solely in terms of persecution and pogroms. The planners of Beth Hatefutsoth have sought to offer a balanced reconstruction of the Jewish past so that the Diaspora can also be viewed as a remarkable achievement.

The culture of Yad Vashem and the Museum of the Jewish Diaspora is echoed in Jewish museums across the world. It is subtly present in the impressive New York Jewish Museum on Manhattan's Fifth Avenue. Although this museum is a living history of Jewish traditions, its exhibition programming reflects Holocaust preoccupations, relying frequently on the curators of Yad Vashem. Indeed, the Holocaust is integral to Jewish life and therefore, *ipso facto*, it is a prime ingredient of Jewish museums. The key issue is how it is portrayed. Traditionally the tendency has been towards introspection, but many curators are experimenting with the Holocaust experience in the context of global suffering. Evidently, the New York museum is now embarking on this latter approach.

A concept metamorphosed

The first institution dedicated to the Holocaust to be built outside Israel is Detroit's Holocaust Memorial Center, which opened in 1984. Proposed some twenty years earlier by prominent Holocaust survivors, it reflects a mutual obligation to remember and learn from the tragedy. The Center not only documents the horrors of this period but highlights the rich history of the Jewish people. Nevertheless, the themes are primarily those of Yad Vashem. Its entrance diorama (representing the historical persecution of the Jews) echoes Yad Vashem's bas-reliefs, while the galleries are scale versions of the exhibitions in Jerusalem.

The founder of the Detroit Memorial Center, Rabbi Charles Rosenzveig, conceived the idea from a concern that the Holocaust was not fully recorded in documentary form in the United States. The United States Holocaust Memorial Museum, which opened in April 1993, is a more innovative product of such commitment. The US Holocaust Memorial Council was established in 1980 by a unanimous act of Congress and was mandated with the task of creating 'a living memorial to the six million Jews and millions of other victims of Nazi fanaticism who perished in the Holocaust'. These are key words, for the Holocaust Memorial Museum represents a significant departure from traditional views. This major national museum, occupying a prominent spot along Washington's 'museum mile', articulates a less introspective perspective on the Jewish tragedy.

The museum is centrally concerned with relating the Jewish experience to the persecution of other minority groups by the Nazi regime. Its permanent exhibition tells the story of state-sponsored genocide of Jews, Gypsies, Poles, homosexuals, the handicapped, Jehovah's Witnesses, political and religious dissidents and other minorities. Although the central theme is the destruction of the European Jews, their tragic story is told through the broader lens of Nazi persecution. Visitors who enter this museum will learn that many groups, along with Jews, were systematically excluded from society in Nazi Germany. Whereas Yad Vashem is principally envisaged as a shrine, the Holocaust Memorial paints a broader tapestry. As its first director Jeshajahu Weinberg puts it: 'The Museum is not intended to be a Jewish museum . . . there were millions of other victims. Their stories will be told as well.'

Weinberg insists that the universality of the Holocaust is one of its important lessons and museum staff hope that visitors will respond. In April 1991 the Holocaust Memorial Council appealed to the President 'to stop the slaughter of the Kurdish minority by the Iraqi government'. In 1992 the Council wrote to the Acting Secretary of State protesting about German deportations of Gypsies, and issued a statement condemning the actions of the government of Serbia. In that year the museum was the site of a rally organized by Jewish organizations protesting about war atrocities in Bosnia-Herzegovina. The Holocaust Museum has been at the forefront in opposing oppression throughout the world.

The stress on transposing concern with the memories of the Holocaust into a broader platform of human rights issues is even more apparent in the Beit Hashoah Museum of Tolerance in Los Angeles. Dedicated in February 1993 to international acclaim, this world center for remembrance and vigilance is part of the Simon Wiesenthal Center. As President Clinton said at its inauguration: 'This internationally renowned human rights organization . . . has stood up to hatred and bigotry . . .

that is embodied not only in the Holocaust but in the continuing problems we have today with racial and religious and ethnic bigotry.'

A similar view was expressed by the Director-General of UNESCO, Federico Mayor: 'I would have hoped that this museum recorded a past which was now closed and no longer of immediate relevance to the world we inhabit. This is not the case. Intolerance, narrow-mindedness, prejudice, bigotry, anti-Semitism and all forms of hatred persist here and around the world.'

The Director-General went on to characterize the new museum as a 'superb teaching tool, perhaps the most advanced research and educational facility in the world on all forms of intolerance . . . a fitting tribute to the life and work of Simon Wiesanthal'. For although Simon Wiesenthal spent a lifetime locating Nazi war criminals, the museum's strongest emphasis is on the achievement of international dialogue and peace. It conceives of tolerance in the broadest terms and attempts to move the Holocaust from a singular event to a worldwide concern with geno-cide prevention.

The museum is a hi-tech experiential centre which focuses on two primary themes – the dynamics of racism and prejudice in the United States, and the Holocaust. Its film programme covers genocide around the world and thereby seeks to empha-size the universality of human suffering. Through the latest in touch-screen techno-logy and multimedia learning, this museum makes a poignant appeal for tolerance, nationally and internationally. It is not a museum pre-occupied with the insularity of the Jewish experience, but with translating the horrors of the Holocaust so that they have resonance for the promotion of world tolerance today. As Wiesenthal himself puts it: 'I hope that visitors to the Museum of Tolerance will realize that to all they can see here, there is only one alternative: tolerance towards all mankind.'

The Holocaust museum concept of today is grounded equally in the tragic experi-ence of the Jewish community and in the worldwide movement for human rights. The metamorphosis of the concept so that it has moved towards a fundamentally universal concern has marked a sea-change in thinking. With the Holocaust Memorial Museum, the Beit Hashoah Museum of Tolerance, and in the museums that will follow their example, the Holocaust experience has quickened the heart of the inter-national community without losing any of its integrity in the unique culture of the Jewish world.

Note

Terence Duffy taught Peace Studies at the University of Ulster, Magee College in Northern Ireland and was Director of the Irish Peace Museum Project.

Further reading

Readers interested in exploring this topic further might wish to consult the following publications:

Yad Vashem: The Holocaust Martyrs' and Heroes' Remembrance Authority, Jerusalem, Yad Vashem, 1990.

M. Berenbaum, *The World We Must Know: The United States Holocaust Memorial Museum*, Boston, Little Brown, 1993.

Beit Hashoah Museum of Tolerance, Los Angeles, Simon Wiesenthal Center, 1994.

The Art of Memory: Holocaust Memorials in History, Munich/New York, Prestel-Verlag, The Jewish Museum, 1994.

Chapter 33

Mapping the Memories

Politics, place and identity in the District Six Museum, Cape Town

Charmaine McEachern

Introduction

IN POST-APARTHEID SOUTH AFRICA, 'the new South Africa' is the most obvious way in which people in all kinds of locations and structural positions confront and seek to give some name to both the obvious and massive political changes which have occurred and the hopes for cultural and social change which have accompanied them.[1] That the label 'the new South Africa' is perhaps the dominant form of an overall identity for this national polity obscures the uncertainty, and precariousness, of this act of confrontation. Just what is 'new' in post-apartheid South Africa? And what does it mean to be South African in the 'new' South Africa? How can this identity achieve some kind of stability, some form of integrity? Can the past be used to establish not just the fact of 'newness', but also to think about what it is, or can be, by reference to what it is not. In the past and its struggles lies the impetus for the nation conceived as unity in diversity, the principle for knowing or interpreting the past thus being embedded in the present (Boyarin 1994: x). Thus also emerges the enormous significance of memory in South Africa today.

Memory is central in social theorising and critique in contemporary South Africa today (one could compare this with the relationship between nation and memory in Israel; Young 1993: 210, Huyssen 1994). The Truth and Reconciliation Commission is probably the most obvious and visible manifestation, publicly engaging the apartheid regime in terms of its oppressive strategies and human rights violations. Here, one is mindful of Boyarin's close link between the role of memory and identity as nation-state (1994: iix). In South Africa this process must be contextualised through other attempts to provide reconciliation and 'truth' to mark the end of oppressive regimes and signal new beginnings. Post-war Germany (see for example Geyer 1996; Young 1993: Chapter 1) and Argentina's return to

Source: *Social Identities*, vol. 4, no. 3, 1998, pp. 499–521.

democracy after military rule come immediately to mind. South Africa's own particular Truth and Reconciliation process certainly drew on other attempts to heal shattered nations, the public consultation and fact gathering process including input from South American and East European countries. Ultimately, some forms such as El Salvador's internationally organised commission were rejected and, as Andre du Toit put it, South Africa's Truth Commission became a 'project of the state' (1995: 95), a decision which suited the fact that here remembering and accounting for the past are also encompassed and circumscribed within the negotiated political settlement which put an end to the apartheid regime.

Yet, at the same time that the harrowing tales of personal suffering told to the Truth and Reconciliation Commission hearings are being given public form through daily media publicity and commentary, in myriad other locations apartheid is also being engaged through memory, always partial and certainly from the perspective of the present. Numerous exhibitions, seminars and conferences testify to and provide critiques of the plethora of ways in which apartheid operated as a comprehensive system of rule, reaching down into the very minutiae of social life. As an exercise of remembering, the new South Africa's act of self-construction is more than the willed action and rhetoric of a new government and state. It also exists in these many accounts, all of which, though partial and often competing (Young 1993: xi), have something to say about the present, the 'new South Africa', through *their* acts of remembering the past.

These themes of remembering for the understanding of both the present and the future emerge as a central problematic in all kinds of representation generally but also in the lives of ordinary South Africans striving to come to terms with what was done to them or in their name. They demonstrate the profound ways in which all kinds of macro-processes take form and power in the lives of people at the most micro-levels. To appreciate the significance of this situatedness of historical processes of transformation (Comaroff and Comaroff 1992), this chapter considers a case study of one of the places of engagement between past, present and future which characterise contemporary South Africa. The focus of the study is the District Six Museum in Cape Town, which was established in December 1994. The study is based on two periods of participant observation in 1996 and 1997. Observation was supplemented by and interrogated through interviews and informal talks with museum staff and visitors.

The museum is a powerful engagement with South Africa's past, partly because its remembering is located in the very heart of apartheid philosophy and social engineering, the construction of the apartheid city. Not just an historical account of the harm done through this vision to people and places, the museum also provides for the active construction and performance of memory which is at the same time a critique of apartheid itself. The chapter's study of this constellation of city construction, memory and critique is facilitated using the work of Michel de Certeau (1988). The insights of his work on walking the city are particularly useful for a critical understanding of the relationship between past and present within this constellation as it is manifest in the museum. In particular de Certeau provides a way of thinking about the relationship between place, people and politics in remembering. In turn, we can open up a little more the symbolic terrain of the 'new South Africa' in these very transitional times.

From District Six to the District Six Museum

District Six was the sixth District of Cape Town, an inner city area which from the nineteenth century had housed people from the working and artisanal classes, many of whom worked in the city and at the nearby docks. The District extended from the harbour up into the lower reaches of the Devil's Peak and from the commercial centre of the city to the edge of the suburbs. As one would expect of such an area, District Six had been very heterogeneous for a very long time, an integrated area in which white, coloured and African working-class people all lived (Bickford-Smith 1992), though actual ownership of property was largely concentrated in the hands of white landlords (Western 1981: 155). There are clear indications that such heterogeneity was seen as problematic well before apartheid. As early as 1901 African people were removed from District Six to a new township, Ndabeni, ostensibly because of the outbreak of plague (Goldin 1987: 162). In the twentieth century, rapid population expansion (particularly under the influence of rural in-migration) and the general disinclination of landlords and the Cape Town City Council to maintain and improve housing and general amenities produced what all researchers identify as a grossly overcrowded and rundown area – a 'slum'.

In 1948 the National Party came to power in South Africa, having run on a platform which promised to deal with overcrowded urban areas which resulted from massive and uncontrolled migration into the cities from the country. As Mabin says, 'In some respects apartheid was a (racist) response to previous failure to develop coherent urbanisation policy' (1992: 19). Population control thus became a cornerstone of apartheid policy as it sought to organise and channel capitalist development in South Africa for the benefit of one sector of the population, white South Africans, through what Mamdani calls 'artificial deurbanisation' (1996: 28, 9). This meant that the colour segregation which was already a feature of pre-apartheid South Africa (Pechey 1994; Mamdani 1996)[2] was systematised and legally enforced as race became *the* factor in the distribution of rights (Christopher 1994: 1). Central to the system of enforcement of racially based rights which followed was the Population Registration Act with its classifications of racial identity and the Group Areas Act which sought comprehensively to enforce racial difference by controlling non-white populations in terms of residence. Apartheid was thus a spatial system, which as Christopher notes, worked very much at the local level. In particular, the city, the urban, was central to policy. The city was seen as white,[3] built by whites for whites, so that access to the cities by non-whites for whatever purpose, residential or employment, had to be strictly controlled through the Group Areas Act in order to maintain this correct relationship between whiteness and urbanisation. Non-whites were to live and work in the urban areas only on white terms.[4] The consequences Marks and Trapido record:

> Over the next 25 years nearly 4 million people were uprooted, many of them several times over, in pursuit of the policies of apartheid. (1987: 22)

In 1948, Cape Town was the most integrated city in South Africa (Christopher 1994). The Cape's liberal tradition (Bickford-Smith 1992; Ross 1992; Mamdani 1996: 69) and the relatively high coloured population all meant that, though economics produced segregation of a kind, namely, 'civil inequality' (Mamdani 1996: 69), when it came to working-class areas in particular residential patterns were character-istically integrated. It was these areas which were torn apart as proclamation after proclamation declared areas white or coloured (mostly the former) forcing all other classifications of people out.

District Six was one such area. It has been eulogised as an integrated area of workers and small traders where people of all races and religions and cultures mixed, lived together and shared the hardships of poverty and neglect.[5] There was also a significant degree of intermarriage between groups, which prompted precisely the fear of both miscegenation and the blunting of European 'colour feelings' which Goldin (1987: 170) argues fuelled the National Party's determination to regularise and codify the ad hoc and often economically derived forms of segregation which were already in place in 1948. District Six thus exemplified the articulation of ideo-logical principle and spatial organisation which underpinned the apartheid vision of the city lodged at the very heart of its regime and its way of seeing South Africa as a whole. Under the National Party, space itself was to be racialised and trans-formed, in turn transforming people.

Though the Group Areas Act was legislated in 1950, District Six itself was not proclaimed white until 1966. Over the next 15 years the District was physic-ally destroyed, bulldozed street by street, to make way for white residents. All in all between 55,000 and 65,000 people were moved from District Six, usually relocated in the townships out on the Cape Flats, often separated from closest kin and friends.

In many ways District Six and *this* history of forced removal has come to over-shadow the many, many other areas of forced removal from the urban area of Cape Town, like Mowbray and Claremont. It has become the symbol of the dislocation and harm caused by the Group Areas Act. In part this must be because Zonnebloem (as the apartheid authorities renamed the area) or District Six today was never effect-ively redeveloped. Indeed, in terms of occupation it was the state which took it over, building houses for state employees and a Technikon, originally for whites only. Hart reports that by 1985 'Zonnebloem comprised some 3000–4000 people, predominantly lower-middle class Afrikaans speakers and overwhelmingly state employees' (1990: 133). The white residential development dreamed of by apar-theid authorities never came to fruition. This visibility of the state maintained District Six as a pathological symptom of apartheid and its cities, making visible the relationship between force and dislocation. The rest is emptiness and ruin, in sharp contrast to the overcrowded, urban past. It is a wasteland, marked only by the isolated, untouched churches and mosques of District Six and traces of the old cobbled streets among the weeds and rubbish.

As a wasteland, District Six did not just stand as a 'blot on the conscience of the entire nation' (Hart 1990: 134). The space could still be defended by those who waited for the inevitable demise of the apartheid system. In the late 1980s the Hands Off District Six campaign formed out of the Friends of District Six in order to protect the area from British Petroleum's (BP) intended redevelopment using the private sector (see also Western 1981: 158). Although BP's development plans specified that the area was to be open to people of all races and indeed stated that ex-residents would be given preference, there was strong community opposition.

Hart argues of the campaign, 'Their guiding intention is that District Six be declared "salted earth" and left undeveloped until the demise of apartheid' (1990: 136). As Young observes of the death camps left by the Holocaust, such ruins cannot on their own remember, it is people's 'will to remember' which endows them with meanings and significance (1993: 120). Still, left undeveloped, the wasteland could operate as a space on which such meanings could be inscribed in the imagination and produced as memory. The District Six Museum has become one place where the sense of absence can be linked to the District's presence in people's lives and popular memory.

The District Six Museum is housed in the Buitenkant Methodist Church on the central business district edge of the old District Six. The exhibition covers the ground floor centre space of the church. Down one side are carrels of photographs grouped around streets and areas of District Six.[6] At the altar end, high up, hang representations of the four main religions of District Six people: Hinduism, Islam, Christianity and Judaism, religious polyphony being part of the message of heterogeneity about the district that the museum seeks to convey, despite its housing in a Christian church. Below this, dramatically, a photograph of the skyline of District Six extends across the church, standing for and helping people to envisage the whole District which once stood behind the church. At the other Buitenkant Street end is a display of street signs from the old District and press clippings and information about individuals and events in District Six (and the museum) fill the other wall. Visitors are welcomed at the museum by officers who are themselves District Sixers (the name given to ex-residents) and who willingly talk about their experiences. This makes this museum reminiscent of the Pan Pacific Park Holocaust Museum in the United States described by Young (see also Mithlo 1995: 50) in these terms:

> In fact, as instructive and powerful as the photographic panels were, students and teachers agreed that the exhibition's principal resource was the survivors who led them through the museum. In their presence, the photo montages came alive. (1993: 304)

In fact, the presence of District Sixers as visitors also contributes to this 'coming alive' in the museum.

The Buitenkant Church had been a struggle church during the era of apartheid, a site in the political protest history of the Western Cape. Various trustees of the museum recalled services and meetings to protest the apartheid regime, mentioning names like those of Alan Boesak and Trevor Manuel, in 1996 a government minister. They talked of marches from the church and of deliberately courted arrests. Part of the symbolic power of this particular church is that it is also directly across the road from the security forces' headquarters in the Caledon Square Police Station. Through displayed materials about the church's struggle history, the history of struggle in the Western Cape is made physically to encompass the museum's exhibition in the form of the church, providing one very powerful reading or identification, perhaps a preferred reading, for the exhibition and its visitors. This creates a space for a possible continuity being drawn between the demise of District Six, *remembering* that demise and the struggle itself, which enables the recasting of the relationship between the demise and the struggle.

The museum itself emerged out of the Hands Off District Six campaign of the late 1980s. The possibility of a museum to keep alive the memory of the District Six which the campaign was defending was discussed at the very inception of the campaign (Soudien 1990). But the museum, when it came, took form in 1994, when apartheid had ended and democracy instated. It was established within the 'new South Africa' and bears the marks of this moment in time. This is clear from the words of a central banner which hangs from the rails of the upper floor of the church which reads:

In 1966
District Six
Was declared
A 'White' Group Area
Shortly afterward
The first bulldozers
Moved in and set about
destroying homes in which
generations of families had
lived. Intent on erasing
District Six from the map
of Cape Town the Apartheid
State attempted to Redesign
The Space of District Six,
Renaming it Zonnebloem
Today, only the scars of the
Removals remain. In this
Exhibition we do not wish to
Recreate District Six as much
As to re-possess the history of
the area as a place where people
lived, loved and struggled. It is
an attempt to take back our right
To signpost our lives with those
Things we hold dear. At one
level the exhibition is about signs of
Our past. We would like to invite you
to write your names and addresses and
Make comments in the spaces around the
Exhibits and in our visitors book. This is
important in helping us to trace our past. At
another level, the exhibition is also about
Pointers to our future. We, all of us, need to decide,
how as individuals and as people we wish to retrace and re-signpost the lines of our future. Such a process
Is neither easy nor straightforward. It is not predictable either.

Here we see the museum's envisaging of the possible connections between past, present and future, the connection of apartheid South Africa to the new South Africa at a time when memory is still palpable, 'still almost visceral', providing for it a social power and authority which the passing of time erodes or transforms (Young 1993: 169–75). The chapter will show that the way these themes and connections are played out and given form is very much in the hands of the visitors, many of whom experienced the destruction. And, very much in keeping with the state rhetorics of empowerment, representation and reconciliation, this is how the museum staff want it to be. At this level, the museum is taking on board agendas which coincide with those of the new South African state. But the outcome is not at all assured in these terms. This is precisely because the actual playing out of those processes of empowerment is through the performances of the people. As visitors and new South Africans, the people begin to take over and engage the rhetorics in their own terms. This has never been the kind of museum which seeks to do all of the memory-work and serve it up to the people. Museum staff comment on how they began with a two week exhibition in 1994 but are still there because 'the people wouldn't let us close'. People came to look at the photographs and the old street signs which had been saved from the destruction of the District and retrieved to be put on exhibition here. They came to write their names and old addresses on the long calico cloths hung up for this purpose. They made the exhibition into a space of what Pratt calls 'autoethnography', representations 'in which people undertake to describe themselves in ways that engage with representations others have made of them' (1994: 28). For the rest of this chapter I consider just one of the features of the museum as it facilitates this autoethnography.

The mapping of memory

In the centre of the church, covering much of the floor space is a huge map of the District. The map is decorated with poems to the life of the District as well as linocuts by the artist, Lionel Davis, himself a District Sixer and a political activist who had been jailed on Robben Island.[7] Davis helped put together the exhibition with the map at its centre.

Visibly dominant, the map is used by the museum's education officers to talk about the history and development of the District, to explain different areas, where particular landmarks were and so on. There is some ambivalence about the map, with some trustees and others arguing that it has become reified, setting District Six in stone (or paper and plastic). Certainly in some tours, it is pointed out that the map's impression of boundedness was negated by people, events and relationships spilling out into surrounding districts (the harbour, the commercial area of central Cape Town, nearby districts like Walmer Estate and Woodstock, where some moved after 1966). Few of the District Sixers who come express the same ambivalence.

The director of the museum stresses that their first priority are District Sixers, people whose history they are showing. And for these people the map is very powerful indeed. It is one site in the exhibition where people took over and turned it into something else, something living. Not just content to sign their names and put their old addresses on the cloths, the ex-residents of District Six also wrote their names on the map. They marked in their houses, their family names, shops, bioscopes (cinemas), markets, bus stops and so on. In so doing they wrote themselves into the map; they rendered social the map's physical representation. The map is thus implicated in the declared intentions of the museum to resist apartheid's history by providing the opportunity for people to 're-possess the history of the area as a place where people lived, loved and struggled' and to 'attempt to take back our right to signpost our lives with those things we hold dear'. Through the map, District Sixers make visible the histories which they have carried with them but which were rendered invisible in the destruction of the area.

In his most famous chapter of *The Practice of Everyday Life*, 'Walking in the City', Michel de Certeau argues that walking in the city can operate as resistance to official, authoritative constructions of the city – construct it as place in which meanings slip authorised versions as walkers find new ways through, attach place to memory – turning space into place. This is exactly what District Sixers walking over the map do. The map has a peculiar efficacy in engaging with apartheid. It can be seen as a core symbol of apartheid given the centrality of urban planning to apartheid's particular version of social engineering (Smith 1992; Western 1981). As Christopher (1994) has demonstrated, maps are particularly suitable for analysing the transformative and destructive impact of the apartheid regime's policies and practices. As such, the map in District Six Museum is a particularly powerful ground on which District Sixers can engage with apartheid's interventions into their lives. The map representation is a physical thing, an official text which baldly lays down the basic topographical features of the district. It is empty, devoid of life, able to be manipulated in the interests of those in authority. On the basis of such a representation and armed with the official narrative of District Six which stated that it was a slum, degenerate, crime and poverty ridden, 'a blight on the social landscape' requiring redemption (Soudien and Meltzer 1995: 8), the authorities could organise the systematic destruction of District Six, street by street (see Fortune 1996). The walkers use exactly the same representation, which on the floor of the museum also began as an 'empty' representation, but their articulation of memory and walking provide for it a totally different meaning, one which resists the apartheid regime's judgement, while at the same time criticising its acts of destruction.

People obviously use the map in different ways. Some just stand and stare, often with tears in their eyes, others are looking for specific sites, trying to remember who lived and worked where. They look for old haunts, locate the homes of friends and kin, where they went to school, the swimming baths, places of fun, places of work. Where they come in with others, usually kin, conversation is intense as they exchange memories of who lived where, maybe even disagreeing with each other about places and people. They may meet others on the map and talk about *their* District Six, trying to find connections in people and places and often finding them in shared shopkeepers or school teachers and principals. They may look to see from the marks on the map who of their old neighbourhood has also been here. In the summer of 1996–97 the museum saw a lot of District Sixers visit from new homes overseas in Canada, the United States and Australia. Many of these used the map to show their children who had never seen District Six where they had lived and what it was like. Many come to the museum officers who are always interested, always encourage them to tell of their relationship to District Six, to narrate their District Six. They swap stories, remember different aspects of the same event or person's history. There is a constant movement here; between differentiated histories and memories which signify many District Sixes and the more homogenised District Six, the symbol of a history greater than the District itself. Both are present in the map walking and the narratives, so that Soudien and Meltzer are right to call these popular narratives, the assertion of 'humanity, dignity and creativity' (1995: 10), but they also seem to be particular narratives of identity.

Obviously walking on the map in these ways is a different exercise at many levels from de Certeau's walking in the city. He speaks of 'walking rhetorics' (1988: 100) whereby 'pedestrian speech acts' like taking shortcuts or detours or refusing to take particular routes are appropriations of urban space, at the same time bringing this space into being – as place. Such an act of appropriation and begetting is no longer given to ex-District Six residents. Though they do visit and attend churches and mosques in the District still, there is little left to 'walk in' in the way de Certeau speaks of. There are no houses, shops, parks, just rank weeds, the odd group of squatters with little fires and the ubiquitous lines of washing, rubbish, a huge Technikon complex and some housing on the fringes. What the ex-residents do have is the spatial representation of the district, in the form of the map.

It is the map that allows the walkers to bring 'District Six' into being again as physical space; but this time it is not so much in relation to the intentions of builders, architects and urban designers as de Certeau has it. Rather than the *creators* of this urban space, the map allows them to engage with its *destroyers*. Here the map fulfils both of the roles of the modern museum which Huyssen (1994: 15) notes make museums *the* paradigmatic institution of modernisation; collecting that which modernisation has destroyed but also serving as a site of possible resurrections. Certainly the discourse of apartheid when it decreed the destruction of District Six was that of modernisation, progress whatever its politics, so the museum 'collects, salvages' that which apartheid as modernisation destroyed. But, as Huyssen also notes, museums like memory itself, 'construct the past in the light of the discourses of the present and in terms of present-day interest', and in the light of this we see that the walkers turn the museum into a site of resurrection in an act which directly counters apartheid meanings with *post*-apartheid, regardless of the political persuasion of the walkers themselves. The walkers' practices of appropriation and enunciation (de Certeau 1988: 97) bring District Six into being as something morally greater than space – place. Rather than speaking the possibilities of the space, the map works as a mnemonic, which both allows the recall of the place but also puts the rememberer back into it, as they literally have put their names back into District Six by writing them on the map. It produces a re-identification.

The map also works through and enables the play of synecdoche and asyndeton and the movement between them, for de Certeau, primary expressive forms operating to provide the walked through city with its texture and form – its reality. The map of course does stand for the whole, but just what that whole is, is provided by the walkers (and the other exhibits of course). For each, District Six starts from the epicentre of *their* home, *their* street, *their* place. It is this that they always write in first and then move out from their own place in District Six to the whole. If synecdoche 'replaces totalities by fragments' (de Certeau 1988: 101), then this too is the tropic process to construct District Six as a reality that the walkers go through. As they walk over the map, pausing here or there, passing over whole blocks or retracing their steps to stop again, they speak life and form back into the destroyed District of the map. The map is transformed from a graphic representation on two planes into the repository of experiences, relationships, life; another layer is laid down over the lines and shapes by the walking feet and the spoken memories/stories which accompany them. But the life that this represents is in fragments, a mosaic of specific parts – this shop, this bioscope, this street, places and relationships which come within the direct orbit of ex-residents, so that the collective remembered whole is constructed out of overlapping mosaics. Then there are other fragments which all used to speak the special character of the District – places like the Seven Steps and the Fish Market which everyone relates to and remembers. Proper names, like Hanover Street especially, also have this power of synecdoche to be far more than simply the name of a topographical feature. Even for non ex-resident Capetonians visiting the museum, Hanover Street seems to connote District Six as an identity, a place. De Certeau argues that 'Synecdoche makes more dense: it amplifies the detail and miniaturises the whole' (1988: 101). This is exactly what happens to the District Six of the walkers. Their strategies exactly make District Six more dense, which is probably why they are accused at times of sentimentality and nostalgia. These processes which operate as synecdoche make the whole district accessible while focusing its identity powerfully through significant parts to stand for that whole. And in this process the foreshortening, the breaking of continuity and selecting of parts that is asyndeton, enlarge and make the chosen parts even more significant and powerful. The power of asyndeton, even when District Six was in existence, meant that certain parts of it, like the Seven Steps, were broken up and taken by people who could then take District Six with them. This is how the Museum was able to acquire the small piece of one step which is in its display.

These are then all strategies to construct the metaphorical city out of the reimagining and re-membering of this particular use of the represented city – the map. In a sense they become central devices in ex-residents' performance of their popular narratives of District Six on the map. Through the operation of synecdoche and asyndeton on the map, events and relationships in the memory merge into places as they are identified or re-found cartographically, to be re-created in the vocalisation of those memories as parts of the narratives of the people who lived in these places in the past. Such tellings make District Six exist, not again or as it was, but within a larger encompassing narrative about identity and South Africa in the 1990s post-apartheid society; that is in metaphorical form which is politically inflected in particular ways.

A significant part of this metaphorical form of District Six is in the characterising of this place as lost community. Though in a sense we do get different District Sixes in the mosaics of the visitors, there are striking similarities in the kinds of things that people say about life in District Six, life making District Six a particular kind of place.

> You knew everybody in District Six; it was like one big family, we knew whites and blacks, everyone.

> You were safe in District Six – girls could walk in the streets at night, the kids could play on the street.

People respected each other, you could discipline someone else's child if you saw it misbehave (this also was often linked to being able to leave doors unlocked).

Street life was important — we used to sit on the *stoep* and talk to people going past.

These are just a few of the kinds of comments made over and over in some form, constituting the museum as a location for the construction of 'common meaning' (White 1991: 6). What they seem to be doing is clearly drawing District Six as community. They are projecting from their remembered lives there out into the entire district, characterising it as a community. And, they are certainly constructing this as a favourable form of social organisation, which as Bozzoli (1987: 5) notes, using Raymond Williams' work, is always the case with the concept of 'community'. Further, her insights about this positive valorisation also seem applicable to the above kinds of comments:

The good connotations of 'community' rest in its ability to conjure up images of supportiveness; of a place of kinship ties, of rest and rejuvenation; of cross-class cooperation.

People also used particular places and experiences to evoke a sense of community as shared place. Stories around the Fish Market abounded; first remembered as a place where you could meet everyone else and which everyone shared in common, but second, articulating value and synecdoche by recounting it as a place where the supportiveness of the District was made manifest by the Market making scraps available to the poor at the end of the day. The bioscopes also seemed to feature in many people's narratives, often being the sites that were looked for on the map. While this gave the bioscopes too a synecdochal quality, at the same time loyalty to different bioscopes also seemed to signal difference within the District.

These evocations of community are in fact often accused of nostalgia or sentimentality and certainly it is hard to see anything culturally specific in the comments above. They might be heard in a multitude of places around the world, especially where the impact of modernisation and the more recent fragmentations of postmodern society are seen as destroying meaningful collectivities, producing alienation and dislocation. In a way, the cultural specificity is offered in the kinds of explanations which follow from *criticisms* of such evocations of community. Many people have argued that such evocations ignore the negative aspects of living in the District. One of the few critical comments on the cloths accused the museum of turning District Six into a 'myth' because of this.[8] Critics point out the existence of gangs, of crime and violence; they stress the poverty, the overcrowding; they demonstrate the divisions, the prejudices and the inequalities; they question whether or not there *was* community in District Six. Dullah Omar, Minister of Justice and himself a District Sixer, has taken up this issue in a variety of contexts, one of which was a television talk programme, *Felicia*, about District Six which was recorded in the museum itself during its first week. In another place Omar puts his objection like this:

> There has been a tendency to isolate District Six from its social milieu.
> To regard it as a special case and to mystify its history . . . There appeared
> to be some degree of 'racial harmony'. Families lived closer together
> within reach of each other. A community spirit built up over genera-
> tions lived on. There was the life in Hanover Street, the fish market
> and the many shops and hawkers. Landmarks such as the Star cinema,
> the Avalon, the National and the British. But there has been a tendency
> to romanticize [the] life of that period. Even the gangsterism – the Globe
> gang, the Jesters and the Killers, etc are portrayed in a romantic light
> together with 'The Seven Steps' and the characters who graced District
> Six during its lifetime. And so history will want to record District Six
> and its people as having been a people who enjoyed life and who were
> carefree – 'until the Nats came along and destroyed it all'. (Jeppie and
> Soudien 1990: 192)

This too is the kind of scepticism with which some people greet the narratives which
emerge in walking the map or looking at the photographs. They will ask questions
about elements of disharmony, usually crime or violence as Omar suggests, but
maybe also collaboration with the apartheid state.

Bozzoli argues that one way in which community forms is in terms of opposition to something – and it seems clear that, however illusory community is, however much one can point to serious rifts, differences, evidence of non-harmony and
so on, this oppositional construction is exactly what is happening. In a sense this
is community *post-facto* (Western 1981: 163–201), community retrospectively ascribed
to ways of living in District Six in opposition to what came after. As it is evoked
at the museum (Western 1981: 163–201) this may be far less community as the
form of remembered social organisation and far more a moral community brought
into being as critique of apartheid or at least some of the planning consequences
of apartheid, given the divided political affiliations of those dislocated.[9] Clearly people were asserting their subjectivity and experience in contrast to a time in which
such assertions were devalued, even impossible, making identity itself problematic
(White 1991). And here I will ultimately argue that people are talking about their
identity and forms of sociality in relation to *city* as much as they are talking about
community (Bickford-Smith 1990: 35).

The cosmopolitan community: a politics of memory

The memories on the map and the stories which people tell aren't just stories of
some past, perfect place. Rather they are stories of a people transformed, turned
into somebody else – from the critical perspective of who they feel they have become.
The past recounted from the standpoint of the present is then a strategy of identity
construction (White 1991: 8) which here provides a way of criticising that transformation, narratives becoming morality tales as much as they are history. Regardless
of how romanticised it has become, District Six seems most certainly to have been
a place of generational depth; Western claims seven generations. The history which
was sedimented into the District as place, in part lived in the people as the map

walking reveals. Then too, most accounts suggest that people did *not* live as isolated nuclear units. Rather they all had kin, as well as friends, living close-by. This is certainly borne out by the stories and map commentaries where people will also point out where their aunties, uncles and grandparents lived, with their children or others of the family and how they could as readily as freely walk into these homes, sit down and talk or eat as in their own. This takes on very particular significance when one considers that poverty also characterised the people of District Six. Kinship links were critical in coping with this poverty at a day to day level (Pinnock 1987: 426; see also Western 1981). Again this is embedded in the help, support, redistribution and care which features in many of the stories and it is also in part the context for the integrated nature of the District. As many observers note, integration in urban Cape Town was a feature of poor, working-class areas more than any other (Goldin 1987; Bickford-Smith 1992). So the negative *urban* features many note, poverty, overcrowding, poor facilities and so on are exactly those things which seem to have generated the forms of sociality, the social relationships, which people today are representing as community. Then in memory, it is the sociality which dominates rather than the structural conditions which produced it.

In keeping with Bozzoli, the remembered community which people then build on these social accommodations of poverty and self help is also opposition. It is community as a kind of critique – a remembered community based on stories of the sociality which is brought into being from the perspective of where they are now, in order to criticise the transformations of their lives under apartheid. Two examples help make the point. First, it is clear that, for many of the coloured population, particularly those moved early, the standard of housing into which they were moved was superior in many ways to their District Six accommodation (Western 1981). Though small and very basic, the houses were clean, had full facilities, small plots of land and people were able to have modern conveniences. At the same time, they remained poor, and now they had to spend more money on commuting to work, as well as the often higher prices that shops and services with monopolies in the townships could charge. But, because of the way in which the Group Areas Board (often called 'the Board', see also Rive 1989: 93–104) allocated new housing, more often than not people were now living far away from kin and neighbours with whom they had built up long-term networks of support and cooperation. Now they were isolated in their poverty, made to feel it much more, and despair (see for example Adams and Suttner 1988: Chapters 15–18; Western 1981: Chapters 7–9). This was particularly hard on women left isolated and some women talked of walks of several miles that they made across townships to visit mothers and sisters similarly isolated. So forms of sociality changed; as they recount it, to their impoverishment.

The second example concerns the most contentious claim of the map walkers, that District Six was safe. This, as indicated, is the thing that people most often pick up. It is a question often asked of the education officers when they are conducting tours of the museum. What of violence and crime? What of the gangs? This is hardly a surprising question given the amount of media attention to this feature of the new South Africa, but it is very valid as an historical question also (Pinnock 1987). The position that District Sixers seem to take is that, yes there were gangs, but they were mostly a problem for each other or outsiders, not the people of the

District who could mostly keep out of their way. Further, they fought with knives and fists rather than today's full arsenals. Now part of the context for this must be the activities of the organisation People Against Gangsterism and Drugs (PAGAD) which had greatly heightened people's awareness of these things in 1996 and 1997.[10] But, as Pinnock reports, this also seems to be the perception of gangsters themselves at the time. He quotes Stone, the leader of the Mongrels gang in Grassy Park:

> It was tough then. But you knew where you stood. You were never short of kroon (money) or people who would pull in to help you. Ja, we had our fights, but there wasn't all the killing. The families were big, you know, and you knew everybody. They would all help you when you fell in the shit. (1987: 427)

Here gangs and community (or communal families as Pinnock argues) go together rather than being incompatible. There seem to be two kinds of things being brought out in these accounts. First the narratives seem to deny a place in District Six for the level of violence they experience today (Hanover Park was one township often used to exemplify this), for its randomness and the possibility of being murdered which meant that not for the townships but the life on the *stoep* or the streets. People stayed inside and kept their children inside almost from the moment of moving out into the Cape Flats, testimony I think to their fears of a place where they did not know the people they were living among, an alien residential experience for them (Fortune 1996: 105). Their memories of street life then are not just expressions of community which was symbolically constituted on the street (Soudien and Meltzer 1995) but also seem to be constructed with the intention of testifying to changing social patterns of violence. And this is as much directed at today's post-democratic rule as it is at apartheid, particularly where the speaker is anti-ANC. Yesterday's violence had a kind of social meaning which for them is denied in the experiences of contemporary violence and crime in the townships. Implicated in this, echoed in Stone's comments in a way too, are the changing forms of sociality which ultimately changed coloured subjectivity and identity. Life, and people, became more individualised. Instead of living in large communal families, they turned inwards, into the nuclear family, into the house, not going out, not knowing their neighbours, isolated as many walkers said, 'out on the Cape Flats'. Comments echo the words of a Mowbray coloured resident forcibly removed to the Cape Flats under the Group Areas, to whom Western spoke:

> I was really living then, now I'm not sure I am. I mean, I live for my job. That is the money I can make so we can make the home comfortable for the family and to invite people in and be proud of it. But it's very rarely we can get up a party and go out dancing or to a movie. In Mowbray there was *too* much to be done outside – people would participate with you – here we live *too* much in our houses. (1981: 239)

This comment has the diasporic structure of feeling which Small (1986: 11) argues characterised District Sixers removed to the townships of the Cape Flats.

These big questions of who people feel they became under apartheid, are the crux to both the narratives of memory and the critical engagement with apartheid that the map encourages. And here the relationship between map and city is crucial. The map walkers demonstate that, for them, both identity and history are space. This is very much as one would expect, given that space was central to apartheid, its ideology and its transformations of South Africa in terms of this ideology and the interests it served. The map on the floor symbolises the social emptiness of District Six as inner city which was necessary to make Cape Town into a quintessentially apartheid city, the city which Christopher (1994) argues was most transformed under apartheid's social engineering. And the people walking the map respond to this, criticising apartheid's policies and actions in making Cape Town an apartheid city, by repeopling, resocialising, the inner city with their stories, their presence as coloured people, however momentarily.

Living in District Six gave coloured people an identity located in two things; the inner city and Cape Town itself, the Mother City. It is the first of these that Western's informant seems to be engaging. He was living then, on the Cape Flats he's not so sure . . . What people lost by being shipped out to mono-race spaces was the experience of city living itself, an experience which had become part of their very identity. They lost the heterogeneity, the openness, what Hannerz (1992: Chapter 1 and p. 173) calls the 'cultural complexity' of the city and city living, which had shaped who they were, as people. We need only to think of the short story 'Moon over District Six', by Richard Rive (1989), a writer who *did* talk about District Six as a 'slum', in which the same New Year moon shines on 'the teaser-man', the 'young buck and his girlfriend', the 'early celebrator' drinking from a paper cup reading KISS ME SWEETIE who is chastised by the 'prim, light-brown lady who lived in Walmer Estate and only spoke English at home', the 'dandy in pink socks' at the cinema, the 'housewife' out on the town, the 'Cheeky, yellow youth' playing dice, a guitar-playing 'cuuuuulid' serenader, the full cast of a fight including the white policeman armed with revolver who came to break it up and the 'street-corner Jesus-jumper' preaching to the drunks. No wonder the Cape Flats seemed so alien. They didn't necessarily like their co-residents in the District and the map walkers show that they carved out their own spaces within the whole, but these other lives, these other spaces and times (Pechey 1994) of District Six were also part of their District Six and part of *them* as District Sixers, an identity which became all the more poignant when they lost it.[11] These people were cosmopolitans, forced into a racialised kind of suburbia, a mode of living and an identity which was not of their own choosing. And in doing so they lost a significant element of their identity as South Africans. They lost their right to determine their own identities. And they lost their place in Cape Town itself. As Small says, from now on they lived in the diaspora, the Cape Flats. There is such a strong sense of this in many of the stories visitors and officials tell, as they recount their lives in District Six as city, cosmopolitan lives. They talk about how they used to use the whole city, the harbour, Canal Gardens, the Mountain, the sea. All of these places were theirs, part of their space, who they were. As they talk, it is clear that difference was also important in the city, that structural and category differences, around religion and class for example, constituted part of the knowledge about people which they negotiated in their social relationships with them (see Hannerz 1980: 149).

They also talk of life around the harbour and the people from overseas who came into the District from the ships. Some speak of their 'colouredness' as a result of this as seamen and adventurers landed and established relationships with local women. Their whole 'differentness' is bound up in Cape Town the seaport, the cosmopolitan city connected to the other side of the Atlantic by sea and ship.

Cape Town is called the Mother City, the city of origin for both whites and coloured people, both of whom made it, despite apartheid's claims to the contrary when it annexed the cities for whites. The location of District Six close-by the original city centre with its monuments to colonialism, the Art Gallery, the House of Parliament, the Natural History Museum and so on elided its identity with that of Cape Town proper, while Table Mountain also drew the two into one, by encompassing them both as horizon. As Western notes:

> By removing Coloureds from District Six, the Whites are doing more than clearing slums or underpinning their exclusive claim to central Cape Town's sacred space. *They are also destroying one of the symbols of whatever Coloured identity may exist, a space in parts at least seven generations deep and one with associations with the emancipation of the slaves.* (1981: 150, italics in the original)

In so doing the apartheid authorities transformed Cape Town as they had always intended, but at the same time they diminished it historically, since they destroyed Cape Town, the coloured city. They removed part of the sedimentation of history which *was* Cape Town. And museum people want to argue that they were an important part. One of the trustees expressed this through architecture.[12] Using also the photographs on the museum walls, he talked of how his home, an old nineteenth-century two storey house, had been destroyed and of how an important part of Cape Town's history disappeared in this and other such demolitions. Obviously, its early establishment gave District Six a deep sedimentation of historical material culture. As coloured people were diminished then, so too was their city. This they are also saying in their stories of the lost jazz clubs, dance halls and cinemas, the lost street life, the colour, the noise, the vibrancy. They lost their cosmopolitan identity, but so in a way did Cape Town, since white society did not replace these things, these forms of sociality, these kinds of relations and practices.

This transformation of city and coloured identity has also to be seen as betrayal, something reflected in the stories of how people felt in their interactions with 'the Board' (see also Rive 1989; Fortune 1996; Adams and Suttner 1988). People talk about shame in being told that they had to go, of being told where to live. In part this is shame at the interference of authority into the lives of people who deeply valued 'respectability'. Many analysts (see Western 1981; Ross 1992; Goldin 1987 for example) have noted the importance of respectability in coloured culture, and it is possible that this had its roots in a mimetic response to dominant white, particularly English, culture, where in Taussig's terms (1993) mimesis is part of an appropriation of dominant culture which is all about coping with domination (see also Ross 1992). Within a deep need for respectability, apartheid's residential control was shaming, diminishing. Several people told with enormous satisfaction how they had got together enough money to resist such control by buying a house of their own choosing. Further, the townships were places of control and surveillance, built in such a way that they could be sealed off and scrutinised in times of unrest (Christopher 1994). The self-determination which accompanies respectability was undermined by the Group Areas Act. At the same time, the home and family seems to have been a crucial site of respectability so that the assault on respectability featured particularly in women's stories and the distinctions they made between themselves and others. Apartheid's Group Areas thus attacked coloured people at the very site of respectability – their residence, their home.

Another context of perceptions of betrayal is the privileging of the coloured population over the African population, particularly in the Western Cape, where coloureds were seen both as being more like the whites, and also useful as a buffer between whites and Africans. Afrikaans speaking in the main, coloured people were cultivated by those who in the 1950s appeared to turn on them and cast them out. Thus we find things like coloured people never having to carry passes as Africans did and in the Cape jobs were reserved for coloured people under the Coloured Employment Protection Act (Goldin 1987; Humphries 1992). Yet at the same time that a special relationship between white and coloured was being encoded in law, urban coloured people were decreed a threat and forcibly removed to the Cape Flats, as Africans had been before them.

Apartheid's betrayal provides a reconciliation function for the museum, which criticises apartheid at a collective and structural level through its focus on community.[13] And interestingly here, we find a final engagement with the state rhetorics of the new South Africa.

At one level the museum does provide a site in which people may express a relationship of identity between themselves and a new South Africa. They often assert that District Six already was what ideologues in the 'new dispensation' argue South Africa should strive to be today – a unity in diversity. Here they stress heterogeneity and respect for differences in culture, religion and race. For them the state rhetorics and narratives of nation are given concrete form, reality through memory and District Six somehow stands for 'the new South Africa'.

To understand walkers in the museum as playing out state rhetorics though is problematic if it implies necessary intention. For, even in the museum, but certainly outside, there is real ambivalence, are real divisions among coloured people, about the new South Africa and particularly the ANC government. Particularly in the Western Cape, there are also very real differences of opinion about and support for the National Party and its role in the apartheid past. Even among a group of people who share the experience of dispossession and disloca-tion under apartheid, people have different histories of response to the apartheid regime (James *et al.* 1996). So it is also people with these different political his-tories who walk the map, constituting their pasts through similar processes.

In many ways, it is the encompassment of the walking within the museum with its overarching critique of apartheid which constitutes these acts as political acts of resistance. It is this encompassment in a post-apartheid South Africa which refigures the remembering of disruption and dispossession from within a variety of orientations towards apartheid as an act of protest. Within the overarching critical narrative suggested through the museum, apartheid is interrogated through one of its policies which was central to its entire ideological project. Yet this does not necessarily accompany or indeed constitute a full, overt or radical political critique on the part of the walkers. It certainly does not entail automatic approval of the regime today. And here again, it is the Cape Town identification which emerges as having potential in an identity politics which is characterised through such uncertainty, ambivalence and differentiation.

Imagining a South African identity for themselves *is* radical, though not necessarily thought of as such, in the context of a past in which a South African identity was denied to non-whites who were expected to develop an identity in terms of their racial category and 'South African' was reserved for whites (again coloureds were somewhat ambiguous in this regard, harder to see as a separate nation, since they had no separate space which was not also claimed by whites).

What is *also* radical in the context of apartheid's declaration of the city as white is the way in which some visitors and staff also saw themselves as Capetonian, occasionally even privileging this over South African. Here identity involved a reappropriation of the city which was taken from them. But this is only one side of such an appropriation. It can certainly be *made* radical in the context of the exclusions of the past, but if one shifts the context to the present and the building of a national identity, post-apartheid, this embracing of a Capetonian identity may also involve something different, more troubling and precarious. First, Capetonian may obscure the very real differences and conflicts among coloured people, particularly around current political allegiances. But second, and related to this, people seemed to be suggesting that, within South Africa, the content of 'South African' seemed to be uncertain and that 'Capetonian' was somehow clearer, less uncertain, easier. Given the massive obstacles in the way of delivering the 'brave new world', of overturning the inequalities of apartheid, just what is really 'new' is still problematic. And the TRC itself has contributed to this, demonstrating clearly the different worlds and realities inhabited by those today who would be South African.

It is not clear from the comments of the District Six walkers whether all South African people can yet imagine sharing history and memory to the point where they can embrace a clear new *South African* identity. This leaves something lesser (or different) available as identity. Because of the exclusions of apartheid, to embrace the identity of Capetonian *is* new, *is* engaging with present and future in a new polity, so it is also attractive, and attainable, as a position. It is radical, precisely because it is a re-appropriation, a demand for inclusion and the claiming of an identity taken away by apartheid as a fundamental principle of that regime. Maybe here too we have 'Capetonian' synthesising the work of reconciliation which many feel is necessary *before* South Africa can become a single nation. Here, as Boyarin (1994: 2; see also Geyer 1996) suggests, is a *politics* of memory in which memory actually constitutes the politics of national identity, rather than only the process of mobilising the past for political purposes, though of course this is *also* happening in South Africa today.

Conclusion

Geoffrey White (1991) notes that stories of the past are always discourses of identity. We see this in the stories which people recount prompted by the map in District

Six Museum, but we also see operating White's corollary, that stories of the past actually constitute identity. This is a political process, producing a politics of memory which is fundamentally a construction of the present through an engagement with the apartheid regime. Post-apartheid is a substantial dimension of the politics of South Africa today.

Operating as one location in which South Africans contemporarily can make their own meanings and their own accommodations to state rhetorics about country and nation, the District Six Museum suggests that what the 'new South Africa' is constituted out of is a variety of identities, a variety of engagements with the past, a variety of pasts (Pechey 1994). In the politics of memory enabled, generated by the map, South Africans who were ex-residents of District Six seem to be first asserting the social constitution of this area that apartheid managed to define in asocial terms, either as a problem, a desirable position for whites or simply a physical space to be managed and redeployed. Second they criticise, through recollection and comparison, the forms of collectivity and sociality which apartheid policies and administrators thought desirable for non-white people. Third, the retrieval of a more desirable past provides a way into new identity for them in post-apartheid South Africa as they take back urban citizenship, their identity as Capetonians. What is new is imagined in terms of, in engagement with, how they recollect the past.

Notes

Charmaine McEachern wrote this article while a member or the Department of Anthropology, University of Adelaide, Australia.

1   This article is based on a 10-week period spent in Cape Town in the first half of 1996 and a follow-up visit in December 1996 and January 1997.

2   Mamdani argues that the focus on territorial segregation in South Africa can be traced back to Smuts and that the way in which such policies were first and foremost political, generated by what was seen as 'the native question', which was a question of minority control over a majority population, links South Africa under apartheid to colonialism in Africa generally, rather than differentiating South Africa from the rest of the continent.

3   Interestingly, in the case of a much earlier Cape Town, 1894, whites taking advantage of their generally greater wealth and moving into the suburbs had prompted some speculation that Cape Town's city could be left for coloureds, so producing the residential separation of white and coloured (Bickford-Smith 1992: 48).

4   As many writers have stressed (see for example Smith 1992; Lemon 1995; Marks and Trapido 1987), this enforcement was only ever imprecise, as non-white people resisted and evaded the controls, ultimately causing the breakdown of strict influx controls and residential segregation which was so central to apartheid's conception of the city.

5   People classified as coloured made up the largest grouping, but there were smaller populations of whites and Africans living in the area.

6   The museum from time to time mounts exhibitions which require the modification of this first layout. This initial format is important for the way in which it made clear the assumptions and aims of the museum creators.

7   When in January 1997 Robben Island was opened to tourists, as a one-time prisoner, Lionel Davis was one of the tour guides appointed.

8   Another visitor expressed great anger at the exhibition, seeing it as romanticism and declaring that this was not what the struggle was for. He gave the poverty, overcrowding and lack of life chances for the children as factors to counter what he saw as an overly romantic view.

9   The similarities in the comments of Western's (1981) informants a short time after coloured people were moved from Mowbray seem to confirm this identification of critique as much as described past.

10   A Cape Town movement of mainly the Islamic coloured population, PAGAD set itself up to oppose the gangs and drug pushers in the townships. Its activities have been highly visible in the media and full of controversy as gun-related deaths have marked various demonstrations. Despite this, there has been approval that some action is being taken, the perception being that the police are unable to control violence and the possession of guns and drugs in the townships. In January 1997, a PAGAD demonstration which ended at the Caledon Square Police Station, outside the Museum created enormous interest and sympathy among visitors to the Museum.

11   One woman expressed this perfectly when she said that she had not really realised what was happening until the day they had to move and then she cried and cried.

12   Architecture was very topical at this time, since the Museum was mounting an exhibition of a photographic record made of District Six architecture as it was being destroyed. This exhibition actually straddled the map and was a source of some contention, since for some it undermined the power of the map. Certainly people had to crawl under the exhibited photographs to find their streets on the map.

13   Here it speaks to another dimension of apartheid not much covered by the Truth Commission with its focus on human rights violations to individuals.

References

Adams, H. and H. Suttner (1988) *William Street, District Six*, Diep River: Chameleon Press.

Bickford-Smith, V. (1990) 'The Origins and Early History of District Six to 1910', in S. Jeppie and C. Soudien (eds) *The Struggle for District Six: Past and Present*, Cape Town: Buchu Books.

—— (1992) 'A "Special Tradition of Multi-racialism"? Segregation in Cape Town in the Late Nineteenth and Early Twentieth Centuries', in W.M. James and M. Simons (eds) *Class, Caste and Color: A Social and Economic History of the South African Western Cape*, New Brunswick (USA) and London: Transaction Publishers.

Boyarin, J. (ed.) (1994) *Remapping Memory: The Politics of Time Space*, Minneapolis and London: University of Minnesota Press.

Bozzoli, B. (ed.) (1987) *Class, Community and Conflict: South African Perspectives*, Johannesburg: Ravan Press.

Braude, S. (n.d.) *People Were Living There: Sandra Braude Interviews Sandy Prosalendis*, Project Directory of the District Six Museum, Cape Town (distributed by District Six Museum).

Christopher, A.J. (1994) *The Atlas of Apartheid*, London and New York: Witwatersrand University Press.

Comaroff, J. and J. Comaroff (1992) *Ethnography and the Historical Imagination*, Boulder: Westview Press.

de Certeau, M. (1988) *The Practice of Everyday Life*, Berkeley: University of California Press.

Fortune, L. (1996) *The House in Tyne Street: Childhood Memories of District Six*, Cape Town: Kwela Books.

Geyer, M. (1996) 'The Politics of Memory in Contemporary Germany', in J. Copjec (ed.) *Radical Evil*, London: Verso.

Goldin, I. (1987) 'The Reconstitution of Coloured Identity in the Western Cape', in S. Marks and S. Trapido (eds), *The Politics of Race, Class and Nationalism in Twentieth Century South Africa*, London: Longman.

Hannerz, U. (1980) *Exploring the City: Inquiries Toward an Urban Anthropology*, New York: Columbia University Press.

—— (1992) *Cultural Complexity: Studies in the Social Organization of Meaning*, New York: Columbia University Press.

Hart, D.M. (1990) '"Political Manipulation of Urban Space" The Razing of District Six, Cape Town', in S. Jeppie and C. Soudien (eds) *The Struggle for District Six: Past and Present*, Cape Town: Buchu Books.

Humphries, R. (1992) 'Administrative Politics and the Coloured Labour Preference Policy during the 1960s', in W.M. James and M. Simons (eds) *Class, Caste and Color*, New Brunswick and London: Transaction Publishers.

Isaacson, M. (1996) 'Sharpen those Pencils, Roll up those Sleeves – the Stuggle may be Over but the Book is not Closed', *Sunday Independent*, 26 May.

James, W., D. Caliguire and K. Cullinan (1996) *Now That We are Free: Coloured Communities in a Democratic South Africa*, Cape Town: Institute for Democracy in South Africa.

James, W.G. and M. Simons (eds) (1992) *Class, Caste and Color: A Social and Economic History of the South African Western Cape*, New Brunswick (USA) and London: Transaction Publishers.

Jeppie, S. and C. Soudien (eds) (1990) *The Struggle for District Six: Past and Present*, Cape Town: Buchu Books.

Lemon, A. (ed.) (1995) *The Geography of Change in South Africa*, Chichester: John Wiley and Sons.

Mabin, A. (1992) 'Dispossession, Exploitation and Struggle: an Historical Overview of South African Urbanization', in D. Smith (ed.) *The Apartheid City and Beyond*, London and New York: Routledge and Witwatersrand University Press.

Marks, S. and S. Trapido (eds) (1987) *The Politics of Race, Class and Nationalism in Twentieth Century South Africa*, London: Longman.

Mithlo, N.M. (1995) 'History is Dangerous', *Museum Anthropology*, 19 (2): 50–7.

Pechey, G. (1994) 'Post-apartheid Narratives', in F. Barker, P. Hulme and M. Iversen (eds) *Colonial Discourse/Postcolonial Theory*, Manchester and New York: Manchester University Press.

Pinnock, D. (1987) 'Stone's Boys and the Making of a Cape Flats Mafia', in B. Bozzoli (ed.) *Class, Community and Conflict: South African Perspectives*, Johannesburg: Ravan Press.

Prosalendis, S. (1995) 'Foreword', in South African National Gallery, *District Six: Image and Representation*, Cape Town: South African National Gallery and the District Six Museum.

Rive, R. (1986) *'Buckinghan Palace', District Six*. Cape Town: David Philip.

—— (1989) *Advance, Retreat. Selected Short Stories*, Cape Town: David Philip.

Ross, R. (1992) 'Structure and Culture in Pre-industrial Cape Town: A Survey of Knowledge and Ignorance', in W.M. James and M. Simons (eds) *Class, Caste and Color*, New Brunswick and London: Transaction Publishers.

Rossouw, R. (1996) '"District Six" under Threat Again', *Mail and Guardian*, Thursday 25 April.

Small, A. (1986) *District Six*, Linden: Fontein Publishing Co. Ltd.

Smith, D.M. (ed.) (1992) *The Apartheid City and Beyond: Urbanization and Social Change in South Africa*, London and New York: Routledge and Witwatersrand University Press.

Soudien, C. (1990) 'District Six: From Protest to Protest', in S. Jeppie and C. Soudien (eds) *The Struggle for District Six: Past and Present*, Cape Town: Buchu Books.

Soudien, C. and L. Meltzer (1995) 'Representation and Struggle', in South African National Gallery and the District Six Museum, *District Six: Image and Representation*, Cape Town: South African National Gallery.

Taussig, M. (1993) *Mimesis and Alterity: A Particular History of the Senses*, New York: Routledge.

Western, J. (1981) *Outcast Cape Town*, London: George Allen and Unwin.

White, G.M. (1991) *Identity Through History: Living Stories in a Solomon Islands Society*, Cambridge: Cambridge University Press.

Young, J. (1993) *The Texture of Memory: Holocaust Memorials and Meaning*, New Haven and London: Yale University Press.

Challenges: Museums and Communities in the Twenty-first Century

Introduction to Part Five

THESE CHAPTERS CONSIDER SOME of the key challenges facing museums in the twenty-first century as they reflect on, and work towards, more equal and inclusive relationships with the communities they serve. While some of them offer tentative models or part solutions, they all acknowledge that working with, and for, all types of communities is difficult. Nevertheless, they encourage all those engaging with museums to think creatively and constructively about what it means to be a museum in the twenty-first century.

Ashley tackles the difficult issue of power and control within the museum, particularly within the context of national meaning-making and 'social cohesion'. She draws together many of the issues considered by other authors in this volume and examines an exhibit on the Underground Railroad and African-Canadian history at the Royal Ontario Museum in Toronto. She considers a method of power sharing within the process of exhibition making. Such power sharing is all too rare in museum exhibitions and provides us with a model of how museums can move from being instruments of the state to 'sites of public identity discourse and social inclusion' (Ashley 2005 'Abstract': 5).

Ashley refers to the way in which museums are trying to bring about 'structural change' within their institutions as a method of supporting community inclusivity (2005: 9, this volume p. 490). 'Structural change' is complex and is dealt with in another reader in this series. However, one particular issue should be raised here – the composition of the museum community itself and the lack of diversity within the workforce in many institutions. If we take the United Kingdom as a case study, Sandell (2000) has posited a museum-specific model of diversity management and points to some initiatives here that attempt to create a profession more representative of a multicultural nation. While Sandell is mainly concerned with cultural diversity he also indirectly highlights another factor within the museum profession that discourages people from certain sectors in society from seeing museum work as something they can aspire to do. Competition for jobs is intense and 'the model candidate emerges as a person with a good first degree, often in a traditional discipline, a commitment to a museum career demonstrated through often extensive voluntary work and, with limited and diminishing funding opportunities, the ability to pay for course fees and subsistence for a year' (2000: 219). In other words, if you are relatively wealthy or have support networks to help you through the education system you are far more likely to be able to contemplate a museum career than if you are poor. Ironically at a time when museums with paid staff are becoming more aware of their local audiences and communities, and the need to engage with them, they are tending to recruit from outside the community. When I started my museum career I met several distinguished and respected community curators and officers who had been recruited locally many years before at a time when higher educational opportunities were fewer. They did not have first degrees. They did, however, have a deep understanding of the locality in which they had been born and subsequently lived and worked and had links to many communities within it. Their expertise and knowledge was widely respected by their peers inside and outside the museum walls and by the communities they served. Most of these have retired and have been replaced by people with first and second degrees recruited from outside the area. I was one of those replacements. Despite working in one location for fourteen years, when I left I was aware I had only begun to understand the cultural complexities and aspirations of its many communities. I was fortunate to stay in one place and receive promotion. For many in the museum sector promotion means a geographical move. Thus many museums are staffed by people serving communities with whom they have to struggle to make even the first tentative links. This is one of the key challenges facing museums in the twenty-first century.

Van den Bosch's chapter discusses the impact of globalisation on the concept and practice of community identity and relationships. While she looks specifically at art museums she considers a range of issues such as the way in which, with a global culture, 'shared understandings' (van den Bosch 2005: 84, this volume p. 504) can no longer be assumed, how history, memory, culture and the search for identities are complex. She looks at how museums play a key part in supporting individual and community understanding of these issues. She reminds us that museums need to consider their audiences and evaluate what is happening in the museum today.

With Cuno we return to the question of authority and power. Cuno reminds us that consultation and audience-focussed exhibitions can appear to threaten scholarship and that professionals 'will be asked instead to research and present what others want to know, or rather what others know they want to have confirmed as true' (Cuno 1997: 7, this volume p. 572). He calls for a return to 'scholarship' and a greater confidence among curatorial staff to defend their commitment to this. He challenges us to consider who decides 'on what terms and whose authority' (Duncan 1991: 98, cited Cuno 1997: 8, this volume p. 514) groups such as women, African Americans and Irish Americans are seen or not seen on museum walls. He poses some interesting questions. Perhaps the most interesting question of all is, however, not aired. Cuno suggests that there is a tension between scholarship and community involvement in exhibitions. Certainly his two examples (*Gaelic Gotham* the exhibition about *Enola Gay*) illustrate forcefully the damage that can be done to curatorial confidence and museum independence when certain lobby groups mobilise. However, consultation does not have to be about loss of scholarship and independence. Individuals within communities have knowledge that can be invaluable to museums. Consultation with a wide range of individuals, groups and communities can provide opportunities for different perspectives in an exhibition, not just the most vocal one. Thus an important question to ask is how do museums support those members of staff who feel threatened by community consultation and empowerment?

However, as Peers and Brown point out, consultation is not enough. In an overview of museums' relationships with source communities[1] they remind us that consultation can be about unequal power relations with resulting tensions. All too often it is about providing support 'for the maintenance of institutional practices' (2003: 2, this volume p. 520). They argue that 'involving and sharing power with source community members means that staff must unlearn much of what they know, or think they know . . .' (2003: 7, this volume p. 525). However, this does not necessarily happen even when close relationships with source communities have been established. The purpose of the collections is often seen very differently by source communities. Artefacts are opportunities for the communities to gain knowledge and develop their ideas about themselves. Rarely are the objects passive. They become active agents in identity making.

Working with communities requires immense patience and a great deal of time. Peers and Brown remind us that it is an ongoing process that should not be abandoned once a project has been completed. They point out that often a museum establishes links with a community for a purpose such as an exhibition or to reach, through a programme of events, a group that does not use the museum. Then the imperative to continue this work with that particular community disappears. The exhibition opens; the funding for the outreach programme is spent. The community's expectations have been raised and its members feel abandoned. Some museums are now working towards a change in museum practice that ensures that source communities are involved in an ongoing way as an integral part of a new kind of museum practice.

Peers and Brown focussed on relationships between museums and indigenous groups and with diaspora communities but many of the points they make are equally valid for communities everywhere. Community empowerment is not just a matter for those working with indigenous peoples. Barnard's brief account of the Greater Pollock Kist project in Glasgow illustrates a successful project where local people were encouraged to develop their own exhibitions with the help of museum staff. It also raises an issue that has yet to be debated in the museum world: 'What if the stories the volunteers want to tell in the future make the museum service uncomfortable' (Barnard 2002: 37, this volume p. 556)? Peers and Brown point out how there is very little in print about the difficulties experienced by communities and museums and most of the literature focusses on the positive benefits for both partners, resulting in serious omissions in the literature. Thus some of the key challenges facing museums in the twenty-first century are to debate this issue, to be honest about the implications of community involvement, and to decide just how far museums are prepared to relinquish control to the communities they serve.

Museums are sometimes partners in economic regeneration schemes. Frequently such projects are proposed on the grounds that cultural elements within their schemes are not only good for tourism but also for the local community. All too often such community benefits are neither measured nor evaluated. However, there are some examples of good practice. In his description of the development of the archaeology of Fiji, in partnership with among others the local museum service, Crosby describes a community led eco-tourism project that had benefits for the local people and the museum. Glasgow's Greater Pollock Kist scheme, part of the city's strategy of regeneration through culture, provided opportunities for communities to curate exhibitions in their own localities (Barnard 2002). Both these examples demonstrate a refreshingly open attitude towards consultation, an understanding that such work is time-consuming, difficult and has to be done in a true spirit of equal partnership.

Note

1   Source communities or originating communities are terms used to refer to 'indigenous peoples in the Americas and the Pacific, but apply to every cultural group from whom museums have collected: local people, diaspora and immigrant communities, religious groups, settlers and indigenous peoples whether those are First Nations, Aboriginal, Maori, or Scottish' (Peers and Brown 2003: 2, this volume p. 520).

References

Ashley, S. (2005) 'State authority and the public sphere: Ideas on the changing role of the museum as a Canadian social institution', *Museum and Society*, vol. 3, no. 1, 5–17.

Barnard, M. (2002) 'Kist and Tell', *Museums Journal*, vol. 102, no. 2, February.

Crosby, A. (2002) 'Archaeology and *vanua* development in Fiji', *World Archaeology*, vol. 34, no. 2, 363–78.

Cuno, J. (1997) 'Money, power and the history of art', *Art Bulletin*, vol. 79, 6–7.

Duncan, C. (1991) 'Art museums and the ritual of citizenship' in I. Karp and S.D. Levine (eds) *Exhibiting Cultures: The Poetics and Politics of Museum Display*, Washington D.C.

Peers, L. and Brown, A.K. (2003) 'Introduction', *Museums and Source Communities*, London: Routledge, 1–16.

Sandell, R. (2000) 'The strategic significance of workforce diversity in museums', *International Journal of Heritage Studies*, vol. 6, no. 3, 213–30.

Van den Bosch, A. (2005) 'Museums constructing a public culture in the Golden Age', *Third Text*, issue 1, January, 81–9.

Chapter 34

State Authority and the Public Sphere

Ideas on the changing role of the museum as a Canadian social institution

Susan Ashley

Introduction

MUSEUMS ARE IMPORTANT PUBLIC SITES for the authentication and presentation of 'heritage' in Western cultures. Heritage can be defined as the legacy of the natural and human world that society wishes to pass on to future generations. The authority of museums is derived from their long history as repositories of material culture and as agents of identity formation, nationalism and most recently, social inclusion. As influential sites, what is shown and what is not shown can have a major impact on how society sees itself and presents itself to others. But in a country like Canada, where global economics and popular culture combine with an unprecedented influx of immigrants, how society imagines itself and how the nation articulates its community and its heritage is changing radically. Issues of power, meaning, authenticity and citizenship have threatened the museum's representational authority. How are Canadian museums responding to these changes, and is their authority now up for debate? Or is the need to assert authority a problem in itself and can Canadian museums evolve a new type of discourse about heritage?

This chapter considers the nature of the public sphere in which museums operate, and investigates museum authority as a contested issue inherent in its simultaneous roles as voice of the state articulating identity and nationalism, and as a public space for opinion and meaning-making. It looks at how the museum's power to determine the national narrative, and limit voices, has changed over the years in Canada. It focuses attention on Canadian federal policies that have influenced the authority of museums, in particular, theoretical implications of the current policy drive for 'social cohesion'. It describes how Canadian museums are gradually moving away from acting for and about diverse communities, and are instead

Source: *Museum and Society*, vol. 3, no. 1, March 2005, pp. 5–17.

offering their expert voice as one among many. An exhibit on the Underground Railroad at the Royal Ontario Museum in Toronto is examined to consider how museums as instruments of the state can be re-tuned as sites of public identity discourse and social inclusion. Through this exhibit, Canada's National Historic Sites reworks its traditional approach to exhibition planning and design in order to open up the process of national identity-building and to focus instead on the social process of citizenship. A product of a collaborative process that encouraged networking among African-Canadians and openness by heritage professionals, the exhibit paved the way for both formal and substantive changes in designating and commemorating Canadian heritage sites.

The museum as authority

Traditionally, the museum is one of those institutions holding 'symbolic power,' acting as important places for the accumulation of information, communication, material and financial resources, and shaping the ways in which information and symbolic content are produced and circulated in society (Thompson 1995). Harold Innis (1951) would express such an institution as a 'monopoly of knowledge', a centralized structure of power, situated in an imposing city building, controlling the preservation of historical knowledge and identity of the dominant culture, and also world knowledge seen through the lens of the dominant culture. In terms of Marxist cultural theorists, such as Gramsci, Althusser, Williams and many others, museums would be considered a means by which ideology, that unconscious bias by which we live, is reinforced, not only through its overt communications but through its very way of being in the world. It could be seen as hegemonic, one of the ways in which the cultural ideologies of the ruling class are made acceptable to the masses. There is always some resistance to the hegemony when subcultures develop their own meanings, as we shall see outlined in the case study below. But through its physical structure, its categorization of knowledge, the flow of visitors and information through its halls and its determination of what themes and subjects are displayed and discussed, the museum institution, our society's custodian of historical artifacts, supports hegemonic rule. In the public mind, the museum is where history is kept; we agree that these public institutions represent us and can speak for us in matters of history and national identity. The very act of representing history in a building like a museum assigns significance to those events – an historical occurrence is raised from a first order meaning to mythic signification when it is depicted in a museum.

Several key authors laid the groundwork for the discussion of power and authority and nationalism in museums. In his important work *The Birth of the Museum* (1995), Tony Bennett writes that museums were not just expressions of history or science as defined in the Enlightenment, but closely wrapped up in nineteenth century efforts to define nations. Bennett links the birth of museums to the rise of bourgeois culture and capitalism, and the need to present the dominant society and economic system as the correct way of being within a nation. He shows how public museums and galleries played an important role in the formation of the modern nation-state by acting as hegemonic educative and civilizing agencies to bring order to an unruly public. He further demonstrates how museum exhibitions embedded modern ideals of the 'universal history of civilization', with European audiences positioned at the pinnacle of this march of history. Benedict Anderson's (1983) discussion of nation-states as imagined political communities details the use of museums as repositories and narrators of 'official nationalism' and symbols of those imagined communities. He envisions museums as tools for remembering and narrating national identity. Evans (Boswell & Evans 1999) echoes this idea in her introduction to *Representing the Nation*: 'The point about "imagining" is that nations have to be imagined in a particular and selective style. [This style] achieves tangible and symbolic form through traditions, museums, monuments and ceremonies' (1999: 2). Sharon Macdonald (2003) also discusses the role of museums in establishing an imagined, sentimentalized nation, stressing the importance of this emotional underpinning. The sentimental idea of belonging to a group and experiencing an emotional identity with the group carries a greater charge and leads to a sense of passion and involvement that, Anderson points out, commands a profound emotional legitimacy. The manipulation of this sense of belonging, this nationalism, could be seen as a great achievement of modern capitalism – the dominant society and economic system is legitimized through this non-rational emotional attachment. The dominant culture's economic and political interests are thus secured with the consent of the masses.

The museum as public space

But while the museum is clearly seen as a hegemonic agent for the state, at the same time, the institution is also considered an important space in the public sphere for the discussion, construction and contestation of ideas. In Habermas' (2001) understanding of the public sphere, all members of society come together as a unified group to discuss ideas about the common good in an objective, rational manner. The museum fulfills this role by the nature of its scientific, objective stance on knowledge and its position as a public forum, theoretically accessible to all, where large numbers of people gather for events, programs and lectures. Charles Taylor (2002) sees the public sphere as an essential part of the modern 'social imaginary' where individuals come together to voice opinion in a public space that exists outside state power. In his view, the 'extrapolitical' status of the public sphere is essential so that ideas and opinions can be expressed outside of the state, and political power can be 'supervised and checked by something external . . .' (Taylor 2002: 114).

The extrapolitical nature of the modern public sphere is key to our discussion of the role of the museum and the nature of the public sphere in which it operates, and where its conflicted nature becomes evident. If we are to accept the writings of theorists who demonstrate the integral place of the museum as a hegemonic agent of dominant culture, how can we reconcile this with the concept of the museum as a public forum disengaged from state power? The use of the medium of museums as a voice of the state is highly manipulative, and is a source of disaffection among non-dominant groups when they think about museums. Crooke (2004), for instance, cites the anxiety of Northern Irish communities who fear that local expression of heritage will be 'taken over' by state museums. African-Canadians voice a discomfort in entering museums because of the overwhelming official presence (Ashley

2004). Henry has written extensively on the case of the Royal Ontario Museum in Toronto where a controversial exhibit, *Into the Heart of Africa*, caused outrage among some African-Canadians who interpreted the exhibit as a perpetuation of dominant culture racism. In these cases their fears relate to loss of control of and participation in the dialogue within the museum walls – the museum space is not theirs, it belongs to someone else. The museum is clearly not a public space equally accessible to all.

The traditional bourgeois concept of the public sphere implies the troubling assumption that the public sphere is *not* accessible to all. And, in order to participate in this space, any difference is cast aside in order to act in unity with the group (Fraser 1993). The limited nature of the public sphere has been pointed out by many scholars who agree that Habermas' original notion excluded access on the basis of gender, race and other characteristics, and implied participation in a unity based on the characteristics of European white males. Thus the public sphere shares with the notion of state authority the issue of power – domination and exclusion are implied here too. So we can add another layer to the problem of authority in museums: not only does authority and domination exist in the use of the museum as a voice of the state, but this power of exclusion can creep into its alternative use as a public site of contestation and dialogue. The theme of exclusion runs through Stuart Hall's work, and is linked by most writers to the core values of nationalism: the state defines its identity through closure or exclusion and buys acceptance to this closure from those of its citizens who share some of its characteristics. Hall writes about the formation of identity, and the role of the nation-state in the creation of national identity. He points out how a nation-state is represented as homogenous and imagined as stretching back in time (Hall 1996). To Hall, this homogeneity or unity which identity treats as natural, or an 'inevitable totality', is not natural, it is a constructed form of closure, constructed within the 'play of power and exclusion' (Hall 1993: 5).

Within the museum world, the exoticization of Others and the exclusion of Others is a much-discussed issue from the colonial era and even survives now in post-colonial times. Non-dominant players now ask that the post-colonial museum respond to criticisms of gender, class and racial exclusion by opening up and reflecting upon the process of representation. While admitted in theory, in practice some institutions and professionals have not even considered that the act of displaying is an act of power. Yet authority is exercised throughout the process of planning museum displays – what gets discussed at exhibit planning meetings, how the theme is framed and positioned, what media are used, which objects and visuals are shown or not shown, as well as how the content is expressed in written texts. In the post-modern museum all of these steps would be open to negotiation by many parties outside the mainstream.

How to open up the process of representation has been a source of constant debate in the museum community (for example Boswell & Evans 1999; Carr 2001; Clifford 1997; Karp *et al.* 1992; Sandell 2002). It was Clifford (1997) who introduced the notion that the museum should move away from presentation with its implication of vested authority, towards multi-cultural exchange in a public space with community dialogue and ongoing construction of meaning. But essential to this move was the rejection of the ideas of authority and exclusion inherent not only in state representations but in participation in the public sphere. To accomplish this would have a major impact on how society sees itself and its heritage.

The state and Canadian museums

The movement towards non-authoritative representation and inclusive participation has been only a recent concern for Canadian museums, indicative of the slow evolution of state policies in their articulation of nationalism and the imagining of community. Scientific collections formed the basis of early Canadian museums in the nineteenth century, as governments and universities responded to increased concern about the preservation of important scientific, anthropological and archaeological artifacts and knowledge. While scholarly interest was the primary focus, museums at that time were also the only medium through which citizens could get a sense of their own shared history, and the strange and exotic people and countries which lay beyond their personal experience. These early institutions offered an academic, disciplinary and Anglo-centred view of history and the world (Gillam 2001).

Canada's Massey Report of 1951 was the first major policy document that closely scrutinized Canadian museums. It laid out the concern of the federal government with the Americanization of Canada, and sought to stem the tide through the support of arts and culture, and through an emphasis on universities and education. The report recommended that museums redefine their role from collecting and research to vehicles of adult education – education with the intent of achieving nationalist goals. Their language bore a striking resemblance to that of British Victorian museums that sought to 'civilize' the lower classes (see Bennett 1995). It supported the creation of state facilities that would serve the express purpose of defining and presenting Canadian natural history and cultural history, beginning a trend of government agency and authority in the life of museums. Canada's centennial year in 1967 was the next defining moment in museum history when many local and provincial centres of identity were created to boost a sense of Canadian nationalism. Following this, the Trudeau/Pelletier policies of 'democratization and decentralization' saw the establishment of the National Museums of Canada and various travelling programs like the Museumobiles which depicted an imagined, romantic Canadian nation, and sought to unite the country in a unified, state-sponsored vision of heritage. National unity was a central feature of the political agenda in the following years, and by the late 1980s and early 1990s the battle between separatists and federalists in Quebec played out in its museums (Ruddel 2004). Quebec developed the Musée de la civilization and other heritage facilities such as *la maison des patriotes* to tell patriotic *québéquois* political and social history narratives. On the federal side, the Canadian Museum of Civilization (CMC) in Hull countered with a Canadian history hall that told an official, celebratory vision of the past. There, the story of Quebec was represented by a quaint, pre-conquest village; an imagined simulacra, with no mention here of difficult social issues in history such as the expulsion of the Acadians or the 1837–38 rebellion (Ruddel 2004).

The nationalistic imagining of Canada was surprisingly monolithic outside of Quebec. Permanent exhibits in national, provincial and regional institutions reflected a similar mix of displays about Anglo settlement history. Until the 1970s the treatment of First Nations and non-Anglo cultures was either anthropological or non-existent. Canadian First Nations narratives were often isolated either in detached spaces within natural history museums, or in separate anthropological museums, effectively separating native collections and stories from mainstream representations of national narratives (Ruddel 2004). But it was in the anthropological museum, and specifically dealing with First Nations issues, that museum practice in Canada began to change. In western Canada, museums like the Glenbow began to include some native input into programming, staffing and some exhibits as a response in many cases to native activism and a heightened public awareness of First Nations' social issues. As well, cultural pride and activism resulted in the creation, by First Nations groups, of museums specifically devoted to expressing indigenous perspectives on culture and heritage, such as the Woodland Cultural Centre of the Six Nations. By the 1990s, when ownership, protection and repatriation of indigenous cultural property became an international issue, some significant collaborations were under-taken in public museums both in Canada and other Western countries (see Haas 1996; Phillips 2003).

At this time, Canadian museums began to deal with another aspect of national culture that surfaced as an issue for Canadian society – ethnic diversity. International flows of people, money and information had stirred up a number of social issues in Canada and throughout the world. On a political level, the needs of immigrants to Canada were addressed through the Multiculturalism Act of 1988 that defined programs to support the symbolic cultures of new Canadians. But the integration of the heritage of minorities into actual museum programs and practices was more challenging. Indigenous peoples and diasporic minorities are two very different categories in Canada, and have been dealt with differently in Canadian museums. A basic technical problem is that while material objects relating to First Nations are available in abundance in most museums, rarely are there any collections connected to ethnic communities in Canada. On the level of public opinion, First Nations' rights are officially acknowledged in the Canadian Charter, and they have a sympathetic place in the minds of average Canadians since they were the 'first' Canadians. New Canadians however, especially 'visible minorities', have a differ-ent place in the Canadian imagination (Bannerji 2000), and their inclusion in museum representations and institutional practices has been problematic. Following the lead of many Western museums, the Canadian Museums Association encouraged its members to fundamentally question their values, assumptions and purpose in society, and to consider the inclusion of more diverse voices in all aspects of museum practice. But translating the professional interest into structural change and a more inclusive imagining of Canadian-ness on the institutional level has been slow. At the Canadian Museum of Civilization, for example, ethnic diversities are still rep-resented in permanent collections by a vision of managed multi-culturalism – a Chinese laundry and a Ukrainian church are all that contribute to the overall, progressive national story that omits troubling issues. A more significant example of myopic vision was the *Into the Heart of Africa* exhibit of 1989–90 which became the most controversial show in the history of the Royal Ontario Museum (ROM), and a touch-stone in the Canadian imagination for future museum exhibits about minority groups. Vocal and violent objections emerged from divergent readings of that exhibit, which told the story of nineteenth century collecting by Canadians in Africa to address colonial attitudes and interpret histories of minority groups not previously exhibited. African-Canadians protested that the exhibit presented instead a story of white people in Africa, and perpetuated racism through its texts and visuals. They blamed a lack of consultation by the ROM and its curator. The ROM responded defensively against what they saw as interference in curatorial professionalism, independence and academic freedom – what others saw as inherent white privileges (Tator & Frances 2000). Instead of taking the opportunity to interact with current and historic social issues in the museum forum, either through planning consultation, by representing the complexity of the subject in the exhibit itself or by other means, the contestation had to take place on the street outside the museum walls.

In the late 1990s the Canadian government initiated a significant policy shift that opened the door for more diverse imagining of Canadian stories, and, to borrow from Stephen Weil (1999), the re-positioning of heritage institutions away from being *about* unity and nationalism and being *for* its citizens. Canadian arts, culture and museums were framed instead as social goods that supported cohesion in society. At this time, preliminary efforts to collaborate with Canadian ethnic communities to develop exhibitions were undertaken, for example at the CMC (Phillips 2003). The primary federal department responsible for articulating nationalism/unity since the mid-1990s was Canadian Heritage, the umbrella department for arts, culture, heritage and multicultural programs on the federal level. When this department's mission and objectives were re-aligned in 2001 away from talk of identity and nationalism, and into 'social cohesion', the resulting departmental mission statement became 'towards a more cohesive and creative Canada'. The parlance in the policy planning context became: how can Canadians, including new ethnic Canadians, make a social investment or acquire social capital through participation in cultural/heritage programs? The strategic policy objectives responding to these questions named four essential elements of cohesion that Canadians should share and support: connections; stories and symbols; inclusion and participation; and values.

Unity or cohesion?

While federal policy researchers defined social cohesion as 'how to build a sense of connectedness and belonging in Canadian society' (Baeker 2002), the idea suffers from the underlying suspicion that we were again discussing issues of power – that social cohesion was a means of nationalism or unification or assimilation that did not resolve the social issues of inequality or exclusion. In fact, the Canadian government's Final Report of Social Cohesion in 1999 warned that the concept of social cohesion does not convey the same awareness of exclusion or inequity as policy concerns like 'social justice'. The report pointed out the tendency to confuse social cohesion with national unity and concluded that these fuzzy ideas of 'shared values and traditions' should not be allowed to overshadow ongoing challenges associated with social justice (Canada 1999). Supporters maintain that cohesion is an internal sharing and bonding of diverse participants in society that brings a sense of mutual aid and passion once devoted to nationalism. Critics contend that cohesion is an external imposition of unity in order to ensure authority and social control. Bannerji (2000) asserts that Canadian federal multi-culturalism language and policies still serve white elitist goals rather than the interests of visible minorities. She writes that non-whites might be citizens but they do not 'belong' in the imagining of the nation. Henry (2002) points out that social cohesion policies rely on concepts of tolerance and unity within a paradigm of diversity that presumes that justice and equality exist in Canada. She maintains that these policies only address symbolic not transformative change. Baeker (2002) also cautions that cohesion policies must do more than offer surface change, and points out that the use of what he calls 'affirmative' strategies try to correct inequitable social arrangements without disturbing underlying and generative structures or frameworks. Bernard (1999) calls this the formal aspects of cohesion that are state-driven and passive and tend to be framed in words like 'shared values' and 'tolerance'. Such words imply that a paternalistic national culture is bestowing inclusion upon the minority cultures, or that visible minorities are now being asked to participate in the culture of their superiors. He maintains that official versions of cohesion merely mask growing social inequalities, and are very different from what he calls the Substantial day-to-day aspects of cohesion such as social justice, active participation and real dialogue about values.

Is social cohesion a new term for assimilation or social control, or are we now at the point where these Canadian Heritage objectives mean true equality and sharing of power? What would Canadian museums need to do, on the ground, to develop cohesive policies and practices in a truly equitable manner, to step back from their position as arbiters of content, and develop as accessible public forums? Cohesion must be seen as a social force that goes beyond official or formal identity, and incorporates substantive change, a definition that straddles and incorporates the two positions of 'state authority' and 'public forum'. An essential element lies in seeing these two positions as a communicative dialectic. The concept of authority implies, on one hand, a communicative effect that is top-down, official, unitary, symbolic and one-way or transmissive. The concept of public forum, on the other hand, suggests a communicative effect that is horizontal or multi-level, everyday, complex, constructivist and two-way or dialogic. It is possible to relate the concepts of 'state authority' and 'public space' to the 'formal' and 'substantial' of Bernard's analysis. The formal level of cohesion carries with it the authoritative power of the state with its symbolic and transmissive characteristics. The substantial level imparts the give-and-take life of citizens participating in the constructivist dialogues of the everyday. In a truly cohesive society, museums would act as part of the social process of citizenship where all citizens encounter and interact with heritage on both formal/symbolic and substantial/everyday levels. As state institutions, they have a monopoly or the power to formally define citizen membership through representation – but definitions become fixed in the process of exhibition. The fluidity of the substantial sphere of participation, interaction and contestation is essential to respond to and overcome that fixation.

Much of the recent museological literature about concrete attempts to make museum practices more inclusive on both formal and substantial levels stress two methods: deep structural and policy change, and collaboration (for example Baeker 2002; Phillips 2003; Sandell 2002). Many museums have, internationally, taken on this challenge, especially in the UK where social inclusion is a major government policy initiative. Macdonald (2003) cites the study of a museum in Bradford, England, that redesigned its Transcultural Gallery. There an East Indian curator integrated various ethnic communities in selecting the objects for display, defining local narratives, and encouraged connections between groups. Macdonald offers the strategy of 'leaving objects to speak for themselves' as key to opening up how identities are represented. Crooke (2004) describes how museums in Northern Ireland are building their exhibits from the bottom-up in an attempt to include all. She points out that no overarching national narrative was ever offered in museums because of 'the Troubles' and conflicting imaginings of Northern Ireland's history. Instead, museums there are beginning to serve as grassroots spaces for sharing private memories and stories – a multiplicity of versions of history offered in the public sphere with the intent of community building. Whether non-white minorities will be invited to share this space is an unanswered question. Sandell (1998) discusses nation-wide organizational changes in British museums that would enhance the inclusivity of their programs. While the overall approach recommends deep structural change, the process itself seems to exclude people in poverty from the structural analysis, seemingly reinforcing a hegemonic stance in which insiders decide what is right for disadvantaged people. Despite their limitations, all three examples demonstrate that some museums are willing to share authority in the process of conceptualizing and presenting heritage, using both collaborative and organizational methods.

Canadian museums and social cohesion

Some Canadian museums have stepped away from authoritative practices and have tried to initiate policies, operations and programming that integrate both formal and substantial cohesion. This has been especially successful in attempts to feature First Nations' perspectives in the national narrative. Examples of First Nations collaborations, and the integration of First Nations managers and staff, exist throughout the Canadian museum world (see Phillips 2003). The First Peoples Hall at the Canadian Museum of Civilization, for instance, was opened in 2003 at the Canadian Museum of Civilization after an 11-year process of collaboration. A sharing of management and curatorial power between aboriginal and CMC participants resulted in a unique exhibition that juxtaposes standard ethnographic treatment and First Nations' perspectives on living cultures. But examples of significant participation of ethnic communities, not First Nations, in Canadian museums are more difficult to find. Oral histories and projects such as community mapping related to multicultural communities, as well as outreach programs and travelling exhibits developed with community input on diversity topics can be found in museums of all sizes. But notable expenditures or changes to institutional structure to incorporate visible minorities have not been documented. One institution that has devoted resources to changing its relationship to minority citizens is Canada's National Historic Sites. Their recent exhibit, *The Underground Railroad: Next Stop Freedom*, tested the process of collaboration and led to a re-orientation of priorities and approaches within the agency. A closer look at the process of planning this exhibit, undertaken over a three-year period, illustrates how changes on both formal and informal levels are required for a true paradigm shift in this social institution.

The Underground Railroad: Next Stop Freedom

The Underground Railroad: Next Stop Freedom (UGRR) was installed at the Royal Ontario Museum from 2002–3, and is currently on view at the Black Creek Pioneer Village in Toronto. The show is a multi-media exhibition that interprets the story of the escape of many Black slaves from the US into Canada through the early 1800s, and the urban experience of these Underground Railroad settlers in Toronto. The history of the exhibit's development illustrates how this federal heritage agency, under the Department of Canadian Heritage, was obliged to confront the substantive issues of participation and belonging, with the potential of contributing in a small way to the long-term issue of equality. The department was dragged into this position by the US government through its National Parks Service, who, in 1997, requested the participation of Canadian Heritage in increasing the number of UGRR-related museums and historic sites in the US and Canada. Their aim was to correct a perceived imbalance of African-American stories in American cultural institutions. Since Canada was the destination for UGRR refugees, Canadian Heritage, through the National Historic Sites and Monuments Board (NHSMB) and the Board's operational agency, National Historic Sites (NHS), was asked to join the network of institutions interpreting this story. In December 1998, NHSMB recommended designation of several new national historic sites and persons of national historic significance to commemorate the Underground Railroad in Canada. One specific recommendation addressed the need for a presentation in Toronto on UGRR urban settlers. Subsequently, Historic Sites historians and project staff took on the planning of an exhibit, something they were accustomed to doing. But in their efforts to ensure a product that would not receive public condemnation, they asked key stakeholders to sit on a consultative committee that would direct the production of the exhibit – African-Canadians were invited to sit at the table. This was an unprecedented move for the agency, a direct result of the violent reaction to ROM's *Into the Heart of Africa* exhibit (Watt, personal comment, 2004).

The invitation to the consultative committee to have substantive input into the end product took the exhibit beyond the traditional Canadian exhibit form and into an evolutionary hybrid. The production moved from being a controlled, in-house representational project, to a very public project with great symbolic meaning to the minority group it depicted. The original intent of the NHSMB was undoubtedly a formal commemoration of an event that would show Canada as a liberal nation that rescued slaves. What evolved in this production was a very real and very precarious relationship of power as the project became politicized and its claim to authenticity became a thing of negotiation. The dynamic of the consultative committee forced NHS to address the new social cohesion objectives of the department – on both formal and substantial levels. The process removed the heavy hand of official state interpretation and presented a point of view that was human, rooted in the everyday and offering a face-to-face negotiation of national narrative both for the producers and the audience. The project entered the public sphere not as the authoritative work of a particular museum, but as a collaborative dialogue between a range of minority stakeholders, and in a broader sense initiated agency-wide deep structural and policy changes.

Siting the exhibit, researching and framing the story, selecting media and exhibit materials, consulting with related Black history sites in other locations, and maintaining relations with the African and Caribbean communities in Toronto emerged as areas of particular concern to the consultative committee (NHS 1999–2002). Their first task was to find an appropriate site for the exhibition, and the Royal Ontario Museum was the only suitable space available – a choice that did not sit comfortably with several committee members. From the beginning, the *Into the Heart of Africa* exhibit loomed in their discussions. Both government representatives and 'civilian' committee members trod carefully around subjects related to 'the ROM's past record' (1 December 2000). When it was discovered that the museum had offered a small, basement location, one member refused to accept the site (27 October 2000) and commented how this symbolically placed them 'in the back of the bus again'. After intense negotiation, an invitation for a ROM representative to sit on their committee and letter writing to political supporters, they compromised on additional square footage at the museum and a series of satellite messaging sites.

Committee minutes reveal some of the collaborative dynamic in which the heritage professionals ceded power to the committee at large. The Underground Railroad was an entirely new subject matter for NHS, and unlike most aspects of Canadian history and prehistory, the agency had little internal expertise. This was an advantage since there were no preconceived notions of white expertise, and it allowed the committee to take a fresh approach. They hired several African-Canadian historians (one of whom was involved in the *Into the Heart of Africa* protests) to undertake original and secondary historical research (Watt 2004). The committee members themselves and their extended communities were also seen as sources of knowledge for stories, artifacts and photos. How to frame the story was also a source of contention: was it to be a social and political history featuring the hardships of slavery that implicated Canada as a slave-owning nation, or was it to be a celebration of the accomplishments of the refugees when they arrived in Toronto? The committee was divided, but settled on a celebratory tone. Some might call this a false harmony, but the decision was born of the committee's desire to counter the myth that Blacks were victims (Canada 2000). They also wanted to assert through this public medium that African-Canadians and their history had achieved status in Canadian society. They developed a specific planning objective that the presentation, 'instill in audiences a sense of personal connection to the stories of Black immigrants and refugees' (2000: 14). Preliminary studies of audience reaction undertaken in 2003 reveal that the exhibit engendered not only a recognition of the specific history of a minority group, but a recognition that the story told was one involving all Canadians (Ashley 2004). Whether this implied that audiences were ignoring the narrator's 'otherness' and appropriating her story as the 'same' as theirs, or instead recognized the intrinsic inequality of this minority history, is a subject for further study. But the group hoped to sensitize audiences to the Black experience and affirm their history as an integral part of Canadian national identity.

The consultative committee pushed for a non-typical museum exhibition technique – a story-telling mode with a holographic female narrator in a dramatic theatre setting. It is interesting to see how the exhibit approach originally taken by consultants – with panels, artifacts and graphics reflecting the NHS's Western museological approach – did not sit well with the group and was reworked over the course of the project to arrive at the final object theatre. The team wanted to shift the making of meaning from a didactic representation of standard historical information to the affective telling of an individual's story. Audiences were not presented with knowledge so much as experience, dangerous in its potential to alienate some audience members. Indeed, some visitors reacted to the presentation with the question, 'where is the "real" exhibit?' (Ashley 2004). But to clearly indicate that this exhibition was their point of view, the committee members, the researchers and the consultative process were fully acknowledged at the entrance to the theatre, an admission of authorship and dialogic process, as well as, undoubtedly, a confirmation of the internal politics of the committee. And, while the first-person, multimedia heritage approach was criticized by some as promoting a synchronous, populist past to nostalgic audiences (for example Hodgins 2004), preliminary audience research has indicated that the public (children and adults of many ethnicities) were willing to sit through this 25-minute presentation and invest in it intellectually and emotionally (Ashley 2004).

The collaborative approach brought new voices into decision-making for this exhibit, installed a new type of media at the 'stodgy' ROM, and resulted in strong networking with other African-Canadian museum workers, heritage sites and members of the diverse Black community of Toronto. From the outset, the team felt that the collaboration had a broader educative function, derived more from the process not just the final product. A process to identify, research and commemorate a range of 'satellite' sites across Toronto, and to relate the Toronto exhibit to Black history sites in Ontario, was seen as essential to the planning process (NHS, 6 July 2001). This also included drawing Toronto's African-Canadian community into the exhibit at all stages from planning; to creative design, scripting, music and visuals; to ancillary programming; to coming to see the show. The committee room became a neutral meeting place where a diverse group of African-Canadians, some of whom had been here for generations and some of whom were born on another continent, could assemble and share experiences, work together, disagree, come up with solutions and find a vision to present to other Canadians.

On a deep organizational and policy level, the UGRR project propelled both formal and substantial changes. To undertake the terms of the designation, NHS was compelled to draw active input from a range of minority stakeholders both on the committee and within a network of communities in Ontario. This led to a re-assessment of their internal practices of planning and designations on the policy level, contributing to a reassessment of the agency's System Plan (which sets thematic criteria for commemorations) and a new agency-wide emphasis on 'ethno-cultural communities' (NHS, 1 December 2000). A specific result of the project was the continued employment of several African-Canadian historians to work on this and other projects. The agency also integrated Canadian government-wide equity hiring procedures which promoted the hiring of First Nations and 'visible minority' candidates, for example the hiring of an African-Canadian superintendent at a NHS military historic site (Watt 2004). But efforts to ensure diversity and inclusion have not yet permeated the system at individual museums and sites to a great extent, other than through individual projects, interpretive programs and at new sites specifically devoted to minority histories. It is easier for NHS to change the way they do business and meet cohesion objectives on small, semi-independent projects and programs than on the basis of a deep structural change. Whether changes initiated by the UGRR exhibit will gain momentum agency-wide in the coming years is a subject for future longitudinal research.

State authority and the public sphere

This chapter argues that Canada's museums, as supporters of equality, must view the world as an ongoing construction in a dialogue among participants. Substantial cohesion in all its dimensions – social, economic and political – involves an admission that our world can be constructed by all. Whether this has permeated the outlook of practitioners in Canadian museums is an ongoing question. The idea of the museum as authority and state agent in representing unitary narratives of the past has been discredited in theory but only slowly undermined in practice. Elite ways of looking at heritage, and practices that reflect unitary ideologies continue at all levels.

Some critics see the abandonment of the grand narrative and its replacement by multiple narratives of minorities or populist representations of ordinary people as another form of tyranny. Instead of the public depicted as uniform citizens, it becomes individuals and communities of difference that are isolated, depoliticized and made digestible for mass consumption (Hodgins 2004). Others voice the danger that in favouring new or minority perspectives museums might trade 'one set of exclusionary practices for another' (Phillips 2003: 165), as old audiences and practitioners are cut out of the process of communication in an effort to over-compensate for past domination.

But small measures such as the *Underground Railroad* exhibit can point to future directions. The success of the UGRR exhibit with visitors is the *perception* of dialogue: that the presentation was clearly developed as a result of dialogue and that reaction to it can be a thing of dialogue. This was unusual in Canada where museums have traditionally acted as state agents of national culture, rather than spaces for the contestation of state authority. National Historic Sites was an agency where state control normally dictated an official message, usually a dominant-culture narrative. The idea of inviting participation, dialogue, involvement and the construction of community, all essential elements of true social cohesion, would suggest that agencies like NHS are beginning to turn away from statist or elitist points of view towards serving a non-exclusive public sphere. Projects such as the UGRR exhibit demonstrate that museum policies and methodologies have the potential to be egalitarian and cohesive, and in the long term will result in a negotiated view of Canadian identity. The key in this case was the removal of an authoritative voice and its functioning as one voice among many. Those voices, offering their own version of history, admitted their authorship, their own interpretation, thus offered up to audiences a choice of reactions – much like any conversation among equals or discourse in the public sphere. It reinforces the idea that the museum does not need only to focus on representation and exhibition – acting 'in public', but can serve as meeting place or community centre – acting 'of the public'.

Hilde Hein's (2000) thoughtful conclusion to her philosophic book on museums focuses on the dilemma that post-modern museums have 'descended from the heaven of authoritative certainty' (2000: 142) and are now consumed with doubt about their role in the world. The need to reinvent themselves has brought 'progressively more uniformity as museums hedge their bets by covering all possibilities' (Hein 2000: 142). She is concerned about the desire to manipulate and control the visitor's experience and laments the loss of the selective, individual, haphazard viewing experience that involved personal relationships with the objects. She writes, 'the challenge facing contemporary museums, therefore, is not to seal themselves off from multiplicity, nor to unify and sanitize it, but to invest its complexity with moral breadth, cognitive significance, and aesthetic pleasure' (Hein 2000: 148). Carr (2001) sees the answer as recognizing the museum as 'an open work' and he writes, 'to see the museum as an open work is to recognize that it is always discovered by its users in an unfinished state, not unlike seeing it as a laboratory, or a workshop for cognitive change' (2001: 182). Both writers echo the same challenge: the museum must be more open to ways that will temper the authoritative agency and certainty; remove homogeneity and single points of view, reject exclusion, encourage complexity and pluralism, and ensure conversation, dialogue and true cohesion.

Note

Susan Ashley is a postgraduate student in the Communication and Culture program at Ryerson University in Toronto, Canada.

References

Anderson, B. (1983) *Imagined Communities: Reflections on the Origins and Spread of Nationalism*, New York: Verso.

Ashley, S. (2004) 'Power and Presentation: The Visual Effects of Museum Display', unpublished paper presented at Canadian Communications Association Conference, Winnipeg, 3 June.

Baeker, G. (2002) 'Sharpening the Lens: Recent Research on Cultural Policy, Cultural Diversity, and Social Cohesion', *Canadian Journal of Communication*, 27, 179–196.

Bannerji, H. (2000) *The Dark Side of the Nation: Essays on Multiculturalism, Nationalism and Gender*, Toronto: Canadian Scholar's Press.

Bennett, T. (1995) *The Birth of the Museum: History, Theory, Politics*, London and New York: Routledge.

Bernard, P. (1999) 'Social Cohesion: A Dialectique Critique of a Quasi-Concept', Strategic Research and Analysis, Department of Canadian Heritage, SRA-491e.

Boswell, D. & Evans, J. (eds) (1999) *Representing the Nation: A Reader – Histories, Heritage and Museums*, London & New York: Routledge.

Canada (1951) Royal Commission on National Development in the Arts, Letters, and Sciences, *Report*, Ottawa: King's Printer.

—— (1999) 'Final Report On Social Cohesion', The Standing Senate Committee on Social Affairs, Science and Technology <http://www.parl.gc.ca/36/1/parlbus/commbus/senate/com-e/soci-e/rep-e/repfinaljun99-e.htm>.

—— (2000) 'Interpretation Concept Plan: Toronto UGRR Presentation', unpublished report.

Carr, David (2001) 'A Museum is an Open Work', *International Journal of Heritage Studies*, 7(2), 173–183.

Clifford, J. (1997) 'Museums as Contact Zones', in *Routes: Travel and Translation in the Late Twentieth Century*, 186–219, Harvard: Harvard University Press.

Crooke, E. (2004) 'Negotiating a way forward: Representing a contested history in Northern Ireland's Museums', paper presented at (Re)Visualizing National History: Museology and National Identities in the New Millennium Conference, University of Toronto, 5 March.

Fraser, N. (1993) 'Rethinking the Public Sphere: A Contribution to the Critique of Actually Existing Democracy', in Bruce Robbins (ed.) *The Phantom Public Sphere*, 1–32, Minneapolis: University of Minnesota Press.

Gillam, R. (2001) *Hall of Mirrors: Museums and the Canadian Public*, Banff: The Banff Centre Press.

Haas, J. (1996) 'Power, Objects and a Voice for Anthropology', *Current Anthropology*, 31, Supplement.

Habermas, J. (1995) 'Multiculturalism and the Liberal State', *Stanford Law Review*, 47(5), 849–853.

—— (2001) 'The Public Sphere: An Encyclopedia Article', in Meenakshi Gigi Durham and Douglas M. Kellner (eds) *Media and Cultural Studies: Key Works*, 102–107, Oxford: Blackwell.

Hall, S. (1993) 'Culture, Community, Nation', *Cultural Studies*, 7, 349–363.

—— (1996) 'Introduction', in Stuart Hall and P. DuGay (eds) *Questions of Cultural Identity*, 1–17, London: Sage Publications.

Hein, H.S. (2000) *The Museum in Transition: A Philosophical Perspective*, Washington: Smithsonian Institution Press.

Henry, F. (2002) 'Canada's Contribution to the "Management" of Ethno-Cultural Diversity', *Canadian Journal of Communication*, 27, 231–242.

Hodgins, P. (2004) 'Our Haunted Present: Cultural Memory in Question', *Topia: Canadian Journal of Cultural Studies*, 12, 99–108.

Innis, H. (1951) *The Bias of Communication*, Toronto: University of Toronto Press.

Karim K. (1996) 'Postmodernist Debates on Cultural Pluralism', Strategic Research and Analysis, Department of Canadian Heritage, SRA-158.

Karp, I., Mullen Kreamer, C. and Lavine, S. (eds) (1992) *Museums and Communities: The Politics of Public Culture*, Washington, D.C.: Smithsonian Institution Press.

Katriel, T. (1993) 'Our Future is Where our Past is: Studying Heritage Museums as Ideological and Performative Arenas', *Communication Monographs*, 60(1), 69–75.

Lang Rottenberg, B. (2002) 'Museums, Information and the Public Sphere', *Museum International*, 54(4), 21–28.

Macdonald, S. (2003) 'Museums, national, postnational and transcultural identities', *Museum and Society*, 1(1), 1–16.

Mason, R. (2004) 'Conflict and Complement: An Exploration of the Discourses Informing the Concept of the Socially Inclusive Museum in Contemporary Britain', *International Journal of Heritage Studies*, 10(1), 49–73.

National Historic Sites (1999–2002) Minutes of Meetings Underground Railroad Consultative Committee, 5 November 1999 to 5 March 2002.

Phillips, R. (2003) 'Introduction: Community Collaboration in Exhibits', in Laura Peers and Alison Brown (eds) *Museums and Source Communities*, 155–170, London and New York: Routledge.

Ruddel, T. (2004) 'Negotiating National Narratives in Canadian Museums', unpublished paper presented at (Re)Visualizing National History: Museology and National Identities in the New Millennium Conference, University of Toronto, 5 March.

Sandell, R. (1998) 'Museums as agents of social inclusion', *Journal of Museum Management and Curatorship*, 17(4), 401–419.

Sandell, R. (ed.) (2002) *Museums, Society, Inequality*, London and New York: Routledge.

Stanley, R. (2003) 'The three faces of culture: Why culture is a strategic good requiring government policy attention', Strategic Policy and Research, Department of Canadian Heritage, SRA-771.

Stevenson, N. (ed.) (2001) 'Introduction', in *Culture and Citizenship. Theory, Culture and Society*, 1–21, London: Sage.

Tator, C. and Frances, H. (2000) 'The role and practice of racialized discourse in culture and cultural production', *Journal of Canadian Studies*, 35(3), 120–137.

Taylor, C. (2002) 'Modern Social Imaginaries', *Public Culture* 14(1), 91–124.

Thompson, J.P. (1995) *The Media and Modernity: A Social Theory of the Media*, Stanford: Stanford University Press.

Weil, Stephen (1999) 'From Being About Something to Being for Somebody: The Ongoing Transformation of the American Museum', *Daedalus*, 28(3), 229–258.

Interview

Watt, Rob (2004) Personal Interview with Manager, Underground Railroad project, April 2.

Chapter 35

Museums

Constructing a public culture
in the global age

Annette van den Bosch

GLOBALISATION DOES NOT JUST REFER to new technologies and the economy; it affects the way people live and how they attempt to make meaning out of their lives. It affects the ways in which cultural narratives are created and used by audiences. Communication by means of new and complex systems and the global spread of mass-mediated imagery changed the expectations of people in all areas, including culture. Globalisation accelerated the mass movements of people as refugees, as migrants, and as cultural tourists. Concepts of place, such as the national and the local, and even concepts of memory and history, which were represented in the museum, have become subjects of debate. Some concepts and theories of globalisation can be linked to new ways of conceptualising the museum audience. The challenge for public museums is to develop more complex concepts of the audience, and to formulate research that takes account of the transformation of identity and the concept of diverse interpretive communities. Although the new museology produced major changes in museum practices, few museums have provided clear policy statements that acknowledge the challenges posed by globalisation.

Museums are linked through cultural tourism

Museums are social institutions that are part of, as well as dependent on, changes in society. The globalisation of economies has even affected museums all over the world. Consequently, the corporatisation of institutions and declining public-sector funding has led to increased autonomy for institutions and closer liaisons with business. The vexed relationships between culture and business are intrinsic to change in the arts and museums.[1] A ground-breaking examination of cultural tourism

Source: *Third Text*, vol. 19, no. 1, January 2005, pp. 81–9.

undertaken by UNESCO in 1997 explored the relationships between culture, tourism, and development, and showed that museums and tourism are the fastest growing industries in the modern world.[2] All museums are now competing for funding and audiences so that creating networks and links between museums to develop policies, and to identify strengths and strategies, will become a necessity in the twenty-first century.

All museums are affected by the growth of cultural tourism but some cities and countries are better placed to capitalise on its potential. Developed countries have exploited the potential of cultural tourism most strategically. The development of an economic-cultural macroproject in Paris in which the major museums – the Louvre, the Musée d'Art Moderne and the Pompidou Centre – were incorporated has also benefited the two thousand other museums administered by the Ministry of Culture. The key role of the museum in urban development and tourism is recognised in cities as far apart as Bilbao and Bendigo, resulting in the building of a new museum or the renovation and extension of an older building. The Frank Gehry-designed Guggenheim Museum in Bilbao has become an international icon, a logo for the marketing of the city similar to that of the Sydney Opera House. New architecture performs the same function as the big travelling exhibitions and retrospectives of great artists that bring a museum or city into the limelight of the worldwide media. As an integral component of the network of a globalised economy, the major museum today has an impact on the market value of a city comparable to the quality of its airports, trade-fair centres, headquarters, shopping centres, or gentrified districts.[3] Richard Meires's design for the Museum of Contemporary Art (MACBA) in Barcelona and Arata Izozaki's design for the Museum of Contemporary Art (MOCA) in Los Angeles have transformed the older precincts in their inner cities. Culture and the economy, cultural practices, and patterns of consumption are linked by service providers who understand that they are explicitly interwoven with the financial investments of a globalised economy.

There is a change in audience expectations, which is reflected in museum architecture. The Galerie du Carrousel in the Louvre, designed by I.M. Pei, Macary and Wilmotte, initially attracted controversy but its function as a shopping mall and visitor orientation centre were influential for museums across the world. The quality of the permanent collection is no longer sufficient to attract the masses to museums. Like a shopping mall, museums are seeking to attract a broad range of visitors who will stay as long as possible, and who are less interested in originality, or in art itself, than in the additional opportunities for consumption and interaction. The changes in architecture also reflect more relaxed attitudes in the modern museum visitor, who is less intimidated by the museum and art. These changes that have occurred in the OECD countries also characterise cultural tourism in developing countries.

Indeed, the values common to tourism and the middle classes are characteristic of modernity itself. They include: a secular education, the conservation of the past for its own sake, the enhancement of social status, aesthetic appreciation, entertainment, and the fostering of social relationships. These values underline the connections between religious institutions, museums, and tourist attractions and between the social organisation of tourism and of pilgrimage.[4] Since 1945, UNESCO has institutionalised these relationships by developing a long list of world heritage sites, some of which are museums that we now regard as belonging to all humanity. However, in an age of global mass tourism and pilgrimage, conservation and access may be mutually exclusive concepts as tourism still remains a predominantly middle-class activity. Ames has suggested that World Heritage Sites in developing countries have become possible sites for hegemonic class-based worldviews that effectively exclude local people.[5]

The questions of heritage and ownership are now a focus for debate. Graburn points out that between one's personal family heritage and world heritage are a variety of identities and heritages at the level of ethnicity, class, and nation, which differ and may conflict with each other, complicating the efforts of museum planners and curators.[6] Traditionally, the museum's primary function was seen as the preservation and display of the heritage of the specific social groups who formed its clientele. Nowadays, it is understood that heritage is culturally constructed and historically contingent. Museums' collection and exhibition policies have become political issues. Many world-class museums contain materials from all the great civilisations of the world owing to the collection practices that characterised colonialism. Demands for the return of art and artefacts to their countries of origin are now common. In multicultural societies such as Australia, whose heritage is complex and whose geographical position is part of a region of great cultural diversity, museum collection and exhibition policies have to be strategically targeted and open to public scrutiny. The Queensland Art Gallery, for example, collects and exhibits contemporary art of the Asia-Pacific region, while the National Gallery of Australia, with its greater fiscal resources, collects and exhibits twentieth-century European and North American art.

One of the most obvious problems created by mass cultural tourism is conservation, of both the physical integrity of a space, an environment, or a place, and its integrity in a non-material sense.[7] In order for works of art and sites of cultural heritage to be respected, the public needs to be taught to understand them. Conservation, public programmes, and information are all crucial to the continued maintenance of collections and sites. While modern scientific conservation has developed in the last forty years these developments are costly; new media, materials, and their associated conservation problems are also changing. Patterns of tourist behaviour that have enormous technical, social, and economic repercussions are created by globalisation. From an anthropological point of view, tourism is itself a cultural activity, and one that has been inadequately researched. In his book, *The Great Museum: The Representation of History*, Donald Horne points out that some museum objects have become sacred relics and tourism is a new form of pilgrimage.[8] The challenge for museum planners and educators is to identify diverse audiences with different social and cultural knowledge and habits in order to develop targeted information and public programmes that ensure the preservation of all cultural heritage.

Nation and region

The art museum that emerged in the modern nation-building era is now experiencing dramatic discontinuities in the global era. The renovation and expansion of

Australian art institutions from the 1960s was based on the same narratives of art and the nation that characterised nineteenth-century institutions. However, the transformations of becoming global mean that notions of citizenship and national identity are being re-negotiated in response to contemporary patterns of global migration and cultural globalisation, and that in many cases the trajectory of such negotiations is far from clear.[9] In the last three decades or so, global relations have become more extensive and intensive, facilitating new forms of identity, community, and action. This period was also characterised by the increasing mobility of people for purposes of business and labour, migration and study, creating a more complex cultural mix and cosmopolitan and hybrid identities.[10] Appadurai shows that, in this environment, people undergoing new cultural influences use media, communications, and return travel to maintain contact with their previous place-locations, their previous selves.[11] The complex mix of cultural identity and knowledge among contemporary audiences provides a challenge for art museums and other cultural industries. The shared understandings that may have been assumed between artists, curators, and audiences in the past can no longer be assumed, so that exhibition and display practices need to become more reflexive in what is presented and how it is presented.

The museum is a crucial site of cultural reproduction, which is why the critique of indigenous communities, women, and minority cultures has centred on museum practices. The museum is important in the public life of a nation-state, in the education of its citizens, especially new citizens, and increasingly in the representation of national identity to cultural tourists and global media audiences. The production of local and national subjectivities and cultures is now intersected by a complex set of migrant diasporas, population mobility, and global media possibilities that make the reproduction of local culture more fragile and contradictory, even before the question of the specific effects of the global economy on cultural industries are taken into account.

The art museum in particular stands between two contradictory tendencies: one is the dominant art historical narrative, and the other is the new sense of cultural diversity. The international art market and its influence on art practice since the 1960s have led to a rapid turnover of styles and the institutionalisation of art galleries and museums. Much of what is described as new involves the recycling of art practices attached to a few novel signs. Perpetual re-invention is also one of the markers of globalisation, creating ever-new products and markets, while basic relations of power remain unchanged. A cultural globalisation that loses locality, identity, and cultural context in a world culture that lays claim to the universal does not constitute a complete break from the past.[12] The means of transmitting this model are global, the reach of the model is global, yet the model has a local first world – a Northern and particularly North American identity. Other national and cultural identities do not vanish; they become subordinated. The main problem for the art museum is the homogenisation of practices, collections, and attitudes to the audience through the internationalisation of the art market. Oyen has shown that the emphasis in any comparative analysis needs to change from the search for sameness or unity that reproduces the global first world model to an inclusion of difference, and an analysis of why some differences appear more pronounced.[13] Differences appear more pronounced in the Asia-Pacific region, for example, because

the histories of cultural modernisation are different within the region, and in relation to the countries of Western Europe and the United States.

The challenge for national museums is to recognise that population mobility
often makes them part of a larger regional entity that is not homogenous. Regionalism can be conceptualised as a terrain in between a geographic reality and a
constructed discursivity. For example, Arif Dirlik argues that regionalism is an essential component of globalisation rather than a systemic effect.[14] If the new phase of
global capitalism, or the postmodern, is distinguished by space rather than by time,
then it is symbolic exchanges that are important rather than economic and political ones. Regionalism in Asia can be articulated on cultural grounds rather than
economic ones, as in North America (NAFTA), or political, as in Western Europe
(the EU).[15] Australia's position as a predominantly European settler society in the
Asia-Pacific region can be understood as marked by processes of immigration,
policy, and cultural change, engendered by its regional position and cultural
difference. Australia is a member of APEC (Asia-Pacific Economic Cooperation),
which includes the United States, but has not been accepted as part of ASEAN
(Association of South East Asian Nations) in which its European cultural origins
and Western political values are viewed suspiciously. In this region, the images
and ideologies produced in the national media of each country are political and
economic forces that can be recognised as part of the processes of exchange in which
national, territorial, and regional discourses are contending within the region,
and against other regional formations.[16] Museums have to develop policies for collections and audiences, particularly online audiences, which take account of their
regional localities and their contending discourses.

While Euro-American hegemony may have declined relatively in the economic
realm in the Asia-Pacific region, its cultural influence, in the form of mass culture
from the United States, has not. In any concept of regional culture the practices
of the dominant mass culture industry have to be taken into account. For example,
Star TV, which broadcasts from Hong Kong, reaches a potential audience of
2.7 billion people from Japan to Israel and Papua New Guinea, making it the largest
regional television market in the world. Star TV's programming, from Cantonese
soap opera to Japanese films, music videos from India, China, and Korea, sporting
events from cricket to sumo wrestling, fragments any regional identity as it works
to standardise media products. The concept of the Oriental, the East, and Asia that
existed within Western high culture and which still justifies some museum collections has no equivalent in the regional mass culture. The challenge for artists and
cultural institutions within the region is to establish partnerships and to provide
cultural links, such as online links, to reach audiences in ways that enable the audience to actively create new meanings – meanings that differ from the commodified
Asianism produced by the media corporations.

Migration, cultural tourism, and regionalism challenge old concepts of the local
and the national that were represented in the national museum. The loosening
of the holds between people, wealth, and territories (called deterritorialisation),
fundamentally alters the basis of cultural reproduction.[17] At the same time, it creates
new markets that affect local populations through the transfer of commodities and
the transformation of consumer taste. Deterritorialisation makes the nature of locality more problematic and more subject to change. Images, ideas, and opportunities

that come from elsewhere make previous practices of cultural reproduction less effective, thereby posing a problem for the representation of social life in the museum. Appadurai argues that there has been a general change in the global condition of life-worlds: where once improvisation came from the habitus,[18] habitus now has to be painstakingly reinforced in the face of life-worlds that are frequently in flux. In contemporary art, possibilities and meanings are often conveyed to audiences who have barely begun to imagine or articulate them, yet these audiences for contemporary art need forms of interpretation that will enable them to participate and relate these meanings to their own lives. A similar need for narrative and interpretive elements exists in the form of the museum exhibition. If audiences are involved in far more complex narratives and debates, in relation to current issues, then traditional contents and discipline boundaries will disappear, and so will simple conceptions of local, national, modern, and international.

History, memory, culture, and the search for identity

The contemporary dilemma is that people demand more of the arts and museums in order to understand authentic truths about the worlds of the past, the other, and their own predicament. Andreas Huyssen argues that memory emerged as a cultural and political phenomenon that stands in direct contrast to the privileging of the future so characteristic of twentieth-century modernity.[19] David Harvey shows that the separation of time and space imperils a full understanding of either modern or postmodern culture.[20] Museums offer a unique opportunity to represent the historical past in ways that create a dialogue with contemporary issues and possible futures.

The question of discrepant temporalities and differently paced modernities is key to new understandings of the long-term processes of globalisation, which supplant rather than merely adjust the paradigms of Western modernisation.[21] For example, the successful marketing of memory by the Western culture industry takes a more political inflection in other parts of the world. Fundamental questions of human rights were addressed in debates around the stolen generation of Aboriginal children and its documentation in the report *Bringing Them Home* (Canberra, 1997). These issues have been the subject of contemporary art, and of museum installations, such as at the Bunjalika Galleries in the Melbourne Museum. The political site of memory practices is still national, not post-national or global, although local debates are always shot through with the effects of global media and their focus on themes such as genocide, victimisation, and accountability.

The worldwide phenomenon of memory is the result of a desire to locate identity in a world characterised by an increasing instability of time and the fracturing of lived space, while knowing that the strategies or remembering and memorialisation may be transitory and incomplete.[22] Huyssen's observation that the past is currently selling better than the future is pertinent because we cannot be sure for how long this will be so. His conclusion that the desire for the past is a response to the slow but palpable transformation of temporality in our lives, brought on by the complex intersections of technological change, mass media, and new patterns of consumption, work, and global mobility, suggests that history, memory, and culture, fulfil an important function in this transformation but do not provide a guarantee of cultural stability. Museums play a central role in the re-creation and reproduction of history, memory, and culture, in the search for identity and understanding of the other, which is taking place as a result of accelerated change. What museum professionals, policy-makers, and funding agencies need to know is a lot more about the changes in audiences and the uses they make of the museum.

Hybrid cultural identities

Globalisation has created new hybrid cultural identities and patterns of consumption that pose a major challenge for audience research and evaluation in the museum. Experimental ethnography, where the visitor is put in the position of asking or learning about his/her own culture, in comparison with other cultures, is one obvious approach to take in a period of globalisation when the close interrelationships between different cultures, resulting from the rapid changes in communications technology and tourism, are producing a universalising culture.

In her research, Patricia Gillard explores the potential of audiences to construct their own text, by recording the many interpretations that they construct as part of their museum experiences.[23] Her approach draws on specific studies of groups (or fieldwork ethnographic studies), to enable visitors to respond to the layered meaning and content of exhibitions in their own words, and to gain some insight into the ways people use their experiences. Gillard also points out that visitor research of online museum audiences – on the number of visitors to a website, or particular web pages, and the location of the server from which contact has been made – has not been systematically addressed beyond statistical information.

One of the problems with empirical evaluation is that evaluation processes are often kept at arm's length from the creative design and exhibition work within museums, and only used in public programmes and marketing. A review of museum marketing literature and research has also indicated that 'What is missing is knowledge about the pattern of visitor encounters with an object or exhibition'.[24] Nightingale has argued that the audience is not a person or group but a relation.[25] Audiences are formed through their engagement with the content or site of a museum, and it is this relationship that needs to be understood. Art and other cultural activities create audiences, and audiences, in turn, are part of the processes that are represented.

One of the most useful concepts is that of an 'interpretive community', a social group formed through consistent cultural practices. Tony Bennett, in *The Birth of the Museum*, has observed that 'contemporary societies with advanced media systems are shot through with diverse and coexisting interpretative communities'.[26] Once a more complex understanding of the social contexts and practices of the audience and museum relationship are put into play, then it is possible to understand what audiences brings to the object, exhibition, or site and how this affects what they make of it. Any artist, teacher, or curator knows that understanding is layered and diverse and that some people recognise one aspect of what is being communicated, while others have more complex perceptions. One way to conceptualise this is to conceive of the audiences as engaging in a narrative practice in which they construct their own text.[27] Audience members are sites of meaning construction, and it is their choices rather than the exhibition or site that bring a narrative structure into being. The idea of audiences constructing narratives places the emphasis on the interpretive activity of audiences, for example, what attracts or hold their attention, their paths through an exhibit, their responses or participatory activities, become the focus of the study rather than the curatorial rationale.

This approach to evaluation promotes a subtle shift in power between the institution and its audience that may be enormously productive. It enables the curator or education officer to understand what is being learnt, and what other museum activities may attract its audience. It facilitates exhibition and programme planning and may assist sponsorship and funding proposals. It could suggest intra-institutional and collaborative ventures as ways to enhance audience experience. Most importantly, it enables museums to evaluate their own strengths and weaknesses and to focus on them. In this approach, the use of websites, databases, and CD-ROMs by museums and cultural institutions to reach audiences and to supplement exhibitions, conferences, or public programme activities forms part of a total mix from the planning stage to evaluation. These new approaches are essential because audiences that access worldwide media webs migrate and travel extensively, and are different from those of the past. Globalisation is a constellation of effects that interact to create a whole new cultural dynamic, which we cannot afford to ignore.

Notes

Annette van den Bosch taught in the Department of Visual Culture, Monash University, Australia.

1   Denis Bayart and Jean-Pierre Benghozi, 'Le tournant commercial des musées en France', *Culture Francophone*, La Documentation Française, Paris, 1992.
2   *Culture, Tourism, Development: Crucial Issues for the XX1st Century*, UNESCO, Paris, 1997.
3   Claus Käpplinger, 'Architecture and the Marketing of the Museum', *Museum International*, no. 196, 49:4, 1997, pp. 6–9.
4   Nelson Graburn, 'A Quest for Identity', *Museum International*, no. 199, 50:3, 1998, pp. 13–18.
5   Michael M. Ames, *Cannibal Tours and Glass Boxes: The Anthropology of Museums*, University of British Columbia Press, Vancouver, 1992.
6   Graburn, 'A Quest for Identity', op. cit., p. 15.
7   Yani Herreman, 'Museums and Tourism: culture and consumption', *Museum International*, no. 199, 50:3, 1998, p. 11.
8   Donald Horne, *The Great Museum: The Representation of History*, Sydney, Pluto, 1984.
9   David Held, Anthony McGrew, David Goldblatt and Jonathan Perraton, *Global Transformations: Politics, Economics and Culture*, Polity Press, Cambridge, 1999, p. 326.
10 Homi K. Babbha, *The Location of Culture*, Routledge, London, 1994, p. 193.
11 Arjun Appadurai, *Modernity at Large: Cultural Dimensions of Globalisation*, University of Minnesota Press, Minneapolis, 1996, p. 6.
12 Simon Marginson and Marcela Mollis, 'Comparing National Education Systems in the Global Era', *Australian Universities Review*, 42/43:1, 2000, p. 57.

13 E. Oyen, 'The Imperfection of Comparisons', in *Comparative Methodology: Theory and Practice in International Social Research*, Sage, London, 1990.

14 Arif Dirlik, *After the Revolution: Waking to Global Capitalism*, University Press of New England for Wesleyan University Press, Hanover, NH, 1994, p. 322.

15 Leo Ching, 'Globalizing the Regional: Regionalizing the Global: Mass Culture and Asianism in the Age of Late Capital', *Public Culture*, 12:1, Winter 2000, p. 238.

16 Fredric Jameson, 'Notes on Globalisation as a Philosophical Issue', in *The Cultures of Globalisation*, eds Fredric Jameson and Masao Miyoshi, Duke University Press, Durham, NC, 1998, pp. 54–77.

17 Appadurai, *Modernity at Large*, op. cit., p. 48.

18 Pierre Bourdieu, *Outline of a Theory of Practice*, Cambridge University Press, Cambridge, 1977, pp. 72–95.

19 Andreas Huyssen, 'Present Pasts: Media, Politics, Amnesia', *Public Culture*, 12:1, Winter 2000, p. 21.

20 David Harvey, *The Condition of Postmodernity: An Inquiry into the Origins of Cultural Change*, Basil Blackwell, Oxford, 1989.

21 Appadurai, op. cit.

22 Huyssen, 'Present Pasts: Media, Politics, Amnesia', op. cit., p. 31.

23 Patricia Gillard, 'Shaping Audiences Online: Principles of Audience Development for Cultural Institutions', *Media Information Australia (Incorporating Culture and Policy)*, no. 94, February 2000, pp. 117–30.

24 Nobuko Kawashima, 'Knowing the Public: A Review of Museum Marketing Literature and Research', *Museum Management and Curatorship*, 17:1, p. 30.

25 Virginia Nightingale, 'Shifty Characters and Shady Relations', *Media Information Australia*, no. 73, August 1994, p. 40.

26 Tony Bennett, *The Birth of the Museum: History, Theory, Politics*, Routledge, London, 1995, p. 103.

27 Virginia Nightingale, *Studying Audiences: The Shock of the Real*, New York, Routledge, 1996, p. 107.

Chapter 36

Money, Power, and the History of Art

Whose money? Whose power? Whose art history?

James Cuno

IN A CLUMSY CONCLUSION to an otherwise tightly argued case, James Beck recently imputed dishonesty of motive to the National Gallery, London, for attributing its *Entombment* to Michelangelo.[1] He implied that institutional vanity and commercial interests might play a role in the gallery's sustaining an attribution he finds so obviously wrong. After all, the attribution to Michelangelo rather than to, say, Baccio Bandinelli (to whom it once was attributed) might hold greater appeal for the gallery and, not least of all, Beck noted, for its marketing of 'knickknacks, video disks, CD-Roms, books and other publications, tee-shirts, slide [*sic*] and deals with vast international computer industries.' '[M]useums have become big business,' he argued, 'and big business has a healthy stake in its image and especially the public's reception of its activities.'[2]

Not long ago, Beck's colleague Richard Brilliant wrote of an art museum's obligations to its nonscholarly public as a debilitating constraint on museum-based art historical scholarship. 'Professor and curator diverge in their respective engagement in the artworks they (re)view, in the interpretations they advance, in their resorting to display or publication to make their ideas known, and in the historical dimensions and objectives of their scholarship.' This is in part, he argued, because the curator must serve the museum as 'collector, guarantor of authenticity, conservator, inventory manager, recorder, journalist, exhibitor, and asset protector and enhancer.' If in addition, he or she seeks to 'raise the residual cultural value of the artworks in popular esteem, no wonder, then, that museum curators have less and less time and energy to give to research, scholarly-critical writing, the production of scholarly exhibitions (however defined), and the creation of meaningful historical perspectives.' Rarely if ever can a curator present the sophisticated and nuanced context within which a work of art from 'another site and another time' ought to be considered.[3]

Source: *Art Bulletin*, vol. 79, 1997, pp. 6–9.

From Beck's point of view, a curator's scholarly work suffers from reflexive institutional self-boosterism in the name of 'big business,' while for Brilliant it is compromised by the myriad of public responsibilities he or she has to perform in the name of 'public access.' Although naive and cynical, these charges are not without interest.[4] If nothing else, they raise the question of museums – the professional 'other' to university-based art historians – and the problems we face at the end of the twentieth century.[5] I use the opportunity of writing for these pages to discuss what I consider to be far more real and urgent problems.

Coercive philanthropy and social agendas

Museums are and have been for some time in financial crisis. Without consistent government support, we are forced to rely on notoriously fickle sources of income – admission and rental fees, museum shop profits, and individual and corporate gifts – all of which are, as they say, 'market driven.'

We've all heard weird stories of commercial incidents in museums: most recently, and most bizarre, the Montreal Museum of Fine Arts' partnership with Oldsmobile in the presentation of a Magritte exhibition. For the duration of the exhibition an Aurora, the latest Oldsmobile model, was parked in the museum lobby because, as Glenn Lemmerick, manager of advertising and promotion, Oldsmobile, for GM of Canada, put it, 'With the Aurora, Oldsmobile was seeking to demonstrate a new and unexpected look for the division. That is why the visual elements, produced for the Aurora's participation in the exhibition, were developed to highlight the natural fit between the car and Magritte's works.'[6] But these are just plain weird; they are not a harbinger of things to come, and there is no sign that they have affected scholarship in the ways that Beck imagines.

More influential and problematic are the constraints placed on museum activities by federal, corporate, and foundation granting agencies. In an op-ed piece in the *New York Times* two years ago, theater director and cultural critic Robert Brustein quoted an unidentified contributions manager as stating in the newsletter *Corporate Philanthropy Report*, 'We no longer "support" the arts. We use the arts in innovative ways to support the social causes chosen by our company.' He also quoted the stated purpose of the Lila Wallace-Reader's Digest Fund's three-year grant program for resident theaters as '[t]o expand their marketing efforts, mount new plays, broaden the ethnic makeup of their management, experiment with colorblind casting, increase community outreach activity and sponsor a variety of other programs designed to integrate the theaters into their communities.' Nowhere did the fund express the desire to expand, broaden, or support an artistic goal, only to encourage art's *presumed* social effects.

Brustein is right to call these developments in cultural funding coercive. And he is right to suggest that the limited resources available for both social and cultural programs in our country encourage humanitarian agencies to believe that 'a single dollar can fulfill a double purpose' and that 'by forcing artistic expression to become a conduit for social justice and equal opportunity instead of achieving these goals through basic humane legislation, we are distracting our artists and absolving our politicians.'[7]

The emerging consensus

Indeed, the biggest problem facing art museums today – and the gravest threat to the quality of their scholarship – is not Beck's vision of the art museum as money-grubbing and quick to compromise, or Brilliant's view of a curator as an over-worked sometime-journalist/sometime-housekeeper, but the emerging 'consensus' among politicians, community activists, funding sources, and engaged academics that the art museum is first and foremost a social institution, an active educational center with a mandate to encourage therapeutic social perspectives for learning about and appreciating the visual arts.

This is made clear in the 1992 American Association of Museums' report *Excellence and Equity: Education and the Public Dimension of Museums*, which claims, 'Museums perform their most fruitful public service by providing an educational experience in the broadest sense: by fostering the ability to live productively in a pluralistic society and to contribute to the resolution of the challenges we face as global citizens.'[8] No longer, it argues, can museums 'confine themselves simply to preservation, scholarship, and exhibition independent of the social context in which they exist.' They must 'help nurture a humane citizenry equipped to make informed choices in a democracy and to address the challenges and opportunities of an increasingly global society.'[9]

Whew! What a responsibility! How are we to decide how to do this? What exhibitions, programs, and publications should we offer to nurture such citizenry? And how should we implement them? The report calls on us to develop a new model for decision making, one that 'encourages internal dialogue, transcends the intellectual hierarchy often imposed on staff, stimulates cross-fertilization of ideas, and may even provoke argument and dissent.' In addition, the 'perspectives of the museum audience and potential audience must be represented as an important ingredient in planning and decision making.'[10] Can one imagine the same model being imposed on a university faculty trying to decide how it is going to allocate its resources for teaching and research: administrative and support staff as well as students joining professors in planning the curriculum, scheduling sabbaticals, and deciding on equipment purchases and library acquisitions? Our colleagues would run screaming from the room.

By broadening the decision-making process in this way – by inviting our stakeholders to participate in ways we would not allow our individual or corporate sponsors – museum-based scholars will be less free to pursue 'disinterested' scholarship. They will be asked instead to research and present what others want to know, or rather what others know they want to have confirmed as true. Take two recent examples.

The museum as a site of self-commemoration

Last year, after loud and sustained opposition from representatives of the Veterans of Foreign Wars and from leaders in the United States Senate and House of Representatives, the Smithsonian Institution canceled a controversial exhibition marking the fiftieth anniversary of the flight of the *Enola Gay*, the airplane that dropped the atomic bomb over Hiroshima. At issue was the exhibition's intention to raise the question of whether it was necessary to drop the bomb, a question more easily debated than answered. After considering the protests (by the stakeholders – that is, the veterans' groups and the politicians), Michael Heyman, secretary of the Smithsonian, concluded, 'Bringing off a celebration and commemoration of the 50th anniversary and doing a historical analysis at the same time is very hard; it is exceedingly difficult to do this and be fair to the millions of veterans who believe that dropping the bomb saved their lives.' So he decided to cancel the original exhibition and present one that 'every American can be proud of'; the original exhibition was replaced by a simple display of portions of the restored plane with text labels honoring the mission uncritically. Museums, it would seem, are more suited for commemoration than for critical inquiry.[11]

A second example involves the Museum of the City of New York and its exhibition *Gaelic Gotham: A History of the Irish in New York*. Marion Casey, at the time an archivist and Ph.D. student at New York University, was the exhibition's guest curator. When, according to director Robert McDonald, the museum began to renegotiate a new contract with Ms. Casey, she demanded final say in the exhibition, claiming that the original exhibition proposal derived essentially from her Ph.D. research. Casey later claimed that she only wanted a share in the show's copyright, a condition from a previous contract. Her request was denied and she was offered a lesser role and then, ultimately, she was told she was no longer on the exhibition team.[12]

This brought a storm of protest from scholars serving as consultants on the exhibition, from several Irish-American groups like the Order of the Hibernians and the Irish-American Cultural Institute, which declined to loan objects to the show, and from Irish-American performers who refused to participate in its events. They objected to the replacement of Casey and the consultants with specialists in the history of ethnic relations in New York who were not specialists in Irish-American history. They believed that they, as Irish-American specialists, had a stake in the exhibition and a right to influence its content. As Emmett Cory, former professor at St. Johns University and past president of the New York History Round Table, argued, 'It's a public trust responsibility for a community to have input in the portrayal of its own history' because, as Walter Walsh, the Samuel I. Golieb Fellow in Legal History at New York University and the current president of the Round Table, put it, 'How a community is portrayed affects how it's treated.' In other words, because museum exhibitions have a clear social effect – because their subjects will be treated in life as they are represented in exhibitions – the museum's stakeholders have a claim on the museum, its programs, and purpose. Ms. Casey expressed it more bluntly, saying, 'the community has a voice and has a right to say what goes on the museum's walls.'[13] The museum, in other words, is not only a site for commemoration but also for *self-commemoration*, by and for its 'stakeholders' themselves.

Identity-defining machines

The challenge to the museum's traditional authority over its own affairs, as represented by these exhibition controversies, has been embraced and theorized by many of our academic colleagues. In a recent article, for example, Carol Duncan, who has frequently criticized art museums for masquerading as neutral when we are said to be in fact highly ideological, wrote:

> . . . museums can be powerful identity-defining machines. To control a museum means precisely to control the representation of a community and some of its highest, most authoritative truths. It also means the power to define and rank people, to declare some as having a greater share than others in the community's common heritage – in its very identity. Those who are in the greatest accord with the museum's version of what is beautiful and good may partake of this greater identity. . . . In short, those who best understand how to use art in the museum environment are also those on whom the museum ritual confers this greater and better identity. It is precisely for this reason that museums and museum practices can become objects of fierce struggle and impassioned debate. What we see and do not see in our most prestigious art museums – and on what terms and whose authority we do or don't see it – involves the much larger questions of who constitutes the community and who shall exercise the power to define its identity.[14]

'What we see and do not see' and 'on what terms and whose authority': there's the rub. It's not just that certain peoples – say, African Americans, Hispanics, Chicanos, Asian Americans, and women, even Irish Americans – are not 'seen' on our museums' walls, but on what terms would they be seen? As, for example, Irish-American painters? Or as Irish-American subjects? Or as Irish-American painters of Irish-American subjects? And if as subjects, as subjects representative of only the noblest achievements of that community? Or as representative of the full complexity of that community? Is a portrayal of the less than noblest achievements – indeed, the downright horrible achievements – of a particular community insulting to that community and thus off-limits to museums? Are we only to be sites of community *self-celebration*? And of all communities equally?

Do the Veterans of Foreign Wars have the same rights to self-representation in an exhibition of the *Enola Gay* that Chicanos have in an exhibition of Chicano art? And can one say of all such 'stakeholder'-driven exhibitions, as Richard Kohn of the University of North Carolina, Chapel Hill, said of the *Enola Gay* controversy, that '[it] may constitute the worst tragedy to befall the public presentation of history in the United States in a generation' because it may cause historians and museum professionals to conclude 'that responsible scholarship and the pursuit of truth on controversial topics are too dangerous to attempt in public forums'?[15]

Authority and power

The problem is really one of authority and power. Who has authority and power over museums? In a recent address to a meeting of the Association of Art Museum Directors, Amalia Mesa-Bains, the San Francisco commissioner of fine arts, put it like this:

Exhibitions have to be formulated with expertise, and that has to be shared. Power – the ability to self-define in a way upon which we can act – must entail shared decision-making, leadership, empowerment, scholarship, and curatorial expertise between the diverse communities and mainstream institutions.[16]

If all 'stakeholders' have the power to exercise their right to self-definition, what role the museum? Or, as Neil Harris noted in his remarks to the symposium 'Presenting History: Museums in a Democratic Society,' organized by the Smithsonian Institution and the University of Michigan following the *Enola Gay* controversy, over the past few decades, museums have suffered a widespread 'loss of expertise,' and suddenly anyone 'could become a significant critic of the museum, not merely artists and professionals.' As a result, he said, we are supposed to 'define more clearly and self-consciously [our] actions and goals, [our] relations to truth-seeking, and to learn more about how exhibitions function as sources of opinion.' But then how do we respond to the audience member who queried the symposium panelists with this remark and question?

Controversy now not merely happens but is deliberately provoked by museum staff who want to agitate for their own superior social and political views, yet they are bureaucratically remote and inaccessible to the views of the ordinary citizen whose values the cosmopolitan staffs deride and even ridicule. What can museums do to ensure that lay perspectives can be heard effectively and given respect?

Not surprisingly, the panelists had no clear answer. Elizabeth Broun, director of the Smithsonian's National Museum of American Art, explained, 'Not every good idea belongs in a public exhibition. Once you determine to do an exhibition, there are ways to bring the general public into the planning process. What cannot be institutionalized in a process is a fundamental sense of respect for other people's experiences.' And Neil Harris pointed out, 'It is a complex balancing act.'[17]

Now that anyone could become a significant critic of the museum – isn't that what is troubling museums today? A loss of authority over our own field of expertise? An inability to defend our purpose on our own grounds – on the grounds of sophisticated scholarship and nuanced presentations of works of art – and the acceptance of grounds more easily identified, measured, and defended: the number of young children who come to our museums, the diversity of our audience, the range of our programs, the extent of our community outreach, the breadth of the ethnic makeup of our management, and other ways we integrate ourselves into our communities? Aren't those the kinds of things our funding sources, government agencies, and popular and academic critics are looking for when they examine the state of museums today and hold out the promise of financial support and popular and critical acclaim?

In light of the widespread 'loss of expertise' among museums and the ongoing challenges to our authority, where is the defense of our scholarly mission? Who among us – museum professionals and university-based art historians alike – is calling for greater support of museum-based scholarship at the expense of increased public service? The silence is deafening. We have surrendered to our challengers and withdrawn behind the shield of arrogance. We need to defend the support of scholarship with clear, forceful, and convincing arguments. Most academic pronouncements on museums are not helpful in this regard. At best they offer a rich and entertaining panoply of intellectual fantasies far removed from the experience of art museums, and at worst they constitute direct assaults on museums as elitist playgrounds for the rich and powerful. Almost never do they call for strengthening art museums as sites for scholarship.[18]

I should be clear. I am not calling for art museums to neglect their public mission. I am proposing that we include within that mission the production and distribution of scholarship. This means spending today's money for tomorrow's benefit. And at a time of severe financial constraint, few government or philanthropic agencies are likely to take this long view. Not even the National Endowment for the Arts, which continues to defend itself on the basis of the popularity of the arts and how much they improve the quality of life, and certainly not the American Association of Museums, which demands in its report *Excellence and Equity* that museums 'help nurture a humane citizenry equipped to make informed choices in a democracy and to address the challenges and opportunities of an increasingly global society.'

No, only we – both museum-based and university-based scholars – can make the case for scholarship. And to date we have failed. The real and urgent problems facing museums today are not those caricatured by Beck and Brilliant, but the far more real and urgent ones raised by the questions: Whose Money? Whose Power? Whose Art History? To these, we have yet to give convincing answers.

Notes

James Cuno has been Director of Harvard University Art Museum and Professor of History of Art and Architecture at Harvard, Director of the Courtauld Institute of Art, London, and is currently Director and President of the Art Institute of Chicago.

1   James Beck, 'Is Michelangelo's *Entombment* in the National Gallery, Michelangelo's?' *Gazette des Beaux-Arts*, CXXVII, May–June 1996, 181–98.
2   Ibid., 195. Beck's concern that art museum-based scholarship might be influenced or inhibited by the financial pressures felt by museums is similar to his worry that restoration of works of art has become big money and that the politics of sponsorship might play an inappropriate role in deciding whether or not or just how to proceed with restoration. In Michael Daley and James Beck, *Art Restoration: The Culture, the Business, the Scandal*, London, 1993, Beck and his coauthor criticize the National Gallery's restoration of the *Entombment*. A spirited defense of the restoration was published in the *Art Newspaper*; see Helen Glanville, 'Vandals or Saviors (the Conservation Debate),' *Art Newspaper*. no. 37, Apr. 1994, 25.
3   'Out of Site, Out of Mind,' *Art Bulletin*, LXXIV, Dec. 1992, 551, an editorial written when Brilliant was editor-in-chief of these pages.
4   In a letter to Beck, my colleague Ivan Gaskell, the Fogg Art Museum's Margaret S. Winthrop Curator, pointed out that universities 'have their own financially inspired preferences and inhibitions that can affect conditions of scholarship and

scholarship itself.' He could have added, 'and almost certainly do.' That's what I mean about Beck's and Brilliant's charges being naive: both perpetuate the fiction that museum work is soiled by its contact with the public marketplace while the university's is not (as if professors with literary agents, consulting contracts, full speaking calendars, and regular columns in magazines and appearances on television news shows are free of market-driven temptations).

5   It always surprises me that university-based art historians speak and write about art museums as if they were not implicated in their successes and failures. The participation of numerous scholars, of all ideological perspectives, in programs and publications sponsored by museums (not to mention those consulted on attributions by museums or provided information on and access to works of art in support of their research) would argue against such independence of the academy from the affairs of the museum. For additional remarks on this and related matters, see Ivan Gaskell's contribution to 'A Range of Critical Perspectives: Writing (and) Art History: Against Writing,' *Art Bulletin*, LXXVIII, Sept. 1996, 403–6.

6   Oldsmobile also developed an advertising campaign that showed the Aurora head-on, as if printed on canvas, with the words 'Ceci n'est pas une Oldsmobile' in Magritte-like script. Of this, the museum's communications director said, 'With all of our shows, we try to find sponsors for whom the connection is so obvious that it would be impossible to refuse such partnership. Both GM and the Museum agreed that this is certainly the case with *Magritte* and Aurora.' 'Aurora and Magritte at the Montreal Museum of Fine Arts: An Excellent Business Opportunity,' *Collage* (calendar of the Montreal Museum of Fine Arts), July–Aug. 1996.

7   Robert Brustein, 'Culture by Coercion,' *New York Times*, Nov. 29, 1994, sec. A, 25.

8   Excellence and Equity: Education and the Public Dimension of Museums, A Report from the American Association of Museums, Washington, D.C., 1992, 6.

9   Ibid., 8.

10   Ibid., 21.

11   Michael Heyman, quoted in Paul Goldberger, 'Historical Shows on Trial: Who Judges?' *New York Times*, Feb. 11, 1996, sec. 2, 26.

12   Charisse Jones, 'Museum's Walls Tell a Story of Division: Exhibition on the Irish in New York Sparks a Bitter Battle over Content,' *New York Times*, Feb. 1, 1996, sec. B, 1–2.

13   Ibid., 2.

14   Carol Duncan, 'Art Museums and the Ritual of Citizenship,' in *Exhibiting Cultures: The Poetics and Politics of Museum Display*, ed. Ivan Karp and Steven D. Lavine, Washington, D.C., 1991, 101–2.

15   Richard Kohn, quoted in Goldberger (as in n. 11), 26.

16   Amalia Mesa-Bains, 'The Real Multiculturalism: A Struggle for Authority and Power,' in *Different Voices: A Social, Cultural, and Historical Framework for Change in the American Art Museum*, New York, 1992, 98. This book contains the proceedings of a two-part symposium of the same title, which took place at the June 1990 and January 1991 meetings of the Association of Art Museum Directors.

17   *Presenting History: Museums in a Democratic Society*, Washington, D.C., 1995, 4, 9. This summary was prepared for the Smithsonian Institution by Keens Company.

18   For a perceptive review of recent critical literature on art museums, see Ivan Gaskell's review article in *Art Bulletin*, LXXVII, Dec. 1995, 673–75. As an

example of the fantastic, I would have to include Donald Preziosi's 'Museology and Museography,' in 'A Range of Critical Perspectives: The Problematics of Collecting and Display, Part 1,' *Art Bulletin*, LXXVII, Mar. 1995, 13–15, which includes the point that the 'modern museum of art may also be understood as an instrument of compulsory heterosexuality: one of the chief productions of the institution, after all, is the engendered subject. The topologies of gender positions are among the museum's effects: the position of the museum user ("viewer") is an unmarked analogue to that of the (unmarked) male heterosocial pose/position. So much has been clear; what may be less apparent is that *all* art is drag, and that hegemonic heterosexuality is itself a continual and repeated imitation and reiteration of its own idealizations. Just as the viewer's position in exhibitionary space is always already prefabricated and bespoken, so also is all gender (a) drag.' If this is true, the AAM, which is hoping to 'nurture a human citizenry equipped to make informed choices in a democracy,' has its work cut out for itself!

Chapter 37

Museums and Source Communities

Laura Peers and Alison K. Brown

HERE WE EXAMINE ONE of the most important developments in the history of museums, a dramatic change in the nature of relationships between museums and their source communities, the communities from which museum collections originate. During the great age of museum collecting which began in the mid-nineteenth century, this was a one-way relationship: objects and information about them went from peoples all over the world into museums, which then consolidated knowledge as the basis of curatorial and institutional authority. Often this relationship was predicated on another set of relationships, between museums as institutions within imperial powers and source communities in colonised regions. Within this context, ethnographic collections, in particular, were built up on the premise that the peoples whose material heritage was being collected were dying out, and that the remnants of their cultures should be preserved for the benefit of future generations (Cole 1985; Griffiths 1996; Schildkrout and Keim 1998; Krech and Hail 1999; O'Hanlon and Welsch 2000). That those future generations might be the descendants of those with whom early collectors interacted was undoubtedly inconceivable at the time collections were assembled: museum collections were thought to be 'for' dominant-society audiences, whether of specialist researchers or the general public.

In recent years, however, the nature of these relationships has shifted to become a much more two-way process, with information about historic artefacts now being returned to source communities, and with community members working with museums to record their perspectives on the continuing meanings of those artefacts. Museums have begun to see source communities as an important audience for exhibitions, and to consider how museum representations are perceived by and affect source community members. In some parts of the world this shift has occurred

Source: *Museum and Source Communities*, London: Routledge, 2003, pp. 1–16, 252–73.

in the context of changing relations of power, so that source community members have come to be defined as authorities on their own cultures and material heritage. These changes have been given impetus by new forms of research and relationships which involve the sharing of knowledge and power to meet the needs of both parties. This new approach to research, which also informs curation and display, involves museums and community members working towards building a relationship of trust, often in cases where none has existed before and where there may be a significant legacy of distrust as a result of the dynamics of earlier anthropological and museum research projects. The desire and processes used to build such trust and to share power are the most important manifestations of a new curatorial praxis which incorporates source community needs and perspectives. . .

The term 'source communities' (sometimes referred to as 'originating communities') refers both to these groups in the past when artefacts were collected, as well as to their descendants today. These terms have most often been used to refer to indigenous peoples in the Americas and the Pacific, but apply to every cultural group from whom museums have collected: local people, diaspora and immigrant communities, religious groups, settlers, and indigenous peoples, whether those are First Nations, Aboriginal, Maori, or Scottish. Most importantly, the concept recognises that artefacts play an important role in the identities of source community members, that source communities have legitimate moral and cultural stakes or forms of ownership in museum collections, and that they may have special claims, needs, or rights of access to material heritage held by museums. In this new relationship, museums become stewards of artefacts on behalf of source communities. They are no longer the sole voices of authority in displaying and interpreting those objects, but acknowledge a moral and ethical (and sometimes political) obligation to involve source communities in decisions affecting their material heritage.

In the initial stages of realising that their relationships with and representations of source communities were no longer adequate, museums began to consult with members of those communities, and are still doing so. However, consultation is often structured to provide outside support for the maintenance of institutional practices, and source community members are wary of contributing to museum-led consultation exercises which do not lead to change within museums or benefits to their people. Indeed, as Michael Ames has observed, while 'partnering' and 'collaboration' are terms commonly used in museums, they describe arrangements that most frequently reflect the perspective of the museum (Ames 2003; see also Ames 1991). Similarly, James Clifford has remarked that unless museums do more than consult, they will continue to be 'perceived as merely paternalistic by people whose contact history with [them] has been one of exclusion and condescension' (Clifford 1997b: 208). While consultation with source communities is fundamental to the new ways of working that we describe, it is of a kind that goes beyond simply asking for knowledge and advice, but not otherwise altering the traditional relations of power between museums and source communities. It asks for partnership rather than superficial involvement.

At the core of these new perspectives is a commitment to an evolving relationship between a museum and a source community in which both parties are held to be equal and which involves the sharing of skills, knowledge, and power to produce something of value to both parties. This is very different from the traditional curatorial approach in which museum staff, on the basis of professional knowledge and authority, control exhibition content, storage facilities, and other museological functions. It involves learning from source community representatives what they consider appropriate to communicate or to display, or about traditional care practices, and implementing those desires and suggestions. Aspects of what in the social sciences has come to be known as co-management or collaborative or community-based research are part of this new way of working between museums and source communities (Notzke 1996; Ryan and Robinson 1990; Warry 1990), which includes the concept of heritage 'stakeholders', so that projects are sometimes determined by community members themselves and facilitated by a team of museum staff and community people in a negotiated process. This process, and the intent and ownership of its products, may be formally codified, and the partnership element acknowledged at the outset of a project by the negotiation of a Memorandum of Understanding, or other document, by the appropriate representatives of the source community and the museum (Ames 2003). However, relationships between museums and communities vary widely by degree of involvement and commitment, by goals and focus, and by longevity: we explore these differences through a range of case studies.

These shifts represent a radical re-envisioning of the nature of museums, and while obviously challenging, have been of tremendous benefit to all parties. Bringing source community members into museums turns these ordinarily dominant-society institutions into arenas for cross-cultural debate and learning, and can lead to extraordinary exchanges of knowledge as well as opportunities for people from all walks of life to begin to understand the views of someone from another cultural group.

Development and diversity

The development and form of these new relationships have depended in part on the nature of the source community, on the political relationship between the source community and museums (and the need to resolve conflict between them), and on the geographical proximity of museums to these communities. The greatest changes have emerged in relationships between museums and local source communities, whether these are indigenous populations (in, for example, North America and the Pacific), or local, settler, or immigrant groups (such as the social history initiatives in the United Kingdom and elsewhere). There have, however, also been significant attempts to forge new bridges between museums and overseas source communities. . .

Projects between Maori and New Zealand museums, Aborigines and Torres Strait Islanders and Australian museums, and First Nations/Native Americans and museums in Canada and the United States have set the standard for new relationships and forms of research. These have been born out of indigenous critiques of museum curation and representation, and from a growing sense of frustration by scholars and museum professionals with many of the same issues. They are given impetus by the growing expertise of indigenous peoples at pursuing their agendas, both locally and on the world stage, and by changing political relations between their communities and settler societies. Lobbying for and implementing changes in museum practice have (even where staff are co-operative) involved much conflict and tension within museums because of the challenges these changes create for curatorial authority, as well as for the essential functions of museums. Nor have such changes been evenly adopted across North America and the Pacific: they have emerged out of endeavours between particular museum personnel and particular source communities on a project-by-project basis.

Collaborative projects between museums and geographically distant source communities have been much more sporadic. The extensive face-to-face inter-action between community members and museum staff necessary for relationship-building and central to these new processes is even more expensive and logistically difficult when the museum is in England and the source community is in the Torres Strait. Combined with a sense of political distance from source communities that such situations lead to, these factors have made museums in the United Kingdom and Europe slower to adopt the new attitudes and processes associated with community-based research that museums in the Pacific and North America have begun to assume are necessary, even though costs in these countries are also often restrictive (for example, if the museum is in New York City and the community is in Alaska). In the United Kingdom, while there has been a long tradition of social history curators developing consultation procedures with diaspora communities (e.g. Poovaya Smith 1991; Giles 2001), curatorial authority and institutional procedures have not shifted much at all as far as overseas communities are concerned: for exam-ple, source community members are not necessarily consulted when research or exhibition proposals are submitted, exhibit labels are written, or catalogues published, whereas these have become fairly common procedures in Canada and Australia. In these places, too, as Ames (2003) remarks, funding for research and exhibition development may now be dependent on approval from the source com-munity, which is not the case in the United Kingdom or Europe (and see, on such differences in praxis, Peers 2000, 2001; King 2001). Nevertheless, individual cura-tors and institutions have initiated change, usually on a project level. . . .

Diversity in museums and source communities has been an important factor in the process of developing new relationships between them. The changing nature of what constitutes a heritage institution means that these relationships do not always involve traditional museums with ethnographic collections (which themselves range from university museums to national museums), but may also involve local museums with social history collections, tribal keeping houses, cultural centres, or eco-museums founded and maintained by the local community (Bolton 2003). Furthermore, just as the nature of museums is diverse, so is that of the commun-ities involved in these new relationships. Communities are not homogeneous, and source community members inevitably represent a range of perspectives. Museums entering into research projects need to deal with this diversity and ensure that dif-ferent community voices are represented on project teams.

Artefacts as 'contact zones'

One of the most frequently referenced articles documenting some of these chang-ing relationships has been James Clifford's 'Museums as contact zones' (1997b), which begins by describing a consultation session, and the tensions that emerged in a museum space as it became evident that the museum's agenda for consulting with a Native American group – to gain knowledge about its collections – was being ignored as the source community members used the opportunity to pursue their own agendas. This article is a useful starting point from which to consider the meanings of material heritage to source communities today, as well as the relationships that can be created around artefacts. The term 'contact zone', borrowed by Clifford from Mary Louise Pratt (Pratt 1992), refers to a 'space in which peoples geographically and historically separated come into contact with each other and establish ongoing relations' (Clifford 1997b: 192). Pratt located this in the context of unequal colonial relations, which would equate to the traditional relationship between museums and source communities, but it could equally be taken to mean relations within source communities, where the histories and politics of the past several centuries have often led to gaps in knowledge across generations. Artefacts function as 'contact zones' – as sources of knowledge and as catalysts for new relationships – both within and between these communities.

Artefacts in museums embody both the local knowledge and histories that produced them, and the global histories of Western expansion which have resulted in their collection, transfer to museums, and function as sources of new academic and popular knowledge. As 'sites of intersecting histories' (Edwards 2001: 2), artefacts have overlapping, but different, sets of meanings to museums and source communities – and tend to be interpreted very differently by each group. Particularly for indigenous peoples, for whom the effects of colonisation have produced rapid and wrenching change, museum artefacts represent material heritage and incorporate the lives and knowledge of ancestors. They are also crucial bridges to the future. For peoples whose way of life has changed dramatically but whose identity rests on historical cultural knowledge, artefacts offer the possibility of recovering a broad range of cultural knowledge for use in the present and future. Some of that knowledge may have been deliberately suppressed by policies of assimilation, or lost as a result of dislocation from familiar landscapes. Still, knowledge surrounding historic artefacts tends to live on in source communities even without their presence, sometimes for many decades, and can be reinvigorated and used for new purposes when those artefacts are encountered again. Aldona Jonaitis describes such a scenario in the volume that accompanied the American Museum of Natural History exhibition *Chiefly Feasts: The Enduring Kwakiutl Potlatch* (Jonaitis 1991), recalling the responses of Kwakiutl people to the Museum collections: the evocation of song, of story, of dance, of laughter (Jonaitis 1991: 68). Jonaitis's work foreshadowed that of Clifford (1997) and Ann Fienup-Riordan, whose moving account of the visit by Yup'ik elders to a collection of Yup'ik material culture at a German museum describes both their determination to take home the knowledge embedded in the objects, but also the way that the objects, even in that very foreign context, triggered songs, stories, memories, biographies, histories, laughter, and traditional social behaviour. As Fienup-Riordan notes, what the group sought was 'the return of the knowledge and stories, the history and pride'; they saw the artefacts as 'opportunities to affect the future' (Fienup-Riordan 2002, 2003).

For source community members, gaining access to their material heritage is vital. Work with museums has enabled communities dealing with the legacy of

colonisation to engage with objects and images in ways that bolster cultural identity and foster healing. Artefacts prompt the re-learning of forgotten knowledge
and skills, provide opportunities to piece together fragmented historical narratives,
and are material evidence of cultural identity and historical struggles. They also
prompt the transmission of cultural knowledge across generations: the songs and
stories evoked by the artefacts documented by Jonaitis, Clifford, and Fienup-Riordan
might not have been told within their local communities if not prompted by the
sight of the artefacts to which they were tied. Within museums, source community research with collections and consultation for exhibition developments provides
opportunities to articulate perspectives and narratives denied by the dominant
society. In other instances, through loans or repatriation, objects and archival
collections leave museum buildings and are reincorporated into source community
life so that the knowledge they embody can be transferred across the generations
(Tapsell 1997, 2003). Repatriation may in fact, be thought of as one end of the
spectrum of actions which result from the changing relations between museums
and source communities.

Photographs, whether of people or of artefacts, have the same capacity as
artefacts to evoke knowledge, spark lively debates on the identity and stories of
the people or makers involved, and the cultural knowledge and intention encoded
in them, and function as links between past and present. Though projects, that
link communities with archival photographs and film footage of their ancestors or
of artefacts in museums known as photo-elicitation or visual repatriation, raise their
own sets of problems which overlap with other kinds of collaborative methodologies, they are proving to be a meaningful way for museums to give back to source
communities and to build relationships of trust (see A.K. Brown 2001; Brown and
Peers 2005; Kingston 2003; Peers and Brown 2002; Stanton 2003).

The stories that emerge when copies of film or photographs are shared with
the communities in which they were taken are often local histories that have been
denied by official narratives constructed by Europeans (Bell 2003; Binney and Chaplin
2003; Edwards 1994). The sight of these images can trigger the telling of counter-
narratives, often for the first time in generations, and are used as visual proof of
a community's account of past events. (This can, of course, be a very difficult and
emotional process for source community members who find themselves facing dis-
tressing histories.) This work also leads to conversations within communities about
issues such as cultural identity, the uses of historic knowledge in the present, the
shifting meanings of artefacts, and the nature of change and cultural continuity. In
some indigenous communities, working with historic artefacts and photographs
becomes part of a strategy to preserve the emotional, psychological, cultural, and
physical health of members through the dissemination of knowledge about identity
and history. Educational materials designed by community members which utilise
museum and archival resources, for instance, have become a means through which
people can learn about the diversity of materials available to them and about how
the histories related to these resources are relevant today. Such projects include
curriculum materials produced by the Kainai Board of Education to address social
issues such as drug and alcohol abuse based on interviews with elders and historic
photographs (Fox 2001) and a CD-ROM, *Our Grandmothers' Voices: East Cree material
culture in museums* (Oberholtzer 2001), which presents images of historic northern

Cree beaded artefacts, and associated information, for use by beadworkers in northern Cree communities. Some museums are also developing educational programmes aimed at indigenous school children which provide them with an opportunity to explore their own culture and history, and to learn about museums more broadly (e.g. Alger and Welsh 2000; Christal *et al.* 2001; Kahnapace and Carter 1998). In turn, such work has brought new sources of knowledge into the museum, has re-attached information to artefacts, and has re-vivified museum collections: objects gain fresh meanings and acquire new interest for the public when viewed through the eyes of source community members (Clifford 1997b: 188–91; Dunstan 1999; Philp 1998).

Recognition of the very personal connections that can be made between families, communities, images, and artefacts has also made museum professionals aware of the ways in which museums are expressions of Western culture, and has helped them to re-think the intentions and procedures of their institutions to become more responsible to source communities. Poignant (1996: 12), working with photographs, found herself cutting up copies of prints in order not to show images of recently deceased people to their close kin; archivists and curators are working with source communities to find mutually acceptable solutions to curating sacred and sensitive information and artefacts. Following consultation, access to these materials may be limited: sensitive information is generally not placed on publicly available catalogues, and researchers may require permission from elders or community councils to study or publish certain collections (Edwards 2003; Macaulay 1999; Rosoff 2003). Some of the most successful solutions have emerged from projects involving the hiring of source community members to assist in-house and to act as liaisons between their communities and heritage institutions (Rosoff 2003; Stanton 2003). Such projects have been very little published about, however, and the museum profession requires opportunities for training in such new attitudes. Museums have their own traditions of knowledge about the items in their collections, their own professional culture, their own ways of caring for and classifying artefacts, and their own goals of education and entertainment that they wish to realise from their collections in their work with the public. By and large, these differ dramatically from the perspectives and goals of source communities. Involving and sharing power with source community members means that staff must unlearn much of what they know, or think they know, about collections and museums, and begin to see these from very different perspectives. Fienup-Riordan's account (2003) of Yup'ik elders reordering and correcting attributions of a Yup'ik collection in Germany according to their own detailed knowledge, only to have the museum staff place things back in their long-established but incorrect order and categories, hints at some of the issues, problems, and implications of cross-cultural work within museum institutions.

In many cases, museum staff have made a commitment to collaborative work, most often through exhibition development, but also through the involvement of source community members in developing new storage and conservation practices (Rosoff 2003; Clavir 2002). Beyond specific procedures, however, is a willingness to seek community involvement at as many levels as possible. The selection of artefacts for display, the writing of label text, the enhancement of database entries, the storage and conservation of collections, the establishment of procedures for approving research projects involving museum collections, the design of special storage facilities for sacred/sensitive materials and human remains, the development of educational programmes, the selection of gift shop stock, the choice of logo designs, are all areas where source community members should be consulted and where their input is invaluable. These are specific points at which overlapping museum and source community rights in historic artefacts can and should be recognised. To involve community members in these ways does take additional time and money. But for museums committed to addressing issues of access and ethics, to exploring a new model in which they are forums for discourse between peoples (Ames 1991: 14) – in which they act as contact zones – it is critical that such involvement begin.

Relationships and power: learning and unlearning

To do this, of course, rests on establishing relationships between museums and source communities, a process in which we all have much to learn. At the core of the new approaches . . . is a series of crucial issues including power and authority, commitment, control, and learning. Without addressing these, new relationships and outcomes between museums and source communities cannot develop. As noted earlier, museums and source communities bring very different goals and needs to a working relationship. They almost certainly have different expectations about how matters will proceed, about the appropriate division of labour and credit, and about the nature of authorship or control. A museum's obligations to its publics, to its governance structure, and to the museum profession may be quite different to the community, kinship, and cultural obligations felt very keenly by source community consultants. Combined with the cross-cultural factors involved, partnerships are prone to strains resulting from these differences. It is all too easy to misread a partner's intentions and perceptions from one's own perspective, or to interpret community input as fitting easily into existing museological practice. Margaret Hanna, a curator at the Royal Saskatchewan Museum, Canada, who was involved in the redisplay of its First Nations gallery in the early 1990s, for example, writes candidly about the 'patience and persistence' needed to overcome deeply entrenched attitudes of some staff, who were committed to 'the traditional view of the museum world', whereby the curators were the experts and 'asking the spiritual leaders was a nice formality, but we didn't really have to follow their advice if it didn't fit with our plans' (Hanna 1999: 44). Hanna observes that as the gallery developed, attitudes changed; staff learned to listen and sought ways to get round some of the bureaucratic and institutional constraints.[1]

For such change to happen, relationships of respect and trust must develop between museum staff and community members, and for this reason, in the process of working with members of other cultures within the museum space, relationships are foregrounded at least as much as the artefacts themselves (Bolton 2003). Conaty's essay on Glenbow's Blackfoot Gallery (2003) explains that the efforts of community members and museum staff over the past decade to nurture mutual trust *before* the gallery development process got underway were essential to the project. In developing relationships, museums may have to put their agendas aside temporarily to first address community concerns regarding, for instance, the handling of secret sacred objects or the disposition of human remains, before community members agree to participate in projects such as exhibition development. Shifting priorities in this way reflects community desires to see issues of importance to them effectively dealt with and is also, of course, a test of the institution's commitment to the community, rather than to its own needs. One of the most important elements of the new way of working with source communities is that trust-building is considered integral to the process, and creating respect or healing the effects of the past is seen as being as important as co-writing labels or enhancing the database.

In the process of developing relationships and dealing with community needs, larger issues must also be addressed. Clifford's description of Tlingit elders examining historic artefacts in the Portland Museum of Art focused on the elders' call for the museum to support the families whose material heritage it held, 'to act on behalf of Tlingit communities, not simply to represent the history of tribal objects' (Clifford 1997b: 193). Museums have claimed they are neutral spaces, and have tended to resist lending political support to source communities; Clifford, however, notes that, 'when museums are seen as contact zones, their organizing structure as a *collection* becomes an ongoing historical, political, moral *relationship* – a power-charged set of exchanges' (1997b: 190). One of the effects of working with source community members is realising the political nature of museums, their histories, and their functions, as well as the need to acknowledge and address these dynamics when creating new relationships.

None of this is easy to do in practice. Some of the core dynamics of new approaches pose great challenges which are often not realised by museum staff until well into a project. For many source communities, collaboration means full and equal partnership in all stages of a project; it is a recognition of their expertise and their attachment to objects that are central to their culture, and their participation will often be based upon expectations of community benefit. Furthermore, the more a community invests in a project, the greater their expectations for continued involvement will be. Though many relationships begin with a specific project (the creation of a new gallery, or collections research), community expectations are that such projects are vehicles to developing long-term relationships, while museums may assume their responsibilities are over when one project ends. Project teams need to give thought to what happens once the exhibition opens or the initial project concludes: what are the long-term goals for the relationship? Who sets these goals? Who is intended to benefit from the partnership? How best can museum and community partners make use of a relationship which starts very tentatively, and then deepens and strengthens as participants get to know one another, work through problems, and enjoy the successes of collaborative projects? At one level, this work involves allocations of money, time, and human resources which are too significant for one-off projects; at a more fundamental level, it is about changing the attitudes and goals of museums so that they are committed to long-term relationships involving mutual support and learning.

Conaty (2003) describes how the primary goal of Glenbow's Blackfoot community team was to develop a gallery in which their children could learn about their culture and history from the perspectives of their own people. In comparison with needs such as this, a museum's goals for a collaborative project may appear more superficial and be based upon the need to gain knowledge of collections or a desire to 'do things the right way' and gain political credibility. Such goals may be achieved by what communities regard as a 'hit and run' policy, whereby the museum comes in search of information and then leaves to work on its projects, but is less prepared to address the community's needs (Lorne Carrier cited in A.K. Brown 2000: 242). Museums and source communities need to accept that while they may have some shared goals, others will simply be different, requiring compromise. Similarly, working with source communities may illuminate the multiple agendas that are played out within museums, for instance, balancing the conservation needs of an object with its cultural use (Bernstein 1992; Clavir 2002).

With notable exceptions (Kreps 1998; Dunstan 1999), most of the existing case studies of museum/source community collaboration have focused on the positive benefits for both partners and have tended to skim over the problems encountered and how these were overcome. There are fairly obvious reasons why this has happened, largely relating to confidentiality. However, this has led to serious omissions in the literature; methodological, institutional and cross-cultural difficulties have been glossed over, despite the fact that such challenges are inherent in this kind of work. Furthermore, few writers have been prepared to comment on those situations whereby their hopes for collaboration have failed, due to insufficient resources, lack of planning, problems communicating, or disagreements within the community. Indeed, there are times when a collection or a museum's history may have so many negative associations for a community, that it simply is not possible for that community to work with the museum.[2]

Typically, anthropology curators are the interface between the museum and a source community, while few other museum employees may be involved in co-managed projects. This can be interpreted by source community members as a sign of a museum's lack of institutional commitment, putting the researchers in a difficult position if their efforts to engage their institution in a closer relationship with the community fail. Gift shop managers, educational programmers, conservators, registrars, and administrators should all ideally have some involvement in a collaborative project and be prepared to think through the implications of relationships as well as to support innovative projects administratively. Their participation heightens institutional awareness of the legitimacy and importance of cultural protocols when developing new relationships (see Fienup-Riordan 1999: 353–4), for instance sponsoring feasts and giving gifts as well as honoraria to source community partners, in addition to the more traditional costs involved in museum work.

Many staff, and many institutions, who have learned to cope with such new dynamics, have found them rewarding and stimulating. One of the most important elements of new relationships between museums and source communities is the extent to which they promote learning and growth for the museum profession. By viewing collections through the eyes of source communities, museum staff are able to think more broadly about the meanings of objects and their continued significance for communities today, alerting them to new possibilities for interpretation. As the roles are reversed and museum staff find that they are being educated by community members, they begin to see in a new light the assumptions embedded in traditional museum training, and become open to alternative ways of doing things. This is particularly so for those staff who have been privileged to attend ceremonial events involving objects that, at some point during their social lives have been part of the museum's collection. Seeing artefacts in their cultural context, hearing stories of frustration and pain caused by inappropriate scholarly inquisitions or museum representations in the past, understanding a community's dreams for the future, all make clear the importance of developing new ways of thinking and of working.

Contexts and literatures

Developments between museums and source communities have been part of a broad pattern in the social sciences of questioning relations between scholars and those whom they study. Anthropology has proved something of a lightning rod for such questioning, and many scholars have felt the need to move away from a praxis based on colonial relations of power to one in which power is more equitably shared. At the same time, source communities have begun to insist that their participation in research and exhibition projects is conditional on forms, goals, and outputs of work which are acceptable to them as well as to the museum or scholarly researcher. Various forms of community based research are part of this new way of working between museums and source communities. Applied and advocacy anthropology are part of this new approach, as are participatory action research and collaborative research, in which forms of research and their outcomes are mutually determined and controlled by researcher and source community alike (Hall 1979; Ryan and Robinson 1990; Warry 1990, 1998) . . . Some of this material is difficult to access: the still-emerging nature of work between museums and source communities means that much is yet unpublished, and other materials have been produced either for in-house use by individual museums or are only known within a particular nation. . .

One of the most powerful bodies of literature . . . has critiqued museum representation and the historical relations of power it embodies. These works includes James Clifford's essays 'Histories of the tribal and the modern' (1988), 'Four Northwest Coast museums: travel reflections' (1991), 'Paradise' (1997a) and 'Museums as contact zones' (1997b), which address the complex relationships between museums, their audiences, and their collections. Other critiques include Coombes's *Reinventing Africa* (1994), Barringer and Flyn's *Colonialism and the Object* (1998), and several case studies in Phillips and Steiner's edited volume *Unpacking Culture* (1999). These explore how objects have been used by scholars to construct notions of indigenous identity, culture and history for consumption by audiences in the West. Such analyses have drawn on parallel works in ethnography which have problematised the history of relations between anthropologists and the peoples they have traditionally studied and the role of colonialism in those relations (e.g. Clifford and Marcus 1986; Fabian 1983; Stocking 1985) and explored the often problematic relations of power inherent in these histories. These have extended, in museum contexts, to the ethnographic tendency to turn a blind eye to the realities of the present in favour of the idealised pasts of their subjects – part of a broader pattern of scholars fulfilling their intellectual and career needs rather than their research subjects' often more pressing ones, and a pattern against which the new relationships are reacting.

Indigenous museum professionals and other source community voices have made important contributions to these critiques, and have especially questioned the right of museum staff to represent their communities in Western academic modes. They have expressed concern at the re-contextualisation of their objects according to Western values, and have pointed out the political meanings and implications of museum display. This literature is still emerging as a genre, but there are powerful pieces by writers such as Deborah Doxtator (1985, 1988), Gerald McMaster (1992, 1993), Gloria Frank (2000), Richard W. Hill (2000), Richard Handler and Eric Gable (1997), Paul Tapsell (1997, 2000), Deborah Eldridge (1996), and Henrietta Fourmile (1990), which convey a range of source community responses to tradi- tional ethnographic museum practice and attitudes (and see also interviews in Clavir 2002). Indigenous curators are also publishing on their approaches to museum work and on the changes they are making within their own institutions, whether they work in mainstream museums or community-managed facilities (Mauger and Bowechop 1995; Tamarapa 1996), and while this body of work is still slender, it is very much welcomed to provide guidance for the museum profession.

Another branch of the literature has emerged from source communities' protests against traditional museum practice and particular exhibitions. The heated and highly publicised conflict surrounding the Lubicon Lake Cree's 1988 boycott of *The Spirit Sings* exhibition in Canada – a protest, in part, against an exhibition that was firmly focused on the past while being funded by a corporation felt to be damaging First Nations communities in the present – made visible the rifts between First Nations peoples and museums in Canada, as well as within the museum community. Other exhibitions, such as the Royal Ontario Museum's 1990 exhibit, *Into the Heart of Africa*, which was perceived by many in the African-Canadian public to have racist overtones, have proven equally contentious for related reasons (Butler 1999; Harrison 1993; A.L. Jones 1993). Responses to such conflicts have led to the creation of working groups in several countries which have made recommendations for change in museum practice designed to meet the needs of source communities and to encour- age better working relations with them. In Canada, for instance, following the controversy over *The Spirit Sings*, a joint Task Force was established by the Canadian Museums Association and the Assembly of First Nations, which met with repres- entatives of museums and First Nations communities to 'develop an ethical frame- work and strategies for Aboriginal Nations to represent their history and culture in concert with cultural institutions' (Task Force 1992). The resulting *Report* sug- gested recommendations to make museums more accountable to First Nations com- munities, relating to issues of access to and interpretation of collections, the repatriation of human remains, and increased training opportunities for Aboriginal staff (Task Force 1992; Nicks 1992).[3] Similarly, Museums Australia has produced a policy document that explicitly states that Aboriginal and Torres Strait Islander people have rights to self-determination in matters relating to cultural heritage and that museums have obligations to support them.[4] The document goes beyond repatri- ation of secret/sacred objects and human remains and outlines ways in which museums can incorporate indigenous Australian and Torres Strait Islander perspectives into their daily management and exhibition strategies (Museums Australia 1996). More publications, which both reflect and explain the new ways of thinking about and working with collections, are needed by museums as a starting-point to begin developing relationships with source communities. For museums that are geographic- ally distant from some of their source communities, such documents are especially valuable resources, revealing as they do the new standards and expectations, and consolidating existing experience as a springboard for learning and change elsewhere.

In order to address the challenges raised by critics, many museums, especially in North America and the Pacific, have generated institutional documents and policies that encapsulate the guidelines of the national strategy documents referred to above and recognise indigenous interests (e.g. Kawharu 2002). A number have developed community advisory councils which advise museum staff on a range of issues such as selecting objects for loan to other institutions, assessing shop stock, and providing suggestions for educational programming (Conaty 1996). Policies that are developed in conjunction with source communities allow both partners to negoti-ate their different understandings and expectations, reducing the possibilities for misunderstandings. They also ensure that museums put into writing assurances that they will adhere to the wishes of the community involved, a point that can be extremely important in developing trust where none has existed before. Some museums are beginning to make these policies available in abbreviated format on their websites, or on request, a move that is helpful not only to indigenous groups planning research, but also to museum professionals seeking guidance on drafting policies for their own organisations.[5]

The implementation of new curatorial processes cannot, however, be done on the basis of documents alone; it requires consultation with source communities. Curators who ask whether, for instance, small bags of tobacco should be placed with some Native American or First Nations collections as offerings to show respect, or whether one should burn sweetgrass or other purifying herbs before handling these artefacts, need to understand that such procedures can only be respectful when they are performed by people who have been trained by the source community, who have begun to understand community perspectives and histories at a deep level, who have built relationships and trust with members of the source com-munity, and who have been authorised to act by community elders (Rosoff 2003). The actions taken within the museum storeroom need to happen within the context of relationships in the present with the community: the consultation, the human interaction, the willingness to learn, and the investment of time, effort, and money are far more important, and genuinely respectful, than gestures learned from books.

These relationships are the most important manifestation of the new curator-ial praxis, but the process of establishing them has not received much attention in the critical literature. Nor has the concept of 'source community' and its special needs in and rights to material heritage held in museum collections been a focus in the literature. The one volume that stands out as a forerunner to the present work in exploring some of these concepts is Karp, Kreamer, and Lavine's anthology *Museums and Communities: the politics of public culture* (1992), which explores museum/community relationships. In an essay in that volume, 'Audience, ownership, and authority: designing relations between museums and communities', Steven Lavine observed that by 1992 'many museums [had] taken up the challenge of responding to their various constituencies and relating to them more inventively; many have even begun to reimagine who those constituencies might be' (Lavine 1992: 137). A number of the essays in that anthology presented projects based on partnerships of various kinds between museums and local communities.

Notes

Laura Peers is curator for the Americas Collection, Pitt Rivers Museum, lecturer in
the School of Anthropology, and fellow of Linacre College at the University of Oxford.
Alison K. Brown is research manager (Human History) at Glasgow Museums and
was formerly a researcher at the Pitt Rivers Museum and junior research fellow at Wolfson
College, University of Oxford.

1   For discussion of this project from the perspective of a Plains Cree participant,
    see Goforth (1993).
2   Laura Peers (Peers 2003) has written about such a project dealing with children's
    hair samples taken at schools in an Ojibwe community in Minnesota in the 1920s
    which have since been part of the collections of the Pitt Rivers Museum, University
    of Oxford, and are sensitive to the Ojibwe for cultural and historical reasons.
    While community members were pleased to be contacted and told about the
    collection, and asked for advice about its curation, they have not so far been
    willing either to work further with the museum or to request repatriation of the
    hair.
3   In the United States, the process of negotiating the Native American Graves
    Protection and Representation Act (NAGPRA, 1990) and the effects of that
    legislation in enforcing consultation between museums and Native Americans has
    produced similar results, though in a more confrontational way.
4   This statement is closely related to parts of the draft Declaration of the Rights
    of Indigenous Peoples, which affirm the rights of indigenous peoples to their
    heritage and traditions, and urges states to take appropriate steps to ensure the
    preservation of these. Work on this important document has also assisted indi-
    genous source communities to codify their feelings regarding heritage and out-
    side institutions which curate it.
5   Examples of museums which provide on-line guidance of this nature include
    the Museum of Anthropology at the University of British Columbia, and the
    Australian Museum's Aboriginal Heritage Unit.

References

Alger, A. and Welsh, P.H. (2000) 'Creating hybrid space: the Native American high
    school student guide program at the Heard Museum', *Journal of Museum Educa-
    tion*, 25 (3): 14–19.
Ames, M.M. (1991) 'Biculturalism in exhibitions', *Museum Anthropology*, 15 (2): 7–15.
—— (1992) *Cannibal Tours and Glass Boxes: the anthropology of museums*, Vancouver:
    University of British Columbia Press.
—— (2003) 'How to decorate a house: the renegotiation of cultural representations
    at the University of British Columbia Museum of Anthropology', in L. Peers
    and A.K. Brown (eds) *Museums and Source Communities*, London and New York:
    Routledge, 171–180.
Barringer, T. and Flyn, T. (1998) *Colonialism and the Object*, London: Routledge.
Bell, J.A. (2003) 'Looking to see: reflections on visual repatriation in the Purari Delta,
    Gulf Province, Papua New Guinea', in L. Peers and A.K. Brown (eds) *Museums
    and Source Communities*, London and New York: Routledge, 111–122.

Bernstein, B. (1992) 'Collaborative strategies for the preservation of North American Indian material culture', *Journal of the American Institute of Conservation*, 31 (1): 23–9.

Binney, J. and Chaplin, G. (2003) 'Taking the photographs home: the recovery of Māori history', in L. Peers and A.K. Brown (eds) *Museums and Source Communities*, London and New York: Routledge, 100–110.

Bolton, L. (2003) 'The object in view: Aborigines, Melanesians, and museums', in L. Peers and A.K. Brown (eds) *Museums and Source Communities*, London and New York: Routledge, 42–54.

Brown, A.K. (2000) 'Object encounters: perspectives on collecting expeditions to Canada', unpublished DPhil thesis, University of Oxford.

—— (2001) 'Artefacts as "alliances": perspectives on First Nations collectors and collecting', *Journal of Museum Ethnography*, 13: 79–89.

Brown, A.K. and Peers, L. (2005) *'Pictures Bring us Messages': Photographs, Histories, Reconnections*, Toronto: University of Toronto Press.

Butler, S.R. (1999) *Contested Representations: revisiting* Into the Heart of Africa, London: Gordon and Breach.

Chaat Smith, P. (1995) 'The ghost in the machine', in *Strong Hearts: Native American visions and voices*, New York: Aperture.

Christal, M., Roy, L., Resta, P. and Cherian, A. (2001) 'Virtual museum collaborations for cultural revitalization: the Four Directions model', paper presented at the Museums and the Web 2001, Seattle, March 2001. Online. Available http://www.archimuse.com/mw2001/papers/christal/christal.html (accessed 23 March 2002).

Clavir, M. (2002) *Preserving What Is Valued: museums, conservation and First Nations*, Vancouver: University of British Columbia Press.

Clifford, J. (1988) 'Histories of the tribal and the modern', in *The Predicament of Culture: twentieth century ethnography, literature, and art*, Cambridge, Mass.: Harvard University Press.

—— (1991) 'Four Northwest Coast museums: travel reflections', in I. Karp and S.D. Lavine (eds) *Exhibiting Cultures: the poetics and politics of museum display*, Washington, DC: Smithsonian Institution Press.

—— (1997a) 'Paradise', in J. Clifford, *Routes: travel and translation in the late twentieth century*, Cambridge, Mass.: Harvard University Press.

—— (1997b) 'Museums as contact zones', in J. Clifford, *Routes: travel and translation in the late twentieth century*, Cambridge, Mass.: Harvard University Press.

Clifford, J. and Marcus, G.E. (1986) *Writing culture: the poetics and politics of ethnography*, Berkeley, Ca.: University of California Press.

Cole, D. (1985) *Captured Heritage: the scramble for Northwest Coast artefacts*, Norman: University of Oklahoma Press.

—— (1996) 'Working with Native advisory groups', *Alberta Museums Review*, 22 (2): 52–3.

Conaty, G.T. (1996) 'Working with Native advisory groups', *Alberta Museums Review*, 22 (2): 52–3.

—— (2003) 'Glenbow's Blackfoot Gallery: working towards co-existence', in L. Peers and A.K. Brown (eds) *Museums and Source Communities*, London and New York: Routledge, 227–241.

Coombes, A.E. (1994) *Reinventing Africa: museums, material culture, and popular imagination in late Victorian and Edwardian England*, New Haven and London: Yale University Press.

Doxtator, D. (1985) 'The idea of the Indian and the development of Iroquoian museums', *Museum Quarterly*, 14 (2): 20–6.

—— (1988) 'The home of Indian culture and other stories in the museum', *Muse*, 4 (3): 26–8.

Dunstan, C. (1999) 'Fostering symbiosis: a collaborative exhibit at the California State University Sacramento Museum of Anthropology', *Museum Anthropology*, 22 (3): 52–8.

Edwards, E. (1994) 'Visualizing history: Diamond Jenness's photographs of D'Entrecasteaux Islands, Massim, 1911–1912 – a case study in re-engagement', *Canberra Anthropology*, 17 (2): 1–26.

—— (2001) *Raw Histories: photographs, anthropology and museums*, Oxford: Berg.

—— (2003) 'Introduction', in L. Peers and A.K. Brown (eds) *Museums and Source Communities*, London and New York: Routledge, 83–99.

Eldridge, D. (1996) 'Aboriginal people need to control their own heritage', *Curatorship: indigenous perspectives in post-colonial societies*, Proceedings, Mercury Series 8, Hull: Canadian Museum of Civilization with the Commonwealth Association of Museums and the University of Victoria.

Fabian, J. (1983) *Time and the Other: how anthropology makes its object*, New York: Columbia University Press.

Fienup-Riordan, A. (1999) 'Collaboration on display: A Yup'ik Eskimo exhibit at three national museums', *American Anthropologist*, 101 (2): 339–58.

—— (2002) 'Inuguat, iinrut, uyat-llu: Yup'ik dolls, amulets and human figures', *American Indian Art Magazine*, 27(2): 40–7.

—— (2003) 'Yup'ik elders in museums: fieldwork turned on its head', in L. Peers and A.K. Brown (eds) *Museums and Source Communities*, London and New York: Routledge, 28–41.

Fourmile, H. (1990) 'Possession is nine tenths of the law – and don't Aboriginal people know it', COMA, 23: 57–67.

—— (1991) 'The case for independent but complementary Aboriginal cultural institutions', *Extending Parameters*: 35–40.

Fox, L. (2001) *Kipaitapiiwahsinnooni. Alcohol and Drug Abuse Education Program*, Edmonton: Duval House Publishing and Kainai Board of Education.

Frank, G. (2000) '"That's my dinner on display": a First Nations reflection on museum culture', *B.C. Studies*, 125/6: 163–78.

Giles, S. (2001) 'The great circuit: making the connection between Bristol's slaving history and the African-Caribbean community', *Journal of Museum Ethnography*, 13: 15–21.

Goforth, L. (1993) 'First Nations and museums – a Native perspective', *Muse*, 11 (1): 14–16.

Griffiths, T. (1996) *Hunters and Collectors: the antiquarian imagination in Australia*, Cambridge: Cambridge University Press.

Hall, B. (1979) 'Knowledge as a commodity and participatory research', *Prospects*, 9 (4): 393–408.

Handler, R. and Gable, E. (1997) *The New History in an Old Museum: creating the past at Colonial Williamsburg*, Durham, N.C.: Duke University Press.

Hanna, M.G. (1999) 'A time to choose: "us" versus "them" or "all of us together"', *Plains Anthropologist*, 44 (170): 43–52.

Harrison, J.D. (1993) 'Completing a circle: *The Spirit Sings*', in N. Dyck and J.B. Waldram (eds), *Anthropology, Public Policy and Native People in Canada*, Montreal: McGill-Queens University Press.

Herle, A. (2003) 'Objects, agency and museums: continuing dialogues between the Torres Strait and Cambridge', in L. Peers and A.K. Brown (eds) *Museums and Source Communities*, London and New York: Routledge, 194–207.

Hill, Sr., R.W. (2000) 'The museum Indian: still frozen in time and mind', *Museum News*, 79 (3): 40–74.

Jonaitis, A. (1991) 'Chiefly feasts: the creation of an exhibition', in A. Jonaitis (ed.) *Chiefly Feasts: The Enduring Kwakiutl Potlatch*, New York: American Museum of Natural History.

Jones, A.L. (1993) 'Exploding canons: the anthropology of museums', *Annual Review of Anthropology*, 22: 201–20.

Kahnapace, G. and Carter, B. (1998) '*Circle of Honour*: a unique partnership between Glenbow and the Plains Indians Cultural Survival School', *Alberta Museums Review*, 24 (1): 39–42.

Karp, I., Kreamer, C.M., and Lavine, S.D. (eds) (1992) *Museums and Communities: the politics of public culture*, Washington, D.C. and London: Smithsonian Institution Press.

Kawharu, M. (2002) 'Indigenous governance in museums: a case study, the Auckland War Memorial Museum', in C. Fforde, J. Hubert and P. Turnbull (eds) *The Dead and Their Possessions: repatriation in principle, policy, and practice*, One World Archaeology, 43, London: Routledge.

King, J.C.H. (2001) 'Native museums. A response to Laura Peers', *Anthropology Today*, 17 (1): 22–3.

Kingston, D.P. (2003) 'Remembering our namesakes: audience reactions to archival film of King Island, Alaska', in L. Peers and A.K. Brown (eds) *Museums and Source Communities*, London and New York: Routledge, 123–35.

Krech, III, S. and Hail, B.A. (eds) (1999) *Collecting Native America, 1870–1960*, Washington, D.C.: Smithsonian Institution Press.

Kreps, C. (1998) 'Museum-making and indigenous curation in Central Kalimantan, Indonesia', *Museum Anthropology*, 22 (1): 5–17.

Lavine, S.D. (1992) 'Audience, ownership, and authority: designing relations between museums and communities', in I. Karp, C.M. Kreamer and S.D. Lavine (eds) *Museums and Communities: the politics of public culture*, Washington, D.C. and London: Smithsonian Institution Press.

Macaulay, S.P. (1999) '"Keeping Taonga warm": museum practice and Maori guardianship', *Journal of Museum Education*, 24 (3): 14–17.

McMaster, G. (1992) 'Colonial Alchemy: reading the boarding school experience', in L.R. Lippard (ed.) *Partial Recall: photographs of Native North Americans*, New York: The New Press.

—— (1993) 'Object (to) sanctity: the politics of the object', *Muse*, 11 (3): 24–5.

McMaster, G. and Martin, L. (eds) (1992) *Indigena: contemporary native perspectives in Canadian art*, Vancouver and Hull, Quebec: Douglas & McIntyre in association with the Canadian Museum of Civilization.

Mauger, J.E. and Bowechop, J. (1995) 'Tribal collections management at the Makah Cultural and Research Center', *Perspectives: a resource for tribal museums*, 2: Washington, D.C.: American Indian Studies Program, Smithsonian Institution.

Museums Australia (1996) *Previous Possessions, New Obligations: a plain English summary of policies for museums in Australia and Aboriginal and Torres Strait Islander peoples*, Melbourne: Museums Australia.

National Museum of the American Indian (NMAI) (1991) 'National Museum of the American Indian policy statement on Native American human remains and cultural materials', *Museums Anthropology*, 15 (2): 25–8.

—— (2000) *The Changing Presentation of the American Indian. Museums and Native Cultures*, National Museum of the American Indian Smithsonian Institution in association with University of Washington Press.

Nicks, T. (1992) 'Partnerships in developing cultural resources: lessons from the Task Force on Museums and First Peoples', *Culture*, 12 (1): 87–93.

Nightingale, E. and Swallow, D. (2003) 'The Arts of the Sikh Kingdom: collaborating with a community', in L. Peers and A.K. Brown (eds) *Museums and Source Communities*, London and New York: Routledge, 55–71.

Notzke, C. (1996) 'Co-managing Aboriginal cultural resources', *Muse*, 14 (3): 53–6.

Oberholtzer, C. (2001) *Our Grandmothers' Voices: East Cree material culture in museums*, CD-ROM. Copyright Cree Regional Authority.

O'Hanlon, M. and Welsch, R.L. (eds) (2000) *Hunting the Gatherers: ethnographic collectors agents and agency in Melanesia, 1870s–1930s*, Methodology and History in Anthropology 6, Oxford and New York: Berghahn Press.

Peers, L. (2000) 'A review of the Chase Manhattan Gallery of North America', *Anthropology Today*, 16 (6) 8–13.

—— (2001) 'Author's response', *Anthropology Today*, 17 (1): 23.

—— (2003) 'Strands which refuse to be braided: Beatrice Blackwood's Ojibwe collection at the Pitt Rivers Museum', *Journal of Material Culture*, 8 (1): 75–96.

Peers, L. and Brown, A.K. (2002) 'Sharing knowledge', *Museums Journal*, 102 (5): 24–7.

Phillips, R.B. and Steiner, C.B. (eds) (1999) *Unpacking Culture: art and commodity in colonial and post-colonial worlds*, Berkeley: University of California Press.

Philp, J. (1994–5) 'About friendship; about trade: about photographs', *Voices: Quarterly Journal of the National Library of Australia*, 4(4): 55–70.

—— (1998) 'Owning artefacts and owning knowledge: Torres Straits Island material culture', *Cambridge Anthropology*, 20 (1–2): 7–15.

Poignant, R. with Poignant, A. (1996) *Encounter at Nagalarramba*, Canberra: National Library of Australia.

Poovaya Smith, N. (1991) 'Exhibitions and audiences: catering for a pluralistic public', in G. Kavanagh (ed.), *Museum Languages: objects and texts*, Leicester: Leicester University Press.

Pratt, M.L. (1992) *Imperial Eyes: travel writing and transculturation*, London: Routledge.

Rosoff, N.B. (2003) 'Integrating Native views into museum procedures: hope and practice at the National Museum of the American Indian', in L. Peers and A.K. Brown (eds) *Museums and Source Communities*, London and New York: Routledge, 72–79.

Ryan, J. and Robinson, M. (1990) 'Implementing participatory action research in the Canadian North: a case study of the Gwich'in language and culture project', *Culture*, 10 (2): 57–71.

Schildkrout, E. and Keim, C.A. (eds) (1998) *The Scramble for Art in Central Africa*, Cambridge: University of Cambridge Press.

Shelton, A. (2003) 'Curating *African Worlds*', in L. Peers and A.K. Brown (eds) *Museums and Source Communities*, London and New York: Routledge, 181–193.

Stanton, J.E. (2003) 'Snapshots on the dreaming: photographs of the past and present', in L. Peers and A.K. Brown (eds) *Museums and Source Communities*, London and New York: Routledge, 136–151

Stocking, G.W., Jr. (1983) *The Ethnographer's Magic: fieldwork in British anthropology from Tylor to Malinowski*, Madison: University of Wisconsin Press.

—— (ed.) (1985) *Objects and Others: essays in museums and material culture*, History of Anthropology 3, Madison: University of Wisconsin Press.

Tamarapa, A. (1996) 'Museum *Kaitiaki*: Maori perspectives on the presentation and management of Maori treasures and relationships with museums', *Curatorship: indigenous perspectives in post-colonial societies*, Proceedings, Mercury Series 8, Hull: Canadian Museum of Civilization with the Commonwealth Association of Museums and the University of Victoria.

Tapsell, P. (1997) 'The flight of Pareraututu: an investigation of *Taonga* from a tribal perspective', *Journal of the Polynesian Society*, 106 (4): 323–74.

—— (2000) *Pukaki: a comet returns*, Auckland: Reed.

—— (2003) 'Afterword: beyond the frame', in L. Peers and A.K. Brown (eds) *Museums and Source Communities*, London and New York: Routledge, 242–251.

Task Force on Museums and First Peoples (1992) *Turning the Page: forging new partnerships between museums and First Peoples*, Ottawa: Assembly of First Nations and the Canadian Museums Association.

Warry, W. (1990) 'Doing unto others: applied anthropology and Native self-determination', *Culture*, 10: 61–73.

—— (1998) *Unfinished Dreams: community healing and the reality of Aboriginal self-government*. Toronto: University of Toronto Press.

Chapter 38

Archaeology and *Vanua* Development in Fiji

Andrew Crosby

Introduction

THERE IS AN IMPORTANT DIVIDE between archaeology that attempts to incorporate or involve local communities into externally devised projects and those that are initiated by the communities themselves.[1] On one side, the community may influence and participate in the timing, operation and goals of the project, and may benefit from it, but the project's *principal* objectives will be to generate publications that serve external interests. On the other side, there are usually no academic publications at all: the *point* of this sort of community archaeology is that it is entirely local, uncompromised by the interests of a broader academy. At their extremes, the two types of archaeology are of little relevance to each other, the two types of archaeologist seldom mix and there is a certain amount of name-calling that goes on between them. Nearer the centre, however, post-colonial archaeology is less polemical and busies itself with genuine communication and accommodation of external and local community interests and attempts to reach a quid pro quo – a mutually beneficial exchange of services and resources.

This chapter is based on the author's experiences in Fiji over the period 1990–4 conducting anthropological research into the construction of the modern chiefly system during the colonial period. Having previously conducted archaeological research in Fiji, I was frequently asked during my stay to advise and assist the Fiji Museum on projects ranging from field survey and excavation to fund-raising, which I was only too happy to do. And it is in this capacity – as an unpaid adviser to the Fiji Museum and participant in a number of community archaeological projects – that this article is written. My anthropological research supports the proposition that a once fluid and balanced set of relationships between Fijian chiefs and commoners

Source: *World Archaeology*, vol. 34, no. 2, 2002, pp. 363–78.

was transformed and then ossified into a system of fixed class relationships. Despite this, the chiefly system is a famously beloved institution in Fiji and is a key ethnic marker that serves to define ethnic Fijians from the other main population groups: Fijian Indians, Europeans and Chinese. During the course of my parallel involvement in community archaeology projects, therefore, it surprised me to what degree Fijians in rural communities were disenchanted with their chiefs and were prepared to mobilize community development projects that directly challenged the chiefs' authority and provided local people with a measure of economic independence from them. Some years later I find it ironic that these projects have been considerably more effective in challenging the iniquitous chiefly system of Fiji than my self-consciously critical academic analysis. They have also raised more interesting questions. Perhaps I now understand what it means to be a post-colonial archaeologist.

Problems

Fiji is a precarious economy for which the conservation of the natural and cultural heritage resource is an ill-afforded luxury. As with most 'developing nations' the resources – forestry, agriculture and tourism – have been sold to the highest bidders, mostly overseas consortiums. Although this has provided the metropolitan government with the rental, licensing and tax revenues to square the balance sheet, there have been considerable costs to the environment and to the sense of self-determination and economic well-being of people in the rural communities. A series of quite specific problems emerged during the 1980s to bring some of these costs to near crisis point.

Problem 1: cultural resource management

Fiji is like most developing nations around the post-colonial world: the departing colonial administration bequeathed a toothless and ill-funded heritage management structure to an apathetic and nearly destitute beneficiary – one that was barely able to raise a mortgage for society's essential services, let alone the luxury of an archaeological past. In Fiji, the management of the archaeological resource was commended to the combined care of the Fiji Museum, the National Trust and the Department of Town and Country Planning, which, authorized and empowered by various Acts, have discharged their responsibilities with great dedication but negligible support.

Of primary significance is the Fiji Museum, which carries statutory responsibility for preserving and maintaining archaeological objects and monuments. Under the Preservation of Objects of Archaeological and Palaeontological Interest Act 1978, the museum is authorized to declare sites to be national monuments and to acquire those monuments where appropriate. The museum, however, lacks the authority to prohibit the disturbance of archaeological sites that have not been declared monuments and cannot oblige the owner to enter into a preservation agreement. Severe funding restrictions ensure that compulsory purchases of monuments are unheard of and the legislation languishes untested and unused. Fiji has only one declared national archaeological monument – Wasavulu – which survives in a dilapidated and vandalized state (Watling and Chape 1992: 144). The museum instead focuses on maintaining a register of sites and on the custodial care of the portable components of heritage: objects, archives and oral histories. Where sites *have* been acquired, they are owned by the independently funded National Trust, which maintains them in consultation with the Fiji Museum. The number of properties, however, is few, the most significant being the archaeologically spectacular Sigatoka Sand Dunes (Marshall *et al.* 2000).

Of equal importance is the Department of Town and Country Planning, which is authorized by the Town Planning Act, 1946 to consider items and areas of historic interest in drawing up local planning schemes. Such schemes – such as at the old capital Levuka – *have* provided for the preservation of historic buildings of Fiji's post-European period (Watling and Chape 1992: 144; Takano 1996). But these are structures of colonialism, and it is therefore poignant that the inherited colonial legislation has been most effective in protecting its own architectural edifice. I am aware of only one or two occasions where the 1946 Act has been invoked to prevent the destruction of indigenous Fijian sites (Wood *et al.* 1998: 16–17).

The problem is only partially one of funding. By far the greatest destruction to the Fijian archaeological heritage is caused by the indifference, ignorance or commercial avarice of ethnic Fijians themselves. This occurs at a very small scale through repeated clearance, planting and occasional bulldozing of sites for crops by villagers and independent farmers. But it also occurs on a massive scale through the operations of commercial planters and foresters. The field officers of the Fiji Museum are well aware that the most effective course of action is not to enforce protection but to work with Fijians – especially villagers and farmers – to educate them about the very existence of the archaeology and of its value.

Problem 2: economic inequality

There is a very uneven distribution of wealth among Fijians (Spate 1959; Burns *et al.* 1960; Fisk 1970). This is only partially to do with the colonial creation of 'Three Fijis', which for many decades has seen the ethnic Fijians as the majority landowners, subsistence farmers and political élite, the Fijian Indians as the predominant cash croppers, labourers, merchants and owners of small industry, and the ethnic Europeans and Chinese as the owners and managers of large manufacturing and service industries (Fisk 1970: 33–48; Knapman and Schiavo-Campo 1983). It is also to do with the inequities of the land ownership system instituted by the Colonial Government and enshrined at independence in 1970 that recognizes majority communal land ownership by ethnic Fijians and vests control of communal lands in chiefs. Traditionally, chiefs would exercise their control for the benefit of the *mataqali* and *vanua* (landowning groups) (Ravuvu 1983, 1987, 1988). However, in the post-independence neo-colonial state the chiefs emerged as an élite class, dominating the House of Representatives and using their control over the vast majority of the land resources to form a hegemonic alliance with European capital (France 1969; Nayacakalou 1975; Durutalo 1985, 1986; Hau'ofa 1987: 10–11). Within the ethnic Fijian population, this resulted in the concentration of political power and economic wealth in the hands of chiefs generally and the chiefs of Eastern Fiji in particular.

The relevance for this paper is in several dimensions. Eighty-three per cent of Fijian lands, and therefore 83 per cent of the archaeological resource, lies in ethnic Fijian ownership. The usage of that land is steadily moving away from low-intensity subsistence use (Overton 1987, 1988). The chiefs have taken increasing amounts of communally owned lands – those nominally considered waste or excess to subsistence requirements – and leased them to yield a cash dividend: typically through forestry, farming or tourism. Few of the cash proceeds of those enterprises have found their way into the ethnic Fijian villages where the chiefs are also seldom to be found these days. The chiefs now form a new urban élite, whereas those Fijians remaining in the villages are forced to intensify their use of the remaining land for both subsistence and income. In the absence of the chiefs, the formal protocols surrounding land use are relaxing. In particular, much of the knowledge of the locations of ancestral sites has been forgotten or ignored and sites previously considered *tambu* (sacred) are now being cultivated, built upon and even bulldozed. The problem is one of outright apathy: the increasingly disenfranchised rural Fijians have little incentive to care for archaeological sites that take up valuable agricultural land, and the incentive to maintain the traditional 'customs of respect' (Nation 1978) is diminishing with the migration of the chiefs to the towns.

Problem 3: diversification of land use

The Native Land Trust Board (NLTB) administers the 83 per cent of all Fijian lands owned by ethnic Fijians (429,000 hectares). Approximately 65 per cent of this land is leased for agricultural purposes – including commercial sugar and rice cultivation. The remainder is leased for a variety of purposes including tourism and forestry. The total rental pay out to ethnic Fijians in 1988 was very low, only F$6.5 million at the rate of just over F$15 per hectare. Of this, agricultural leases contributed approximately F$12 per hectare compared to F$20 per hectare for non-agricultural leases. The NLTB has come under increasing pressure to increase the rental returns on land (Volavola 1993), but, with the collapse of world sugar prices, cannot significantly increase the land rents paid by Indian sugar farmers. In an effort to stimulate income growth, land managers at the NLTB have been asked to meet income quotas and to diversify the uses for which land has been leased. This could perhaps be most easily achieved by increasing the area leased for forestry. However, environmental concerns over forestry and other environmentally damaging land uses have placed increasing scrutiny on the NLTB to allocate land leases to more environmentally sustainable uses.

The problem for the NLTB, then, is that it has come under simultaneous pressure to increase the returns from land leases and diversify its rentals away from low earners, such as sugar cultivation, and environmentally damaging operations, such as forestry. Apart from the damage caused to the natural and cultural heritage, the brunt of the forestry and other extractive operations has been felt by ethnic Fijians in the villages. Although forestry activities have typically been confined to relatively remote and steep areas unsuitable for arable or even subsistence agriculture (Watling and Chape 1992: 31), they have eroded the important resource available for traditional agro-forestry (Thaman 1994) and damaged the capacity of Fijians to manage production systems holistically (Clarke 1994). When questioned, many rural Fijians have expressed to me that they have met resistance and animosity when they have challenged the NLTB for issuing leases to forestry. As they explain it, the NLTB itself consists of too many 'ratus' (chiefs), who indeed made up 50 per cent of the membership in 1988. Given that many of these chiefs are also principal shareholders, directors or beneficiaries of forestry enterprises, a clear conflict of interests exists (Durutalo 1985, 1986).

Problem 4: conservation of native forests

According to *The National State of the Environment Report* (Watling and Chape 1992: 54), Fiji has just under half of its total land area (1.83 million hectares) under forest. Of this, approximately 25 per cent (237,000 hectares) comprises areas of native hardwoods exploited for timber production with a further 85,000 hectares of plantation forests managed by the Fiji Pine Commission and the Forestry Department. Between 1967 and 1992 an estimated 11–16 per cent of the nation's forests were converted to non-forest use, with deforestation occurring at a rate of between 0.5 and 0.8 per cent a year. This is particularly problematic for the Forestry Department, the government agency principally responsible for managing the forest resource. Although Fiji appears to be well forested, the resource is rapidly dwindling. In particular, there is a severe imbalance in the distribution of forest, with the drier parts of the larger islands and many smaller islands suffering the most severe deforestation.

The result has been something of a partitioning of the nation's forest resources and a separation of the forests away from the people, increasingly relegating the native hardwoods to inaccessible zones on steep lands and specially designated conservation areas. The effect is to increasingly remove agro-forestry – a traditionally important subsistence strategy – from everyday village life for ethnic Fijians (Thaman 1988, 1994; Thaman and Clarke 1983). Moreover, some within the Department of Forestry itself have expressed concern over the dividing off of forested areas from the traditionally holistic Fijian conceptualization of the *vanua* as a world in which the land, the people and the gods – the physical, cultural and spiritual spheres – are fully integrated (Ravuvu 1988: 6; Crosby 1994; personal communication Alivereti Bogiva 1992). The problem is the simultaneous contraction of the natural forest resource and its gradual removal from the everyday lives of ethnic Fijians. While the creation of forest conservation areas is beneficial in preserving native forest plant and animal species, there is great dissatisfaction that this has occurred at the expense of an important component of the traditional Fijian concept of community.

Problem 5: diversification of tourism

The Fijian tourism industry is floundering. Second only to sugar as a revenue earner, tourism has been hit hard by political instability in Fiji and the recent world economic recession. More significantly, the market for selling 'sun, sea and surf' – Fiji's traditional tourism marketing strategy – is a highly competitive one, with many other comparable holiday destinations offering weaker currencies and cheaper flights from North America and Europe. Fijian operators have recognized that the Fijian tourism industry needs to diversify to appeal to a wider range of holidaymakers, and to accentuate the cultural uniqueness of Fiji among the otherwise ubiquitous glossy beach brochures. This has been accomplished partially by modelling resort architecture on traditional Fijian building styles, by having displays of Fijian artefacts and textiles in hotel lobbies and by putting on cultural performances of Fijian dance groups and string bands. Since the early 1980s hotels and small independent tour operators have been increasingly guiding the more adventurous visitors out of the hotels to visit waterfalls and other natural beauty spots, to go on horse-riding and walking treks and to visit Fijian villages.

Successful to a degree, the problem is that there has been little involvement of ethnic Fijians in this new venture, and little additional money has found its way into the pockets of Fijian villagers, who consider themselves the rightful custodians of Fijian culture and the environment. The problems are how to increase the overall tourism revenue through diversification and to distribute the benefits more evenly, particularly so that those who are the caretakers of Fijian culture past and present are more active stakeholders in its exploitation.

Problem 6: overseas development assistance

Overseas development agencies have consistently been criticized for failing to deploy their assistance in ways that are culturally appropriate, sustainable and targeted to the areas that most need stimulation. The domination of regional development ministries and departments by self-interested locals – frequently the chiefly élite – has exacerbated the problem and has led to the deployment of development funds in ways that have actually been damaging to local communities and their environments (Watters 1987). There have been many instances involving the implementation of rural development projects that have served only to increase the class domination of the urban élite, allowing them to exercise long-distance control over an increasingly disenfranchised rural labour force. Such projects, far from being culturally sensitive, have accelerated the break-up of community as defined by the traditional *vanua* concept. The proceeds and benefits of the land have not been shared evenly, the physical environment has not been managed sustainably, and there has been a breakdown of the pathways of communication between members of the community. This has become increasingly embarrassing for overseas governments.

Summary

The various problems outlined above, although disparate, demonstrate just some of the economic, political, social and environmental strands that weave together the context of Fijian heritage management. In essence, ethnic Fijians make much of their traditional concept of community: the *vanua*. It differentiates them ethnically from Fijian Indians, Europeans and others. In their view, it is what makes them *traditional*, it is what justifies their vast majority claim over the landholdings, it is the foundation of their political élite – their chiefs, it is what binds ethnic Fijians together into a social system and it is the source and repository of the historical knowledge and cultural understandings by which those social knots are tied. In reality, the *vanua* is somewhat different. The weave is nowhere near so tight, more an assemblage of threads from which any number of patterns can be woven, some exploitative and self-serving, others a determined effort by groups of villagers to develop a rural economy and preserve their local resources, both human and environmental.

Solutions

Some ethnic Fijians recognize the heritage as a key resource, one that can be conserved, managed and sold to tourists in a way that would also re-awaken an interest in the past by villagers themselves – especially the youth. They hope that the preservation of archaeological sites for economic gain may also reinforce the historical knowledge of past social relationships and genealogical connections by which the *vanua* adheres as a community. During the 1990s several rural village communities, supported by sympathetic government agencies, initiated a momentum for community-led archaeology development projects.

Waikatakata

As far as I am aware, Waikatakata is the first *vanua*-based archaeology development project in Fiji. It is situated near to the heart of Fiji's 'Coral Coast', a string of resorts along the south-west coast of Viti Levu (Fig. 38.1). It includes an area of virgin native forest, hot springs, streams and waterfalls and is interspersed with several pre-European village and ceremonial *naga* sites – spectacular stone-walled enclosures in which initiation rituals are thought to have taken place. The archaeological sites were badly overgrown and dilapidated, threatened by logging and by guided horseback treks operated by private entrepreneurs.

The Department of Town and Country Planning initially proposed the project in 1986 with the following objectives:

- To widen the scope of visitor attractions within Fiji and, in particular, to develop an aspect of cultural tourism which to date has been largely neglected.
- To encourage greater participation of the local community in culturally oriented tourism development and to raise incomes through the creation of employment opportunities and visitors returns.
- To ensure, through controlled access and protective measures, that the archaeological (scientific), educational and cultural value of the sites is adequately preserved and in no way debased or impaired.
- To promote a general awareness and interest in Fiji's archaeological sites and monuments and an appreciation of the need to conserve/preserve this important aspect of Fiji's heritage.

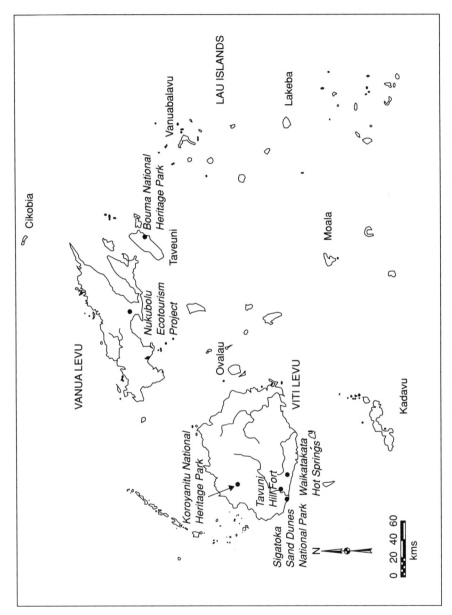

Figure 38.1 Map of Fiji showing the archaeology and eco-tourism projects discussed in the text

Several similar projects were also proposed for the vicinity should the Waikatakata pilot scheme prove successful.

Initial progress was highly promising, with meetings by representatives of the Fiji Museum, the Department of Town and Country Planning, the NLTB, Forestry Department and other agencies with members of the local landowning communities. The proposal was for an integrated forest/tourism park, managed by the NLTB but operated by local villagers who would gain from employment in the park and a share of the tourism revenues. The local community would eventually take over management of the project. A trained archaeologist was appointed by the NLTB to complete a site survey, the archaeological sites were cleared of vegetation and partially rebuilt, and a plan was drawn up of walking/trekking routes, signage and shelters, with the prospect of building tourist accommodation in or adjacent to the park in the future. It seemed that Waikatakata would pave the way for a new kind of community-based archaeological development in which the archaeological and natural environments would be preserved to the benefit of the local ethnic Fijian community.

Too good to be true? Of course. To this day Waikatakata is again overgrown, undeveloped and threatened by logging. The Waikatakata project failed because it was imposed from afar by metropolitan bureaucrats. A cash cow was presented to the local community before any degree of consensus was achieved over vital questions such as who actually owned the land, how the proceeds should be divided, who should provide the labour and who should oversee and control the whole affair. It soon became clear that those individuals who had wholeheartedly backed the initial proposals did not represent the wider group. The project stalled permanently through the classic Fijian strategy of passive resistance. Worse, acrimonious feuds erupted between villagers and the net result appears to have been to further split an already riven community.

Bouma, Taveuni

Waikatakata, however, is a hearth from which several other more successful projects have risen. Paramount among these is a project located at Bouma at the north-eastern end of Taveuni Island (Figs 38.1 and 38.2). The crucial difference with this project is that it proceeded from a request for assistance by the local landowning community itself. Bouma forms part of the Fijian chiefly confederacy of Cakaudrove, the paramount chief of which – Tui Cakau – resides on the other side of Taveuni at Somosomo. In 1988, when the project was initiated, the people of Bouma had been asked by Tui Cakau (who at that time was Ratu Sir Penaia Ganilau, President of Fiji) and his cousin at the Provincial Office to participate in a Korean forestry scheme. The Bouma people were attracted by the promised benefits of land rentals and employment, but felt bullied by the Somosomo chiefs and concerned about the unsustainability of forestry for future generations. They were aware of the Waikatakata project and requested the NLTB's assistance in initiating a similar programme of landowner-based tourism development.

Initially, the NLTB was approached by representatives of Nakorovou village to assist in establishing a forest park on their land. The area included the Tavoro falls,

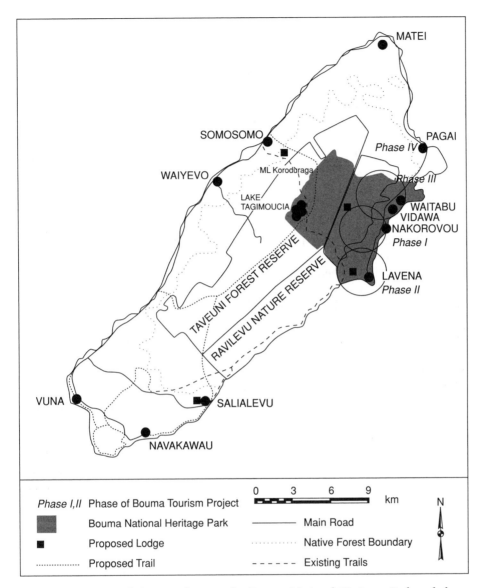

Figure 38.2   Map of Taveuni showing the Bouma National Heritage Park and the four phases of the Bouma Tourism Project

a series of spectacular waterfalls set within native forest. The Nakorovou villagers had obtained a modest and ad hoc income from guiding tourists to these falls for some time and now wished to develop the attraction. As stated, their aims were conserving and protecting their forest and cultural heritage resources while providing employment and income-generating opportunities. These aims were commensurate with the ideals of sustainability lying at the heart of eco-tourism — conserving and preserving the resource in a way that provides some practical gain (Seroma 1995).

Their interests went further, however, and emphasized the development of the *vanua*, seeking to enhance their prosperity in spiritual and cultural dimensions as well (Ravuvu 1983: 76, 1988: 6; Crosby 1994). They were particularly concerned at the breakdown of traditional cultural values within the community. As they saw it, this was demonstrated by their own paramount chief's disregard for the natural resources of the forest, and by a widespread breakdown of social taboos marked by increased drunkenness and decreased co-operation within the village. They wanted a prosperity that also included social and spiritual harmony.

It became clear in preliminary discussions that *vanua* development should involve the co-operative effort of villagers communally sharing their skill and labour resources to create the forest park themselves under the leadership of their own village leaders. The process of creating the park would be developmentally beneficial in itself. What was required was outside support, advice and skill in implementing trails, visitor centres, conservation programmes and effective management practices. It also emerged that *vanua* development required preserving not just the natural heritage of the forest, but also the cultural heritage of *koro makawa* – the ancient settlements of the ancestors located in the forest. These sites had become damaged by gardening and neglect, and would have been destroyed by forestry, but they represented the historical foundations of the communities and are considered by some to be the spiritual abode of the ancestors themselves. The preservation of the old settlements and the remembrance of oral histories associated with those sites were seen as crucial to the rejuvenation of the spirituality of the *vanua*. Ever pragmatic, the Bouma people also saw the *koro makawa* as a further attraction for tourists.

Having learnt from the divisiveness of Waikatakata, the NLTB insisted on the full participation of all four *yavusa* (landowning groups) that constitute the wider *vanua* of Bouma under the overall patronage of the *vanua* chief, the Vunisa of Bouma. To avoid future disputes, they recommended that each *yavusa* should control separate parts of the project, each of which could stand as a self-contained, independently managed concern (Fig. 38.2). Accordingly, a four-phase eco-tourism project was devised covering 1,603 hectares of land extending from the coast to the island's mountainous central plateau and including Fiji's largest lake, Tagimoucia (Native Land Trust Board 1989, 1993). The bulk lies under tropical rainforest, some of which was already designated Forest Reserve. Phases 1–3 were designed to focus on three areas easily accessible from the coastal road and centred on attractions close to each of the main villages. Phase 1 would see the development of the Tavoro Falls based on Nakorovou. Phase 2 was a coastal walking trail and lodge based at Lavena. Phase 3 was an archaeological and forest trail based between Vidawa and Waitabu. Phase 4 was a longer-distance trail network accessible from all four villages. Each phase was to proceed at one-year intervals, to be overseen by a steering committee drawn principally from the NLTB, the Department of Forestry, the Fiji Museum, the Ministry of Fijian Affairs and the Department of Tourism. The New Zealand Government funded the establishment of the first three phases. The villagers voluntarily supplied labour, and expertise was provided by the agencies forming the steering committee.

Phase 1 was opened in April 1991 and Phase 2 in June 1993. Both have since been operating as successful commercial ventures, charging tourists five Fiji dollars per visit. Phase 3, the Vidawa forest and heritage trail, was initiated with a formal management plan in 1991 (Wakelin 1991) and an archaeological survey in 1993

(Crosby and Marshall 1994). Oral histories were also recorded and a series of site plans and detailed recommendations were put forward, which culminated in a network of signposted walking trails linking two hill fortifications – Nasau and Navuga – with walks through native rainforest. All stages, from the archaeological survey to the construction of the trails and signs, were completed as a co-operative effort between outside experts and local villagers convened under the leadership of the village chiefs. After some delay, the Vidawa Forest Walk is now open for visitors and, for sixty Fiji dollars, visitors are guided on a full-day walk taking in the fortifications, bird watching and the Tavoro falls. On the way, visitors are informed about the basic principles of the Fijian *vanua* philosophy and about the traditional history of the Bouma people. Phase 4 is less formally structured but is now also completed and includes guided walks up to Lake Tagimoucia.

The project has not been without its problems. Proposed accommodation lodges were cancelled, partly due to fears over the intrusive effects of visitors staying near to the villages. And there have been disagreements over procedure and allocation of resources. By and large, however, the project has been successful and is promoted aggressively as the Bouma National Heritage Park by the Fiji Visitors Bureau and by independent tour operators. In its promotional literature, the Fiji Visitors Bureau proclaims: 'The Park . . . wouldn't exist if it wasn't for the shared vision of four local villages, the Fiji and New Zealand Governments and other conservation organisations' (http://www.fijifvb. gov.fj/activity/listing/bouma.htm). The park is a major tourism resource that is being used to brand the whole tourism industry in Fiji as eco-friendly. Last but not least, the financial backers of the project – the New Zealand Government – are delighted to be able to demonstrate their investment in a rare commodity: a culturally appropriate and environmentally friendly overseas development project.

Other projects

The success of Bouma and the commitment of the Steering Committee have had immediate spin-offs elsewhere in Fiji. On the western side of Viti Levu, the Koroyanitu National Heritage Park (Fig. 38.1) – a more complex project involving 25,000 hectares of unlogged rainforest and fifty *mataqali* landowning groups – was initiated in 1993. This project, again, occurred at the request of the five villages that bounded the area, and began with ground and air-photo surveys of the forest and archaeological resources. The first stage of the project, the Abaca Village and Recreation Park, has been completed with the development of simple accommodation and a series of hiking trails taking in native forest, mountain walks and archaeological sites. As with Bouma, labour and expertise were all voluntarily provided as a co-operative effort between the landowning communities and government agencies.

A more explicitly archaeological project has also been completed at Tavuni Hill Fort near Sigatoka (Fig. 38.1), also initiated at the request of the local community: the four surrounding villages, each of which regard Tavuni as their ancestral settlement. Long abandoned and neglected, the hill-fort was first cleared using community labour and, following the advice of the Fiji Museum, parts of the site were repaired and a network of trails constructed to guide visitors around remnants of the fort's fifty-six structures. The Fiji Museum conducted oral historical research and prepared a guide to the site. Funding was received to construct signs, a car park and a combined visitor centre and museum. As with Bouma and Koroyanitu, the project has proved highly successful, is actively marketed and continues to provide the local community with income and employment.

Other projects are also being negotiated throughout Fiji, although not all have the degree of community agreement and leadership, the quality of physical or cultural attractions or the necessary tourism infrastructure to allow them to proceed at this time. Perhaps most advanced is the Nukubolu Ecotourism Project on Vanua Levu: a series of ring-ditch fortifications and hot-springs surrounded by rivers and rainforest (Fig. 38.1). The project is planned in three phases of trails and accommodation and is again being conducted as a community-led project.

Summary

Community-led and community-operated eco-tourism projects in Fiji appear to successfully resolve many of the problems outlined at the start of this chapter. They take areas of natural and archaeological importance that would otherwise have been lost to forestry or neglect and develop them as tourism alternatives to sandy beach resorts. Crucially, control over the implementation and final operation of the projects has at all times remained with the local community, allowing a degree of resistance to bureaucratically imposed development and a buffer to the economic exploitation of the chiefs. The common denominators of the various projects are:

- They are initiated by local communities seeking alternative income and employment-generating opportunities.
- They are based on the Fijian concept of the *vanua* and seek to integrate sustainable economic development of the natural and cultural heritage with less tangible cultural benefits that include the development of community co-operation, the rejuvenation of a sense of history and the reassertion of 'traditional' Fijian values.
- They are expertly guided and assisted by a loose conglomerate of government and non-government agencies now formalized as the National Steering Committee. This is made up of representatives from all organizations involved in conservation, forestry and tourism, including the NLTB, the Departments of Forestry, Tourism, Lands, Fijian Affairs, Co-operatives and Economic Planning, the Environment Unit, the Development Bank, the National Trust of Fiji and the Fiji Museum.
- They are financially supported by government and overseas development assistance programmes that recognize the contribution to the national economy of sustainable and culturally appropriate development.

The benefits have extended beyond each individual project. The crucial involvement of the National Steering Committee has provided a forum for exchange and liaison between normally autonomous agencies that has effected a more integrated national conservation policy and has been to the great benefit of heritage conservation in particular.

Conclusions

In Fiji, a series of apparently dislocated problems is being tackled jointly at grass-roots level by community-led development projects aimed at sustainably promoting the natural and cultural heritage. Community archaeology has featured in all of these projects through the clearance, survey and repair of ancient sites and the collection and recording of oral historical information. This has usually been accomplished with the involvement and assistance of the Fiji Museum and visiting foreign archaeologists, but has in all cases led to a rejuvenation of local interest in the cultural heritage and the training of community members to manage the archaeological resource. Without exception, all projects have led to improvements in the economic fortunes of the villagers and to the condition of the archaeological sites concerned. In all cases, the projects have also empowered the communities to reclaim their local histories in ways that sometimes directly challenge the historical underpinnings of the Fijian chiefly élites.

There is nothing academic about these projects aside from the affiliations of the visiting archaeologists. Indeed, in some cases the archaeological interpretations that have ended up in the visitor guides and signs contravene orthodox academic understandings. Community archaeology in Fiji represents the claiming of the heritage resource by local Fijian communities to make of it what they will. But conventional academic archaeology is also the winner here. Apart from the conservation of the resource, the whole profile of archaeology has been raised in Fiji. The museum's funding and staffing levels have increased, the Fiji Government has taken cultural heritage much more seriously and the level of local debate about prehistory has risen to a level never previously attained.

In a post-colonial world this is the key message for archaeologists. For institutional and academic archaeologists the tendency has been to pay lip service to community-based archaeology – to entertain it, patronize it, exploit it in the name of appearing to be post-colonial, but to distance it from the 'real' work of archaeology and to fear or ridicule the sometimes unorthodox or counter-hegemonic claims it may make. Perhaps, with a little more imagination, archaeologists will see that anything that raises the level of the debate and increases the involvement of people in the past will ultimately challenge and thereby enrich their own interpretations. Certainly for this archaeologist – labouring to understand the processes of state formation and the emergence of a political élite in Fijian history – it has been illustrative to be immersed in the present reality of political economy and the creative reinvention of tradition.

Notes

Andrew Crosby was visiting research fellow in Pacific archaeology at the University of Southampton, UK.

1   The ideas put forward in this paper are the result of discussions with many people in Fiji more visionary and committed than myself. In particular I should like to thank Stefan Cabaniuk, Alivereti Bogiva and Sepeti Matararaba, whose single-minded zeal paved the way for the projects outlined above. More generally, I should like to thank everybody who participated on the projects for their kind assistance and hospitality, and the Fiji Museum, the Native Land Trust Board, the Department of Forestry and the New Zealand Government Nature Tourism Funding Programme for supporting community archaeology in Fiji. I am especially indebted to Yvonne Marshall who conducted much of the archaeology at Bouma and generously commented on an earlier draft of this paper.

References

Bogiva, A. 1993. Personal communication, Department of Forestry Fiji, June.

Burns, Alan et al. 1960. Report of the Commission of Enquiry into the Natural Resources and Population Trends of the Colony of Fiji. London: The Crown Agents for Overseas Governments and Administration on behalf of the Fiji Government.

Clarke, W. C. 1994. Traditional land use and agriculture in the Pacific Islands. In Science of Pacific Island Peoples, Vol. II, Land Use and Agriculture (eds J. Morrison, P. Geraghty and L. Crowl). Suva: Institute of Pacific Studies, pp. 11–38.

Crosby, A. D. 1994. Fijian cosmology, vanua, development and ecology. In Science of Pacific Island Peoples, Vol. IV, Education, Language, Patterns and Policy (eds J. Morrison, P. Geraghty and L. Crowl). Suva: Institute of Pacific Studies, pp. 55–78.

Crosby, A. D. and Marshall, Y. M. 1994. Archaeological sites and development recommendations for Phase III, Bouma Environmental Tourism Project. Report prepared for The Native Lands Conservation and Preservation Projects Steering Committee, Suva.

Durutalo, S. 1985. Internal colonialism and unequal regional development: the case of Western Viti Levu, Fiji. MA thesis. Department of History and Politics, University of the South Pacific, Suva.

Durutalo, S. 1986. The Paramountcy of Fijian Interest and the Politicization of Ethnicity. South Pacific Forum Working Paper Number 6. Suva: University of the South Pacific Sociological Society.

Fisk, E. K. 1970. The Political Economy of Independent Fiji. Canberra: Australian National University Press.

France, P. 1969. The Charter of the Land. London: Oxford University Press.

Hau'ofa, E. 1987. The new South Pacific society: integration and independence. In Class and Culture in the South Pacific (eds A. Hooper, S. Britton, R. Crocombe, J. Huntsman and C. Macpherson). Auckland and Suva: University of Auckland and University of the South Pacific, pp. 1–12.

Knapman, B. and Schiavo-Campo, S. 1983. Growth and fluctuations of Fiji's exports, 1875–1978. Economic Development and Cultural Change, 32: 97–119.

Marshall, Y. M., Crosby A. D., Matararaba, S. and Wood, S. 2000. Sigatoka: The Shifting Sands of Fijian Prehistory. University of Southampton Department of Archaeology Monograph Number 1. Oxford: Oxbow Books.

Nation, J. 1978. Customs of Respect: The Traditional Basis of Fijian Communal Politics. Canberra: Australian National University Development Studies Centre.

Native Land Trust Board 1989. A forest park and reserve proposal for Mataqali Naituku and the Vanua of Bouma, Taveuni. Plan prepared by the Native Land Trust Board, Suva.

Native Land Trust Board 1993. Taveuni environmental tourism project: concept plan. Plan prepared by the Native Land Trust Board, Suva.

Nayacakalou, R. R. 1975. *Leadership in Fiji*. Melbourne: Oxford University Press.

Overton, J. 1987. Fijian land: pressing problems, possible tenure solutions. *Singapore Journal of Tropical Geography*, 8: 139–51.

Overton, J. 1988. A Fijian peasantry: galala and villagers. *Oceania*, 58: 193–211.

Ravuvu, A. 1983. *Vaka i Taukei: the Fijian Way of Life*. Suva: University of the South Pacific.

Ravuvu, A. 1987. *The Fijian Ethos*. Suva: Institute of Pacific Studies.

Ravuvu, A. 1988. *Development or Dependence: The Pattern of Change in a Fijian Village*. Suva: University of the South Pacific.

Seroma, L. 1995. Ecotourism: the Fijian experience. In *Beyond Timber: Social, Economic and Cultural Dimensions of Non-Wood Forest Products in Asia and the Pacific: Proceedings of a Regional Expert Consultation 28 November–2 December* (eds P. B. Durst and A. Bishop). Regional Office for Asia and the Pacific Publication 1995/13. Bangkok: Food and Agriculture Organization of the United Nations, Regional Office for Asia and the Pacific.

Spate, O. H. K. 1959. *The Fijian People: Economic Problems and Prospects*. Council Paper Number 13 of 1959. Suva: Government Press.

Takano, G. T. 1996. Learning from Levuka, Fiji – preservation in the first colonial capital. *CRM*, 19(3): 15–17.

Thaman, R. R. 1988. Fijian agroforestry: trees, people and sustainable polycultural development. In *Rural Fiji* (ed. J. Overton). Suva: Institute of Pacific Studies of the University of the South Pacific, pp. 31–58.

Thaman, R. R. 1994. Pacific Island agroforestry: an endangered science. In *Science of Pacific Island Peoples*, Vol. II, *Land Use and Agriculture* (eds J. Morrison, P. Geraghty and L. Crowl). Suva: Institute of Pacific Studies, pp. 191–222.

Thaman, R. R. and Clarke, W. C. 1983. Pacific Island agrosilviculture: systems for cultural and ecological stability. Paper presented to the Fifteenth Pacific Science Congress, Dunedin, 1–11 February.

Volavola, Ratu M. 1993. NLTB and landowner – in the same team, says general manager. *Vanua*, June: 1–4.

Wakelin, D. 1991. A management plan for Bouma Forest Park, Taveuni, Fiji Islands. Report prepared for the New Zealand Ministry of External Relations and Trade, Wellington.

Watling, D. and Chape, S. P. (eds) 1992. *Environment Fiji: The National State of the Environment Report*. Gland, Switzerland: IUCN – The World Conservation Union.

Watters, R. 1987. Mirab societies and bureaucratic elites. In *Class and Culture in the South Pacific* (eds A. Hooper, S. Britton, R. Crocombe, J. Huntsman and C. Macpherson). Auckland and Suva: University of Auckland and University of the South Pacific, pp. 32–55.

Wood, S., Marshall, Y. M. and Crosby, A. D. 1998. Mapping Sigatoka, Site VL 16/1: the 1992 field season and its implications. Report prepared for the Fiji Museum and the New Zealand High Commission, Suva.

http://www.fijifvb.gov.fj/activity/listing/bouma.htm.

Chapter 39

Kist and Tell

Matt Barnard

AMONG THE BUOYANCY AIDS AND coke machines in the leisure centre on Glasgow's Greater Pollok Housing estate on the south side of the city, residents can now find a suit of armour from the sixteenth-century Battle of Langside, a Bronze-Age axe-head and picture cards collected from 1960s tea packets. They are all part of the first entirely volunteer-run museum set up by the Glasgow Museum Service through its Open Museum scheme.

Described as a 'mini-museum', the Greater Pollok Kist opened in October last year and was curated by a team of local volunteers with help from Open Museum staff. 'Kist' is a Scottish word meaning treasure chest, the kind of box a bride would keep her wedding linen in. It was a name that they hoped would resonate with local residents and describe the kind of museum it would be – somewhere to display important elements of local history.

The Open Museum was set up by the Glasgow Museum Service in 1990. It was a response to critics of Glasgow's strategy of regeneration through culture which was attacked as highbrow and socially exclusive. In responding to those concerns the service anticipated the focus on tackling social exclusion that became a priority when Labour came to power in 1997.

The Open Museum was given teeth by being set up on the principle that 'no part of the museum collections was to be considered too precious or important for use in community venues'. This means that theoretically the Open Museum has a mandate to loan out any item from the Glasgow Museum Service collections, which includes the famous Burrell Collection, provided security and conservation issues are addressed.

The service had been organising temporary exhibitions for ten years in collaboration with community groups. But it wanted to set up a permanent exhibition space

Source: *Museums Journal*, Feb. 2002, pp. 36–7.

to be run by local volunteers and with the help of an £87,000 grant from the Heritage Lottery Fund's Access Fund it was able to make that happen. The grant covers the set-up costs and the Open Museum has committed to funding at least one exhibition per year after that.

The first hurdle was to get local people involved. This was particularly difficult as Greater Pollok was specifically chosen because few people from the area visit museums. Laura McGugan, the acting head of the Open Museum, explains: 'It was an area where there was little interest in museums and museums did very little for them. We wanted to set up something that allowed a better link between the local community and particularly the Burrell Collection which is nearby.'

The Open Museum set up a stand in the leisure centre and invited people who expressed an interest to come to a meeting. However, at least one of the volunteer curators, Mary Macbride, a retired bank clerk, remembers the process being a little more proactive than the Open Museum lets on. Macbride says: 'I started talking to the girls and they asked me if I wanted to come to a meeting, and I think they'd admit that they didn't say they wanted to shanghai us. So I went along and suddenly found myself part of a team to set up a local museum.'

Any initial reluctance disappeared as the volunteers began the process of putting the museum together. The six volunteers at the first meeting were joined later by seven others who made up the Kist management team and they met every fortnight over a period of about a year, doing research between meetings. They decided on the theme of 'Greater Pollok from the big bang to the present day', partly to incorporate all the various interests of the team, and divided topics suggested by the Open museum staff among them. These ranged from the persecution of witches, to the local World War I hero John Meikle, recipient of the Victoria Cross, to the nineteenth-century mining disaster in the local area.

Esther Baxter, a member of the management team who combines motherhood with working as a caretaker and is also a part-time actress, says that to begin with she was not enthusiastic about her subjects. 'Initially I wasn't interested in witches or Mary Queen of Scots', she says. 'But then I saw that it would be interesting to see how women were persecuted in the past. And when you start doing something like this, all sorts of things turn up, like a coin my daughter found in the market which had Mary on it.'

The management team were taken around the city's museums to meet curators and learn how to put together a display and were also sent on local history courses. Security at the mini-museum, which is not staffed, was dealt with by bringing in three large display cases that are of very high specification, which McGugan describes as 'bandit proof'. As well as the three cases, which display items borrowed from museums and donated by local residents, the exhibition has two interactive displays, including a model of a volcano.

There is something almost magisterial in the historical sweep that the exhibition achieves in such a small space. The section on the disaster in one of Britain's best ventilated mines in 1851 is particularly touching. The disaster is close enough in time to be alive in the community memory particularly, as the exhibition explains, given that the bodies of the 62 miners who died were buried in a mass grave, a fate normally reserved for paupers. They were later exhumed and buried individually.

The volunteers clearly got a great deal from working on the museum. Macbride comments: 'Considering the small space and the limited time, I think the team is justly proud of what we have achieved. I'm much more aware of what goes on behind museums now and it has made us all appreciate the effort that goes into producing the city's wonderful museums.' It has also made them want to get other people involved. Baxter says: 'We want to help people start to think for them-selves, to give them a push like we were given a push.'

But the project also raises questions about social inclusion that have not yet been addressed. The Open Museum has agreed to support the Kist in the future, and allow the volunteers to curate it. But what if the stories the volunteers want to tell in the future make the museum service uncomfortable? What would happen if a similar museum in Oldham told the history of 'white Britain'? McGugan says of the Kist museum: 'It is their stories and their words, and it would be wrong for anyone in the service to change them.' Like the museum world more generally, the Open Museum does not seem prepared for the possibility that local history might be highly controversial.

Some, like Sue Davis, the museum development officer for Hertfordshire Museum Service, think that social inclusion should be about letting people tell their own stories whatever they want to say: 'Let everyone in Oldham have a gallery to tell their history. It would be a great exhibition. I think that just because we don't know what is going to happen, that is not a reason not to have a go.' The Kist is an example of giving real power to the local community. It remains to be seen what happens when community museums start to flex their muscles and how the sponsoring museums will respond.

Note

Matt Barnard is a freelance journalist.

Index